Teacher's Wraparound Edition

ARTTALK

THIRD EDITION

Rosalind Ragans, Ph.D.

Associate Professor Emerita
Georgia Southern University

 **Glencoe McGraw-Hill**

New York, New York   Columbus, Ohio   Woodland Hills, California   Peoria, Illinois

About the Author

Rosalind Ragans

Rosalind Ragans is the author of Glencoe's senior high school art text, *ArtTalk*. She served as senior author on the elementary program *Art Connections* for the SRA division of McGraw-Hill, and was one of the authors of Glencoe's middle school/junior high art series, *Introducing Art, Exploring Art,* and *Understanding Art.* She received a B.F.A. at Hunter College, CUNY, New York, and earned a M.Ed. in Elementary Education at Georgia Southern University and Ph.D. in Art Education at the University of Georgia. Dr. Ragans was named National Art Educator of the Year for 1992.

About Artsource®

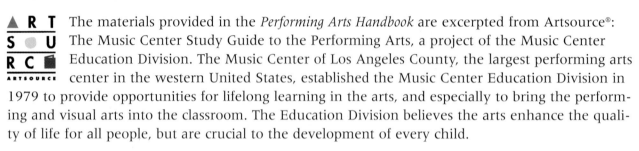

The materials provided in the *Performing Arts Handbook* are excerpted from Artsource®: The Music Center Study Guide to the Performing Arts, a project of the Music Center Education Division. The Music Center of Los Angeles County, the largest performing arts center in the western United States, established the Music Center Education Division in 1979 to provide opportunities for lifelong learning in the arts, and especially to bring the performing and visual arts into the classroom. The Education Division believes the arts enhance the quality of life for all people, but are crucial to the development of every child.

Cover/Title Page Credit:

Cover Photo by Kazu Okutomi/theStockRep

Glencoe/McGraw-Hill

A Division of The **McGraw·Hill** *Companies*

Send all inquiries to:
Glencoe/McGraw-Hill
21600 Oxnard Street, Suite 500
Woodland Hills, CA 91367

ISBN 0-02-662434-6 (Student Edition)
ISBN 0-02-662435-4 (Teacher's Wraparound Edition)

Printed in the United States of America.

1 2 3 4 5 6 7 8 9   004/043   05 04 03 02 01 00 99

Table of Contents

New Directions in the Visual and Performing Arts

Welcome to *ArtTalk*—a lively, inviting, comprehensive art program written and designed for beginning and advanced level art classes. This popular program has been updated and expanded to include more interactive student activities, new multicultural studio projects, integrated computer options, and over two hundered artworks representing a wide range of cultures, artistic styles, and art media.

You know that a quality, comprehensive art program enriches student's lives and allows for discovery and creative problem solving. It provides students with a broader perception of their environment and a greater understanding of historical and cultural perspectives. In the process, a quality art program cultivates learners who are able to make positive contributions to society.

ArtTalk Addresses the New Directions

ArtTalk answers the new directions in art education by providing this comprehensive program designed specifically for the high school student. This comprehensive program is structured around the belief that students learn best in a classroom that is engaging, meaningful, and focused on art as a core curriculum subject, one that is built on their everyday experiences and enriches their learning in all areas.

Providing a Comprehensive Art Program

ArtTalk is based on the following key concepts:

- In order for students to comprehend art concepts, it is important to provide meaningful, hands-on learning experiences that allow for personal growth and creative expression.
- A comprehensive art program integrates the areas of aesthetics, art criticism, art history, and studio production.
- A quality art education program provides students with experiences that are sequentially planned, building on previous concepts, and provides learning opportunities that incorporate a variety of media, artistic styles, and historical periods.
- An up-to-date art program includes information and practice on the computer and other new technology including the use of scanners, digital cameras, CD-ROMs, and the Internet.

Integrating the Four Components

- **ARTISTIC PERCEPTION**   At the very center of arts instruction is the process of being able to talk about works of art and learning the basic skills and knowledge neccessary to communicate in each art form. By learning the elements and principles of art, working with various media, and evaluating master artists' works, students develop an awareness of and appreciation for the presence of art both within the classroom and in their everyday experiences.
- **CREATIVE EXPRESSION**   Studio projects and studio activities give students the opportunity to create works of art using various media and techniques, including computers.
- **HISTORICAL AND CULTURAL CONTEXT** Throughout the program, works of art from various periods, styles, and cultural groups develop a broad base for students to celebrate cultural diversity and understand various global views.
- **AESTHETIC VALUING**   As students explore, theorize, and apply the principles of aesthetics and art criticism to their own artwork and the artwork of others, they formulate a lifelong appreciation of, and satisifying experience in, the arts.

Linking the Performing Arts and Other Curriculum Areas

■ **MUSIC, DANCE, THEATRE**   The visual and performing arts are mutually reinforcing. *ArtTalk* is designed to underscore that unity by presenting the exploration of art as it correlates to the performing arts. Students experience how the foundation of all areas of art, including dance, theatre, and music, are built upon corresponding concepts.

■ **CROSS-CURRICULUM CONNECTIONS**   The art classroom provides an exciting opportunity to make connections between the visual arts and other curriculum areas. Students learn how concepts in one subject area, in this case art, can enhance and increase their interest in and knowledge of other subject areas. Throughout *ArtTalk*, students make connections that translate across a wide range of curriculum areas including math, science, social studies, and language arts.

Addressing The National Standards for Arts Education

The National Standards for Arts Education provide guidelines that set benchmark standards for grade-appropriate competency in the performing and visual arts. *ArtTalk* is correlated to the National Standards (see the Scope and Sequence on pages 22–28), and helps teachers design their lessons around the National Standards.

Expanding the Arts Through Technology

Advances in technology offer exciting opportunities to art teachers and students. Through videodiscs, CD-ROMS, and the Internet, students can sharpen their visual perception. With computer art programs, students expand the limits of their creative expression. New activities and resource components provide a range of technology options that encourage exploration of new possibilities both in art education and production.

Including Assessment Strategies

Throughout *ArtTalk*, students are encouraged to keep sketchbooks and to develop a portfolio featuring their selected works of art. In addition, the frequent self-examination of completed artworks provides ongoing evaluation of each student's progress, fostering a sense of accomplishment and a commitment to high standards of art production, and preparing them for the transition to excellence in the work place.

Meeting the Needs of All Students

ArtTalk includes activities and teaching strategies that help teachers adapt the art classroom to the specific needs of students. This inclusive approach reinforces the universal value of art education for all students.

THE STUDENT EDITION

Engaging the Students

The *ArtTalk* student text introduces students to a comprehensive art program emphasizing the elements and principles of art. From line and color to rhythm, movement, and unity, the 14 chapters interweave studio production with narrative lessons on the elements and principles of art, techniques, art history, and criticism.

CHAPTER OPENING   Each chapter opens with a full-color motivational reproduction of a work of art related to the chapter's contents. A brief introduction helps students focus on the chapter. Chapter objectives are listed as well as vocabulary terms that will appear in the chapter.

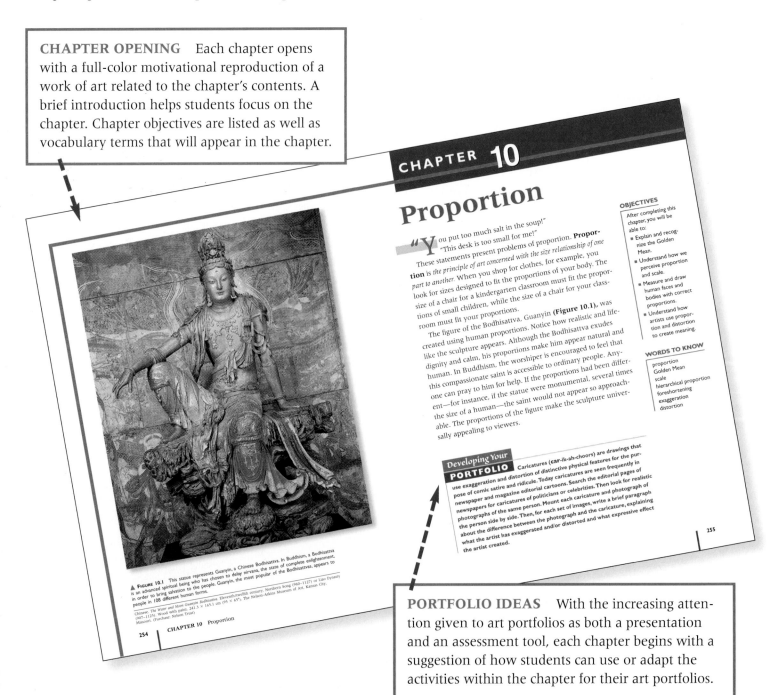

PORTFOLIO IDEAS   With the increasing attention given to art portfolios as both a presentation and an assessment tool, each chapter begins with a suggestion of how students can use or adapt the activities within the chapter for their art portfolios.

ArtTalk is a visually oriented program incorporating reproductions of master's works and student artworks. These examples enable students to expand their appreciation and understanding of various artists, works of art, and artistic styles. Each reproduction is discussed within the narrative portion of the text. The teaching captions and credit lines reinforce chapter content and can be used as effective learning tools.

Artwork for this edition has been carefully selected from museums and private collections throughout the world. Each work of art has been reproduced in a size large enough to be visually "read" by the reader. The artists who have been selected represent a variety of historical and cultural contexts.

The text is written in a friendly, informal style giving students practical information about art concepts without overloading them with theoretical concepts. This style gives students the confidence and skills they need to comfortably discuss works of art and critique their own works of art.

NARRATIVE LESSONS   Art concepts are presented and reinforced in accessible, easy-to-understand language, using relevant examples from art, from students' daily lives, or from history. Check Your Understanding provides a short review at the end of each lesson.

STUDIO ACTIVITY   Hands-on activities found in narrative lessons explore ways for students to quickly grasp ideas presented in the lessons. They are specifically designed to require minimal time and resources.

COMPUTER OPTION   Where appropriate, technology alternatives for Studio Activities are offered. They give students an opportunity to use the computer as an art tool, and learn how it can be used with traditional media and methods of creating art.

LESSON 1

What Is Art?

A work of art is the visual expression of an idea or experience created with skill. Visual art is more than paintings hanging on a wall. Visual art includes drawing, printmaking, sculpture, architecture, photography, filmmaking, crafts, graphic arts, industrial and commercial design, video, and computer arts.

Art Is Communication

When you talk to someone or write a letter, you communicate. You share your ideas and feelings by using words. You can also communicate through the arts. Art is a language that artists use to express ideas and feelings that everyday words cannot express. Through the arts, artists can convey ideas in ways that go beyond describing and telling. But in

order to understand the meaning of a work of art, you must do more than simply look at it with your eyes. In order to experience art fully, you must develop the ability to perceive. To look is to merely notice and label an object with a name such as "chair" or "house." To **perceive** *is to become deeply aware through the senses of the special nature of a visual object.* A perception is a sensation to which you attach a meaning. To understand and receive communication from a work of art you must train yourself to perceive.

The arts cross language barriers. You do not need to be able to speak English to perceive what Meyer Straus is expressing in his painting, *Bayou Teche* **(Figure 1.2).** If you concentrate on his image you can feel the humid atmosphere of the Louisiana swamps and hear

▲ **FIGURE 1.2**   Straus painted this bayou scene while working for the Academy of Music in New Orleans painting backdrops for major productions. He captured the feel of the bayou by including details such as the flowers in the foreground and the gray Spanish moss overwhelm them. What do the live oak trees. Look at the figures in the boat. The trees and swamp overwhelm them. What do you think the figures are doing? What atmosphere does the painting capture?

Meyer Straus. *Bayou Teche.* 1870. Oil on canvas. 76.2 × 152.4 cm (30 × 60″). Morris Museum of Art, Augusta, Georgia.

6   CHAPTER 1   Art in Your World

the mosquitoes buzzing. You can understand how it feels to be enclosed by branches dripping with Spanish moss. You can almost hear the water lapping at the boat.

Activity — Learning to Perceive

Applying Your Skills. Select an everyday object such as one that might be found in the classroom. Closely examine the object. Don't just look at it—turn it over, walk around it, touch it. Allow yourself two or three minutes to perceive the object. Then put the object where you can't see it and make a list of all the attributes of the object that you can think of. Then look at the object again and add at least three more attributes or characteristics to your list.

The Purposes of Art

People created art to record ideas and feelings long before they had written words. They used art then as we use it today. The following are some of the most common functions of art.

- **Personal Functions.** Artists create art to express personal feelings. Edvard Munch had a tragic childhood. His mother died when he was very young, and one of his sisters died when he was 14. His painting *The Sick Child* **(Figure 1.3),** shocked viewers who were used to seeing happy paintings with bright colors. The work was meant to remind viewers of personal family tragedies. Perhaps the artist wanted to tell them to appreciate what they had. Often people who have suffered a loss remind

others to live each day as if it were their last. That is what Munch is saying with his striking image.

- **Social Function.** Artists may produce art to reinforce and enhance the shared sense of identity of those in a family, community, or civilization (Figure 12.17, page 332). That is why many families commission or hire an artist or photographer to produce a family portrait. Art produced for this purpose also may be used in celebrations and displayed on festive occasions. Think of the many forms of visual art that might be seen in a parade—costumes, band uniforms, floats, and dances are all forms of visual art that might be included in the public celebration of a parade to commemorate an important holiday or event.

- **Spiritual Function.** Artists may create art to express spiritual beliefs about the destiny of life controlled by the force of a higher power. Art produced for this purpose may reinforce the shared beliefs of an individual or

▶ **FIGURE 1.3**   The child in the painting appears pale and calm. She is not looking at her mother. What is she staring at? Notice the exaggerated drooping of the woman's head. What has the artist done to focus your attention on the sick child?

Edvard Munch. *The Sick Child.* 1907. Oil on canvas. 118.7 × 121 cm (46¾ × 47⅝″). Tate Gallery. London, England.

LESSON 1   *What Is Art?*   7

THE STUDENT EDITION

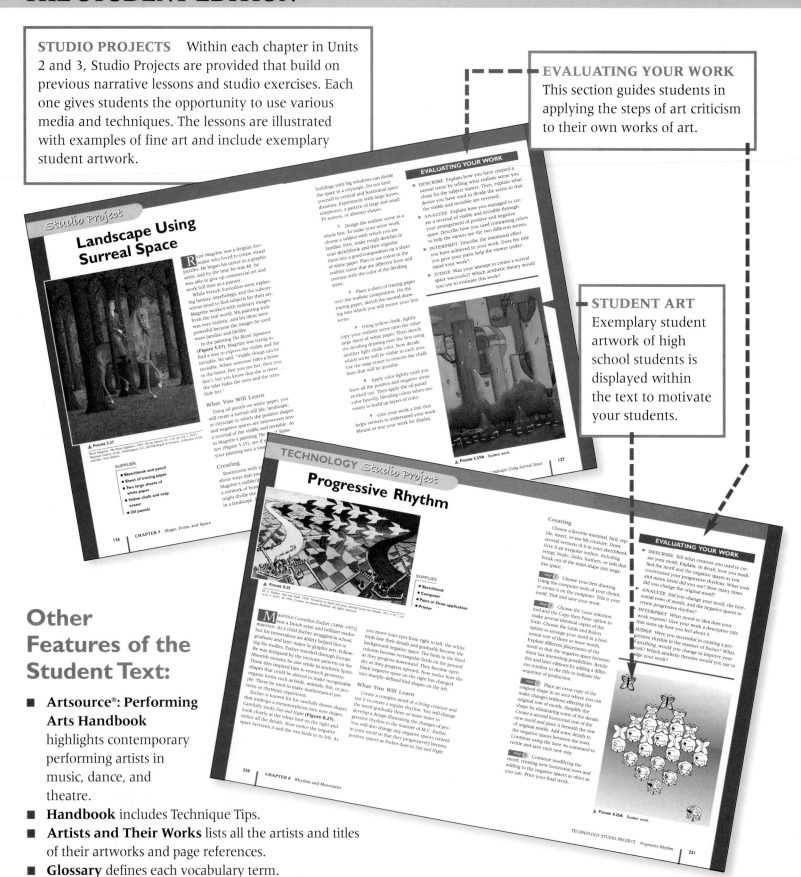

Other Features of the Student Text:

- **Artsource®: Performing Arts Handbook** highlights contemporary performing artists in music, dance, and theatre.
- **Handbook** includes Technique Tips.
- **Artists and Their Works** lists all the artists and titles of their artworks and page references.
- **Glossary** defines each vocabulary term.
- **Index** provides a study aid and assists students in finding particular topics.

Integrating the Performing Arts

The Artsource®: Performing Arts Handbook is an exciting new addition to *ArtTalk*. It features 14 artists or groups from the three fields of performing arts—dance, music, and theatre. The artists and groups are specifically chosen to correlate to the chapters in the book. Responding to the national direction for arts education to include an integration among the four arts disciplines—visual arts, music, drama, and theatre—*ArtTalk* provides this handbook as an opportunity for students to recognize and appreciate the connections that exist between the four arts disciplines. You are invited to use them as supplements to your lessons, or to have students work independently with the features as extension activities.

MUSIC

Vocalworks

Vocalworks. Bruce Cooper, Michael Geiger, Timand Debbie Reeder, and Dave Eastly perform "Vocalworks Radio Hour." Photo: Richard Hines, © 1998.

Since 1983, Bruce Cooper, Michael Geiger, Tim and Debbie Reeder, and Dave Eastly of Vocalworks have brought the music of the 1930s and 1940s to audiences throughout the United States and abroad. Singing the music of the swing era, they are proud to note that Vocalworks has lasted longer than the swing era itself. In the "Vocalworks Radio Hour," the group recreates a live radio broadcast from the period when home entertainment meant gathering around the radio in the living room to hear news, music, drama, or comedy programs. The Depression and World War II were very difficult times for the American people. They were concerned about their future and what would become of their country. Swing music was a wonderful escape that allowed people to lift their spirits and forget their troubles for awhile. Vocalworks shows the importance of music in that role and how it can still function in the same way today.

■ Discussion Questions
1. Improvisation is one of the characteristics of swing jazz. Look at the photo on this page. Identify the instruments. Which one is improvised?
2. Swing music was characterized by its positive message during the Depression in the 1930s and during World War II in the 1940s. Swing dance and music has had a resurgence today. How do you account for its renewed popularity?

■ Creative Expression Activities
LANGUAGE ARTS. Read about the Harlem Renaissance and its influence on jazz musicians and poets. Working in groups, present a choral verse reading of one of the following Langston Hughes poems to show how he was influenced by jazz: "The Weary Blues," "The Negro Speaks of Rivers," or "Afro-American Fragment."

SOCIAL STUDIES. Each of three groups will research one of the following periods: 1930–1935, 1936–1940, 1941–1945. Use the group period as a title and divide the paper into three sections: World, United States, and Swing Music. Group members should fil...

DANCE/MUSIC

Ballet Folklorico de Mexico

Amelia Hernández, director of Ballet Folklorico de Mexico, decided at the age of eight to make dance her life's work. Her parents made her dream possible, and her training and experiences inspired her artistic vision. For over 30 years she has researched the roots of Mexican folklore and traditions. Her intention has been to create a contemporary show based on Mexican themes, and to convey the heart and spirit of the Mexican people. From the time of the Olmec Indians to the birth of modern Mexico, more than thirty distinct cultures have influenced Mexican culture. The Spanish brought horses to Mexico and introduced the caballero, or rancher, lifestyle. The dance shown in this photo is called "Danza de la Reata" and celebrates the beauty and harmony of life on the ranchero, or Mexican ranch.

Ballet Folklorico de Mexico. "Danza de la Reata." Amalia Hernández, artistic director. Courtesy of Ballet Folklorico de Mexico.

■ Discussion Questions
1. Look closely at the photo of the male and female dancers inside the lariat, or lasso. Describe the costumes and what you think the dance is about.
2. What do you know about Mexican culture and dance? Can you think of any other styles of Mexican dance? Describe the costumes and movements.
3. What dances, songs, or paintings can you think of that refer to the work of a group of people, or to a specific culture?

■ Creative Expression Activities
LANGUAGE ARTS. Look at the photo on this page and use your imagination to write a description about what is taking place. Describe the relationship between the two people and the types of movements that would be done.

SOCIAL STUDIES. The Spanish brought horses and the Catholic religion to the indigenous people of Mexico and taught them a new way of life. The word "Mestizo" is used to refer to the unique blend of European and native cultures and races that make up the majority of the Mexican people of today. Research what other European cultures influenced the people of Mexico.

416 | *Performing Arts Handbook*

THEATRE

Faustwork Mask Theater

Faustwork Mask Theater. "The Mask Man." Robert Faust, artistic director. Photo: Craig Schwartz, © 1993.

Robert Faust is an actor, athlete, dancer, choreographer, mask-maker, and the artistic director of his company, Faustwork Mask Theater. Born and raised in New Orleans, he experienced the color and pageantry of the Mardi Gras celebration throughout his youth and college years. Through his studies he came to realize that the carnival characters that annually paraded the streets of his hometown were actually works of art rooted in theatrical traditions. His one-man show, "The Mask Man," provides insights into the artistic, psychological, and historical aspects of masks. In his performance, Faust transforms himself into more than 20 different characters. Some characters speak, wearing *commedia dell'arte* style half-masks. Other characters are created with full masks worn on top of the head or on the back of the head. These masks can transform the performer into creatures on all fours or create distortions that baffle or surprise. Masks, found in many cultures throughout the world, are worn at festivals, celebrations, and rituals. In whatever ways they are used, masks have the power to transform an ordinary person into someone or something else.

■ Discussion Questions
1. The photo on this page shows Robert Faust with masks from "The Mask Man." Study the expression of the masks. What kinds of personalities are being shown? What can you tell about the character's age, culture, and personality traits from the mask alone?
2. The first Greek masks were used in plays to impersonate gods. What Greek gods and goddesses can you name? What were their attributes or symbols?

■ Creative Expression Activities
LANGUAGE ARTS. Read Greek myths such as "Theseus and the Minotaur" or "The Golden Fleece." How might masks be used in these works?

ART. Create a two-sided mask showing contrasting feelings on each side. You might choose happy and sad or good and evil. Think of movements to go with your mask to express each emotion.

Performing Arts Handbook | 413

Cross-Curriculum Links

Your visual arts classroom comes to life with Connections features, new to this edition of *ArtTalk*. These self-contained pages weave the study of art with that of science, math, literature, and social studies.

You will find the Connections feature at the end of each chapter, just before the chapter review page. Use it as a culminating activity that will deepen students' understanding of the links between what they learn

in the art classroom with lessons and concepts from other curriculum areas. If your school encourages interdisciplinary teaching, this feature is a worthwhile place to invite a teacher from the featured curriculum area to team teach with you. Each feature concludes with a series of questions, as well as an extension activity.

Special Features

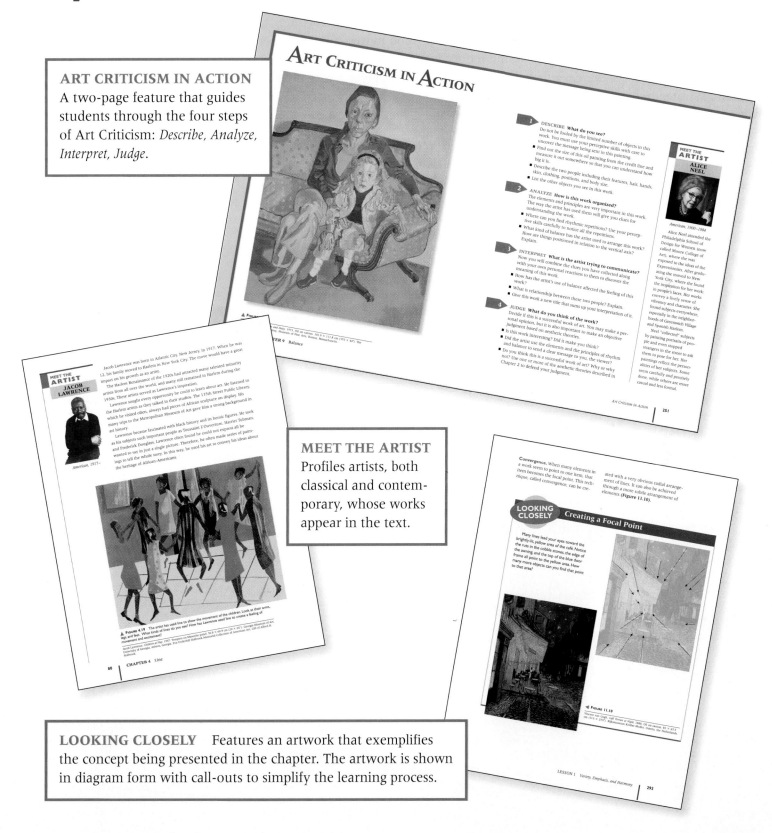

ART CRITICISM IN ACTION
A two-page feature that guides students through the four steps of Art Criticism: *Describe, Analyze, Interpret, Judge*.

MEET THE ARTIST
Profiles artists, both classical and contemporary, whose works appear in the text.

LOOKING CLOSELY Features an artwork that exemplifies the concept being presented in the chapter. The artwork is shown in diagram form with call-outs to simplify the learning process.

Support for the Art Teacher

The Teacher's Wraparound Edition provides complete lesson plans, teaching suggestions, supplemental information, cross-references, and more—all conveniently "wrapped" around every page of the reduced student text. Teachers will discover that the consistent, easy-to-follow lesson plan format gives a variety of teaching strategies to motivate students; to introduce, teach, and reinforce concepts; and alternative teaching strategies for adapting the program to your own teaching style and to the learning styles of your students.

CHAPTER OPENER includes the following:
- Chapter Scan
- Resource Cross-reference
- Artsource®: Performing Arts Handbook reference
- Chapter Overview
- Examining the Artwork
- National Standards for the Visual Arts correlation
- Featured Artists
- Developing a Portfolio

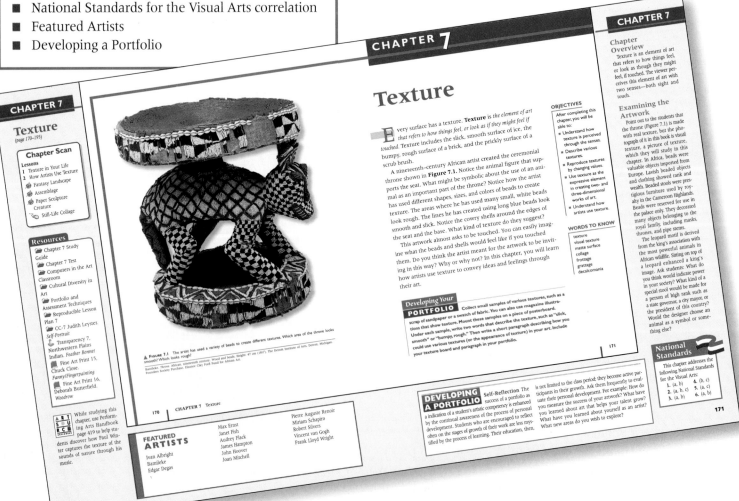

Organized with the Teacher in Mind

LESSON PLANS The teaching material follows a consistent, easy-to-use pattern. The complete lesson cycle—*Focus, Teach, Assess,* and *Close*—make it easy for you to plan a lesson.

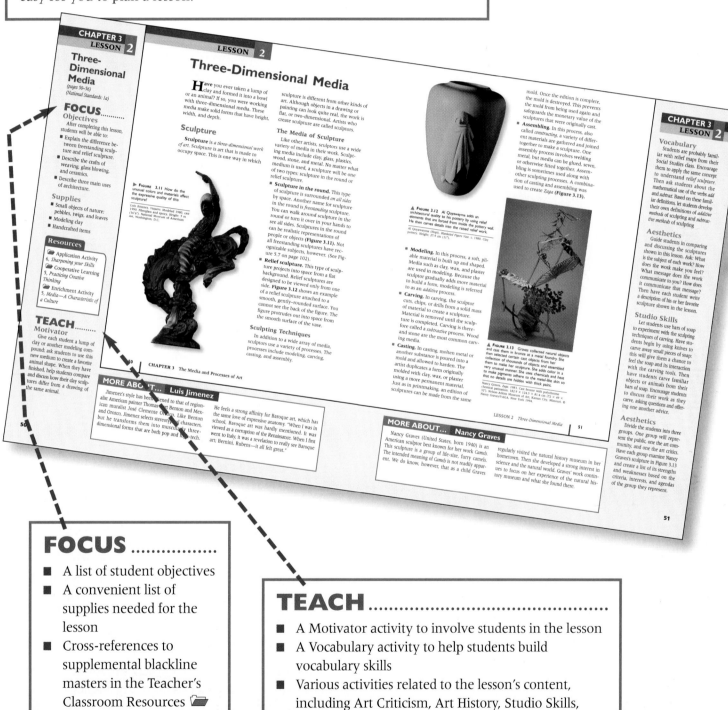

FOCUS ....

- A list of student objectives
- A convenient list of supplies needed for the lesson
- Cross-references to supplemental blackline masters in the Teacher's Classroom Resources 📁

TEACH ....

- A Motivator activity to involve students in the lesson
- A Vocabulary activity to help students build vocabulary skills
- Various activities related to the lesson's content, including Art Criticism, Art History, Studio Skills, Promoting Discussion, and Aesthetics

ASSESS

- Assessment techniques, including strategies for reteaching students who have difficulty mastering the important lesson concepts
- Extension activities designed for students who are able and willing to explore the content further

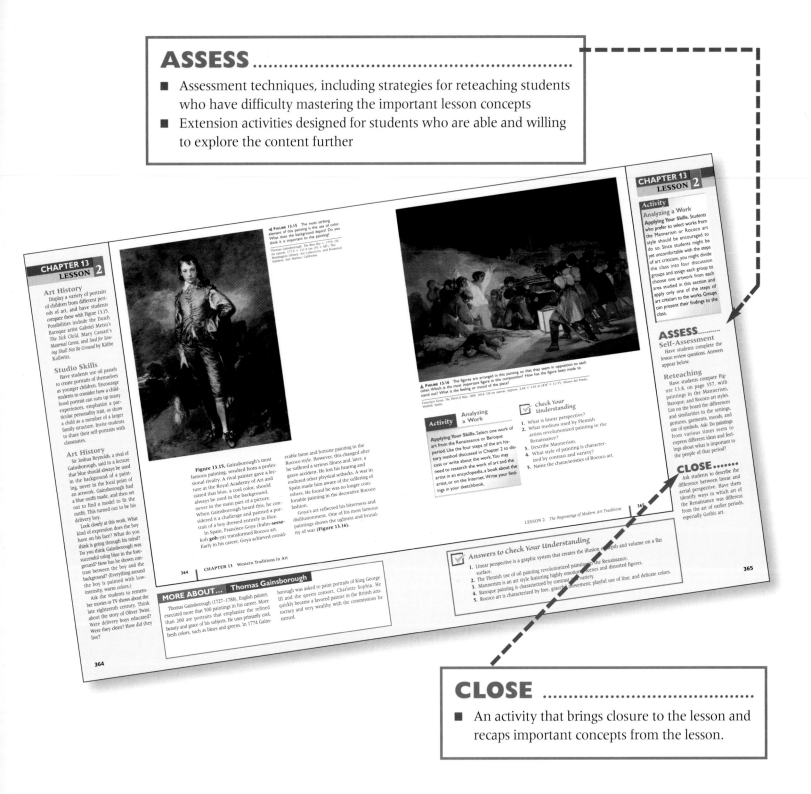

CLOSE

- An activity that brings closure to the lesson and recaps important concepts from the lesson.

As the core of the Teacher's Wraparound Edition, this lesson cycle provides you with complete suggestions for introducing each chapter and lesson and allows you to tailor the lesson to your own style and to the specific needs of your students.

SPECIAL BOXED FEATURES Stimulating and creative ideas to help you manage your classroom and help students recognize the presence of art all around them are available in three types of boxes set off from the lesson cycle. *Art on a Shoestring* provides suggestions for stretching your school's art budget. *Sparking Creativity* reminds students that the creative imagination can be expanded to new and exciting dimensions when they perceive and respond creatively. *Art in Everyday Life* demonstrates that art is the life experience touching every aspect of our existence.

MAKING ART ACCESSIBLE FOR ALL STUDENTS Teaching strategies in the *Cultural Diversity* and *Meeting Individual Needs* boxes incorporate cultural perspectives, strategies for special needs students, and strategies for addressing different learning styles.

BOTTOM COLUMN ANNOTATIONS Boxes at the bottom of the page give you additional information related to the content of the Student Text. This information supplements the core lesson plan by focusing on various areas of interest. The categories include:

- More About. . .
- Teacher Talk
- Curriculum Connection
- Meeting Individual Needs
- Technique Tips
- Safety Note
- Developing a Portfolio
- Technology Options
- Internet Connection
- Answers to Check Your Understanding

STUDIO ACTIVITY Each activity in the Student Text has a corresponding box in the Teacher's Wraparound Edition that provides alternative ways for students to address the hands-on activity.

INTERNET CONNECTION The Internet Connection, found at the bottom of the page, offer ways for teachers to access and make use of Glencoe's new Fine Arts Web site. Additionally, the feature offers strategies for implementing safe, educational Internet exploration in the classroom.

Art on a Shoestring

Ask students to bring in textured materials from home to complete the exercises in this chapter. You might prepare a list of suggested materials, which could include the following: aluminum foil, plastic wrap, wrapping paper, ribbons, wax paper, paper napkins, paper towels, tree bark, sandpaper, screening, foam plates, paper plates, loose sand (in a bag), scrap fabrics, gum wrappers, grasses, pine straw, and so on.

Sparking CREATIVITY

Want students to think creatively about shapes? Suggest this: Put a spoonful of cooking oil and a few drops of food coloring in a shallow dish of water. Use a stick to move the oil and watch the shapes it takes. Try putting small quantities of oil, water, and color in a sealed plastic bag and place it on an overhead projector. Gently move the bag and watch the projected shapes change.

Art in Everyday Life

To foster students' awareness of expressive shapes in everyday life, suggest this: Look for ways in which cultures that do not have a written language express ideas in the shapes of visual images, ritual, music, and dance. Native American totem poles tell whole family histories in symbolic animal forms. Designs on African warriors' shields warn their enemies of their power. Hopi Kachinas are used to teach Hopi children the rich stories of their heritage. The geometric shapes of Navajo woven blankets have symbolic meaning. The Inuit (Eskimo) sculptor holds the chunk of soapstone to his or her ear to let the spirit in it speak, then carves away just enough to let the spirit out.

MEETING INDIVIDUAL NEEDS

Visually Impaired For students who are blind, cut shapes from a stiff paper such as oak tag. Keep the outline simple. Students will then be able to feel the outline and form a mental image of the shape. The student can sort the different shapes into categories and then trace around them onto a foam meat tray which will leave an indented line. This tracing could then be printed to make greeting cards or note cards.

MORE ABOUT... Lost Wax Method

In the lost wax process, an exact model of the object to be produced is made in wax. Skillful modeling and scratching enable the artist to make works with fine surface details. After modeling, wax extensions called ther layers of increasingly coarse clay are added. The mold is heated. This fires the outer clay and melts the inner wax. When the wax is poured out it leaves an empty space which is filled by pouring in molten brass. [...] clay mold is broken, [...] the original wax model.

Time & Place — Sixteenth-Century Islamic Art

This scene from an Islamic manuscript was made in 1524-25. Some other events that happened in 1524:

Politics: Persia's Shah Ismail died and was succeeded by his ten-year-old son Tahmasp.

Social Studies: Chile peppers and cayenne from the Americas were introduced to India by the Portuguese and became staple ingredients in curry.

Curriculum Connection

Language Arts Just as the visual arts are concerned with shape and form, certain language arts are based on specific forms as well. For example, poetry has a long tradition of precision in its composition. The sonnet is always fourteen lines of iambic pentameter; the ballad is four lines of iambic verse alternating tetrameter and trimeter; the Spenserian stanza is eight lines of iambic pentameter followed by one of iambic hexameter. Free verse is unrhymed iambic pentameter; the haiku is based on exact syllable count. Often, students of literature are so familiar with poetic forms that they can identify the type of poem by looking at its shape on the printed page!

TECHNOLOGY OPTIONS

National Gallery of Art Videodisc Use the following to show examples of how artists use shape, form, and space.

Use Glencoe's *Correlation Bar Code Guide* to the National Gallery of Art to locate more artworks.

Jan Steen
The Dancing Couple

Search Frame 924

John Thomas Biggers
Starry Crown

Search Frame 5670

---

inter**NET** CONNECTION

ART ON THE WEB You and your students are invited to take a trip through Glencoe's Fine Arts Site on the World Wide Web. Your class can explore *Studio Cyberspace*, full of art activities: *Glencoe Student Galleria*, a changing showcase of student artworks; links to adventures through art museums, worldwide cultural treasures, and contact with other art teachers and classrooms. To reach the Glencoe Fine Arts page, visit us at: **http://www.glencoe.com/sec/art**

There you will also find a rich array of teacher resources waiting for you. Check the Internet Activity Booklet included with the ArtTalk program for more information.

The Teacher's Classroom Resources

A separate *ArtTalk* Teacher's Classroom Resources provides you with correlated supplemental materials. It contains a wealth of additional handouts, teaching strategies, and resource material designed for more effective teaching. You can choose the materials that complement the skill level, time framework, and interest level of your class. The Teacher's Classroom Resources is organized into individual booklets. These include:

APPLICATION ACTIVITIES worksheets make the teaching and application of aesthetics and art criticism meaningful and enjoyable. As aestheticians and art critics, students explore, theorize, and apply the principles learned in the text to practical solutions.

ARTIST'S PROFILES feature biographical information on over 40 master artists.

COMPUTERS IN THE ART CLASSROOM provides activities that reinforce the concepts of the chapter using the computer.

COOPERATIVE LEARNING ACTIVITIES promote team-work, cooperation, and responsibility. As students work in small groups or in teams of three or four, they help each other master skills, solve problems, and find creative solutions. In this type of classroom environment students are encouraged to share ideas, interpret material, and cooperate to help each other learn.

CULTURAL DIVERSITY IN ART worksheets are presented for each chapter to help students celebrate cultural diversity and understand various global views.

ENRICHMENT ACTIVITIES expand and extend the information presented in the student edition.

REPRODUCIBLE MASTER provides supplementary material for your students. They can be used to create an overhead transparency master, which visually reinforces information, or they can be used as blackline masters and distributed as handouts to students.

REPRODUCIBLE LESSON PLANS provide an easy-to-use checklist format.

RETEACHING ACTIVITIES include both concept maps and study guides.

STUDIO ACTIVITIES offer a variety of activities that help students develop and practice art production skills. These field-tested activities can be used in place of, or in addition to, the studio projects in the Student Text.

TESTING PROGRAM AND ALTERNATIVE ASSESSMENT provides a chapter and unit testing program.

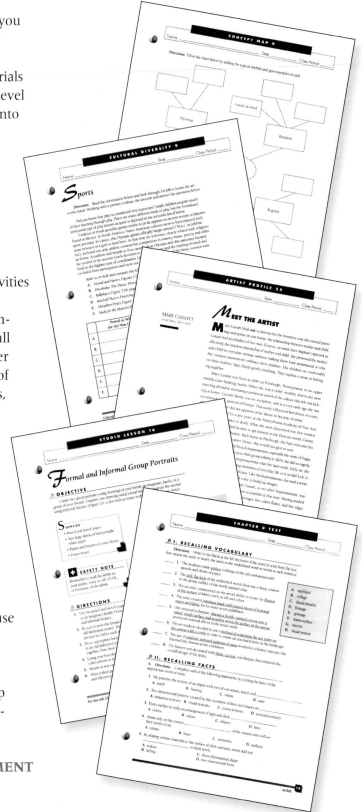

Portfolio and Assessment Techniques

All subject areas recognize the importance of measuring individual student performance in attaining specified goals and objectives. A booklet titled *Portfolio and Assessment Techniques* is designed to address basic information used in portfolio assessment for visual art. Why is portfolio assessment important? Portfolio assessment provides

- Tangible evidence of anticipated student outcomes
- Contextual information on student growth as an artist
- An opportunity for students to reflect on their work, acknowledge their accomplishments, and evaluate personal artistic goals
- Consistency and objectivity in the evaluation process for the instructor.

Fine Art Transparency Package

The ready-to-use overhead color transparency package contains 32 full-color fine art overhead transparencies. Accompanying the transparencies is an Instructor's Guide with background information and student activity sheets to assist the teacher in guiding discussion, all in a convenient 3-ring binder.

Fine Art Print Package

Twenty quality art masterpieces are printed on sturdy self-supporting stock to supplement the artwork appearing in the student text. The laminated prints are resistant to wear and are presented in a durable portfolio for convenient classroom use and storage. This package includes an Instructor's Guide with a page for teaching strategies and a student worksheet.

Media and Technology Support

National Gallery of Art Videodisc

This full-length videodisc features 1,645 artworks from the National Gallery of Art collection, along with a tour of the gallery. Glencoe has published a separate *Correlation Bar Code Guide to the National Gallery of Art* for your convenience, including 300 artworks from the entire videodisc collection. For your convenience, selected bar codes are reprinted in the Teacher's Wraparound Edition that correlate to lesson contents. The videodisc is available on loan free of charge by
contacting: Department of Education Resources
Extension Programs Section, Education Division
National Gallery of Art
Washington, D.C. 20565

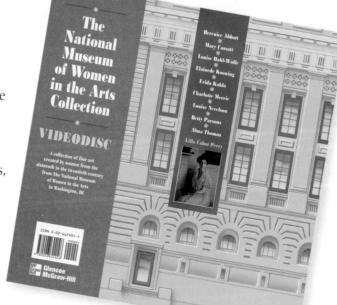

The National Museum of Women in the Arts CD-ROM and Videodisc

This videodisc of 200 art works from the collection of The National Museum of Women in the Arts includes a video introduction to the museum itself. The videodisc includes a 24-page bar code guide for all images. The CD-ROM provides multi-media access and activities for the 200 works, including an assessment tool to test students' knowledge of artist, time, location, media, and subject.

ArtTalk and the Performing Arts

This new performing arts package provides a multi-media resource for further exploration of artists and groups within the three performing arts areas—dance, music, and theatre. The units within the package supplement the Artsource®: Performing Arts Handbook in the Student Text, and include an Instructor's Guide that provides additional information about each artist and group and their performances. The media package includes both video and audiocassettes.

Pacing Chart

To assist with the planning and development of your individual course, this Pacing Chart is included in this section. These are only intended as suggested guidelines. Individual teachers will need to make necessary adjustments and modifications as required by their local, state, and national curriculum guidelines, and by the ability level and learning styles of their students.

		Total Days	9 wk 45 days	18 wk 90 days	36 wk 180 days
Chapter 1	**Art in Your World**				
Lesson 1	What Is Art?		1	1	1
Lesson 2	Why Do Artists Create?		1	1	1
Lesson 3	The Language of Art		1	1	1
		Total	3	3	3
Chapter 2	**Art Criticism and Aesthetic Judgment**				
Lesson 1	Art Criticism: Learning from a Work of Art		½	1	2
Lesson 2	Aesthetics: Thinking about A Work of Art		½	1	2
Lesson 3	Art History: Learning about A Work of Art		1	1	1
		Total	2	3	5
Chapter 3	**The Media and Processes of Art**				
Lesson 1	Two-Dimensional Media		1	1	2
Lesson 2	Three-Dimensional Media		1	1	2
Lesson 3	Technological Media		1	1	2
		Total	3	3	6
Chapter 4	**Line**				
Lesson 1	The Element of Line		1	1	1
Lesson 2	The Expressive Qualities Of Line		1	2	2
Studio Projects:	Contour Wire Sculpture		1	1	2
	Imagination Landscape		0	1	2
	Drawing Expressing Movement		0	1	2
	Expressive Line Design		0	0	0
		Total	3	6	9
Chapter 5	**Shape, Form, and Space**				
Lesson 1	Shapes and Forms		½	1	1
Lesson 2	Space		½	1	1
Lesson 3	How We Perceive Shape, Form, and Space		½	1	2
Lesson 4	How Artists Create Shapes and Forms in Space		½	1	2
Lesson 5	What Different Spaces, Shapes, and Forms Express		1	2	2
Studio Projects:	Drawing an Outdoor Scene		1	2	3
	Clay Plaque with High Relief		0	2	5
	Landscape Using Surreal Space		0	0	3
	One-Point Perspective Drawing		0	0	3
		Total	4	10	22
Chapter 6	**Color**				
Lesson 1	The Properties of Color		1	1	2
Lesson 2	Color Schemes		1	1	2
Lesson 3	Understanding the Nature and Uses Of Color		1	1	2
Studio Projects	Photo Collage and Mixed Media		1	2	3
	Photo Enlargement		0	2	3
	Using Color to Create an Expressive Statement		0	1	3
	Expressive Portrait		0	0	3
		Total	4	8	18
Chapter 7	**Texture**				
Lesson 1	Texture in Your Life		1	1	1
Lesson 2	How Artists Use Texture		1	1	1
Studio Projects:	Fantasy Landscape		1	1	2
	Assemblage		0	2	3
	Paper Sculpture Creature		0	1	3
	Still-Life Collage		0	1	3
		Total	3	7	13

PACING CHART

		Total Days	9 wk 45 days	18 wk 90 days	36 wk 180 days
Chapter 8	**Rhythm and Movement**				
Lesson 1	Rhythm and Repetition		½	1	1
Lesson 2	Types of Rhythm		½	1	1
Lesson 3	How Artists Use Rhythm to Create Movement		1	1	2
Studio Projects:	Painting with a Rhythmic Activity		0	2	2
	A Pattern Collage		0	2	3
	Coil Baskets		0	3	5
	Progressive Rhythm		0	2	3
		Total	2	12	17
Chapter 9	**Balance**				
Lesson 1	Visual Balance		1	1	1
Lesson 2	Natural Balance		1	1	1
Lesson 3	The Expressive Qualities of Balance		1	1	2
Studio Projects	Formal Portrait		2	2	3
	Informal Group Portrait		0	3	3
	Linoleum Print Using Radial Balance		0	4	5
	Invent an Inside View of a Machine		0	0	3
		Total	5	12	18
Chapter 10	**Proportion**				
Lesson 1	The Golden Mean		1	1	2
Lesson 2	Scale		1	1	2
Lesson 3	How Artists Use Proportion and Distortion		1	1	2
Studio Projects	Storyteller Figure		1	2	2
	Papier-Mâché Mask		0	3	4
	Soft Sculpture		0	2	4
	Hybrid Creature		0	0	2
		Total	4	10	18
Chapter 11	**Variety, Emphasis, Harmony, and Unity**				
Lesson 1	Variety, Emphasis, and Harmony		½	1	1
Lesson 2	Unity		½	1	1
Studio Projects	Assemblage with Handmade Paper		1	2	4
	Clay Sculpture Unifying Two Ideas		0	0	4
	Designing a Mural		0	0	5
	School Web Page Design		0	2	3
		Total	2	6	18
Chapter 12	**Art Traditions from Around the World**				
Lesson 1	Art of Earliest Times		1	1	3
Lesson 2	Art of Asia and the Middle East		1	1	4
Lesson 3	The Art of Africa		1	1	4
Lesson 4	Art of the Americas		1	1	4
		Total	4	4	15
Chapter 13	**Western Traditions in Art**				
Lesson 1	The Beginnings of Western Art Tradition		½	½	2
Lesson 2	The Beginnings of Modern Art Traditions		½	½	3
Lesson 3	The Nineteenth Century		1	1	3
Lesson 4	Early Twentieth Century		1	1	3
Lesson 5	Art After 1945		1	1	3
		Total	4	4	14
Chapter 14	**Careers in Art**				
Lesson 1	Careers in Business and Industry		1	1	2
Lesson 2	Environmental and Education Careers		1	1	2
		Total	2	2	4

National Standards for the Visual Arts

The National Standards for Art Education represents, in part, the results of a 2-year effort by the Consortium of National Arts Education Associations to set standards for arts education in the United States. These six standards listed below are designed specifically for students in grades 9–12.

1. **Content Standard:** Understanding and applying media, techniques, and processes
Achievement Standard, Proficient:
Students
a. apply media, techniques, and processes with sufficient skill, confidence, and sensitivity that their intentions are carried out in their artworks.
b. conceive and create works of visual art that demonstrate an understanding of how the communication of their ideas relates to the media, techniques, and processes they use.
Achievement Standard, Advanced:
c. communicate ideas regularly at a high level of effectiveness in at least one visual arts medium.
d. initiate, define, and solve challenging visual arts problems independently using intellectual skills such as analysis, synthesis, and evaluation.

2. **Content Standard:** Using knowledge of structures and functions
Achievement Standard, Proficient:
Students
a. demonstrate the ability to form and defend judgments about the characteristics and structures to accomplish commercial, personal, communal, or other purposes of art.
b. evaluate the effectiveness of artworks in terms of organizational structures and functions.
c. create artworks that use organizational principles and functions to solve specific visual arts problems.
Achievement Standard, Advanced:
d. demonstrate the ability to compare two or more perspectives about the use of organizational principles and functions in artwork and to defend personal evaluations of these perspectives.
e. create multiple solutions to specific visual arts problems that demonstrate competence in producing effective relationships between structural choices and artistic functions.

3. **Content Standard:** Choosing and evaluating a range of subject matter, symbols, and ideas
Achievement Standard, Proficient:
Students
a. reflect on how artworks differ visually, spatially, temporally, and functionally, and describe how these are related to history and culture.
b. apply subjects, symbols, and ideas in their artworks and use the skills gained to solve problems in daily life.
Achievement Standard, Advanced:
c. describe the origins of specific images and ideas and explain why they are of value in their artwork and in the work of others.
d. evaluate and defend the validity of sources for content and the manner in which subject matter, symbols, and images are used in the students' works and in significant works by others.

4. **Content Standard:** Understanding the visual arts in relation to history and cultures
Achievement Standard:
Students
a. differentiate among a variety of historical and cultural contexts in terms of characteristics and purposes of works of art.
b. describe the function and explore the meaning of specific art objects within varied cultures, times, and places.
c. analyze relationships of works of art to one another in terms of history, aesthetics, and culture, justifying conclusions made in the analysis and using such conclusions to inform their own art making.
Achievement Standard, Advanced:
d. analyze and interpret artworks for relationships among form, context, purposes, and critical models, showing understanding of the work of critics, historians, aestheticians, and artists.
e. analyze common characteristics of visual arts evident across time and among culture/ethnic groups to formulate analyses, evaluations, and interpretations of meaning.

5. **Content Standard:** Reflecting upon and assessing the characteristics and merits of their work and the work of others
Achievement Standard, Proficient:
Students
a. identify intentions of those creating artworks, explore the implications of various purposes, and justify their analyses of purposes in particular works.
b. describe meanings of artworks by analyzing how specific works are created and how they relate to historical and cultural contexts.
c. reflect analytically on various interpretations as a means for understanding and evaluating works of visual arts.
Achievement Standard, Advanced:
d. correlate responses to works of visual arts with various techniques for communicating meanings, ideas, attitudes, views, and intentions.

6. **Content Standard:** Making connections between visual arts and other disciplines
Achievement Standard, Proficient:
Students
a. compare the materials, technologies, media, and processes of the visual arts with those of other arts disciplines as they are used in creation and types of analysis.
b. compare characteristics of visual arts within a particular historical period or style with ideas, issues, or themes in the humanities or sciences.
Achievement Standard, Advanced:
c. synthesize the creative and anlytical principles and techniques of the visual arts and selected other art disciplines, the humanities, or the sciences.

(1), (2), (3) etc. = Lessons; (R) = Chapter Review; (SP) = Studio Project; (AC) = Art Criticism in Action; (CC) = Curriculum Connections	Chapter 1 Art in Your World	Chapter 2 Art Criticism and Aesthetic Judgment
NATIONAL STANDARDS FOR THE VISUAL ARTS	**2.** (b) **4.** (b) **6.** (a, b) **3.** (a) **5.** (a, c)	**2.** (a, b) **4.** (a, c) **6.** (a, b) **3.** (a, c) **5.** (a, b, c)
ARTISTIC PERCEPTION	Understanding art as communication (1) Perceiving art defined (1) Activity: Learning to Perceive (1) Artist defined (2) Comparing Picasso's, Velazquez's art (2) Subject, composition, content defined (3) Non-objective art defined (3) Activity: Credit line information (3) Art Criticism in Action (AC)	Art criticism defined (1) Value of studying art criticism (1) Identifying steps of art criticism (1) Using aesthetics to think about art (2) Combining aesthetic theories (2) Identifying purpose of art history (3) Individual style defined (3) Art Criticism in Action (AC)
CREATIVE EXPRESSION	Purposes of sketchbook (2) Activity: Keeping a Sketchbook (2) Activity: Create a Symbol (3)	
HISTORICAL/CULTURAL CONTEXT	Identifying five purposes of art (1) Meet the Artist: Grant Wood (2) Recognizing influence of past artists (2) Credit line defined (3) Meet the Artist: Marc Chagall (3)	Meet the Artist: Georgia O'Keeffe (1) Identifying steps of art history (3) Die Brucke defined (3) Meet the Artist: Faith Ringgold (3)
AESTHETIC VALUING	Understanding why artists create (2)	Using art criticism (1) Aesthetic qualities defined (2) Activity: Classifying Aesthetic Theories (2) Judging own artwork (2)
ELEMENTS AND PRINCIPLES OF ART	Use of color, van Gogh (1) Understanding elements, principles (3) Symbol defined (3) Elements and principles of art defined (3)	Line, color, texture in painting (1, 2)
ART FORMS	Painting (1, 2, 3) Pottery (1) Silkscreening (1)	Painting (1, 2, 3)
MEDIA, TOOLS, TECHNIQUES, AND PROCESSES	Artistic innovation—Pollock (2)	
CURRICULUM AND PERFORMING ARTS CONNECTIONS	Connections: Social Studies (CC) Artsource®: Dance (R)	Connections: Language Arts (CC) Artsource®: Dance (R)
CAREERS/PORTFOLIOS	Portfolio idea (1)	Portfolio idea (1)

Chapter 3 The Media and Processes of Art	Chapter 4 Line	Chapter 5 Shape, Form, and Space
1. (a, b) 5. (a, b, c) 2. (a, b) 6. (a, b)	1. (a, b, c) 3. (a, b, c) 5. (b, c) 2. (a, b, c) 4. (b, c) 6. (a, b)	1. (a, b, c) 3. (a, b, c) 5. (b, c) 2. (a, b, c) 4. (b, c) 6. (a, b)
Two-dimensional media introduced (1) Understanding effect of media, processes on art (1) Using sketchbooks (1) Identifying qualities of drawing, painting media (1) Recognizing printmaking steps (1) Three-dimensional media introduced (2)	Dimension defined (1) Understanding relation of line and value (1) Looking Closely: Line types, variations (2) Understanding expressive qualities of line (2)	Identifying expressive qualities of geometric and free-form shapes (1) Expressive qualities of positive, negative space (2) Understanding perception (3) Understanding illusion of depth (4) Perspective, vanishing point defined (4) Looking Closely: Identifying perspective techniques (4) Expressive qualities of space, shape, form (5)
Activity: Watercolor experiments (1) Activity: Making a printing plate (1) Activity: Assembling (2) Activity: Redesigning a building (2) Activity: Comparing media (3)	Activity: Identifying lines; creating varied lines; using line for value (1) Activity: Using lines expressively; contour lines; gesture drawing; calligraphic lines (2) Studio Projects: Contour Sculpture; Imagination Landscape; Expressing Movement Technology Studio: Expressive Line Design	Activity: Experimenting with space (2) Activity: Shape, point of view (3) Activity: Shading; creating depth (4) Activity: Active and static shapes (5) Studio Projects: Outdoor Scene; Clay Plaque; Landscape with Surreal Space Technology Studio: Perspective Drawing (5)
Meet the Artist: Winslow Homer (1) Origins of crafts (2) Technological innovations create new media (3) History of photography (3) History of filmmaking (3) Meet the Artist: Miriam Schapiro (3)	Meet the Artist: Jacob Lawrence (2) Meet the Artist: David Malangi (2)	Meet the Artist: M. C. Escher (2) Meet the Artist: Christo (5)
Effects of shading techniques (1) Effects of painting media (1) Crafts, fine art, applied art defined (2) Art Criticism in Action (AC)	Evaluating Your Work (SP) Art Criticism in Action (AC)	Evaluating Your Work (SP) Art Criticism in Action (AC)
Line, shape, form in drawing (1) Line defined (1)	Line introduced (1) Recognizing kinds of lines (1) Variation of line appearance (1) Line movement (2)	Relationship of space, form, shape (1) Positive, negative space defined (2) Natural and manufactured shapes (4) Qualities of outline, surface, and density (5)
Drawing, Painting, Printmaking (1) Crafts (2) Architecture (2) Photography, film, video (3)	Drawing (1, 2) Calligraphy (2) Sculpture (2) Painting (2)	Painting (1, 3, 4, 5) Drawing (1, 4, 5) Sculpture (1, 2, 3, 5) Printmaking, Architecture (2) Crafts (5)
Drawing, painting, and printmaking (1) Sculpting media and techniques (2) Processes of crafts (2) Innovations in architecture (2) Photography, film, video, and computer (3)	Media, tools affect line (1) Crosshatching defined (1) Contour line defined (2) Gesture drawing defined (2) Computer media (2)	Freestanding, bas (low) relief, high relief defined (2) Holograms defined (2) Chiaroscuro defined (4) Techniques used to create perspective (4)
Connections: Science (CC) Artsource®: Dance (R)	Connections: Social Studies (CC) Artsource®: Dance (R)	Connections: Math (CC) ArtSource®: Dance (R)
Portfolio idea (1)	Portfolio idea (1)	Portfolio idea (1)

ARTTALK SCOPE AND SEQUENCE

(1), (2), (3) etc. = Lessons; (R) = Chapter Review; (SP) = Studio Project; (AC) = Art Criticism in Action; (CC) = Curriculum Connections	Chapter 6 Color	Chapter 7 Texture
NATIONAL STANDARDS FOR THE VISUAL ARTS	1. (a, b, c) 3. (a, b, c) 5. (b, c) 2. (a, b, c) 4. (b, c) 6. (a, b)	1. (a, b, c) 3. (a, b, c) 5. (b, c) 2. (a, b, c) 4. (b, c) 6. (a, b)
ARTISTIC PERCEPTION	Recognizing expressive qualities of color (1, 3) Color spectrum, color wheel defined (1) Afterimage defined (1) Identifying expressive qualities of value (1) Color schemes introduced (2) Understanding expressive qualities of color schemes (2) Understanding purpose of color (3) Looking Closely: Value and movement (3)	Perceiving texture (1) Understanding texture choices (1) Looking Closely: Visual texture combinations (1) Understanding how artists use texture (2)
CREATIVE EXPRESSION	Activity: Making a color wheel; creating value; using intensity (1) Activity: Using color schemes (2) Activity: Mixing colors; using colors for effect (3) Studio Projects: Photo Collage and Mixed Media; Photo Enlargement; Using Color Expressively Technology Studio Project: Expressive Portrait (3)	Activity: Creating textures (1) Activity: Contrasting textures (1) Activity: Inventing textures (2) Studio Projects: Fantasy Landscape; Assemblage (2); Paper Sculpture (2) Technology Studio Project: Collage (2)
HISTORICAL/CULTURAL CONTEXT	Meet the Artist: Elizabeth Murray (3) History of pigment (3) Impressionist use of color (3) Meet the Artist: Romare Bearden (3)	Meet the Artist: Edgar Degas (2) Meet the Artist: Audrey Flack (2)
AESTHETIC VALUING	Evaluating Your Work (SP) Art Criticism in Action (AC)	Evaluating Your Work (SP) Art Criticism in Action (AC)
ELEMENTS AND PRINCIPLES OF ART	Properties of color (1) Hue, value, intensity introduced (1) Primary, secondary, intermediate hue defined (1) Tint, shade defined (1) Intensity, high and low key, defined (1) Monochromatic, analogous, complementary colors defined (2) Primary triads, split complements, warm and cool colors defined (2) Optical, arbitrary color defined (3)	Texture defined (1) Visual texture, simulated and invented, defined (1) Relationship of texture and value (1) Rough, smooth, matte, shiny textures introduced (1) Color, value create texture (2) Using real texture in painting (2) Texture in three-dimensional art (2)
ART FORMS	Painting (1, 2, 3) Crafts (2, 3) Mixed media (3) Multi-media (3)	Crafts (1, 2) Painting (1, 2) Collage (2) Architecture (2) Sculpture (2)
MEDIA, TOOLS, TECHNIQUES, AND PROCESSES	Pigment, dye, binder, solvent defined (3) Qualities of painting media (3) Computer media (3)	Assemblage (2) Found objects, natural objects (2) Bronze casting (2) Craft techniques create texture (2)
CURRICULUM AND PERFORMING ARTS CONNECTIONS	Connections: Science (CC) ArtSource®: Storytelling (R)	Connections: History (CC) Artsource®: Music (R)
CAREERS/PORTFOLIOS	Portfolio idea (1)	Portfolio idea (1)

Chapter 8 Rhythm and Movement	Chapter 9 Balance	Chapter 10 Proportion
1. (a, b, c) 3. (a, b, c) 5. (b, c) 2. (a, b, c) 4. (b, c) 6. (a, b)	1. (a, b, c) 3. (a, b, c) 5. (b, c) 2. (a, b, c) 4. (b, c) 6. (a, b)	1. (a, b, c) 3. (a, b, c) 5. (b, c) 2. (a, b, c) 4. (b, c) 6. (a, b)
Understanding rhythm, movement (1) Looking Closely: Rhythm creates movement (1) Recognizing types of rhythm (2) Expressive qualities of rhythm (2) Understanding how rhythm creates movement (3)	Recognizing expressive qualities of symmetry (1) Understanding qualities of natural balance (2) Effects of art elements on balance (2) Expressive qualities of balance (3) Looking Closely: Formal balance (3) Thinking Critically about Art (R)	Recognizing harmony, beauty of proportion (1) Understanding relationship of Golden Mean to human body (1) Looking Closely: Golden Mean organizes painting (1) Expressive qualities of scale (2) Foreshortening defined (2) Understanding how artists use proportion, exaggeration, and distortion (3)
Activity: Motif and pattern (1) Activity: Random rhythm; alternating rhythm; progressive rhythm (2) Studio Projects: Painting with a Rhythmic Activity; Pattern Collage; Coil Basket Technology Studio Project: Progressive Rhythm (3)	Activity: Using symmetry; creating radial balance (1) Activity: Using informal balance (2) Activity: Identifying balance (3) Studio Projects: Formal Portrait; Informal Group Portrait; Radial Balance Technology Studio Project: Invent an Inside View of a Machine	Activity: Experiment with scale; human proportions; drawing a head (2) Activity: Distorting proportion (3) Studio Projects: Storyteller Figure; Papier–Mâché Mask; Soft Sculpture Technology Studio Project: Hybrid Creature
Meet the Artist: Rosa Bonheur (1) Futurists capture movement (3) Meet the Artist: George Bellows (3)	Meet the Artist: Diego Rivera (1) Meet the Artist: Alice Neel (3)	History of proportion (1) Meet the Artist: Pablo Picasso (3) Meet the Artist: Isabel Bishop (3)
Evaluating Your Work (SP) Art Criticism in Action (AC)	Evaluating Your Work (SP) Art Criticism in Action (AC)	Evaluating Your Work (SP) Art Criticism in Action (AC)
Rhythm, visual rhythm defined (1) Repetition, motif, module, pattern introduced (1) Random, regular, alternating, flowing, progressive rhythm introduced (2) Visual movement defined (3)	Balance introduced (1) Relationship of axis to balance (1) Symmetry, approximate symmetry introduced (1) Radial balance in nature, architecture (1) Informal balance (asymmetry) defined (2) Identifying factors that influence visual weight (2) Balance organizes composition (3)	Proportion, Golden Mean defined (1) Organizing artwork using Golden Mean/proportion (1) Scale defined (2) Hierarchical, symbolic proportion introduced (2) Understanding proportions of human body, human head (2) Distorting proportion (2) Exaggeration, distortion defined (3)
Drawing and Painting (1, 2, 3) Photography (1) Crafts (1, 2, 3) Architecture (2) Sculpture (2, 3)	Painting (1, 2, 3) Architecture (1, 3) Crafts (1) Stained glass (2) Printmaking (2, 3)	Painting (1, 2, 3) Sculpture (2, 3) Architecture (2) Drawing (2, 3) Mixed media and Crafts (3)
Kinetic sculpture (mobile) (3) Computer media (3) Rhythm in other arts (1)	Computer media (3)	Drawing human proportions (2) Creating a clay sculpture (SP) Papier–Mâché Mask (SP) Soft Sculpture (SP)
Connection: Dance (CC) Artsource®: Dance (R)	Connections: Language Arts (CC) Artsource®: Theatre (R)	Connection: Math (CC) Artsource®: Theatre (R)
Portfolio idea (1)	Portfolio idea (1)	Portfolio idea (1)

(1), (2), (3) etc. = Lessons; (R) = Chapter Review; (SP) = Studio Project; (AC) = Art Criticism in Action; (CC) = Curriculum Connections	Chapter 11 Variety, Emphasis, Harmony, and Unity	Chapter 12 Art Traditions from Around the World
NATIONAL STANDARDS FOR THE VISUAL ARTS	1. (a, b, c) 3. (a, b, c) 5. (b, c) 2. (a, b, c) 4. (b, c) 6. (a, b)	3. (a, b) 5. (a, b, c) 6. (a, b) 4. (a, b, c)
ARTISTIC PERCEPTION	Recognizing variety adds interest (1) Understanding use of emphasis (1) Looking Closely: Creating focal point (1) Identifying how harmony is achieved (1) Understanding how artists create unity with variety, emphasis, harmony (2)	Recognizing symbolism (1, 3, 4) Identifying purpose of art, architecture (1, 3) Interpreting Indian sculpture, architecture (2) Recognizing how culture affects subject matter (2, 3) Recognizing pre-Columbian contributions (4)
CREATIVE EXPRESSION	Activity: Variety and contrast; using emphasis (1) Activity: Creating unity (2) Studio Projects: Assemblage; Clay Sculpture; Designing a Mural Technology Studio Project: Web Page Design	Activity: Creating a writing system (1) Activity: Constructing a mask (3) Activity: Sketching an event (4)
HISTORICAL/CULTURAL CONTEXT	Meet the Artist: Allan Houser (2) Meet the Artist: Henri Rousseau (2)	Mesopotamian culture described (1) Ancient Egyptian life introduced (1) Understanding Indian culture (1, 2) Chinese culture introduced (1, 2) Meet the Artist: Andö Hiroshige (2) Identifying influence of Islam (2) Recognizing African cultural traditions (3) Pre-Columbian defined (4) Native American cultural traditions (4) Meet the Artists: Persian Artists of Islam (4)
AESTHETIC VALUING	Evaluating Your Work (SP) Art Criticism in Action (AC)	Ceremonial uses of art (3) Identifying Inuit picture writing (4) Interpreting ceremonial masks (4) Art Criticism in Action (AC)
ELEMENTS AND PRINCIPLES OF ART	Variety, emphasis, harmony, unity introduced (1) Value of contrast (1) Focal point defined (1) Unity defined (2)	Harmony, balance in sculpture (3) Color, principles of art in crafts (4)
ART FORMS	Architecture (1, 2) Crafts (1, 2) Painting (1, 2) Sculpture (2)	Architecture (1, 2, 3, 4) Painting (1, 2, 4) Sculpture (1, 2, 3, 4) Crafts (2, 3, 4) Printmaking (2)
MEDIA, TOOLS, TECHNIQUES, AND PROCESSES	Assemblage (2) Computer media (2)	Scroll defined (2) Woodblock printing (2) Jewelry, metalworking (3) Assemblage, natural fibers (3, 4) Clay modeling and Weaving (4)
CURRICULUM AND PERFORMING ARTS CONNECTIONS	Connection: Theatre (CC) Artsource®: Music (R)	Connection: Social Studies (CC) Artsource®: Music, Dance (R)
CAREERS/PORTFOLIOS	Portfolio idea (1)	Portfolio idea (1)

Chapter 13 Western Traditions in Art	Chapter 14 Careers in Art
3. (a, b) **5.** (a, b, c) **6.** (a, b) **4.** (a, b, c)	**5.** (a, b, c) **6.** (a, b)
Understanding contributions of Greek, Roman art, artists (1) Recognizing Gothic style (1) Plurality of art styles since 1945 (5) Twentieth-century artistic trends (5)	Logos defined (1) Skills needed for art-related careers (2)
Activity: Gothic style (1) Activity: Analyzing style (3)	Activity: Critiquing animation (1) Activity: Using design for display (2)

Western art, culture introduced (1)
Identifying the Middle Ages (1)
Byzantine and Renaissance art (1)
Meet the Artist: Michelangelo Buonarroti (2)
Contributions of women artists (2)
Baroque and Rococo defined (2)
Neoclassic, Romantic, and Realism (3)
Impressionism, Post-Impressionism (3)
Twentieth-century art styles (4)
Meet the Artist: Leonardo da Vinci (5)
	Art careers introduced (1)
	Graphic designer, Illustrator, Web artist, Product/package designer,
	    Fashion designer, Animator, Special effects designer, Art director,
	    Computer, arcade, video game designer (1)
	Multimedia designer (1)
	Urban planner, Architect (2)
	Meet the Artist: I.M. Pei (2)
	Art teacher, Art therapist, Museum curator and designer,
	    fine artist (2)

Harmony, proportion in Greek art (1) Influence of photography on art (3) Aesthetics of Expressionism, Cubism, Surrealism (4) Non-objective art (4, 5) Art Criticism in Action (AC)	Critiquing industrial design (1) Understanding environmental planning, development (2) Art Criticism in Action (AC)
Colors, line in Byzantine art (1) Light, shape, color in Impressionism (3) Harmony, form in architecture (4) Color, shape, design in Pop art (5) Space in Color-field painting (5)	Artistic design in art-related careers (1) Layout in graphic design (1)
Printmaking (1) Architecture (1, 4, 5) Sculpture (1, 2, 4) Painting (2, 3, 4, 5) Photography (3)	Painting and drawing (1, 2) Photography, film, video (1, 2) Mixed media (1, 2) Multimedia (1, 2) Architecture (2)
	Technology in art-related careers (1) Storyboard defined (1)
Connection: Language Arts (CC) Artsource®: Dance (R)	Connection: Technology (CC) Artsource®: Storyboard art (R)
Portfolio ideas (1)	Portfolio idea (1)

(1), (2), (3) etc. = Lessons; (R) = Chapter Review; (SP) = Studio Project; (AC) = Art Criticism in Action; (CC) = Curriculum Connections	Handbook
NATIONAL STANDARDS FOR THE VISUAL ARTS	**6.** (a, b)
ARTISTIC PERCEPTION	Discussion Questions (pp. 413, 414, 415, 416, 417, 418, 419, 420, 421, 422, 424, 425)
HISTORICAL/CULTURAL CONTEXT	Faustwork Mask Theater (p. 413) Martha Graham (p. 414) Merce Cunningham Dance Company (p. 415) Ballet Folklorico de Mexico (p. 416) Lewitzky Dance Company (p. 417) Joanna Featherstone (p. 418) Paul Winter (p. 419) African American Dance Ensemble (p. 420) Eth-Noh-Tec (p. 421) Eugene Friesen (p. 422) Vocalworks (p. 423) Korean Classical Music and Dance Company (p. 424) Kurt Jooss (p. 425) John Ramirez (p. 426)
AESTHETIC VALUING	Discussion Questions (pp. 414, 415, 416, 420, 425, 426)
ELEMENTS AND PRINCIPLES OF ART	Discussion Questions (p. 417)
CURRICULUM AND PERFORMING ARTS CONNECTIONS	Theatre (pp. 413, 418, 421, 425) Dance (pp. 414, 415, 416, 417, 420, 424) Music (pp. 416, 419, 420, 422, 423, 424, 426) Creative Expression Activities: Language Arts (pp. 413, 416, 418, 419, 420, 422, 423, 425, 426) Art (pp. 413426) Science (pp. 414, 417) Technology (p. 415) Social Studies (pp. 415, 416, 419, 421, 423, 424) Theatre/Movement (p. 417) Dance (pp. 417, 424) History (pp. 420, 421)

Safety in the Art Classroom

Art teachers and their students are often in contact with potentially harmful materials, although many may be totally unaware of the danger. Lead poisoning, cancer, nervous system disorders, anemia, silicosis, chemical pneumonia, asthma, dermatitis—all of these as well as others are recognized as industrial diseases caused by hazardous chemicals. However, many fail to recognize that these same diseases are found among artists, craftspeople, theater technicians, teachers, and students using art and craft materials without adequate precautions.

Although studies have been conducted and the findings published, many teachers remain unaware that toxic substances may be in some of the art materials they use routinely in their teaching. Other teachers, aware of the problem, feel that they are exercising adequate precautions by referring to the labels on the art products they use.

Labeling of Art Materials

The labeling of art materials continues to be limited in many ways. Ingredients that caused laboratory animals to perish within two weeks after a single dose was administered were identified as "acutely toxic" and must bear a warning label. However, if fewer than half the animals die, the product may be labeled "nontoxic." In addition, when products are imported or repackaged, the hazards may not be listed or properly described on the label.

Teachers should be aware of the fact that the Federal Hazardous Substances Act and other legislation introduced at the federal level, have not been entirely successful at rectifying problems of this kind. Some worrisome inadequacies persist.

Industry Safety Standards

Not to be overlooked is the fact that the art-materials industry has, for many years, supported the use of voluntary safety standards. These standards have been developed with the cooperation and input of various manufacturers. The Art and Craft Materials Institute (ACMI) has for some time adhered to a voluntary program designed to ensure the safety of younger students working with art materials. Most art teachers are familiar with the two ACMI safety labels—AP indicating Approved Product, and CP specifying Certified Product. These labels certify that the products on which they are placed have been found to contain no ingredients in sufficient quantities to be toxic or harmful to users. In addition, products bearing a CP seal abide by certain quality standards pertaining to workmanship, working qualities, and color.

While the AP/CP seal applies to art products intended for use by younger students, a Certified Label (CL) is used to identify products considered to be more appropriate for older students and adults. The CL seal on a label indicates that the product's ingredients have been examined by toxicologists. The label lists any safety precautions required by law and by labeling standards developed by the American Society of Testing and Materials. Teachers are advised to read and adhere to the safety precautions listed on these labels.

Material Safety Data Sheets and Their Use

Teachers should realize that they may request a Material Safety Data Sheet (MSDS) from manufacturers pertaining to any art products they are unsure of. Among the items included on the MSDS are a listing of all the ingredients for which industrial standards exist, health-hazard information, fire-hazard data, and the chemicals with which the product might react dangerously.

In most school systems, central ordering procedures are—or should be—developed as a means of ensuring that all art materials entering the school are approved by appropriate authorities (for example, the Health Department or Board of Education). Requiring Material Safety Data Sheets from suppliers as a condition of purchase should effectively eliminate many of the toxic materials that might otherwise be brought into the classrooms by unsuspecting teachers.

Protection from Exposure

Considerable protection from exposure to toxic materials can be achieved by promoting good hygiene in the classroom. Safe storage and proper labeling of art and craft supplies, keeping dust to a minimum by damp mopping rather than sweeping, and thorough cleanup after use of art and craft materials will help prevent toxic exposures. Personal hygiene also plays a role in the prevention of potentially harmful exposures. Students should refrain from eating or drinking while engaged in art projects, and they should wash their hands thoroughly when finished. Another general safety practice is to ensure proper ventilation in the art classroom so that contaminants may be diluted and eventually removed from the air. Exposure to hazardous dusts and fumes will be minimized if the instructor premixes dry materials with water (for example, tempera, wheat paste, and so forth) and fires ceramic products when students are away from the kiln area. If an art material has been transferred to an unlabeled container and its identity is unknown, it should be disposed of. For specific information on the proper disposal of art and craft materials, please contact your local county health department. (From the California Department of Education Program Advisory # CIL: 94(95-01).

Safety Precautions for Students

In order for a chemical in an art material to harm a student, it must first come into contact with or enter the body. Teachers should be aware of the following three ways in which this can occur.

SKIN CONTACT. Some chemicals such as those used in etching, or solvents like lacquer and paint thinners, can irritate the skin on contact and result in a variety of skin problems. Other chemicals, known as sensitizers, can cause skin allergies. Examples of these sensitizers include formaldehyde found in some color photography solutions, turpentine, epoxy glues and resins, nickel and chromium compounds, and many tropical woods.

However, the danger with regard to skin contact does not end here. Many toxic chemicals do not just damage the skin itself. They can also be absorbed through the skin into the bloodstream where they can affect other organs. Examples include methyl alcohol found in some shellacs, toluene found in lacquer thinners and silk screen inks, and glycol ethers found in photoetching materials.

INHALATION. Dusts, powders, vapors, gases, aerosols, and other airborne substances may be readily inhaled and, therefore, represent a health hazard. Examples include solvent vapors from paints, inks, and thinners; spray mists from air brush or aerosol spray cans; gases from photographic baths; pottery kiln firing; metal fumes from soldering, welding, and metal casting; and dusts from dyes and pigments, pottery glazes, and woodworking. Some of the chemicals in these materials can result in lung damage from inhalation while others can be absorbed into the bloodstream, where they can lead to a variety of problems including lead poisoning, nerve damage, and kidney damage.

INGESTION. Ingestion is of particular concern with younger students who are inclined to experiment and put things in their mouths. However, ingestion of hazardous substances can occur in the case of older students as well. These students can be affected if they eat, drink, or apply make-up in a classroom where art materials can contaminate these items.

Precautions in Selecting and Using Art Materials

Although some products on the market are labeled "nontoxic," they should not be purchased for use by students in grades K-6 unless assurance is obtained from the manufacturer. A major reason for this is that the product may have been tested for acute toxicity only. Chronic hazards, cancer-causing potential, and other sensitivities are not included in acute toxicity testing. The "nontoxic" label can thus be misleading, and products identified with such labels should not always be regarded as safe for use by children.

There are certain safety precautions that all teachers should take when selecting art materials for use in their classrooms. Included in these precautions are the following:

■ Make certain that the materials obtained for younger students (age 12 or under) have an AP or CP seal of approval; materials secured for use by older students should have a CL seal.

- Incorporate into the art curriculum written information on the potential hazards of art materials and techniques; students should be tested on this information just as they are tested with regard to other aspects of curriculum content. Documentation of this type of instruction should be made and filed.

- Carefully supervise students in the classroom, making certain that safety rules are understood and observed. Teachers must also remember to obey these safety rules themselves in order to impress upon their students the seriousness of these regulations. Students should never be allowed to work in the classroom, during or after school hours, without direct teacher supervision.

- Avoid using solvents or products containing solvents in the art room. These include turpentine, lacquer, shellac, paint thinner, rubber cement, and rubber cement thinner, permanent markers, and solvent-based inks such as silk-screen printing ink.

- Do not use acids, alkalies, or bleaches.

- Do not use aerosol spray cans in the classroom, since the inhalation of the spray mist can cause injury to lung tissue.

- Use dust-causing products with care in a well-ventilated area. This precaution applies to the use of pastels, chalks, plaster and clays in dry form, copper enamels, glazes, papier-mâché mixtures, and powdered tempera paints.

- Place kilns in a separate room, outdoors, or if this is not possible, in an out-of-the-way part of the room where students are not likely to come into contact with them when they are in operation. In addition, all kilns should have local exhaust ventilation.

- Remember that good ventilation is an absolute necessity whenever using any art or craft material.

- Be prepared for emergencies by having written emergency procedures prepared, posted, and explained to students. This includes fire-drill procedures and the use of fire extinguishers.

- Report all accidents, even minor ones such as a small cut. Illnesses suspected of being related to art materials should be reported in writing to the school principal or other designated authority at once so that an investigation can be conducted and corrective action determined.

A 1992 bulletin from the Consumer Product Safety Commission stated that art materials with any warning labels whatever are not suitable for use by students in grade 6 and under. These students cannot be expected to understand the hazards of toxic substances or to carry out precautions effectively or consistently. A teacher must "childproof" the art room to prevent either intentional or unintentional access to toxic materials or dangerous machinery.

At the beginning of each school year or new term, teachers are urged to determine if any of their students are asthmatic, visually impaired, hearing impaired, or on prescribed medication. If asthmatic students are enrolled in the art class, they should not be exposed to dusts, fumes, or vapors because of their breathing difficulties. Visually impaired students understandably operate very close to their art work and, as a consequence, are more likely to inhale harmful dusts, vapors, and fumes. Students with hearing impairments should not be exposed to activities requiring loud hammering or noisy machinery, because this can aggravate their condition. If students are found to be on medication, the teacher should seek their physician's advice regarding the potentially harmful interaction between their prescribed medicine and the art materials they might use in class.

Similar precautions are recommended in situations involving students who are physically handicapped in other ways or who may be learning disabled or emotionally disturbed. These students are at an even greater risk from toxic materials and require special care and attention. In some instances, they might not be able to use the same materials and processes as other students. Careful evaluation is needed in each case to determine what special precautions might be necessary.

Clearly, the need to direct time and effort to safeguarding the health and safety of students in the art classroom is essential. Art teachers, aware of their responsibilities in this regard, recognize that assistance may be needed. In order to properly inform and train their students, teachers need specially tailored hazard communication (HAZCOM) training. The curriculum must include formal health and safety training at levels far above the basic information required by the law. This is not only proper, it provides an opportunity for the school to develop training materials for which there is a demand.

Steps to Incorporate Training into Your Program

First find out which law applies to you. There are state and federal HAZCOM laws and they differ somewhat in their requirements. Ask your employer, but do not stop there! Call your Department of Labor's Occupational Safety and Health Department to be absolutely sure whose jurisdiction you are under. Ask for a copy of the law and any additional free materials they may have.

Learning the Rules

1. Spend a few moments looking at the HAZCOM file. If you do not know where this file is kept, ask your school administrator. OSHA requires employers to include the file's location in HAZCOM training.
2. Look at the condition of the file. OSHA requires that it is organized and easy to read. Included in the file should be:
   a. A written program telling how the school will comply (including names of parties responsible for each compliance activity).
   b. A survey of all the potentially toxic substances in the school and their locations.
   c. An organized collection of material safety data sheets (MSDSs) on these substances.
   d. A record of training sessions, which usually includes dates of training, lists of participants, qualifications of trainers, results of quizzes given, and so on.

3. Check your classroom/shop.
   a. Are there any containers that do not have the following information:
      • identity of the substance (must be the same as on the MSDS)
      • hazard warnings, if needed
      • name and address of the manufacturer (required for transport)
   b. If children grade 6 and under ever have access to your classroom/shop, be sure there are no materials with warnings on them of any kind, no sharp tools, and no hazardous equipment. Look under sinks, in drawers, and so on. Children's classrooms, like homes, must be childproofed.
   c. Be sure you have a dilution ventilation system separate from the ventilation in the rest of the school if you work with solvents or solvent-containing products, black-and-white photo developing, resin casting, or any other process requiring it.
   d. Be sure you have local ventilation systems (e.g. spray booth, and flexible ducts) for any process that puts substances into the air such as spraying, air brushing, machine sawing, sanding, soldering, welding, mixing clay or glazes, and so on.

REMEMBER: No amount of training will make up for teaching without the proper safety equipment. If you cannot demonstrate a process with all proper precautions, safety equipment and ventilation, eliminate the project from the curriculum. Don't ever let students see you violate safety rules or the law.

ARTTALK

THIRD EDITION

Rosalind Ragans, Ph.D.
Associate Professor Emerita
Georgia Southern University

Glencoe
McGraw-Hill

New York, New York   Columbus, Ohio   Woodland Hills, California   Peoria, Illinois

About the Author

Rosalind Ragans

Rosalind Ragans is the author of Glencoe's senior high school art text, *ArtTalk*. She served as senior author on the elementary program *Art Connections* for the SRA division of McGraw-Hill, and was one of the authors of Glencoe's middle school/junior high art series, *Introducing Art, Exploring Art,* and *Understanding Art*. She received a B.F.A. at Hunter College, CUNY, New York, and earned a M.Ed. in Elementary Education at Georgia Southern University and Ph.D. in Art Education at the University of Georgia. Dr. Ragans was named National Art Educator of the Year for 1992.

About Artsource®

 The materials provided in the *Performing Arts Handbook* are excerpted from *Artsource®: The Music Center Study Guide to the Performing Arts*, a project of the Music Center Education Division. The Music Center of Los Angeles County, the largest performing arts center in the western United States, established the Music Center Education Division in 1979 to provide opportunities for lifelong learning in the arts, and especially to bring the performing and visual arts into the classroom. The Education Division believes the arts enhance the quality of life for all people, but are crucial to the development of every child.

Cover/Title Page Credit:

Cover Photo by Kazu Okutomi/theStockRep

Glencoe/McGraw-Hill

A Division of The **McGraw·Hill** Companies

Printed in the United States of America.

Send all inquiries to:
Glencoe/McGraw-Hill
21600 Oxnard Street, Suite 500
Woodland Hills, California 91367

ISBN 0-02-662434-6 (Student Edition)

1 2 3 4 5 6 7 8 9   004/043   06 05 04 03 02 01 00

Editorial Consultants

Cris E. Guenter, Ed.D.
Specialist, Portfolio and Assessment
Professer, Fine Arts/Curriculum and Instruction
California State University, Chico
Chico, CA

Holle Humphries
Assistant Professor
The University of Texas at Austin
Austin, TX

Faye Scannell
Specialist, Technology
Bellevue Public Schools
Bellevue, WA

Contributors/Reviewers

Lea Burke
Art Instructor
Bartleville High School
Bartleville, OK

Patricia Carter
Assistant Professor of Art Education
Georgia Southern University
Statesboro, GA

Randy Hayward Jolly
Art Instructor
Warren Central High School
Vicksburg, MS

Audrey Komroy
Art Instructor
Akron High School
Akron, NY

Jack Schriber
Supervisor of Fine Arts
Evansville-Vanderburgh School Corporation
Evansville, IN

Nancy Shake
Art Instructor
Center Grove High School
Indianapolis, IN

Steve Thompson
Visual Art Instructor
Henry County Middle School
McDonough, GA

Performing Arts Handbook Contributors

Joan Boyett
Executive Director
Music Center Education Division
The Music Center of Los Angeles County

Susan Cambigue-Tracey
Project Coordinator

Melinda Williams
Concept Originator and Project Director

Arts Discipline Writers:
Dance — Susan Cambigue-Tracey
        Diana Cummins
        Carole Valleskey
Music — Ed Barguiarena
        Rosemarie Cook-Glover
        Connie Hood
Theatre — Barbara Leonard

Studio Lesson Consultants

Acknowledgements: The author wishes to express her gratitude to the following art coordinators, teachers, and specialists who participated in the field test of the Studio Projects with their students.

Donna Banning
El Modena High School
Orange, CA

Karen Nichols
Reseda High School
Reseda, CA

Barbara Cox
Glencliff Comprehensive High School
Nashville, TN

Roberta Sajda
Klein Forest High School
Houston, TX

Audrey Komroy
Akron High School
Akron, NY

Faye Scannell
Bellevue Public Schools
Bellevue, WA

David Long
Akron High School
Akron, NY

David Sebring
Dobson High School
Mesa, AZ

Student Contributors

The following students contributed exemplary works for Studio Projects and Technology Studio Projects.

Figure 4.29a, Julia Stout, Dobson High School, Mesa, AZ; Figure 4.32a, Xenia Nosov, International School, Bellevue, WA; Figure 5.36a, Victoria Purcell, Glencliff Comprehensive High School, Nashville, TN; Figure 5.38a, Alex Penescu, Reseda High School, Reseda, CA; Figure 6.35a, Mike Nachtrieb, Akron High School, Akron, NY; Figure 7.19a, Binyam Jimma and Jacob Egler, International School, Bellevue, WA; Figure 8.22a, Ruben Garcia, Reseda High School, Reseda, CA; Figure 8.25a, Reed Hague and Myia Bloomfield, International School, Bellevue, WA; Figure 9.25a, Danielle Gupton, Klein Forest High School, Houston, TX; Figure 9.26a, Nena Guin, Glencliff Comprehensive High School, Nashville, TN; Figure 9.28a, Kyoko Kurasawa, International School, Bellevue, WA; Figure 10.30a, LeaAndrea Glover, Klein Forest High School, Houston, TX; Figure 10.31a, Sarah Rosenfeld, International School, Bellevue, WA; Figure 11.26a, Kristen Bruyere, Akron High School, Akron, NY.

TABLE OF CONTENTS

Credit line on Page 6.

UNIT 1   THE WORLD OF ART

Credit line on Page 26.

Credit line on Page 51.

UNIT 2   THE ELEMENTS OF ART

Credit line on Page 80.

 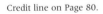

Credit line on Page 107.

Credit line on Page 136.

Credit line on Page 174.

UNIT 3   THE PRINCIPLES OF ART

Credit line on Page 209.

Credit line on Page 230.

Credit line on Page 270.

Credit line on Page 292.

UNIT 4 ART THROUGH THE AGES

Credit line on Page 324.

Credit line on Page 358.

Credit line on Page 402.

UNIT 5 HANDBOOKS

A R T
S O U
R C

FEATURES

Art Criticism in Action

CONNECTIONS

Activities

Listing of Studio Projects by Media

I

THE WORLD OF ART

Unit Overview

Learning about the language of visual art is a key to understanding, appreciating, and creating works of art. In Unit 1, students are introduced to the elements and principles of art, to the steps of art criticism and art history, and to the media and processes used to create works of art.

CHAPTER 1—Art in Your World

In chapter 1, students will sharpen their perceptual skills while learning more about the language of art. They will identify sources of inspiration that artists might use to get ideas and they will be introduced to the elements and principles art.

CHAPTER 2—Art Criticism and Aesthetic Judgment

Chapter 2 helps students analyze and evaluate artworks based on aesthetic qualities and the steps of art criticism—*describe, analyze, interpret,* and *judge.* They also learn about the art history operations.

CHAPTER 3—Media and Processes of Art

In chapter 3, students learn about the various media and processes used to create works of art and create their own artworks using several media.

Unit Resources

📁 Artist's Profile 36, Georgia O'Keeffe

📙 Print 1, Faith Ringgold. *The Church Picnic Story Quilt.*

📁 Unit 1 Test

📁 Portfolio and Assessment Techniques

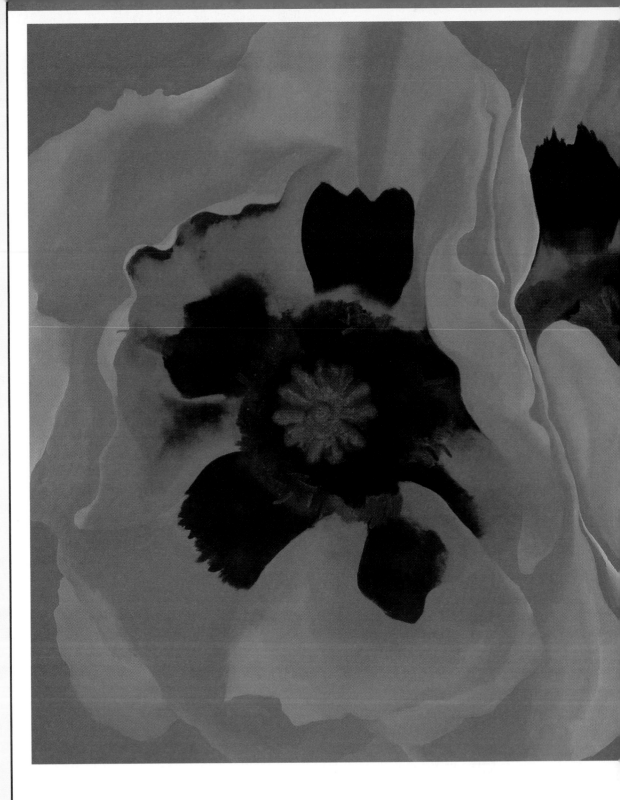

2

MORE ABOUT... Georgia O'Keeffe

Georgia O'Keeffe is famous for her paintings of parched bones and flowers. She forced viewers to take a new and different look at everyday objects. Have students experiment with O'Keeffe's style by choosing an object that is ordinary. Examine the lines, shapes, and details of the object so that it fills the paper. Instruct them to pay particular attention to the elements of line, space, texture, and shape. Also, remind them to consider how they will arrange the shape to create a pleasing balance. Have them display their finished artworks.

THE WORLD OF ART

"So I said to myself—
I'll paint what I see—
what a flower is to me
but I'll paint it big and
they will be surprised
into taking time to look at
it—I will make even
busy New Yorkers take
time to see what I see
of flowers."

Georgia O'Keeffe
1887–1986

◄

Georgia O'Keeffe. *Oriental Poppies*. 1927. Oil
on canvas. 76.2 × 101.9 cm (30 × 40⅛")
University Art Museum, University of
Minnesota, Minneapolis.

3

Introducing the Unit

Ask students to go through the artworks in Chapters 1 through 3 and ask them to choose their favorite artwork. Have them discuss their preference and give reasons to support their choices.

Unit Motivator

Ask students to brainstorm terms that are synonymous with *artist* and to record their responses on the board in the form of a word web. For example, if students call out painter, circle the term and ask: What types of tools does this artist use?

Discussing the "Quotation"

Ask students to describe their usual reaction to flowers and discuss what new appreciation is possible after viewing O'Keeffe's flowers. Have students note the formal devices she uses to attempt to change our perception of flowers. (Answers should include how she frames her subject and fills the canvas completely; uses intense, contrasting colors; and emphasizes petals as abstract forms.)

National Museum of Women in the Arts

You may wish to use the National Museum of Women in the Arts videodisc and/or CD-ROM. The videodisc features a bar code guide.

interNET CONNECTION **CURRICULUM LINKS** Explore World Wide Web links related to the content of each chapter of *ArtTalk*. These preselected links can be found under Curriculum Links in the Teacher Resources section of Glencoe's Fine Arts Site. Find the chapter you are studying in the Table of Contents and click on one of the highlighted or underlined "hot links" that will transport you to an appropriate, previewed site guaranteed to expand your students' experience. Many of these sites offer views of extensive art collections from museums and art galleries. Cultural connections will link students to Internet sites around the world. Visit us at: **www.glencoe.com/sec/art**

Art in Your World

(pages 4–23)

Resources

📁 Application Activity 1

📁 Artist's Profile 28, Vincent van Gogh

📁 Chapter 1 Study Guide

📁 Chapter 1 Test

📁 Computers in the Art Classroom

📁 Cultural Diversity in Art

📁 Portfolio and Assessment Techniques

📁 Reproducible Lesson Plan 1

🎮 Transparency CC-1, Norman Rockwell. *Triple Self-Portrait.*

🎮 Transparency 1, Antonio Ruiz. *The Bicycle Race.*

📕 Fine Art Print 2, Dong Kingman. *Skaters in New York.*

 While studying the chapter, use the Performing Arts Handbook page 413 to help students discover other alternative art forms of dance, music, and theatre.

▲ **FIGURE 1.1** Notice how the artist has used color to connect the houses to the environment. See if you can find the same blues in the houses, on the road, and in the sky. The bright colors and strokes of paint indicate that the houses are full of life. The curved strokes of paint connect the person, plants, and clouds.

Vincent van Gogh. *Houses at Auvers.* 1890. Oil on canvas. 75.5 × 61.8 cm (29¾ × 24⅜″). Courtesy, Museum of Fine Arts, Boston, Massachusetts. Bequest of John T. Spaulding.

4   **CHAPTER 1**   Art in Your World

FEATURED ARTISTS

Romare Bearden
Roger Brown
Pieter Bruegel
Marc Chagall

Janet I. Fish
Hans Holbein
George Inness
Edvard Munch
Gabriele Münter
Pablo Picasso
Jackson Pollock

Meyer Straus
Leo Twiggs
Vincent van Gogh
Diego Velàzquez
Vigil Family
Grant Wood
Yup'ik

Art in Your World

The urge to create art has been with people throughout history. The visual arts satisfy human needs for celebration, personal expression, and communication. We use the visual arts to enhance our environment, to express our deepest feelings about life, and to record events.

Art tells us about places we may never go and people we might never know. Vincent van Gogh painted *Houses at Auvers* **(Figure 1.1)** more than 100 years ago. He painted more than the colors he saw; he selected colors that expressed how he *felt*. He applied paint in short, layered strokes to create a sense of movement. Van Gogh's choices of color and his use of texture in the painting seem to visually echo his intention to replicate his love for the spirit and energy of nature.

The painting tells a story that you can understand if you look closely, even though the landscape and objects in it might be unfamiliar to you. What unusual shapes and colors do you notice? What ideas or feelings do you think the artist was attempting to express by using these colors?

Developing Your PORTFOLIO

Most people have opinions about what makes an artwork successful and they have reasons why they like certain works of art. List your favorite works of art. Provide the title of the artwork and the name of the artist. Then describe why you like the artwork and what meaning it has for you. Include your list in your portfolio.

OBJECTIVES

After completing this chapter, you will be able to:

- Explain what is meant by *perceive*.
- Understand the purposes of art.
- Name sources of ideas that artists might use for inspiration.
- Identify the elements and principles of art.
- Identify the subject, composition, and content in a work of art.

WORDS TO LEARN

perceive
artists
symbol
elements of art
principles of art
subject
nonobjective art
composition
content
credit line
medium

Chapter Overview

In Chapter 1, students sharpen their perceptual skills while learning more about the definitions of art and artists. They learn some of the reasons or functions of creating art and identify sources of inspiration for artists. This helps students become better artists. In this chapter, they will learn there is a language of art. This language is a visual one, and communication is accomplished through the successful use of the elements and principles of art.

Examining the Artwork

Ask students to study Figure 1.1 and identify the unusual colors. Have them notice the bright yellow road and have them point to the figure on the road. Tell them it must have been painted while the under paints were still wet because you can see how the blue of the road, the green of the grass, and the brown of the building were picked up with the brushstrokes of black for the skirt and white for the shirt. Ask students to count the different kinds of greens and browns that are brushed into the thatched roof. Point out that all these colors look as if they have not been mixed on the palette before Vincent van Gogh applied them with brushstrokes of thick paint to the canvas.

National Standards

This chapter addresses the following National Standards for the Visual Arts:

- **2.** (b)   **5.** (a, c)
- **3.** (a)   **6.** (a, b)
- **4.** (b, c)

5

DEVELOPING A PORTFOLIO

Choosing a Project Tell students that a portfolio should exhibit strong, confident examples of their work. Typically, evaluators would rather see fewer competent works than many that are mediocre and would call into question the student's overall ability. However, a diversity of artistic skill is also critical, so they must learn to balance both objectives. Encourage students to approach each assignment throughout the course as a potential project for their portfolios and as a method of isolating their strengths and weaknesses. Then students can concentrate on improvement in those areas that are weaker while continuing to develop the stronger ones.

What Is Art?

FOCUS............

Objectives

After completing this lesson, students will be able to:

- Explain what is meant by *perceive*.
- Identify the purposes of art.

Supplies

- Large photograph or reproduction of an artwork
- Drawing paper, pencil
- Everyday objects

Resources

📁 Cooperative Learning 1, *Designing a Classroom Gallery*
📁 Enrichment Activity 1, *Developing Your Portfolio*

TEACH..........

Motivator

Briefly display a large photograph or reproduction of an artwork. Then cover it and let students discuss what they saw. Display the artwork again and leave it in view as students continue to discuss it. Ask: How does looking closely help you understand what is in this artwork? What purposes do you think the artist had in creating the artwork?

Vocabulary

Tell students that the prefix *per* means "thoroughly" and *–ceive* means to "take in." Ask: How might the meaning apply to the art experience? *(They learn to enjoy and understand art by looking closely.)*

What Is Art?

A **work** of art is the visual expression of an idea or experience created with skill. Visual art is more than paintings hanging on a wall. Visual art includes drawing, printmaking, sculpture, architecture, photography, filmmaking, crafts, graphic arts, industrial and commercial design, video, and computer arts.

Art Is Communication

When you talk to someone or write a letter, you communicate. You share your ideas and feelings by using words. You can also communicate through the arts. Art is a language that artists use to express ideas and feelings that everyday words cannot express. Through the arts, artists can convey ideas in ways that go beyond describing and telling. But in order to understand the meaning of a work of art, you must do more than simply look at it with your eyes. In order to experience art fully, you must develop the ability to perceive. To look is to merely notice and label an object with a name such as "chair" or "house." To **perceive** is *to become deeply aware through the senses of the special nature of a visual object.* A perception is a sensation to which you attach a meaning. To understand and receive communication from a work of art you must train yourself to perceive.

The arts cross language barriers. You do not need to be able to speak English to perceive what Meyer Straus is expressing in his painting, *Bayou Teche* **(Figure 1.2).** If you concentrate on his image you can feel the humid atmosphere of the Louisiana swamps and hear

▲ **FIGURE 1.2** Straus painted this bayou scene while working for the Academy of Music in New Orleans painting backdrops for major productions. He captured the feel of the bayou by including details such as the flowers in the foreground and the gray Spanish moss hanging from the limbs of the live oak trees. Look at the figures in the boat. The trees and swamp overwhelm them. What do you think the figures are doing? What atmosphere does the painting capture?

Meyer Straus. *Bayou Teche.* 1870. Oil on canvas. 76.2 × 152.4 cm (30 × 60″). Morris Museum of Art, Augusta, Georgia.

MEETING INDIVIDUAL NEEDS

Visually Impaired Students who are blind can think deeply about what they are perceiving. They can feel an object and describe what it seems like. They can model it in clay. If some students have limited vision, they can draw an object's shape into a plastic foam meat tray or onto a piece of heavy aluminum foil with a pad of paper beneath, making an embossed line which can be felt. Blind students can draw an object's outline shape into white sand on black paper. Students with partial vision can draw using a bold black marking pen.

the mosquitoes buzzing. You can understand how it feels to be enclosed by branches dripping with Spanish moss. You can almost hear the water lapping at the boat.

Activity	Learning to Perceive

Applying Your Skills. Select an everyday object such as one that might be found in the classroom. Closely examine the object. Don't just look at it—turn it over, walk around it, touch it. Allow yourself two or three minutes to perceive the object. Then put the object where you can't see it and make a list of all the attributes of the object that you can think of. Then look at the object again and add at least three more attributes or characteristics to your list.

The Purposes of Art

People created art to record ideas and feelings long before they had written words. They used art then as we use it today. The following are some of the most common functions of art.

■ **Personal Functions.** Artists create art to express personal feelings. Edvard Munch had a tragic childhood. His mother died when he was very young, and one of his sisters died when he was 14. His painting, *The Sick Child* **(Figure 1.3),** shocked viewers who were used to seeing happy paintings with bright colors. The work was meant to remind viewers of personal family tragedies. Perhaps the artist wanted to tell them to appreciate what they had. Often people who have suffered a loss remind

▶ **FIGURE 1.3** The child in the painting appears pale and calm. She is not looking at her mother. What is she staring at? Notice the exaggerated drooping of the woman's head. What has the artist done to focus your attention on the sick child?

Edvard Munch. *The Sick Child.* 1907. Oil on canvas. 118.7 × 121 cm (46¾ × 47⅖″). Tate Gallery, London, England.

others to live each day as if it were their last. That is what Munch is saying with his striking image.

■ **Social Function.** Artists may produce art to reinforce and enhance the shared sense of identity of those in a family, community, or civilization (Figure 12.17, page 332). That is why many families commission or hire an artist or photographer to produce a family portrait. Art produced for this purpose also may be used in celebrations and displayed on festive occasions. Think of the many forms of visual art that might be seen in a parade—costumes, band uniforms, floats, and dances are all forms of visual art that might be included in the public celebration of a parade to commemorate an important holiday or event.

■ **Spiritual Function.** Artists may create art to express spiritual beliefs about the destiny of life controlled by the force of a higher power. Art produced for this purpose may reinforce the shared beliefs of an individual or

LESSON 1 *What Is Art?* **7**

Promoting Discussion

Direct students' attention to Figure 1.2 and have them write one paragraph describing the sights, sounds, and smells a person might experience if he/she were placed in that setting. Have students read their descriptions to the class and compare similarities of adjectives and phrases used to describe the atmosphere.

Activity

Learning to Perceive

Applying Your Skills. Throughout *ArtTalk*, activities have been interspersed to provide students with immediate hands-on application of key concepts. When appropriate, computer options have also been added and may be optional or used as extension activities for those students who have access to a computer. Assure students that these assignments will not be graded and are intended for diagnostic purposes only. You can use the information you collect to evaluate what students need to learn.

Aesthetics

Refer students to Figure 1.3, *The Sick Child* and ask them: What is your first reaction to this work of art? What questions come to mind as you look at this painting? Explain that pictures like this shocked viewers when the paintings were first seen. Munch's figures seemed crude and grotesque when compared to the colorful and lighthearted visions of the Impressionists, who were enjoying popularity at the time. Munch's works, however, were in keeping with the period in which he lived, a period when writers and artists were turning their attention inward. Like Munch, they were interested in exploring feelings and emotions rather than describing outward appearances.

MORE ABOUT...	Edvard Munch

The childhood of Edvard Munch was marked by tragedy. His mother died when he was five, and one of his sisters died when he was fourteen. His father was a doctor in a poor district, and Munch's own health was never strong. The fear, suffering, and death of loved ones that he experienced in his own life became the subject matter for his art. Ask: How

much of his suffering that contributed to his work can be seen in Figure 1.3, *The Sick Child?* He returned to this subject several times in paintings and was no doubt inspired by the death of his older sister. In the painting, Munch captures the pale complexion, colorless lips and hopeless stare of a child weakened and finally conquered by illness.

Art History

Have students review Figure 1.4, *Pueblo Scene: Corn Dancers and Church*. This painting shows a traditional Hopi dance. Explain that in the Hopi culture, only a small number of dances are considered social events. The majority occupy an important place in rituals celebrating their people's oneness with nature. Have students examine the painting. Ask: Did you find your eyes drawn by the ceremonial procession on the right side? Notice the traditional clothing. Have the students find the feathered headdress standing on top of the pueblo. Ask: Who do you think this person is?

Promoting Discussion

Tell students that every culture finds ways to express their beliefs, rituals, and ideas. The materials they use for this expression can range from feathers, shells, and dye, to stitchery. Each material shows the ingenuity of the people who use it. Often, the chosen material can be found only in their particular locale and reveals the feeling for beauty that is a rich part of every culture. For example, feathers and shells are common to the art of the Native American, South Pacific, and African cultures. Silk thread is a feature of Asian, Chinese, and European stitchery. Have students bring in examples of art from various cultures and display them.

Critical Thinking

Bring to class a manufactured product you use everyday, such as Figure 1.5, a necklace, or a hair dryer or a toothbrush. Ask students to study the object, then think of one change in the product's design that would make it easier to use or more aesthetically pleasing.

8

a human community. In *Pueblo Scene: Corn Dancers and Church* **(Figure 1.4),** the artists have created a three-dimensional representation of a religious festival that connects two cultures and two religions. Works of art have been created for religious purposes throughout history. Many experts believe that the prehistoric cave paintings of animals had ceremonial purposes, which means they were more than simple records of events. The Greek Temples were built to honor the ancient gods. During the Middle Ages in Europe, almost all art was created for the Catholic Church.

- **Physical Functions.** Artists and craftspeople constantly invent new ways to create functional art. Industrial designers discover new materials that make cars lighter and stronger. Architects employ new building materials such as steel–reinforced concrete to give buildings more interesting forms. In **Figure 1.5,** notice how the artist has combined a variety of precious and semiprecious materials to create a unique necklace.

- **Educational Function.** In the past, many people could not read and art was often created to provide visual instruction. Artists produced artworks, such as symbols painted on signs, to impart information. Viewers could learn from their artworks. In the Middle Ages, artists created stained-glass windows, sculptures, paintings, and tapestries to illustrate stories from the Bible or about rulers of a kingdom.

▲ **FIGURE 1.4** The figures and buildings for this scene were made by a family of artists. Look closely and you will notice that some of the figures are made of painted clay, while others have hair made from yarn and clothing made of fabric. What do the different figures appear to be doing? What does the procession in the foreground seem to be about?

Vigil Family, Tesuque Pueblo, New Mexico. *Pueblo Scene: Corn Dancers and Church.* c. 1960. Painted earthenware. Girard Foundation Collection at the Museum of International Folk Art, a unit of the Museum of New Mexico, Santa Fe, New Mexico.

MORE ABOUT... Fine Art and Applied Art

The controversial distinction between fine art and applied art, or functional art, has been made only in modern times. In Europe, until the later part of the Middle Ages, painters, sculptors, and others we now consider artists were regarded as skilled craftspeople. During the Renaissance, these artists and their works gained new prestige and their art began to be dis-tinguished from crafts, or applied arts. For example, some artists and critics regard certain paintings as merely decorative, and therefore, categorize these works as applied art. On the other hand, some artists and craftspeople insist that art is valid only if it is functional and can be used in daily life.

Earl Pardon. Necklace 1057. 1988. 43.1 × 2.8 × 3 cm (17¼ × 1⅛ × ⅛"). Sterling silver, 14k gold, ebony, ivory, enamel, mother of pearl, ruby, garnet, blue topaz, amethyst, spinel, and rhodolite. National Museum of American Art, Smithsonian Institution, Washington, D.C. Renwick collection.

In addition, when we look at art from the past, we learn from it. Art from other places and other times can tell us what people did. Paintings such as *Anne of Cleves* **(Figure 1.6)** show us people from the past, what they wore, and how they looked. Objects such as pottery and arrowheads show us how people worked and survived in the past. Art from other cultures helps us to understand the beliefs and values of those cultures. We know that the ancient Chinese valued nature from the scrolls we have seen.

In this book you will learn to understand and recognize all the visual arts. You will become familiar with a variety of works that range in size from skyscrapers to tiny feather ornaments. The art in this book will take you through time and space to tell you about places and people you might never know.

 ### Check Your Understanding

1. What does it mean to *perceive?*
2. Name the five purposes of art.
3. Describe two of the purposes of art.

▲ **FIGURE 1.6** This portrait of Anne of Cleves, one of the wives of Henry VIII, shows what a royal person in the sixteenth century might have worn for special occasions. The portrait was created before the wedding because King Henry wanted to know what his intended wife looked like. He had never met her. Notice the unusual jewelry on her hat and the rich fabrics of her dress. How many different fabrics can you identify? How does her clothing indicate her social position?

Hans Holbein. *Anne of Cleves.* 1539. Tempera and oil on parchment. 65.5 × 47.5 cm (25⅝ × 18⅞"). The Louvre, Paris, France.

Promoting Discussion

Direct students to Figure 1.6, *Anne of Cleves.* Have students describe the woman's appearance, expression, and clothing. Have them point out and describe the different textures noted in the painting. Ask: Do you think this is an important person? How do you know? Tell students that Hans Holbein is now best-known as a portraitist. This painting is a portrait of one of the wives of Henry VIII.

ASSESS..........
Self-Assessment

Have students complete the review questions on this page. Answers are provided below.

Reteaching

Have students look through the text and identify works of art that fulfill the following purposes: *personal, social, spiritual, physical,* and *educational.* Then help students explain the value of looking at art made by others.

Enrichment

Have students research other dance rituals and celebrations of Native American groups, such as the Buffalo Dance, Rain Dance, War Dance, and the Hoop Dance. Then have them compare Native American traditions to those of other cultural groups.

CLOSE............

Ask: What can you do to become more perceptive of your environment? *(Look closely for details and notice how objects affect emotions.)*

 ## Answers to Check Your Understanding

1. To become deeply aware through the senses of the special nature of a visual object.
2. The five purposes of art include: personal functions, social functions, spiritual functions, physical functions, and educational functions.
3. Answers vary, but should show the students' understanding of the function of art.

Why Do Artists Create?

(pages 10–15)
(National Standards: 3a, 4b, 5a)

FOCUS............

Objectives

After completing this lesson, students will be able to:

■ Name sources of ideas that artist's might use for inspiration.

■ Describe the benefits of keeping a sketchbook.

Supplies

■ Drawing paper, pencils

■ Newspapers and magazines

■ Aesop fable or short tale

Resources

📁 Artist's Profile 1, Pablo Picasso

📁 Artist's Profile 37, Grant Wood

📁 National Gallery of Art Correlation Bar Code Guide

TEACH..........

Motivator

Hold up a blank sheet of drawing paper. Direct students: Imagine that you are a professional artist. What do you see when you look at this piece of paper? Encourage a variety of responses. Then explain that in this lesson students will discuss where artists find ideas.

Why Do Artists Create?

The urge to create is universal. Artists are driven by their sense of wonder and curiosity. The creative impulse is often suppressed if one becomes afraid of making mistakes. Artists exhibit the courage to take risks. They are able to see their surroundings in new and unusual ways. They are willing to work intensely for long periods of time to achieve their goals. Some artists are self-taught and have been called folk artists because they are not educated in traditional artistic methods. Most artists learn skills and techniques from other artists. Eventually artists develop their own unique styles.

The impulses that drive artists to create vary. Both Roger Brown and Leo Twiggs created art in response to a devastating natural catastrophe: Hurricane Hugo. Twiggs, who lives in South Carolina and witnessed the hurricane, used strong lines to represent the force of the winds **(Figure 1.7)**. Brown, who lives in Chicago, responded to the same tragedy in a different way. He illustrated only the aftermath of the hurricane. He turned the event into a giant postcard in which he depicted the fury of the storm by showing the trees in neat rows, broken off at exactly the same level **(Figure 1.8)**.

◄ **FIGURE 1.7** Identify the door named in the title. Look at the dark shape near the center of the painting. How many figures are standing in the door? What part of this work tells you about the destructive force of the hurricane?

Leo F. Twiggs. *East Wind Suite: Door*. Hugo Series. 1989. Batik: Dyes and wax resist on cotton. 61 × 51 cm (24 × 20″). Private collection.

TECHNOLOGY OPTIONS

National Gallery of Art Videodisc Use the following to discuss how artists get ideas for their artworks.

Bartolomé Esteban Murillo *The Return of the Prodigal Son*	Edward Hicks *Penn's Treaty with the Indians*	Martin Johnson Heade *Cattleya Orchid and Three Brazilian Hummingbirds*
Search Frame 549	Search Frame 1854	Search Frame 1946

Use Glencoe's *National Gallery of Art Correlation Bar Code Guide* to locate more artworks.

◄ **FIGURE 1.8** This painting depicts the same event as shown in Figure 1.7. The two artists represent the hurricane in very different ways. What does this painting remind you of? Does it resemble an advertisement or a postcard? Why do you think the artist chose humor to present such a devastating event?

Roger Brown. *Hurricane Hugo.* 1990. Oil on canvas. 121.9 × 182.9 cm (48 × 72"). Morris Museum of Art, Augusta, Georgia.

Where Do Artists Get Ideas?

Artists are *creative individuals who use imagination and skill to communicate in visual form.* They use the materials of art to solve visual problems. Artists look to many sources for inspiration. Some look outward to their natural and cultural environment for ideas. Others look within themselves for creative motivation.

Nature

Sometimes artists look to their natural surroundings and record them. The first group of landscape artists in the United States was called the Hudson River School because most of them lived near that river in New York. They painted the world around them, paying meticulous attention to realistic detail. One Hudson River School artist, George Inness, lived in Newburgh, New York. His early work depicted the vast American landscape in a romantic manner **(Figure 1.9).**

◄ **FIGURE 1.9** This painting celebrates nature and industry, although the two are not necessarily compatible. If you look carefully, you can see the town of Scranton, Pennsylvania, accurately depicted in the distance. Why do you think the artist has included all the tree stumps in this painting? What symbols of industrialization has he used?

George Inness. *The Lackawanna Valley.* c. 1856. Oil on canvas. .860 × 1.275 m (33⅞ × 50¼"). National Gallery of Art, Washington, D.C. © 1998 Board of Trustees. Gift of Mr. and Mrs. Huttleston Rogers.

LESSON 2 *Why Do Artists Create?*   **11**

Art Criticism

Let pairs of students choose and discuss one of the artworks shown in this lesson. The partners should discuss their responses to these questions: What do you think the specific inspiration for this work could have been? What do you imagine the artist saw, did, or thought about before creating this work? How do you think the artist reacted to that experience? How successfully does the work communicate the artist's reactions to the experience? Then have each student write a short paragraph summarizing the discussion.

Promoting Discussion

After comparing Figures 1.7 and 1.8, distribute several newspapers and newsmagazines to students and ask them to find examples of recorded events. Discuss the kinds of images that can be used to record events. Compare the variety of media and techniques used by artists to capture events.

Promoting Discussion

Ask students to think of a favorite activity or event spent outdoors—perhaps a family picnic, a hike in the woods, a special soccer game, watching the sunset, or some other regular or occasional outdoor happening. Have them close their eyes and visualize an image of that event. Ask: What aspect of nature contributed to your enjoyment of that event? In general, what do you enjoy most about nature? Explain that nature has long been the focus of artists.

Cross-Curriculum: Language Arts

Bring in another example of Grant Wood's artworks, *The Ride of Paul Revere* (Transparency CC-4). Tell students the descriptive recording of events is not limited to the visual arts. Poets are also noted for adding color and immediacy to events from history. Find a copy of the ballad "Paul Revere's Ride" by Henry Wadsworth Longfellow. Read this colorful poem aloud to appreciate its rhythm and compare it to Grant Wood's "visual record" of this historical event.

Studio Skills

Have students study Figure 1.11. Then read one of Aesop's fables or another short tale aloud to the class. Have students draw illustrations to go with the fable. Remind the class that the function of a story illustration is to reinforce the message of the story. When they have finished, help students compare and discuss their illustrations.

MEET THE ARTIST
GRANT WOOD

American, 1892–1942

Grant Wood. *Self-Portrait.* 1932. Oil on Masonite panel. 36.9 × 30.9 cm (14¾ × 12⅛"). Collection of The Davenport Museum of Art, Davenport, Iowa.

Grant Wood grew up on a farm and drew with whatever materials could be spared. Often he used charcoal from the wood fire to sketch on a leftover piece of brown paper. He was only ten when his father died, and his mother moved the family to Cedar Rapids, Iowa, where Wood went to school. He studied part-time at the State University of Iowa and attended night classes at the Art Institute of Chicago. When he was 32, he went to Paris to study at the Academie Julian. In 1927, he traveled to Munich, Germany, where some of the most accomplished artists of the period were working. While there, he saw German and Flemish artworks that influenced him greatly, especially the work of Jan van Eyck. After that trip, his style changed to reflect the realism of those painters.

▲ **FIGURE 1.10** This painting is familiar to most Americans because it has been used and parodied countless times. Because of this, it can be easy to overlook the message Wood intended. Symbols tell a story: the Gothic window represents the couple's European heritage, and the pitchfork stands for their determination. Can you identify other symbols in the painting and tell what they might mean?

Grant Wood. *American Gothic.* 1930. Oil on beaverboard. 74.3 × 62.4 cm (29¼ × 24½"). Friends of American Art Collection. All rights reserved by The Art Institute of Chicago, Chicago, Illinois and VAGA, New York, New York. (1930.934)

People and Real World Events

Another artist, Grant Wood, captured the essence of the Midwestern American spirit during the Great Depression in his work, *American Gothic* **(Figure 1.10)**. The stern, small town citizens posed before their house. The couple's determination was meant to reassure those shaken by the stock market crash during the Great Depression.

Myths and Legends

Some artists borrow ideas from famous works of literature. Romare Bearden interpreted one part of an ancient Greek legend, *The Odyssey,* in his painting *Return of Ulysses* **(Figure 1.11)**. The Greek legend, written by the poet Homer, describes the adventures that befall a hero returning home from war. Bearden used his unique style to portray an important scene from this story.

Spiritual and Religious Beliefs

Visual artists in every culture use their skills to create objects and images to be used to express spiritual beliefs. Many non-Western cultures do not even have a word for "art." Those who

TEACHER TALK

Sources of Ideas for Inspiration A filing system can be made to provide a source to students when conducting research or looking for ideas. Use four file folders and label them with the following: *people, places, objects,* and *designs.* When you or your students see an interesting magazine picture, cut it out and place it in the appropriate file. Later, when students need another source of inspiration they can use the file. Postcards, photos, or prints of artworks can be included.

Promoting Discussion

Tell students that everyone has dreams and fantasies. Artists have the creative ability to turn dreams, and even nightmares, into the illusion of reality. Direct students to Figure 5.37 on page 126 to see one of René Magritte's paintings.

Critical Thinking

Point out to students that the Abstract Expressionist movement brought with it an expanded definition of art. There was a sense that art is as much the act of creation as the object resulting from that act. Have students work in small groups to discuss this idea, specifically as it applies to Figure 1.13 on page 14.

Art History

This may be a good time to have students become familiar with Chapter 12 and 13. These chapters explore the non-Western and Western art traditions. In Chapter 13, students will explore creative techniques used by artists from prehistoric to contemporary times.

◀ **FIGURE 1.12** This bird mask was created for a dance ceremony. Notice how the artist has used natural earth pigments to color the wood, plus natural materials like feathers and sinew to decorate it.

Yup'ik. *Bird Mask.* 1988. Wood, feathers. Height: 65 cm (25½"). Robert H. Lowie Museum, University of California, Berkeley, California.

create objects do the best work they can because it is important. The mask in **Figure 1.12** was made to be worn during ceremonial winter dances by the Yup'ik people who lived in northwestern Alaska.

Creative Techniques

Many artists founded new art movements and developed new techniques to create art. Jackson Pollock was a leader of the Abstract Expressionist movement. He studied painting in the 1930s with Thomas Hart Benton as his teacher. Benton was an American regionalist who painted realistic paintings and murals that celebrated American life (Figure 13.29, page 376). Pollock's earliest works were in the realistic style of his teacher. After 1947, he developed the action-painting technique of dripping and splashing paint onto canvases

MORE ABOUT... Romare Bearden

Romare Bearden enrolled at the Art Students League in New York City. There he met and studied under the German Expressionist George Grosz. Because Bearden wanted to make a social statement about his African-American heritage, Grosz introduced him to the work of Daumier, Goya, and Kollwitz and led him to study composition through the analysis of Brueghel and the great Dutch masters. Grosz also pushed Bearden to refine his draftsmanship by studying the work of Ingres, Dürer, and Holbein. In 1938, Bearden left the Art Students League, but he continued to paint while working at the New York City Department of Social Services.

Art History

Tell students that early European artists were known as journeymen who traveled from country to countryside drawing and painting in their journals. Their subjects included people, landscapes, and events. Artists learned by becoming apprentices to master artists while they worked in their shops as trade workers.

Promoting Discussion

Have students brainstorm a list of events in their daily lives that could serve as inspiration for their artwork. Such events might be family celebrations, sports, hobbies, or music.

▶ **FIGURE 1.13** Pollock wanted to express his personal feelings when he created his art. He allowed his feelings to influence his choice of colors and the manner in which he applied them to the canvas.

Jackson Pollock. *Cathedral.* 1947. Enamel and aluminum paint on canvas. 181.6 × 89.1 cm (71½ × 35¹/₁₆″). Dallas Museum of Art, Dallas, Texas. Gift of Mr. and Mrs. Bernard J. Reis.

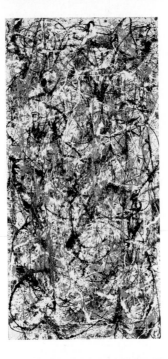

stretched on the floor **(Figure 1.13).** The idea for this style of painting, which influenced many who came after him, came from within himself.

Artists of the Past

Art is not made in a vacuum. Artists of a particular time period often influence each other. Artists also learn from and build on the work of artists who came before them. Pablo Picasso based his 1957 painting, *Las Meninas* (after Velázquez) **(Figure 1.14),** on *Las Meninas (The Maids of Honor)* by Diego Velázquez **(Figure 1.15),** which was painted in 1656. Although Picasso changed the colors and used his own Cubist style, you can recognize some of the figures and objects that are in the realistic Velázquez painting. How many figures and objects can you find that appear in both works?

▲ **FIGURE 1.14** This painting is based on Diego Velázquez's *Las Meninas (The Maids of Honor)* (Figure 1.15). Similar figures and objects are present in both paintings—the artist, the easel with the unfinished painting, the child who appears to be the subject of the artwork in progress, the dog, the figure in the door. Compare these objects with the ones depicted in Velázquez's work. What has Picasso done to make the work uniquely his own? Do you think he was exhibiting a sense of humor?

Pablo Picasso. *Las Meninas* (after Velázquez). 1957. Oil on canvas. 2 × 2.6 m (6′4³/₄″ × 8′ 6³/₈″). Musee Picasso, Barcelona, Spain.

14 | **CHAPTER 1** Art in Your World

COOPERATIVE LEARNING

Setting Expectations As you incorporate cooperative learning into your classroom, keep in mind that some students may have little experience working cooperatively. Take time in the beginning to explain what will be expected of every group member's participation, such as listening, sharing opinions, and respecting other opinions. Your role is one of coach.

You introduce the project, set the parameters, create the teams, provide materials, offer support, monitor the progress of the students, and provide meaningful closure. Monitoring is an essential part of your relationship with learning groups. Otherwise, skepticism, distrust, or lack of self-discipline will be reinforced.

FIGURE 1.15 This painting was interpreted by Picasso, another Spanish artist, three centuries after Velázquez completed it. Explain what is happening in the painting. The princess, in white, has a regal bearing. She is clearly the center of attention. Do you see the king and queen in the picture? Who is the person in the doorway? Can you describe the roles of the other people in the painting?

Diego Velázquez. *Las Meninas (The Maids of Honor)*. 1656. Oil on canvas. 3.18 × 2.8 m (10'5¼" × 9'3¼"). Museo del Prado, Madrid, Spain.

Has Picasso used everything that you see in the Velázquez work?

Ideas Commissioned by Employers

Many artists are hired by individuals or companies to create works of art. Liz Kingslein is a graphic artist who has worked for many years as a commercial artist. **Figure 14.6** on page 392 is an example of images that she designed for an employer, in this case a restaurant. She used a computer draw program to create the art.

Ideas for Your Own Artwork

In the coming chapters, you will need to come up with ideas of your own for original works of art. Like all other artists, you may at times find yourself at a loss for ideas. You can look to the sources listed in this lesson for inspiration. You will also find that keeping a sketchbook can be an enormous help. In addition to recording images in your sketchbook, you may jot down ideas that come to you after participating in other art events such as concerts, movies, and theatre productions. You will also find that a sketchbook can be used to practice skills and techniques you learn in class.

Activity — Keeping a Sketchbook

Applying Your Skills. Artists develop perception and artistic skills by constantly sketching the world around them. Begin keeping a sketchbook of your own. Choose a notebook with unlined paper. Make sure it is easy to carry around. Practice drawing anything that catches your eye. The more you draw, the better you will "see" objects. Make written notes about your sketches, such as the quality of light, the colors you notice, or the mood of a scene.

 Check Your Understanding

1. Define the word *artist*.
2. Identify four different sources for artistic ideas.
3. Why do artists keep sketchbooks?

ASSESS...........
Self-Assessment
Have students complete the review questions on this page. Answers are provided below.

Reteaching
Work with groups of students to review and discuss artists' sources of inspiration. Ask questions that will lead students to consider their own use of the sources listed in the text. For example: What story, myth, or legend would you like to use as the basis for an artwork? What creative techniques would you like to explore? Give all the group members a turn to answer each question, and encourage discussion of the students' ideas. Finally, have students imagine and draw their own artworks.

Enrichment
Have pairs of students show Figure 1.13 to at least three people who are unfamiliar with Abstract Expressionist art and ask their interpretation. Students should compare the various responses and categorize them according to the three main aesthetic theories. Conclude with a discussion of whether people's opinions correlated with their age, gender, or personality.

CLOSE.............
Ask students to identify two sources of inspiration in their own lives for creating artworks.

 Answers to Check Your Understanding

1. Artists are creative individuals who use imagination and skill to communicate in visual form.
2. Sources for artistic ideas may include: nature, people and real world events, myths and legends, spiritual and religious beliefs, artists of the past, creative techniques, and ideas from employers.
3. A sketchbook helps an artist record ideas and practice skills and techniques.

The Language of Art

The Language of Art
(pages 16–19)
(National Standards: 2b, 3a)

FOCUS............

Objectives

After completing this lesson, students will be able to:

- Name the six elements of art.
- Identify the principles of art.
- Explain how subject, composition, and content relate to works of art.
- Identify the information presented in a credit line.

Supplies

- Pencil, drawing paper
- Magazines, scissors

Resources

📁 Application Activity 2, *Sharpening Your Skills*

📁 Cooperative Learning Activity 2, *Campaigning for the Elements*

📁 Concept Map 1

📁 Enrichment Activity 2, *Learning the Language of Art*

TEACH.........

Motivator

Ask students to write a description of the main entrance to the school. Challenge students to remember lines, shapes, forms, spaces, colors, and textures. Ask volunteers to read their descriptions aloud, then display a picture of the entrance, or, if possible, take the class to the entrance. Ask them to suggest ways that they can train themselves to observe more closely the elements of art found in their environment.

People throughout the world speak many different languages. Spanish, Swahili, Japanese, Hindi, French, English, and Apache are just a few of the 3,000 different languages that are spoken. Each language has its own system of words and rules of grammar. To learn a new language, you need to learn new words and a new set of rules for putting those words together.

The language of visual art has its own system. All that you see in a work of art is made up of certain common elements. They are arranged according to basic principles. As you learn these basic elements and principles, you will learn the language of art. Being able to use the language of visual art will help you in many ways. It will increase your ability to understand, appreciate, and enjoy art. It will increase your ability to express yourself clearly when discussing art. It will even help you improve your ability to produce artworks.

The Elements of Art

A **symbol** is *something that stands for, or represents, something else*. In a spoken language, words are symbols. The word chair stands for a piece of furniture that has a seat, a back, legs, and sometimes arms. In the language of art, we use visual symbols to communicate ideas.

The *basic visual symbols in the language of art* are known as the **elements of art.** Just as there are basic kinds of words—such as nouns and verbs—there are basic kinds of art elements. These are *line, shape* and *form, space, color, value,* and *texture.* The elements are the visual building blocks that the artist puts together to create a work of art. No matter how a work is made, it will contain some or all of these elements.

When you look at a visual image, it is difficult to separate one element from another. For example, when you look at **Figure 1.16,** you see a shiny, round bowl outlined with a thin yellow line

Activity — Create a Symbol

Applying Your Skills. In visual art, symbols can be concrete representations of abstract ideas, such as a heart standing for love. Create a visual symbol that represents something important to you, such as an activity you participate in or an organization you belong to. Share your symbol with your classmates. Can they identify what it represents?

Computer Option. Design a visual symbol using a computer application. Choose from the tools and menus to represent this idea with line, shape, or color. Hold down the Shift key when making straight lines or restricting shapes to circles or squares. Title, save, print, and display your best example. Include a short explanation about your symbol.

Curriculum Connection

Literature Writers use words like artists use the elements of art to communicate ideas. By explaining details about color and line, by describing the texture of objects, their shape and form and how they take up space, a writer enriches a story and captures the interest of readers. Rather than simply naming an object or a scene, the writer may use descriptive phrases to vary his or her style and create a certain mood or impression. Writing is enhanced by effective use of description. Ask students to think of a book that uses vivid descriptions. Probably the author used the elements of art to create the memorable images.

◄ **FIGURE 1.16**
Notice how the artist has used color and texture to direct the viewer's eye through this artwork. Look at the number of different surfaces she depicts. How many different textures can you identify? Although the shiny surfaces catch your attention, notice the matte, or dull, surfaces as well.

Janet I. Fish. *Raspberries and Goldfish.* 1981. Oil on canvas. 182.9 × 162.6 cm (72 × 64"). The Metropolitan Museum of Art, New York, New York. Purchase. The Cape Branch Foundation and Lila Acheson Wallace gifts, 1983. (1983.171)

filled with bumpy, red raspberries. However, rather than seeing the elements of texture (shiny and bumpy), color (red), shape (round), and line (thin and yellow) separately, you see the bowl of raspberries as a whole. You visually "read" the elements together.

Sometimes the differences between the elements are not clear-cut. A line may be so wide that it looks like a shape, or an artist may manipulate light and dark values to indicate different surface textures. Look at the variety of textures Janet Fish has created in *Raspberries and Goldfish* (Figure 1.16).

When you first learned to read, you did not begin with a full-length novel. You learned by reading one word at a time. That is how you will start to read the language of art: one art element at a time.

The Principles of Art

After you have learned to recognize the elements of art, you will learn the ways in which the elements can be organized for different effects. When you learn a language, you learn the rules of grammar by which words are

Studio Skills
Tell students that to learn how a clock works, they might take it apart and study the pieces. The same is true of a work of art. By studying the elements, or "pieces," you learn what makes the work "tick." One tool that can help students sharpen their awareness of the elements of art is a viewing frame. They can easily make a frame by following the directions in Technique Tip 6, Using a Viewing Frame, on page 451. Have them make a viewing frame and use it to focus on familiar objects in their environment, such as a tree or a building. Have them keep a sketchbook in which they record their findings.

Art Criticism
Have students review Figure 1.16 and write a short description of the work, the elements of art that they see, and the effect that those elements create. Encourage them to point out how the artist used the elements of art to create variety in the artwork.

LESSON 3   *The Language of Art*   **17**

COOPERATIVE LEARNING

Building Collaboration As an initial drawing experience, this exercise helps students become comfortable with collaborative efforts and peer review: Give each student a blank sheet of drawing paper. Instruct them to begin a drawing with one object or shape. Have them pass the drawing to the next person who adds

something to the drawing. Continue the process until everyone has added something to every drawing. Hang the drawings and have everyone examine the final results. Ask: How did this approach affect the composition? How did it affect the subject? The content? Are any drawings stronger than others? Why?

Promoting Discussion

Remind students that although many artists may begin with the same subject, each will bring a different background and a different style to his or her interpretation. That interpretation becomes the content or meaning of the work. That meaning is like a metaphor; the work of art represents something more than just the subject of the work. The meaning of the work depends upon two key factors: the way the artist has manipulated the elements using the principles; and the emotions and knowledge the viewer brings to the work. Choose an artwork from this chapter and ask students to explain what the work means to them.

Art Criticism

Have students choose an artwork from the textbook and write a description of how the artist used the elements and principles of art. Ask them to decide which is most important in developing the work's composition and mood.

Developing Perceptual Skills

Have students work in small groups to practice visualizing metric measurements. First, have them estimate the metric measurements of these objects around them: a doorframe, a textbook, a shoe, a desk, a pen or pencil, and a piece of notebook paper. Then, using a ruler or meter stick, have them measure the items and compare their estimate to the actual measurement.

---

organized into sentences. Without these rules, people would find it difficult to communicate.

Visual images are also organized according to rules. The *rules that govern how artists organize the elements of art* are called the **principles of art.** They also help artists organize the art elements for specific effects. The principles you will learn about are *rhythm, movement, balance, proportion, variety, emphasis, harmony,* and *unity.*

The Work of Art

In art, it is important to understand the three basic properties, or features, of an artwork. These are *subject, composition,* and *content.*

The Subject

The **subject** is *the image viewers can easily identify in a work of art.* The subject may be one person or many people. It may be a thing, such as a boat. It may be an event, such as a dance. What are the subjects in Gabriele Münter's painting, *Breakfast of the Birds* **(Figure 1.17)**?

Some artists choose to create nonobjective artwork. **Nonobjective art** is *art that has no recognizable subject matter* (Figure 1.13, page 14). In these types of works, the elements of art themselves become the subject matter.

The Composition

The second property of a work of art is the composition of the work. The

▲ **FIGURE 1.17** Gabriele Münter was one of the founders of modern German Abstract Expressionism. In 1911 she joined with other radical artists to form the group known as Der Blaue Reiter ("The Blue Rider") group. She stayed in Germany through World War II but was forced to work in secret during the Nazi era, when German Expressionism was outlawed. Since this was painted in 1934, it is one of her "secret" paintings.

Gabriele Münter. *Breakfast of the Birds.* 1934. Oil on board. 45.7 × 55.2 cm (18 × 21¾"). National Museum of Women in the Arts, Washington, D.C. Gift of Wallace and Wilhelmina Holladay.

COOPERATIVE LEARNING

Peer Review Peer review emphasizes an interdependence that does not interfere with the learning process. Students are apt to experience more success with their creative ideas when they interact with peers who represent a nonthreatening source of feedback. The following activity involves peer review and is successful when used midway through an assignment: Have students get up, walk around, and look carefully at everyone's work. Next, have them trade artwork with one other person, study the work carefully, and suggest one change that would improve the design. Allow time for the pairs' discussion and encourage them to use the vocabulary and concepts emphasized in the chapter.

composition is *the way the principles of art are used to organize the elements of art.* Notice how Münter has used the reds to separate indoors from outdoors, yet she ties the woman to the birds by using related colors. The woman is placed with her back toward the viewer, so that the viewer looks in the same direction as the woman, toward the birds. As you learn more about the elements and principles of art, you will discover how to control the composition of your artwork.

The Content

The third property of a work of art is the content. The **content** is *the message the work communicates.* The message may be an idea or a theme, such as patriotism or family togetherness. It may be an emotion, such as pride, love, or loneliness. Sometimes you know what the intention of an artist might have been when he or she created the work, therefore the meaning of the work may be clear. However, at other times, you may not be certain of what the work might mean, and you have to consider all possibilities. Many artists can paint the same subject, a woman looking out a window, but each painting may have a different message. What do you think is the content of Münter's painting?

The Credit Line

Look at Figure 1.17. The credit line appears beneath the caption. A **credit line** is *a list of important facts about a work of art.* Every artwork in this book has a credit line.

Most credit lines contain at list six facts. They are as follows:

- **Name** of the artist.
- **Title** of the work. This always appears in italics.

- **Year** the work was created. Sometimes, in the case of older works, "c." appears before the year. This is an abbreviation for *circa*, a Latin word meaning "about" or "around."
- **Medium** used by the artist. This is *the material used to make art.* If more than one medium is used, the credit line may read "mixed media."
- **Size** of the work. The first number is always the height, the second number is the width, and if the work is three-dimensional, the third number indicates the depth.
- **Location** of the work. The location names the gallery, museum, or collection in which the work is housed and the city, state, and country. The names of the donors may also be included.

 Activity | Using Credit Line Information

Applying Your Skills. Who is the artist of the work in Figure 1.9 on page 11? What is the title of the painting by Vincent van Gogh (Figure 1.1, page 4)? Which work in this chapter was completed most recently? Which is the largest work in this chapter? Which works in this chapter are not housed in the United States?

Check Your Understanding

1. List the elements of art.
2. Name the principles of art.
3. How do subject and composition differ?
4. Name the six facts most credit lines include.

Activity

Using Credit Line Information

Applying Your Skills. Students should identify the following answers: (Figure 1.9) George Innes. (Figure 1.1) *Houses of Auvers.* (Figure 1.8) Roger Brown's *Hurricane Hugo.* (Figure 1.15) Diego Velázquez's *Las Meninas.*

ASSESS...........
Self-Assessment
Have students complete the review questions on this page. Answers are provided below.

Reteaching
- Review the definitions of the terms *subject, composition,* and *content* as they relate to works of art. Then, have volunteers select works of art from this book that they find appealing and identify whether their choices were based primarily on subject, composition, or content.
- Distribute *Concept Map 1* in the TCR to help students understand the elements and principles of art. 📁

Enrichment
- Distribute Enrichment Activity 2, *Learning the Language of Art.* 📁

CLOSE............
Go around the room and have each student identify one example of an element of art in the classroom.

 ### Answers to Check Your Understanding

1. The elements of art are: line, shape and form, space, color, value, and texture.
2. Rhythm, movement, balance, proportion, variety, emphasis, harmony, and unity.
3. The subject of an artwork is the image viewers can easily identify in a work of art. Composition is the way the principles of art are used to organize the elements of art.
4. The name of the artist, title of the work, year the work was created, medium, and size and location of the work.

Because students have not yet been introduced to the steps of art criticism (these are presented in chapter 2), the instructions in this lesson direct students to study the credit line of the work.

Critiquing the Work

▶ Describe

What do you see?

■ The artist is Marc Chagall. The artwork is called *Paris Through the Window.*

■ It was created in 1913 and done with oil on canvas.

■ Because there are many objects to list, suggest that the students start at the bottom and work upward.

■ Most of the shapes represent objects, but some shapes are just areas of color.

▶ Analyze

How is the artwork organized?

■ Colors: All the rainbow colors are repeated around the painting. The one that is repeated the most is the dull yellow. Red: the jacket, the dots in the black triangle, and the bottom window frames. Orange: the heart on the hand, and the area around the parachutist. Yellow: Some of the right side of the two faces, the body of the cat, some of the window frame, and in some buildings above the man's head. Green: The man's collar, the cat's bottom, the leaves on the windowsill, and one piece of the window frame. Blue: the left side of the two-faced head,

ART CRITICISM IN ACTION

▲ **FIGURE 1.18**

Marc Chagall. *Paris Through the Window.* 1913. Oil on canvas. 135.8 × 141.1 cm (53½ × 55¾"). Solomon R. Guggenheim Museum, New York, New York. Gift, Solomon R. Guggenheim, 1937.

MORE ABOUT... Marc Chagall

Late in his life, Marc Chagall began to collaborate with skilled artisans in various media. With their help and guidance, he was able to realize his designs in monumental forms such as ceramic murals, tapestries, and stained-glass windows. Although he continued to make traditional oil paintings and watercolors, his work in stained glass was the major focus of the last twenty-five years of his career. One of his most important works was done in 1959 for a newly built medical center in Jerusalem. To fill twelve windows, Chagall chose as his theme the Twelve Tribes of Israel.

Art criticism is a four-step procedure for helping you use perception to get deeply involved in a work of art. You will learn more about these four steps in Chapter 2.

1 DESCRIBE What do you see?
During this step you will collect information about the subject of the work. List all of the information found in the credit line and then describe the things you see in the visual image.
- List the objects you see in the painting. Where they are located? Do they seem close to the viewer or in the distance?
- Is this a nonobjective work, or do the shapes in this work represent objects?

2 ANALYZE How is this work organized?
The second step in art criticism deals with the composition of the work. During this step you will use the knowledge you will learn in each chapter about the elements and principles of art to understand the composition of the work.
- Describe where you find rainbow colors in this work.
- Are the colors in this work bright or dull?
- Does this work look like a realistic painting, such as the George Inness painting in Figure 1.9 on page 11, or does it look like a dream scene with real objects in unusual places?

3 INTERPRET What is the artist trying to communicate?
The third step in art criticism focuses on the content of the work. This is where you will make guesses about the meaning.
- Why do you think the head has two faces?
- Why does the cat have a human face? What do you think it represents?
- What tells you, besides the title, that this takes place in Paris?

4 JUDGE What do you think of the work?
The fourth step in art criticism is when you decide if the work of art is successful or not. In Chapter 2 you will learn about theories that will help you to make objective decisions about artworks. When you have studied these theories, return to this painting and make a judgment about the work.

MEET THE ARTIST

MARC CHAGALL

Russian, 1889–1985

Marc Chagall was born in a small town in Russia. He studied art in St. Petersburg and then in Paris. From 1919 to 1922, Chagall was the art director of the Moscow Jewish State Theater. He painted murals in the theater lobby and created sets for the shows.

Chagall was one of the first artists to paint pictures that looked like dreams. He is sometimes called an early surrealist because of his dream-like style and the element of fantasy in his work. His work also shows the strong influence of his home and Jewish heritage. Childhood memories and religious images are often found in his work. Chagall's artworks combine memories with folklore and fantasy.

the hand, the top of the window frame, a triangular shape seen through the window pane, and an area to the right of the parachutist. Violet: one area through the bottom windowpane, some dashes of color through the top windowpanes, and dots inside the white triangle in the upper right corner of the painting.
- Most will say it looks like a dream-like scene.

▶ **Interpret**
What do you think the artist is trying to communicate?
- Answers will vary. Some may say that the man has two faces because he is looking at Paris and thinking about someplace else. The blue on one face may indicate sadness at being in Paris. The yellow on the other face looking away from Paris may be thinking about happy memories.
- The yellow cat with the feminine face may be someone he remembers from the other place. Since the heart is almost the same color it may indicate a love from the other place.
- The Eiffel Tower suggests Paris.
- Answers will vary. Some may say to make this look like a dream.

▶ **Judge**
Is this a successful work?
Answers will vary.

Time & Place   Early Twentieth Century

Point out that *Paris Through the Window* was painted by Marc Chagall in 1913. Some other events that happened the same year:

Music: Russian composer Igor Stravinksky's ballet *The Rite of Spring* opened in Paris to a hostile audience.
Technology: Henry Ford pioneered new assembly-line techniques in the manufacture of cars.
Politics: United States suffragettes marched down Pennsylvania Avenue demanding the right to vote. Success came in 1919 with the passage of the 19th Amendment to the Constitution.

CONNECTIONS
SOCIAL
STUDIES

The Games Children Play

(National Standards: 6a, 6b)

Objectives

After completing this feature, students will be able to:

- Identify a number of games portrayed in the painting.
- Discuss the importance of child's play.
- Analyze the relationship between children's games and society.

Teaching the Connection

1. Have students read the feature on this page.
2. Ask students to describe additional games they remember playing as small children.
3. Tell students that Pieter Bruegel was a metaphorical painter. While there is a realistic dimension to the children portrayed in the painting, the artist is also making a statement about human behavior. *Children's Games* calls attention to the strangeness of some social behaviors and may even suggest, ironically, that human society is based on games and childish activities.

The Games Children Play

◀ **FIGURE 1.19**

Pieter Bruegel, the Elder. *Children's Games*. 1560. Oil on oakwood. 118 × 161 cm (46½ × 63⅓"). Kunsthistorisches Museum, Vienna, Austria.

What were some of your favorite games as a young child? Did you like playing hide-and-seek or capture-the-flag or were you more interested in dressing up or having make-believe tea parties? Although games differ from culture to culture, virtually all children play in ways that captivate the imagination and exercise the body.

However, games also have a social dimension. While at play, children often imitate adult behaviors and activities. Games introduce children to social customs and practices. In addition, many games have rules that must be followed or require specific techniques that must be mastered.

By playing games, children also learn important social skills, such as cooperation and competition. At the same time, games may allow us to act out imaginary scenes that are not likely to take place in reality. By stretching our imaginations as children, we learn to be creative and resourceful as adults. So, whether you liked to play with dolls or toy dinosaurs or to pretend you were a parent or a superhero, the games that occupied your childhood helped you to develop into the person you are today.

Making the Connection

1. How many different games can you identify in **Figure 1.19**?
2. Many of these games involve children imitating adult activities. How do children's games prepare us for the activities of adulthood?

Answers to Making the Connection

1. There are over seventy different games depicted in this painting. These include: blowing bubbles, dressing up, swinging, turning somersaults and cartwheels, rolling hoops, throwing knives, playing tug-of-war, leapfrog, and kick-the-pot, walking on stilts, climbing, wrestling, and playing hide-and-seek and follow-the-leader.

2. Many of the games help to develop important physical skills, such as hand/eye coordination, aim, flexibility, and balance.
3. There are over 100 children in this painting. Rather than portraying realistic children enjoying their play, Bruegel depicted gnomelike creatures with serious expressions.

Building Vocabulary

On a separate sheet of paper, write the term that best matches each definition given below.

1. To become deeply aware through the senses of the special nature of a visual object.
2. Something that stands for, or represents, something else.
3. The basic visual symbols in the language of art.
4. The rules that govern how artists organize the elements of art.
5. Art that has no recognizable subject matter.
6. The way the principles of art are used to organize the elements of art.
7. A list of important facts about a work of art.
8. A material used to make art.

Reviewing Art Facts

Answer the following questions using complete sentences.

1. Describe the five purposes of art.
2. Name and describe four sources of inspiration for artists.
3. Explain the relationship between the elements of art and the principles of art.
4. Select a work of art in this chapter and name the subject.
5. Read the credit-line information of an artwork from any chapter and list the figure number, the title, the year the work was created, and the medium.

Thinking Critically About Art

1. **Analyze.** Look at the different artworks in this chapter. They represent many different artists and many different time periods. Pick out three or four of your favorites and write a brief paragraph explaining your opinion. Are there similarities among the artworks you selected? What does this tell you about your preferences?

2. **Compare and contrast.** Study Figures 1.14 on page 14 and 1.15 on page 15. List the similarities you find in the two paintings. Then identify the qualities that make each of the paintings unique and different.

3. **Analyze.** Find two artworks in this chapter that were created within a few years of each other. List the similarities and differences. Do you think works of art made in the same time period have more similarities than those created at different times? Find another artwork created at a much earlier or much later time. How is it similar and different from the first two artworks you chose?

Use the Performing Arts Handbook to discover the art of masks and the many ways this art form has been created and worn throughout the world's cultures. Faustwork Mask Theatre presents the message of masks on page 413.

Use fun, interactive activities to help you learn the language of art and understand the elements and principles of art. Visit the Glencoe Fine Arts Site at: **www.glencoe.com/sec/art**

Answers to Building Vocabulary
1. perceive
2. symbol
3. elements of art
4. principles of art
5. nonobjective art
6. composition
7. credit line
8. medium

Answers To Reviewing Art Facts
1. The five purposes of art include personal functions, social functions, spiritual functions, physical functions, and educational functions.
2. Answers may vary, but could include: nature, people and world events, myths and legends, spiritual and religious beliefs, exploring creative techniques, and artists of the past.
3. The principles of art are used to organize the elements of art.
4. Answers will vary.
5. Answers will vary, but should demonstrate students' knowledge of reading a credit line.

Reteaching
■ Distribute and have students complete *Chapter 1 Study Guide* in the Reteaching booklet. Have students use the guide to review key concepts in the chapter. 📁

CLOSE............
Display an artwork or choose one from the text. Go around the room and ask each student to identify one aspect of the artwork that is an example of one of the concepts learned in the chapter.

ASSESSMENT ✓

Evaluate
■ Have students complete the *Chapter 1 Test* in the TCR. 📁
■ Alternative Assessment teaching strategies are provided in the *Testing Program and Alternative Assessment* booklet. 📁

Extension
Have each student choose an artwork created during the study of this chapter. Instruct them to include a credit line for the work. In small groups, have students discuss their completed works, focusing on the subject, composition, and content.

Art Criticism and Aesthetic Judgment

(pages 24–39)

Resources

📁 Chapter 2 Study Guide

📁 Chapter 2 Test

📁 Computers in the Art Classroom

📁 Cultural Diversity in Art

📁 Portfolio and Assessment Techniques

📁 Reproducible Lesson Plan 2

🔊 Transparency CC-2, Romare Bearden. *Three Folk Musicians*

🔊 Transparency 2, Käthe Kollwitz. *Seed for Sowing Shall Not Be Ground*

📖 Fine Art Print 3, Jan Steen. *The Dancing Couple*

📖 Fine Art Print 4, Peggy Flora Zulacha. *Map Still Life with Carnation, Keys, and Glasses*

📖 Fine Art Print 5, Pieter Bruegel. *The Tower of Babel*

 Use Performing Arts Handbook page 414 to help students discover how Martha Graham uses aesthetics in her modern dance movements.

24

▲ **FIGURE 2.1** Henri Matisse is known for his spectacular use of color. How would you describe this painting? Can you identify the different objects in the painting? What appears to be the subject of the painting?

Henri Matisse. *Purple Robe and Anemones.* 1937. Oil on canvas. 73.1 × 60.3 cm (28¾ × 23¾"). The Baltimore Museum of Art, Baltimore, Maryland. The Cone Collection, formed by Dr. Claribel Cone and Miss Etta Cone of Baltimore, Maryland.

FEATURED ARTISTS

Leo and Diane Dillon
John Dunnigan
Ernst Ludwig Kirchner
Julio Larraz

Henri Matisse
Georgia O'Keeffe
José Clemente Orozco

Faith Ringgold
Alma Thomas
Leo Twiggs

Art Criticism and Aesthetic Judgment

Have you ever recommended a new music CD to your friends? If you have, you were judging the music and making decisions about why it was a success and not a failure. You were acting as a critic.

Have you ever become so absorbed in watching a wonderful play or movie that you forgot about the passing of time? If you have, you were deeply involved in a work of theatrical or cinematic art and you were having an aesthetic experience. Understanding criticism and aesthetics as they apply to art is the purpose of this chapter.

When you look at Matisse's *Purple Robe and Anemones* **(Figure 2.1),** you may have difficulty understanding what you see because everything looks so flat. Notice that you can see both the top and sides of the table. The artist has used the same effect in painting the woman. Every area of the painting is filled with patterns of lines or shapes. Where do you see patterns in this work? Most of the colors are very bright because Matisse used color to express his emotions and ideas. He was more concerned with visual pleasure through color and pattern than with realism in his paintings.

Developing Your
PORTFOLIO

The act of creation may be satisfying for an artist. The act of appreciating an artwork—having an aesthetic experience—can be satisfying for a viewer. Select an artwork in the book that attracts your eyes. Study it for several minutes. Read the caption and answer any questions. Give yourself time to perceive the artwork instead of just looking at it. Then write a short paragraph about the experience and what you learned from it. Be sure to list the title of the artwork as well as the artist.

OBJECTIVES

After completing this chapter, you will be able to:

- Explain the purpose of art criticism.
- Use the steps of art criticism.
- Explain the three aesthetic theories of art.
- Know what to look for when judging functional objects.
- Use the steps of art history operations.

WORDS TO LEARN

criteria
aesthetics
art criticism
aesthetic experience
description
analysis
interpretation
judgment
literal qualities
design qualities
expressive qualities
Imitationalism
Formalism
Emotionalism
individual style

Chapter Overview

Chapter 2 explains the importance of art criticism and introduces students to the sequential procedures of art criticism. It then examines the three aesthetic theories of art—Imitationalism, Formalism, and Emotionalism and introduces students to the operations of art history.

Examining the Artwork

Ask students to review Figure 2.1, and emphasize that this is a painting of patterns and colors, not just a woman in a decorative room. Point out the numerous patterns and repetitions such as, the flowers in the vase are a repetition of black shapes surrounded by round flower shapes of different colors. The vase has two sets of patterns: black straight lines at the neck, and black curved lines repeated on the bottom. The green table is decorated with patterns of curved lines. The black floor has a pattern of white lines creating diamond shapes. The purple robe has repetitions of curved white lines. The white blouse has a design of repeated gray shapes. Ask: What other patterns do you notice?

Tell students that Matisse was the leader of a group of painters called the "Fauves" (wild beasts) who believed in using color for the pure joy of seeing.

National Standards

This chapter addresses the following National Standards for the Visual Arts:
  2. (a, b)   **5.** (a, b, c)
  3. (a, c)   **6.** (a, b)
  4. (a, c)

25

DEVELOPING A PORTFOLIO

Art Criticism Entries Whether students critique their own artwork, the work of another student, or the work of a famous artist, art criticism entries kept in their portfolios provide excellent opportunities to demonstrate their knowledge of the elements and principles of art. It also allows them to share their personal interpretation of works of art in a nonthreatening, written format. Remind students that interpretations and judgment may vary from person to person. There are no right or wrong answers. It's up to the students to provide facts and evidence to support their opinions. Encourage students to periodically review their art criticism entries to determine whether they have seen any growth in their art knowledge since they first evaluated the artwork.

Art Criticism: Learning from a Work of Art

(pages 26–30)
(National Standards: 2b, 3a)

FOCUS...........

Objectives

After completing this lesson, students will be able to:

■ Name and define the four steps used in art criticism.

■ Apply art criticism to a work of art.

Supplies

■ Fine art reproduction

■ Variety of objects, fabric, paper, yarn; magnifying glass

■ Markers, magazine illustrations

■ Art reviews

Resources

📁 Artist's Profile, Georgia O'Keeffe

📁 Concept Map 2A, *Art Criticism Approach*

📁 *National Gallery of Art Correlation Bar Code Guide*

TEACH.........

Motivator

Ask students to identify the titles of several current movies and explain why each movie was, or was not, considered a successful one. Encourage them to recognize how different people might have a set of criteria for "successful" that is not the same as another's criteria. Tell them that in Chapter 2 they will learn more about art criticism and aesthetic judgment.

Art Criticism: Learning from a Work of Art

There are professional critics who appear on television or write reviews about new movies, plays, television shows, videos, books, art exhibits, and music. These critics describe their responses to various forms of art, and give you their assessment of the merits of the works. You may not always agree with their opinions because your **criteria,** or *standards of judgment,* may be very different from those of the professional critic. In this chapter you will learn about **aesthetics** (es-**thet**-iks), *the philosophy or study of the nature and value of art.* This will allow you to form your own intelligent opinions about works of art. You will also learn about art criticism. **Art criticism** is *an organized approach for studying a work of art.*

Why Study Art Criticism?

What do you think of when you hear the word *criticism*? Do you think it means saying something negative? This is not true. A criticism can be a positive statement. For example, when you shop for clothes, you try on many things. You act as a critic using personal criteria to determine which pieces of clothing look good on you and which pieces do not suit you. You have developed your own criteria for choosing clothing through personal experience.

When you look at Alma Thomas's painting, *Iris, Tulips, Jonquils, and Crocuses* **(Figure 2.2),** you may experience confusion. You may not have had enough experience to develop a set of criteria to judge a work that has no recognizable subject. If you are like most people who are new to art, you may not know what to say. You may be afraid that you will say the wrong thing.

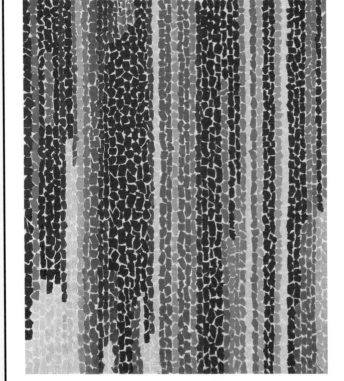

◄ **FIGURE 2.2** At first glance, this painting appears to consist of simple shapes and bright colors. The title of the work, however, should help you understand what the dabs of color represent. Notice how large the painting is. How big does that make each dab of color? Can you imagine the garden these flowers would grow in?

Alma Thomas. *Iris, Tulips, Jonquils, and Crocuses.* 1969. Acrylic on canvas. 152.4 × 127 cm (60 × 50″). The National Museum of Women in the Arts, Washington, D.C. Gift of Wallace and Wilhelmina Holladay.

TECHNOLOGY OPTIONS

National Gallery of Art Videodisc Use the following to help students practice the art-criticism process.

Peter Paul Rubens	Honoré Daumier	Eugène Delacroix
Daniel in the Lions' Den	*Wandering Saltimbanques*	*Columbus and His Son at La Rábida*

Search Frame 776	Search Frame 1164	Search Frame 1128

Use Glencoe's *Correlation Bar Code Guide to the National Gallery of Art* to locate more artworks.

Art criticism is not difficult. In fact, it can be a lot of fun. At the very least, it can make the study of art less mysterious and more logical. Art criticism is a sequential approach for looking at and talking about art.

Your own life experiences may also help you understand the meaning of each work of art. No one has done or seen exactly the same things you have, so no one will see exactly what you see in a work of art. No one can think exactly the way you think. You may see ideas in a work of art that were never dreamed of by the artist. This does not mean that you are wrong; it simply means that the work of art is so powerful that it has a special meaning for everybody.

Learning art criticism will help you interpret works of art. It will give you the confidence to discuss works of art without worrying about what other people might think. It will help you to organize your thoughts. You will develop the courage to speak your mind and make sound aesthetic judgments.

As you learn the language of art, you will be able to "dig deeper" into the layers of meaning of each art object. The deeper you dig, the more important your feelings for that work of art will become. This will make your **aesthetic experience,** or *your personal interaction with a work of art,* more meaningful and memorable. The work will then become a permanent part of your memory.

The Steps of Art Criticism

When you become involved in the process of art criticism, you learn *from* the work of art. Critiquing an artwork is like playing detective. You must assume the artist has a secret message hidden

within the work. Your job is to find the message and solve the mystery.

In this chapter you will learn a special four-step approach that will help you find the hidden meanings in art. The four steps, which must be taken in order, are *Description, Analysis, Interpretation,* and *Judgment.* By following these steps you will be able to answer the following questions:

- What do I see? (*Description*)
- How is the work organized? (*Analysis*)
- What is the artist trying to communicate? (*Interpretation*)
- Is this a successful work of art? (*Judgment*)

As you go through the steps of *description* and *analysis,* you will collect facts and clues. When you get to *interpretation,* you will make guesses about what you think the artist is trying to say. Finally, during *judgment,* you will make your own decisions about the artistic merit of the work.

Step One: Description (What do I see?)

In the first step of art criticism, **description,** you carefully *make a list of all the things you see in the work.* These include the following:

- The size of the work, the medium used, and the process used.
- The subject, object, and details.
- The elements of art used in the work.

During the description step, notice the size of the work and the medium used. You will find these facts in the credit line. This information will help you visualize the real size and look of the work. Notice that Figure 2.1 on page 24 and Figure 3.1 on page 40 are about the same size as reproduced in this book. Read both credit lines and notice the difference in the actual size of each work.

Vocabulary

Ask students to think about the way they use the word *criticism.* Ask volunteers to find a definition for the word in the dictionary. Tell them that although artists may be offended by what critics might say about their art, art criticism is not necessarily a negative evaluation.

Promoting Discussion

Direct students' attention to *Iris, Tulips, Jonquils,* and *Crocuses,* Figure 2.2 by Alma Thomas. Inform students that the artist was a painter, teacher, and gallery director who is considered one of the leaders of African-American abstract art. Alma Thomas began creating art in the 1920s, using the media of sculpture. Then in the 1950s she began painting, but it was not until the 1960s and at the age of 74 that she developed her own personal style. She chose abstract art as her form of expression.

Direct students to the title of this work. It will help the viewer identify the abstract images as flowers. Explain that the flat rows of bright colors painted with short brushstrokes give the viewer an illusion of these three kinds of flowers.

Point out that Alma Thomas establishes a visual rhythm by repeating strokes in the same direction and by using the white background to clearly define a series of repeating columns. Explain how the white background also allows the viewer's eye to rest between the bright patches of color and helps the viewer move in and out of the design.

Curriculum Connection

Performing Arts If possible, show a video excerpt from an appropriate musical production that includes dance, music, and drama. Ask students to identify how a critic might evaluate the production using a process similar to the steps of art criticism. For example, describing a dance performance might include identifying the number of dancers and the type of dance steps used. Analyzing the dance would focus on how the dancers use space and props. Interpreting would focus on the mood created by the dance and finally, judging the dance would determine whether or not it was successful. The same process could be used to discuss the music and dramatic scenes in the piece. Challenge students to be performing art critics for a movie, video, or song they like.

Promoting Discussion

Have students show the painting in Figure 2.2 to at least three people outside the class. Ask each person to think about and interpret the work of art. Have students record the responses they receive. Ask those people who did not think this work was aesthetically pleasing to give reasons why. Have students report their findings during class discussion.

Developing Perceptual Skills

Have students mentally picture the school cafeteria or other common room. Agree on a single vantage point from which the room is being pictured. Ask them to write down a detailed description of what is seen from that viewpoint. Read the descriptions aloud. Discuss the similarities and differences. Why do some people see details that others miss?

Art Criticism

Select a large, clear reproduction of a fine art print that shows plenty of detail. Ask students to write down two or three descriptive phrases about the artwork. Then, using their sketchbooks, have them sketch the artwork. Ask them to list items in their sketchbook that they only noticed after sketching the work. Did they see details that they initially overlooked? Discuss the importance of careful observation in art criticism.

Look at the painting by José Clemente Orozco called *Barricade* **(Figure 2.3).** Notice that the work is 55 inches tall. How does that compare to your own height? If this artwork were standing on the floor, would the figures be larger or smaller than you? What materials were used to create this work?

During the description step, you must be objective. In describing Orozco's painting, you can say that you see five people. You could not say they are all men. That would be a guess. You can describe the person crouched on the ground as wearing a blue shirt and holding a large knife. You can describe the tense muscles that are bulging on the other four figures, but at this point in the criticism process, you should not try to guess why they are tense.

Look again at Figure 2.3. Line and color are two of the art elements that

play an important part in this work. Can you identify the other art elements used?

Look at Figure 2.2 on page 26. This is a nonobjective work. In nonobjective works, the art elements become the subject matter.

Step Two: Analysis (How is the work organized?)

During this step, you are still collecting facts about the elements and principles of art that are used in the artwork. In **analysis** you *discover how the principles of art are used to organize the art elements of line, color, shape, form, space, and texture.* You will learn how the artist has used the elements and principles to create the content of the art, which is known as the theme or the message. Look at *The Blue Wall* by Leo Twiggs **(Figure 2.4).** Notice the curved lines that outline the two figures. Where do you see the darkest colors? Where are the lightest colors? What textures do you see? Notice how the head of one figure is cut off at the top, and the body of the other is cut off at the waist. As you learn more about the elements and principles you will be able to collect more clues that you can use to interpret each work.

Step Three: Interpretation (What is the artist trying to communicate?)

During Step Three, you will answer the question, "What is the artist trying to communicate?" In **interpretation** you will *explain or tell the meaning or mood of the work.* It is here that you can make guesses about the artwork, as long

◀ **FIGURE 2.3** Orozco was one of the Mexican Muralists who combined the solid forms of ancient Mexican art with the powerful colors of European Expressionism. This work depicts the peasants fighting for freedom during the Mexican Revolution in 1910. What could you do to find out more about the event this painting depicts?

José Clemente Orozco. *Barricade.* 1931. Oil on canvas. 140 × 114.3 cm (55 × 45"). The Museum of Modern Art, New York, New York. Given anonymously.

28 **CHAPTER 2** Art Criticism and Aesthetic Judgment

Curriculum Connection

Science Present students with a variety of objects that yield interesting images when magnified (fabric, plant leaves, paper, yarn). Have students draw an object and write a careful description of it. Then have students examine their objects under a microscope or magnifying glass and write a second description. Have them look at their first drawing and ask them if they see the object differently. Does the experience of seeing the item magnified make it look different than its unmagnified state?

FIGURE 2.4 Your interpretation of this work will depend on the clues you have collected during the first two steps of art criticism—description and analysis—plus your personal life experiences. People have different experiences which will produce a variety of interpretations, all of which could be acceptable.

Leo Twiggs. *The Blue Wall.* 1969. Batik painting. 61 × 76.2 cm (24 × 30″). Private collection.

as they appear to be supported by what you see in the work. Interpretation can be the most difficult step in art criticism, because you must dare to be adventurous in stretching the range of your thought processes and imagination. It can also be the most creative and the most rewarding step.

You must use your intelligence, imagination, and courage. You must not be afraid to make an interpretation that is different from someone else's. After all, you are different from other people. Your interpretation will be influenced by what you have experienced and seen in your life.

Your interpretation must be based on the visual facts and clues you collected during your first two steps. Your interpretation can be based on your feelings, but your feelings must be backed up by observation of what you actually see in the artwork.

When you look at the two boys in Figure 2.4, you notice that the boys are

frowning and looking away from each other, but you also notice that there is one point in the work where they are touching. What do you think is happening? What is the artist telling you about these two boys?

Step Four: Judgment (Is this a successful work of art?)

In Step Four you will judge whether or not the work is successful. In **judgment** you *determine the degree of artistic merit.* This is the time to make your own decisions. There are two levels of judgment to be made. The first is personal. Do you like the work? No one can ever tell you what to like or dislike. You must make up your own mind. To make a fair judgment, you must be honest with yourself. Only you know why you feel the way you do. Otherwise, you may close yourself off from experiencing different kinds of art. The second level of judgment you must make is also subjective, but it is somewhat different. At this

Promoting Discussion

Discuss how people in different occupations analyze or break down their object of study in order to better understand it. For example, a chemist analyzes a compound to discover its ingredients. A stockbroker analyzes the stock market to find out which factors cause the market to rise or fall. Relate these practices to that of art critics, who analyze an artwork to figure out how it is organized.

Promoting Discussion

Select a candid photo from a recent school yearbook. Choose an image that includes ambiguous emotions or activities. Have students write a paragraph interpreting the photo. Discuss how the interpretations differ. Do students who know the people in the photograph interpret it differently? What other factors influence someone's interpretation of a picture?

Art Criticism

Be very sure that students understand that interpretation is much more than storytelling. Literature students must interpret and generalize from the given data. This process is also required in art if they are to perceive more than superficial qualities. During step three, each student must go beyond storytelling to generalize, to find the metaphor or allegory in the work. To say that Figure 2.4, *The Blue Wall,* is about two boys by a wall is not enough. Study the relationship between the two boys. Notice that even though the boys look away from each other as if they are angry or frightened, their bodies touch ever so slightly. Ask students what they think the touching may mean. They must see the touching and sense the relationship between the boys.

ASSESS...........

Self-Assessment

Have students complete the review questions on this page. Answers are provided below.

Reteaching

■ Have students select a studio project that they completed in this class and write a short critical review of it. Have them clearly label the four steps of art criticism in their review.

Enrichment

■ Have students read short art reviews that you have gathered from local newspapers or national magazines, such as *Art in America, ArtNews, New Art Examiner, Arts,* and *Artforum.* Select the simplest and most clearly written examples and have the students try to identify the first three steps of art criticism in each review.

■ Ask students to share any experiences they have had where listening to others or learning new ideas helped them develop new or different standards of judgment. Ask: How can learning about art help them make more informed judgments about art in its many forms?

CLOSE............

Have students select one of the artworks in this text, briefly state whether they think it is a successful work of art, and give reasons to support their decision.

30

MEET THE
ARTIST
GEORGIA O'KEEFFE

American, 1887–1986

From the time she was a child, Georgia O'Keeffe knew she was going to be an artist. She studied with several teachers and began creating the flower paintings that made her famous. She painted her flowers big so that they would take viewers by surprise. In 1915, however, she realized that she had ideas for art that were not like anything she had been taught. She decided at age 29 to focus totally on nature and she burned her earlier works in order to start fresh, emphasizing shapes and forms. She continued following her own vision throughout her long life, never being pulled into any of the many movements that have dominated the American art scene during the twentieth century.

O'Keeffe loved to see "connections" in the shapes of ordinary things. After painting a shell and shingle many times, she painted a mountain. It was only later that she realized that she had given the mountain the same shape as the shell and the shingle. She saw beautiful forms everywhere, even in the most unusual places, such as the vast desert spaces and parched bones found near her home in New Mexico.

point, you use aesthetics to help you decide whether the work is successful. A work can be very successful aesthetically, but you might not want to live with it.

To make a judgment, you must take your time. **Figure 2.5** is a painting by Georgia O'Keeffe. To judge this painting, first think about how you would describe the subject of the painting. Then consider how the artist has arranged the art elements according to

the art principles in order to create the composition. Notice how she has used shading to make the skull look solid and the drapery look like a hanging banner. However, she has painted the red borders and the black shape behind the skull flat. Then, think about the feeling the painting gives you. By taking time to look at and describe, analyze, and interpret what you think the meaning of the painting might be, you will be able to make an intelligent judgment. Ask yourself, is this a work of artistic merit? Is it successful?

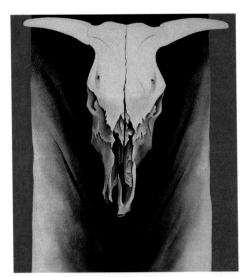

 Check Your Understanding

1. What is aesthetics?
2. Name and describe the four steps of art criticism in order.

◀ **FIGURE 2.5** Georgia O'Keeffe loved the West. She shocked the public with paintings of objects from her environment that people were not used to seeing hanging on a wall. She painted *Cow's Skull: Red, White, and Blue* because she wanted to create something uniquely American. Do you think she succeeded?

Georgia O'Keeffe. *Cow's Skull: Red, White, and Blue.* 1931. Oil on canvas. 101.3 × 91.1 cm (39⅞ × 35⅞"). The Metropolitan Museum of Art, New York, New York. The Alfred Stieglitz Collection, 1952.

30 | **CHAPTER 2** Art Criticism and Aesthetic Judgment

 Answers to Check Your Understanding

1. Aesthetics is the philosophy or study of the nature and value of art.
2. The four steps of art criticism are *Description, Analysis, Interpretation,* and *Judgment. Description,* in art criticism, consists of making a list of all the things you see in a piece of art. In *analysis,* you discover how the principles of art are used to organize the art elements of line, color, shape, form, space, and texture. In *interpretation,* you will explain or tell the meaning or mood of the work. The final step, *judgment,* consists of determining the degree of artistic merit in the work of art.

Aesthetics: Thinking about a Work of Art

Aesthetics is a branch of philosophy concerned with the nature and value of art. Physical beauty was once the only criterion for judging the quality of art. Today, artwork is judged by a different set of criteria and instead of being called "beautiful," a good work of art is called "successful." Some successful works of art may not look pretty, but they may be well-organized, and/or elicit emotional responses from viewers. If a work of art contains strange, disturbing images, yet makes you think, it may be successful.

Aesthetic Theories and the Quality of Art

The aesthetic qualities that are discussed most often by *aestheticians* (specialists in aesthetics) are the literal qualities, the design qualities, and the expressive qualities. These are directly related to the properties of art discussed in Chapter 1 on pages 18 and 19: subject, composition, and content. The **literal qualities** are *the realistic qualities that appear in the subject of the work.* For instance, if the artist depicts a realistic figure of a man on a horse, the literal qualities of the work are the images of a man on a horse. The **design qualities,** or *how well the work is organized,* are found when you look at the composition of the work. Does it look balanced? Is there a rhythmic quality? Is there variety? Has the artist made a unified work of art? These are the types of questions one must ask to determine how well organized a work is. The **expressive qualities,** or *those qualities that convey ideas and moods,* are those you notice when you study the content of a work. Is there something in the work that makes you feel a certain emotion or conveys an idea to you?

The three aesthetic theories of art criticism are most commonly referred to as Imitationalism, Formalism, and Emotionalism.

Imitationalism and Literal Qualities

Some critics think that the most important thing about a work of art is the realistic presentation of subject matter. It is their opinion that a work is successful if it looks like and reminds the viewer of what he or she sees in the real world. People with this point of view feel that an artwork should imitate life, that it should look lifelike before it can be considered successful. This aesthetic theory, called **Imitationalism,** *focuses on realistic representation.*

Formalism and Design Qualities

Other critics think that composition is the most important factor in a work of art. This aesthetic theory, called **Formalism,** *places emphasis on the design qualities,* the arrangement of the elements of art using the principles of art.

Emotionalism and Expressive Qualities

This theory is concerned with the content of the work of art. Some critics claim that no object can be considered art if it fails to arouse an emotional response in the viewer. The expressive

Aesthetics: Thinking about a Work of Art
(pages 31–33)
(National Standards: 2a, 2b, 3a, 5c)

FOCUS...........
Objectives
After completing this lesson, students will be able to:
- Define the term *aesthetics.*
- Discuss three different aesthetic viewpoints.

Supplies
- Functional objects
- Furniture/housing catalogs

Resources

- Application Activity 3, *The Critic's Choice*
- Application Activity 4, *Sharpening Your Skills*
- Cooperative Learning Activity 3, *The Great Aesthetic Debate*
- Cooperative Learning Activity 4, *You Be the Judge*
- Enrichment Activity 3, *Examining Critical Reviews*

TEACH.........
Motivator
Ask students to go through the book and select artworks that they like. Then ask volunteers to display their choices in turn and ask the class: Do you consider this work true to life? Why would someone find it visually interesting? What message, idea, or feeling does this work communicate to you?

Remind students that the goal of using aesthetics in art is discovering an answer to the question "What is art?"

TECHNOLOGY OPTIONS

National Gallery of Art Videodisc Use the following images to discuss aesthetics in artworks.

Jan van Huysum
Flowers in an Urn

Search Frame 968

Claude Monet
Ships Riding on the Seine at Rouen

Search Frame 1380

William M. Harnett
My Gems

Search Frame 1972

Use Glencoe's *Correlation Bar Code Guide to the National Gallery of Art* to locate more artworks.

Art Criticism

Have students write a description of what they see in Figure 2.6 and how they react to it. Next, have them share and discuss their response. Finally, have students focus on describing and evaluating the content of Figure 2.6. Ask: What message do you think the artist wanted to communicate with this work? (Answers will vary.) Do you think he/she succeeded in communicating that message? Why or why not?

Art Criticism

Refer students to Figure 2.7 or bring some functional objects to class such as, cookware, a chair, eating utensils, or a drinking glass. Then ask the students to criticize the object. As they begin interpretation, remind them that they must try it out. At the judgment stage they must make two decisions: Is the object aesthetically pleasing? Does it function properly?

Sparking CREATIVITY

Want students to think creatively about aesthetics? Suggest this: We need a critical eye and aesthetic judgment in many aspects of our daily life. Skim through a catalog for furniture and housewares to see the many different tastes it shows. Test your own aesthetic sense. Cut out from catalogs the furnishings of what you consider a well-designed living room, bedroom, or den. Look for furniture, drapes, bedspreads, rugs, lamps, and decorative pieces. Cut out shapes for each room and arrange them on a sheet of paper. Then share your ideas with classmates.

qualities are the most important to them. Their theory, called **Emotionalism,** *requires that a work of art must arouse a response of feelings, moods, or emotions in the viewer.*

Look at *Papiamento* by Julio Larraz **(Figure 2.6).** You may use the theory of Imitationalism to judge this work as successful because the artist has painted everything very accurately. You can recognize the texture of the freshly-pressed, white cotton dress, the light flickering on the large, tropical leaves, the texture of the trunk of the palm tree, the palm fronds, the yellow sand of the beach, and the beautiful blue of the Caribbean waters. Someone else may choose the theory of Formalism to judge the work as successful because the artist has arranged the objects so that the

foreground is in shadow and the background glows brightly with sunshine. A third person may choose the theory of Emotionalism because of the mysterious mood created by hiding the woman in the shadow of the tree, or because the painting may arouse in the viewer emotional associations with memories of a vacation on a Caribbean island.

You can judge art using just one aesthetic theory or more than one, depending on the type of art and your own purposes. If you limit yourself to using only one theory, however, you may miss some exciting discoveries in a work. Perhaps the best method is to use all three. Then you will be able to discover as much as possible about a particular piece of art.

▲ **FIGURE 2.6** Notice how the artist has blended the woman into the painting. You don't see her until you look carefully. What may have been the artist's reasons for doing this? The title of this work, *Papiamento*, is the name of a language spoken in the Antilles. What else could you find out about the work and its artist that might help you to understand it better?

Julio Larraz. *Papiamento.* 1987. Oil on canvas. 143.5 × 209.5 cm (56½ × 82½″). Courtesy of Nohra Haime Gallery, New York, New York.

Curriculum Connection

Performing Arts Encourage students to relate the aesthetic response to a music, theatre, and dance experience. Ask them to describe how music creates an auditory response, while theatre and dance include visual, kinesthetic, and auditory stimuli. Remind them that all art forms provide an opportunity to respond aesthetically both as a participator and as an observer. Then ask them to list the kinds of art, performing and visual, that they respond to most strongly. Ask volunteers to describe an experience they have had either as a performer or observer in musical, theatre, or dance performances.

Activity — Aesthetic Theories

Applying Your Skills. Select one large work of art in this book. Show the picture to at least three people outside of class. Ask them whether they like the work. Then ask them to tell you why they like or dislike the work. Classify their answers according to the three aesthetic theories of art: Imitationalism, Formalism, or Emotionalism.

Judging Functional Objects

You can use art criticism to make aesthetic judgments about functional objects such as cars, shoes, or fine china. The objects in **Figure 2.7** are an example. In criticizing functional objects, you follow the first two steps of art criticism—description and analysis—as described earlier. However, during the third step, interpretation, you must consider the purpose of the object as its meaning. Does a silver soup ladle look like it will transfer liquid from one container to another without dripping and splashing? That is, does it look like it will function properly? In the last step, judgment, you must consider if the object works when it is used. A chair may look beautiful, but if it is not comfortable to sit in, then it does not function properly. It is unsuccessful.

Judging Your Own Artwork

Art criticism will help you use critical thinking to analyze your own works of art. The four steps of art criticism will help you be as honest and unbiased as possible. When you apply all four of the steps of art criticism to your work, you should find out why your work either needs improvement or is a success.

✓ Check Your Understanding

1. What are the three aesthetic qualities most often discussed by art critics?
2. What is Imitationalism?
3. How are Formalism and Emotionalism different?
4. How does judging functional objects differ from judging fine art?

▲ **FIGURE 2.7** These chairs are appealing to the eye, but are they successful as functional objects? To find out, you will have to apply the steps of art criticism. Do they appear to be the right height for sitting? Would they provide enough back support? Is the padding thick enough for comfort?

John Dunnigan. *Slipper Chairs*. 1990. Purpleheart wood with silk upholstery. Left: 66.9 × 63 × 57.5 cm (26¼ × 25½ × 23″). Right: 110.5 × 66.7 × 61 cm (43½ × 26¼ × 24″). © John Dunnigan. Renwick Gallery, National Museum of American Art, Smithsonian Institution, Washington, D.C.

ASSESS
Self-Assessment
Have students complete the review questions on this page. Answers are provided below.

Reteaching
■ Have students work in pairs to explore one assigned aesthetic view, focusing on subject, composition, or content. Partners should look through the text, noting artworks that especially appeal to a person who prefers their aesthetic view. Ask each pair of students to select four artworks to share and discuss with the other members of the group.

Enrichment
■ Help students discuss the distinctions between the aesthetic viewpoints.

CLOSE
Ask students to identify the aesthetic view that most appeals to them individually, then have each write a paragraph explaining reasons for that preference.

✓ Answers to Check Your Understanding

1. The aesthetic qualities that are discussed most often by aestheticians are the literal qualities, the design qualities, and the expressive qualities.
2. *Imitationalism,* an aesthetic theory, focuses on realistic representation.
3. *Formalism,* an aesthetic theory, places emphasis on the design qualities. *Emotionalism* requires that a work of art must arouse a response of feelings, moods, or emotions in the viewer.
4. To judge functional objects, one must also determine whether the object functions as it is intended to, as well as is it aesthetically pleasing.

Art History: Learning about a Work of Art

(pages 34–35)
(National Standards: 3a, 4a, 4c, 5b)

FOCUS...........

Objectives

After completing this lesson, students will be able to:
- Define art history.
- Tell how time and place influence a work of art.

Resources

📁 Concept Map 2B, *Art History Approach*

📁 Enrichment Activity 4, *At the Museum*

TEACH..........

Motivator

Have students bring in a photograph of themselves. Discuss what someone might think about a person in a photograph if that were the only information available about the subject. Ask: What if a series of photographs were available that ranged from a person's infancy through adulthood? Point out to students that much would still remain unknown about the person. Ask students how they could collect more information on the subject of a photo. Relate their responses to an art historian's use of interview, letters, diaries, and knowledge of the culture in which an artwork was made.

Art History: Learning about a Work of Art

You can develop your appreciation for a work of art by gathering information about the artist and the time period in which the work was created. There is a four-step approach for organizing the way you gather information about a work of art. The four steps make up *art history operations*. The names for the four steps of art history operations are the same as the four steps for art criticism: *Description, Analysis, Interpretation,* and *Judgment.* For art history operations, however, there are different definitions for the terms and different questions to be answered.

- **Description.** When, where, and by whom was the work done?
- **Analysis.** What is the style of the work and can the work be associated with an art movement?
- **Interpretation.** How did time and place affect the artist's style, in terms of subject matter, composition, and content?
- **Judgment.** Is the work considered to be significant in the history of art?

Step One: Description

During this step you will look for information *about* the work of art. You want to know who did it, when, and where it was done. If you were looking at an original work of art, you would look for the artist's signature and the date on the work itself. In this book, because the works have been reduced to fit on the page, you will probably not be able to see the artist's signature or the date on the work. You will find that information in the credit line, however. If you look at the credit line for **Figure 2.8,** you will discover that this

▲ **FIGURE 2.8** The objects in this work are easy to recognize—trees, mountains, and night sky—but the colors are not what you might expect. Why do you think the artist used these colors? What does he appear to be saying?

Ernst Ludwig Kirchner. *Winter Landscape in Moonlight.* 1919. Oil on canvas. 120.7 × 120.7 cm (47½ × 47½"). The Detroit Institute of Arts, Detroit, Michigan. Gift of Curt Valentin in memory of the occasion of Dr. William R. Valentiner's 60th birthday.

TECHNOLOGY OPTIONS

National Gallery of Art Videodisc Use the following images to provide a closer study of the art-history processes.

Jasper Francis Cropsey
Autumn—On the Hudson River

Search Frame 1926

Auguste Renoir
Regatta at Argenteuil

Search Frame 1294

Claude Monet
The Artist's Garden at Vétheuil

Search Frame 1388

Use Glencoe's *National Gallery of Art Correlation Bar Code Guide* to locate more artworks.

painting was created by the same artist who painted **Figure 2.9,** Ernst Ludwig Kirchner. Figure 2.9 was painted in 1907. Compare that date to Figure 2.8. Which was painted earlier? To learn more about Kirchner, such as where and when he lived, you would need to do some further research.

Step Two: Analysis

During analysis, you examine the work and look for information about the artist's style. Style is like handwriting. No two people have exactly the same handwriting and no two artists have exactly the same style. **Individual style** is *the artist's personal way of using the elements and principles of art to express feelings and ideas.* To analyze the style of one artist, you will need to see several works by the same artist. When you look at Figure 2.8 and Figure 2.9, you can easily see the unique aspects of the artist's style: his unusual use of color and his exaggeration of shapes for expressive effect.

Step Three: Interpretation

In order to find the answers for this step you will have to do some research. You will discover that the artist was active in a group of young, adventurous artists in Germany who called themselves Die Brücke (The Bridge) and that their work was part of a larger movement known as German Expressionism. In order to interpret his work, you would need to find out what other artists influenced him, details about his life, and information about his surroundings.

Step Four: Judgment

Once again you must research to find out the importance of this work in the history of art. You must discover what different art historians have to say about

▲ **FIGURE 2.9** Spend a few moments describing this work. What is its most unusual feature? What is the subject matter? Then compare it to Figure 2.8, also by the same artist. What are the similarities and differences between the artworks? Can you draw any conclusions about Kirchner's individual style?

Ernst Ludwig Kirchner. *Seated Woman.* 1907. Oil on canvas. 80.6 × 91.1 cm (31¾ × 35⅞"). The Minneapolis Institute of Arts, Minneapolis, Minnesota. The John R. Van Derlip Fund.

Kirchner and use their assessments to help you shape your own. You can also discover if Kirchner influenced other artists, which would help you judge his importance.

As you study the information in this book and learn more about the language of art, you will begin to acquire information from works of art. You will learn more about the artists who created the works. In Chapters 12 and 13, you will find a brief overview of art history. Refer to these chapters to learn more about art movements and time periods as you encounter them throughout the book.

 ### Check Your Understanding

1. What are the art history operations?
2. Describe each of the steps of art history operations.
3. What is individual style?

 ## Answers to Check Your Understanding

1. The art history operations are *Description, Analysis, Interpretation,* and *Judgment.*
2. The *Description* step consists of when, where, and by whom the work was done. The *Analysis* step consists of the style of the work and if the work could be associated with an art movement. The *Interpretation* step is that of how the time and place affected the artist's style. The *Judgment* step answers the question of whether the work could be considered significant in the history of art.
3. *Individual style* is the artist's personal way of using the elements and principles of art.

Art Criticism

Encourage students to keep an open mind when observing a work of art. In the history of art, historians have often disagreed about the importance of particular styles of art. For example, art from third world countries has been traditionally assigned to exhibits in natural history museums, rather than art museums. Now art historians are more knowledgeable about the cultures from which these artworks come. They agree that an open mind is essential to developing an appreciation of all styles of art.

Art History

Have students look at artworks in the book and choose one from each of three time periods: one that is over two hundred years old, one from the nineteenth century, and one from the last thirty years. Then have them write five descriptive adjectives about each of the selected works. Next, make a list of the three time periods on the board and ask students to call out the artworks and adjectives from their sketchbooks. What general statements can be made concerning the ways artistic expression was used at different times in art history.

ASSESS..........
Self-Assessment

Have students complete the review questions on this page. Answers are provided below.

Enrichment

■ Assign *Enrichment 4* in the TCR. 📁

CLOSE.............

Ask students to briefly state which artist or art historical period they think is the most fun for an art historian to research.

(National Standards: 2a, 2b, 5a, 5b, 5c)

Critiquing the Work

▶ Describe
What do you see?

- The information is in the credit line. The acrylic on canvas is the painting that is sewn in the quilt.

- The fabric frame is a pieced quilt with two strips of beige fabric sewn onto it. The beige strips have the narration of this event printed by hand on them. There are ten people, all of whom are African-American. We see a side view of them, while we have a bird's eye view of the table. In the front of the painting there is a young girl wearing a white dress. The standing woman is dressed in a brightly colored costume. She holds an African mask in her right hand, and she is wearing a headdress.

▶ Analyze
How is this work organized?

- The standing woman is emphasized, because of her brightly colored costume.

- The table, plates, and rug have been painted from a bird's eye view. The chairs and the people are painted from a side view.

- Repetition is shown in: the triangle shapes of the quilt, the rectangle areas of the writing on the beige strips, the rectangle chair backs, the round plate shapes, and the design on the rug. The arrangement of the people is also a repetition.

36

▲ **FIGURE 2.10**

Faith Ringgold. *Bitter Nest Part II: Harlem Renaissance Party.* 1988. Acrylic on canvas, printed, tie-dyed, and pieced fabric. 238.8 × 208.3 cm (94 × 82″). National Gallery of Art, Washington, D.C. © 1998 Board of Trustees.

MORE ABOUT... Faith Ringgold

When Faith Ringgold was a little girl, she was often confined at home with asthma. Her mother, a fashion designer and dressmaker, gave her daughter bits of fabric to play with during the long hours of recuperation. When Ringgold grew up and became an artist, her study of African art coincided with the memory of her mother's use of beautiful fabrics. With her mother's help, Ringgold began to make portrait masks and doll-like soft sculptures of women in Harlem and heroes such as Martin Luther King Jr. She also began making quilts on which she wrote stories, telling of the lives of African-American women.

Notice that the work of art in **Figure 2.10** is a quilt. The center of the work is painted with acrylics on canvas. The frame is made of quilted squares.

 DESCRIBE What do you see?
During this step you will collect information, or clues, about the subject of the work. Use your perception skills to study what you see in the work. If you are not sure of something, do not guess.

■ List the information found in the credit line.

■ Describe the fabric frame around the painting. List and describe the people you see in the painted center. Explain the setting.

 ANALYZE How is this work organized?
The second step in art criticism deals with the composition of the work. This is also a clue-collecting step. Do not make guesses. During this step you will use what you will learn in each chapter about the elements and principles of art.

■ Which person is emphasized? How?

■ What is unusual about the arrangement of objects and people?

■ Where do you see repetition in this work? Describe and locate the objects that are repeated.

 INTERPRET What is the artist trying to communicate?
The third step in art criticism is concerned with the content of the work. You are allowed to make guesses about the meaning of the work during this step. Remember that you do not need to know what the artist meant. Instead, decide what this painted quilt says to you.

■ What does the clothing tell you about this scene?

■ What do you think is happening in this scene? What has happened before this moment, and what will happen next?

■ Why do you think the artist has illustrated this scene on a quilt?

4 JUDGE What do you think of the work?
Now you are ready to make an aesthetic judgment about this work.

■ Do you think this is a successful work of art? Why or why not? Use one or more of the three aesthetic theories explained in this chapter to defend your judgment.

Faith Ringgold, an African-American artist, was born in New York City in 1934. She grew up in a close-knit family in Harlem.

Ringgold taught high school art in New York City for almost twenty years. In 1985, she joined the faculty at the University of California, San Diego.

During the Civil Rights Movement in the 1960s, she focused on political themes in her oil paintings. Then one of her students challenged her to "practice what she preached" and use traditional African materials. Her painting style changed to reflect this. She felt that she could not paint African-Americans using the techniques of shading to achieve realism, and so she changed to painting people to appear as flat shapes.

➡ Interpret
What is the artist trying to communicate?

■ Everyone is dressed for a dinner or a party. The man at the head of the table is wearing a bow tie and a flower in his lapel. Everyone is very dignified except the standing lady. She is wearing a wild costume and does not match the other people.

■ Answers will vary. Most will assume the standing lady is performing for the others. The girl in white has a look of disgust and embarrassment. Answers will vary about the next step. Some may guess that there will be conflict between the girl in white and the standing lady. Some may guess that everyone will sit through the performance politely.

■ Answers will vary. Some may say the artist wanted to know the meaning of every symbol in the work.

➡ Judge
What do you think of this work?

■ Answers will vary. Some will use Emotionalism, because there is a strong undercurrent of feelings obvious in the work. Some may cite Formalism, because of the way the artist has organized three separate parts, the quilt, the written story, and the painting, into a whole composition. Few will choose Imitationalism.

Extension
Tell the students that some of the figures at the table are leaders of the Harlem Renaissance: Alaine Locke, Countee Cousin, Langston Hughes, and Aaron Douglas. Have students research these people and find out more about the Harlem Renaissance.

Time & Place Late Twentieth Century

Tell students that *Dancing on the George Washington Bridge* was created by Faith Ringgold in 1988. Some other events that happened the same year:

Politics: Soviet leader Mikhail Gorbachev instituted *perestroika* (restructuring), transferring economic responsibility from government to private enterprise. A year later, the Berlin Wall came down.
Art: Sculptor Louise Nevelson died in New York at the age of 88.

How Does Imagery Help Us Interpret a Story?

(National Standards: 6a, 6b)

Objectives

After completing this feature, students will be able to:

■ Discuss the imagery of the illustration.

■ Define artistic and literary imagery.

Teaching the Connection

1. Have students read the feature on this page.

2. Ask: How does literary imagery resemble the visual imagery of a book cover? (Both help the reader visualize the characters, setting, and theme of a story.) In what ways might an image in a work of literature express more than a literal meaning? (Imagery can be literal or figurative. Figurative imagery draws comparisons between objects or sensations in the world of a story and something outside that world. Similes, metaphors, symbols, and personification are examples of figurative imagery.)

3. Tell students that Meg and her brother, Charles, are visited by an unearthly time-traveler. He tells them the story of the tesseract. It so happens that Meg's and Charles's father had been experimenting with time travel when he mysteriously disappeared. As the story unfolds, the characters journey through space and time, battling the forces of evil as they try to rescue him.

38

How Does Imagery Help Us Interpret a Story?

▲ FIGURE 2.11

Leo and Diane Dillon. Book cover illustration for *A Wrinkle in Time*. 1979. Watercolor and pastel on paper. 48.4 × 33 cm (19⅛₆ × 13"). Private collection.

Writers and painters are both engaged in forms of artistic expression. Writers help us to connect with the characters and "see" their story using vivid imagery. When you look at a painting, you will not always find characters, but you will usually see images that convey visual ideas and moods. In art, imagery refers to the representation of the visible world as well as the mental impressions evoked by such a representation. In literature, imagery refers to the language that a writer uses to convey a visual picture as well as the sensory and emotional experiences of a particular character or situation.

The cover illustration for Madeleine L'Engle's novel *A Wrinkle in Time* **(Figure 2.11)** suggests the story's themes and introduces its main characters using visual imagery. If you have read this novel, then you may already recognize the characters and their predicament as portrayed in the illustration. Even a reader unfamiliar with the text, however, can interpret the imagery in this painting. To interpret literary imagery, we must listen carefully to the writer's words and visualize the images that those words convey.

Making the Connection

1. Describe the composition of this illustration. How does the design of the picture convey the themes of time and time travel?

2. What emotion or mood does this illustration seem to express? How does it compare with the story?

3. Read (or reread) *A Wrinkle in Time*. How does L'Engle use language to paint a mental picture of the characters and their story? Write a short essay explaining your answer.

Answers to Making the Connection

1. Answers will vary. Students may discuss the geometric shapes and postures of the people. The elements of the illustration lead our eyes to the figures at the center as well as the world contained in the orb. The horizontal and vertical lines that frame or intersect the frame suggest motion or transition. The dark earth tones and deep black convey mystery.

2. Answers will vary. Students may describe the sense of something ominous in the illustration.

3. Answers will vary. Encourage students to define figures of speech such as a symbol or a metaphor and to explore the larger themes of the book.

Building Vocabulary

On a separate sheet of paper, write the term that best matches each definition given below.

1. Standards of judgment.
2. An organized approach for studying a work of art.
3. The art-criticism step in which you make a list of all the things you see in a work of art.
4. The art-criticism step in which you discover how the principles of art are used to organize the art elements of line, color, shape, form, space, and texture.
5. The art-criticism step in which you explain or tell the meaning or mood of the work.
6. The art-criticism step in which you determine the degree of artistic merit of the work.
7. The aesthetic theory that focuses on realistic representation.
8. The aesthetic theory that places emphasis on the design qualities.
9. The aesthetic theory that requires that a work of art must arouse a response of feelings, moods, or emotions in the viewer.

Reviewing Art Facts

Answer the following questions using complete sentences.

1. What will learning the steps of art criticism help you develop?
2. Define the four steps of art criticism.
3. Describe the three aesthetic theories.
4. If the organization of an artwork is most important to an art critic, which aesthetic theory would he or she hold?
5. When criticizing functional objects, what must you consider during interpretation besides beauty?
6. In what ways are the steps of art criticism different from the steps of art history operations? In what ways are they similar?

Thinking Critically About Art

1. **Apply.** Select something from your home that is used solely for aesthetic purposes. Critique it using the four steps of art criticism. When you are finished, ask yourself if the object seems different than it did before. Has your opinion of the object changed?
2. **Analyze.** Find a movie critic's review of a current film in a newspaper or magazine. Read it carefully. Try to find statements that fit each of the four steps of art criticism.
3. **Extend.** Do you think you can appreciate the qualities of a work of art even if you don't like it? Explain your conclusions.

 Dance pioneer Martha Graham uses the principles of aesthetics in the development of her modern dances. See how Graham uses literal qualities, design qualities, and expressive qualities through the use of body movement on page 414.

 Challenge yourself and test your knowledge of art history. Visit the Glencoe Fine Arts site (**www.glencoe.com/sec/art**) and discover information about artworks and famous artists.

Answers to Building Vocabulary
1. criteria
2. art criticism
3. description
4. analysis
5. interpretation
6. judgment
7. imitationalism
8. formalism
9. emotionalism

Answers to Reviewing Art Facts
1. The courage to speak your mind and make sound aesthetic judgments.
2. Description, analysis, interpretation, judgment.
3. Imitationalism, Formalism, Emotionalism.
4. Formalism.
5. How will the object work when it is used.
6. Answers will vary
7. They both use the steps of describe, analyze, interpret, and judge. During art criticism you learn how the work is organized and why. In art history you discover, when, where, and by whom it was created.

Reteaching
- Have students complete *Concept Map 2A* and *Concept Map 2B* in the Reteaching booklet.
- Distribute and have students complete *Chapter 2 Study Guide.*

ASSESSMENT ✓

Evaluate
- Have students complete the *Chapter 2 Test* in the TCR.
- Alternative Assessment teaching strategies are provided below or in the *Testing Program and Alternative Assessment* booklet.

Extension
Challenge students to assume the role of a person whose job requires him or her to make value judgments about a work of art (for example, a museum curator or art critic). Allow each student to select an artwork from the textbook that he or she likes. Ask each student to discuss the artwork from the point of view of the person they have chosen.

The Media and Processes of Art

(pages 40–65)

Resources

📁 Chapter 3 Study Guide

📁 Chapter 3 Test

📁 Computers in the Art Classroom

📁 Cultural Diversity in Art

📁 Portfolio and Assessment Techniques

📁 Reproducible Lesson Plan 3

📌 Transparency CC-3, Pol Bury. *Sphere on a Cylinder*

📌 Transparency 3, Veranda Post. Olowe of Ise

📖 Fine Art Print 6, Joseph Mallord William Turner. *Burning of the Houses of Parliament, 1834*

📖 Fine Art Print 7, Mattie Lou O'Kelley. *Sundown on the Snow*

📖 Fine Art Print 8, Henri de Toulouse-Lautrec. *Au Moulin Rouge*

 While studying this chapter, use Performing Arts Handbook page 415 to help students discover how performing artists use various techniques and media processes to create their work.

40

▲ **FIGURE 3.1** This is an early example of Murray's transition from traditional painting to paintings that have three dimensions. Although this work is still flat, what has she done with space that makes the artwork different?

Elizabeth Murray. *Painters Progress.* 1981. Oil on canvas in 19 parts. Overall 294.5 × 236.2 cm (9'8" × 7'9"). The Museum of Modern Art, New York, New York. Acquired through the Bernhill fund and gift of Agnes Gund.

FEATURED
ARTISTS

Eugene Berman
Isabel Bishop
Edith Bondie
Canaletto

Elizabeth Catlett
Nancy Graves
Rhoda Grossman
Jessica Hines
Winslow Homer
Luis Jimenez
Dorothea Lange

Judy Kensley McKie
Elizabeth Murray
Al Qoyawayma
Miriam Schapiro
Louis Sullivan
Leonardo da Vinci

CHAPTER 3

The Media and Processes of Art

Artists use a variety of tools and techniques to create art. These different tools and techniques affect the look of each individual artwork. For example, a watercolor painting and an oil painting of the same outdoor scene will look very different. A photograph of a baby will look very different from a video of the same baby. The watercolor paints, the oil paints, the photograph, and the video tape are art **media,** *the materials used to make art.*

Painters Progress **(Figure 3.1)** was designed using 19 shaped canvases. The artist's selection of media influenced the effect of the artwork. For instance, the art would appear much different if it had been done using a flat, rectangular piece of canvas. The use of many separate shaped canvases changes the impact of the work. The artist could have drawn on the canvas with chalk or charcoal, but instead she chose brightly–colored paints. Decisions like these about the tools and techniques of art determine the final impression of a work of art. In this chapter, you will learn about many of these tools and techniques—called *media* and *processes*—and how to use them in your own art.

Developing Your
PORTFOLIO
Select some lines from a favorite poem or song. Make sketches of objects and scenes to go with the words. Look through magazines and cut out interesting shapes, letters, or printed words that illustrate your text. Attach the found objects and cutouts around the sketches that you have created. Use a variety of media to draw and paint the remaining images and words of the poem or song. Write a paragraph about how the different media used affect the art. Place your completed work in your portfolio.

OBJECTIVES

After completing this chapter, you will be able to:
- Identify four different shading techniques.
- Name the kinds of painting media.
- Follow the basic steps of printmaking.
- Identify the four sculpting techniques.
- Recognize the media of functional crafts.
- Understand how new media influenced the development of architecture.
- Use the media of technology to create artworks.

WORDS TO KNOW

media/medium
shading
printmaking
print
reproduction
edition
sculpture
photography
analog system
digital system
multi-media programs

41

Chapter Overview
Chapter 3 guides students in understanding that an artist's "tools of the trade" include all of the physical objects necessary to create a work of art. In this chapter, they will learn about these tools and create their own artworks using several media.

Examining the Artwork
Ask students to examine Figure 3.1. Point out that the artist began by creating 19 shaped canvases. Next, she moved the nonobjective shapes around until she was satisfied with the arrangement of pure shapes on the wall. Only then did she consider adding color.

Explain that the three orange shapes represent paint brushes. The green shape looks like a painter's palette. The violet shape might be part of the palette, or it might represent the profile of the painter's face or a distorted human form. Tell students this work was created in 1981— a time when art critics were saying that "painting is dead." One interpretation might be that Murray was using the symbols of the painter and the painter's tools to show that the painting was falling apart, but still holding together because the materials of paint are so appealing.

National Standards

This chapter addresses the following National Standards for the Visual Arts:
1. (a, b)	**5.** (a, b, c)
2. (a, b)	**6.** (a, b)

DEVELOPING A PORTFOLIO
Presentation When making decisions about the appearance of artworks in a portfolio, encourage students to pay attention to important concerns such as the mounting for paintings and protective jackets for pastels and chalk drawings. Remind them to label individual pieces sufficiently to avoid loss. Use slides for projects too large to include and show multiple viewpoints of three-dimensional artworks. Tell students that when photographing a work of art the investment in quality film and careful lighting is worthwhile as it will enhance the finished slide. For more information refer to the separate booklet *Portfolio and Assessment Techniques* that accompanies the *ArtTalk* program. 📁

FOCUS...........

Objectives

After completing this lesson, students will be able to:

- Define the term *medium of art.*
- Name the different kinds of media used in drawing.
- Identify the three basic ingredients found in all paints.
- Explain the three basic steps of the printmaking process.

Supplies

- Pencils, charcoal, crayons, inks, and brushes
- Paints and palette
- Watercolors, brushes, palette knives
- Utility knives, paper, ink

Resources

- 📁 Application Activity 5, *Experimenting with Media*
- 📁 Artist's Profile 3, *Leonardo da Vinci*
- 📁 Artist's Profile 21, *Winslow Homer*

TEACH..........

Motivator

Display an assortment of media and artist's tools such as pencils, charcoal, crayons, inks, and brushes. Ask students to experiment with the media and tell them that in this lesson they will learn more about art media.

Two-Dimensional Media

Elizabeth Murray applied oil paint onto shaped canvases in Figure 3.1. Leo Twiggs used dyes and wax resist on cotton in Figure 1.7 on page 10. Each of these artists created a two-dimensional work of art using different materials. Any material used to create art is called a medium. The plural form of medium is *media*. A medium can be something as ordinary as a graphite pencil or as exotic as gold leaf gilding. In two-dimensional works, such as drawing and painting, artists use media such as crayons, paints, pastels, and pencils.

Drawing

In baseball, a pitcher throws warm-up pitches before facing a batter. Musicians tune their instruments or warm up their voices before a performance. Artists must also prepare before creating art. By drawing, artists become better at perceiving, or carefully noticing, the lines, shapes, and forms of an object.

Many artists use sketchbooks to record their surroundings and to produce studies of objects. Artists also record ideas for later use. The Renaissance artist Leonardo da Vinci filled more than 100 sketchbooks with his drawings and ideas. His sketchbooks included everything from perceptions of people, to his notations on the movement of water **(Figure 3.2),** to his plans for flying machines.

Drawing is usually the first step in producing artworks. Rough sketches, or studies, are often done before creating a work in another medium such as paint or clay. Fashion designers draw their ideas for new styles long before any fabric is cut. Stage designers, graphic designers, and architects

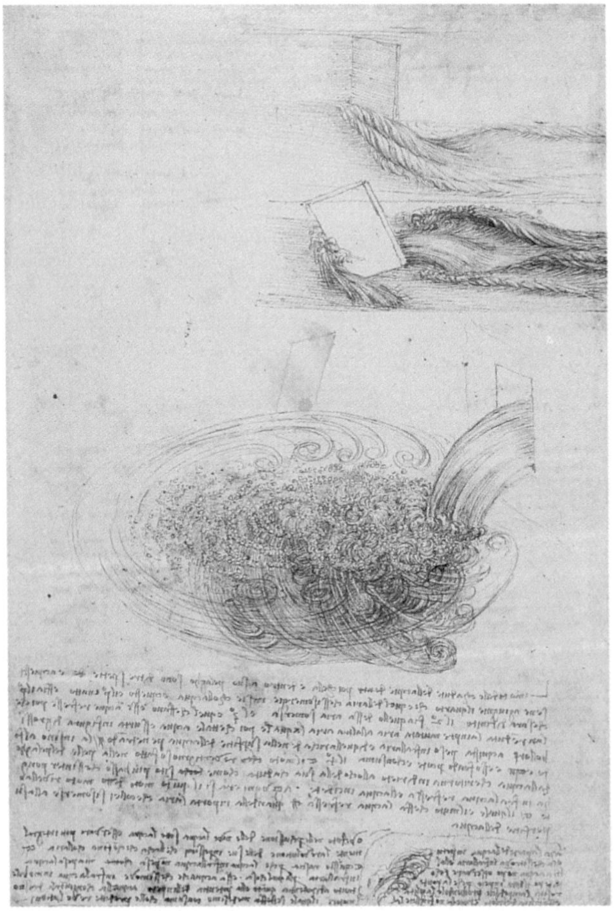

◀ **FIGURE 3.2** Da Vinci's observations of moving water were confirmed as accurate in this century when fast cameras could photographically freeze the action of the water. Da Vinci filled his notebooks with observational sketches and notes. His writing was backward and could only be read when held up to a mirror.

Leonardo da Vinci. Page from his sketchbook showing movement of water. Royal Library, Windsor Castle, London, England. The Royal Collection 1993, Her Majesty Queen Elizabeth II.

TECHNOLOGY OPTIONS

National Gallery of Art Videodisc Use the following to help students analyze other artworks that use drawing, painting, and printmaking media.

Wassily Kandinsky	Honoré Daumier	Mary Cassatt
Improvisation 31 (Sea Battle)	*Two Lawyers*	*The Letter*

Search Frame 2249

Search Frame 2920

Search Frame 3296

Use Glencoe's *National Gallery of Art Correlation Bar Code Guide* to locate more artworks.

must show presentation drawings for a client's approval. **Figure 3.3** is a costume design for a comic ballet, *The Devil's Holiday*. The designer modeled the costumes and stage designs based on the eighteenth-century paintings of Venice by the artist Canaletto.

Although drawings are often used as guides for other artworks, sometimes an artist's drawing *is* the finished artwork. One example of a drawing as a work of art is Canaletto's *Ascension Day Festival at Venice* (**Figure 3.4**).

Drawing Media

Drawing is the process of moving an instrument over a smooth surface to leave a mark, called a line. In drawing, line is the most important element of art. The characteristics of a line are determined, in part, by the medium used to draw it. The most popular drawing media are graphite pencils, colored pencils, crayons, colored markers, pens, pastels, and chalk. Pen and ink, pen and brush, and brushes with watercolors are also used to make drawings.

▲ **FIGURE 3.3** How does this sketch let you know that this character is in a comedy? What makes him look humorous?

Eugene Berman. *Vendeur de Chapeaux.* 1939. Gouache on paper. 31.7 × 24.1 cm (9¾ × 12½"). Wadsworth Atheneum, Hartford, Connecticut. Gift of Mr. and Mrs. James T. Soby. 1939.697.

▶ **FIGURE 3.4** Look closely at this meticulous drawing. Can you tell what city is depicted in this work? What helped you decide?

Canaletto. *Ascension Day Festival at Venice.* 1766. Pen and brown ink with gray wash, heightened with white, over graphite on laid paper. 38.6 × 55.7 cm (15⅛ × 21¾"). National Gallery of Art, Washington D.C. © 1998 Board of Trustees. Samuel H. Kress Collection.

Vocabulary
Have students define *medium* and *media*. Stress the uniqueness of the Latin plural form and ask for examples of similar words that form plurals by changing spellings, rather than adding *s/es*, (for example, foot/feet).

Art Criticism
Invite students to study the effects of various media on drawings. Students should develop a sensitivity to media so that they can make an informed choice when they begin a drawing. Encourage shading and the use of hatching, crosshatching, or stippling to show volume and shadows.

Studio Skills
As an initial drawing experience, the following exercise helps students become comfortable with collaborative efforts and peer review. Give each student a blank sheet of paper. Instruct them to begin a drawing with one object or shape. Have them pass the drawing to the next person who adds something to the drawing. Continue the process until everyone has added something to every drawing. Hang the drawings and have everyone examine the final results. Ask: How did this approach affect the composition? How did it affect the subject? The content? Are any drawings stronger than others? Why?

MORE ABOUT... Drawing Media

The common pencil is still the most often used medium for drawing. Drawing pencils come in 17 degrees of hardness; they are made of graphite, carbon, or charcoal. Colored pencils are also widely used. Wax crayons are another popular choice for students and amateur artists.

Visit Glencoe's art site (**www.glencoe.com/sec/art**) to view a variety of drawings done by famous artists, as well as different drawing techniques that students can put into practice.

x

Critical Thinking

Direct students' attention to the title of the chapter, and in particular to the phrase "two-dimensional." Have them consider the works in Figures 3.7 and 3.9 (pages 45 and 46). Are the scenes in these works meant to appear two-dimensional? After affirming that both artists were striving for a sense of three-dimensional depth, ask students if they can pinpoint the technique used to convey this impression. Finally, ask students to consider why artists might go to the trouble of creating the illusion of depth in two-dimensional works, rather than create three-dimensional works (e.g., sculptures in the round) in the first place.

Studio Skills

Following the above discussion of three-dimensional space in two dimensions, have students try this experiment. Ask them to create a simple geometric shape. Have them make four copies of the object and paste each so that it slightly overlaps the one created before it. Ask them to fill the original object with a deep shade of red and fill each clone with a progressively lighter value. Ask students to comment on the illusion of depth created by the change in value.

Each drawing medium has its own qualities. Chalk and crayon, for example, produce rough lines. Pens, by contrast, make smooth lines. **Figure 3.5** shows lines made with different drawing media.

Crayon
Pastel
Hard pencil
Soft pencil
Watercolor pencil
Color pencil
Thin marker
Wide marker
Wet brush
Dry brush

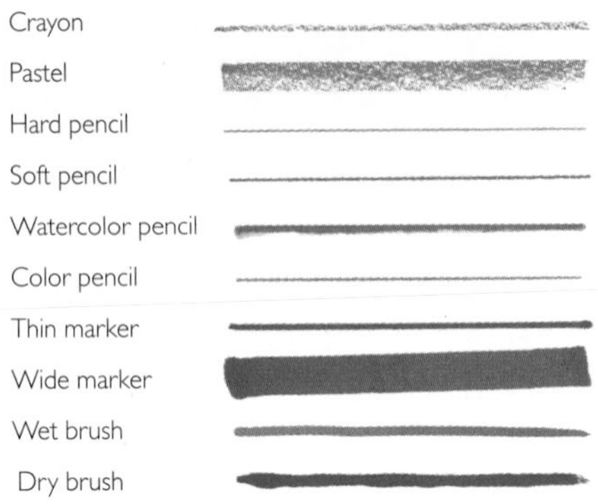

▲ **FIGURE 3.5** Drawing media.

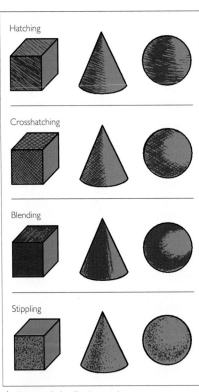

▲ **FIGURE 3.6** Shading techniques.

Hatching
Crosshatching
Blending
Stippling

Shading Techniques

Shading is *the use of light and dark values to create the illusion of form.* There are four main shading techniques:

- **Hatching.** This technique consists of drawing thin lines that run in the same direction. Find the form in **Figure 3.6** that uses hatching.
- **Crosshatching.** Shading created using crisscrossing lines is called crosshatching. Look at the form in **Figure 3.6** that demonstrates this technique.
- **Blending.** Artists perform blending by changing the color value little by little. Find the form in **Figure 3.6** that is shaded using blending.
- **Stippling.** Shading that creates dark values by means of a dot pattern is referred to as stippling. Locate the form in **Figure 3.6** that shows stippling.

Look at the drawing in **Figure 3.7.** Isabel Bishop used three different drawing media to create a drawing that has the look of three dimensions. The artist accomplished this through shading.

Which shading technique was used in Figure 3.4?

Painting

Painting is the process of applying color to a surface using tools such as a brush, a painting knife, a roller, or even your fingers. The surface is the material to which the paint is applied. Canvas, paper, and wood are frequently used as surface material.

All paints have three basic ingredients:

- **Pigments.** Pigments are finely ground colored powders. Pigments come from natural or synthetic materials. Natural pigments include indigo,

---

TEACHER TALK

Sketchbooks To help students gauge their progress, you may find it useful to have them keep a sketchbook of their drawings. Encourage students to look through their sketchbooks from time to time during the term and compare their most recent drawings with earlier efforts. If necessary, help students recognize how their work has matured by "walking" them through critiques of early efforts, then more recent drawings. Periodically, ask students to write a reflection of their progress after this comparison as a record of their artistic growth. Discourage students from using the progress of other students as benchmarks of their own growth.

Isabel Bishop. *Head #5.* No date. Graphite, crayon, and chalk on paper. 29 × 22.6 cm (11¾ × 8¹³/₁₆″). Wadsworth Atheneum, Hartford, Connecticut. Gift of Henry Schnakenberg. 1953.217

Studio Skills

Give students an opportunity to mix paints on palettes. Give each student a palette; old white plates, microwave trays, or foam trays can easily be used in place of palettes. Then let students use acrylic paints on their palettes. Have them work with partners to practice mixing paints before applying them to paper. Encourage partners to discuss and compare the colors and effects they can create. Tell students that in Chapter 6 they will learn more about how artists combine colors to achieve certain effects.

Art History

Tell students that Renaissance artists mixed pigments, which they had to grind up with a mortar and pestle, with linseed oil to make their paint. Turpentine had to be used as a solvent instead of water. An advantage was that the oil dried much slower than egg tempera or fresco, allowing the artist to work much longer. With the extended time available to work, artists could blend with a brush and add layers of transparent glazes, made by thinning the paint with turpentine.

Have students compare the works of Renaissance artists Leonardo da Vinci (Figure 13.41, page 384), Giotto (Figure 10.13, page 263), and Sandro Botticelli (Figure 5.19, page 113).

a vegetable, and the cochineal beetle, an insect. Natural pigments can also be made from minerals or clay. Synthetic pigments are artificially made from chemicals.

■ **Binder.** A binder is a material that holds together the grains of pigment. The binder allows the pigment to stick to the painting surface. Egg yolks mixed with water have long been used as a strong binder for professional artist's tempera paints.

Other binders are linseed oil and wax.

■ **Solvent.** A solvent is a liquid that controls the thickness or the thinness of the paint. Different painting effects require different thicknesses of paint. Using thin watercolor paint gives a light, washed-out appearance; using thick watercolor paint produces a more intense appearance. Solvents are also used to clean paintbrushes and other applicators.

LESSON 1 *Two-Dimensional Media* **45**

! SAFETY NOTE

Safety Labels When using tempera paint or other materials, make certain that the container or package bears one of the following safety labels; *AP* (Approved Product); *CP* (Certified Product); or *HL* (Health Label). The *AP* and *CP* labels certify that the product contains no material in sufficient amounts to be toxic or dangerous to the user. The *CP* label also indicates that the product meets specific quality standards. A *HL* seal is used to certify art products that are appropriate for older students.

Cross-Curriculum: Science

Point out to students that many improvements in paint technology have arisen out of advances made in the field of chemistry in the last 60 years. For example, since 1946, chemists have developed synthetic materials to use as binding vehicles. Some synthetic resins, like the acrylic polymer used in acrylic paint, are often stronger, more flexible, and more water resistant than some natural binders such as egg yolk (used in tempera paints) or gum arabic (used in watercolors). Ask students to examine the labels on paints they use to find out the chemical make-up of each.

Art History

You may wish to distribute *Artist's Profile 21,* Winslow Homer in the TCR and have students keep it in their art notebooks. 📁

Studio Skills

Take this opportunity to explain how to clean and care for brushes and palette knives, and the differences between cleaning up oil paint and water-soluble paint.

MEET THE ARTIST
WINSLOW HOMER

American, 1836–1910

Winslow Homer is considered one of the artists who has captured the true feelings of the United States in his works. Homer developed an appreciation and love for the outdoors while growing up with his two brothers in Cambridge, Massachusetts. By the age of ten, his interest in art began and his talent for drawing became obvious. When he was 19, Homer was accepted as an apprentice at a large printing firm in Boston, even though he had little formal art training.

When his apprenticeship was over, Homer worked as a draftsman, specializing in woodblock engraving. Soon he began illustrating magazines. By the 1860s he was contributing regularly to *Harper's Weekly* magazine as an illustrator of events occurring in the Civil War. After the Civil War ended, Homer traveled to Europe. There, he was influenced by the works of French artists Édouard Manet and Gustave Courbet.

By the 1880s, Homer had begun painting the subject that was to become his trademark—the sea. He loved nature and spent hours outdoors. He felt at home on the sea although he knew its dangers as well. Because he was able to capture the elemental forces of nature, Homer is considered a Realist. His unique talent enabled him, as few others have done before him, to express the reality of the United States.

The look of a finished painting depends on the combination of media, tools, and the surface the artist chooses. In **Figures 3.8** and **3.9,** you can see how Winslow Homer has created two images that are almost exactly alike. However, he has used different media. Figure 3.8 is made with thin, wet, flowing watercolor on white paper. The white in this painting is the white of the paper showing through. Figure 3.9 is painted with thick, creamy oil paint on canvas. The white in this painting is opaque white paint.

Painting Media

As with drawing media, there are many different kinds of painting media, each with its own unique qualities. The artist chooses the paint based on personal preference and the purpose of the work.

Oil-Based Paint. First used in the 1400s, oil paint remains a popular medium today. True to its name, oil paint uses linseed oil as its binder. Its solvent is turpentine.

One advantage of oil paint is that it dries slowly. This allows the artist to blend colors right on the canvas. The work in Figure 3.9 is an oil painting. Notice how smoothly the colors blend.

Water-Soluble Paint. The most popular of water-based painting media, watercolor takes its name from its solvent, water. The binder is gum arabic. Compare the watercolor in Figure 3.8 with the oil painting in Figure 3.9. What differences do you see?

Tempera is another water-based paint. It dries more quickly than oil paint, and it has a more opaque finish than watercolor.

Acrylic paint, which first appeared in the 1950s, uses an acrylic polymer as a binder. The solvent used for acrylic paint is also water. However, once professional acrylic paint dries, it cannot be dissolved. School acrylics have been developed, however, that can be dissolved with soapy water after they dry.

MORE ABOUT... Paints

Paints made with water and gum arabic have been used since ancient times. One form of water paint was used on the illuminated manuscripts of the Middle Ages. Albrecht Dürer (Germany, 1471–1528) used another form of water paint as a wash. Watercolor as we know it now did not develop until the late eighteenth century.

Watercolor has its own characteristics that demand certain ability and knowledge to handle. Watercolor relies on painting thin layers of transparent colors over each other, allowing the paper to give light to the painting. Watercolorists usually use special papers that have grains ranging from smooth to rough and weights ranging from heavy and thick to light and thin.

◄ FIGURES 3.8 AND 3.9 One of these paintings was a sketch made at the scene, and the other was done in the studio based on the first work.

◄ FIGURE 3.8

Winslow Homer. *Sketch for 'Hound and Hunter.'* 1892. Watercolor. 35.4 × 50.7 cm (13¹⁵⁄₁₆ × 20″). National Gallery of Art, Washington, D.C. ©1998 Board of Trustees. Gift of Ruth K. Henschel in memory of her husband, Charles R. Henschel.

◄ FIGURE 3.9

Winslow Homer. *Hound and Hunter.* 1892. Oil on canvas. 71.8 × 122.3 cm (28¼ × 48¼″). National Gallery of Art, Washington, D.C. © 1998 Board of Trustees. Gift of Stephen C. Clark.

Activity | Experimenting with Watercolor

Applying Your Skills. Using watercolor paint, choose one bright color and paint several shapes on a dry sheet of watercolor paper. Then thoroughly brush water on both sides of a sheet of watercolor paper and repeat the process. Share and compare your results with those of classmates.

Computer Option. Drawing with color on the computer is like drawing with light. Light as the computer's pigment can vary in opacity from opaque, like tempera paint, to transparent, like watercolors. Find the menu in the application you are using which controls opacity. Explore the settings. Remember, these qualities change as you paint on different surfaces. If available, investigate rough, smooth, or textured papers.

Studio Skills

Have students experiment with painting media. Have them gather as many different kinds of paint of one hue as they can. For example, they should look for red watercolor, red poster paint, and red acrylic. Have them draw several shapes on a sheet of white paper. Draw one shape for each paint and paint each shape with a different kind of paint. Have them display their results alongside those of their classmates. Then discuss differences and similarities among the different paints. Compare the texture, intensity, value, and reflective quality of each paint.

Art Criticism

Have students work in small groups and select and discuss two paintings from this book. Ask: What idea or feeling do you think the painters of these artworks intended to communicate to viewers? Which painting medium did each artist use? How do you think that choice of medium affects the message of the painting?

Activity

Experimenting with Watercolor

Applying Your Skills. Using a primary hue of watercolor, draw several shapes on a dry sheet of watercolor paper. Repeat the process, this time using paper that has been brushed thoroughly on both sides with water. Demonstrate and discuss your results with students.

Curriculum Connection

Social Sciences Remind students that colors are considered to be warm or cool. (See page 148–149.) Knowing this, commercial decorators and designers attempt to manipulate colors to create certain moods in their designs. Ask: Have you thought that the colors that surround you every day might have an effect on you? Have students write responses to the following questions: Would you return often to a restau-rant that has unappealing color in its décor? What colors do the fast-food chains use? What colors should an employer choose for a work area that will encourage activity and cheerfulness rather than gloom and fatigue? Should a hospital choose warm or cool colors for a restful atmosphere? Encourage responses in terms of the expressive qualities of paint.

Studio Skills

Let students practice their printmaking skills by creating printing plates from various vegetables and erasers. Have students use small knives, utility knives, or potato peelers to slice away parts of the flat cut surface, leaving a simple shape with which to print. Then have students brush tempera paints onto their printing plates and use them to print on sheets of newsprint. Encourage students to plan and create patterns as they print.

Promoting Discussion

Help students review and discuss the four different kinds of printmaking techniques. Ask: How is the image created on each kind of plate? Where and how is the ink applied? How does the printmaker transfer the inked image to paper? Then have the students look at all the artworks in this chapter and identify which kind of printing process was used to create each print.

Activity

Making a Printing Plate

Computer Option. Another computer option includes: Use a line design to make a glue print. Have students look through their sketches. Have them select one to redraw on the computer or make a new drawing that can be used for a glue print. Use line only to make the drawing. Print and transfer the design to cardboard with carbon paper. Follow the lines in the drawing with glue. Dry. Apply ink evenly to the surface with a brayer. Lay a sheet of paper over the ink plate and apply even pressure. Carefully peel back the print.

Printmaking

Printmaking is a *process in which an artist repeatedly transfers an original image from one prepared surface to another.* Paper is often the surface to which the printed image is transferred. *The impression created on a surface by the printing plate* is called a **print.** A print is not the same thing as a reproduction, although sometimes people confuse the two. A print is an original work of art. A **reproduction,** such as the artwork shown in this book, is *a copy of a work of art.*

The Basic Steps of Printmaking

While prints may be made using many different media, processes, and surfaces, all require three basic steps.

- **Creating the printing plate.** A printing plate is the surface on which the desired image is created. In producing a printing plate, the artist

makes a mirror image of the final print. Letters and numbers must be made backward on the plate.

- **Inking the plate.** The artist applies ink to the plate. This is done with a *brayer,* a roller with a handle. For a multicolor print, one plate must be made for each color. The ink creates the image on the print.

- **Transferring the image.** The paper or other material is pressed against the inked plate, and the ink is transferred to the new surface. Sometimes this is done by hand. Other times a printing press is used.

Usually, more than one print is made from a single plate. Together, *all the prints made from the same plate, or set of plates,* form an **edition.** Each print in an edition is signed and numbered by the artist. The printmaker signs the work in the bottom margin and writes the title on each print of an edition as well as the number of each print. The number 10/200 indicates the tenth of 200 prints.

Printmaking Techniques

There are four main techniques artists use to make prints: relief, intaglio, lithography, and screen printing.

- **Relief printing.** In this method, the artist cuts away the sections of a surface not meant to hold ink. As a result, the image to be printed is raised from the background. In **Figure 3.10,** Elizabeth Catlett has controlled the light and dark areas of her linoleum-cut relief print by the amount she has cut away. Notice that

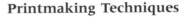

◀ FIGURE 3.10 Catlett has devoted her artistic career to a socially-conscious art that represents the struggles of African–Americans.

Elizabeth Catlett. *Sharecropper.* 1970. Linoleum cut on paper. 45.2 × 43 cm (17¹³⁄₁₆ × 16¹⁵⁄₁₆″). National Museum of American Art, Washington, D.C.

MORE ABOUT...   Printmaking

Artists have been using printmaking techniques for thousands of years. Handprints have been found on the walls of a number of caves. The prints were formed simply—a hand smeared with paint was pressed against the wall. Negative prints were also formed by dotting paint on the wall around a hand.

The meaning of these handprints remains unclear. Since a certain level of skill was involved in this printmaking, a shaman or healer might have been involved, and the prints may have been part of an initiation rite. Another possibility is that the prints are signatures or a form of identification.

the white lines are wider in the very light areas.

- **Intaglio** (in-**tal**-yo or in-**tal**-ee-o). This name comes from the Italian word meaning "to cut into." Intaglio is a process in which ink is forced into lines that have been cut or etched on a hard surface such as metal or wood. Then the plate's surface is wiped clean and the prints are made. You can actually feel the lines of raised ink on an intaglio print.

- **Lithography.** In lithography the image to be printed is drawn on limestone, zinc, or aluminum with a special greasy crayon or pencil. Ink is attracted to this material. When the drawing is completed, the areas that should remain blank are etched with a special solution that repels ink. Then, when the surface is inked, the greasy area alone holds the ink. Because the process is complicated, new materials are being developed to make lithography easier. There are kits for schools that use paper instead of limestone or zinc for the printing plate.

- **Screen Printing.** This is the newest method for making prints. It uses a stencil and screen as the printing plate. The stencil is placed on a fabric screen stretched across a frame. The screen is placed flat on the printing surface. Ink is pressed through the fabric screen where it is not covered by the stencil. If more than one color is used, a separate screen is made for each color. Another term for screen printing is *serigraphy*.

LESSON 1   *Two-Dimensional Media*   **49**

Activity — Making a Printing Plate

Applying Your Skills. You can make your own relief printing plate. Begin by cutting a 4-inch square from a sheet of cardboard. Cut a variety of smaller geometric shapes from the same sheet. Arrange these on the surface of the square. Form an interesting design.

Glue the shapes in place. Let them dry overnight. Apply printing ink to the surface with a brayer. Lay a sheet of paper over your inked plate. Apply pressure evenly. Carefully peel back the print.

Computer Option. Explore the Shape and Line tools in your application. Change line thickness, color menus, gradients, and opacities. Arrange several shapes to make an interesting design. Print onto color transfer paper that is made for your printer. Remember to flip the image before printing if necessary because shapes and letters may be reversed. Follow the instructions on the printing paper package to transfer your design onto paper, cloth, or another surface. (An iron sets some transfer papers while others require more elaborate equipment.)

Check Your Understanding

1. Name four of the most popular media used in drawing.
2. What are the three ingredients found in every type of paint?
3. What are the three basic steps of printmaking?
4. What is an edition?

Answers to Check Your Understanding

1. The most popular drawing media are graphite pencils, colored pencils, crayons, colored markers, pens, pastels, and chalk.
2. Pigment, binder, and solvent are the three ingredients found in every type of paint.
3. The three basic steps of printmaking are: creating the printing plate, inking the plate, and transferring the image.
4. An edition is a series of prints made from one plate or series of plates.

ASSESS..........
Self-Assessment
Have students complete the review questions on this page. Answers are provided below.

Reteaching

- Have the students work with partners to review the four shading techniques. Give each pair of students a photocopy of a drawing in which several shading techniques have been used. Ask the partner to identify and discuss the different techniques. Then let them outline all the areas that have been shaded, using a different color around each shading technique.

- Display several of the students' prints and ask: What kind of artworks are these? *(original prints)* How can you tell? *(the texture of the printing media can be felt on the paper)* If we wanted to make reproductions of these prints, what would we have to do? Be sure students recognize that by photographing or digitizing the print they can make a reproduction of it.

Enrichment
Ask groups of students to work together to learn more about the development of printmaking in Japan. Ask students to find out when Japanese artists began making prints; who some of the most famous Japanese printmakers are; what materials are used in Japanese prints; and how Japanese prints have influenced European artists.

CLOSE............
Have students browse through art books and identify at least one example of a drawing, a painting, and a print.

Three-Dimensional Media
(pages 50–56)
(National Standards: 1a)

FOCUS............
Objectives
After completing this lesson, students will be able to:

- Explain the difference between freestanding sculpture and relief sculpture.
- Describe the crafts of weaving, glass blowing, and ceramics.
- Describe three main uses of architecture.

Supplies
- Small objects of nature: pebbles, twigs, and leaves
- Modeling clay
- Handcrafted items

Resources
📁 Application Activity 6, *Sharpening your Skills*
📁 Cooperative Learning 5, *Practicing Creative Thinking*
📁 Enrichment Activity 5, *Media—A Characteristic of a Culture*

TEACH..........
Motivator
Give each student a lump of clay or another modeling compound; ask students to use this new medium to create a favorite animal shape. When they have finished, help students compare and discuss how their clay sculptures differ from a drawing of the same animal.

Three-Dimensional Media

Have you ever taken a lump of clay and formed it into a bowl or an animal? If so, you were working with three-dimensional media. These media make solid forms that have height, width, and depth.

Sculpture

Sculpture is *a three-dimensional work of art.* Sculpture is art that is made to occupy space. This is one way in which sculpture is different from other kinds of art. Although objects in a drawing or painting can look quite real, the work is flat, or two-dimensional. Artists who create sculpture are called sculptors.

The Media of Sculpture

Like other artists, sculptors use a wide variety of media in their work. Sculpting media include clay, glass, plastics, wood, stone, and metal. No matter what medium is used, a sculpture will be one of two types: sculpture in the round or relief sculpture.

- **Sculpture in the round.** This type of sculpture is surrounded *on all sides* by space. Another name for sculpture in the round is *freestanding* sculpture. You can walk around sculpture in the round or turn it over in your hands to see all sides. Sculptures in the round can be realistic representations of people or objects **(Figure 3.11).** Not all freestanding sculptures have recognizable subjects, however. (See Figure 5.7 on page 102).

- **Relief sculpture.** This type of sculpture projects into space from a flat background. Relief sculptures are designed to be viewed only from one side. **Figure 3.12** shows an example of a relief sculpture attached to a smooth, gently–rounded surface. You cannot see the back of the figure. The figure protrudes out into space from the smooth surface of the vase.

Sculpting Techniques

In addition to a wide array of media, sculptors use a variety of processes. The processes include modeling, carving, casting, and assembly.

▶ **FIGURE 3.11** How do the unusual colors and materials affect the expressive quality of this sculpture?

Luis Jimenez. *Vaquero.* Modeled 1980, cast 1990. Fiberglass and epoxy. Height: 5 m (16′6″). National Museum of American Art, Washington, D.C.

MORE ABOUT... Luis Jimenez

Jimenez's style has been likened to that of regionalist American painter Thomas Hart Benton and Mexican muralist José Clemente Orozco. Like Benton and Orozco, Jimenez selects stereotypical characters, but he transforms them into muscularly three-dimensional forms that are both pop and high-tech.

He feels a strong affinity for Baroque art, which has the same love of expressive anatomy. "When I was in school, Baroque art was hardly mentioned. It was viewed as a corruption of the Renaissance. When I first went to Italy, it was a revelation to really see Baroque art; Bernini, Rubens—it all felt great."

▲ **FIGURE 3.12** Al Qoyawayma adds an architectural quality to his pottery by using relief elements that are forced from inside the pottery wall. He then carves details into the raised relief work.

Al Qoyawayma (Hopi). *Blanketed Figure Vase.* c. 1980. Clay pottery. Height: 27.9 cm (11").

■ **Modeling.** In this process, a soft, pliable material is built up and shaped. Media such as clay, wax, and plaster are used in modeling. Because the sculptor gradually adds more material to build a form, modeling is referred to as an *additive* process.

■ **Carving.** In carving, the sculptor cuts, chips, or drills from a solid mass of material to create a sculpture. Material is removed until the sculpture is completed. Carving is therefore called a *subtractive* process. Wood and stone are the most common carving media.

■ **Casting.** In casting, molten metal or another substance is poured into a mold and allowed to harden. The artist duplicates a form originally molded with clay, wax, or plaster using a more permanent material. Just as in printmaking, an edition of sculptures can be made from the same

mold. Once the edition is complete, the mold is destroyed. This prevents the mold from being used again and safeguards the monetary value of the sculptures that were originally cast.

■ **Assembling.** In this process, also called *constructing,* a variety of different materials are gathered and joined together to make a sculpture. One assembly process involves welding metal, but media can be glued, sewn, or otherwise fitted together. Assembling is sometimes used along with other sculpting processes. A combination of casting and assembling was used to create *Zaga* **(Figure 3.13).**

▲ **FIGURE 3.13** Graves collected natural objects and cast them in bronze at a metal foundry. She then selected certain cast objects from her collection of thousands of objects and assembled them to make her sculpture. She adds color in a very unusual manner. She uses chemicals and heat to make pigments adhere to the metal-like skin so that no details are hidden with thick paint.

Nancy Graves. *Zaga.* 1983. Cast bronze with polychrome chemical patination. 182.9 × 124.5 × 81.4 cm (72 × 49 × 32"). Nelson-Atkins Museum of Art, Kansas City, Missouri. © Nancy Graves/VAGA, New York 1994.

LESSON 2   *Three-Dimensional Media*   **51**

Vocabulary

Students are probably familiar with relief maps from their Social Studies class. Encourage them to apply the same concept to understand *relief sculpture.* Then ask students about the mathematical use of the verbs *add* and *subtract.* Based on these familiar definitions, let students develop their own definitions of *additive methods* of sculpting and *subtractive methods* of sculpting

Aesthetics

Guide students in comparing and discussing the sculptures shown in this lesson. Ask: What is the subject of each work? How does the work make you feel? What message does the work communicate to you? How does it communicate that message? Then have each student write a description of his or her favorite sculpture shown in the lesson.

Studio Skills

Let students use bars of soap to experiment with the sculpting techniques of carving. Have students begin by using knives to carve away small pieces of soap: this will give them a chance to feel the soap and its interaction with the carving tools. Then have students carve familiar objects or animals from their bars of soap. Encourage students to discuss their work as they carve, asking questions and offering one another advice.

Aesthetics

Divide the students into three groups. One group will represent the public, one the art community, and one the art critics. Have each group examine Nancy Graves's sculpture in Figure 3.13 and create a list of its strengths and weaknesses based on the criteria, interests, and agendas of the group they represent.

MORE ABOUT... Nancy Graves

Nancy Graves (United States, born 1940) is an American sculptor best known for her work *Camels.* This sculpture is a group of life-size, furry camels. The intended meaning of *Camels* is not readily apparent. We do know, however, that as a child Graves

regularly visited the natural history museum in her hometown. Then she developed a strong interest in science and the natural world. Graves' work continues to focus on her experience of the natural history museum and what she found there.

CHAPTER 3
LESSON 2

Promoting Discussion

Have students bring examples of hand-crafted items from home. These may be objects they have made, that a friend of family member has made, or something purchased from a professional craftsperson. Display all of the items and have students spend some time examining them. Discuss how the items were made and identify the materials that were used. Ask students why the handcrafted pieces could be considered works of art.

Crafts

Before machines were invented, people made everything by hand. Today, artists are still creating one-of-a-kind items. Some objects are created for practical use, and others are made purely for decorative purposes. Art made to be experienced visually is called *fine art.* Art made to be functional as well as visually pleasing is called *applied art.* Today the distinction between fine art and applied art is fading.

Artists are currently creating both functional and decorative craft objects. Weavings are made from natural wool, linen, silk, cotton, and manufactured fibers. Quilts are stitched from fine fabrics to be hung on the wall like paintings. Baskets are woven from natural materials such as reeds and wood slats **(Figure 3.14),** as well as manufactured fibers. Pottery is made with clay from the earth. Handmade glass objects are formed by forcing air through a tube to shape globs of melted glass. Jewelry is crafted using expensive materials such as precious stones and gold, but it can also be made using paper. As wonderful as technology has become, we still appreciate having an object that is one-of-a-kind and made by hand.

The Media of Crafts

The most commonly used craft media are clay, glass, wood, fiber, and metal. Clay and glass can be used to make plates and cups, vases, and jars. Wood can be used to make furniture or containers. Fiber is used to weave cloth and to make baskets. Metal is used to make utensils and jewelry.

Each craft contains an almost unlimited number of choices. An artist using clay can choose stoneware, earthenware, or porcelain. A weaver can select natural

◄ **FIGURE 3.14** Imagine the skill it took to make this basket and lid perfectly round and to make each twist of the warp just the right size to create points in proportion to the shape of the basket. Notice that the points are smaller at the top and bottom and larger near the center.

Edith Bondie. *Porkypine Basket.* ca. 1975. Wood. 20 × 21.6 × 21.6 cm (7⅞ × 8½ × 8½"). National Museum of American Art, Smithsonian Institution, Washington, D.C.

MORE ABOUT... Quiltmaking

The earliest known evidence of quilting is on a carved ivory figure of an Egyptian pharaoh that dates back to around 3400 B.C. In 1924, a quilt was found on the floor of a tomb in Mongolia. It is a quilted carpet that was made between the first century B.C. and the second century A.D.

The art of quilting was brought to America by the colonists. Because fabric was so precious, every scrap had to be used and reused. The patchwork quilt, made from cotton, calico, silk, and linen fabrics was an American invention. With the arrival of the sewing machine, quiltmaking declined until the last part of the twentieth century.

▶ **FIGURE 3.15** This settee reminds us of an Asante stool from Africa because it incorporates animal totem forms into its structure.

Judy Kensley McKie. *Monkey Settee.* 1995. Walnut and bronze. 90.2 × 182.2 × 61 cm (35½ × 71¾ × 24″). Renwick Gallery, National Museum of American Art, Smithsonian Institution, Washington, D.C.

Art Criticism

Have students form small groups and assign each group one of the works shown in Lesson 2. Ask the group members to examine and discuss the work using the following question. What do you see here? Which visual elements—color, line, texture, shape, form, space—can you identify? How would you describe the use of each element? How are the principles of art used to organize those elements? What idea or feeling does the work suggest? What purpose do you think the work is intended to serve? How successfully does it serve that function? Let one group member summarize the discussion for the rest of the class.

fibers or synthetic fibers. A woodworker can choose among oak, ash, mahogany, rosewood, ebony, cedar, and pine.What media were used to create **Figure 3.15**?

The Processes of Crafts

The techniques and processes a craft artist uses depends on the media selected. Clay, for example, can be modeled, carved, and assembled. It can also be *thrown* on a potter's wheel. Clay is finished by firing it in a *kiln*, a furnace that reaches high temperatures.

Glass can be mold-made or blown. Blown glass requires a process in which the artist, using special tools, blows air into molten glass in order to shape it.

Wood is worked using techniques such as carving and assembling, turning, and bending. In turning, a piece of wood is rotated on a machine called a lathe. The machine may have a fixed tool that shapes the piece, or the artist may use a special tool. Bending is another shaping process. A piece of wood is soaked in water or another liquid to make it pliable. Then it is slowly manipulated into place.

Fiber can be woven into cloth or baskets. It can be embroidered, sewn, or quilted. Metal can be shaped in molds or it can be cut with special shears. Pliable metals can be hammered or filed into shape. Pieces can be assembled by linking them together or by soldering them together. Soldering is a process using a handheld tool called a soldering iron that melts small areas of the metal. When the metal cools, the pieces are joined. Assembling larger pieces of metal, a process called welding, requires a larger, more powerful tool with an open flame.

Teacher Notes

Promoting Discussion

On the board, briefly describe a few buildings in your community. Then, have each student sketch a different building, preferable one of interest to him or her. Let students share their finished works. Students should then consider how their building could be made more attractive or more functional—perhaps by including more windows, or putting a name on the front door. Ask students to put these changes into their sketches and share the results.

Activity

Redesigning a Familiar Building

■ **Computer Option.** Recent computer software makes three-dimensional forms from two-dimensional shapes. Simple CAD applications allow students to design buildings beginning with geometric shapes and automatically include additional sides and tabs for assembling. If this kind of application is not available, design a building. Use simple cylindrical, cube, or pyramid forms. Choose the Grids and Rulers option to guide your measurements.

Your building can include a combination of forms such as: a rectangular base, square middle section, and perhaps a pyramid for the top. Experiment. Print out and assemble initial forms to test them. When satisfied, add doors, windows, and textures to the surfaces.

Architecture

Of all the arts, architecture has the greatest impact on our daily lives. The quality of the architecture we use for shelter, for gatherings, and for worship affects the quality of our lives. Architecture is the planning and creation of buildings. Because a well-designed building is a shelter as well as a work of art, architecture is considered both an applied art and a fine art. An artist who works in the field of architecture is an architect. To be certified, an architect studies engineering because a structure must be designed to hold its own weight and withstand the physical forces placed on it. An architect also studies the visual arts in order to create buildings that are well-proportioned and pleasing to the eye. Architects design for individuals as well as for the public. The needs of each group must be considered and met before a building can be called a success.

The Media of Architecture

From the earliest times people have been creating shelters from materials found in their natural environment. Huts constructed from sticks and bark were covered with mud. Nomadic people constructed movable shelters from wood poles and covered them with animal skins. In the north, ice was cut and formed to make shelters. In the tropics, leaves and grasses were woven together. Gradually, people developed skills to make better use of available materials for permanent structures that were used for gathering as well as shelter. People learned to make bricks by firing clay to

Activity Redesigning a Familiar Building

Applying Your Skills. Architects are often hired to renovate an old structure. Look for a building in your community that you would like to see improved. Study it by making sketches from different points of view. Identify and list in your sketchbook the media that were used in the construction of the building you have selected. Think about the media you have just studied. List some that would harmonize with the surrounding buildings and the environment. Using pencil, draw one face of the building. Include the existing doors and windows. Then redesign the look of that side using the media that you believe will improve the look of the building. Use watercolors to indicate the colors of the new construction media.

Computer Option. Use a computer application to redesign the façade of a building in your community. Choose the Grids and Rulers option to guide your drawing so you can maintain scale and proportion. Consider how you can create harmony by repeating the materials, colors, or architectural features of other buildings in your community. Begin by drawing the front view. Hold down the Shift key to draw straight lines or restrict shapes. Use the copy and paste functions to make duplicates of features such as doors and windows. Save and title the line drawing. Then use your choice of brushes, textures, and gradients to simulate natural materials. Use the Save As option to retitle and save. Print and display your work.

54 | **CHAPTER 3** The Media and Processes of Art

▶ COOPERATIVE LEARNING

Developing Perception Tell students that it is important for architects to be able to visualize how three-dimensional objects appear from different angles. Have students work in small groups. In front of each group place several different objects, such as boxes in various sizes, a ball, a jar, a pencil, and a roll of tape. Explain to students that it is their task to draw the top, bottom, and side views of all these objects—without touching any of them.

Encourage group members to work together, but be sure each student draws three different views of at least one object. Give group members time to discuss their completed drawings. Then have group members select several of their drawings to share. Ask: Which object does each drawing show? From which angle is it drawn?

make it hard. They stacked the bricks to build walls. Stonecutters develop methods for cutting stone so smoothly that one could be stacked on top of the next without anything to hold them in place **(Figure 3.16).** Others learned how to balance one long stone on top of two posts and developed the post-and-lintel method of construction (Figure 12.35, page 348). Today this is called post-and-beam construction because architects use wood or steel beams instead of stone lintels.

Later, architects learned to form an arch with stone. The arch carried the weight of walls and roofs without buckling. Arches led to vaults, or arched roofs that connect walls. Vaulted halls enabled architects to create more open space. A dome is a round roof, as if an arch had been extended into a full circle. Using more advanced construction techniques architects developed a pointed stone arch and supported it with buttresses. This allowed large openings to be made in the walls which were filled with stained-glass windows.

Wood was always a popular material, because it was plentiful. Balloon framing allowed builders to use heavy beams of wood to support thin walls. The truss supported a sloped roof. This technique is still being used today.

Technology has given us steel and reinforced concrete. Steel frames enabled us to cover the outside of skyscrapers with glass. The development of new materials has not eliminated the use of the older materials. New ways of using them are always being developed.

◀ **FIGURE 3.16**
The builders of Machu–Picchu were excellent stone masons. They cut the stones to fit together so perfectly that the buildings have survived to this day without any mortar to hold the stones in place.

David Borsky. Wall of Machu–Picchu. Photograph. Courtesy of the artist.

Art Criticism

List the elements of art—color, line, shape, form, space, and texture—on the board. Then help students examine Louis Sullivan's skyscraper shown in Figure 3.17 on page 56. Ask: What colors can you identify in this work? How would you describe the lines here? Are they vertical, horizontal, diagonal? Can you identify any repeated shapes? Are the shapes geometric or organic? Do you see open areas or recesses allowing for the feeling of deep space, or does the space appear more shallow? How would you describe the texture on the surface of the building? After a class discussion, have each student write a short description of the work.

Promoting Discussion

Tell students to assume that they are architects and have been asked to design a house or apartment building. What must they take into account when working on a design like this? Explain that architects must first make certain that their buildings are tailored to meet the practical purposes for which they are intended. A house, for example, must provide adequate space for the daily needs of the family. However, there is no reason why a design cannot be *both* functional and attractive.

Aesthetics

Ask each student to identify on a sheet of paper a building in their community that they feel is both functional and attractive. Collect and list these on the board. Did the list include buildings serving a variety of different functions? Was one building mentioned more than others? If so, discuss reasons why this building proved to be so highly regarded.

TEACHER TALK

Beyond the Classroom City tours are a fruitful way to discuss architecture; they help students understand that this form of art surrounds them all the time. Each region has certain specialties that are common throughout the area. Eastern cities often have excellent examples of colonial architecture; southern cities often have well-maintained examples of antebellum architecture. Many towns have Victorian homes that are of interest to art students, and even more towns have examples of "classical" architecture—Greek and Roman buildings with stately columns and formal gardens.

ASSESS...........

Self-Assessment

Have students complete the review questions on this page. Answers are provided below.

Reteaching

Divide the class into small groups and have them locate other examples of sculpture, crafts, and architecture in other parts of the textbook and explain the media and processess used to create the artwork.

Enrichment

Local crafts shows and museums offer an opportunity to see—and even buy—the handmade work of skilled craftspeople. Have students explore these resources for seeing and learning more about crafts. Encourage students to visit any museums or shows they discover. If local museums or shows are not available, have students read more about the exhibits at crafts museums in major cities and, if necessary, write to several museums for information and catalogs.

CLOSE.............

Ask students to write a short paragraph explaining the differences between two- and three-dimensional artwork.

When Louis Sullivan built the Wainwright Building **(Figure 3.17),** he first created a large frame, or cage, made with steel beams. To cover the frame he used brick which blended in with the surrounding buildings.

An architect is concerned with the environment into which the structure will be placed as well as the purpose of the building. The success of a building is the combination of the right media with good design. The Sydney Opera House (Figure 11.1, page 286), sits on a peninsula in the bay. It looks like a ship sailing into the harbor because the architect was able to design the unusually–shaped walls using steel–reinforced concrete.

Check Your Understanding

1 What are the two main types of sculpture?
2. What are the four basic sculpting methods?
3. Define crafts. Name three categories of functional crafts.
4. Define architecture.

◄ **FIGURE 3.17** This skyscraper echoes its internal steel frame in its exterior design. Sullivan emphasized the height of the skyscraper by stressing the vertical lines that move the viewer's eyes upward, and underplaying the horizontal elements in the window area.

Louis Sullivan. Wainwright Building. St. Louis, Missouri. 1890-91.

56 | CHAPTER 3 The Media and Processes of Art

 ## Answers to Check Your Understanding

1. Relief sculpture and sculpture in the round are the two main types of sculpture.
2. The four basic sculpting methods are: modeling, carving, casting, and assembling.
3. Crafts are functional objects that are made using artistic media and processes. The categories of crafts include weaving, pottery, quilts, baskets, jewelry, glassmaking, and metal.
4. Architecture is the planning and creation of buildings.

Technological Media

Artists try to communicate ideas through their art and as they do so, they constantly seek out new media. In recent times, technological advances have allowed artists to create new and exciting forms of art. In this lesson you will learn about photography, film, video, and computer art.

Photography

Photography is *the technique of capturing optical images on light-sensitive surfaces.* Photographs are all around us. Newspapers, magazines, and books are full of them. Almost everyone has a collection of snapshots that they've taken. It is hard to imagine that photography started out as an expensive, difficult process only 150 years ago.

Although anyone can point a camera and trip the shutter, photography as art requires more than simply recording images. As photographic media and processes have improved, some photographers have begun exploring photography's potential as art. They have gone beyond simply taking pictures of interesting images. Works by Dorothea Lange **(Figure 3.18)** and other photographers are carefully composed, just as a painter composes an artwork. This artistic composition makes photography a fine art, like painting or sculpting.

In recent years some artists have combined painting and photography to create a new kind of visual expression. Look closely at **Figure 3.19.** Notice how the artist has modified a black-and-white photograph of an automobile in front of a house. The finished work combines familiar images from the real world with ideas and feelings originating in the mind of the artist.

The Media of Photography

The idea of capturing an image on film is very old. Attempts to do so date back to the Renaissance, but the first permanent photograph was not made until the nineteenth century. L.J.M.

 FIGURE 3.18 Dorothea Lange did more than take a snapshot of this family. By moving her camera to get just the right image, she tells us all about the family. What does the expression on the mother's face tell you? What emotions do the children convey with their body language?

Dorothea Lange. *Migrant Mother.* 20.3 × 25.4 cm (8 × 10"). Courtesy of the Library of Congress, Washington, D.C.

Technological Media
(pages 57–61)
(National Standards: 1a)

FOCUS............
Objectives
After completing this lesson, students will be able to:
- Describe the history of photography.
- Tell how movies are made.
- Describe the characteristics of computer art programs.

Resources

📁 Cooperative Learning 6, *Designing a Sculpture*

📁 Enrichment Activity 6, *More About Digital Media*

TEACH..........
Motivator
Make a display of photographs and ask students to describe some of the photographs without identifying or describing the subjects. Encourage them to use the same kinds of descriptions they might use in discussing a painting.

Vocabulary
Help students use dictionaries to examine the word *photography* more closely. Ask: What are the two main parts of the word? (*photo* and *graph*) What is the meaning of the ancient Greek word from which each of those parts is derived? (*light* and *write*) In what sense is photography "writing with light"?

TECHNOLOGY OPTIONS

National Gallery of Art Videodisc Use the following to help students analyze other artworks that use photography.

Alfred Stieglitz
The Steerage

Search Frame 3300

Alfred Stieglitz
Georgia O'Keeffe

Search Frame 3302

Use Glencoe's *National Gallery of Art Correlation Bar Code Guide* to locate more artworks.

Aesthetics

Have students select several of their own photographs and, in small groups, discuss the subject, composition, and content of each photo. Then ask: Do you consider any of these photographs to be works of art? Why or why not? How are these photos similar to, and different from, those shown in Figures 3.18 (on page 57) and 3.19?

Promoting Discussion

Tell students that Dorothea Lange (1895–1965) was an American photographer who is best known for her documentary photographs. During the 1930s, she worked for the Farm Security Administration. Lange documented the social, economic, and personal toll that the Great Depression took on migrant farm workers. Have students study Figure 3.18 (on page 57) and discuss their emotional response to the photo.

Art in Everyday Life

Have students think about some of their favorite entertainment forms (e.g. television, movies, and computer games). Ask them to speculate about careers in industries related to these areas that require training in art and design basics. Traditional responses include a photographer or camera operator, stage and set designers, costume designers, storyboard artists, animators, and so forth. Expand their lists to include promotional material for movies, album covers, and music videos, packaging and advertising for computer products, and color graphics.

▲ **FIGURE 3.19** This work is based on a black-and-white photo taken by the artist. After printing it, she covered the areas she wished to stay black-and-white with rubber cement to protect them. Then she dipped the photo into an acid bath that changed the unprotected portions into tints and shades of brown. The final step was the addition of color, using paints designed for use on photographs.

Jessica Hines. *Dream Series.* Hand-colored black-and-white photograph. 40.6 × 50.8 cm (16 × 20"). Private collection.

Daguerre invented a process of creating silvery, mirrorlike images on a copper plate. This was called a daguerreotype. Daguerreotype was a time-consuming and very expensive process. In the 1850s, the wet plate method was invented. It used glass coated with chemicals to record the image, which was then transferred to paper or cardboard. As with contemporary photographs, the wet plate photos used *negatives*, the reverse image of the object photographed. Today newer and better methods of making film have been invented. The process is simpler and less expensive. Photographers have many media and processes available to affect the look of a finished photograph.

Film

A movie is like any other work of art; it is created by people for others to appreciate. When you watch a movie, you rarely see all the work that went into it. However, filmmaking is a complicated, expensive process involving many people and considerable technology.

The very first films were silent, and even with all of our technological advances, those films are still appreciated today for their aesthetic value. In the 1920s, sound was added. Color came next. Today, many old, faded films have been digitally enhanced by computers to restore color and improve sound. Computers have also aided filmmaking by allowing computer animation and special effects that would have been impossible in the past.

The Media of Film

Filmmaking only became possible about 100 years ago, after photography began to catch on with amateur hobbyists and professional artists. This encouraged the development of different types of film. In 1899, a crude flexible film base called celluloid was introduced. Celluloid could be used to shoot multiple images in a row. When these images were shown in a rapid sequence, they gave the illusion of movement. Early films suffered from jumpy action, flickering light, and other flaws. As cameras, film, film printers, and projectors improved, so did the quality of movies. Cinematographers—artists who use movie cameras—now have the ability to choose from many different film media and production processes to create visually–exciting, artistic films.

Curriculum Connection

Performing Arts Pretend to be delighted about something you have just picked up or be disapproving or angry and perhaps slam a book onto your desk. When you have students' attention, ask them to discuss how actors can use gestures, movement, sound, and music to help them communicate messages in ways that traditional visual artists cannot.

Point out how exaggeration helps a message to be understood quickly and easily, as in the early silent films. Have the students prepare for the following activity by dividing into groups. Have each group prepare a pantomime demonstrating an emotion, mood, or activity that features one or more people, then present the pantomime to another group.

Video

Videotape records and stores images and sounds as magnetic impulses. Patterns of light beams and wavelengths of sound are translated into electric waves, which are then imprinted magnetically on the videotape. *A system that uses electromagnetic energy to imprint both sound and pictures* is called an **analog system.**

Television studios were the first to record programs on videotape because the method was more efficient and less expensive than traditional cinematography. Gradually, videotape and video cameras made their way into homes, so that anyone could tape television broadcasts, watch movies of their choice, or make and view their own home movies.

The Media of Video

Why is videotape such a remarkable development? Videotape does not require special processing or printing. A person can record an event on videotape and immediately view the results. Video artists record the sights, sounds, and scenes of nature or they create totally new environments with moving and still images and sound. This technology allows an artist to paint a visual story or communicate a message, just like an artist who paints on canvas. Perhaps more importantly, video can be combined with the tools available on computers in order to create artwork never before possible.

▶ **FIGURE 3.20** This artist has used humor to create a parody of Escher's drawing while making a statement about computer art. What do you think she is saying to you, the viewer?

Rhoda Grossman. *Self-Portrait After Escher.* 1992. Electronic. Salzman International, San Francisco, California.

Computers

A computer uses a **digital system,** or *a system that processes words and images directly as numbers or digits.* Digital systems are more precise than analog systems. Thanks to digital technology, today's computers are becoming faster and smaller. Tiny computers, called *microprocessors,* can now operate computer programs that once required a computer the size of your classroom!

Using Computers to Create Art

Software programs are computer tools for working, learning, and entertaining. With paint or draw programs, artists can draw, paint, manipulate, and design images. The artwork in **Figure 3.20** was created with a software program. More recent digital technologies, including scanning devices and virtual reality, provide even more exciting ways to stimulate an artist's imagination.

When you use a computer to create art, the art images can be stored as files in the computer's memory. Once saved, they may be opened in a new file and reworked. The advantage is that while the original art is saved, you can try as many variations as you wish, saving

Promoting Discussion

Encourage students to discuss silent motion pictures they have seen, either in theaters or on television. If possible show a short silent film. Ask: What black-and-white movies have they seen? What silent movies have they seen? How do these movies help them understand the history and development of motion pictures?

Aesthetics

Photography and video are two technologies that can make self-expression faster than other art tools or media. Ask students to discuss whether a portrait painted on canvas requires an extended length of time to execute. Encourage students to identify reasons to support their opinions.

Aesthetics

Instruct students to study Rhoda Grossman's self-portrait (Figure 3.20) and speculate what materials were used to create it. Discuss computer scanning techniques. Ask students how much drawing skill was required to make the self-portrait. Have students imagine that the portrait was painted with oils or acrylics instead of the computer. Ask: Would the artwork still be considered as important or valuable? Why or why not?

MEETING INDIVIDUAL NEEDS

Kinesthetic Learners Have students design a set of illustrated cards for each of the four media discussed in this lesson—photography, film, video, and computers. They might gather information for each medium and then create a card for each one showing equipment that is specific to the media, examples of the type of art created by it, and names of artists associated with the media.

Verbal/Linguistic Learners Have students research the life of a contemporary artist in any of the four media discussed in this lesson. Have them prepare interview questions they would like to ask this artist about his or her works, lifestyles, and cultural ties and traditions. The final presentation could take the form of a question-and-answer format or a simulated interview with the help of another student.

Art History

Bring in a reproduction of M.C. Escher's lithograph *Drawing Hands*. Point out how Rhoda Grossman was inspired by the Escher drawing and adapted the idea for her computer self-portrait in Figure 3.20. Ask students how she changed his concept and what she did to bring it into the present.

Activity

Digital Art

Computer Option. The computer's tools not only save time and effort but also allow students to make alterations and many changes quickly. Have them scan a line drawing from their sketchbook using a handheld scanner, flatbed scanner, or digital camera. Have them save the scanned image in a file format compatible with the draw or paint application they will be opening. Have them import the drawing and explore changes in line. Select a mood and add color. Include pattern or texture. Make three or four different versions. Save and print the most successful results.

each as a new file. You never change or lose the original work.

Most computer art applications are one of two main types: paint programs and draw programs.

- **Paint programs.** In paint programs, images are stored as bitmaps, which are a series of tiny dots, or *pixels*. The advantage is the ability to edit pixel by pixel. In general, paint programs are capable of producing more lifelike pictures than draw programs.

- **Draw programs.** In draw programs, images are stored as a series of lines and curves. Each line or curve results from a mathematical formula and is known as an object. An advantage of draw programs over paint programs is that objects can be "resized"—made larger or smaller—without distortion. Recently, the differences between paint and draw programs have begun to blur. Many paint programs today do jobs that were once performed only by draw programs, and vice versa.

Computer Art Tools

In computer art, the physical tools that the artist actually handles are called hardware. Hardware includes equipment such as the monitor, keyboard, printer, and mouse (the point-and-click device). Along with these pieces of hardware, some other tools used by professional computer artists include the following:

- **Digital Camera.** A digital camera works like a regular camera except that the images are recorded digitally; that is, they are recorded as numbers or digits. The camera usually has a viewer that allows you to see what each picture you have taken looks like. The images a digital camera records are downloaded, or transferred, to a computer. Then they can be printed out, or they can be manipulated with special photography software programs. The digital images can be altered and enhanced in unlimited ways, and each version can be saved as a separate file.

Activity — Digital Art

Applying Your Skills. Artists use computers as sketchbooks, design tools, and as painting and collage media because they can store and retrieve artwork quickly. Images can be easily combined and altered which allows the artist to explore many ideas without wasting time or materials. Compare the difference between the media. First, select drawing paper, pencil, pen, brush, and watercolor, tempera, or acrylic paint. Draw a large rectangle or circle on the paper. Explore a mood with a variety of lines made with the pencil, pen, and brush. Change length, thickness, and texture. Arrange a few lines to make a pleasing composition. Choose a color scheme and add color.

Computer Option. Now, repeat the same activity in an art application. Select a Shape tool and draw a large open rectangle or circle on the page. Explore the Pencil and Brush tools. Consider a mood or feeling. Arrange a variety of lines, changing length, thickness, shape, and texture to match this mood. Use the Eraser and Fatbit or Zoom tool, if available, to eliminate unneeded marks. When you are satisfied, title and save with your name or project. Now choose a simple color scheme. Apply color with the Bucket or Brush tools. Select the Save As command to retitle. Add a number behind the original title to indicate a new edition.

MEETING INDIVIDUAL NEEDS

Logical/Math Learners Have students use a Venn diagram to compare and contrast the analog and digital systems. Venn diagrams are constructed by using two or more overlapping geometrical figures, such as a circle, that share an area in common. Have students list those characteristics unique to each system in the areas of the circle not shared, and elements that are common to both systems in the commonly shared area of the circle. This visual organization of information will give students an opportunity to focus on the contrasts and comparisons between the two systems.

Tool		Description	Type of Program
🔍	Zoom tool	Magnifies part of painting or drawing.	Paint or Draw
🖌	Brush tool	Paints lines of different thicknesses.	Paint
✏	Pencil tool	Draws lines and curves.	Draw
🖊	Color eraser	Changes one color to another.	Paint
🪣	Fill tool	Adds color to closed objects or shapes.	Paint or Draw
⬚	Rectangle tool	Creates rectangles and squares.	Paint or Draw

◀ **FIGURE 3.21**
Common on-screen tools.

- **Stylus and graphics tablet.** In simplest terms, a stylus and graphics tablet are electronic answers to the pencil and paper. In recent years, these tools have been improved. The stylus now responds to pressure from the hand to make thick and thin lines, much like a real pencil, pen, or brush.
- **Scanner.** A scanner is a device that "reads" a printed image. It then translates the image into a language the computer can use to make a visual image on the screen or print with a printing device.

On-Screen Tools. Another category of tools that computer artists work with is on-screen tools. These mimic handheld tools used by conventional artists. On-screen tools include pencils, pens, assorted brushes, and erasers.

The set of on-screen tools varies from program to program. The table in **Figure 3.21** shows some common on-screen tools and the type of program in which each is found. It also shows the *icon*, or picture symbol, used to represent each tool.

Multi-media Art

Combining technologies on the computer is made easier by the development of **multi-media programs.** These are *computer software programs that help users design, organize, and combine text, graphics, video, and sound in one document.* With a little imagination, you can make reports, presentations, and art portfolios come alive. Multi-media art combines different media to create a new type of art. For example, an artist might scan a photograph into the computer, then use a paint or draw program to enhance it. The artist might also add sounds to the art that help evoke a feeling or communicate an idea. He or she could add text or quotations to add meaning. The artist might use a special program to make the art appear to move or to take different forms as the viewer watches. Multi-media art expands the boundaries of art by including more sensory experiences.

 Check Your Understanding

1. What is photography?
2. Name the kind of film that made movies possible.
3. What advantage does video have over photography?
4. What is the difference between an analog system and a digital system?
5. What is the advantage of a multi-media program?

LESSON 3 *Technological Media* | **61**

 Answers to Check Your Understanding

1. Photography is the technique of capturing optical images on light-sensitive surfaces.
2. Celluloid, developed in 1899 by the Kodak company, made moviemaking possible.
3. Video can be viewed immediately without any special developing or processing.
4. An analog system uses electromagnetic energy to imprint both sound and pictures, whereas a digital system processes words and images directly as numbers or digits.
5. The artist can combine many different sensory experiences and many different kinds of media to make unique works of art.

ASSESS ....
Self-Assessment
Have students complete the lesson review questions. Answers are provided below.

Reteaching
- Work with small groups of students to gather and examine photographs depicting local history. Ask: What do these photographs show? What was the purpose of the photographers who took them? What message do they communicate to you? Do you consider these photographs works of art? Why or why not?
- Ask students to review ways to use the computer to create art.

Enrichment
- Photography was developed along with other forms of technology. Encourage students to find out more about how earliest cameras worked. How has the camera changed? What are the most recent refinements in cameras and the film used in them? How have the changes in cameras affected photographers and their work? Ask volunteers to work together to research these questions and summarize their findings in short written or oral reports.
- Invite a computer teacher or architectural draftsperson to demonstrate a high-end graphics program.

CLOSE ....
Have students define and discuss the two types of computer art applications.

Critiquing the Work

➡ Describe
What do you see?

- Have the students change inches to feet so that they can realize the painting is probably taller than any-one in the class, and al-most as wide as it is high: 7 feet high and almost 6½ feet wide. Have them measure and mark the size on the floor or wall so they can see concretely how large it is.

- It is difficult to tell from the reproduction, but the skirt, both sleeves, the cutout flowers in her hair and at her waist, the lace buckles, the boots, and the border of light colored squares with diamonds are probably cut paper.

- In the center of the paint-ing there is a dancing woman with a flower and curved lines radiating out from the flower. She is the subject of the work. Her face and neck are red. She has no features, but a round blue earring hangs from the place where her ear would be. Her arms are outstretched. The left hand is red-orange, the right is hot pink. That is the only place in the work where we see hot pink. Her lower arms have tight sleeves. The left is blue, the other is red with a printed design on it. The upper sleeves are full. The left is divided by a diago-nal line into brown and black, and the right is red with a print on it.

ART CRITICISM IN ACTION

▲ **FIGURE 3.22**

Miriam Schapiro. *Personal Appearance.* 1985. Acrylic, fabric, and paper on canvas. 215.9 × 195.6 cm (85 × 77″). Courtesy of Steinbaum Krauss Gallery, New York, New York. Collection of Mr. and Mrs. Irvin Arthur.

MORE ABOUT... Miriam Schapiro

Miriam Schapiro's art celebrates art forms tradi-tionally thought of as "women's work," like quilt-ing, embroidery, and appliqué. Many of these activities were practiced by groups of women working together, and Schapiro's art consciously extends this tradition. In 1972, she and artist Judy Chicago began a project called Womanhouse. This was a mansion located in Los Angeles that the two restored and transformed with the help of many other women artists into an on-going series of environments and performances. Schapiro has also collaged the work of woman artists of the past, such as Mary Cassatt, into her own work and considers this another form of collaboration.

1 DESCRIBE What do you see?

List all the information you can find in the credit line, and then list the things that you can describe and recognize in the work. This is a clue-collecting step. If you are not sure of something, do not guess.

■ How big is this work? Describe everything you recognize in the work.

■ Can you tell which parts of the work were made of cut paper and which parts are painted?

■ What is the subject of this work?

2 ANALYZE How is this work organized?

During this step, you will use the knowledge you learn in each chapter about the elements and principles of art to understand the composition of the work. Even though you have not studied them yet, there are some obvious questions you can answer.

■ Where has Schapiro placed the figure? Does it look calm or active?

■ How many places can you find squares used in this work?

■ Does the background look calm or active? Explain.

3 INTERPRET What is the artist trying to communicate?

You will make guesses about the meaning of the work during this step. It is not necessary to know what the artist meant. Instead, you will decide what this image says to you.

■ What is the figure doing? Why is it within all the squares?

■ Who is the figure? Whom does it represent?

■ Give the work a new title that sums up your feelings about it.

4 JUDGE What do you think of the work?

Now you are ready to make an aesthetic judgment about this work.

■ Do you like the way the artist has made use of the materials? Can you think of other media that might be used to create a work with the same effect?

■ Do you think this work is successful? Why or why not? Use one or more of the theories of art explained in Chapter 2 to defend your decision.

MEET THE ARTIST

MIRIAM SCHAPIRO

American, 1923–

Miriam Schapiro is an American artist who was born in Toronto, Canada. She grew up in the Flatbush section of Brooklyn, New York. Her parents encouraged her interest in art and sent her to art classes at the Museum of Modern Art.

Schapiro has produced work that connects to women artists of the past who made items for household use such as lace and quilts. She invented the word "Femmage" to describe her new style. She felt that collages were made by men who roamed the streets at night, collecting discarded materials for their work. Her materials came from the world of women.

Analyze
How is this work organized?

■ The figure is in the center of the work. It looks very active.

■ Both large and small squares are all behind the figure. We can even see some through her skirt.

■ Because of the squares, the background is fairly calm except for the design in the wide black border that has dotted lines that swirl and swoop.

■ The background looks very active with a variety of swirling patterns and with the horizontal and vertical checkerboard patterns.

Interpret
What is the artist trying to communicate?

■ Answers will vary. Some may say the woman is dancing wildly, trying to get away from her restrictive, square life.

■ Answers will vary. Some may say it represents anyone trying to break free from unwanted restrictions.

■ Answers will vary.

Judge
What do you think of the work?

■ Whether or not students like the painting is a personal decision. Accept all possible answers.

■ Answers will vary. Some will say Formalism, some will choose Emotionalism. Accept positive or negative answers as long as the student applies aesthetic theory to defend his or her answer.

Art Criticism in Action | 63

Time & Place — Late Twentieth Century

Miriam Schapiro created *Personal Appearance* in 1985. Some other events that happened the same year:

Music: "Live Aid" rock festival held in Philadelphia raised 70 million dollars for African famine relief. Performers included Bob Dylan, Paul McCartney, Madonna and others.

Science: British scientists reported a giant hole in the earth's ozone layer widening each spring over Antarctica.

Art: Artist Marc Chagall died in St. Paul de Venne, France at the age of 98.

Pottery and Clay

(National Standards: 6a, 6b)

Objectives

After completing this feature, students will be able to:

- Describe the elemental composition of clay.
- Discuss different uses of clay.

Teaching the Connection

1. Have students read the feature on this page.
2. Ask students to imagine how these figures were made. Do they appear to be sculpted or cast? Are they most likely hollow or solid? (They are almost certainly hollow, since solid clay objects are likely to explode when fired at high temperatures.)
3. Tell students that there are a number of different kinds of ceramic products. Pottery generally refers to all fired clay ware. Unglazed pottery is usually buff-colored and capable of absorbing moisture. *China* is the term used to refer to glazed or unglazed and nonabsorbent white ware. The china-making process involves firing the object until it hardens, after which it is glazed and fired again at a lower temperature. Porcelain and china are interchangeable terms, but the original high-fired porcelain, first produced in China, was brought to Europe by Marco Polo and named for its translucent qualities similar to the sea shell porcellana.

Pottery and Clay

◀ **FIGURE 3.23**

Life-size clay soldiers from the tomb of the first Emperor of a united China, Qin Shihuangdi (c. 246–210 B.C.) discovered in 1974. Terra–cotta. Xian, China.

About 25 years ago, a group of men were digging a well in central China when they uncovered the ancient, enormous tomb of China's first emperor. Imagine the well diggers' astonishment when they found a standing army of life-size clay soldiers, horses, and attendants—at least 7,000 figures in all!

Clay is the perfect medium for such an ambitious artistic project because it can be molded and designed easily. The artist's ability to control and manipulate the density of clay makes possible the creation of large, sturdy pieces. The firing process hardens clay into a permanent, tightly–bonded substance, allowing the sculpture or ceramic work to withstand the test of time, as these figures have.

Clay is produced on the Earth's surface by the weathering and erosion of rocks. The three elements that make up over 80 percent of the Earth also come together in clay: oxygen, silicon, and aluminum. Pottery clay is approximately 40 percent aluminum oxide, 46 percent silicon oxide, and 14 percent water. The presence or absence of particular minerals or impurities in clay makes possible the many variations in pottery, ranging from delicate porcelain Chinese vases to solid Hopi earthenware pots.

Making the Connection

1. Why do you think the people who buried the first emperor of China placed so many life-size statues in his tomb?
2. What allows for the variations in pottery?
3. Using a science textbook, an encyclopedia, or online resources, find out more about oxygen, silicon, and aluminum. Write down your findings.

Answers to Making the Connection

1. Answers will vary. Students may speculate about ancient Chinese beliefs regarding an afterlife.
2. Answers will vary
3. Oxygen is the most abundant gaseous element on Earth. Free or chemically bound oxygen is required by all life forms. The symbol for oxygen is O. Silicon is a nonmetallic element from the carbon family. It is present in stars and meteorites. As the second most abundant element, it constitutes 26 percent of the Earth's crust. The symbol for silicon is Si. Aluminum is the most abundant metallic element, making up 8 percent of the earth's solid crust. The symbol for Aluminum is Al.

Building Vocabulary

On a separate sheet of paper, write the term that best matches each definition given below.

1. Any material used to create art.
2. The use of light and dark values to create the illusion of form.
3. A process in which an artist repeatedly transfers an original image from one prepared surface to another.
4. The impression created on a surface by a printing plate.
5. A copy of a work of art.
6. All the prints made from the same plate or set of plates.
7. A three-dimensional work of art.
8. The technique of capturing optical images on light-sensitive surfaces.
9. A system that uses electromagnetic energy to imprint both sound and pictures.
10. A system that processes words and images directly as numbers or digits.
11. Computer software programs that help users design, organize, and combine text, graphics, video, and sound in one document.

Reviewing Art Facts

Answer the following questions using complete sentences.

1. What is the difference between two- and three-dimensional art?
2. Describe the four shading techniques.
3. Name and define the three main ingredients of paint.
4. What are the three basic steps of printmaking?
5. What is the difference between sculpture in the round and relief sculpture?
6. Why are crafts called the applied arts?
7. How is videotape technology an improvement over cinematography?
8. What are the similarities and differences between paint and draw programs?

Thinking Critically About Art

1. **Analyze.** List all the art media you have used. Which media do you prefer? Write a brief paragraph including two or more reasons for your personal preference.
2. **Compare and contrast.** Study Figures 3.13 (page 51), 3.14 (page 52) and 3.15 (page 53). List the similarities you find in all three artworks. Then identify the qualities that makes each work of art different from the others.
3. **Analyze.** Compare Figures 3.3 and 3.4 on page 43. Berman, the costume designer, based his designs on Canaletto's drawings of eighteenth-century Venice. Look at the Berman costume. Can you see this influence? Explain your answer.

Use the Performing Arts Handbook, page 415, to see how choreographer Merce Cunningham uses the computer and other technology to help him create his renowned ballets.

Take a trip through Glencoe's Fine Arts Site on the World Wide Web. Explore **Glencoe Student Galleria** and see student artworks that were created in two- and three-dimensional media. Then find out how you can submit your own quality works of art for display on the Internet. Visit us at **www.glencoe.com/sec/art**

Chapter 3 Review **65**

Answers to Building Vocabulary

1. medium
2. shading
3. printmaking
4. print
5. reproduction
6. edition
7. sculpture
8. photography
9. analog system
10. digital system
11. multimedia programs

Answers to Reviewing Art Facts

1. Two-dimensional art has length and width but no depth. Three-dimensional art is solid, having length, width, and depth.
2. See page 44 for answer.
3. The three main ingredients of paint are pigment, binder, and solvent. Pigment is a finely ground powder that gives paint its color. Binder is a liquid that holds the grains of pigment together. Solvent is a liquid used to control the thickness or thinness of the paint.
4. Creating the printing plate, inking the plate, and transferring the image.
5. Sculpture in the round has space on all sides. Relief sculpture extends into space from a flat background.
6. Because they are art objects applied to or used for everyday living.
7. Videotape technology is more efficient, less expensive, and requires no special processing, or printing.
8. See page 60 for answer.

ASSESSMENT ✓

Evaluate

- Have students complete the *Chapter 3 Test* in the TCR. 📁
- Alternative Assessment teaching strategies are provided or in the *Testing Program and Alternative Assessment* booklet. 📁

Extension

Have students browse through art books and identify at least one example of a drawing, a painting, a print, a photograph, a sculpture, and a craft. Instruct students to explain how they were able to determine the medium used.

UNIT 2

THE ELEMENTS OF ART

Unit Overview

Unit 2 focuses specifically on the individual elements of art. Because the elements of art are the basic visual symbols in the language of art, students are encouraged throughout the unit to recognize the presence of the elements in the world around them.

Chapter 4—Line

In chapter 4, students explore the expressive qualities of line and how to use lines to make contour, gesture, and calligraphic drawings.

Chapter 5—Shape, Form, and Space

In Chapter 5, students examine the elements of shape, form, and space in two- and three-dimensional artworks.

Chapter 6—Color

Chapter 6 concentrates on the properties of color—hue, value, and intensity, and students examine various color schemes.

Chapter 7—Texture

In Chapter 7, students recognize the difference between real and simulated textures.

Unit Resources

 Print 9, John James Audubon. *The Mocking Bird.*
📁 Unit 2 Test
📁 Portfolio and Assessment Techniques

66

*inter*NET CONNECTION **ON-LINE AND MULTI-MEDIA RESOURCES** Visit the Teacher Resources area to find lists of helpful *On-Line and Multimedia Art Resources*. Here you can click on World Wide Web links to find out about art media and reference materials, image libraries, and art-history resources. Locate distributors of computer art software, art-related CD-ROMS, and art media and supplies you can use in your art classroom. You may even have your own favorite resources that you would like to add. Simply click on the *Contact Us* button to send us information about resources you think would be useful to other art teachers. We welcome your feedback on this and other resources of our site. Find us at **www.glencoe.com/sec/art**

THE ELEMENTS OF ART

"Is there a more mysterious idea for an artist than to imagine how nature is reflected in the eyes of an animal?"

Franz Marc
1880–1916

◄

Franz Marc. Detail from *Stables* (inset). 1913. Oil on canvas. 73.6 x 157.5 cm (29 x 61"). Solomon R. Guggenheim Museum, New York, New York.

67

UNIT 2

Introducing the Unit

Open a discussion with students about situations that require a person to learn a specialized vocabulary. For example, what special vocabulary is part of the game of tennis? Tell them that learning about the elements of art is the first step in speaking the language of the artist.

Unit Motivator

Ask students to identify the uses of the word *element*. If necessary, ask: What do you know about chemical elements? Do you know what a heating element is? Tell students that in this unit they will learn about the use of line, shape, and form, as well as other elements that are specific to the world of art.

Discussing the "Quotation"

Inform students that Marc found a spiritual purity in nature, and that for him, animals possessed a godlike quality that humans lacked. Have students think about the quote and discuss why the artist worked in such an abstract style. Discuss whether or not abstraction allowed him to convey his feelings about animals and nature better than if he had painted in a more naturalistic style.

National Museum of Women in the Arts

You may wish to use the National Museum of Women in the Arts videodisc and/or CD-ROM. The videodisc features a bar code guide, and the interactive CD-ROM provides stimulating activities.

Teacher Notes

_____

_____

_____

_____

_____

Line

(pages 68–95)

While studying this chapter, use Performing Arts Handbook page 416 to help students discover how line is used in dance.

▶ **FIGURE 4.1** This painting of the Brooklyn Bridge was one panel in a series of five paintings that Joseph Stella created as a visual symphony expressing the excitement and energy of New York City. He tried to capture the feeling of steel skyscrapers with straight lines and show light and movement with dynamic, flowing curves.

Joseph Stella. *The Voice of the City of New York Interpreted: The Bridge.* 1920–1922. Oil and tempera on canvas. 224.8 × 137.2 cm (88½ × 54"). Collection of the Newark Museum, Newark, New Jersey.

FEATURED ARTISTS

Abrasha
Thomas Hart Benton
Alexander Calder
Carolyn Clive
Albrecht Dürer

Audrey Flack
Keith Haring
Edward Hopper
Yvonne Jacquette
William H. Johnson
Jacob Lawrence
David Malangi
Gu Mei

Dan Namingha
Alice Neel
Albert Raymond Paley
Diego Rivera
Georges Rouault
Joseph Stella
Jacopo Tintoretto
Charles White

Line

Lines are everywhere. You use lines to write words, numbers, and symbols. You read lines of printed words. The lines on a map help you find the best route from one place to another. You stand in line to get into a movie theater. When actors are studying a new role, they say they are memorizing their lines. You use lines to draw pictures.

The painting *The Voice of the City of New York Interpreted: The Bridge* **(Figure 4.1)** is by Joseph Stella, an Italian-American artist who came to the United States at the beginning of the twentieth century. He was obsessed by the movement and lights of New York City, and he painted several versions of the Brooklyn Bridge. In this work, you can see how the sweeping lines of the suspension cables dominate the scene. Through the Gothic arches of the great pylons that hold the cables you can see abstractions of skyscrapers. Stella uses many different kinds of line and line variations to capture the excitement of the city. Can you find the lines that represent walkways for pedestrians, roadways for cars, and train tracks for the subway?

Developing Your PORTFOLIO

To keep them in order, each entry in your portfolio should be marked clearly for identification. Make sure each piece includes your name and the date you completed the artwork. Any notes about the assignment are valuable and should be kept with your artwork. Make it a point to use the names of the elements of art as you write about your artwork. That way you will demonstrate your growth as an artist and communicate to your readers in the language of art.

OBJECTIVES

After completing this chapter, you will be able to:

- Observe the lines in your environment more closely.
- Name the different kinds of lines.
- Tell the five ways lines can vary in appearance.
- Use lines to change values.
- Understand the expressive qualities or meanings of different lines in works of art.
- Use lines to make contour, gesture, and calligraphic drawings.

WORDS TO KNOW

line
dimension
outline
implied lines
value
crosshatching
contour line
gesture
calligraphy

Chapter Overview

Chapter 4 examines the element of line. Students become aware that line is common to both the natural and the manufactured environment. Additionally, students study and practice techniques of drawing with lines.

Examining the Artwork

Explain to students that Joseph Stella painted his impression of the Brooklyn Bridge several times. Stella had been strongly influenced by the Futurists who had denounced traditional art in favor of the dynamic forces of the twentieth century: machines, subways, automobiles, skyscrapers, and the bright color of neon lights. To Stella, this bridge, the first suspension bridge on which steel wires were used for cables, was a symbol of modern life. Have students notice the shape of the great pylon that supports the cables. The openings look like arches from a Gothic cathedral. Stella emphasizes it to express his reverence for things modern and it gives the work a spiritual quality. The five paintings in *The Voice of the City of New York Interpreted* takes the viewer on an expressive tour of Manhattan Island. *The Bridge* is the fifth panel in the work and it represents the Brooklyn Bridge crossing the East River from Manhattan to Brooklyn on the east side of Manhattan Island.

69

National Standards

This chapter addresses the following National Standards for the Visual Arts:

1. (a, b)   **4.** (a, b, c)
2. (b, c)   **5.** (a, b)
3. (a, b)   **6.** (a, b)

DEVELOPING A PORTFOLIO

Choosing Artworks Ultimately, students must come to terms with the limitations set on the number of artworks included in a portfolio; they cannot submit everything they have done. Consequently, they learn to be qualitatively sensitive about their work. Stress the value of setting standards, especially through informed judgments, that is, developing the ability to assess their own work on the basis of accepted criteria. Through self-evaluation, students take control of decision-making and feel increasingly responsible for the quality of their work.

The Element of Line

(pages 70–76)
(National Standards: 2b, 3a)

FOCUS...........
Objectives

After completing this lesson, students will be able to:

■ Observe the lines in their environment more closely.

■ Name the different kinds of lines.

■ Tell the five ways lines can vary in appearance.

■ Use lines to change values.

Supplies

■ Overhead projector, found objects

■ Reproduction art print, acetate

■ Natural objects: seed pods, leaf, shells; magnifying glass

■ Variety of pencils and pens, paper

The Element of Line

Lines are everywhere. You can see lines in the grain of a piece of wood or in the cracks on a sidewalk. Lines are used to create words, numbers, and symbols. They are also used to create art. In drawing, **line** is *an element of art that is the path of a moving point through space.*

▲ **FIGURE 4.2** The artist has used the line of the highway to pull your eyes into and through this artwork. Identify the kinds of line the artists has used in this painting. How do they convey movement and feeling?

Yvonne Jacquette. *Town of Skowhegan, Maine V.* 1988. Oil on canvas. 198.6 × 163 cm (78³⁄₁₆ × 64¹⁄₁₆″). Courtesy Brooke Alexander Gallery, New York, New York.

What Is Line?

Artists use line to lead your eyes through a work of art. This is because it takes movement to make a line. When you see a line, your eyes usually follow its movement. Lines can lead your eyes into, around, and out of visual images, as in the painting in **Figure 4.2.** Notice how the artist uses the line of the highway to pull your eyes into the artwork.

A line has width as well as length, but usually the width of a line is very small compared with its length. In fact, a line is thought of as being one-dimensional. Its one dimension is length. **Dimension** means *the amount of space an object takes up in one direction.* Two-dimensional objects have height as well as width. A painting is two-dimensional. Three-dimensional objects have height, width, and depth. A sculpture is three-dimensional. You will learn more about dimensions in the next chapter when you study shape, form, and space.

Artists create lines in many ways. A line can be drawn on paper with a pencil or scratched into wet clay with a stick. Of

---

TECHNOLOGY OPTIONS

National Gallery of Art Videodisc Use the following to help students see line variations in other artworks.

Vincent van Gogh
Farmhouse in Provence, Arles

Search Frame 1524

Paul Klee
The Old Steamer

Search Frame 2770

Albrecht Dürer
Melancholia

Search Frame 3125

Albrecht Dürer
Apocalypse: The Four Horsemen

Search Frame 3119

Use Glencoe's *Correlation Bar Code Guide to the National Gallery of Art* to locate more artworks.

course, the world is full of lines that were not drawn with a tool. Some thin, solid objects look like lines. Examples are tree trunks, yarn, spiderwebs, and wires **(Figure 4.3).** These items look like lines because length is their most important dimension.

Some lines that we think we see in nature really do not exist. For instance, when you look at the edges of shapes, you think of lines. In the photo of the dogwood blossom **(Figure 4.4),** notice that there are no black lines around the outside of each petal. However, in a drawing of that same blossom in **Figure 4.5,** lines are used to show the edges of each shape. *A line that shows or creates the outer edges of a shape* is an **outline**.

Implied lines are *a series of points that the viewer's eyes automatically connect.* Implied lines are suggested rather than real lines. A series of dots or dashes, a line of machine stitches, or a trail of wet footprints can create an implied line. A group of shapes arranged in a row can also create an implied line. In **Figure 4.6** on page 72, Abrasha has created a Hanukkah menorah that holds nine cone-shaped candles. The round tops of the cones create an implied line that leads your eyes across the top of the menorah.

▲ **FIGURE 4.3** What lines do you see around you?

▲ **FIGURE 4.4** What edges do you see?

▲ **FIGURE 4.5** Student work. How have the edges on this picture been created?

LESSON 1 *The Element of Line* **71**

TEACH.........
Motivator

To increase students' awareness of line in everyday life, suggest this: Look for lines in your world, the meandering lines of a vine, the sway of telephone lines from pole to pole, the organic lines of wood grain, or the lines of sorrow, anger, laughter, and age in faces. Find dynamic diagonal lines, rigid verticals, quiet horizontals, and flowing curves. Follow the lines of the movement of birds, the converging lines of railroad tracks, or the squiggly lines of a plate of fettucini. Watch the lines of a dancer's movements or the swinging arms of an in-line skater. Challenge students to identify other examples of line in their environment.

Developing Perceptual Skills

Have students look slowly around the classroom and list the lines they see. Then ask them to identify and describe the lines. For example, they might list the straight, blue lines on their writing paper or the wrinkles around their knuckles. Ask them to identify lines that they only now became aware of as a result of this exercise.

Developing Perceptual Skills

Using an overhead projector, place an assortment of small found objects, jewelry or possessions, or pieces of torn paper, on the projector's table. Challenge students to arrange the items in various ways that create implied lines.

TEACHER TALK

Community Organizations Involving others in your art program is invaluable to its success. Both within the school and the community, teachers find it worthwhile to establish communication and interaction with people and organizations that are interested in maintaining the art programs for students. Just as sports programs often have a booster club, art programs would benefit from a similar organization. Even if you don't hold meetings, work with the journalism instructors to send out newsletters designed by students advising people of art shows, awards, and general student progress in your program.

Promoting Discussion

Divide students into small groups and give them this assignment: As a group, select one of the kinds of line described on this page. Each group should appoint a recorder who will write down all the visual examples of the line type that the students can name in five minutes. For example, for curved lines, they might list sagging telephone wires, an eyebrow, and the trail that a snake leaves in the sand. The purpose of the exercise is to have students generate as many ideas as possible without censoring their responses. At the end of the time limit, each group will read its list to the rest of the class. Duplications are likely; allow students to generate as many examples as possible. Encourage students to realize that generally, collaborative efforts are often more productive than individual efforts.

Sparking ▲► CREATIVITY

Want students to think creatively about lines? Suggest this: Exaggerated lines make caricatures. Look for cartoons that exaggerate features of famous people. Try some of your own. Look for the strongest, or weakest, feature in someone's face or body. Then draw it with exaggeration. Exaggerate gestures to express what your character is saying or feeling. Think about the quality of line you need—thick or thin, nervous or strong, rough or smooth. Using a photograph, caricature a celebrity using in-line skates, someone overeating, showing off on a skateboard, and so on.

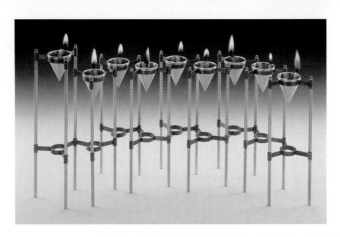

► **FIGURE 4.6** The artist has used implied line to create a sense of movement. How many sets of nine shapes can you find that create implied lines? Describe the lines.

Abrasha. *Hanukkah Menorah.* 1995. Fabricated stainless steel, silver, and gold. 17.5 × 43.8 × 9.8 cm (6⅞ × 17¼ × 2⅞"). Renwick Gallery, National Museum of American Art, Smithsonian Institution, Washington, D.C.

Kinds of Lines

There are five basic kinds of lines: vertical, horizontal, diagonal, curved, and zigzag.

Vertical lines **(Figure 4.7)** move straight up and down—they do not lean at all. A vertical line drawn on a piece of paper is perpendicular to the bottom edge of the paper. It is also perpendicular to the horizon (the line where earth and sky seem to meet). When you stand up straight, your body forms a vertical line.

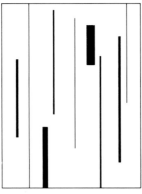

▲ **FIGURE 4.7** Vertical lines move straight up and down.

Horizontal lines **(Figure 4.8)** are parallel to the horizon. They do not slant. When you lie flat on the floor, your body forms a horizontal line.

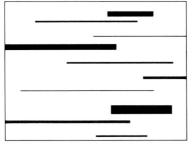

▲ **FIGURE 4.8** Horizontal lines lie parallel to the horizon.

Diagonal lines **(Figure 4.9)** slant. Diagonals are somewhere between a vertical and a horizontal line. Diagonals look as if they are either rising or falling. Imagine you are standing straight up; then, with your body stiff, you fall to the floor. At any point during your fall, your body forms a diagonal line.

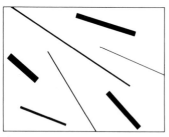

▲ **FIGURE 4.9** Diagonal lines slant.

MEETING INDIVIDUAL NEEDS

Physically or Learning Disabled Students with disabilities may be helped in doing an analysis by taping a sheet of acetate over a large art reproduction. Then the students can trace over certain types of lines with a colored marking pen. They can mark all the vertical lines with one color, all the horizontal lines with another, the diagnol lines with a third, and the curved lines with a fourth color. In this way, students can see how artists carry design elements throughout an artwork and vary them to add interest.

Zigzag lines **(Figure 4.10)** are made from a combination of diagonal lines. The diagonals form angles and change direction suddenly.

▲ **FIGURE 4.10** Zigzag lines are combinations of diagonals.

Curved lines **(Figure 4.11)** change direction gradually. When you draw wiggly lines, you are putting together a series of curves. Other kinds of curved lines form spirals and circles.

▲ **FIGURE 4.11** Curved lines change direction gradually.

Activity — Identifying Lines

Applying Your Skills. Choose one of the following paintings from this chapter: Figure 4.1, 4.12, 4.16, 4.18, or 4.19. Diagram the lines of the painting. Use green for verticals, blue for horizontals, red for diagonals, and violet for curves. Place your diagram on display. Can your classmates identify the painting you represented by looking at the colors?

Computer Option. Use the Line tool to create a series of drawings to illustrate each of the five line types. Vary the widths and lengths of your lines. You may also choose to vary patterns and colors. Label each drawing's line type.

Line Variation

Lines vary in appearance in five major ways:

- **Length.** Lines can be long or short.

- **Width.** Lines can be thick or thin.

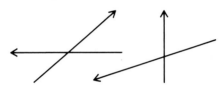

- **Texture.** Lines can be rough or smooth.

- **Direction.** Lines can move in any direction, such as vertical, horizontal, or diagonal.

- **Degree of curve.** Lines can curve gradually or not at all, become wavy, or form spirals.

These five variations can be combined in many, many ways. You can make long, wide lines; rough, short lines; and smooth, curved lines.

Activity

Identifying Lines
Applying Your Skills. To explain this activity, place a large print on the board, cover it with acetate, then demonstrate how to find the different lines.

🖥 **Computer Option.** As an alternative exercise, have students draw five equal-sized rectangles. In these frames, they can use the Line tool to create a series of drawings to illustrate each of the five line types. Vary the widths and lengths. Students may also choose to work in color or use patterns for the lines. Label each drawing with the line type.

Art History

One fascinating way to learn about line is to learn more about Japan's Zen gardens. Explain to students that Zen Buddhism is a religion that emphasizes meditation. Kyoto, Japan, is an important Zen center and the home of more than 2,000 shrines and temples. One of these is the Ryoanji Temple, famous for its garden made entirely of rocks. The garden rocks are raked into straight lines. Zen Buddhists feel that this garden of lines facilitates meditation.

LESSON 1 *The Element of Line* **73**

MEETING INDIVIDUAL NEEDS

Learning Disabled Sometimes we take for granted what might pose a challenge for another person. Different types of lines may challenge some students with mental retardation. Some may be able to make scribbles with little order. Others can conceive of and depict circularity. Still others can show verticality and hori-zontally. Others will be able to draw circles, squares, and triangles. Some students find satisfaction in being able to make a wavy or zigzag line. Some students with mild retardation will take delight in figuring out how to draw such a complicated form as a five-pointed star.

Art History

Inform students that Georges Rouault was associated with the Fauves (wild beasts). These young French painters expressed emotion by creating works that exploded with brilliant colors, bold distortions, and loose brushstrokes. The Fauves were interested in painting scenes with bright colors that expressed happiness and pleasure. Rouault loved the bright colors, but he was interested in serious subjects. He used his art to point out injustices and problems in the world. Probably because he was apprenticed to a stained-glass maker as a young boy, his style reflects the heavy lines that are similar to the lines of solder that join pieces of stained glass. If possible, show other examples of his works such as *The Old King* and *The Italian Woman*. Ask students to discuss the similarities between his paintings and examples of stained glass.

Studio Skills

Collect as many different media and tools as you can for students to experiment with in making lines. After they have experimented, challenge them to go home and find at least one different way to create a line. Ask them to bring the results to school the next day.

▶ **FIGURE 4.12** When Rouault was a boy he was apprenticed to a maker of stained glass. The thick black lines surrounding bright colors in his paintings remind the viewer of stained-glass windows.

Georges Rouault. *Christ and the Apostles.* 1937–38. Oil on canvas. 64.3 × 99.4 cm (25¼ × 39⅛"). The Metropolitan Museum of Art, New York, New York. The Jacques and Natasha Gelman Collection.

▲ **FIGURE 4.13** Although this painting is called a still life, it seems to have movement and activity. This is because of the artist's use of line. How many different line directions and line variations can you find in this painting? Describe them.

Alice Neel. *Still Life, Rose of Sharon.* 1973. Oil on canvas. 101.9 × 76.5 cm (40 × 30"). Collection of Whitney Museum of American Art, New York, New York. Arthur M. Bullowa Bequest.

The media, tools, and surfaces used to make lines affect the way a line looks. As with the combination of various line types, a multitude of possible effects can be created. Some common materials used by artists to make lines are graphite, chalk, crayon, ink, and paint. The material is applied by using a tool. Some tools used for making lines include pencils, markers, pens, brushes, and scissors.

Artists use different tools and materials to create different types of lines. For example, a line drawn with chalk on a chalkboard looks smoother than a line drawn with chalk on a sidewalk. Some artists have discovered very unusual ways of using line, as shown in **Figures 4.12** and **4.13**. In **Figure 4.14**, the artist has used many line types and variations.

MORE ABOUT... Georges Henri Rouault

Born in Paris in 1871, Rouault is often considered the greatest modern religious painter. His work is characterized by clear and glowing reds, blues, and greens; use of impasto (thickly applied pigment); and heavy black outline. This style suggests that of stained glass, which Rouault learned from his mentor, Gustave Moreau. Rouault favors such themes as the Passion of Christ, corrupt judges and prostitutes, and somber portraits of kings and clowns. Such themes reflect his devout Roman Catholicism.

LOOKING CLOSELY

Line Types and Variations

In this painting, the artist has used five different kinds of line and many line variations. Can you find other examples of line and line variation combinations?

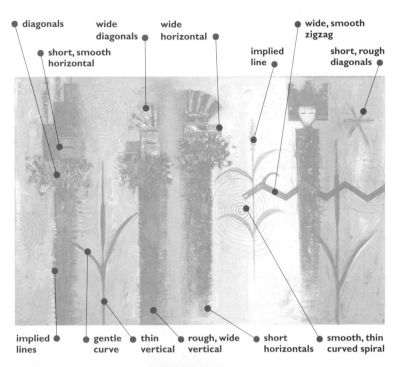

diagonals

wide diagonals

wide horizontal

wide, smooth zigzag

short, smooth horizontal

implied line

short, rough diagonals

implied lines

gentle curve

thin vertical

rough, wide vertical

short horizontals

smooth, thin curved spiral

◀ **FIGURE 4.14**

Dan Namingha. *Blessing Rain Chant.* 1992. Acrylic on canvas. 198 × 305 cm (78 × 120″). Niman Fine Art, Santa Fe, New Mexico.

Line and Value

Value is *the element of art that describes the darkness or lightness of an object.* Value depends on how much light a surface reflects. A surface has a dark value if it reflects little light. It has a light value if it reflects a lot of light. Every time you make a pencil mark on a piece of white paper, you are creating a line with a certain value. The harder you press, the

Studio Skills

Have students do a close-up line drawing in pencil of one of the following: bare twigs on the limb of a tree; pine needles on the end of a branch; feathers of a bird; or similar types of items. Before they begin, demonstrate how to use the sharp point of the pencil for thin lines and the side of the pencil for wide lines. This activity requires some expertise in perception drawing. If your students lack confidence in their ability to draw, you can help. Bring a bicycle into the room. When they complain that it is too hard to draw, agree with them. Then ask if anyone can draw a circle. Ask someone to point out the circles on the bike. Have them find vertical, horizontal, and diagonal lines on the bike. Now challenge the students to forget that this object is a bike and to think of it as a combination of lines. They can draw the bike by drawing the various lines.

Developing Perceptual Skills

Try to provide a variety of pencil hardness and a variety of pens for the students to experiment with. Even if you can only get a few of each kind, students can share them so that they can discover the effects they can create with different pens and pencils.

Studio Skills

Have students make a pencil drawing of a person engaged in an activity and use straight lines in the composition to lead the viewer's eye toward the focal point of action.

MEETING INDIVIDUAL NEEDS

Building Self-Esteem Drawing a dense pattern of lines is a good type of challenge for gifted students. Challenge their skills in elaboration by urging them to include intricate patterns. While elaboration is a key element in creativity, others are fluency, flexibility, and originality. Drawing a dense pattern of lines may need to be simplified for some students with disabilities. For example, the feathers of a bird can be conceived in a schematic way, which communicates the idea of feather just as much as does a realistic feather drawing. It is a sufficient challenge for some students to visually conceive of and draw a single object.

darker the value. A series of closely placed lines can create areas of dark value. The lines may be parallel or they may cross one another. **Crosshatching** is *the technique of using crossed lines for shading.*

The values that line groups create depend on four factors: the number of lines, the size of the spaces between the lines, the media, and the tools. A soft pencil (2B, 4B) makes a wide, dark line. A hard pencil (2H, 4H) makes a thin, gray line. A crayon stroked over a rough surface makes a broken line. A crayon stroked over smooth paper makes a solid line.

Look at the Dürer drawing in **Figure 4.15.** Use a magnifying glass to study the way Dürer has used line combinations to create dark and light values.

▲ **Figure 4.15** The artist has used line to create this drawing. Identify the areas where the artist has used crosshatching to indicate shading. What kinds of line variation has Dürer used?

Albrecht Dürer. *An Oriental Ruler Seated on His Throne.* c. 1495. Pen and black ink. 30.6 × 19.7 cm (12 × 7¾"). National Gallery of Art, Washington, D.C. © 1998 Board of Trustees. Ailsa Mellon Bruce Fund.

Activity   Using Line to Create Value

✓ Check Your Understanding

1. How is line defined in drawing?
2. What are the five basic kinds of lines?
3. In what five ways do lines vary in appearance?
4. Describe the crosshatching technique.

✓ Answers to Check Your Understanding

1. A line is the path of a dot moving through space.
2. The five basic lines are vertical, horizontal, diagonal, curved and zigzag.
3. Lines can vary in appearance by length, width, texture, direction and degree of curve.
4. The crosshatching technique is a method of drawing crossed lines for shading.

The Expressive Qualities of Line

Depending on its direction, a line can express different ideas or feelings. This is why line is an important element in the language of art. Vertical lines can make certain objects look taller. For example, vertical lines on wallpaper can make low ceilings seem higher. Clothing designers use vertical lines to make short people look taller and heavy people look thinner.

Line Movement

Vertical lines are static, or inactive. They appear to be at rest. For this reason,

they express stability. Artists use them to show dignity, poise, stiffness, and formality, as in Figure 4.14 on page 75.

Horizontal lines are also static. They express feelings of peace, rest, quiet, and stability, as in **Figure 4.16.** They give a feeling of permanence or solidarity. Because we stand on solid horizontal ground, horizontal lines make us feel content, relaxed, and calm.

Because curved lines change direction, they express activity. How much activity they express depends on the type and direction of the curve. The less active the curve, the calmer the feeling. Spiral

▲ **FIGURE 4.16** Strong horizontal lines create a sense of calm on this empty street. As you look at this painting, you get the feeling that everyone is sleeping peacefully. How many real and how many implied horizontal lines can you find in this painting?

Edward Hopper. *Early Sunday Morning.* 1930. Oil on canvas. 89.2 × 152.4 cm (35 × 60"). Collection of Whitney Museum of American Art, New York, New York.

LESSON 2 *The Expressive Qualities of Line*   **77**

MORE ABOUT... Edward Hopper

Born in 1882 in Nyack, New York, Edward Hopper is known for his landmark works of American realism. The paintings of this twentieth century American artist are characterized by a style that evokes isolation, melancholy, and loneliness. His early paintings, such as *Le pavillion de flore*, were strongly realistic in style and characterized by large, simple geometric

forms, flat masses of color, and the use of strong vertical, horizontal, and diagonal lines. Many of these elements would be retained in his work throughout his career. However, in 1925, Hopper painted a landmark piece, *House by the Railroad.* This work exhibited an atmosphere of eerie solitude and loneliness.

FOCUS............

Objectives

After completing this lesson, students will be able to:

■ Understand the expressive qualities or meanings of different lines in works of art.

■ Use lines to make contour, gesture, and calligraphic drawings.

Supplies

■ Fine art reproductions representing architectural details

■ Paint brushes, inks, watercolors

Resources

📁 Application Activity 8, *Sharpening Your Skills*

📁 Artist's Profile 35, *Edward Hopper*

📁 Cooperative Learning Activity 8

📁 Enrichment Activity 8, *Calligraphy in the Carolingian Style*

📁 Studio Lesson 2, *Foil Relief*

TEACH.........

Motivator

Have students brainstorm a list of words they think of when they hear the word *line. (path, trail, road, row, curve, slant)* Record their ideas on the board. Discuss what all the words have in common. *(All suggest movement.)* Explain that lines can lead the eyes into, around, and out of visual images.

Art History

To help students further appreciate the life and times of Edward Hopper, whose work is shown in Figure 4.16, assign Artist's Profile 35 in the TCR. 📂

Art Criticism

Divide the class into four groups and assign each one to assume the role of one of the following: art educator, consumer, art patron, and art critic. Then have them brainstorm a list of reasons why their particular person would, or would not, purchase a painting like Hopper's *Early Sunday Morning.* List the reasons on the board and discuss the results.

Art on a Shoestring

Students' capacity to appreciate works of art or architecture that contain an abundance of fine or intricate detail, such as Figure 4.17, can be enhanced by displaying the works as slides or overhead transparencies. A common, but often overlooked, source of such material is vacation slides and photographic negatives that can be processed into slides at a nominal cost. Also, museum gift shops often sell high-quality slides of their major artworks. Prior to lesson time, assemble slides, either from your own collection or from other teachers, friends, and relatives.

◀ **FIGURE 4.17** Notice the many different kinds of curves the artist used to create this luxurious gateway. Identify any straight lines. Follow them through the work. Do they stay straight? Can you think of adjectives to describe the many types of curves used in the artwork?

Albert Raymond Paley. *Portal Gates.* 1974. Forged steel, brass, copper, and bronze. 230.5 × 182.9 × 10.2 cm (90¼ × 72 × 4"). Renwick Gallery, National Museum of American Art, Smithsonian Institution, Washington, D.C.

curves wind around a central point. They are hypnotic and draw the eye to their center. Curved lines are often used in decorative arts to suggest a feeling of luxury, as in **Figure 4.17.**

Diagonal lines express instability, tension, activity, and excitement, as shown in **Figure 4.18.** Since they can appear to be either falling or rising, they sometimes make a viewer feel uncomfortable. Artists use them to add tension or to create an exciting mood. However, when two diagonals meet and seem to support each other, as in the roof of a house, they appear more stable.

Zigzag lines create confusion. They are extremely active and may evoke feelings of excitement **(Figure 4.19,** page 80) and nervousness. The degree of intensity is indicated by the direction of the zigzag. Zigzags that move horizontally, such as those across the top of a picket fence, are less active than the irregular zigzags of a streak of lightning.

Activity	**Using Lines Expressively**

Applying Your Skills. Choose two words from the following list:

swimming	burning	praying
rocking	flowing	jumping
marching	running	growing
dancing	crawling	laughing
wagging	writing	flying

On separate sheets of paper, illustrate the words you have chosen by using line movement only. Do not draw objects.

Choose the medium you think will work best. When you are finished, write the words on the back of each paper. Ask your classmates to look at the lines and guess which words you have illustrated.

Computer Option. Use the Line tool to make two drawings using lines. Let one drawing illustrate quiet, calm piano music, and let the other illustrate loud rock music.

TEACHER TALK 📖

Classroom Management Because the art room is more often used for noisy production activities, classroom arrangement should lend itself to quick manipulation. It is hard to space young people around the room at tables and still keep their attention during a lengthy discussion. Even though you must crowd students together or ask them to move chairs from work stations to a discussion area, some provision must be made so that they can gather, facing the teacher. Consider the need for an area where quiet activities take place—films, slide presentations, lectures, and discussions.

▲ **FIGURE 4.18**   In this print every line that should be static is diagonal. Look at the window, the lamp, the rug, the floor planks, and the fiddler's bench. The diagonal lines fill the work with a sense of excitement. Not only the people but also every corner of the room seems to be alive and dancing to the music of the fiddler.

Thomas Hart Benton. *Country Dance.* 1929. Oil on gessoed canvas. 76.2 × 63.5 cm (30 × 25"). Private collection.

Using Lines Expressively

Applying Your Skills. Have students select a word from the list, or use another word of their choice, to illustrate the concept of the expressive quality of line.

🖥 **Computer Option.** You may wish to provide music from a different culture depending upon which region your students are studying in Social Studies… Africa, Japan, Middle East, South America. This provides a nice comparison for listening and responding to distinct styles of music.

Aesthetics

After students have studied Thomas Hart Benton's painting, *Country Dance,* guide them through the steps of art criticism by asking the following questions: What painting media did Benton use? What do you see in the painting? How has Benton used lines to create a sense of excitement and liveliness? How many horizontal or vertical lines do you see? What is happening in the scene? What is the artist trying to say in the painting? How might a critic respond to the painting?

Studio Skills

Have students work in pairs or small groups to list at least five adjectives that describe moods or activities (for example, playful, sad, mysterious, puzzled, and disagreeable). Then have students independently draw a line that expresses each adjective. Encourage them to use the kinds of lines described in this chapter. Have students select one example to share with the rest of the class.

MEETING INDIVIDUAL NEEDS

Learning Partners Students who may have difficulty following directions or discussion topics may benefit from a learning partner. Choose a partner based on the nature of a student's difficulty, such as hearing, vision, language proficiency, or comprehension. Allow time for partners to confer whenever the partner needing help feels it is necessary. Encourage students to develop an ongoing method of self-directed learning. For example, students with limited English proficiency might routinely make a list of terms that are particularly difficult. They can then ask their learning partners to work with them to clarify the meanings of those terms.

Developing Perceptual Skills

Discuss how the line type affects the expressive quality of each work. To help the student grasp the idea of expressive line qualities, refer to the pull of gravity. Vertical lines are in balance with gravity. When you are standing upright, gravity is pulling through the center of your body. When you are horizontal, you are totally at rest. You are lying flat and gravity is pulling evenly on all parts of your body. However, anyone in a diagonal position must be supported. A diagonal looks as if it is falling or rising; it seems to be in motion. If your students are not too inhibited, ask them to act out the line directions to stand straight as a vertical, for example, and then ask them how they feel.

Exploring Aesthetics

Have students study the painting in Figure 4.19, taking note of the specific kinds of lines the artist used. Ask them to discuss the work and then react to the following questions: How do they think Jacob Lawrence went about creating these lines? What adjectives would they use to describe these lines? What message or mood do they feel is communicated by the use of such lines? Do they feel the painting is successful? Why, or why not?

MEET THE ARTIST

JACOB LAWRENCE

American, 1917–

Jacob Lawrence was born in Atlantic City, New Jersey, in 1917. When he was 12, his family moved to Harlem in New York City. The move would have a great impact on his growth as an artist.

The Harlem Renaissance of the 1920s had attracted many talented minority artists from all over the world, and many still remained in Harlem during the 1930s. These artists served as Lawrence's inspiration.

Lawrence sought every opportunity he could to learn about art. He listened to the Harlem artists as they talked in their studios. The 135th Street Public Library, which he visited often, always had pieces of African sculpture on display. His many trips to the Metropolitan Museum of Art gave him a strong background in art history.

Lawrence became fascinated with black history and its heroic figures. He took as his subjects such important people as Toussaint L'Ouverture, Harriet Tubman, and Frederick Douglass. Lawrence often found he could not express all he wanted to say in just a single picture. Therefore, he often made series of paintings to tell the whole story. In this way, he used his art to convey his ideas about the heritage of African-Americans.

▲ **FIGURE 4.19** The artist has used line to show the movement of the children. Look at their arms, legs, and feet. What kinds of lines do you see? How has Lawrence used line to create a feeling of movement and excitement?

Jacob Lawrence. *Children at Play.* 1947. Tempera on Masonite panel. 50.8 × 60.9 cm (20 × 24″). Georgia Museum of Art, University of Georgia, Athens, Georgia. Eva Underhill Holbrook Memorial Collection of American Art, Gift of Alfred H. Holbrook.

80 | **CHAPTER 4** Line

MORE ABOUT... The Harlem Renaissance

In the late 1920s and early 1930s an African American cultural movement emerged that was centered in the Harlem neighborhood of New York City. Although mainly a literary movement, this period brought great developments in African American music, theater, art, and politics. The Harlem Renaissance marked the first time that mainstream publishers and critics gave serious regard to African American literature and arts. The works that were produced through this movement attracted significant attention throughout the nation. It was the artists from this movement that inspired the work of Jacob Lawrence.

Contour Drawing

A **contour line** *defines the edges and surface ridges of an object.* A contour line also creates a boundary separating one area from another. Learning how to contour draw will add to your drawing skills as well as to your ability to observe and understand objects. See the examples in **Figure 4.20** and **Figure 4.21.**

When drawing contours, let your eyes follow the contour of the object you are drawing. Move your pencil at the same speed as your eyes. Do not lift the pencil from the paper. The line should be continuous. Draw the line slowly and with care. Concentrate in order to draw accurately. See the Technique Tip on page 429 in the Handbook for help in making contour drawings.

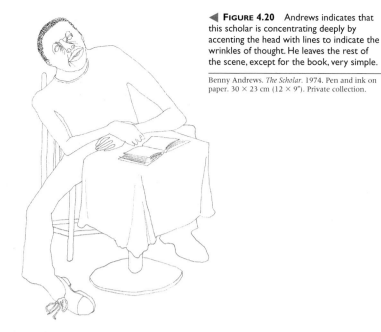

◄ **FIGURE 4.20** Andrews indicates that this scholar is concentrating deeply by accenting the head with lines to indicate the wrinkles of thought. He leaves the rest of the scene, except for the book, very simple.

Benny Andrews. *The Scholar.* 1974. Pen and ink on paper. 30 × 23 cm (12 × 9"). Private collection.

◄ **FIGURE 4.21** Student work. Notice how the line flows through this hospital scene. Look at the difference between the busy zigzag lines that describe the wrinkles in the sheet and the few lines that define the person's face.

Activity — Using Contour Lines

Applying Your Skills. Set up a group of three shoes in an interesting, overlapping composition. Arrange them at different angles so you can view them sideways, head-on, from the top, and from the back. Use a black marker to do a contour line drawing of all the shoes. Use only line. Do not color or shade the drawing. Use line to add details such as laces, stitches, patches, and holes.

Computer Option. Sit at your computer, turn sideways, and look down. Use the Line tool to draw your feet, legs, and free hand. You may start at the feet and work your way up toward your lap, or vice versa. Use the mouse just as you would use a pencil. Be sure to start your drawing near the edge of your screen so you will have room for the entire picture.

Sparking CREATIVITY

Want students to think creatively about drawing? Here is the key to unlock your drawing ability: Let your eyes follow every edge of what you want to draw and let your hand record what your eye is seeing. Trust your eyes. Don't worry about "wrong" lines. Lots of eye training is all you need. Draw your world close up. Record your dreams and ideas. Your own drawing style will develop just as your handwriting style develops into one that is uniquely your own.

Studio Skills

Ask students to do contour drawings as a homework assignment. Have them sketch a pet, an animal at the zoo, objects in their homes, and so on.

Activity

Using Contour Lines

Computer Option. Another alternative for this activity is to have students place an object such as a shoe, hat, or backpack near the computer or hold it in their less dominant hand to view. They should decide where they are going to begin drawing and locate that place on the screen. They should observe the outer edges as well as the interior lines and details that are created by the folds and textures. Have them use a continuous line and only occasionally look at the screen.

TECHNIQUE TIP ✓

Contour Drawing When making contour drawings of a still-life arrangement, be sure to place the arrangement high on a counter or table so that it can be seen by everyone in the class. This may require that you rearrange the seating. Some students may need to lean on drawing boards or sit upon countertops or tabletops so that they can see the arrangement. You will not have discipline problems if you insist upon quiet concentration while drawing is going on. Sometimes playing music on the radio helps students concentrate. The choice of music is up to you. Some prefer classical or easy-listening, while others will want pop and rock. Be sure to get permission from your administrators before you bring a radio into the room.

Developing Perceptual Skills

Encourage students to practice gesture drawing as it makes use of the whole arm, not just the hand. Encourage students to practice this method often, using the same object each time. After several attempts, ask them to evaluate their progress by examining the rough sketches in the order that they were made.

Studio Skills

Have students make chalk gesture drawings using photographs of action figures from sports or fashion magazines. They should then put the photograph away and turn the gestures into a different scene of the student's choice. For example, the gestures of a basketball player could turn into those of a dancer. Make these sketches into finished works using oil pastels or paints.

Activity
Gesture Drawing

Applying Your Skills. The best way to help students understand gesture drawing is to demonstrate it for them. Have a model pose, point out the position to the students, and explain that you are going to draw only the position and not the details of the model. Before you draw, show them that you are observing the curve of the back or the diagonal lines of one leg. Then quickly demonstrate.

Computer Option. Students will have to work quickly. Encourage them to capture the feeling of motion and energy by selecting a different brush color each time the model changes position. They might also overlap their drawings.

▶ **FIGURE 4.22**
Tintoretto describes the gesture and bulk of this figure with just a few rough lines. You can sense the movement of the figure through the looseness of the quickly drawn lines. Why was it unnecessary for the artist to add more detail?

Jacopo Tintoretto. *Standing Youth with His Arm Raised, Seen from Behind.* Black chalk on laid paper. 36.3 × 21.9 cm (14¼ × 8⅝″). National Gallery of Art, Washington, D.C. © 1998 Board of Trustees. Ailsa Mellon Bruce Fund.

▶ **FIGURE 4.23**
The artist used a brush and paint to create this gesture oil sketch. Compare it to Figure 4.22. Describe the similarities and differences between the two pieces of art. Does this painting have more detail?

Audrey Flack. *Self-Portrait: The Memory.* 1958. Oil on canvas. 127 × 86.4 cm (50 × 34″). Miami University Art Museum, Oxford, Ohio. Gift of the artist.

Gesture Drawing

A **gesture** is *an expressive movement.* The purpose of drawing gestures is to capture the feeling of motion. A gesture drawing uses very little detail. (See **Figures 4.22** and **4.23**).

Lines showing gestures are drawn quickly. They should be sketched freely and loosely—even recklessly—in order to capture movement. Unlike contours, they represent the interior of an object. Your gesture drawings may look like scribbles at first, but this is acceptable. Concentrate on showing position and movement.

Activity
Creating Gesture Drawings

Applying Your Skills. Make a series of gesture drawings. (See the Technique Tip on page 429 in the Handbook.) Classmates should take turns posing for one another. Start with thirty-second poses. Shorten the time by five seconds for each pose until the pose is held for only ten seconds. Have the model twist, turn, bend, and kick, trying to avoid doing the same thing twice.

Computer Option. Choose a round, medium-size Brush or Pencil tool. Sit at the computer station, turn sideways, and look at other students who are modeling for gesture drawing. They will be changing positions every 20 or 30 seconds. Try to capture the feeling of motion, not detail. Change color each time the model changes positions. Some of your drawings will overlap.

TEACHER TALK

Classroom Management Set small still-life arrangements around the room in various places so that every student can see one clearly. You might have to place one on each table. Limit the arrangements to three objects each. Try to include one plant in each arrangement. Ask the students to make contour drawings. First, have them point to the objects and draw them in the air. Get them to notice that the bottom of round things, like pots and cylinders, usually curve. Observe when they draw in the air that they are drawing on a flat picture plane and not in depth.

Calligraphic Drawing

The word **calligraphy** means *beautiful handwriting.* Calligraphy is often associated with Asian writing and art. In China and Japan, calligraphy is used to form *characters* that represent the language. However, characters are more than just a letter of the alphabet. They are like pictures. They can represent an idea, an object, or a verbal sound. The Chinese and Japanese use the same types of calligraphic lines and brushstrokes in their paintings **(Figure 4.24).** In fact, in the Chinese language, the words *writing* and *painting* are represented by the same character.

Calligraphic lines are usually made with brushstrokes that change from thin to thick in one stroke. To make a very thin line, use the tip of the brush. As you press on the brush and more of it touches the paper, the line becomes wider. (See Technique Tip 3 on page 429 in the Handbook.)

(See Technique Tip 3 on page 429 in the Handbook.)

Activity — Calligraphic Lines

Applying Your Skills. Practice making calligraphic lines with ink or watercolor paint. Use round, pointed brushes, both thin and thick. Also, try bamboo brushes. Next, use a watercolor brush and ink or watercolor paint to make a series of five calligraphic studies of one natural object, such as a leaf or a vegetable.

Computer Option. Research either Egyptian hieroglyphics or Southwestern pictographs to gain information about "picture writing." Create your own picture writing by making up symbols. Use any computer tools and options available. Remember that the Cut and Paste options are helpful when you want to repeat a symbol without redrawing it.

Check Your Understanding

1. What do vertical and horizontal lines express?
2. How are contour drawings and gesture drawings different?
3. What type of artwork is often associated with calligraphy?

▲ **FIGURE 4.24** Gu Mei was a famous singer, poet, and painter of landscapes and ink orchids. She created this long handscroll containing three sections depicting orchids and rocks. Notice the long curving lines have been made with one brushstroke. Where else can you find lines that seem to have been painted with one brushstroke?

Gu Mei, *Orchids and Rocks.* 1644. Ming dynasty. Detail of handscroll. Ink on paper. 27 × 170.8 cm (10⅝ × 67¼"). Arthur M. Sackler Gallery, Smithsonian Institution, Washington, D.C. Arthur M. Sackler Collection.

Answers to Check Your Understanding

1. Vertical and horizontal lines are static. They express inactivity and can give the impression of dignity, formality, calm and contentment.
2. Contour drawings define the edges and surface ridges of an object. Gesture drawings are different because they capture movement and show the interior of an object.
3. Chinese and Japanese paintings, especially scroll paintings, are associated with calligraphy.

Activity

Calligraphic Lines

Applying Your Skills. Bring in other examples of Oriental calligraphy. Read the Technique Tip directions and study the photographs with the students to help them see how they can gain control over their brushes. This activity will be more successful if you have some nylon sable brushes for them to use.

Computer Option. A program's selection of fonts and styles gives students additional options for this activity. Encourage students to use the options on their programs that they are least familiar with, thereby expanding their knowledge.

ASSESS..........

Self-Assessment

Have students complete the review questions on this page. Answers are provided below.

Reteaching

■ Help small groups of students go through a collection of drawings, identifying the gesture drawings and explaining how those drawings differ from the others.

Enrichment

■ Assign Enrichment Activity 8, *Calligraphy in the Caroligian Style* in the TCR.

CLOSE............

Have students review Figure 4.1 that opened this chapter. Have them identify the kinds of line, line variations, and expressive qualities that were used in the painting.

Contour Wire Sculpture

(National Standards: 1a, 1b, 2b, 2c)

FOCUS............
Objective

After completing this lesson, students will be able to:

■ Design and create a three-dimensional contour sculpture based on a series of contour drawings of a single object.

Supplies

■ Sketchbook and pencil
■ Needle-nose pliers
■ Wire cutter
■ Pliable wire

Optional:

■ Small block of wood
■ Staple gun or staple nail and hammer
■ String

Resources

📁 Artist's Profile 26, *Alexander Calder*

TEACH.........
Motivator

Show large photos of wire sculptures and mobiles by Alexander Calder. Show students how he used line to define shape in space.

Studio Skills

When making contour drawings for ideas, begin by making initial drawings of a variety of objects before choosing one to draw and sculpt. Also, if a jeweler's jig is available, students may benefit by using it to bend the wire. To provide a nice finish, students may want to sand and apply varnish to the block of wood before mounting the sculpture.

84

▲ **FIGURE 4.25**

Alexander Calder. *Varese.* 1931. Wire. 34.2 × 34.9 × 31.1 cm (13½ × 13¼   12⅛"). Whitney Museum of American Art, New York, New York.

SUPPLIES

■ **Sketchbook and pencil**
■ **Needle-nose pliers**
■ **Wire cutter**
■ **Pliable wire**
Optional:
■ **Small block of wood**
■ **Staple gun or staple nail and hammer**
■ **String**

Alexander Calder grew up in the studios of his parents, who were both artists. As a child, Calder made spiral-wire jewelry for his sister's dolls. This family atmosphere of creativity sparked his enthusiasm for art and led him to invent mobile sculpture and wire-line sculptures such as *Varese* (**Figure 4.25**).

While attending the Art Students' League in New York City, Calder would go out into the streets and rapidly sketch people as they passed by. He was well known for his skill in capturing a sense of movement with a single, unbroken line. In these simple contour drawings, he captured the essential characteristics of his subjects. He was able to transfer that talent to sculpture.

As Calder experimented with wire sculptures, his figures became three-dimensional forms drawn in space by wire lines. He made animals inspired by his childhood fascination with the circus, and he created portraits of people such as *Varese*. Many of his wire figures were humorous. Each sculpture drew attention from every angle.

Try your hand at wire sculpture and create a lively and interesting three-dimensional figure.

MORE ABOUT... Alexander Calder

Alexander Calder is most noted for his wind mobiles. These mobiles were made from rods, wires, and delicate shapes made of sheet metal and wire hung from a single point. Air currents set the mobiles in motion, treating the viewer to constantly changing patterns of colors and shapes. Many of Calder's mobiles are based on natural forms—animals, birds, fish, or plants—and the motions were carefully planned to imitate the movement of the subject. His later works show that he became more interested in shapes and movements that had little to do with natural objects.

What You Will Learn

You will design and create a three-dimensional sculpture that defines space and shape through the movement of a wire line through space. Make your contour wire sculpture look interesting from every point of view. Base this sculpture on your own series of contour drawings of a single object. Prepare your finished work for display.

Creating

Brainstorm with classmates to identify objects for this project. Some possibilities are a houseplant, a bicycle, an animal, a person, or a head. Choose something that is interesting to you and that you can observe in person. Do not use a photograph. Study the photo of Calder's wire sculpture. Notice how the wire is used.

Step 1 Make a series of three or more contour studies of the object. Make each drawing from a different point of view.

Step 2 Collect your materials and experiment with some scrap wire. Practice using the tools to bend, twist, loop, and cut the wire so that you understand the way the wire behaves.

Step 3 Create your wire sculpture based on the drawings you have made. Work on all sides of the sculpture so that it looks interesting from every point of view.

Step 4 To prepare your work for display, staple or nail it to a small block of wood, hang it with string from a support, or invent a method of display.

EVALUATING YOUR WORK

▶ **DESCRIBE** Name the object you chose as the subject of your wire sculpture. How many contour line drawings of the object did you make? List the contour line variations you used to create the outlines and ridges of your sculpture. How did you prepare your finished work for display?

▶ **ANALYZE** Do the lines of your work follow the contours and ridges of the object you chose? Is the work interesting from every angle?

▶ **INTERPRET** What kind of mood is created by the use of line in three-dimensional space? Describe the difference between the look of the two-dimensional contour line drawings and the three-dimensional wire sculpture. Give your work a title.

▶ **JUDGE** Have you created a three-dimensional contour sculpture that is interesting from all sides and angles? Does your work successfully represent the object you chose? Is there anything you would change to make the work more successful? Which aesthetic theory would be the best to judge your work?

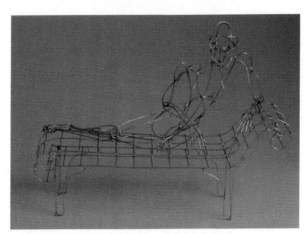

▲ **FIGURE 4.25A** Student work.

Art History

To help students further appreciate the life and times of Alexander Calder, whose work is shown in Figure 4.25, assign Artist's Profile 26 in the TCR. 📁

ASSESS...........

Keeping a Portfolio

Remind students that the preliminary sketches and the final artwork for this Studio Project are likely candidates for their portfolios.

Self-Assessment

■ Have students apply the steps of art criticism to their own artwork using the "Evaluating Your Work" questions on this page.

■ Ask students to display both the sketch for the design and the wire sculpture. Encourage each student to briefly explain how the sculpture defines space with line.

Enrichment

As an optional activity, have students create a nonobjective wire sculpture by bending the wire in different directions to create movement and rhythm. Encourage them to think about how they feel as they bend the wire. They can reflect this emotional reaction in the sharp edges, smooth curves, and straight lines of the sculpture. The final artwork can be freestanding or attached to a base.

CLOSE.............

Ask each student to display both the sketch for the design and the wire sculpture. Encourage each student to briefly explain how the sculpture defines space with line.

▶ COOPERATIVE LEARNING

Brainstorming Ideas Activities such as the Studio Project above lend themselves to collaborative sessions, especially in the planning stage. Often, students have difficulty conceiving an idea when called to do so. Working in groups, students hear the ideas of other students which in turn promotes more ideas. Teachers who have had an opportunity to recognize which students have no problem generating creative ideas are wise to place these students into groups with students who have difficulty. That way, their ideas benefit others. Another approach to brainstorming sessions is to provide examples of previous student work to small groups and instruct them to use the sample as a discussion model for their own designs.

Imagination Landscape

(National Standards: 1a, 1b, 2b, 2c)

FOCUS...........
Objectives

After completing this lesson, students will be able to:

- Create an imaginary landscape using torn paper stencils to make the edges of land masses.
- Imagine living things and objects that belong in the landscape and add them to the design.

Supplies

- Sketchbook
- Oil pastels
- Large sheet of white paper
- Paper towels
- Newspaper for tearing into stencils
- Scissors (optional)

TEACH.........
Motivator

Ask the students to look for lines in their environment that define edges. If necessary, refer to the discussion of contour lines on page 81. Also, take the students outside and ask them to describe the surrounding horizons. What do they see? Mountains? Trees? Flat plains? Buildings and skyscrapers? What kind of lines are created where the sky appears to meet the horizon? What sort of edges and lines do they see between them and the horizon?

Aesthetics

Experiment with different types and thicknesses of paper for varied edges. Cutting the paper with scissors will give a sharp edge. Torn thick, soft paper will result in a rough, yet, softer edge.

86

Imagination Landscape

▲ **FIGURE 4.26**

Carolyn Clive. *Amplitude.* 1987. Oil paint used with stencil brush and torn paper stencil on paper. 61 × 46 cm (24 × 18"). Collection of the artist.

SUPPLIES

- **Sketchbook**
- **Oil pastels**
- **Large sheet of white paper**
- **Paper towels**
- **Newspaper for tearing into stencils**
- **Scissors (optional)**

L ook at *Amplitude* **(Figure 4.26)** and turn your imagination loose. What might this landscape be? Is it a landscape or a seascape? Can you identify mountains, plains, waves, sky? What does the sphere in the rectangle represent? How has the artist used line to create this landscape?

Carolyn Clive was driving through the Georgia countryside one bleak fall day. "The leaves had fallen and the crops were in. I looked out over the land and told myself, 'I don't know what I'm going to do, but I'm going to capture the spirit of this land.'"

Clive developed her own stenciling technique for working with oil paints and used line and value changes to create her abstract landscape. Notice how she has combined geometric shapes with flowing, overlapping waves of color. Observe how she has brought parts of the design outside the image area to provide added interest.

What You Will Learn

In this project, you will use torn-paper stencils to create an imaginary landscape. Use the stencils to create the land mass edges. Then add objects or figures to the landscape.

Creating

Study the stencil painting by Carolyn Clive. Notice how the edges of the shapes are dark on one side and light on the other. The artist did this by holding a stencil in place and pulling oil color gently from the edge of the stencil into the shape with a stippling brush.

CULTURAL DIVERSITY

Visual Elements Across Cultures Visual elements are the ingredients of art. Explain to students that the elements have been analyzed, organized, and used in many ways, but they are not the inventions of artists. They are natural elements that artists have learned to use as an alternative language. For example, Carolyn Clive "translated" the spirit of her photographs into a visual design with a unique medium. Emphasize that the use of visual elements is common to all cultures. Helping students to understand the elements, in this case, line, will give them new methods of applying them and new ways to perceive the environment and the environment of others.

Step 1 First, practice the torn-stencil technique in your sketchbook. Tear a 9 × 6 inch piece of newspaper to create a rough, curving edge that will be your stencil. Draw a heavy line of oil pastel along the rough edge of the stencil. With one hand, hold the stencil firmly on a page of your sketchbook. With the other hand, use a piece of paper towel to pull the color from the stencil onto the paper. Experiment with different techniques until you feel comfortable. Try mixing colors. Compare your results with those of your classmates. Discuss the different effects you have created. For variety, try cutting the edge of your stencil with scissors.

Step 2 Based on your findings from the experiments, make some rough plans in your sketchbook for the final work. Choose your best idea. Now you are ready to create your landscape.

Step 3 Using newspaper or other scratch paper, tear or cut stencils for your finished work. Choose the colors you will use. In order to keep from smudging the pastel lines, work from the top of your page toward the bottom edge. Draw a very heavy line of oil pastel along the edge of your first stencil. Hold the stencil firmly in place and pull the oil pastel color from the stencil onto the large sheet of paper. Repeat this step until you have created the land masses you want.

Step 4 Give your work a title. Mount or mat your finished work for display.

EVALUATING YOUR WORK

▶ **DESCRIBE** Tell what kind of a landscape you have created.

▶ **ANALYZE** How did you create your stencils? What kinds of lines make up the edges of your land masses? How did the stencil technique you used to pull the color from the stencil to the paper affect the look of your work?

▶ **INTERPRET** Describe the mood of your imagination landscape. Did the stencil technique you used contribute to the mood?

▶ **JUDGE** Which aesthetic theory would be best to judge your work? Do you think this work is successful? Is there anything you would change to make it more successful?

▲ **FIGURE 4.26A** Student work.

STUDIO PROJECT *Imagination Landscape* **87**

ASSESS..........
Keeping a Portfolio
Remind students that the preliminary sketches and the final artwork for this Studio Project are likely candidates for their portfolios.

Self-Assessment
Have students apply the steps of art criticism to their own artwork using the "Evaluating Your Work" questions on this page.

Enrichment
Encourage students to create a second version of their imagination landscape, this time using a different medium than the first attempt. For example, they might try colored markers, crayons, or watercolors. When finished, ask them to write a brief evaluation of the media used for the two works. Ask them to consider which medium worked best mechanically for this project. Which was more aesthetically pleasing? What else might they change about the activity that would change the quality and appeal of the finished product?

CLOSE............
Ask each student to express what they learned about the stenciling technique while making this landscape.

MEETING INDIVIDUAL NEEDS

Learning Disabled Students with learning disabilities may have difficulty conceiving a landscape with the method prescribed in this Studio Project. The student may find more satisfaction in a less abstract subject for representation. Use the smear technique on a stencil of a simple or familiar object, such as an animal's outline shape. For even more clarity of conception (a worthwhile goal for students with learning disabilities who are in an early stage of representation), few media surpass painting with a half-inch brush and poster paint on a large sheet of paper.

Studio Project

Drawing Expressing Movement

(National Standards: 1a, 1b, 2b, 2c)

FOCUS............

Objectives

After completing this lesson, students will be able to:

■ Create a drawing that expresses linear movement of people involved in energetic action.

■ Create contrast between active figures and the background.

Supplies

■ Sketchbook, pencil, and eraser

■ Large sheet of white paper

■ Colored pencils or crayons

■ Watercolor paints

■ Variety of watercolor brushes

TEACH..........

Motivator

Have students listen to a variety of fast-paced music while making gesture poses. Suggestions might be popular, rap, rock, or country music. Classical pieces such as *Flight of the Bumblebee* or jazz pieces might also motivate some students. Costumes will release tension and add enthusiasm and fun to the activity. You may want to divide the class into small groups with each student taking a turn posing.

Studio Skills

As an alternative medium, have students use watercolor markers rather than watercolor paints, which give a nice wash when brushed with clear water.

Drawing Expressing Movement

▲ **FIGURE 4.27**

William H. Johnson. *Jitterbugs IV*. c. 1941. Tempera and ink with pencil on paper. 32.7 × 27.3 cm (12⅞ × 10¾"). National Museum of American Art, Smithsonian Institution, Washington, D.C.

SUPPLIES

■ **Sketchbook, pencil, and eraser**

■ **Large sheet of white paper**

■ **Colored pencils or crayons**

■ **Watercolor paints**

■ **Variety of watercolor brushes**

In *Jitterbugs IV* **(Figure 4.27)**, William H. Johnson used diagonal lines to provide energetic movement. Although his dancers are abstract, simple figures, they move. For contrast he used vertical and horizontal lines to show stable, unmoving objects.

Johnson is considered a major African-American artist. He integrated the customs and cultures of New York, Europe, and North Africa into his African-American heritage, finally settling on the abstract forms and limited color palette you see here. In *Jitterbugs IV* Johnson used line and simple shapes to show the expressive movements of the jitterbug dance craze of the 1940s.

What You Will Learn

You will create a drawing that expresses the linear movement of people involved in energetic action. Emphasize the lines that express movement. Base the figures on gesture drawings you make while observing real people in action. If you wish, you may create contrast between the active figures and the background by using static lines for the background objects.

Curriculum Connection

Language Arts Inform students that in addition to the flowering of art during the Harlem Renaissance, significant contributions were made to American literature. Have them research the works of Jean Toomer, Countee Cullen, and Langston Hughes. Although these three writers were known for their poetry, they were truly Renaissance men. Toomer wrote essays on religion and philosophy; Cullen published books for children; and Langston Hughes wrote drama, fiction, popular songs, and movie screenplays.

Creating

Study the painting by William H. Johnson. Notice how he has represented two dancing people with a few geometric shapes and many diagonal lines. Can you find the floor, the drum, and the drumsticks? Observe how the lines of the floor under the dancers are diagonal, while the rest of the floor remains vertical and static.

Step 1 Choose an energetic activity that you could represent using active lines. Ask a classmate to act out the movement of the activity so that you can make several gesture drawings in your sketchbook.

Step 2 Study your sketches. Decide which line directions will best express the movement of the activity. Will you use zigzag, or curved lines? Simplify the figures in your gesture drawings using the lines you have chosen.

Step 3 Decide which objects you will use for the background. Remember that you may use static lines for these objects. Sketch your finished plan on white paper.

Step 4 Go over the lines of your composition with colored pencils or crayons. Press hard to make the colors bright. Vary the lines. Emphasize the action lines by drawing them wide and using bold colors. Make the other lines thinner with softer colors.

Step 5 Color the shapes between the lines and the spaces around the figures with watercolor paints (see Technique Tip 12 on page 433 in the Handbook). Mount or mat the finished work for display.

EVALUATING YOUR WORK

▶ **DESCRIBE** Which energetic action did you choose as the subject of your drawing? Did you make gesture drawings of a real person acting out that movement? How many gesture drawings did you make? How many figures did you put in your finished work? Did you use any objects for the background?

▶ **ANALYZE** Which line directions did you choose to express the action? Which line directions did you choose for the background objects? Which lines did you emphasize and how did you emphasize them?

▶ **INTERPRET** Does your work express the action you were trying to capture? Give your work an expressive title. Do not use the name of the action your figures are doing.

▶ **JUDGE** Have you created a drawing that expresses the movement of people involved in energetic action? Is there anything you would change to make the work more successful? Which aesthetic theory would be best to judge this work?

▲ **FIGURE 4.26A** Student work.

Studio Skills

Have students who are less confident with their creative abilities draw with three or more pencils taped together. This method will create a multiple-line drawing which should automatically loosen the students' fears and apprehensions about drawing.

Art History

Students may want to research the Harlem Renaissance of the 1920s and its influences upon African-American artists, writers, and scholars of the twentieth century. Ask students to research African-American contemporaries of William H. Johnson. Remind students that Romare Bearden (pages 13 and 166–167) and Jacob Lawrence (page 80) were a part of the Harlem Renaissance.

ASSESS..........
Keeping a Portfolio

Remind students that the preliminary sketches and the final artwork for this Studio Project are likely candidates for their portfolios.

Self-Assessment

Have students apply the steps of art criticism to their own artwork using the "Evaluating Your Work" questions on this page.

Enrichment

Have students make life-sized or larger gesture drawings on butcher paper. Suggest that they use colored chalk on dark paper as it creates a nice effect.

CLOSE............

Have students write a paragraph in their sketchbooks explaining what they learned about themselves or the element of line while completing this activity.

MEETING INDIVIDUAL NEEDS

Learning Disabled If the class is drawing for a posed student model, easily discouraged students with behavioral disorders may be inclined to yell out, "Hold still" and "He ruined mine when he moved." Tell this student that it is just the gesture, the essence, the feeling, that is to be captured. Help the student who says, "I messed up," by assisting the student in diagnosing one particular area that is wrong and in coming up with a way to try to fix it. To foster integration, include students with disabilities as models; figures in wheelchairs are particularly good to challenge drawing skills.

Expressive Line Design
(National Standards: 1a, 1b, 2b, 2c)

FOCUS............
Objectives

After completing this lesson, students will be able to:

- Create an expressive contour line design based on the style of Keith Haring.
- Identify computer drawing tools and menu choices that make different kinds of line.
- Apply the steps of art criticism to their expressive line designs.

Supplies

- Sketchbook
- Computer with Paint/Draw application
- Printer

TEACH.........
Motivator

Have students examine Figure 4.28 and discuss how Keith Haring uses expressive lines to depict simplified human and animal shapes. Ask students to observe other ways Haring uses lines. Direct their attention to the patterns and symbols in the painting. Brainstorm and list common symbols made from the simple lines. Tell students that Haring's symbols relate to his personal ideas and responses to the spaces within the drawing. Patterns or rhythms are also created in the painting through the repetition of lines. Ask students to consider other types of lines that can be repeated to create rhythm or visual movement.

Expressive Line Design

▲ **FIGURE 4.28**

Keith Haring. *Untitled.* 1983. Vinyl ink on vinyl tarp. 213.3 × 213.3 cm (84 × 84"). Tony Shafrazi Gallery, New York, New York. From the collection of Mrs. Rita Cecchi Gorl.

SUPPLIES

- **Sketchbook**
- **Computer**
- **Paint or Draw application**
- **Printer**

Keith Haring was born in 1958 and raised in Kutztown, Pennsylvania. Even as a high school student, his work exhibited a distinctive and original way of representing people and objects using line. Haring was also fascinated with symbols and signs. This is not surprising because Kutztown, which hosts an art college, is located in a rural area where Amish farmers decorate their barns with hex signs and symbols to bring them good luck, crops, and love.

Look at Haring's *Untitled* **(Figure 4.28)**. Lines are everywhere. It is hard to distinguish shapes among the lively lines and bright hues that fill all the spaces. Repeated short, black lines cause your eye to move quickly around the page and eventually focus on a single round shape. You discover a human form with a long neck. Haring was influenced by the break dancers he saw in 1983, when this work was created. He watched dancers contort their bodies by bending and stretching backward to touch the floor with their hands, while other dancers went underneath them in moves called the bridge and the spider. The rhythmic, repetitive lines relate to the rap music Haring heard at the time.

What You Will Learn

You will create an expressive line design in the style of Keith Haring's work. Begin by drawing the shape of a person, animal, or object that fills a page, using a continuous contour line. Add more shapes to fill the page. Emphasize one or more shapes by using thicker lines or increasing their size. Fill the space within and around the shapes with different line types and line variations. Add color, but limit yourself to three colors.

MORE ABOUT... Keith Haring

After moving to New York City, Haring was attracted to the graffiti art popular in the streets during the 1970s and 1980s. Drawing with spray paints and chalks, he worked quickly and confidently. Unlike other graffiti artists at the time, who draw on walls and subway cars, Haring chose the black paper that covered empty advertising space. His subjects included crawling babies, the "radiant" child, dancing figures, barking dogs, space saucers and animated appliances. Public acceptance of his playful graffiti paintings energized Haring. He continued to work until his early death at the age of 32.

Creating

Explore the tools on your computer application that make different kinds of lines such as Brush, Pencil, and Line. Experiment with them by selecting menus and options that allow you to change line thickness, shape, direction, and texture.

Step 1 Begin by working only in black and white. Select a small Brush or the Pencil tool. Draw a large person, animal, or object that touches three edges of the screen. Draw the contour of the shape using a continuous contour line that has smooth curves, sharp corners, and flat edges. Add more shapes to fill any empty spaces. The shapes may be nonobjective or realistic. Emphasize the large shape by thickening its outline. Save this design with your name and the project title. As you continue to work, use the Save As command and modify the title by adding a number behind the original title to indicate the second, third, or fourth save.

Step 2 Create variety by filling the shapes and the spaces around them with different patterns of line types and line variations. Make perfectly straight vertical, horizontal, or diagonal lines without jagged edges.

Step 3 Unify the design by selecting a limited color scheme of three colors. Use the Bucket tool to add color to enclosed spaces. When your composition looks complete, select the Save As command to retitle your work. Print and display your work. Compare it with the works of your classmates.

EVALUATING YOUR WORK

▶ **DESCRIBE** What shape did you use to start your design? Did you make it touch three edges of your page? Did you use a continuous contour line that had smooth curves, sharp corners, and flat edges? Did you use realistic or nonobjective shapes to fill the rest of the design?

▶ **ANALYZE** Did you emphasize your large shape by using a thick line? What line types and line variations did you use to create patterns to fill the shapes and spaces? What colors did you use?

▶ **INTERPRET** What idea, feeling, or mood does your work convey to the viewer? How did the addition of patterns of lines affect the look of your work? Create a title that expresses the way you feel about your work.

▶ **JUDGE** Did you use a variety of tools to produce shapes and fill all the spaces with many kinds of lines? Would you change anything to make your work more successful? Which aesthetic theory would you use to judge this work?

▲ **FIGURE 4.28A**   Student work.

TECHNOLOGY STUDIO PROJECT   *Expressive Line Design*   **91**

Critiquing the Work

▶ Describe
What do you see?

- Natural pigments on bark means that pigments made from natural sources such as earth clay, minerals, and plants were painted on a piece of bark that was peeled from the surface of a tree.

- The river is the thin, vertical dark shape in the center of the painting. The river divides the painting into six shapes. In the upper left shape we find five fish and a crab. The lower left shape holds a large conch shell. The lower right corner holds three recognizable fish. There is one fish shape and four tree shapes in the area above that. There are four more tree shapes in the area across the river. Above the trees on the right are some oval shapes and a snake.

▶ Analyze
How is the work organized?

- He has used line to outline every shape. Most of the outlines are white, some are yellow ochre, and a few are a warm brown ochre. Some shapes have triple outlines: white, brown in the center, and white again.

- Implied lines are used within many shapes. He uses them as decorative patterns. They make the colors shimmer. He has painted white dotted lines over warm brown or yellow ochre wide lines. Only the catfish shapes have dark brown dots along with the other earth colors.

92

ART CRITICISM IN ACTION

▶ **FIGURE 4.29**

David Malangi. *Abstract (River Mouth Map)*. 1983. Ochres on stringy bark. 135 × 78 cm (51⅛ × 30¾"). The Art Gallery of New South Wales, Sydney, Australia.

MORE ABOUT... Malangi

Read the following quotation and have students write their interpretation of its meaning:

In his own words Malangi says: "This is no ordinary place. This is my country . . . This is our traditional area and that is why we don't want any mining or balada (European settlers) there . . . The river is where our dreamings are. We have grown up with our culture and have kept it; our sacred sites, our ceremonies, and secret dreamings. My people and ancestors have lived here for a long time . . ." David Malangi, Australian Perspecta 1983, The Art Gallery of New South Wales, p.67.

1 ▶ DESCRIBE What do you see?

- How many dimensions does this work have? List them.
- What media have been used to create this work?
- You know from the title that this is an abstract map of a river mouth. Can you find the river? Try to find the objects in this design that relate to the river. How many familiar objects can you find?

2 ▶ ANALYZE How is this work organized?

- Can you find where Malangi has used line to outline objects? Are all the outlines the same color?
- Can you find implied lines in this work? Where are they? What is unusual in Malangi's use of implied lines?
- Identify all the different kinds of lines (vertical, horizontal, diagonal, curved, and zigzag) in this work. List at least one location for each line type you identify.
- Do you see any line variations such as length, width, and texture in this work? List at least one location for each variation you identify.

3 ▶ INTERPRET What is the artist trying to communicate?
Use the clues you discovered during your analysis to find the secret message the artist is trying to convey to you through this work.

- What does this work say to you?
- Imagine you are the artist. Write a letter to a viewer who may see this artwork. Explain one of your reasons for painting it.

4 ▶ JUDGE What do you think of the work?

- What is your reaction to this work?
- Did it make you think?
- Do you think it is successful? Use one or more of the aesthetic theories of art explained in Chapter 2 to defend your judgment of this work.

MEET THE ARTIST

DAVID MALANGI

Australian, 1934–

David Malangi is an Aboriginal artist in Australia. He was born in Mulanga, near the mouth of the Glyde River, Central Arnheim Land. He is a senior ritual leader and custodian of three tracts of land on either side of the Glyde River.

Malangi has been painting on bark commercially for over 30 years. His works are always created on bark with natural pigments even though other contemporary Aboriginal artists have switched to using acrylics on canvas. The warm brown ochre that he uses is rarely used by other artists in his region. Malangi continues to paint both commercial and ceremonial works.

- Vertical: in the upper right corner. Horizontal: in the upper right corner. Diagonal: the decorative implied lines within the many shapes. Curved: the outline of the conch shell and the outlines of the fish. Zig-zag: The branches of the trees. The longest and widest line is the river. We see short lines on the raga nuts, and across the pointed shapes above them. The thin lines are the outlines. The implied lines create the look of rough texture.

▶ Interpret
What is the artist trying to communicate?

- Answers will vary. Some may say it is rich with life. Some may say the unknown symbols make it mysterious.
- Answers will vary. Some may say he knows his land very well. Some may say this land is very important to him and his people.

▶ Judge
What do you think of the work?

- Answers will vary. Accept positive and negative reactions equally.
- Answers will vary. Accept positive and negative reactions equally.
- Answers will vary. Most will use the theory of formalism to defend a positive response to the work.

Extension Activity

Ask the students to imagine that they are the artist. Have them write a poem to express his feelings about this area of land or write a letter to a viewer explaining the importance of this river and the land that surrounds it to the people who live here.

MORE ABOUT... Aboriginal Art

There are many different layers of meaning to Malangi's work. First, there is the public, aesthetic design. Then there is the political, land deed value of the work. There is also a layer that refers to the cultural heritage of the symbols. Finally, there is a secret, sacred meaning that is known to only a few initiated ones.

Land rights have affected all Aboriginal people and art has been used as a way of making political statements. In the 1960s while the United States was going through its Civil Rights crisis, Australia was having one of its own. The Aboriginal peoples went to court to defend their land rights, and they bought their art as proof of ownership as someone else might bring a deed.

The History of Ink

(National Standards: 6a, 6b)

Objectives

After completing this lesson, students will be able to:

■ Explain the history of ink

■ Describe different types of ink and ink effects

Teaching the Connection

1. Have students read the feature on this page.
2. Ask students to describe different types of inks and pens. If possible, show students different examples of art using ink as the primary medium. Ask students to describe different techniques, and encourage them to imagine how the artists achieved their effects.
3. Tell students that ink is also used in calligraphy, the art of beautiful handwriting. Eastern artists often used calligraphic techniques with brushes to portray spiritual interpretations of nature. Western artists such as Rembrandt, Goya, Manet, Braque, and Picasso have also used ink in their works. Today, artists may even use felt-tip and ball-point pens for drawing.

The History of Ink

◀ FIGURE 4.30

Charles White. *Preacher.* 1952. Ink on cardboard. 54 × 75 cm (21⅛ × 29⅛″). Collection of Whitney Museum of American Art, New York, New York.

Long ago, people made ink from plant dyes and sepia, which is the inky secretion from the cuttlefish, octopus, and squid. The earliest inks were brown in color. By 2500 B.C., the Egyptians and the Chinese were making ink out of carbon or soot suspended in water with a binding ingredient such as gum or mineral oil. Sometimes called india ink, this carbon-based substance is black and permanent. Consequently, many ancient writings and drawings created with india ink are still legible today.

Since the 1940s, inks have evolved rapidly. With the invention of the ball-point pen and the felt-tip marker, new inks were also created. Permanent inks of today usually contain iron sulfate and gallic and tannic acids, which combine to resist both light and water.

Charles White has used the simple technique of ink-drawn lines to create the detailed and vividly expressive drawing in **Figure 4.30.**

Notice how he has built up the dark areas by applying layers of lines that cross each other in different directions. The lines in the gray shadows are clearly visible, while some areas appear totally black. White's use of ink and line adds an interesting sense of texture and consistency to the drawing.

Making the Connection

1. Describe the elements of line and value in Figure 4.30.
2. How do these elements contribute to the meaning of the drawing?
3. Experiment with different inks, pens, and/or brushes. Create as many different effects as you can. How does ink differ as a medium from charcoal, pastel, or paint when it comes to creating shadow and texture?

CHAPTER 4 Line

Answers to Making the Connection

1. White uses intricately layered lines and cross-hatching to create texture, shape, and shadow. The drawing appears strikingly three-dimensional as a result of its values.
2. Answers about the painting's meaning will vary, but students should notice the preacher's concerned demeanor. The position of the man's arms, combined with his facial expression (in the midst of elocution) suggests urgency. The contrasted values heighten this effect.
3. Responses will vary. Ink is usually impossible to blend or alter once it touches paper, so the effects of texture and shadow must usually be achieved through lines or brushstrokes.

Building Vocabulary

On a separate sheet of paper, write the term that best matches each definition given below.

1. An element of art that is the path of a moving point through space.
2. The amount of space an object takes up in one direction.
3. A line that shows or creates the outer edges of a shape.
4. A series of points that the viewer's eyes automatically connect.
5. The element of art that describes the darkness or lightness of an object.
6. The technique of using crossed lines for shading.
7. A line that defines the edges and surface ridges of an object.
8. An expressive movement.
9. A term meaning beautiful handwriting.

Reviewing Art Facts

Answer the following questions using complete sentences.

1. Give an example of an implied line.
2. How does a two-dimensional object differ from a three-dimensional object?
3. Name and describe the five basic kinds of lines.
4. Name five major ways in which lines can vary.
5. What are the four factors that affect the value of a group of lines?
6. Name the kind of line that conveys instability, tension, and action.
7. Tell which kind of line you would use to represent the surface of ridges in an object.

Thinking Critically About Art

1. **Analyze.** Study Figure 4.1 (page 68) Figure 4.14 (page 75), and Figure 4.19 (page 80). What is the common thread that links the three works?
2. **Synthesize.** Explain why the three related works, Figures 4.1, 4.14, and 4.19, belong in a chapter devoted to the concept of line.
3. **Compare and contrast.** In what ways are Figure 4.20 (page 81) and Figure 4.22 (page 82) similar? In what ways are they different? Consider the element of line and the subject matter in your comparison.

Explore the use of line in dance as shown in the performance of "Danza de la Reata" by Ballet Folklorico de Mexico in the Performing Arts Handbook on page 416. One example of the element of line is the use of the lariat, or lasso, during the performance. Identify other examples.

Explore World Wide Web links related to the contents of each chapter of this book. These preselected links can be found under Hot Links at the Glencoe Fine Arts Site (**www.glencoe.com/sec/art**). Find the chapter you are studying in the Table of Contents and click on one of the "hot links."

Chapter 4 Review | **95**

Answers to Building Vocabulary

1. line
2. dimension
3. outline
4. implied lines
5. value
6. crosshatching
7. contour line
8. gesture
9. calligraphy

Answers to Reviewing Art Facts

1. Answers will vary but can include such examples as a trail of wet footprints or any other series of points that a viewer's eyes would automatically connect.
2. Two-dimensional objects have width as well as length. Three-dimensional objects have width, length, and depth.
3. Vertical, horizontal, diagonal, curved, zigzag. Vertical, horizontal, and diagonal lines do not change direction. A curved line changes direction gradually. A zigzag line changes direction suddenly.
4. Length, width, texture, direction, and degree of curve.
5. Number of lines; size of the spaces between the lines; media; and tools.
6. Diagonal lines.

Enrichment

Have students find a book on Oriental brush painting. After they have learned to make some of the brushstrokes, have them demonstrate the technique to the class.

CLOSE............

Have students choose two illustrations from this chapter and compare how the artists use the element of line.

ASSESSMENT ✓

Evaluate

- Distribute *Chapter 4 Study Guide* and have students review the chapter. 📁
- Have students complete the *Chapter 4 Test* in the TCR. 📁

Extension

Ask each student to select one artwork from this book and write a three-paragraph evaluation of the artist's use of line. Their reports should focus on the kinds of line used, the feelings or ideas expressed by the lines, the value of the various lines, and the methods used to create dark and light values in the work.

Shape, Form, and Space

(pages 96–133)

Resources

📁 Chapter 5 Study Guide

📁 Chapter 5 Test

📁 Computers in the Art Classroom

📁 Cultural Diversity in Art

📁 Portfolio and Assessment Techniques

📁 Reproducible Lesson Plan 5

🕹 Transparency CC-5, M.C. Escher. *Other World*

🕹 Transparency 5, Winslow Homer. *A Good Pool, Saguenay River*

📖 Fine Art Print 11, Allan Houser. *Prayer Song*

📖 Fine Art Print 12, Alice Neel. *Mother and Child*

96

▲ **FIGURE 5.1** Tooker's paintings protest the problems of modern technology. He transforms familiar places such as subways, streets, parks, and offices into menacing and alien worlds. The ordinary people in his paintings passively accept his weird world. His works express the powerlessness of people against the bureaucracy of the modern world.

George Tooker. *Highway.* 1953. Tempera on panel. 58 × 45.4 cm (22⅞ × 17⅞″). Courtesy of Terra Museum of American Art, Chicago, Illinois. Terra Foundation for the Arts, Daniel J. Terra Collection.

FEATURED ARTISTS

Marie Apel
John Thomas Biggers
Sandro Botticelli
Constantin Brancusi
Paul Cézanne
Christo and Jeanne-Claude

M.C. Escher
Helen Frankenthaler
Artemisia Gentileschi
Ralph Goings
Barbara Hepworth
Anna Hyatt Huntington
Jasper Johns
William Kurelek
Doris Lee

René Magritte
Michael Naranjo
Ben Shahn
David Smith
Larry Smith
George Tooker
Jan Vermeer
Jane Wilson
Frank Lloyd Wright

Shape, Form, and Space

Y ou live in space, in a world full of objects. Each object—whether it be a car, an apple, this book, or you—has a shape or form. Often it is by their shapes or forms that you recognize objects. You identify a stop sign in the distance by its shape long before you can read the word *stop* on it. You may identify a friend in the distance before seeing his or her face.

Shape, form, and space are all closely related to one another. They are elements of art, and artists use their knowledge of how these elements work together to create art. In this chapter you will learn how to "read" the meaning of these elements and how to use them to express your own ideas and feelings.

Notice how George Tooker has arranged very realistic shapes and forms in a natural, yet impossible space in his painting, *Highway* **(Figure 5.1)**. What shapes and forms has he used to create the feeling of claustrophobic space? Which forms indicate deep space? Where does he use shape to indicate anger? How? What do you think the white arrows indicate?

Developing Your
PORTFOLIO
Draw a series of geometric shapes, such as triangles, squares, and circles. Then, alter these shapes by drawing them at odd angles, stacking them on top of each other, or drawing designs inside of them. In your sketchbook, describe how altering the shapes changed their appearance. Next, list several adjectives that come to mind when you look at the first set of geometric shapes. Keep your answers in your portfolio along with the drawings of the shapes.

OBJECTIVES

After completing this chapter, you will be able to:

- Explain the difference between shapes and forms.
- Create two- and three-dimensional works of art.
- Observe more carefully the shapes and forms in the space around you.
- Use point of view and perspective to create artworks.
- Identify the expressive qualities of shapes, forms, and spaces in artworks.

WORDS TO LEARN

shape
geometric shapes
free-form shapes
forms
space
holograms
chiaroscuro
highlights
perspective

97

Chapter Overview

In Chapter 5 students will examine the relationship between the elements of shape, form, and space.

Examining the Artwork

As students examine Figure 5.1, point out that the objects representing three-dimensional forms use shading to create this illusion. Explain that the diagonally striped wall closes off the space behind the cars and prevents the cars from backing up. The cars cannot move forward because they are blocked by someone holding a stop sign.

Have students notice the shapes of the car grilles that look like angry, turned down mouths and the vertical boards of the grille that give the expressive quality of snarling teeth. Call attention to the chrome design above the grille that gives the car a human facial characteristic. Notice how the steering wheels cross the drivers' faces where their mouths should be. This hides the men's mouths, cutting off their power to speak.

 While studying this chapter, use Performing Arts Handbook page 417 to help students discover how shapes and forms are used in dance.

National Standards

This chapter addresses the following National Standards for the Visual Arts:
1. (a, b, c) 4. (b, c)
2. (a, b, c) 5. (a, c)
3. (a, b, c) 6. (a, b)

DEVELOPING A PORTFOLIO
Peer-Evaluation Peer review helps students establish priorities for revision of their work through feedback from other students. When expected to articulate responses to the work of others, basic concepts are reinforced, and a student learns to trust his or her artistic insights. Often a cooperative environment encourages a mutual exchange of ideas that help students progress at an accelerated rate. Peer review is also a source of ongoing reflection that refines judgment. Students often see the relationship between ideas and design in another's work more easily than in their own; likewise, suggestions from peers are sometimes less intimidating.

Shapes and Forms

(pages 98–102)
(National Standards: 2b, 3a)

FOCUS...........
Objectives

After completing this lesson, students will be able to:

■ Explain the difference between shape and form.

■ Create two- and three-dimensional works of art.

Supplies

■ Small common objects, such as keys, leaves, paper cups, buttons, construction paper, tempera paint in shallow dishes

■ Overhead or slide projector

■ Newspaper, scissors, rulers, glue, black construction paper

Resources

📁 Application Activity 9, *Shape Up with Imagination*

📁 Concept Map 5, *Shapes and Forms*

📁 Cooperative Learning Activity 9, *Practicing Creative Thinking*

📁 Bar Code Guide to the National Gallery of Art

TEACH..........
Motivator

Give small groups of students several small common objects, one sheet of paper, and tempera paint in shallow dishes. Ask group members to dip the objects into the paint and then press the objects onto the paper, making prints. Help students compare the two-dimensional shapes with the three-dimensional forms used to make them.

Shapes and Forms

All objects are either shapes or forms. Rocks, puddles, flowers, shirts, houses, chairs, and paintings are all shapes and forms. The words "shape" and "form" are often used interchangeably in everyday language but, in the language of art, they have very different meanings.

Shape

A **shape** is *a two-dimensional area that is defined in some way.* A shape may have an outline or a boundary around it, or you may recognize it by its area. For instance, if you draw the outline of a square on a sheet of paper, you have created a shape. You could also create the same shape without an outline by painting the area of the square red.

You see many two-dimensional shapes every day. They are found in most designs, which in turn can be seen on many flat surfaces. Look for shapes on such things as floor coverings, fabrics, and wallpapers. Floors and walls are two-dimensional shapes; so are tabletops, book pages, posters, and billboards. The images you create with your computer and the images in the handheld and computer games you play may have the illusion of depth, but they are also two-dimensional shapes.

Geometric Shapes

All shapes can be classified as either *geometric* or *free-form*. **Geometric shapes** are *precise shapes that can be described using mathematical formulas* **(Figure 5.2)**. The basic geometric shapes are the circle, the square, and the triangle. All other geometric shapes are either variations or combinations of these basic shapes. Some of the variations include the oval, rectangle, parallelogram, trapezoid, pentagon, pentagram, hexagon, and octagon.

Geometric shapes are used for decoration, uniformity, and organization. Notice the decorative quality of the geometric shapes in the artwork shown in **Figure 5.3.** How many different simple and complex geometric shapes can you find in Biggers' painting?

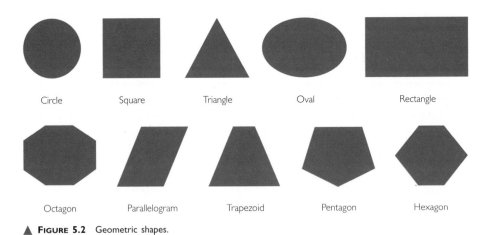

Circle   Square   Triangle   Oval   Rectangle

Octagon   Parallelogram   Trapezoid   Pentagon   Hexagon

▲ **FIGURE 5.2**   Geometric shapes.

98   **CHAPTER 5**   Shape, Form, and Space

TECHNOLOGY OPTIONS

National Gallery of Art Videodisc Use the following to show examples of how artists use shape, form, and space.

Henri Matisse
Beasts of the Sea

Search Frame 2203

Constantin Brancusi
Maiastra
Search Frame 2561

Georges Braque
Leaves, Color, Light

Search Frame 3249

Use Glencoe's *Correlation Bar Code Guide to the National Gallery of Art* to locate more artworks.

Road signs are examples of uniformity. The same kind of sign must always have the same shape. Do you know the shape of a stop sign? Which shape is used for "Yield"? Which shape is used for TV screens? Why do you think ceiling tiles and window panes have geometric shapes?

Free-Form Shapes

Free-form shapes are *irregular and uneven shapes.* Their outlines may be curved, angular, or a combination of both. They often occur in nature. Another word that may be used to describe free-form shapes is "organic." Organic is used when we talk about the shapes that are silhouettes of living things such as animals, people, or trees. Look at the difference between the decorative patterns of geometric shapes in Figure 5.3 and the free-form, organic shapes painted on the vases in **Figure 5.4.** Which looks more organized?

▲ **FIGURE 5.3** Biggers uses the women in this work to represent the African civilizations of Egypt, Benin, and Dogon. The crowns are symbols of these civilizations. The cloth on their laps represents the geometry that has brought order to each culture.

John Thomas Biggers. *Starry Crown.* 1987. Acrylic, mixed media on canvas. 155 × 124.5 cm (61 × 49"). Dallas Museum of Art, Dallas, Texas. Texas Art Fund.

◀ **FIGURE 5.4** Notice the free-form, organic qualities of the dragons and clouds that were painted on this matching pair of vases. Although the forms of the vases are perfectly matched, the paintings are not exactly alike. Look closely to find the differences between the two dragons.

Chinese, *Pair of Vases.* 1426–1435. Ming Dynasty (1368–1644). Porcelain with underglaze blue decoration. 55.2 × 29.2 cm (21¾ × 11½"). The Nelson-Atkins Museum of Art, Kansas City, Missouri. Purchase: Nelson Trust.

Developing Perceptual Skills

One type of shape is the silhouette, which originally meant a profile portrait that looked like a solid shadow. Now it is used to describe any two-dimensional, shadowlike shape. Using a slide or overhead projector, have students make hand shadows. Project the light onto a large piece of white paper. Have one student trace the silhouette on the paper while another "poses" the hand. To take this to the next step, use a slide projector and trace the silhouettes of full-length figures. Remind students that although they are using outlines, they are concerned with the concept that one object can have many different silhouettes.

Cross-Curriculum: Science

Direct students to look at a drop of water through a microscope and sketch the free-form shapes they see. Encourage them to discuss the activity with their science teachers, who may make other suggestions for sources of free-form shapes from the scientific point of view.

Studio Skills

On a sheet of white paper, instruct students to draw a light pencil line from the upper right corner to the lower left corner. Then have them cut out a variety of large and small geometric shapes from colored magazine illustrations. Arrange these shapes along the diagonal line by placing the smaller, more intensely colored ones nearest the line. The remaining shapes should become gradually larger and duller as they are placed farther and farther away from the line. Study the finished composition and add as many new shapes as necessary to make it more unified and visually appealing. Overlap shapes so that no white paper shows.

MEETING INDIVIDUAL NEEDS

Visually Impaired For students who are blind, cut shapes from a stiff paper such as oak tag. Keep the outline simple. Students will then be able to feel the outline and form a mental image of the shape. The student can sort the different shapes into categories and then trace around them onto a foam meat tray which will leave an indented line. This tracing could then be printed to make greeting cards or note cards.

Activity

Geometric and Free-Form Shapes

Applying Your Skills. Have students share and compare their cut-paper designs.

💻 **Computer Option.** Students might vary this exercise by flipping, inverting, rotating, or nudging as they fill the page. Sometimes, an arrangement may create a new shape. This shape or unit may be copied and pasted to form larger units. Suggest that students try varying solid colors, patterns, and gradients. Do not overlap. See *Computers in the Art Classroom* for additional ideas. 🗀

Application

Distribute Application Activity 9, *Shape Up with Imagination,* and have students use their imaginations to create figures based on the geometric shapes provided. 🗀

Sparking CREATIVITY

Want students to think creatively about shapes? Suggest this: Put a spoonful of cooking oil and a few drops of food coloring in a shallow dish of water. Use a stick to move the oil and watch the shapes it takes. Try putting small quantities of oil, water, and color in a sealed plastic bag and place it on an overhead projector. Gently move the bag and watch the projected shapes change.

Activity

Geometric and Free-Form Shapes

Applying Your Skills. Using the printed areas of a newspaper, make two cut-paper designs. Make one design by measuring and cutting precise geometric shapes. Make the second design by tearing free-form shapes. Arrange the shapes and glue them on a sheet of black construction paper. Use a white crayon to print the words *free-form* and *geometric* on the appropriate design. Try to make the letters for *geometric* look geometric, and the letters for *free-form* look free-form.

Computer Option. Use the Shape or Straight Line tools to draw four different geometric shapes. Do not overlap the shapes and space them apart so they can easily be selected and arranged later. Choose a color scheme and make each shape a solid color. Pick the Selection tool and then the Copy and Paste menu to repeat each of the shapes several times on the page. When the page is nearly full, choose a Brush or Pencil tool to draw free-form shapes in between the geometric shapes. Select the Bucket tool to fill these shapes with pattern.

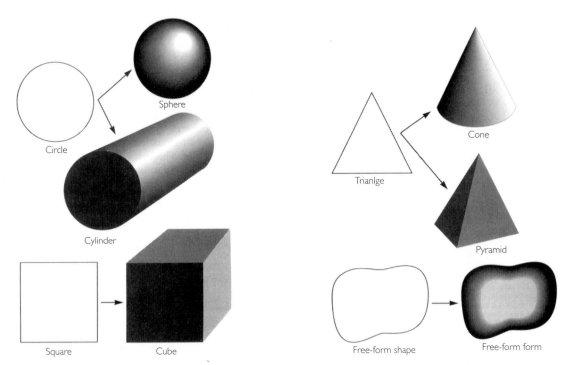

▲ **FIGURE 5.5** What kind of relationship do you see between the two-dimensional shapes and three-dimensional forms?

Curriculum Connection

Language Arts Just as the visual arts are concerned with shape and form, certain language arts are based on specific forms as well. For example, poetry has a long tradition of precision in its composition. The sonnet is always fourteen lines of iambic pentameter; the ballad is four lines of iambic verse alternating tetrameter and trimeter; the Spenserian stanza is eight lines of iambic pentameter followed by one of iambic hexameter. Free verse is unrhymed iambic pentameter; the haiku is based on exact syllable count. Often, students of literature are so familiar with poetic forms that they can identify the type of poem by looking at its shape on the printed page!

◀ **Figure 5.6** This is one of Smith's earliest stainless steel geometric sculptures. It is made of steel plates joined to form rectangular solids. Smith insisted that his monumental sculptures were made to sit in nature, not in buildings. Because the smooth steel reflected light like chrome on a car, he burnished the surface to diffuse the light so the surface would take on the colors of the natural environment.

David Smith. *Cubi IX.* 1961. Stainless steel. 268 × 149 × 111.4 cm (105¾ × 58⅝ × 43⅞″). Collection, Walker Art Center, Minneapolis, Minnesota. Gift of the T. B. Walker Foundation, 1966. © Estate of David Smith/Licensed by VAGA, New York.

Sparking ▲▼
CREATIVITY

Want students to think creatively about our perception of shapes and forms? Suggest this: Look at the shapes in a mountainous landscape. Mountains are not triangles. They flow in a range of shapes. The science of topography shows that land contours were formed as the earth buckled, folded, and eroded. Arrange a sweater or a large piece of cloth on a table in a heap. Direct students to draw the shapes they see. Then have students turn their drawing into a landscape, using their imagination to add roads, lakes, and tree clusters.

ASSESS..........
Self-Assessment

Have students complete the review questions on page 102. Answers are provided at the bottom of page 102.

Reteaching

■ Have each student work with a partner to make a simple four-column chart with these headings: *Geometric Shapes, Free-form Shapes, Geometric Forms,* and *Organic Forms.* Then name various items and have students, working with their partners, record the items in the correct columns. Examples of items to name: cloud, ice-cream cone, stop sign, softball, leaf, mountain, key. Finally, encourage students to compare and discuss their charts.

■ Distribute Concept Map 5, *Shapes and Forms* to help students understand the vocabulary used in this lesson. 🗁

Forms

Although the words *shape* and *form* are often used interchangeably in everyday language, they have different meanings in the language of art. **Forms** are *objects having three dimensions.* Like shapes, they have both length and width, but forms also have depth. *You are a three-dimensional form; so is a tree or a table.*

Two-dimensional shapes and three-dimensional forms are related **(Figure 5.5)**. The end of a cylinder is a circle.

One side of a cube is a square. A triangle can "grow" into a cone or a pyramid.

Like shapes, forms may be either geometric **(Figure 5.6)** or free-form **(Figure 5.7 on page 102)**. Geometric forms are used in construction, for organization, and as parts in machines. Look around you. What forms were used to build your school, your church, your home? Look under the hood of a car. What forms were used to build the motor? Did you know that common table

⚠ SAFETY NOTE

Knives and Sharp Blades Be sure to emphasize safety if you let students use sharp blades to score paper. (See Activity: Creating Forms, page 102.) If you use construction paper, the scoring can be done easily with the point of a pair of scissors. The purpose of scoring is to weaken the paper along one line and make it thinner so it will give when bent.

If you have never tried scoring before, do so before you work with the class. You need to discover how much of a curve you can score before it gets too tight to bend without wrinkling the rest of the paper. If you wish to make a semicircular curve, you will have to make a cut from the open side of the curve to that edge of the paper.

Enrichment

- Have students find a geometric object that is three dimensional. Have them draw its contours using a pencil and ruler. Next, have them find a three-dimensional free-form object. Then, have them draw it with flowing calligraphic contour lines using brush and ink. Have them share their final products with the class.

- Distribute Cooperative Learning 9, *Practicing Creative Thinking*. 📁

CLOSE............

Have each student select one artwork in this textbook and briefly describe the use of shape or form in the work.

Activity

Creating Forms

Applying Your Skills. Students are always surprised when they realize they can make curved forms from flat paper. Have them experiment with scratch paper before making their final paper sculpture.

💻 **Computer Option.** Students who wish to draw a cylinder might try this: Draw an oval high on the screen. Select it, then Copy and Paste another oval, placing the second one directly below the original but some distance apart. Connect the two ovals using two straight lines. Erase the top half of the lower oval to make a solid-looking cylinder. Use the Airbrush or Gradient Fill and a consistent light source to add shading to the shapes to create a form.

For additional ideas see *Computers in the Art Classroom.* 📁

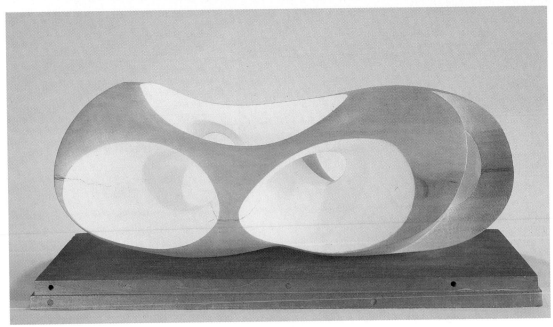

▲ **FIGURE 5.7** An example of free-form sculpture.

Barbara Hepworth. *Pendour*. 1947–48. Painted plane wood. 30.8 × 74.6 × 23.8 cm (12⅛ × 29⅜ × 9⅜"). Hirshhorn Museum and Sculpture Garden, Smithsonian Institution, Washington, D.C. Gift of Joseph H. Hirshhorn, 1966.

salt is made of a series of interlocking cubes? You can see these cubes when you look at salt through a microscope.

Free-form forms are irregular and uneven three-dimensional objects such as stones, puddles, and clouds. Your own body and the bodies of animals and plants are free-form forms.

Activity

Creating Forms

Applying Your Skills. Make a flat sheet of construction paper into a three-dimensional paper sculpture by using cutting and scoring techniques. (See Technique Tip on page 436 in the Handbook.) Give your sculpture a minimum of five different surfaces. Do not cut the paper into separate pieces. Use only slots and tabs if you wish to join any parts. Experiment with scratch paper before you make your final paper sculpture.

☑ *Check Your Understanding*

1. List three geometric shapes.
2. What is another word for free-form shapes?
3. Is a house a shape or a form? Explain your answer.

Computer Option. Use the Round Shape tool to draw a circle or oval on the screen. Choose the Airbrush to gently add shading around the edges to make the shape appear as a solid form. Draw a free-form shape. Apply shading with the airbrush to represent a form. Consider adding a surface for the three-dimensional forms to sit on and then apply shadows.

☑ **Answers to Check Your Understanding**

1. Geometric shapes are the circle, square, triangle, oval, rectangle, parallelogram, trapezoid, pentagon, hexagon, or octagon.
2. Another word for free-form shapes is *organic.*
3. A house is a form because it is an object having three dimensions—height, width, and depth.

Space

Space refers to both outer space and inner space. Rockets move through outer space to explore other planets. People move through the inner space of rooms and buildings. Space can be flat and two-dimensional, such as the space of a window. Space can also be three-dimensional, such as the space filled with water in a swimming pool.

Space and Its Relationship to Shape and Form

Shapes and forms exist in space. **Space** is *the element of art that refers to the emptiness or area between, around, above, below, or within objects.* All objects take up space. You, for example, are a living, breathing form moving through space.

Shapes and forms are defined by the space around and within them. They depend on space for their existence. This is why it is important to understand the relationship of space to shapes and forms.

Positive and Negative Spaces

In both two- and three-dimensional art, the shapes or forms are called the *positive space* or the *figure.* The empty spaces between the shapes or forms are called *negative spaces* or *ground.* Look at **Figure 5.8** and read the caption for an

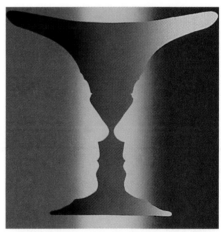

▲ **FIGURE 5.8** Do you see a vase or do you see two profiles of Picasso? Johns has deliberately organized this lithograph as a visual puzzle to confuse the viewer. One minute the faces are very clear and they seem to be the figure while the space between the profiles is the ground. The next moment the vase between the profiles becomes the figure and the space around the vase becomes the ground.

Jasper Johns. *Cups 4 Picasso.* 1972. Lithograph. 57 × 82 cm (22½ × 32¼"). The Museum of Modern Art, New York, New York. Gift of Celeste Bartos. © Jasper Johns/VAGA, New York.

Space
(pages 103–107)
(National Standards: 2b, 3a, 4b)

FOCUS...........
Objectives
After completing this lesson, students will be able to:

■ Explain the difference between positive and negative space.

■ Describe depth perception and point of view.

Resources

📖 Transparency CC-5, M.C. Escher. *Other World*

📖 Studio Lesson 3, *Photogram*

🗀 Artist's Profile 39, M.C. Escher

TEACH..........
Motivator
To introduce the concept of space, use a cardboard box. Color each set of parallel lines on the box form with different colors. Label one set "length," the second set "width," and the third set "depth." Show students how length and width just outline a flat shape, but when you add the dimension of depth, the box takes up space.

Aesthetics
Ask students to look through the text for examples of two-dimensional works that (1) illustrate obvious distinctions between figure and ground, (2) make negative space as important as the positive space, and (3) reverse the figure and ground.

TECHNOLOGY OPTIONS

National Gallery of Art Videodisc Use the following to show examples of how artists use shape, form, and space.

Jan van Eyck
The Annunciation

Search Frame 580

Marino Marini
Horseman

Search Frame 2569

Use Glencoe's *Correlation Bar Code Guide to the National Gallery of Art* to locate more artworks.

103

Studio Skills

Have students create their own figure/ground. Fold a small piece of paper in half. On one side of the fold have the students draw a profile with a pencil. Go over the line of the profile with a dark crayon, pressing heavily to lay down a thick layer of wax. Then fold the paper again and rub heavily over the area of the profile line to transfer it to the other half. Unfold the paper and go over the transferred line. Then have some students color in the center shape and others color in the two outside shapes. Display these so that the class can see how the different designs keep reversing as students look at them.

Activity

Experimenting with Space

Applying Your Skills. Remind students that part of this exercise is to set up objects so that the negative spaces create interesting designs.

💻 **Computer Option.** Encourage students to experiment with space on the screen by first filling the area with a solid black color. Then have them use the Eraser tool to create varying sizes of white shapes that change the appearance of the remaining black areas. Students can Save and title their work when satisfied. Invite them to continue to explore other arrangements and fill some of the erased shapes with patterns or gradients. Remind students to use the Save As command to save and retitle new editions. Have students select the best results, print, and display their artwork.

example of figure and ground. In a portrait, the image of the person is the positive space; the negative space is the area surrounding the person.

The shape and size of negative spaces affect the way you interpret positive spaces. Large negative spaces around positive spaces may express loneliness or freedom. When the positive spaces are crowded together, you may feel tension or togetherness **(Figure 5.9).** The full meaning of a work depends on the interaction between the positive and negative spaces. It is not always easy to tell which are the positive spaces and which are the negative spaces in two-dimensional art. Sometimes it is difficult to identify the negative space. This is because some artists give equal emphasis to both the figure and the ground.

Sometimes artists even try to confuse the viewer. They create positive and negative spaces that reverse themselves while you are looking at them. These visual puzzles fascinate some viewers **(Figure 5.10).**

▲ **FIGURE 5.9** In this sculpture, Brancusi goes beyond the realistic representation of love. He uses the lack of space between the two figures to symbolize the concept of the togetherness, the unity, of a couple in love. The rectangular solid of their combined form reminds us of the solidity of their union.

Constantin Brancusi. *The Kiss.* c. 1908. Stone. Height 50.2 cm (19¾"). Musee National d'Art Moderne, Centre Georges Pompidou, Paris, France.

Activity — Experimenting with Space

Applying Your Skills. Select a group of objects to draw. Make an arrangement with a variety of negative spaces between the shapes. Draw the arrangement lightly with pencil or chalk. Finish the work by (a) coloring only the negative spaces with crayons or paint, or (b) filling the negative spaces with closely drawn sets of parallel lines. Leave the positive spaces empty. What shapes did the negative spaces take?

Computer Option. Use the Rectangle shape tool to draw a solid rectangle approximately 3" x 4" in the center of the screen. Explore the different shapes of Selection tools to select and move parts of the rectangle away from the original shape. Continue selecting and moving until the rectangle has been broken into many smaller parts with varying spaces in between. Save and Title your work when you have created an interesting composition by adding space within the form.

MORE ABOUT... Constantin Brancusi

Constantin Brancusi (1876–1957), a Romanian sculptor, trained as a carpenter and a stone mason. In 1904, he settled in Paris where his early influences included African and Oriental art. Rodin was also an early influence. Around 1909, Brancusi abandoned modeling for direct carving. His craftsmanship was masterly and he would often let the nature of the stone dictate stylizations. Brancusi's originality in reducing natural forms to their ultimate—almost abstract—simplicity had profound effects on the course of twentieth-century sculpture.

MEET THE ARTIST
M.C. ESCHER

Dutch, 1898–1972

Born in Leeuwarden, Holland, M. C. Escher (**esh**-ur) studied graphic art at Harlem's School of Architecture and Ornamental Design. He concentrated on illustrating his eccentric inner visions and his fascination with the laws of nature. In his lithographs, he explored a variety of visual jokes and trickery, such as optical illusions and distorted or impossible perspective.

Escher's works achieve their visual puzzles through his clever manipulation of positive and negative space. They skillfully switch forms into places where the viewer would logically expect space, or what appears to be the outer surface of an object reverses into an inner space.

Escher also created designs using positive and negative space to transform one object to another. A flock of birds on the left side of the picture becomes a school of fish on the right side. Each time a change takes place, the negative space becomes dominant and transforms into the new object.

▶ **FIGURE 5.10** At first this print looks normal. Water is falling to turn a water wheel. However, follow the water from the base of the fall. It runs uphill! Escher has created a visual puzzle using the mathematics of perspective.

Promoting Discussion

Use the fine art transparency, CC-5, M.C. Escher, *Other World* and have students compare the similarities and differences to Figure 5.10.

Art on a Shoestring

If you are planning an art project that involves foam containers or empty food cartons, you might investigate organizations that bring food to elderly and confined people, such as the "Meals on Wheels" program. These organizations may be able to supply you with clean, recyclable supplies. Also, ask students and parents to send in unneeded mail-order catalogs to use for collages. The coating of the paper used in these catalogs usually makes them nonrecyclable, but in the art classroom they still have some life left in them!

Studio Skills

Have students cut a large geometric shape from a sheet of black paper. Then have them cut the shape into nine or more separate pieces and re-form the pieces into the original shape on a large sheet of white paper. Have them expand the shape by gradually sliding the pieces apart. Experiment by creating different amounts of space between the pieces, then glue down the best arrangement. Explain that they may not add or subtract any pieces from the original number, and the original shape must be recognizable. Emphasize to the students that the shapes will not change, but the negative space must vary, and that the negative space will control the final look of the design.

MORE ABOUT... M.C. Escher

Have students examine Figure 5.10. Explain that Escher was well-known for creating optical illusions and interlocking patterns in his work. Tell students that much of Escher's early work consisted of landscapes and townscapes, but later in his career he changed his style to spatial illusions. Point out that although Escher used an analytical approach to his artwork, he had no formal training in math or science.

Space in Three-Dimensional Art

Over, under, through, behind, and *around* are words that describe three-dimensional space. Architecture, sculpture, weaving, ceramics, and jewelry are three-dimensional art forms. They all take up real space. You can walk around, look through, look behind, peer over, and reach into three-dimensional art.

▲ **FIGURE 5.11** The interior of this cathedral was designed so that the stained glass and the vertical columns would pull your eyes upward toward the heavens.

Reims Cathedral (interior). Reims, France. Begun c. 1225.

Architects shape space. They design structures that enclose a variety of spaces for people. They create large spaces for group activities, such as the one you see in **Figure 5.11**. They also create small spaces for privacy. Landscape architects and city planners are also involved in planning spaces for people to use.

Negative areas in three-dimensional art are very real. Most three-dimensional works are meant to be *freestanding*, which means they are surrounded by negative space **(Figure 5.12)**. The viewer must move through this negative space to see all of the different views of a three-dimensional work.

Relief sculpture is not intended to be freestanding. It projects out from a flat surface into negative space. You can find relief sculpture on ceramic pots and plaster ceilings. When the positive areas project slightly from the flat surface, the work is called *bas relief,* or *low relief* **(Figure 5.13)**. When the positive areas project farther out, the work is called *high relief.*

Most jewelry is planned as relief sculpture to decorate human surfaces. The inside of a ring or the back of a pendant is smooth. It is not meant to be seen; it simply rests on the person's surface.

Today many artists are experimenting and changing traditional art forms. Printmakers are creating relief prints. Some printmakers are molding relief designs in handmade paper. Painters are adding a third dimension to the painted surface. Some painters are cutting or tearing real negative spaces in two-dimensional surfaces.

Weaving has also gone in new directions. It started as a practical craft, with weavers making two-dimensional fabrics for clothing, and has evolved into an art form. Today hand weavers are

---

creating relief hangings and three-dimensional woven sculptures.

Photographers are creating **holograms**, *images in three dimensions created with a laser beam.* Sculptors are making *kinetic,* or moving, sculpture.

▶ **FIGURE 5.12** This example of folk art from Peru is a freestanding sculpture. Look carefully and you can see forms peeking out from the back. To see them you would have to walk around to the back of the work.

Artist unknown. *Church Quinua,* Ayacucho, Peru. 1958. Painted earthenware. Girard Foundation Collection at the Museum of International Folk Art, a unit of the Museum of New Mexico, Santa Fe, New Mexico.

 **Using Three Dimensions**

Applying Your Skills. Make a freestanding, three-dimensional design that projects into negative space on all sides. Using pieces of cardboard tubing and small boxes, join the design pieces with glue and tape. Paint the finished work in one color to emphasize its form.

Set up a spotlight on one side of your free-standing sculpture. In your sketchbook draw the contours of the sculpture and the shape of its shadow. Move the spotlight to another angle. Draw the sculpture and its shadow. Notice how the changing light changes the shadow's shape.

Computer Option. Draw a solid cube or rectangular form so the top, side, and front are visible. Add shading by filling each surface with a different value of a color, texture, or gradient. Remove an area within the form by using the Eraser or Selection tool. Explore adding shadows and lines to accurately depict the inner space you see.

 Check Your Understanding

1. Define positive space and negative space.
2. What words specifically describe three-dimensional art?
3. What are the two types of relief sculpture?

▲ **FIGURE 5.13** An example of low relief. Since the design was for the back of a chair, the relief has to be low relief or the chair back would be too uncomfortable to lean against.

Queen Ankhesenamun and King Tutankhamon. Egypt, Eighteenth Dynasty. Wood overlaid with gold, silver, semiprecious stones, and glass paste. Egyptian Museum, Cairo, Egypt. Scala/Art Resource, New York.

LESSON 2   *Space*   **107**

Enrichment

■ Have students complete Studio Lesson 3, *Photogram,* to work with positive and negative space.

■ Have students use a viewing frame to help them study the negative spaces around an ordinary chair.

CLOSE............

Ask students to give a definition of the word *space* and explain how it compares to shape and form.

Activity

Using Three Dimensions

Applying Your Skills. Unless students do this activity at home, it will be wise to start collecting cardboard tubes and boxes about a week before they construct their forms. The paint is not necessary, but it enhances the forms. At home any lamp will serve as a light source to create the shadows as long as the other lights in the room are dim. In school, students might have to share the light, so they might select one of the pieces in the group to draw.

Computer Option. Using the same steps, students can draw a cylinder, cube, or pyramid. Use the Gradient Fill to make the form appear three-dimensional. Use the Copy and Paste commands to make multiple copies. The sizes of each copy can be varied by using the Scale Selection or Resize tool. An environment with three or more dimensional forms can be arranged in the same manner by storing the original copies in the Scrapbook. The invisible Clipboard saves a copy when you use the Copy and Paste commands, but it only holds one image at a time.

Answers to Check Your Understanding

1. In both two- and three-dimensional art, the shapes or forms are called the positive space of the figure. The empty spaces between the shapes or forms are called the negative spaces or ground.
2. Over, under, through, behind, and around are words that describe three-dimensional art.
3. The two types of relief sculpture are low relief and high relief.

How We Perceive Shape, Form, and Space

(pages 108–110)
(National Standards: 2b, 3a)

FOCUS...........
Objectives

After completing this lesson, students will be able to:

■ Explain how the eyes perceive depth.

■ Define *point of view.*

Resources

📁 Studio Lesson 4, *Plaster Sculpture*
📁 Studio Lesson 5, *Soft Sculpture*

TEACH..........
Motivator

To help students understand that they have stereoscopic vision, bring in an example of stereography (three-dimensional photography) and the special glasses required to merge the two pictures into one. Tell students that in this lesson they will learn about how the eyes perceive.

Cross-Curriculum: Science

To help students determine their eye dominance, have them do the following: Place your hands together so that your fingers are crossed but a small space is created between the overlapping thumbs and fingers. Select an object in the room. Use this open space as a viewfinder. Center an object within the opening. Then close one eye at a time. The right or left eye that clearly views the whole object through the viewfinder is the dominant eye.

How We Perceive Shape, Form, and Space

Look up from this book to an object across the room to see if you can feel the movement of your eye muscles. If you didn't feel anything, try again until you become aware that your eyes are working to refocus.

You have just taken a trip through visual space. Your brain measured the amount of space between you and the object and sent a message to your eye muscles to adjust. The muscles then refocused your eyes so that you could clearly see the object.

Perceiving Depth

Your eyes and brain work together to enable you to see in three dimensions—*length, width,* and *depth.* Each eye sees an object from a slightly different angle. The brain merges these two separate and slightly different views into one, creating a three-dimensional image.

To see how this works try the following experiment. Close your right eye. Point to a specific spot in the room. Without moving your pointing finger, open your right eye and close your left eye. It will appear that you have moved your finger, even though you know you have not.

Point of View

The shapes and forms you see depend on your *point of view.* Your point of view is the angle from which you see an object. Another person at another location will see the same shape or form differently. For example, a person looking down on a circle drawn on the sidewalk sees a round shape. If that person lies on the ground beside the circle and looks at it, the circle will appear to have an oblong shape. A person looking at the front end of a car will see a form different from the one seen by a person looking at the side of that same car. **Figure 5.14** shows three different views of a sculpture.

Activity — Shape and Point of View

Applying Your Skills. Look through magazines for three or more different views of one type of object. Look for TV sets, sofas, spoons, toasters, cars, or shoes. Cut out the objects and mount each one on a sheet of white paper. Emphasize the changes in shape by drawing around each outline with a crayon or marker.

Computer Option. Divide the page into three equal sections. Use the Grids and Rulers menu to guide you if available. Choose an interesting but simple object such as a cup, a screw, pliers, a book, or a paint container. Observe and draw three views of the same object using the Pencil, small Brush, Crayon, or Marker tool. After drawing the contour or outer edges of the object, add shading to emphasize the form and surface from different views.

MORE ABOUT... Binocular Vision

No photographic technique has been able to duplicate the human brain and eyes in creating images of objects in space. Stereoscopic photography captures some of the illusion, but this photography is limited. The principle of binocular vision has also been used to design optical range finders for mapmaking and tank gunnery.

Double-image (or 3-D) movies are produced by making one print of the film in warm colors and one print in cool colors. The audience is given glasses that filter out the warm colors for one eye and cool colors for the other eye. The brain lays one image on top of the other so that viewers see a third dimension, depth.

Michael Naranjo. *Spirits Soaring.* 1985. Bronze. Height 51 cm (20"). Private collection.

Shape and Point of View

Applying Your Skills. This activity requires drawing skills and the perception necessary to find different silhouettes of a similar object.

💻 **Computer Option.** The Grids and Rulers menu can be found on many software programs. These guidelines are visible only on the computer screen to assist you and do not appear on printed copy. Many art applications also include a Perspective tool that varies from simple to complex. Simple perspective tools provide handles that allow you to pull, tilt, or "extrude" a shape onto a horizontal or vertical plane, which gives the effect of linear perspective.

See *Computers in the Art Classroom* for other computer options. 📁

Experiments in Point of View

You can learn about point of view by doing the following experiments. Place your hand flat on the desk and spread your fingers apart. The shape and form you see are the shape and form you would probably draw. They are part of the mental image you have of the object "hand." Now lift your hand and let your fingers relax. Notice how the shape and form of your hand change. Turn your hand and watch what happens. Your hand is still the same hand. Only its shape and form are different.

Next, look at a rectangular table. What shape does the top have when you are sitting at the table? Look at the top through a rectangular viewing frame. Are the edges of the table parallel to the edges of the frame? You know the top is a rectangle, but does it really look rectangular now? What shape does the top seem to take if you are sitting across the room from it? What would the shape look like if you viewed it from the top of a tall ladder? Do you think the shape you see will change if you lie on the floor directly under the table?

Critical Thinking

Help students understand depth perception by following this experiment carefully:

- Cover your right eye. Point with your finger to a specific spot in the room. Note the position of the spot.
- Without moving your pointing finger, cover your left eye. Note how the spot looks now.
- Again, without moving your pointing finger, uncover both eyes and focus on the tip of your finger.
- Describe exactly what you saw in each step of this experiment. Based on your experience, what can you conclude about someone who is blind in one eye? Can this person function as well as someone with two good eyes? Explain your conclusions.

MORE ABOUT... Michael Naranjo

Just like every other sculptor, Michael Naranjo feels the need to study the works of other artists. When he looks, however, he sees with his hands. In 1968, while serving in the army, he was blinded by a grenade in Vietnam.

Naranjo has always been interested in art. He was born near Santa Fe, New Mexico, a Tewa Indian of the Santa Clara Pueblo. Naranjo gets ideas from the things he saw in his past. He has to visualize the image in his mind. Then he models his idea in wax or carves it from stone. Wax carving is easier, because he can correct mistakes. He has to keep the whole of the image in his mind so he knows how much he has taken away.

ASSESS..........

Self-Assessment

Have students complete the review questions on this page. Answers are provided below.

Reteaching

If students are having trouble with the changing table top exercise on this page, bring a safe ladder into the room and let them use a viewing frame to see how the shape changes as they move up and down. A simpler but less dramatic method is to bring in a rectangular solid similar to a table and hold it at different levels while students study it through viewing frames. The viewing frame is important because it acts as the picture plane. Students can note how the angles of the edges of the table change in relationship to the edges of the viewing frame.

Enrichment

- Distribute Studio Lesson 4, *Plaster Sculpture* and have students create a free-standing, lifelike form that looks interesting from every point of view.
- Have students complete Studio Lesson 5, *Soft Sculpture* to make a humorous soft sculpture of a common object.

CLOSE............

Have students write a definition of depth perception and point of view.

▲ **FIGURE 5.15** In this painting the viewer can see all the tabletops easily. All the serving dishes and the food in them are clearly visible. Can you tell what kind of a party this is? Why was this point of view a good one for this painting?

William Kurelek. *Manitoba Party*. 1964. Oil on Masonite. 121.9 × 152.6 cm (48 × 60″). National Gallery of Canada, Ottawa, Canada.

When you looked at your hand, your eyes stayed in the same place, but your hand moved. When you studied the table, it remained in one place, but you moved. In both cases, what you saw changed because your relationship to the object changed. Your point of view depends on where you are and where the object is. Look at **Figure 5.15**. Where is the artist's point of view in relation to the tables in that picture?

 Check Your Understanding

1. What three dimensions are we able to see?
2. Define point of view.
3. Why may people who are looking at the same object see different shapes and forms?

110 | **CHAPTER 5** Shape, Form, and Space

Answers to Check Your Understanding

1. The three dimensions we are able to see are length, width, and depth.
2. Point of view is the angle from which you see an object.
3. The shapes and forms you see depend on your point of view. Point of view depends on where the viewer is and where the objects are.

How Artists Create Shapes and Forms in Space

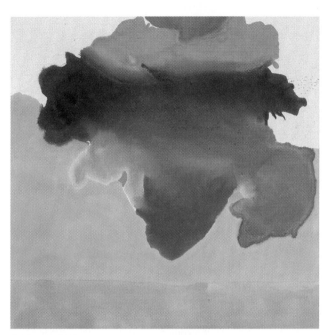

▲ **FIGURE 5.16**
Frankenthaler is an action painter who creates shapes by pouring thinned acrylic paint onto a canvas that is placed flat on the floor.

Helen Frankenthaler. *The Bay.* 1963. Acrylic on canvas. 201.1 × 207 cm (79⅜ × 81½"). The Detroit Institute of Arts, Detroit, Michigan. Founders Society Purchase with funds from Dr. and Mrs. Hilbert H. DeLawter.

Shapes and forms can be classified as *natural* or *manufactured*. Natural shapes and forms are made by the forces of nature. For instance, animals, plants, and stones are natural forms. Manufactured forms are those created by people, whether mass-produced by the thousands in factories or made by hand.

Artists use many materials and techniques to make shapes. They concentrate on both outline and area. Some artists outline shapes in drawings and paintings. Others may paint shapes by placing brushstrokes together without using even a beginning outline. Some may cut shapes and print shapes and some may pour paint to create shapes **(Figure 5.16)**.

Like shapes, three-dimensional forms can be made in many ways. Artists model clay forms, mold metal forms, and carve forms from wood or stone. They use glass, plastic, bricks, and cement to create forms as well as shapes.

The Illusion of Form

Artists can create the illusion of three-dimensional form on a two-dimensional surface. They can give the impression of depth and solidity by using changes in value. **Figure 5.17** is an example of this illusion.

◀ **FIGURE 5.17** Artemisia Gentileschi was a Baroque artist who used the arrangement of contrasting light and dark to create a dramatic effect in her work. Notice how the light seems to be coming from a single candle.

Artemisia Gentileschi. *Judith and Maidservant with the Head of Holofernes.* c. 1625. Oil on canvas. 184.2 × 141.6 cm (72½ × 55¼"). The Detroit Institute of Arts, Detroit, Michigan. Gift of Mr. Leslie H. Green.

LESSON 4 *How Artists Create Shapes and Forms in Space* | **111**

**CHAPTER 5
LESSON 4**

How Artists Create Shapes and Forms in Space
(pages 111–116)
(National Standards: 2b, 3a)

FOCUS...........
Objectives
After completing this lesson, students will be able to:
- Describe the meaning of *chiaroscuro.*
- Explain techniques used to create perspective in artworks.

Resources

📁 Artist's Profile 13, Sandro Botticelli
📁 Cooperative Learning Activity 10, *A Perspective Treasure Hunt*
📁 Enrichment 9, *Drawing in One-Point Perspective*
📁 Enrichment 10,

TEACH.........
Art Criticism
After students have studied Figure 5.16, have them cut photographs of geometric or freeform shapes from magazines. For example, they may consider cans, boxes, tires, gears or other objects and arrange the shapes to create a mechanical creature. Instruct students to glue the design onto paper, then draw or paint a mechanical, geometric environment for the creature. Have them use the four steps of art criticism to evaluate their work individually.

COOPERATIVE LEARNING

Research and Report Point out that, although the practice of modeling figures in light and shadow was certainly a hallmark of Baroque art (the word *chiaroscuro* was itself coined in 1686), the technique had its roots in works of art as early as the Renaissance. Divide the class into research committees and ask them to choose one of the following topics as the basis for an oral presentation: (1) the origins of chiaroscuro (i.e., who coined the term?); (2) the history of chiaroscuro in art; and (3) different color models (e.g., process color, the RGB model) and its role in gradations of light and dark. Set aside time for committees to present their findings.

Art History

Refer students to Figure 5.17 on page 111 and tell them this is a good example of the artist's strong use of value to create drama in her work. Tell students that this painting was done by Artemisia Gentileschi, who studied under the master of chiaroscuro, Caravaggio. Explain that Artemisia Gentileschi was the first woman in the history of Western art to have a significant impact on the world of art in her time.

Activity

Using Shading

Applying Your Skills. Set up a still life in the classroom as described in this activity. Turn off as many of the overhead lights as you can and place a strong spotlight on one side of the still life. Before students start to draw, help them analyze the values they perceive by finding the darkest and lightest areas. Help them see the difference between gradual changes of value on rounded forms and jumps in value on angular surfaces. Insist that they use all of the values from white to black in their works. Many students try to stay in the safe gray areas of value and need to be pushed to go to black.

Computer Option. Have students try this: use any drawing or shape tool to design a large vase. Choose the Brush Symmetry menu if available to ensure a symmetrical shape or, draw half the vase, then Select, Copy, Paste, and Flip the copy to match the original side and complete the vase. Determine the light source and use any of the tools or menus you have explored such as the Pencil, Brushes, Airbrush, Texture, and Gradients to shade the vase leaving highlighted areas. Draw a horizon line and other lines to create a sense of space and a setting.

FIGURE 5.18 The artist has represented shadows and highlights with photographic reality. Notice how he has made the objects seem to look solid. The seats of the stools look round. The reflections on the metal ceiling indicate rounded form. How does he use light to create the effect of a cool, air-conditioned interior against a hot outdoor scene?

Ralph Goings. *Diner With Red Door.* 1979. Oil on canvas. 112.4 × 153.7 cm (44¼ × 60½"). Courtesy of OK Harris Works of Art, New York, New York.

The arrangement of light and shadow is called **chiaroscuro** (**kyah**-roh-**skoo**-roh). In Italian *chiaro* means "bright," and *oscuro* means "dark." Chiaroscuro was introduced by Italian artists during the Renaissance. Today, chiaroscuro is often called *modeling* or *shading.*

Look, for instance, at an object with angular surfaces, such as a cube. You will see a large jump in value from one surface of the cube to the next. One surface may be very light in value and the next very dark. Now look at an object such as a baseball. The curved surfaces of spheres and cylinders show gradual changes in value.

The area of a curved surface that reflects the most light is, of course, the lightest in a drawing. **Highlights** are *small areas of white used to show the very brightest spots.* Starting at the highlights, the value changes gradually from light values of gray to dark values of gray. The darkest values are used to show areas that receive the least light. An area that is turned completely away from a light source is almost black. Look at **Figure 5.18** to see the different ways an artist has created the illusion of form.

Activity

Using Shading

Applying Your Skills. Set up an arrangement of geometric forms. Use boxes, books, balls, and cylindrical containers. Study the way light reflects off the surfaces of the objects. Draw the arrangement. Give the shapes in your drawing the illusion of three dimensions by using the medium and shading technique of your choice. Use values that range from black to white, and employ many value steps in between.

Computer Option. To perfect your shading technique, experiment with the Pencil, Brush, Line, Gradient, and Airbrush tools. Several programs include a Smudge or Blending tool, which softens edges. The Pencil, Line, and small Brush tools can be used with shading techniques you use when working with pen and ink. To explore these options, draw a small square shape. Select, copy, and paste seven more copies of the square in a row across the screen. Then choose from a variety of tools, textures, and settings to create different values from light to dark in the squares.

CULTURAL DIVERSITY

Space in Artworks There are many different ways of organizing space in works of art. Show students examples of how other, non-Western cultures show depth in their works of art. For example,

1. In Egyptian art, both front and side views of an object or figure are shown at the same time.
2. Asian artists often show distance by using atmos-

pheric perspective to differentiate the foreground, middle ground, and background.
3. Ancient Egyptian wall paintings found in Egyptian tombs are divided into geometric areas, often to allow the important figures to be drawn larger.
4. In an Egyptian painting, stories can be told with each part presented in a separate panel.

The Illusion of Depth

In paintings, artists often create the illusion of depth. When you look at these paintings, you see objects and shapes, some of which seem closer to you than others. You seem to be looking through a window into a real place **(Figure 5.19)**. This idea—that a painting should be like a window to the real world—has dominated traditional Western art since the early Renaissance.

There are several terms that will help you as you talk about and create depth in a painting or drawing. The surface of a painting or drawing is sometimes called the *picture plane*. The part of the picture plane that appears nearest to you is the *foreground*. The part that appears farthest away is the *background*. The area in between is called the *middle ground*.

Perspective is *a graphic system that creates the illusion of depth and volume on a two-dimensional surface*. In the following

▲ **FIGURE 5.19** Everything is carefully placed within the frame of this scene. In the foreground, figures dressed in bright robes kneel before the Christ Child. Beyond the human activity there is a background of calm, rolling, green hills. Notice how the artist tries to focus your attention on the child. After reading about perspective, see if you can find examples of each of the six devices used for creating perspective in this painting.

Sandro Botticelli. *The Adoration of the Magi.* Early 1480s. Tempera and oil on panel. 70.1 × 104.1 cm (27⅝ × 41"). National Gallery of Art, Washington, D.C. © 1998 Board of Trustees. Andrew W. Mellon Collection, 1937.

Art History

Display reproductions of paintings created by European artists before the Renaissance. Then add to the display several reproductions of paintings by some of the great artists of the Renaissance, such as Leonardo da Vinci, Michelangelo, and Raphael. Help students see the contrast between the flat figures and lack of depth in the first set of paintings and the rounded, more realistic figures and the illusion of depth created in the Renaissance paintings. Ask students to identify examples of specific techniques used to give the feeling of depth.

Aesthetics

It is important that students understand the use of value in creating illusions of three-dimensional form. This is much more difficult for them to grasp than contour drawing. They have been drawing lines all of their lives, but they may not be as aware of values. After helping them become aware of different values, let them practice shading techniques without looking at real objects.

Studio Skills

Have students cut out seven magazine photos of objects that are all related to each other, such as animals, food, cars, shoes, furniture, and so on. Each object should be of a different size. Instruct students to arrange the cutouts on a dark sheet of paper using overlapping, differing sizes, placement, varying detail, and color to create the illusion of depth. Remind students that they can blur details and lighten colors in a magazine photograph by rubbing it lightly with an eraser. Have students share their work in small groups and explain how their choices create the illusion of depth.

CULTURAL DIVERSITY

Christianity Some of the students in your class may not be familiar with Christianity and may need an explanation of the figures who appear in *The Adoration of the Magi.* Point out to them that an aisle bordered by kneeling figures leads the viewer to the Holy Family consisting of Joseph, Mary, and the Christ Child. The Holy Family is surrounded by the Magi and their atten-

dants who are dressed in garments worn during Botticelli's time. The Magi are presenting their gifts to the Christ Child who is seated on Mary's lap. To help students further appreciate the life and times of Sandro Botticelli, whose work is shown in Figure 5.19 assign *Artist's Profile 13* in the TCR. 🗀

113

Critical Thinking

To help students understand picture plane, bring in a rectangular piece of glass taped on the edges to prevent cuts. Have the students hold the glass perpendicular to the table and draw on the glass. The glass represents the surface of the painting. If you have windows in your room, several students at a time may draw what they see outside directly on the panes of glass. The windows can be cleaned afterward with any commercial household glass cleaner.

Developing Perceptual Skills

When discussing the six perspective techniques, be sure to have available large prints of realistic paintings, or use those in the book, so that students can identify the techniques and understand how artists used them.

Art History

When linear perspective was first used, Renaissance artists were able to give exciting visual reality to their artworks. Today, perspective is used by many kinds of artists. Video game designers use perspective to provide three-dimensional effects for auto-racing games. Graphic artists design logos for television that zoom into the foreground and rotate in space. Computer games have been designed that provide the experience of piloting and landing a plane; the perspective changes as the plane changes altitude.

Remind students that the concept of linear perspective is so common to us that we take it for granted. Ask them to imagine how Renaissance artists might react to the many ways it is used today.

pages you will learn techniques artists use to give their paintings and drawings perspective.

Overlapping. When one object covers part of a second object, the first seems to be closer to the viewer, as in **Figure 5.20**.

▲ **Figure 5.20**   Overlapping.

Size. Large objects appear to be closer to the viewer than small objects, as in **Figure 5.21**. The farther an object is from you, the smaller it appears. Cars far down the road seem to be much smaller than the ones close to you. If you stand at the end of a long hallway and raise your hand, you can block your view of a whole crowd of people. You know that each person is about your size, but at a distance the crowd appears to be smaller than your hand.

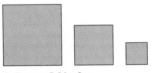

▲ **Figure 5.21**   Size.

Placement. Objects placed low on the picture plane seem to be closer to the viewer than objects placed near eye level. The most distant shapes are those that seem to be exactly at eye level **(Figure 5.22)**.

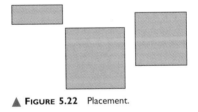

▲ **Figure 5.22**   Placement.

Detail. Objects with clear, sharp edges and visible details seem to be close to you **(Figure 5.23)**. Objects that lack detail and have hazy outlines seem to be farther away. Look closely at your own hand. You can see very tiny lines clearly. Now look at someone's hand from across the room. You have trouble seeing the lines between the fingers. All the details seem to melt together because of the distance between you and what you are seeing.

▲ **Figure 5.23**   Detail.

Color. Brightly-colored objects seem closer to you, and objects with dull, light colors seem to be farther away **(Figure 5.24)**. This is called *atmospheric* perspective. The air around us is not empty. It is full of moisture and dust that create a haze. The more air there is between you and an object, the more the object seems to fade. Have you ever noticed that trees close to you seem to be a much brighter green than trees farther down the road?

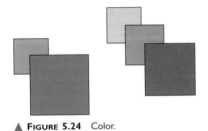

▲ **Figure 5.24**   Color.

MORE ABOUT...   Linear Perspective

Because linear perspective is fundamental to our understanding of art, we often take it for granted. Our familiarity with complex computer graphics could make us forget that earlier cultures did not understand the concept. Does the lack of linear perspective in the art of earlier generations diminish its significance?

Ask students to choose an illustration from an earlier chapter and sketch the same subject using linear perspective to create the illusion of depth; for example, an Egyptian hieroglyphic, a frieze from the Parthenon, or a Byzantine painting.

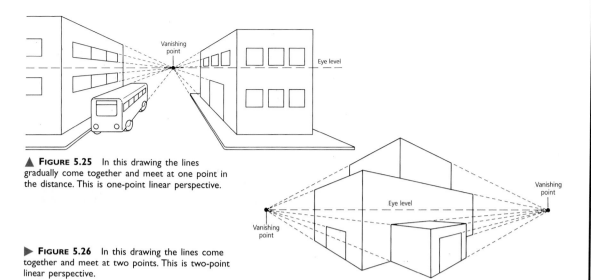

▲ **FIGURE 5.25** In this drawing the lines gradually come together and meet at one point in the distance. This is one-point linear perspective.

▶ **FIGURE 5.26** In this drawing the lines come together and meet at two points. This is two-point linear perspective.

Have students find a newspaper or magazine photograph of rectangular solids, such as the exterior of buildings or interior rooms of a building. Instruct students to use tracing paper to trace the main shapes in the photograph. Then, using a ruler and pencil, extend any parallel lines that recede into the distance. Ask them to identify the vanishing point(s) and the horizon line.

Activity

Creating Depth

Applying Your Skills. Accurately measured linear perspective is not a subject of this course. It is, however, very important that students recognize and identify that perspective is always mathematical. Remind students to look at Shading Techniques on page 430 of the *Handbook* to help them use shading techniques to create illusion of three dimensions. To further challenge them, ask them to plan a light source and then draw shadows on the ground.

Computer Option. Students can create a simple landscape by choosing the Pencil or Brush tool to draw overlapping lines representing mountains, hills, and fields. Use the foreground, middle ground, and background space on their screen. Add winding roads or roaming streams and fences that change size and direction as they move higher on the picture plane. Draw trees, houses, barns, bridges, animals, or other details. Use the Copy and Paste commands and Scale Selection or Resizing tool to repeat these shapes in varying sizes, overlapping occasionally. Add color and patterns using the Bucket Flood-fill tool.

Converging Lines. *Linear* perspective is one way of using lines to show distance and depth. As parallel lines move away from you, they seem to move closer together toward the horizon line **(Figure 5.25)**. When you look at the highway ahead of you, the sides of the road appear to move closer together. You don't worry, though, because you know this is an illusion. The sides of the road ahead of you are actually just as far apart as they are in your present position.

Sometimes lines appear to meet at a point on the horizon line called the *vanishing point*. In two-point linear perspective, different sets of parallel lines meet at different vanishing points **(Figure 5.26)**. Because two-point perspective creates more diagonal lines in a painting,

Activity **Creating Depth**

Applying Your Skills. Create three different designs on three separate sheets of paper. Each design should contain five shapes. Use the same five shapes in each design as follows:

- Draw all of the items as close to the foreground as possible.
- Draw one item close to the foreground and make the others look as if they are slightly farther back.
- Draw one item close to the foreground, one far in the background, and the other three in the middle ground.

Computer Option. Use the Brush or Pencil tool to draw a landscape that includes a foreground, middle ground, and background. Draw several medium size trees in the middle ground. Draw at least one large tree in the foreground. This tree should touch two or three edges of the paper, and overlap the smaller trees. It should display the most detail. Add other objects and details that might include plants, animals, water, and objects made by hand. Remember the methods for creating the illusion of depth that were discussed earlier in the chapter.

Curriculum Connection

Math Renaissance fascination with mathematics and with representation led artists into devising mathematical approaches to drawing. Leon Battista Alberti (1404–1472), an Italian artist, published the first written account of the system of perspective. From this, mathematicians developed projective geometry.

German artist Albrecht Dürer (1471–1528) experimented with perspective by looking at his subject through a pane of glass and seeing how receding lines seemed to angle inward and narrow. Think of the glass as the picture plane and the depth you show as the picture space. The point where your eye rests in the distance is the vanishing point.

ASSESS..........

Self-Assessment

Have students complete the review questions on this page. Answers are provided below.

Reteaching

■ Working in small groups, have students complete Co-operative Learning Activity 10, *A Perspective Treasure Hunt,* to recognize and review perspective techniques in their environment. 📁

Enrichment

■ Duplicate and distribute Enrichment Activity 9, *Drawing in One-Point Perspective,* to help students understand the way the eye perceives size and linear movement in space. 📁

■ Distribute Enrichment Activity 10, *Building a 3-D Space Construct,* and have students design and construct a box, frame, or platform to contain or support a three-dimensional arrangement of simple forms that create and exaggerate the illusion of deep space. 📁

CLOSE.............

Have each student select one of the artworks in this lesson and briefly describe the use of shape, form, or space in the work.

it seems more active. Renaissance artists used strict mathematical formulas to calculate perspective. Most of today's artists rely on visual perception rather than mathematical formulas. Notice the ways in which Doris Lee has used perspective to show depth in her busy kitchen scene **(Figure 5.27)**.

Check Your Understanding

1. How are shapes and forms classified?
2. What effect does chiaroscuro create in artworks?
3. List and describe three techniques artists use to give their works perspective.

LOOKING CLOSELY

Identifying Perspective Techniques

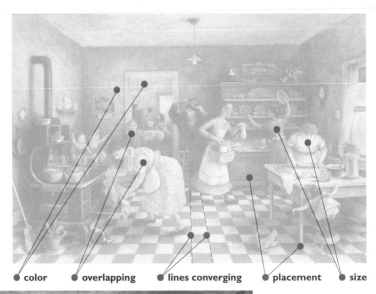

In this painting about the preparations for an old-fashioned Thanksgiving feast, Doris Lee has used all six perspective techniques. The lines in the diagram of the painting indicate one example of each technique. Can you find more examples of the six techniques in the painting?

● color   ● overlapping   ● lines converging   ● placement   ● size

◀ **FIGURE 5.27**

Doris Lee. *Thanksgiving.* 1935. Oil on canvas. 71.4 × 101.6 cm (28 × 40"). The Art Institute of Chicago, Chicago, Illinois. Mr. and Mrs. Frank G. Logan Prize Fund (1935.313).

 Answers to Check Your Understanding

1. Shapes and forms can be classified as natural or manufactured.
2. Chiaroscuro affects the arrangement of light and shadow.
3. Overlapping is when one object covers part of a second object and the first one appears to be closer to the viewer. Size is when large objects appear to be closer to the viewer than smaller objects. Placement is when objects that are placed low on the picture plane seem to be closer to the viewer than objects placed higher on the picture plane.

What Different Spaces, Shapes, and Forms Express

Shapes, forms, and spaces in art convey certain feelings. This is possible because you associate them with similar shapes, forms, and spaces in real life. When you see a certain shape or form in a work of art, you may think of an object from real life. Any feelings you have about that object will affect your feelings about the artistic work. Artists use this relationship between art and the environment to generate these feelings in the viewer.

◀ **FIGURE 5.29** This painting shows contrast between the static, solid form of the man and the active movement of the stems and thorns. This is a moment of tension. The viewer can imagine the pain that will occur when the blind botanist moves his hands to study the plant.

Ben Shahn. *The Blind Botanist.* 1954. Tempera on Masonite. 132 × 78.8 cm (52 × 31"). Wichita Museum of Art, Wichita, Kansas. The Roland P. Murdock Collection. © Estate of Ben Shahn/Licensed by VAGA, New York.

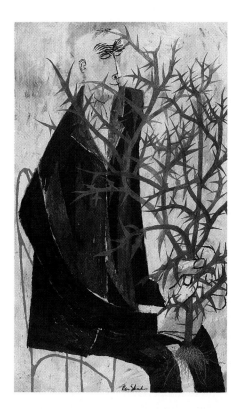

Outline and Surface

The outline of a shape and the surface of a form carry messages. Artists often use free-form shapes and forms to symbolize living things. When they want to please and soothe viewers, they use shapes and forms with smooth, curved outlines and surfaces **(Figure 5.28)**. Forms that remind us of well-worn river rocks or curled-up kittens tempt us to touch them. These forms are comfortable. They appeal to us through our memories of pleasant touching experiences.

Angular shapes with zigzag outlines and forms with pointed projections remind us of sharp, jagged things **(Figure 5.29)**. We remember the pain caused by broken glass and sharp knives. We would never carelessly grab a pointed, angular form. If we were to touch it at all, we would do so very carefully.

Geometric shapes suggest mechanical perfection. It is impossible to draw a perfect circle freehand. The special

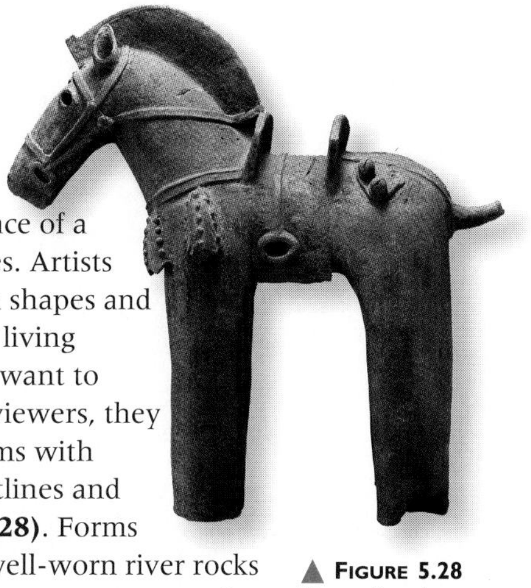

▲ **FIGURE 5.28** The artist who created this horse used rounded forms to make it appealing to look at and to touch.

Haniwa Horse. Japan, Kofun Period, A.D. 300–550. Earthenware. 66 × 71.8 × 22.9 cm (26 × 28¼ × 9"). The Minneapolis Institute of Arts, Minneapolis, Minnesota. The John R. Van Derlip Fund and Gift of anonymous St. Paul Friends.

CHAPTER 5
LESSON 5

What Different Spaces, Shapes, and Forms Express

(pages 117–121)
(National Standards: 2b, 3a)

FOCUS

Objectives

After completing this lesson, students will be able to:

- Identify the expressive qualities of shapes, forms, and spaces in a work of art.
- Explain the differences between static and active shapes.

Resources

T-5, Winslow Homer. *A Cool Pool, Saguenay River*

TEACH

Motivator

To help students learn to recognize the aesthetic qualities of shapes, forms, and space, challenge them with this exercise: Think of examples from their environment to illustrate the concepts of shapes, forms, and space. Ask them to think of smooth objects they like to touch and of sharp angular things that they have learned to handle carefully. Now ask them to look through prints to find examples of works that express each quality.

MORE ABOUT... Ben Shahn

Tell students that Ben Shahn, like many artists of his time, was employed through government programs during the Depression years. Between 1934 and 1938, he was commissioned under the Farm Security Administration to capture images of rural poverty with his paintings and photographs. After World War II, he turned to easel and poster painting, and then was a Charles Eliot Norton Professor of Poetry at Harvard University in 1956–1957, where he published several essays. He is also famous for his illustrations of books about Jewish culture.

▲ **FIGURE 5.30** The artist has transformed the free-form, soft human torso into a metallic, dense, geometric abstraction.

Constantin Brancusi. *Torso of a Young Man*. 1924. Polished bronze on stone and wood base. 45.7 × 27.9 × 17.8 cm (18 × 11 × 7"). Hirshhorn Museum and Sculpture Garden, Smithsonian Institution, Washington, D.C. Gift of Joseph H. Hirshhorn, 1966.

appeal of geometric shapes and forms has been felt throughout the ages. Their lines, contours, and surfaces are clean and crisp. This appeals to people's sense of order.

As used by modern artists, geometric shapes and forms express less feeling than other types. They are unemotional; in fact, they may express a total lack of feeling. Geometric forms in artworks appeal to viewers' minds rather than to their emotions **(Figure 5.30)**.

Density

The *density* or mass of an object refers to how compact it is. Dense materials are solid and heavy. Granite and lead, for example, are very dense. They are so solid and firm that you cannot make a dent on their surfaces when you press on them. Dense forms seem unyielding. They resist impact. For this reason, you may associate them with the idea of protection. In two-dimensional art, you can depict dense objects using shading techniques and hard-edge contours.

Soft, fluffy forms are less dense. When you press on them, you can make a dent. These forms have air inside them, and they look more comfortable than denser forms. In two-dimensional art, you can depict soft forms by using shad-ing techniques and curved contours.

Openness

An open shape or form appears invit-ing. It seems to say, "Come in." You can see into or through it. An armchair is an open form that invites you to sit **(Fig-ure 5.31)**. An open door invites you to enter. An empty cup invites you to fill it. Transparent objects, such as a glass wall, invite you to look inside. When you extend your hand to invite someone to join you, the form of your outstretched hand is an open form.

Open spaces in sculpture invite your

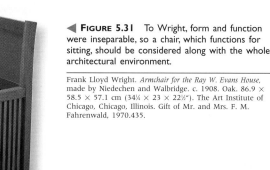

◀ **FIGURE 5.31** To Wright, form and function were inseparable, so a chair, which functions for sitting, should be considered along with the whole architectural environment.

Frank Lloyd Wright. *Armchair for the Ray W. Evans House,* made by Niedechen and Walbridge. c. 1908. Oak. 86.9 × 58.5 × 57.1 cm (34¼ × 23 × 22½"). The Art Institute of Chicago, Chicago, Illinois. Gift of Mr. and Mrs. F. M. Fahrenwald, 1970.435.

◀ **FIGURE 5.32** Notice how the artist has indicated the extreme feeling of isolation one experiences at the loss of a loved one. She has created this effect by using a closed form to represent the grieving person.

Marie Apel. *Grief.* 1940. Bronze. 51 × 17.8 × 15.2 cm (20 × 7 × 6"). National Museum of Women in the Arts, Washington, D.C. Gift of the artist's daughter.

eyes to wander through the work. Weavers leave openings in fabrics and hangings to let you see through them. If you remove an oak table from a room and replace it with a glass table, the room will seem less crowded. Architects use glass walls to open small spaces. Windows open up a building and bring in the outdoors.

Closed shapes and forms look solid and self-contained. Windowless buildings look forbidding. Closed doors keep people out; closed drapes and shades keep light out. When you make a tight fist, your hand is a closed form that seems to say, "Keep away." Folding your arms tightly to your body closes you off from others. Open arms invite people to come closer to you. The woman shown in **Figure 5.32** has wrapped her robes around herself, creating a closed form to repel any contact. She tells you that she wants to be alone without saying a word. Her body language says it all.

Activity and Stability

You have already learned about active and static lines. Shapes and forms, also, can look as if they are about to move or as if they are fixed in one place.

Art in Everyday Life

To foster students' awareness of expressive shapes in everyday life, suggest this: Look for ways in which cultures that do not have a written language express ideas in the shapes of visual images, ritual, music, and dance. Native American totem poles tell whole family histories in symbolic animal forms. Designs on African warriors' shields warn their enemies of their power. Hopi Kachinas are used to teach Hopi children the rich stories of their heritage. The geometric shapes of Navajo woven blankets have symbolic meaning. The Inuit (Eskimo) sculptor holds the chunk of soapstone to his or her ear to let the spirit in it speak, then carves away just enough to let the spirit out.

Promoting Discussion

Have available several architectural magazines or other magazines that feature house and garden designs. Ask students to work together in small groups and find examples of open and closed architectural and landscape designs. Instruct the groups to analyze the pros and cons of each design, paying particular attention to the practical needs of people who would use the building or landscape. If they find a design that is too open or too closed, encourage them to sketch a revision of the design, showing what specific features they would change in order to make the design more appealing.

MORE ABOUT... Frank Lloyd Wright

Frank Lloyd Wright (1867-1959), American architect, is considered one of the greatest contributors to twentieth-century architecture. His philosophy of "organic architecture" is established on the principle that a building should be built based entirely on its natural surroundings. Wright's architecture was developed after having considered all of the intended functions of the structure, its environment, and the materials which were used. The interiors of his buildings emphasized space, color, and texture.

In 1959, Wright completed the Solomon R. Guggenheim Museum in New York City. This curvilinear structure was one of Wright's most highly acclaimed accomplishments.

Art History

Remind students that artists are a product of the historical, cultural, and aesthetic contexts in which they live and work. By understanding more about these areas, students will have a greater understanding and appreciation for any particular artist's style.

Active shapes and forms seem to defy gravity. They slant diagonally, as if they are falling or running. In **Figure 5.33** notice how the back of the wave and all the horse forms are arranged in diagonal, active positions.

Static shapes and forms are motionless, or stable. Their direction is usually horizontal **(Figure 5.34)**. However, if two diagonal shapes or forms are balanced against each other, a static shape results. For instance, if an equilateral triangle rests on a horizontal base, the two diagonal edges balance each other.

Because static shapes and forms are firmly fixed in position, they evoke quiet and calm feelings. For instance, in landscape paintings the land forms are horizontal and the trees are vertical. They look very peaceful. This is probably why so many landscape paintings are chosen for people's homes.

▶ **FIGURE 5.33** The diagonal push of the back of the wave creates an unstable, active feeling. The wave is caught at the moment before it will collapse.

Anna Hyatt Huntington. *Riders to the Sea.* 1912. Bronze. 47 × 61 × 53 cm (18½ × 24 × 21"). The Newark Museum, Newark, New Jersey. Gift of the estate of Mrs. Florence P. Eagleton, 1954.

MEETING INDIVIDUAL NEEDS

Learning Styles The difference between shape and form can be hard to remember. Shape is most commonly defined as, "an area clearly set off by one or more of the other five elements of art." Shape is limited to two dimensions: length and width. Tell students they can think of shape as the outline of an object—what you would trace if you drew a line around it. The two classifications of shape—geometric and organic—can be differentiated and remembered by pointing out that the root of the word "organic" is organ. Our organs—heart, liver, kidney—have curved outlines. Most students will recognize the term "kidney-shaped pool" and will know what a kidney bean looks like. Ask them to suggest other organic shapes from nature (a flower petal, a raindrop, a puddle).

Computer Option. Choose the Shape and Line tool to make a design that creates a static feeling. The Line tool on most applications can be constrained to draw straight horizontal, vertical, or diagonal lines by holding down the shift key while drawing with the mouse. Title and Save the black line static design. Select a color scheme. Pick the Bucket tool to fill the spaces with solid colors. Use the Save As command to Retitle the work by adding a number or letter after the original title. Open the original line design. Apply the same color scheme but explore the tools and menus, which create active flowing edges. Use the Save As command to retitle the active composition.

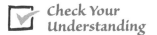
Check Your Understanding

1. What do angular shapes suggest?
2. What do geometric shapes suggest?
3. Define density.
4. List one example each of an open shape or form and a closed shape or form.

ASSESS..........
Self-Assessment
Have students complete the review questions on this page. Answers are provided below.

Reteaching
Have students work in pairs or small groups to find examples of artworks that have active and static shapes and forms in other chapters of the text. Have them make a list that is divided into two columns, one for *active* and the other for *static*. Challenge them to find as many examples as possible in a specific length of time, such as fifteen minutes. Then ask each group to identify their examples and the category where each is placed. A volunteer student could write the figure numbers or titles on the board. Review the list to see how many examples were repeated in the same category. Look for any that were listed in both categories. Choose one or more of these examples to discuss more closely with the entire class.

CLOSE............
Ask students to find an example of an artwork that represents active shapes and static shapes.

▲ **FIGURE 5.34** The strong horizontal shape of the orange wheat at the base of the work creates a calm, stable effect.

Jane Wilson. *Winter Wheat*. 1991. Oil on linen. 101.6 × 127 cm (40 × 50"). Photo courtesy of DC Moore Gallery, New York, New York. Private Collection.

LESSON 5   *What Different Spaces, Shapes, and Forms Express*   **121**

Answers to Check Your Understanding

1. Angular shapes suggest sharp, jagged forms.
2. Geometric shapes suggest mechanical perfection.
3. The density or mass of an object refers to how compact it is.
4. An open shape or form appears inviting. An armchair is an open form that invites you to sit. Closed shapes and forms look solid and self-contained. A tight fist is an example of a closed form.

Drawing an Outdoor Scene

(National Standards: 1a, 1b, 2b, 2c, 3b)

FOCUS...........
Objectives

After completing this lesson, students will be able to:

■ Draw an outdoor scene that creates the illusion of three-dimensional depth.

■ Use shading techniques to create three-dimensional depth.

TEACH..........
Motivator

If possible, take the students on a field trip to a city, state, or national park for a day of drawing. Otherwise, a trip outside or a travel video might provide inspiration. Encourage students to see the values, forms, and composition of the landscape.

Studio Skills

To help students understand the value of the viewing frame, instruct them to be sure that the shape and proportions of the viewing frame are the same as that of the paper they are using.

Art History

Discuss the works of Georges Seurat, particularly his use and invention of pointillism as a method of creating the illusion of solid form and structure in compositions. Ask students to compare Seurat's style to Larry Smith's use of stippling to create shadows in his landscape. Other artists who worked with landscapes to consider for discussion might include photographer Ansel Adams, painter Thomas Eakins, and painter Andrew Wyeth.

Drawing an Outdoor Scene

▲ **FIGURE 5.35**

Larry Smith. *North Georgia Waterfall*. 1993. Pen and ink on paper. 66 × 61 cm (26 × 24″). Collection of the artist.

SUPPLIES

■ **Sketchbook**
■ **Large sheet of white drawing paper**
■ **Drawing board and tape**
■ **Pencils and erasers**
■ **Viewing frame**

L arry Smith is an artist in love with the land. Born and raised in Georgia, he has committed his professional life to capturing its majestic scenery on paper **(Figure 5.35)**.

Smith uses a realistic style to create his artwork. Regionalists such as Winslow Homer (Figures 3.8 and 3.9 on page 46), and Edward Hopper (Figure 4.16 on page 77) inspired him to preserve the historical significance of a building, a landscape, or an environmental treasure. Smith likes to use pencil, colored pencils, or pen and ink to draw the scenes that represent his local environment. He is concerned with capturing light, and in this landscape he has used stippling for the shadows and has left the white of the paper to represent the white froth of the foaming falls.

Observe the different ways in which Larry Smith has created three-dimensional forms and depth in his landscape. Watch how your drawing springs to life when you use shading to create three-dimensional forms and perspective techniques to show deep space.

What You Will Learn

Make a drawing of an outdoor scene that is interesting to you. This scene should have a foreground, middle ground, and background. Create the illusion of three-dimensional forms in the scene by using a variety of shading techniques. Use values that range from black to various grays to white. Create the illusion of deep, three-dimensional space by using one or more perspective techniques. Mount or mat the finished work for display.

COOPERATIVE LEARNING

Landscape Art Remind students that landscape art, such as the example in Figure 5.35 is common to all cultures. To encourage an appreciation for the diversity of styles of landscape art, divide students into small groups and ask them to browse through art books with reproductions of landscapes from various countries. Instruct each group to find at least five examples that represent different cultural groups. They should consider whether each artist tried to create a mirror of the natural world, or tried to evoke a sense of the landscape without copying it. Allow time for each group to share its examples with the class and discuss the styles.

Creating

Larry Smith chooses scenes from his local environment to record for others to enjoy. Find an outdoor scene that is important to you and that you think is important enough to record for the future. Think of the view from your window, a country or park scene, or a view of boats in a harbor. Do not use a photograph or another drawing.

Step 1 Make a viewing frame and use it to help select the exact view you wish to draw. (See Technique Tip on page 431 in the Handbook.) Be sure to include a large shape in the foreground. All parts of the large shape do not have to fit in the picture. Each shape and form will have the same relationship to the edges of the paper as it does to the edges of the frame. Make rough sketches of the scene in your sketchbook.

Step 2 Now look through the frame at the objects in the scene and write notes in your sketchbook about how they are arranged. Pay attention to overlapping, placement, size differences, details, values, and receding parallel lines.

Step 3 Tape your paper to the drawing board and lightly draw in the shapes, paying careful attention to the placement of the major objects on the page. Shade the shapes using a value scale that includes black, white, and all the grays in between. Use a variety of shading techniques to create the illusion of flat and rounded three-dimensional forms.

Step 4 Give your work a title that expresses the mood or meaning of the work. Mount or mat your work for display.

EVALUATING YOUR WORK

▶ **DESCRIBE** What scene did you choose as the subject of your drawing? Tell why you selected this scene. How did the use of the viewing frame affect your work? How did you prepare the work for display?

▶ **ANALYZE** Which shading techniques did you use to create three-dimensional forms? Which perspective techniques did you use to create the illusion of depth?

▶ **INTERPRET** What kind of a feeling does this drawing express? Does the title you chose express the mood or meaning of the work?

▶ **JUDGE** Which aesthetic theory would you use to judge your work? Do you think the work was successful? What would you change to improve it?

▲ **Figure 5.35A** Student work.

Developing Perceptual Skills

To reinforce the concept of perspective for students who are having difficulty, instruct them to draw three or four geometric and organic shapes on white drawing paper. Then show them how to draw converging lines to a vanishing point. Remind them to overlap shapes and forms to create the illusion of depth.

ASSESS...........
Keeping a Portfolio

Remind students that the preliminary sketches and the final artwork for this Studio Project are likely candidates for their portfolios.

Self-Assessment

Have students apply the steps of art criticism to their own artwork using the "Evaluating Your Work" questions on this page. In addition, ask the following: What interested you most about the scene that you chose? How did you incorporate that interest in your scene? Did you use a variety of values ranging from black to white? How does the composition of your piece effect the mood of your drawing? Did the use of a viewing frame improve your ability to concentrate and draw better?

Extension

Divide students into small groups and have one volunteer bring an apple or pear to class. Direct them to eat the fruit but leave the core intact. Instruct the small groups to draw the core by using the shading techniques used in this chapter.

TECHNOLOGY OPTION

Computer Tell students that they can adapt this lesson to the computer. If students have Powerbooks with an art application, they can go outside with the computer to draw. If not, then students can use the viewfinder to focus their composition and to make careful sketches noting details and textures. When they return to the classroom, they can refer to the sketches as they draw an outdoor scene on the computer. If using a light pen and drawing table, students can vary lines by applying more or less pressure. They can also choose from paper surfaces and tools to enhance textures they recreate.

CLOSE............

Give each student a chance to show his or her artwork to the class and explain how the illusion of three-dimensional depth was created.

Studio Project

Clay Plaque with High Relief

(National Standards: 1a, 1b, 2b, 2c, 3b)

FOCUS...........

Objectives

After completing this lesson, students will be able to:

■ Use high and low relief to create a clay plaque.

■ Create a clay plaque depicting a current event.

TEACH.........

Motivator

Ask students to suggest contemporary issues and events. Event topics could relate to current studies in social studies or they could be drawn from world, national, state, local, or family history. Discuss why artists might be inspired to create artworks based on contemporary issues and events.

Art History

Remind students that there is little information on the past of the African nations because of the absence of a written history. However, students may be interested in studying the influences by the people of Africa on colonial Europeans. Likewise, students may also enjoy learning about various artists, such as Picasso and Matisse, who were influenced by African art.

Critical Thinking

Encourage students to choose background patterns that reflect the culture or period represented by the figures they chose. Ask volunteers to describe their methods of deciding how a visual pattern represents a culture or period.

Studio Project

Clay Plaque with High Relief

▲ **FIGURE 5.36**

Warrior Chief, Warriors, and Attendants. Plaque. Nigeria, Edo. Court of Benin. Sixteenth to seventeenth centuries. Brass. Height 48 cm (18⅞"). The Metropolitan Museum of Art, New York, New York. Gift of Mr. and Mrs. Klaus G. Perls, 1990.

SUPPLIES

■ **Sketchbook and pencil**
■ **Clay**
■ **Clay tools and equipment**
■ **Newspaper and scissors**
■ **Slip and brush**
■ **Large plastic bag**
■ **Kiln**
■ **Glaze or acrylic paints and brushes (optional)**

124   CHAPTER 5   Shape, Form, and Space

The Brass plaque shown in **Figure 5.36** was one of many that decorated the walls of the palace of the Oba, the divine ruler of the Benin kingdom (now the capital of Nigeria's Bendel state). *Warrior Chief, Warriors, and Attendants* depicts ceremonies and rituals that were carried out in the court. In fact, because the plaques so accurately documented the costumes, ornaments, hairstyles, weapons, and musical instruments employed in these ceremonies, they were often used in later centuries to answer questions about court procedures.

The techniques of high and low relief, shown here, indicate a person's rank. Notice how the most important figure, located in the center of the plaque, is larger and in higher relief than the others. People of less importance are placed to the side and are shown smaller and in low relief. Many detailed objects are added to the surface and are used to fill the spaces in between.

What You Will Learn

In this studio project, you will create a clay plaque depicting an event from current events or history that you find interesting. You will use high and low relief to illustrate the scene. In the style of the Benin plaque, the most important person should be the largest and in the highest relief. Your finished work will demonstrate what can be learned about people by their relative sizes and the degrees of relief.

MORE ABOUT... The Benin Kingdom

The Benin kingdom exists today as a part of modern Nigeria's Bendel State, with Benin City serving as the capital of the state. It is located in the tropical rain forest of southern Nigeria on a sandy coastal plain west of the Niger River. The people are known as Edo, which is the name also given to their language. Outside of the city, people live as they have always lived—in small villages with an average population of four to five hundred people. The villagers are farmers who grow yams, timber, and rubber trees.

Creating

Do research sketching. Draw examples in your sketchbook of clothing, the setting, and the objects related to the event. Make detail sketches of the most important items. These do not have to be complete drawings. Think of them as visual note taking.

If you have not worked with clay, take time to become familiar with clay and the proper clay-joining techniques. (See Technique Tips on page 434 in the Handbook).

Step 1 Make a complete plan for your plaque in your sketchbook. First, sketch the figures using the Benin style of making the most important figure the largest. Then add objects and a natural setting, if necessary. Finally, plan the shape of the plaque.

Step 2 Draw a pattern for the shape of the plaque on a sheet of newspaper and cut it out. Roll out a slab of clay approximately ½ inch thick. Trace the shape of the plaque pattern onto the slab and cut the slab into the shape of the pattern.

Step 3 Model the figures and objects you have designed for the plaque. Add the figures and the objects to the plaque using scoring and slip. Notice how the Benin plaque has details added to the main figures as well as details that are carved and stippled into the work. Use clay tools to add details to your plaque.

Step 4 Punch holes into the slab for hanging the plaque. Make sure they are more than ½ inch from every edge of the slab. When the clay is bone dry, fire it in the kiln following your teacher's instructions.

EVALUATING YOUR WORK

▶ **DESCRIBE** What is the subject matter of your plaque? Describe the event and identify the people you have included. Did you use proper clay-modeling procedures? Did the clay stay joined, and did it come through the firing process successfully? Which option did you choose to finish the work?

▶ **ANALYZE** Did you follow the style of the Benin relief by making the most important figure larger and in higher relief than the others? What kind of a shape did you make the background slab? Did you fill the negative space with patterns?

▶ **INTERPRET** Can the viewer recognize the event by just looking at your work? What is the mood you were trying to convey? Have you caught the mood of the occasion?

▶ **JUDGE** Were the viewers able to understand the event you were illustrating? Which aesthetic theory would you use to judge this work?

▲ **FIGURE 5.36A** Student work.

The plaque shown in Figure 5.36 had decorated the walls of the palace of the Oba, the divine ruler of the Benin Kingdom. It is one of many rectangular plaques that depict the ceremonies and rituals that were carried out in the daily life of the court. The plaques were used as references when questions about court procedures came up. They were like an etiquette book for the rulers to consult.

ASSESS..........
Keeping a Portfolio

Remind students that the preliminary sketches and the final artwork for this Studio Project are likely candidates for their portfolios.

Self-Assessment

Have students apply the steps of art criticism to their own artwork using the "Evaluating Your Work" questions on this page. In addition, ask the following: How did you choose the subject matter for your plaque? Did you choose a theme close to your personal beliefs or something that you feel strongly about?

Extension

Ask students to research the culture and government of the Benin Kingdom. Have them compare and contrast the Benin Kingdom with another African kingdom that flourished at the same time. Students might also be interested in learning more about Oba Eweka II, who was crowned king after his father's death in 1914.

CLOSE............

Ask each student to write a brief paragraph in response to this prompt: Now that I have studied about shape, form, and space, I am aware that. . . .

MORE ABOUT... Lost Wax Method

In the lost wax process, an exact model of the object to be produced is made in wax. Skillful modeling and scratching enable the artist to make works with fine surface details. After modeling, wax extensions called sprues are added to provide space for the metal to flow into the mold and the gases to escape. The entire wax model is covered with a layer of fine clay, then further layers of increasingly coarse clay are added. The mold is heated. This fires the outer clay and melts the inner wax. When the wax is poured out it leaves an empty space that is filled by pouring in molten metal. After the metal hardens, the clay mold is broken, revealing a metal object identical to the original wax model.

Landscape Using Surreal Space

Landscape Using Surreal Space

(National Standards; 1a, 1b, 2b, 2c, 3b)

FOCUS...........

Objectives

After completing this lesson, students will be able to:

■ Create a surreal still life, landscape, or cityscape using positive and negative spaces.

TEACH..........

Motivator

Ask students to suggest phrases that represent contraries, such as "expect the unexpected," or "achieve the impossible." Likewise, discuss how Magritte could claim to make invisible things visible. Because this activity is challenging as a concept, you might try to push the initial discussions as far as your students' imaginations will go.

Cross-Curriculum: Language Arts

Some of Magritte's paintings could be referred to as a visual paradox. Instruct students to research the meaning of paradox as it relates to literature. Ask them to bring examples of literary paradoxes to class. Also instruct them to make up examples of their own visual paradox. Examples could include a light bulb bearing the weight of a human being or a fish swimming in the desert sand.

▲ **FIGURE 5.37**

René Magritte. *The Blank Signature.* 1965. Oil on canvas. 81 × 65 cm (32 × 25⅛"). National Gallery of Art, Washington, D.C. ©1998 Board of Trustees. Collection of Mr. and Mrs. Paul Mellon.

SUPPLIES

■ **Sketchbook and pencil**
■ **Sheet of tracing paper**
■ **Two large sheets of white paper**
■ **Yellow chalk and soap eraser**
■ **Oil pastels**

René Magritte was a Belgian Surrealist who loved to create visual puzzles. He began his career as a graphic artist, and by the time he was 40, he was able to give up commercial art and work full time as a painter.

While French Surrealists were exploring fantasy, psychology, and the subconscious mind to find subjects for their art, Magritte worked with ordinary images from the real world. His painting style was very realistic, and his ideas were powerful because the images he used were familiar and lifelike.

In the painting *The Blank Signature* **(Figure 5.37)**, Magritte was trying to find a way to express the visible and the invisible. He said, "Visible things can be invisible. When someone rides a horse in the forest, first you see her, then you don't, but you know that she is there . . . the rider hides the trees and the trees hide her."

What You Will Learn

Using oil pastels on white paper, you will create a surreal still life, landscape, or cityscape in which the positive shapes and negative spaces are interwoven into a reversal of the visible and invisible. As in Magritte's painting *The Blank Signature* (Figure 5.37), see if you can turn your painting into a visual puzzle.

Creating

Brainstorm with your classmates about ways that you can create Magritte's visible/invisible effect. Trees, a network of branches, or haystacks might divide the positive and negative in a landscape. Signposts, lampposts, or

---

MORE ABOUT...   Rene Magritte

Magritte did not like to talk about his work. Finding subjects to paint, and then titles for the finished pieces, was a game that was played by Magritte and the Brussel's Surrealists. His paintings can be interpreted differently by each person who sees them. Magritte felt that the image should speak for itself and the titles "protect" the paintings. The titles never explained the images. He said that the titles were an extra protection to discourage any attempt to reduce pure poetry to a trivial game. When he was asked what he painted and why, he would answer, "Life obliges me to do something, so I paint."

buildings with big windows can divide the space in a cityscape. Do not limit yourself to vertical and horizontal space divisions. Experiment with large leaves, telephones, a pattern of large and small TV screens, or abstract shapes.

Step 1 Design the realistic scene as a whole first. To make your scene work, choose a subject with which you are familiar. First, make rough sketches in your sketchbook and then organize them into a good composition on a sheet of white paper. Plan to use colors in the realistic scene that are different from and contrast with the color of the dividing scene.

Step 2 Place a sheet of tracing paper over the realistic composition. On the tracing paper, sketch the second drawing into which you will weave your first scene.

Step 3 Using yellow chalk, lightly copy your realistic scene onto the other large sheet of white paper. Then sketch the dividing drawing over the first using another light chalk color. Now decide which scene will be visible in each area. Use the soap eraser to remove the chalk lines that will be invisible.

Step 4 Apply color lightly until you have all the positive and negative areas worked out. Then apply the oil pastel color heavily, blending colors when necessary to build up layers of color.

Step 5 Give your work a title that helps viewers to understand your work. Mount or mat your work for display.

EVALUATING YOUR WORK

▶ **DESCRIBE** Explain how you have created a surreal scene by telling what realistic scene you chose for the subject matter. Then, explain what device you have used to divide the scene so that the visible and invisible are reversed.

▶ **ANALYZE** Explain how you managed to create a reversal of visible and invisible through your arrangement of positive and negative space. Describe how you used contrasting colors to help the viewer see the two different scenes.

▶ **INTERPRET** Describe the emotional effect you have achieved in your work. Does the title you gave your piece help the viewer understand your work?

▶ **JUDGE** Was your attempt to create a surreal space successful? Which aesthetic theory would you use to evaluate this work?

▲ **FIGURE 5.37A** Student work.

STUDIO PROJECT *Landscape Using Surreal Space* **127**

TECHNOLOGY
Studio Project

One-Point Perspective Drawing

(National Standards: 1a, 1b, 2a, 2b, 2c)

FOCUS...........
Objectives

After completing this lesson, students will be able to:

- Create a one-point linear perspective drawing of an interior space

- Apply other perspective techniques such as: shading and changes in size, detail, and color

TEACH..........
Motivator

Refer to the artworks found in the text that represent one-point perspective. These include Vermeer, Doris Lee, Botticelli, and Escher. Discuss how the use of angled lines that appear to meet at the vanishing point deceive the eye. Ask students to describe outdoor scenes where they have observed this phenomenon. (City street, farmer's field, streets lined with trees or telephone poles.)

Vocabulary

Have students write a definition of their understanding of the word *perspective*. Then have them research the meaning and the origins of the word. Help them distinguish between linear and atmospheric perspective. Challenge students to discover when and how artists began to apply these techniques to their paintings and the importance of painters from Florence: Leon Battista Alberti, Filippo Brunelleschi, Masaccio, Leonardo da Vinci, and Michaelangelo.

One-Point Perspective Drawing

▲ **Figure 5.38**

Jan Vermeer. *The Astronomer*. 1668. Oil on canvas. 51.5 × 45.5 cm (20¼ × 18"). The Louvre, Paris, France. Erich Lessing/Art Resource, New York.

SUPPLIES

- **Sketchbook**
- **Computer**
- **Draw or paint application**
- **Printer**

Jan Vermeer was a Dutch painter, best known for his paintings of dramatically–lit interior scenes. Vermeer used one-point linear perspective to organize the scene in *The Astronomer* **(Figure 5.38)**. If you trace the lines in and around the window, the lines of the chair, the edges of the books on the cabinet, and even the line at the top right edge of the cabinet, you will find that they all meet at one point—on the man's raised wrist. Vermeer pulls your eyes toward the hand on the globe rather than the man's head to indicate that what the astronomer studies is more important than the man himself.

What You Will Learn

You will create a one-point linear perspective drawing of an interior space. The space may be realistic, or you may create a fantasy interior scene. Incorporate as many other perspective techniques as you need. Begin by drawing guidelines. Then use these guidelines to place rectangular objects in the room using one-point perspective. Complete your drawing by adding details, color, and shading that include value changes from dark to white highlights.

Creating

Decide whether you will draw a vertical or horizontal interior. For a horizontal scene, change the view to Landscape under Page Setup in the File menu.

Curriculum Connection

Math Prior to the Renaissance, European artists during the Middle Ages painted symbolic religious images commissioned by the Church. There was no attempt to place people or objects in space using perspective techniques. By contrast, many of the Renaissance artists were engineers, architects, or skilled mathematicians. Several artists invented drawing and sighting tools to help them draw lines and angles of receding objects. Linear perspective is based on the fixed viewpoint of one eye and was planned mathematically to show how the eyes perceive depth. Alberti compared the picture plane to the "open window" in which artists see their subject.

Step 1 Select a tool, such as Line, from your menu to help you make guidelines. Place the eye level and vanishing point in the middle of the page. Make a dot with the Brush tool to represent this point. Begin by drawing the wall farthest from you. Make an open rectangle around the vanishing point to represent this wall.

Step 2 Draw four thin, straight, diagonal lines that start at the vanishing point and continue through each corner of the rectangle and proceed to the edge of the page. These lines will be the guidelines for the walls of your room and define its edges.

Step 3 Define the space by drawing windows or doorways on these walls. Start with a vertical line to represent the side of the door or window nearest you. From the top of the window or door line, draw a diagonal line that converges with the vanishing point to form the top edge. Form the bottom edge by drawing a second diagonal line that begins at the bottom corner of the window or door line and leads to the vanishing point. Now, determine the width of the opening and draw a second vertical line between the two angled lines.

Step 4 Make the interior space look interesting. Keep size relationships in mind as you place objects within the scene. Continue to use the vanishing point when you draw rectangular objects.

Step 5 When your drawing is complete, erase the vanishing point and any unnecessary lines or marks. Consider techniques to emphasize perspective. Consider the light source and apply color, shading, and shadows to enhance the sense of depth. Explore tools to change value. Print and display your final edition.

EVALUATING YOUR WORK

▶ **DESCRIBE** What kind of an interior view did you draw? Describe the objects you placed in the scene. Where did you place your eye level and vanishing point? Explain how you used the vanishing point to create the walls, windows, and objects in the room.

▶ **ANALYZE** Do all of the receding lines meet at your vanishing point? Do the sizes of the objects fit the room? What other perspective techniques did you use? What other drawing tools did you use to enhance the setting? Did you add color and shading?

▶ **INTERPRET** Describe the mood or feeling of your drawing. Create a descriptive title that sums up your ideas and feelings about the room.

▶ **JUDGE** Did you use perspective correctly? Are the objects in your scene the correct size? Have all the unnecessary marks and lines been erased? What, if anything, would you change to improve this drawing? Which of the three aesthetic theories would you use to judge your work?

▲ **FIGURE 5.38A** Student work.

MORE ABOUT... Distortion

Artists who are also talented in math have experimented with illusions created by using distorted grids. During the late 1650s, Dutch artist Samuel van Hoogstraten painted multiple views of one room inside a box. When viewed with one eye through a peephole in a box, a three-dimensional illusion was visible. This distortion is known as an "anamorphic" form. Artists Hans Holbein the Younger and Leonardo da Vinci also created anamorphic art forms by using cone-shaped grids. When cylindrical mirrors are placed on the grid, a realistic three-dimensional image magically appears.

Developing Skills

Ask students to draw a one-inch grid with a fine, black felt-tip pen on a sheet of acetate. This represents a sighting device that artist Albrecht Dürer used during the Renaissance to help him draw the lines and angles of foreshortening and objects as they appeared to change as they receded. Have students go outside or observe a campus scene outside a window. Have them select an object that can be viewed near as well as far away through the sighting device. Compare sizes of the close and distant objects and how the angles and direction of these objects appear to move as they are seen in the distance.

Studio Skills

Before students begin the drawing activity, ask them to find the Grids and Rulers option on their computer application to help guide lines. Ask students to practice making straight lines by holding down the Shift key to restrict lines as they draw. Have them discover whether their application allows them to reduce the size of the eraser in small areas or they can investigate other methods they can use to erase unnecessary lines. Hint: try the Zoom tool or command combined with the pencil tool as an eraser.

ASSESS..........
Keeping a Portfolio

Remind students that the preliminary sketches and the final artwork for this Studio Project are likely candidates for their portfolios.

Self-Assessment

Have students apply the steps of art criticism to their own artwork using the "Evaluating Your Work" questions on this page.

ART CRITICISM IN ACTION

(National Standards: 6a, 6b)

Critiquing the Work

▶ Describe

What do you see?

- After reading the credit line the students may still be confused. It is a temporary work of art. Some call it environmental art, others say that Christo and Jeanne-Claude are creating art that combines all the arts: painting, sculpture, architecture, and the crafts.

- A building called The Reichstag is wrapped with woven polypropylene fabric with an aluminum surface and polypropylene rope.

- The work is a form and it is a freestanding work.

▶ Analyze

How is this work organized?

- This work is a three-dimensional, freestanding sculpted form.

- There are many flat shapes created by the wrapping of the building. They are all geometric. There is a pentagon on the center of a side, rectangles on the sides, many trapezoids covering small areas near the roof of the building.

- The fabric has softened the look of the normally dense building material. It has made brick and stone look like a puffed pillow. The fabric has created a closed form. It looks as though no one could enter or leave the building.

- The vertical and horizontal lines created shapes that look static. The work takes up real space, it is not an illusion of space.

130

▲ **FIGURE 5.39**

Christo and Jeanne-Claude. *Wrapped Reichstag, Berlin, 1971–95.* © Christo 1995. Photograph: Wolfgang Volz.

MORE ABOUT... Christo

Christo's environmental art projects are unique for their scale, their temporary quality, and their interaction with the inhabited environment. *Valley Curtain at Grand Hogback. Rifle, Colorado* (1972) was a translucent orange curtain suspended for 28 hours between two slopes in the Rocky Mountains. The curtain, 1313 feet wide and 365 feet high, crossed a well-traveled highway. *Running Fence* (1976) was a nylon curtain 18 feet high and 24 miles long crossing farmlands, open country, highways, and small towns for a period of two weeks. In 1985 Christo wrapped the Pont Neuf in Paris with 440,000 square feet of gold fabric. The bridge, wrapped for two weeks, had to remain open to both cars and foot traffic.

1 DESCRIBE What do you see?

This work is probably different from anything you have seen before. It is classified as environmental art. This term refers to work done outdoors in both rural and urban settings.

- How big do you think it is? Look at the people to help you determine the size.
- What materials have been used to create this work?
- Is this work a shape or a form? Does it take up space?
- Is it a freestanding or relief work?

2 ANALYZE How is this work organized?

Before you study the organization of the shape, form, and space of this work, describe the lines that you see.

- Is the work two- or three-dimensional?
- Does it have any flat shapes? Are the shapes geometric or free-form? Describe them.
- Can you find changes in value? Describe them.
- Are the forms dense or soft? Open or closed? Active or static?
- What have the artists done with space?

3 INTERPRET What are the artists trying to communicate?

Use the clues you found during your Analysis to help you find a message in this unusual artwork.

- What are the artists communicating to you with this work?
- Why have they wrapped this specific building?
- What has the wrapping done to the forms under the wrapping?

4 JUDGE What do you think of the work?

- Now that you have evaluated this work of art, what do you think about it?
- Do you feel more comfortable with environmental art than before you saw this work?
- Is it a work of art? Why or why not? Use one or more of the theories of art explained in Chapter 2 to defend your decision.

Art Criticism in Action   **131**

MEET THE ARTIST

CHRISTO

Bulgarian, 1935–

Christo was born in Bulgaria in 1935. He studied art at the Fine Arts Academy in Sophia and worked with the Burian theater in Prague. In 1956, he took advantage of the Hungarian Revolution to escape to Paris where he met his future wife, Jeanne-Claude de Guillebon.

Christo's interest in wrapping objects such as bottles and bicycles in plastic, paper, and cord began as a form of social protest against bureaucratic red tape. Before long, he and Jeanne-Claude were wrapping larger objects as well. The planning for *Wrapped Reichstag* **(Figure 5.39)**, began in 1971. The actual wrapping was carried out in 1995 by 90 climbers and 120 installation workers. Two weeks from the day of *completion, the Wrapped Reichstag* was unwrapped. All of the materials were recycled.

▶ Interpret
What are the artists trying to communicate?

- Answers will vary. Some may talk about simplifying the environment. Some may think about hiding old things. Some may talk about bringing an old building into the future with the aluminum covered fabric simplifying the old building materials. Some may know the building and talk about covering up history, even go so far as to refer to hiding Hitler.
- Answers will vary.
- The wrapping has softened the look of the normally sharp edges of the building. It has hidden any decorative relief forms, steps, balconies, windows, arches, and doors. The wrapping has simplified the form of the building.

▶ Judge
What do you think of the work?

- Answers will vary. Insist that the student give a reason for his or her opinion.
- Answers will vary. Insist that the student give a reason for his or her opinion.
- Most students will choose the theory of formalism to defend their decision because this is about changing shapes and forms by adding new materials to an old structure. Some may use the theory of emotionalism because the fabric changes the expressive quality of the building.

Extension Activities

- Ask the students to research the history of the building, The Reichstag, and its relationship the history of Germany.

Time & Place   Twentieth Century

Christo and Jeanne-Claude worked on their project, *Wrapped Reichstag,* between 1971 and 1995. Other events of the time included:

Social Studies: In 1971 cigarette ads were banned from United States television and the twenty-sixth amendment to the Constitution granted 18-year-olds the right to vote.

Technology: The microprocessor became a reality in the mid-1970s, marking the beginning of the home computer revolution.

Social Studies: In 1995 Israeli prime minister, Yitzhak Rabin, was assassinated after attending a peace rally in Tel Aviv.

How Do Artists Use Geometry?

How Do Artists Use Geometry?

(National Standards: 6a, 6b)

Objectives

After completing this feature, students will be able to:

- Understand the presence of geometric shapes in artworks.
- Identify the geometric shapes used in Cézanne's painting.

Resources

📁 Artist's Profile 22, Paul Cézanne

Teaching the Connection

- Have students read the feature on this page.
- Ask volunteers to identify some common geometric shapes. *(Circle, square, oval, triangle, rectangle, hexagon, octagon.)* What are other examples of geometric shapes found in nature? *(Answers will vary.)* How do geometric shapes differ from organic shapes? *(Geometric shapes are precisely drawn, while organic shapes look free-form and natural.)*
- Tell students that Paul Cézanne (1839–1906) experimented with art styles and greatly influenced modern art. Although he began his career as an Impressionist, Cézanne went on to develop his own unique ideas. Unlike the Impressionists, Cézanne not only emphasized color and light in his paintings but also shapes.

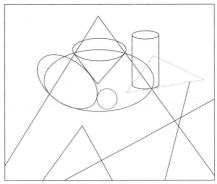

◀ **FIGURE 5.40**

Paul Cezánne. *Apples and Oranges*. Oil on canvas. 74 × 93 cm (29⅛ × 36⅝″). Museé d'Orsay, Paris, France.

I f you look carefully, you can see geometric shapes all around you. For example, the sun, moon, and planets are spherical in shape. Some evergreen trees are shaped like a cone. A shoe box is a rectangular solid and a soft drink is a cylinder. However, did you know that the first use of geometry was a practical one? The word itself comes from Greek words meaning "earth" and "measure." The concept of geometry was originally used by Egyptian surveyors in the fourteenth century B.C. Every year, the Nile River had severe flooding. People who lived close to the river often lost land when the flooding stopped. Surveyors used geometry to reestablish the boundaries of the fields near the river.

Yet people have also been creating geometrically–shaped objects for thousands of years. These shapes appear in ancient pottery, cave paintings, and buildings. The shape of the ancient Egyptian pyramids is an early example of a geometric shape used in architecture.

Over the years, the meaning of geometry has changed and expanded. In art, geometry is often a source of ideas for artists. In *Apples and Oranges* **(Figure 5.40),** Paul Cézanne painted many objects that have natural geometric shapes. In addition to these objects, the overall composition of the painting shows a geometric arrangement. As a result, the painting has a sense of completeness.

Making the Connection

1. Identify the geometric shapes that Cézanne used in this painting.
2. How did Cézanne create a sense of geometry in the overall composition of this work?
3. Why do you think Cézanne called works such as this "constructions after nature"?

132   **CHAPTER 5**   Shape, Form, and Space

Answers to Making the Connection

1. Circles, ovals, spheres, cones, cylinders, and triangles.
2. Cézanne positioned the objects in a triangular shape.
3. Cézanne arranged natural objects in a way that was clearly "constructed," or artificial.

Building Vocabulary

On a separate sheet of paper, write the term that best matches each definition given below.

1. A two-dimensional area that is defined in some way.
2. Precise shapes that can be described using mathematical formulas.
3. Irregular and uneven shapes.
4. Objects having three dimensions.
5. The element of art that refers to the emptiness or area between, around, above, below, or within objects.
6. Images in three dimensions created with a laser beam.
7. The arrangement of light and shadow.
8. Small areas of white used to show the very brightest spots.
9. A graphic system that creates the illusion of depth and volume on a two-dimensional surface.

Reviewing Art Facts

Answer the following questions using complete sentences.

1. Name the two basic types of shapes and tell which is more often used in decoration.
2. What is the difference between shapes and forms?
3. Name the two kinds of space found in art.
4. Using a portrait as an example, name the kind of space the subject occupies.
5. Explain how the eyes and brain enable us to see in three dimensions.
6. Explain how an artist creates the illusion of three-dimensional form on a two-dimensional surface.
7. Name the six devices for creating perspective.
8. Name two kinds of perspective.
9. Give an example of an active shape and tell what makes it look active.
10. Give an example of a static shape and tell what makes it look motionless, or stable.

Thinking Critically About Art

1. **Compare and contrast.** Look at *The Adoration of the Magi* by Sandro Botticelli (Figure 5.19, page 113) and *Thanksgiving* by Doris Lee (Figure 5.27, page 116). Evaluate the artists' use of forms and space. In what ways are these two styles similar? In what ways are they different? List your findings.
2. **Synthesize**. *The Kiss* (Figure 5.9, page 104) and *Torso of a Young Man* (Figure 5.30, page 118) are two of Brancusi's abstract works. Make a list of the similarities and differences between them. Do you think his style has changed over the years? Explain and defend the conclusions you reach in a few paragraphs.

Use Performing Arts Handbook page 417 to find out how dancer and choreographer Bella Lewitzky uses the elements of shape and form in dance to express her impressions of Henry Moore's art.

Many choices await you in activities such as virtual field trips, studio tours, collages and crafts, applied arts experiences, and gallery-hopping adventures. Visit us at: **www.glencoe.com/sec/art/students**

Answers to Building Vocabulary
1. shape
2. geometric shapes
3. free-form shapes
4. forms
5. space
6. holograms
7. chiaroscuro
8. highlights
9. perspective

Answers to Reviewing Art Facts

1. Geometric and free-form; geometric.
2. Forms have depth; shapes do not.
3. Positive and negative space.
4. Positive space.
5. The eyes see an object at slightly different angles. The brain causes these two separate and slightly different views to merge into one.
6. By using shading to show a change in value.
7. Overlapping, size, placement, detail, color, converging lines.
8. Atmospheric and linear.
9. Active shape would be one that had diagonal lines. It looks as if it is falling or rising.
10. A rectangle resting on a horizontal surface. Horizontal lines look stable and static.

Reteaching

■ Have students complete Concept Map 5 in the Reteaching booklet. 📁
■ Encourage students to experiment with materials and techniques to create shapes and forms.

Chapter 5 Review | **133**

ASSESSMENT ✔

Evaluate

■ Have students complete the *Chapter 5 Test* in the TCR. 📁
■ Alternative Assessment teaching strategies are provided in the *Testing Program and Alternative Assessment* booklet. 📁

Extension

Have students choose a manufactured object, such as a telephone, and research the history of its form. Then make a chart showing how and when the form changed over the years. Ask them to consider why these changes occurred. Other items they might choose are ships, TV sets, sewing machines, shoes, eyeglasses, and cars.

Color

(pages 134–169)

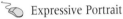
 While studying this chapter, use Performing Arts Handbook page 418 to help students discover how performing artists use the expressive qualities of color in their art form.

134

▲ **FIGURE 6.1** Delaunay wanted the subject of his paintings to be the relationship between colors and round shapes. Look closely at the artwork above. Can you find symbols that represent three objects from the beginning of the twentieth century?

Robert Delaunay. *Sun, Tower, Airplane.* 1913. Oil on canvas. 132 x 131 cm (52 × 51⅝"). Collection, Albright-Knox Art Gallery, Buffalo, New York. A Conger Goodyear Fund, 1964.

FEATURED ARTISTS

Richard Anuszkiewicz
Romare Bearden
Emily Carr
Mary Cassatt
Paul Cézanne

Marc Chagall
Margaret Courtney-Clark
Stuart Davis
Robert Delaunay
Fritz Glarner
Childe Hassam
Franz Marc

Henri Matisse
Claude Monet
Elizabeth Murray
Pablo Picasso
Jaune Quick-to-See Smith
Pat Steir
Rufino Tamayo

Color

Color surrounds us. A blue sky, a lavender sunset, a red brick building—all demand our attention. The expressive qualities of color are so powerful that they can create instant emotional reactions in people. Even the color of a room can affect the way people behave. Blue is thought to have soothing qualities, while red can excite or stimulate people.

In the painting *Sun, Tower, Airplane* **(Figure 6.1),** the artist is moving away from the dull colors of Cubism to a brightly–colored style known as Orphism. Orphism is a variation of Cubism named by the French poet and critic, Guillaume Apollinaire. He was referring to the poetic use of pure color and named the style after the legendary Greek poet, Orpheus.

In Figure 6.1, the artist has used bright colors and circular shapes to express the excitement and dynamic movement of the objects represented on the right side of the work. The circular shapes represent the universe and the bright colors express the movement of the light of the universe. Delaunay was interested in exploring the effects of color and light when they were not restricted within the shapes of objects.

Developing Your
PORTFOLIO
Collect a variety of objects that show different combinations of colors. Use magazine pages, fabric swatches, found objects, and the like. Write a paragraph describing what you think of the different color schemes and how you might use them in your own artwork. Keep the sample color schemes and your paragraph in your portfolio.

OBJECTIVES

After completing this chapter, you will be able to:

- Understand how your eyes see color.
- Name the properties of color and the colors of the spectrum.
- Identify different color schemes.
- Use color as the expressive element in creating two- and three-dimensional artworks.
- Recognize the expressive qualities of color that artists use to create meaning.

WORDS TO KNOW

color
color spectrum
hue
color wheel
tint
shade
intensity
complementary colors
monochromatic
analogous colors
pigments
binder
solvent
dyes

Chapter Overview

Ask students to think about ways that color can communicate a mood or feeling. Suggest they first think of their own favorite color and speculate about the reasons why they prefer it.

Examining the Artwork

Have students examine Figure 6.1. Explain to them that this is an abstract, not a nonobjective work. Point out that near the center of the top of the work is a simple design that is painted with four rectangular forms representing an early airplane called a biplane. The dark black and green lines represent the Eiffel Tower. Ask: "Where do you think the sun is?" (Most will say it is the swirling shapes on the left. Some may name the yellow and orange radiating area at the bottom of the tower.)

It is said that the right half of the painting looks like an actual, realistic photograph that was known to be in the artist's possession at the time this work was done. From the photograph, people have recognized the red and black curved shape on the right to be a Ferris wheel. Let students decide why they think Delaunay chose to use these colors.

National Standards

This chapter addresses the following National Standards for the Visual Arts:
1. (a, b)	**4.** (a, c)
2. (b, c)	**5.** (a, c)
3. (a, b, c)	**6.** (a, b)

135

DEVELOPING A PORTFOLIO

Self-Reflection A well-maintained art journal or sketchbook provides a permanent record of personal and creative growth. Students who routinely write about their work in a journal and use a sketchbook to practice designs have more insights into their progress. These impressions, responses, thoughts, and efforts provide students with a means of understanding how willing they are to be challenged as well as recognizing those areas that need improvement. A regular five-minute writing exercise at the beginning or the end of each class gives students the opportunity to reflect on changes and refinements of their artistic skills.

The Properties of Color

FOCUS...........
Objectives
After completing this lesson, students will be able to:
- Understand how their eyes see color.
- Name the properties of color and the colors of the spectrum.

Resources
📁 Application Activity 11, *Say It With Color*
📁 Artist's Profile 25, Mary Cassatt
📁 Cooperative Learning Activity 11, *Paint a Corrida*
📁 Concept Map 6
📁 Enrichment Activity 11, *Color as a Symbol and Identification*
📁 National Gallery of Art Bar Code Correlation

TEACH..........
Motivator
Direct students to list as many ways as they can think of that color impacts their daily lives. Encourage them to think about how color in their clothing choices can set a mood or make a first impression.

Cross-Curriculum: Science
Tell students that in 1665, Isaac Newton was grinding lenses for a telescope when he found that one of his lenses made blurred rims of color around the edge. He stopped working on lenses and began his study of color.

136

Color is the most expressive element of art. It shares a powerful connection with emotion. That relationship is why we hear people say, "I'm feeling blue," or "She was green with envy." The connection of color to emotion is also illustrated in a question we often ask friends—"What's your favorite color?" Almost everyone has a favorite color. It might remind us of a favorite childhood toy or a piece of clothing that we love to wear. Our appreciation of color affects many of the choices we make.

In this lesson you will learn what color is and how you see it. You will learn the properties of color. You will also learn how to mix colors to create shades you might use in your artwork.

How We See Color

Color is *an element of art that is derived from reflected light.* You see color because light waves are reflected from objects to your eyes **(Figure 6.2).** White light from the sun is actually a combination of all colors.

When light passes through a wedge-shaped glass, called a prism, the beam of white light is bent and separated into bands of color, called the **color spectrum.**

▲ **FIGURE 6.2** Chagall has used many different tints and shades of blue. He has also used a few other colors for emphasis. Identify some of the objects he has emphasized this way. As the light outside changes throughout the day, how do you think the artwork changes? What if the day were stormy or rainy? How do you think the artist planned for this?

Marc Chagall. *The American Windows.* 1977. Stained glass. The Art Institute of Chicago, Chicago, Illinois. Gift of the Auxiliary Board of The Art Institute of Chicago in memory of Richard J. Daley, 1977. 938

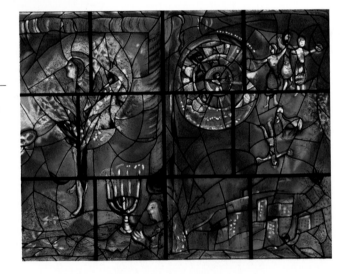

TECHNOLOGY OPTIONS

National Gallery of Art Videodisc Use the following images to show how color is used by artists.

Wassily Kandinsky
Improvisation 31 (Sea Battle)

Search Frame 2247

Piet Mondrian
Lozenge in Red, Yellow, and Blue

Search Frame 2255

Helen Frankenthaler
Wales

Search Frame 2329

Use Glencoe's *Correlation Bar Code Guide to the National Gallery of Art* to locate more artworks.

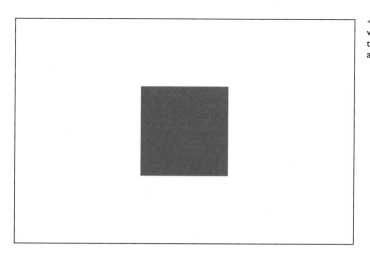

Developing Perceptual Skills

The most effective way to illustrate the relationship between light and color and to explain the spectrum is to use a prism. Science labs will have one if you do not. If you cannot take the students outside, you can use the strong light from a slide projector to demonstrate the spectral colors. Although you will not always get all six colors evenly spaced as they are shown on charts, you can play with the prism and turn it slowly to demonstrate how the color spread occurs.

Studio Skills

One exciting activity you can do with afterimage is to have students draw an American flag and paint it with its opposite colors: green for red, orange for blue, and black for white. Have students stare at the newly colored flag and then stare at a white wall or backdrop. They will see the true colors of the flag in the afterimage. As an alternative approach to the same activity, duplicate a drawing of a flag and have students color it.

Developing Perceptual Skills

Allow students to work in pairs to try this experiment about perception of colors. Students should hold a piece of red cellophane over one eye and a piece of green cellophane over the other eye while looking at a piece of white paper. Instruct them to remember what they see and to speculate about why they see it. Ask the partners to discuss the results and their speculations, then write a short explanation of the results. Encourage motivated students to research more about color perception.

The colors of the spectrum always appear in the same order: red, orange, yellow, green, blue, and violet.

A rainbow is a natural example of a spectrum. Rainbows occur when sunlight is bent by water, oil, or a glass prism. You can find rainbows in the sky after a storm, in the spray from a garden hose, or in a puddle of oil.

We see color because objects absorb some of these light waves and reflect others. A red apple looks red because it reflects red waves and absorbs the rest of the colors. Special color receptors in your eyes detect the color of the reflected light waves. Another type of receptor detects the lightness or darkness of the color. Colors don't change.

Your ability to distinguish between them does. That is why your eyes have trouble seeing colors in dim light. Not enough light is reflected off of objects for you to see their color.

When you are looking at colors, your eyes can sometimes fool you. For instance, stare at the bright red shape in **Figure 6.3** for 30 seconds; then quickly shift your gaze to the white area below it. Did you see a green shape on the white surface? This is called an *afterimage*. It occurs because the receptors in your eyes retain the visual stimulation even after it has ceased. Your brain creates the afterimage as a reaction to the color you stared at originally.

LESSON 1 *The Properties of Color* **137**

MORE ABOUT... Color

For many artists, color has been essential both to the experience of life and to the creation of art. This importance of color has led painters to discuss and write about the subject. During a trip to Tunisia, Paul Klee felt nearly overwhelmed by the intense light. He wrote, "Color has taken possession of me. No longer do I have to chase after it; I know that it has hold of me forever. That is the significance of this blessed moment. Color and I are one. I am a painter."

Aesthetics

Have students choose one hue, then look through magazines and cut out examples of all the variations of that hue they can find. Classify the colors into five groups: (1) pure hue, (2) dull tint, (3) dull shade, (4) bright tint, and (5) bright shade. Glue the examples to a small sheet of white paper and label each group.

Developing Perceptual Skills

Impress upon students that the facts about hue are extremely important. Students must know the primary hues and the order of the spectrum before they can control color. This information is as basic to working with color as simple addition is to mathematics.

Vocabulary

To strengthen students' familiarity and their usage of the terms associated with hue, have them work in pairs and prepare five flash cards on which they write one of the following terms: *hue, primary, secondary, intermediate,* and *color wheel.* On each of five other cards they should write the definition for each of the terms. Then let the partners use their cards to quiz each other on the definitions.

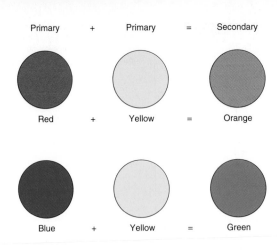

Primary + Primary = Secondary

Red + Yellow = Orange

Blue + Yellow = Green

Red + Blue = Violet

▲ **FIGURE 6.4** Primary and secondary hues.

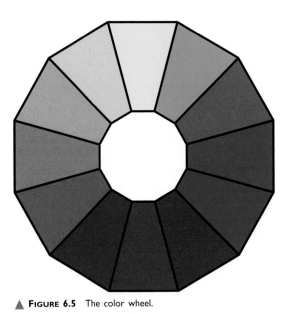

▲ **FIGURE 6.5** The color wheel.

The afterimage of a color is the opposite of that color. Green is the opposite of red. So the afterimage of green is the color red. The afterimage of black is white, and the afterimage of blue is orange. An afterimage isn't a strong color—it is only the ghost of a color. Some artists make use of the way your eyes work when they create optical illusions of color and movement.

Three properties of color work together to make the colors we see. These properties are *hue, value,* and *intensity.*

Hue

Hue is *the name of a color in the color spectrum,* such as red, blue, or yellow. Red, yellow, and blue are the *primary* hues. You cannot make primary hues by mixing other hues together. However, by combining the three primary colors and black and white, you can produce every other color.

The *secondary* hues are made by mixing two primary colors **(Figure 6.4).** Red and yellow make orange; red and blue make violet; and blue and yellow make green. Orange, violet, and green are the secondary hues.

The six *intermediate* colors are made by mixing a primary color with its secondary color. For example, red and orange make red-orange, red and violet make red-violet, blue and violet make blue-violet, and so on. You can make many additional variations by combining the intermediate colors.

A **color wheel** is *the spectrum bent into a circle.* It is a useful tool for organizing colors. The color wheel in **Figure 6.5** is a twelve-color wheel showing the three primary, three secondary, and six intermediate hues.

MEETING INDIVIDUAL NEEDS

Learning Disabled Because the walls of most art rooms are filled with the bright color of artworks, students with attention deficit dysfunction are sometimes overloaded with distractions. Nevertheless, teachers with students who suffer from this disorder can help them to focus on their work by following a few guidelines when arranging class space. Try to have these students face an orderly, uncluttered view, with minimal distracting bright colors. For example, organizing students' desks in a circular study arrangement can block out much of the distractions of other students' movements.

Activity Making a Color Wheel

Applying Your Skills. Design your own unique color wheel, showing the correct color relationships. Use only primary paint colors to mix the secondary and intermediate colors. The wheel does not have to be a circle; use your imagination. Plan a way to distinguish among primary, secondary, and intermediate colors.

Computer Option. Use the tools of your choice to design your own unique color wheel. Show the correct color relationships but explore enticing arrangements of the shapes and spaces. Be creative. Plan some way to indicate the differences among primary, secondary, and intermediate colors. The wheel does not have to be a circle; use your imagination. Plan a way to distinguish among primary, secondary, and intermediate colors. Choose and mix your colors carefully.

Value

Value is the art element that describes the darkness or lightness of a color. The amount of light a color reflects determines its color value. Not all hues of the spectrum have the same value. Yellow is the lightest hue because it reflects the most light. Violet is the darkest hue because it reflects the least light.

Black, white, and gray are *neutral colors* **(Figure 6.6).** When white light shines on a white object, the object reflects all of the color waves and does not absorb any. As a result, you see the color of all the light, which is white. A black object absorbs all of the color waves. Black reflects no light; black is the absence of light. Gray is impure white—it reflects an equal part of each color wave. The more light that gray

▲ **FIGURE 6.6** Neutral colors: black, gray, and white.

Making a Color Wheel

Applying Your Skills. This activity is a creative solution to a rather dull color-wheel exercise. There is no limit to the kinds of objects that the students can use for their wheels. An alternate activity for less creative students, which will help them memorize the order of the spectrum, is to make a picture of whatever they like using the colors of the spectrum in the correct order. The results can be anything from a scene with a rainbow in the sky to an eighteen-wheeler truck decorated with color stripes.

💻 **Computer Option.** Use the Brush, Pencil and/or Shape tools to design a manufactured, imaginary, or natural shape. This shape will be used to create a unique color wheel; therefore, the size should be somewhat small so that twelve copies of this shape can be used on a full page. When a satisfactory shape has been made, use the Lasso Selection tool to tightly select the object. Then choose the Copy command from the Edit menu to make a duplicate on the Clipboard. Use the Paste command to successively copy twelve editions of the shape. These shapes should be arranged without overlapping to form a continuous, but not necessarily a circular, design. Experiment with flipping and reversing some of the shapes. After achieving an interesting arrangement of both positive and negative space with the shapes, assign each shape the appropriate primary, secondary, and intermediate colors using the Bucket-fill tool.

CULTURAL DIVERSITY

Colors as Symbols From an encyclopedia or almanac that illustrates flags of the world, have students work in small groups to choose several colorful or unusual national flags. Have students research the origins and significance of the colors on each flag. Students might want to look further into the importance attached to the color in the nation's culture. For example, does the leader of the nation live in a building associated with a particular color, such as the White House. Encourage students to discuss their findings. Finally, have them work together to create a design and color scheme for a class flag.

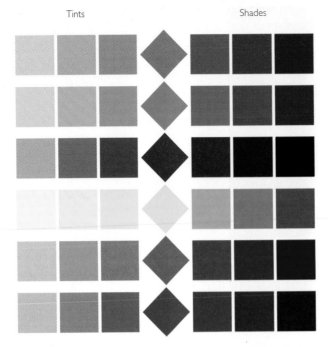

Tints   Shades

▲ **FIGURE 6.7** Color value scales.

reflects, the lighter it looks; the more it absorbs, the darker it looks.

You can change the value of any hue by adding black or white **(Figure 6.7).** *A light value of a hue is called a* **tint,** *and a dark value of a hue is called a* **shade.** The term *shade* is often used incorrectly to refer to both tints and shades. A tint is created by adding white; a shade is created by adding black.

When artists want to show a bright, sunny day, they use tints **(Figure 6.8).** Paintings having many tints are referred to as *high-key* paintings. Cassatt's *Margot in Blue* is an example of a high-key painting. *Low-key* paintings have shades,

◀ **FIGURE 6.8** Everything except Margot's eyes and hair are painted with tints of color. Even the shadow in the upper left corner of the picture has been softened with gray. The white highlights shimmer and create the effect of a sunny day.

Mary Cassatt. *Margot in Blue.* 1902. Pastel. 61 × 50 cm (24 × 19⅝″) The Walters Art Gallery, Baltimore Maryland.

or dark values, which are used when the artist wants to represent dark, gloomy days, nighttime, and dusk. Dark values can add a feeling of mystery to a work. They can also be used to create a sense of foreboding or danger **(Figure 6.9)**.

If the change in value is gradual, the design produces a calm feeling. If the values take large leaps up and down the scale, from almost white to almost black, the artwork has an active, even nervous, effect.

◄ **FIGURE 6.9** The dark values in this work enhance its ominous mood. Every hue in this work has been darkened with the addition of black except one. Which hue has not been changed? Why?

Rufino Tamayo. *Girl Attacked by a Strange Bird.* 1947. Oil on canvas. 177.8 × 127.3 cm (70 × 50¹/₈"). The Museum of Modern Art, New York, New York. Gift of Mr. and Mrs. Charles Zadok.

Art in Everyday Life

To foster students' awareness of the colors of the spectrum in everyday life, suggest this: You can find color wheels in everything. Look in the produce section of a market for a food color wheel. Find color wheels of flowers, cars, packaging, shoes, carpeting, even the sky. Color is everywhere! Watch it change as light changes. A lake can look inky blue, green, gray, or turquoise. Visit your local paint store and be amazed at the endless variations of each color. Look at an article of clothing or paint swatches in artificial light, with your sunglasses on, and then in sunlight. You'll be astonished! Color is reflected light. Even colors you mix will be different at different times of day and under different light conditions.

MORE ABOUT... Rufino Tamayo

Influenced by the great Pablo Picasso, Rufino Tamayo (1899–1991), Mexican artist, was famous for his ability to create color intensified paintings and murals. Tamayo's work can be characterized by vivid color and varied abstract and flattened figures. As a young artist, Tamayo worked for the National Archaeology Museum in Mexico City as head of the Department of Ethnographic Drawing. The experience with working with pre-Columbian artifacts gave Tamayo many ideas for the subject matter of his future artworks. His pieces were also inspired by the pride in his Native American heritage. Tamayo created numerous murals, paintings, and sculptures throughout his career. In 1981, the Rufino Tamayo Museum opened.

Creating Values

Applying Your Skills. Remind students that it takes just a drop of hue to turn white to a light value of the hue. The seven-step value scale in this activity is easier to make using opaque paints than with transparent watercolors. Some teachers prefer that students mix colors on the palette; others prefer that students mix paint on the paper until it looks just right.

Computer Option. Use the full page of the computer program or draw a large rectangle, circle, or square frame that covers most of the page. Select the Brush tool to draw a curved line that connects one side of the paper or frame to the other. Choose the Line tool. Draw a straight line from the curved line to one side of the page or frame. Draw a zigzag line. Draw a wavy line. Add a thick line. Draw a dotted line. Repeat one of the previous lines two more times. Draw one circle, two squares, and three triangles. Thicken some of the lines for contrast.

Add or repeat whatever is necessary to complete the composition. Now choose a monochromatic color scheme. Using the color palettes of the software program, choose the hue and at least one tint and one shade of the color. Flood-fill the individual spaces of the composition with alternating colors of the selected monochromatic color scheme.

If the program allows mixing white or black to the hue, students will be able to make more variations. Continue to fill all the spaces with a hue and its tints and shades until no white remains. Print.

Applying Your Skills. Select a hue. Draw a row of three equal shapes. If you are using an opaque paint, such as tempera, add only a small amount of the hue to white. Fill the first shape with the light value. Paint the second shape with the pure hue. Add a small amount of black to the hue to create a dark value, and paint this in the third shape.

If you are using a transparent watercolor paint, make a light value by thinning the paint with water to let more white paper show through. Make a hue darker by adding a small amount of black. Fill the three shapes as in the above directions.

Computer Option. Look at the color palette of your software program. Choose only the tints and shades of one hue to create a computer drawing of a simple cityscape or underwater scene. Colors do not have to be used realistically. Your software program will determine the number of tints and shades that you can use. If your software has the capabilities, mix your own tints and shades for use in this assignment.

Intensity

Intensity is *the brightness or dullness of a hue* **(Figure 6.10).** If a surface reflects only yellow light waves, for example, you see an intensely bright yellow. If a surface reflects other light waves, the color will appear duller. A pure or bright hue is called a *high-intensity color.* Dull hues are called *low-intensity colors.*

Complementary colors are *the colors opposite each other on the color wheel.* The complement, or opposite, of a hue absorbs all of the light waves that the hue reflects **(Figure 6.11).** Red and green are complements. Green absorbs red waves and reflects blue and yellow waves. (Blue and yellow waves combine to appear green.) Red absorbs blue and yellow waves and reflects red waves.

Mixing a hue with its complement dulls the hue, or lowers its intensity. The more complement you add to a hue, the duller the hue looks. Eventually, the hue will lose its own color quality and appear a neutral gray.

The hue used in the greatest amount in a mixture becomes dominant. For this reason, a mixture might look dull

▲ **FIGURE 6.10** Intensity scale. This scale shows how the intensity of one hue changes as you add its complement to it. The first box is pure, high-intensity green. Each time you add more red, the green becomes duller. Eventually the even mix of green and red creates an interesting, low-intensity gray.

MEETING INDIVIDUAL NEEDS

Learning Disabled Working with color intensities demands that students remember the order of the color wheel. They cannot remember opposites unless they remember what goes where. The colors of the spectrum are pure hues. Explaining the relationships of the complements to the three primaries clarifies the concept for students who have difficulty understanding these concepts. If you start with red, you have blue and yellow left. They combine to make green, and green is the opposite, or complement, of red. This works even with intermediate colors. The opposite of blue-green is the opposite of blue (orange), plus the opposite of green (red) or red-orange.

orange or dull blue, depending on the amount of color used. Orange and blue mixtures usually yield brownish results.

Hue, value, and intensity do not operate independently. They rely on one another to create all of the colors that you see around you. When you observe colors, you will see dull tints and bright tints, dull shades and bright shades, light hues and dark hues. Knowing the three properties of color helps you to understand and use color.

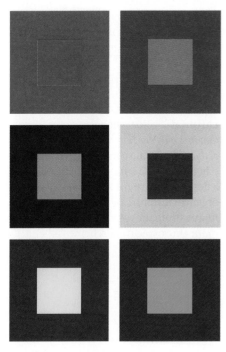

▲ **FIGURE 6.11** Sets of complements. The left column are sets of primary and secondary complements. The right column are sets of intermediate complements.

Activity | Working with Intensity

Applying Your Skills. Contrary to what you may have thought, tree trunks are not really brown. They reflect a variety of light and dark low-intensity grays. Draw seven or more bare trees on a large sheet of white paper. Use real trees as models, if possible; if not, find photographs. Combine varying amounts of one primary color and its complement as well as white and black to create a number of different, low-intensity light- and dark-valued colors. Then use these colors to paint each tree a different color.

Computer Option. Design a simple motif using only two solid colors. Use Copy and Paste options to make five copies of the motif. Fill each motif with one primary color or intermediate color and its complement. If your software has the capabilities, mix the two complements together to create a dull or low-intensity version of each. Label each set of complements and mixture sets.

 Check Your Understanding

1. What are the three properties of color?
2. Define *color wheel*. What does a color wheel show?
3. Describe the difference between tint and shade.
4. What happens when you mix a hue with its complement?

Activity

Working with Intensity
Applying Your Skills. This exercise works best with opaque colors, but it can also be done with transparent watercolors. Students must be careful to control the amount of water used so that the values are consistent. This activity is a creative application of low intensities. It does not need to be limited to trees.

ASSESS...........

Self-Assessment
Have students complete the review questions on this page. Answers are provided below.

Reteaching
Distribute Concept Map 6 to help students review the principles of the color wheel. 📁

Enrichment
■ Have students research the symbolic meanings people have given to various colors. What cultural factors, if any, influence these different meanings? Have them ask their English teacher how poets and writers use color in different ways and report to the class.

■ Ask students to explore how color is used in advertising. Have students choose a common, everyday product such as toothpaste, cereal, or detergent. Have them identify the color used most often and discuss why certain colors are used.

CLOSE............
Call on student volunteers to give one new fact they learned about the properties of color.

 Answers to Check Your Understanding

1. The three properties of color are hue, value, and intensity.
2. A color wheel is the color spectrum bent into a circle, used to organized color. It usually shows the three primary, three secondary, and six intermediate hues.
3. A tint is the light value of a hue created by adding white; a shade is the dark value of a hue created by adding black.
4. When you mix a hue with its complement, you lower the intensity of the hue, making it appear duller.

Color Schemes

Color Schemes

FOCUS............
(pages 144–149)
(National Standards: 2b, 3a)

Objectives
After completing this lesson, students will be able to:
- Identify different color schemes.
- Describe the effect created by different color schemes.

Supplies
- Colored construction paper
- Drawing paper
- Tempera paints
- Colored pencils
- Watercolor paints

Resources
📁 Cooperative Learning Activity 12, *Color Collage*
📁 Studio Lesson 6, *Through the Looking Circle*
📁 National Gallery of Art Bar Code Correlation

TEACH..........
Motivator
The value of understanding color schemes is in knowing how they may be used for specific purposes. Discuss the attributes of various color schemes. Ask students to analyze colors such as the colors they would like to use to decorate a room in their home and the colors they would choose for a car. What color scheme would they use to paint a battle scene, a scene of children playing, or an old couple sitting together on a park bench? Name a color scheme and let the students suggest a scene that would be effective painted in those colors.

Colors are like musical instruments. Each instrument has its own special sound. When you hear an instrument in an orchestra, the sound you hear is affected by the sounds of the other instruments. When the musicians tune up before a performance, you hear confusing, even unpleasant, noises. When they play together in an organized way, they can make beautiful sounds. In the same way, putting colors together without a plan can be confusing and unpleasant to your eyes. Color without organization can look like a visual argument. A plan for organizing colors is called a color scheme.

When two colors come into direct contact, their differences are more obvious. A yellow-green surrounded by a green looks even more yellow. A yellow-green surrounded by yellow, however, appears greener. Grayish-green will seem brighter when it is placed against a gray background. This effect is called simultaneous contrast **(Figure 6.12)**.

A color scheme is a plan for organizing colors according to their relationship on the color wheel. By following a color scheme, you can avoid putting together colors in a confusing or unpleasant way. The following are some of the most frequently used color schemes.

Monochromatic Colors

Monochrome means one color. A **monochromatic** color scheme is *a color scheme that uses only one hue and the tints and shades of that hue.* Because this is such a limited scheme, it has a strong, unifying effect on a design **(Figure 6.13)**. It is very easy to organize furniture or clothing using monochromatic colors. The drawback to a monochromatic color scheme is that it can be boring.

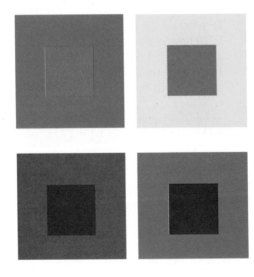

◀ **FIGURE 6.12** Your perception of any color is affected by the colors that surround it. This effect is called simultaneous contrast.

TECHNOLOGY OPTIONS

National Gallery of Art Videodisc Use the following to show how artists use color combinations.

Henri Rousseau	Marsden Hartley	Georges Braque	Mary Cassatt
Tropical Forest with Monkeys	*The Aero*	*Still Life: Le Jour*	*The Boating Party*
Search Frame 1588	Search Frame 2098	Search Frame 2173	Search Frame 2016

Use Glencoe's *National Gallery of Art Correlation Bar Code Guide* to locate more artworks.

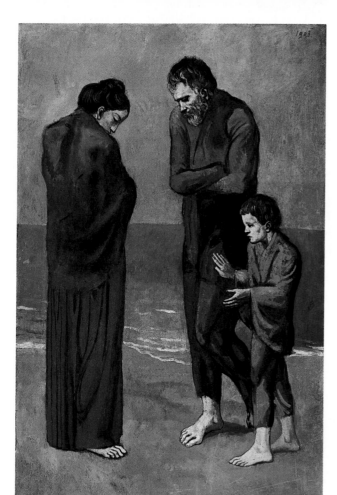

◄ FIGURE 6.13 The artist has captured the sad mood of these people by using a monochromatic blue color scheme. He has kept it interesting by using the full range of tints and shades from white to black. Where are the whitest areas? Where are the blackest areas? Look at the title. Does the painting evoke this feeling?

Pablo Picasso. *The Tragedy.* 1903. Oil on wood. 105 × 69 cm (41½ × 27⅛"). National Gallery of Art, Washington D.C. © 1998 Board of Trustees. Chester Dale Collection.

Vocabulary

Have students research both the Greek and French etymologies of the word *analogous*. What are the differences and similarities? Ask students to suggest other uses of the word in different fields. How does the word relate to similar words such as analog, analogue, and analogy? Ask them to give examples of analogies and explain the parallels between analogous statements and colors.

Aesthetics

Another activity that will help students see the effects of different color schemes would be to have each student find one reproduction in *ArtTalk* that fits one of the color schemes described in this section. Make a rough sketch of the reproduction and then color it using oil pastels in a different color scheme.

Developing Perceptual Skills

Ask students to design a new color scheme for a specific area of the school-hallways, classroom doors, cafeteria, health office, front office, and so on. Using scale model drawings of the selected areas, have students create new color and/or graphic schemes. When they are finished, have them give rationales for the way(s) the new scheme would effect students, faculty, staff, and visitors.

Analogous Colors

Analogous colors are *colors that sit side by side on the color wheel and have a common hue* **(Figure 6.14).** Violet, red-violet, red, red-orange, and orange all have red in common. A narrow color scheme would be limited to only three hues, such as violet, red-violet, and red. An analogous color scheme creates a design that ties one shape to the next through a common color (see Figure 13.34, on page 380).

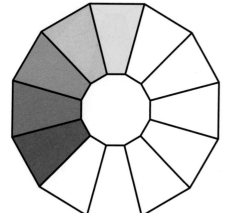

▲ FIGURE 6.14 Analogous colors are related.

COMPLEMENTARY COLORS Have students visit Glencoe's art site (www.glencoe.com/sec/art) and click on the activity: **Hooray for the Cyan, Black, and Yellow!** This activity features an experiment with complementary colors. Invite students to first read the caption, and then try the experiment by staring at the flag for thirty seconds. When students have successfully completed this experiment, ask them to describe what they see. Point out that this physiological phenomenon explains why using complementary colors together creates such intense pictures.

Studio Skills

Give each student a small square of the same piece of construction paper. Let each one take the square home and find a larger square of color on which to glue the small one. (You can dictate a specific size if you wish.) Encourage students to use different materials, such as construction paper, wrapping paper, fabric, paper towels, small pieces of wood, and leather for the larger square. When students bring the squares to class mounted on unique backgrounds, have them glue the squares onto a large sheet of poster board or cardboard. When the color collage is complete, ask them to write a few sentences describing unusual combinations within the collage. The purpose of this activity is to show students how changing a color scheme can change the look of a design.

Cooperative Learning

While discussing color schemes, bring in a chart of a permanent palette so students will recognize colors such as cadmium, cerulean, or manganese. Divide students into small groups and have each group research one manufactured permanent color. Have them find out what it is made of and how it is made.

Studio Skills

Direct students to make line drawings of landscapes, either real or imaginary. Make three photocopies of each student's drawing and have them color all three pictures, using a different set of complementary colors for each one. Then have students compare, contrast, and discuss their work.

Complementary Colors

The strongest contrast of a hue is produced by complementary colors. When a pair of high-intensity complements are placed side by side, they seem to vibrate. It is difficult to focus on the edge where the complements touch. Some artists use this visual vibration to create special effects. They make designs that sparkle, snap, and sizzle as if charged with electricity **(Figure 6.15)**.

Complementary color schemes are exciting. They are loud, and they demand to be noticed. They are frequently used to catch the viewer's attention. How many ways do people use the red-and-green color scheme? Where else have you seen complementary color schemes used to grab attention?

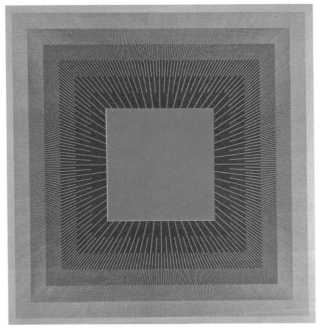

▲ **FIGURE 6.15** This painting is an experiment with the effects of high-intensity, complementary colors. The well-defined squares have been created by precise lines, evenly placed. Notice how the red ground changes color according to the density of the alternating blue and green lines. Stare at this painting. Do the afterimages affect your perception?

Richard Anuszkiewicz. *Iridescence.* 1965. Acrylic on canvas. 152.4 × 152.4 cm (60 × 60″). Albright-Knox Art Gallery, Buffalo, New York. Gift of Seymour H. Knox, 1966.

Not all color schemes based on complements are loud and demanding. If the hues are of low intensity, the contrast is not so harsh. Changing the values of the hues will also soften the effect of the design.

Color Triads

A color triad is composed of three colors spaced an equal distance apart on the color wheel. The contrast between triad colors is not as strong as that between complements. The primary triad is composed of red, yellow, and blue. The secondary triad contains orange, green, and violet **(Figure 6.16)**.

A high-intensity primary triad is very difficult to work with. The contrast between the three hues is so strong that they might make people uncomfortable. A triad can be made more comfortable to the viewer by changing the intensity or values **(Figure 6.17)**. A triad of secondary colors is less disturbing.

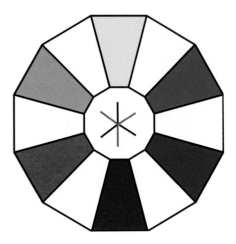

▲ **FIGURE 6.16** Color triads.

MORE ABOUT... **Endowment for the Arts**

During the Depression, the government established a program, called The Federal Arts Projects, to help artists. The program created jobs for artists in all the arts: theater, dance, music, and the visual arts. The artists were able to support themselves and their families on the $23 a week they were receiving. Many artists survived the Depression through this government support. Some of them were Ben Shahn, Alice Neel, Louise Nevelson, Mark Rothko, Stuart Davis, and Jackson Pollack. Some artists painted murals in post offices, some created drawings and paintings that recorded what the country looked like at that time, and some were employed as teachers in community art centers.

◄ **FIGURE 6.17** Even though this painting is based on the primary triad, it is very comfortable to view. What has the artist done with the colors to make this painting easy to look at?

Fritz Glarner. *Relational Painting #93.* 1962. Oil on canvas. 169.9 × 111.8 cm (66⅞ × 44"). Albright-Knox Art Gallery, Buffalo, New York. Gift of the Seymour H. Knox Foundation, Inc., 1966.

Art History

Have students select an artist that created his or her art prior to the twentieth century. Have them write a dialogue between that artist and Richard Anusz-kiewicz, whose painting appears in Figure 6.15 on page 146. The conversation should reveal what is different about life as an artist in the twentieth century and life as an artist in a past century. In particular, the dialogues should touch on such issues as patronage, lifestyles, society's attitudes toward artists, the media and techniques available to artists, and the goals artists bring to their works. If possible, have students work together on this exercise, then use their dialogues as the basis of a skit. Allow time for them to perform the skit for the class.

Aesthetics

Have students study *Relational Painting #93* in Figure 6.17. Then ask these questions: How does Fritz Glarner create interest in the painting by his use of the element of color? What sense, feeling, or mood does he communicate through his use of line? What message do you think he intends to convey? What roles do line, shape, and color play in conveying the painting's message?

Split Complements

A *split complement* is the combination of one hue plus the hues on each side of its complement **(Figure 6.18).** This is easier to work with than a straight complementary scheme because it offers more variety. For example, start with red-orange. Check the color wheel to find its complement, blue-green. The two hues next to blue-green are blue and green. Red-orange, blue, and green form a split-complementary color scheme.

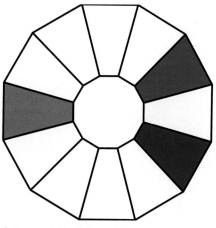

▲ **FIGURE 6.18** Split complement.

LESSON 2 *Color Schemes* | **147**

Want students to think creatively about color intensity? Suggest this: What colors do you like to wear? You can enjoy wearing all the colors of the color wheel, but not necessarily in full hue, intensity, and value. Use clothing catalogs to find a color wheel of clothes that you would like to wear. You might choose a maroon or a pink rather than flag red. Decide whether you like full intensity colors or neutral colors such as tans, browns, and muted greens. Pick light or dark colors. Cut out objects and glue them into a color wheel of your own variation. Then use tempera paint and try to mix the colors you like best.

Studio Skills

Have students select an object in the classroom with a single solid color, such as a wastebasket or a storage cabinet, and make three separate pencil sketches of it. With colored pencils or watercolors, have them select three hues from the color wheel and color one sketch a hue and its complementary colors. A second sketch should be another hue and its analogous colors. The final sketch should be the third hue and its split complement.

Ask students to exchange sketches among themselves and challenge them to identify the position on the color wheel of each of the hues used.

Warm and Cool Colors

Sometimes the colors are divided into two groups, called *warm* and *cool* **(Figure 6.19).** Warm colors are red, orange, and yellow. They are usually associated with warm things, such as sunshine or fire **(Figure 6.20).** Cool colors are blue, green, and violet. They are usually associated with cool things, such as ice, snow, water, or grass **(Figure 6.21).** Warm colors seem to move toward the viewer and cool colors seem to recede, or move away.

The amount of warmth or coolness is relative. Violet on a red background appears much cooler than violet alone. However, the same violet on a blue background seems much warmer than the violet alone.

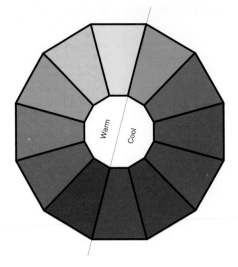

▲ **FIGURE 6.19** Warm and cool colors.

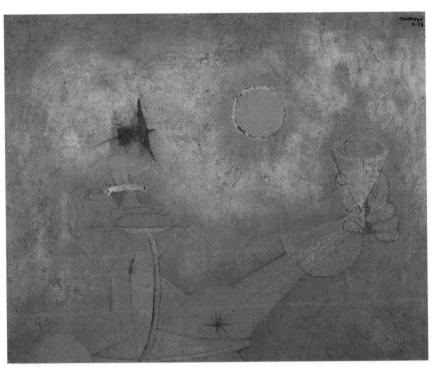

▲ **FIGURE 6.20** The warm colors in this painting tell us the mood the artist is trying to create.

Rufino Tamayo. *Toast to the Sun.* 1956. Oil on canvas. 80 × 99 cm (31½ × 39"). Wichita Art Museum, Wichita, Kansas. The Roland P. Murdock Collection.

MEETING INDIVIDUAL NEEDS

Physical Disabilities Students with neurological and orthopedic disabilities can be helped to control their movements when an activity calls for dipping brushes into paint. One way to do this is to have a holder for the paints, such as a soft drink container. Also, only a small amount of paint in each container will facilitate getting the right amount onto the brush. The holder for the jars of paints can be taped to the desk, as well as the container of rinse water. It may be helpful to enlarge the brush's handle with tape and/or to try taping the brush into the student's hand. Brushes can also be attached to forehead pointers or held in the mouth, depending on a student's capabilities and preferences.

Activity
Using Color Schemes

Applying Your Skills. In your sketchbook, draw several squares. Arrange your initials or the letters of your name in a design in one of the squares. The letters must touch the four edges of the square. Do several different designs using the remaining squares. Play with the letters—turn them upside down, twist them out of shape, make them fat, or overlap them. Consider the letters as shapes. They do not have to be readable.

When you find a design you like, reproduce it on four squares of white paper. Now paint each design using one of the following color schemes: monochromatic, analogous, complementary, triad, split-complementary, warm, or cool. How do the color arrangements affect the design?

Computer Option. Create a design with the initials or letters of your name. The letters must touch the four edges of the screen. Experiment with the letters—make them different sizes and turn them upside down or twist them out of shape. Try making them thin, fat, wide, or overlapping them. Consider the letters as shapes. They do not have to be readable. Use only solid colors and lines, since you will fill them with new colors as you progress through the assignment. You may use any tools or options available on your computer software.

When you find a design you like, save it. Use various tools to fill in all the shapes, lines, and spaces with each of the following color schemes: monochromatic, analogous, complementary, triad, split-complementary, warm, and cool.

Label and save each color scheme separately as you finish it. When you finish all the color schemes, evaluate their effect on the basic design.

▲ **FIGURE 6.21** The artist has used green in the blue sky and blue in the green foliage. What does this use of color accomplish? How does the color scheme affect the mood of the painting?

Emily Carr. *Above the Trees.* c. 1939. Oil on paper. 91.2 × 61 cm (36 × 24″). Vancouver Art Gallery, Vancouver, British Columbia, Canada.

✓ Check Your Understanding

1. Describe a monochromatic color scheme.
2. What types of colors, when placed side by side, seem to vibrate?
3. List two examples of a color triad.

Activity
Using Color Schemes

💻 **Computer Option.** Make a design with the initials or letters of your name. Begin by drawing one letter at a time. Use a Selection tool and experiment with some of the options on your software application. Vary the thickness and size of each letter and try overlapping. The letters do not need to be recognizable. Choose a geometric shape to frame the letters. Save the most satisfying design and title it "Basic Design." Now, begin to make multiple editions (seriations) of the chosen design by opening the original design and using the Bucket Flood-fill tool to colorize each copy. Use the Save As command to label and save each rendition. Represent the various color schemes. Print. Evaluate your results and choose your personal preferences.

ASSESS...........
Self-Assessment
Have students complete the review questions on this page. Answers are provided below.

Reteaching
Have students work in pairs or small groups to collect magazine pictures showing the use of complementary colors. Ask students to cut out the pictures they select, glue them onto construction paper, and label the complementary colors.

CLOSE.............
Ask students to identify one concept about color schemes that they understand better after completing this lesson.

✓ Answers to Check Your Understanding

1. A monochromatic color scheme uses only one hue and the tints and shades of that hue.
2. High-intensity complementary colors seem to vibrate when placed together.
3. A color triad is three colors spaced an equal distance apart on the color wheel, such as red, yellow, and blue or orange, green, and violet.

Understanding the Nature and Uses of Color

Understanding the Nature and Uses of Color

(pages 150–157)
(National Standards: 2b, 3a)

FOCUS...........

Objective

After completing this lesson, students will be able to:

■ Mix paints using different pigments and vehicles.

Supplies

■ Paints such as: acrylics, oils, water colors, gousche, casein, and temperas.

■ Other color media such as: food coloring, dyes, crayons, colored pencils, and pastels.

■ White glue

■ Earth pigments

■ Mortar and pestle

Resources

📁 Application Activity 12, *Sharpening Your Skills*

📁 Artist's Profile 22, Paul Cézanne

📁 Artist's Profile 23, Claude Monet

📁 Studio Lesson 7, *Three-Dimensional Sculpture*

📁 Studio Lesson 8, *Painting with Expressive Colors*

📁 Studio Lesson 9, *Painting One Scene with Two Moods*

TEACH..........

Motivator

Discuss natural pigments with the class. Have any of the students ever heard about natural sources for colors? Invite them to tell what they know.

150

Artists use color to create special effects in art. Not only do they use color to depict objects the way they actually look, but artists also use color to express ideas and emotions **(Figure 6.22).** As a child, you probably learned that adding too many colors together makes a muddy mess. The more you know about color, the easier it is to avoid making that mistake. By experimenting with color, you will learn what it can do and you will learn how to use it so that you achieve the results you want. Understanding the nature and uses of color allows you to express yourself artistically.

Paint

All paints used in art are made up of three basic ingredients: pigment, binder, and solvent. Artists' **pigments** are *finely–ground, colored powders that form paint when mixed with a binder.* Pigment colors cannot match the purity and intensity of the colors of light. The **binder** is *a material that holds together the grains of pigment* in a form that can be spread over some surface. Linseed oil is the binder for oil paints. Wax is used for encaustic paint, gum arabic for watercolor paints, and acrylic polymer for acrylic paints. A chemical emulsion is used to make school tempera paint. Many professional artists use a traditional method of mixing pure pigments with egg yolk for a translucent tempera paint. These binders each give different qualities to the paint.

The **solvent** is *the liquid that controls the thickness or the thinness of the paint.* Turpentine is the solvent for oil paints.

Water is the solvent for watercolors and tempera. Water or acrylic medium is the solvent for wet acrylic paints, but once acrylic paint dries, it is waterproof.

Paint pigments do not dissolve—they remain suspended in the binder. When applied to a surface, the pigments stay on top of the surface and dry there. *Pigments that dissolve in liquid* are called **dyes.** Dyes do not remain on the surface as paints do. Dyes sink into the fabric to which they are applied and color the fabric by staining it.

The pigment, the binder, the solvent, and the surface to which the paint is applied all affect the color you see. Wet colors look brighter and darker than dry ones. Tempera and watercolor paints look lighter and duller after they dry. Oil paints glow even when dry because of their oil binder. If diluted with turpentine, oil paints dry to a dull finish.

The density and color of the surface receiving the paint affects the way the light waves will be reflected back to your eyes. Have you ever applied wax crayon to colored paper? The crayon lets light through to the paper, and the colored paper absorbs some of these light waves and reflects the rest. Only white paper allows the true color of the crayon to show, because it reflects all the light.

Have you ever tried to match colors that are on two different surfaces? A brown leather bag can never truly match a fuzzy brown sweater. A shiny green silk shirt will look brighter than green knit pants even if the same dye is used. Dense surfaces always look brighter because they reflect more light.

! SAFETY NOTE

Natural Dyes Natural dyes are not as safe to use in school as you might imagine. The dye material itself is safe, but many of the mordants are poisonous. Check all the directions carefully and check out the nature of the chemicals before you bring anything into your classroom. Also note that some of the author's experiments with natural coloring materials yielded some horrible aromas, so be careful before you boil them inside the school building. A safe mordant to use when making your own dye is iron. If you boil onion skins in an old iron kettle, the iron acts as a mordant.

MEET THE
ARTIST
ELIZABETH MURRAY

American, 1940–

Elizabeth Murray was born in Chicago in 1940. From an early age, she showed an interest in art that her parents encouraged. In elementary school she sold drawings of elephants, cowboys, and stagecoaches to her classmates for 25 cents apiece. This early success kept her interest in art alive.

A high school teacher recognized her talent and created a scholarship for her at the Art Institute of Chicago. Murray took classes in figure drawing, landscape painting, and traditional techniques. She walked through the exhibit halls of the Art Institute museum. Surrounded by masterpieces, she was inspired to become a painter.

In the 1960s, she was told that painting was dead. Everything that could be done had been done. Murray refused to listen and kept painting. Through her perseverance, she developed a style that combines painting with sculpture. Murray is now considered a master of the shaped canvas.

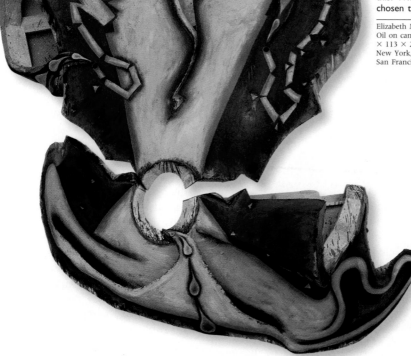

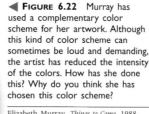

◄ **FIGURE 6.22** Murray has used a complementary color scheme for her artwork. Although this kind of color scheme can sometimes be loud and demanding, the artist has reduced the intensity of the colors. How has she done this? Why do you think she has chosen this color scheme?

Elizabeth Murray. *Things to Come.* 1988. Oil on canvas. 292 × 287 × 71 cm (115 × 113 × 27″). Paula Cooper Gallery, New York, New York. Private Collection, San Francisco, California.

Art History

Because pigments are now commercially produced, the contemporary artist does not have to be concerned with obtaining and preserving a supply of pigments. However, the history of pigments is vitally important to art historians who might need to rely on the presence and composition of specific pigments in an artwork when verifying authenticity. If possible, arrange for a guest speaker to present more information on the specialized training that an art historian receives about the history of pigments.

Developing Perceptual Skills

Present an assortment of different color media, such as acrylic paints, pastels, oil paints, watercolors, gouache, designer paints, casein paints, food coloring, dyes, crayons, colored pencils, and so on. Try to obtain each in the same color, if possible. Then, allow the students to experiment with the various media. If that is not possible, use the paints yourself on one surface and let them guess which paint made which mark.

Studio Skills

Tell students that prehistoric artists used their hands, fur, bark, twigs, moss, and leather to achieve various textures and colors when they used natural pigments. Discuss the advantages and disadvantages of a color palette that uses only earth pigments. Encourage students to make a sketch of an object. Then using only earth tones, color the sketch in a way that makes it interesting and aesthetically pleasing.

LESSON 3   *Understanding the Nature and Uses of Color*   **151**

TECHNIQUE TIP ✓

Using Dyes If you would like to dye something very simply, do the following: Boil onion skins in an enamel pot (do not use aluminum) until the water is strongly colored. Strain out the skins. Add about a teaspoon of alum to the mix to set the dye. (Alum can be found in a grocery store; it is used in making pickles and is safe.) Add white pure-wool yarn or white natural-cotton fabric to the solution and heat it gently. You cannot dye synthetic fabrics with natural dyes. The longer you leave the fibers in the solution, the stronger the color will be.

Sources of Pigment

In the past, pigments came from animals, vegetables, and minerals. A kind of beetle and the root of a certain plant were both sources for red pigment. Another plant produced a deep, transparent blue. Ultramarine blue was made by grinding a semiprecious stone. The color ocher was created by using natural clay colored by iron rust.

Today synthetic (artificially made) pigments have been developed by scientists. The synthetics are brighter and more permanent than natural pigments, but some artists still prefer to use natural colors **(Figure 6.23).** Many weavers color their yarns with natural dyes. Some contemporary painters use only natural earth pigments.

▲ **FIGURE 6.23** This Soninke woman is applying a paste of ground natural pigment and water to the mud wall. All the paints are made from materials found in the local environment. The scratch lines on the unpainted wall are the outlines for the paints that will be applied.

Photo from *African Canvas* by Margaret Courtney-Clarke. Rizzoli, 1990.

The Expressive Effects of Color

Artists use color in the language of art. They use color to express thoughts, ideas, and emotions. There are many ways to use color to convey feelings, and realistic representation is only one of them.

Optical Color

Sometimes artists reproduce colors as they see them. Until the late nineteenth century, this was the way most Western artists painted. Artists would try to capture color as it actually appeared. As we saw earlier in the chapter, colors can change depending on their surroundings. For example, in an automobile dealer's showroom, the color of a blue car is affected by the light, the color of the floor and the walls, and even the colors of the other cars. The car may sparkle as it reflects the showroom lights. Shadows on the car may look dark blue or blue-violet. The red from

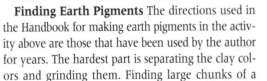

TEACHER TALK

Finding Earth Pigments The directions used in the Handbook for making earth pigments in the activity above are those that have been used by the author for years. The hardest part is separating the clay colors and grinding them. Finding large chunks of a single color simplifies the process. If you teach in the city and have no immediate access to earth pigments, you might be able to collect some different earth colors while on a vacation and bring them back to school to share with your students. Another way to obtain materials is to establish an exchange with teachers in other geographical areas.

the car next to it may cause a red-violet reflection on the blue surface.

A painter who is trying to show the car in its setting will use all the colors involved. He or she will make use of *optical color,* the color that results when a true color is affected by unusual lighting or its surroundings. Optical color is the color that people actually perceive. Compare the two paintings by Claude Monet in **Figures 6.24 and 6.25** to see how the time of day affects color.

The Impressionists were deeply involved with optical color and its relationship to light. They tried to express the sensation of light and atmosphere with their unique style of painting. They applied dots and dabs of colors from the spectrum. They did not mix black with any colors. They made gray, low-intensity colors by putting complements together instead of mixing just black and white. These low-intensity grays, such as dull blue and dull green, are much richer and

▲ **FIGURE 6.24** Monet was one of the first artists to take his paints and canvases outdoors. He realized that the colors of the scene changed as the time of day changed, so he carried several canvases. As the light changed, he moved on to another painting. What time of day was this painting done?

Claude Monet. *Poplars.* 1891. Oil on canvas. 100 × 65.2 cm (39½ × 25¹¹/₁₆″). Philadelphia Museum of Art, Philadelphia, Pennsylvania. Bequest of Anne Thomson as a memorial to her father, Frank Thomson, and her mother, Mary Elizabeth Clarke Thomson.

▲ **FIGURE 6.25** What time of day was this painting done? Compare it to Figure 6.24. What are the similarities and differences in the use of color?

Claude Monet. *The Four Trees.* 1891. Oil on canvas. 81.9 × 81.6 cm (32¼ × 32¹/₈″). The Metropolitan Museum of Art, New York, New York. Bequest of Mrs. H. O. Havemeyer, 1929. The H. O. Havemeyer Collection. (29.100.110)

Art History

To help students further appreciate the life and times of Claude Monet, whose work is shown in Figures 6.24 and 6.25, assign Artist's Profile 23 in the TCR. 🗂

Art History

Claude Monet's style is similar to that of his two friends, Pierre Auguste Renoir and Alfred Sisley. All three began experimenting together, making paintings outdoors in natural sunlight. At first their works were laughed at by critics. Today the works of these three artists are among the most admired in the history of art. Have students research other artworks by Monet, Renoir, and Sisley and find the similarities and differences between the artists' styles.

Cross-Curriculum: Language Arts

After students have studied Monet's paintings in Figures 6.24 and 6.25, ask them to select one painting and write a paragraph describing and analyzing its tone. Remind them that tone is associated with the feeling Monet has about the scene, how he conveys the feelings to the viewer, and how he encourages the viewer to respond with emotions to the scene. Encourage students to first make a list of adjectives for the colors and the forms in the painting. Then begin a paragraph using their lists of words and making specific references to the painting.

LESSON 3   *Understanding the Nature and Uses of Color* | **153**

Born on November 14, 1840 in Paris, France, Claude Monet is best known for his paintings of flowers, especially water lilies. However, he also painted trees, steam engines, churches, mountains, the sea, and people. Because he loved sunlight and was fascinated by the effect it had on the color of objects, he tried to capture a special moment in his paintings. He wanted his paintings to shine, sparkle, and come alive on the canvas. Monet, along with other artists such as Picasso, Renoir, Sisley, and Morisot, were called Impressionists by enraged critics, who viewed their style with contempt. However, Impressionism has had a lasting influence on the course of art history.

Art History

Inform students that Franz Marc, whose painting is shown in Figure 6.26, is remembered as one of the founders of Der Blaue Reiter along with Wassily Kandinsky and Alexei von Jawlensky. His passionate interest in the spiritual nature of animals is reflected in his work. Often he used symbolic colors that were not natural to the animals because he wanted to depict them not as we see them, but as they feel their own existence. His paintings became more abstract as he fell under the influence of the Cubists and Futurists at the beginning of World War I. Perhaps as a foreshadowing of the tragedy that would become the war, his last paintings portrayed a world on the edge of destruction. Marc's life and art were cut short when he died in action during the war.

Art in Everyday Life

To foster students' awareness of expressions of color in everyday life, suggest this: Poets use color in their poetry, sometimes to describe objects but also as metaphors of feelings, moods, or scenes. For example, Matthew Arnold wrote vivid descriptions of Dover Beach, England, at night. Look in Bartlett's Familiar Quotations for literary references to each color. You will find under red, for example, a reference to Percy Bysshe Shelley's "Ode to the West Wind." Find a copy of the poem and locate his description of autumn leaves. Write your own color metaphors.

look more natural in landscapes than do grays made by mixing black and white.

Arbitrary Color

When artists use color to express feelings, they usually ignore the optical colors of objects. They choose the colors *arbitrarily,* that is, by personal preference. They choose arbitrary colors rather than optical colors because they want to use color to express meaning **(Figure 6.26).** In abstract art, color is teamed with the other elements to become the subject as well as the meaning of the work (Figure 6.15 on page 146 and Figure 6.28 on page 156).

Colors affect feelings. Light, bright colors can create happy, upbeat moods.

Cool, dark colors can express mysterious or depressing themes. Warm, low-intensity earth tones seem comfortable and friendly. They are often used to decorate rooms in which people gather. A unique, light value of red-orange has been used to soothe people and has even been successful in calming violent prisoners. Blue is also known for its soothing qualities. Bright yellow is stimulating and pure red excites.

Artists today have put their knowledge of color psychology to work to develop unusual methods for using color. Many of their choices are personal—they make color say what they wish to express.

▲ **FIGURE 6.26** Marc developed his own personal scheme for the symbolic meaning of color. To him, blue represented the spiritual. Red represented matter, and in this work he used it to represent the land. Yellow conveyed comfort, and green served to set off red. The combination of the abstract, curved forms of the horses and the blue, spiritual color reveal Marc's philosophy that animals have a purer relationship with the earth than human beings do.

Franz Marc. *The Large Blue Horses.* 1911. Oil on canvas. 106 × 181 cm (41⅝ × 71¼″). Walker Art Center, Minneapolis, Minnesota. Gift of the T. B. Walker Foundation, Gilbert M. Walker Fund, 1942.

MEETING INDIVIDUAL NEEDS

Visually Impaired If you have students who are blind, rather than shy away from talking about color, be aware of the need for complete descriptions when talking about color. Instead of avoiding references to the subtleties of color, use creative and natural analogies, such as "a light delicate purple color like lilac flowers," or "reds, yellows, and oranges like the color in flames of fire." The age of the onset of blindness governs how many visual memories the person retains. Monet did his greatest paintings while experiencing yellowing of the cornea. El Greco is reported to have had an astigmatism, a condition that caused him to see and draw figures stretched out.

▲ **Figure 6.27** Look at the different objects on the table. Identify the number of colors used for each object. Notice how the artist has used dark blue lines to outline the fruit and make each piece stand out. Does this use of color make the objects seem real?

Paul Cézanne. *The Basket of Apples*. c. 1895. Oil on canvas. 65.5 × 81.3 cm (25¾ × 32″). The Art Institute of Chicago, Chicago, Illinois. Helen Birch Bartlett Memorial Collection. (1926.252)

Space

The placement of warm and cool colors can create illusions of depth. Warm colors advance toward the viewer, and cool colors seem to recede and pull away. The French artist Paul Cézanne was the first to use warm and cool colors to create depth. He painted a cool, blue outline around the shape of a warm, round orange. The fruit seemed to be pushed forward by the surrounding blue background **(Figure 6.27).**

Movement

Color can create a sense of movement. When the values in a work jump quickly from very high key to very low key, a feeling of excitement and movement is created **(Figure 6.28**, page 156). When all the values are close together, the work seems much calmer. Today's artists use color to create movement and depth in abstract art.

When you work with color to create movement, remember to use values of pure hues as well as those of tints and shades. You will need to remember, for instance, that the pure hue yellow is much lighter than red or blue.

Promoting Discussion

Give students this challenge: How many ways can they say this sentence, "I really want to go now"? Encourage them to use voice inflections and body language to accent their delivery. Now tell them that artists use color in order to achieve the same type of impact. Ask them to choose an artwork from the book and describe its use of color with voice inflections that mirror the impact of color on the viewer.

Art on a Shoestring

If your art program participates in a school or community art show, use the following idea to create inexpensive, handmade calendars to sell. Make photocopies of blank calendar pages or, if you have access to computers, print them using a computer program that has a selection of calendar forms. (Do not use any decorative additions either from the original that is photocopied or that are available on the computer program.) Have students use watercolors, tempera, or permanent markers to decorate the calendars in the style of a specific artist. For example, a Monet calendar could include Impressionistic scenes, even a few facts about the artist. Staple or bind the pages at the top. Encourage originality.

Teacher Notes

Looking Closely

Point out the unusual title, *Still Scape*. In this painting, Davis integrates still life (the interior of his studio) with cityscape (impressions of his exterior view of the city). The symbols for his exterior environment are contained within the slanting diamond shape that runs from upper left to lower right. The interior is represented by the one point perspective walls of his studio.

Activity

Using Color for Effect

Applying Your Skills. The purpose of these activities is to show how different uses of color arrangements can change the look of a painting. Encourage students to be creative with their designs.

💻 **Computer Option.** Use the Brush or Pencil tool to sketch a leaf or a tree. Try Brush Symmetry, if available. Either select the object and resize it to fill the page, or select it and make multiple overlapping copies to fill the page. Save and title as "Basic Design." Use the Bucket-fill tool. Choose from available colors and the Mixing, Blending, Transparent, and Gradient options to illustrate one of the following: true color, optical color, arbitrary color that expresses personal feelings, warm and cool colors to show depth, movement through value, and tonality. Use the Save As command to title the work. Open another copy of "Basic Design." Choose and create another edition using a different color scheme. Use the Save As command to title work. Complete three editions. Have students evaluate the results of this series of artworks.

LOOKING CLOSELY
Jumps in Color Value Create Visual Movement

This is one of Stuart Davis's first abstract works that celebrates his love for New York City. Davis has used strong jumps in value (from bright white, pale blue, and yellow to red, black, and orange) to make your eyes jump around the work. He wants you to feel the excitement and movement of the city. This diagram indicates some of the value jumps. Where can you find others?

◀ **FIGURE 6.28**

Stuart Davis. *Hot Still Scape for Six Colors–7th Avenue Style, 1940.* 1940. Oil on canvas. 91.4 × 114.3 cm (36 × 45″). Courtesy, The Museum of Fine Arts, Boston, Massachusetts. Gift of the William H. Lane Foundation and the M. and M. Karolik Collection, by exchange.

Go to the Glencoe art Web page (**www.glencoe.com/sec/art**) and click on the site for Stuart Davis. This site is part of a comprehensive art education and entertainment site called Artchive, produced by Mark Harden. Instruct students to examine three paintings, **Egg Beater #4, G&W,** and **Rapt at Rappaport's.** Ask students to find examples of complementary colors and analogous colors the artist used in these works.

Activity Using Color for Effect

Applying Your Skills. Create four small sketches of trees with leaves. Use a simple color medium such as crayon. Color each sketch to illustrate one of the following: true color; arbitrary color; tonality; optical color; depth through the use of warm and cool colors; or movement through value.

Computer Option. Using the tools of your choice, draw and label six sketches of trees or leaves. Let each sketch illustrate one of the following: true color; optical color; color that expresses personal feelings; depth through the use of warm and cool colors; movement through value; or tonality.

Evaluate the results of your work. Develop your favorite sketch into a finished drawing.

Tonality

Sometimes an artist lets one color, such as blue, dominate a work. In such a case, the work is said to have a blue *tonality* **(Figure 6.29)**. To have a certain tonality, the painting does not have to be monochrome. Other colors may be present. The overall effect of the work, however, will be of one color. Tonality has a unifying effect.

✓ Check Your Understanding

1. All paints are made up of what three basic ingredients?
2. What is the difference between paint pigments and dyes?
3. When might artists use optical color, and when might they use arbitrary color?

◀ **FIGURE 6.29** The blue tonality of this work conveys the cool impression of the water. The jellyfish are in the inlet and swimming close to the rocks. They are spots of contrast in the blue water. Although blue is the dominant color in this painting, other hues are used. What are they?

Childe Hassam. *Jelly Fish.* 1912. Oil on canvas. 51.4 × 61.6 cm (20¼ × 24¼"). Wichita Art Museum, Wichita, Kansas. The John W. and Mildred L. Graves Collection.

ASSESS...........

Self-Assessment
Have students complete the review questions on this page. Answers are provided below.

Reteaching
Working in small groups, allow students to select two paintings from this text. Ask: What idea or feeling do you think the painters of these artworks intended to communicate to viewers? Which painting medium did each artist use? How do you think that choice of medium affects the message of the painting?

Enrichment
Have students make a painting, collage, or mural design that focuses on major events in their lives. Instruct them to use color to indicate the emotional connection they have with each specific event.

CLOSE............
Have students recall the three properties of color.

✓ Answers to Check Your Understanding

1. Paints are made up of pigments, binders, and solvents.
2. Pigments do not dissolve. They stay suspended on the surface of the painting medium. Dyes are absorbed and color the medium by staining it.
3. Artists might use optical color to depict a realistic representation of an object. They might use arbitrary color to express an emotion or idea.

Studio Project

Photo Collage and Mixed Media

(pages 158–159)
(National Standards: 1a, 1b, 2b, 2c, 3b)

Photo Collage and Mixed Media

FOCUS...........

Objective

After completing this lesson, students will be able to:

■ Use cut-out shapes from black-and-white magazine and newspaper photographs to create a composition in the manner of Romare Bearden.

TEACH..........

Motivator

Bring to class examples of African masks so that students can see the relationship between the masks and the faces in the painting. Display the masks and discuss them before you begin this lesson.

Studio Skills

Provide students with magazines that are popular for their photography, such as *Life, National Geographic,* and *Vogue.* Fashion and sports magazines are great sources for facial and body parts. Avoid weekly news magazines unless you are doing current events. Students can also bring their own magazines from home. If a color photograph is desirable, use it.

▲ FIGURE 6.30

Romare Bearden. *Prevalence of Ritual: Baptism, The.* 1964. Photomechanical reproductions, synthetic polymer, and pencil on paperboard. 23.2 × 30.5 cm (9⅛ × 12″). Hirshhorn Museum and Sculpture Garden, Smithsonian Institution, Washington, D.C. Gift of Joseph H. Hirshhorn, 1966.

SUPPLIES

■ **Sketchbook and pencils**
■ **Magazines and newspapers**
■ **Envelope and scissors**
■ **6 × 9″ white paper**
■ **White glue, damp sponge, paper towels**
■ **Photocopy machine and paper**
■ **Crayons**
■ **Oil pastels**
■ **Colored pencils**
■ **Acrylic paints, gloss medium, and brushes**
■ **Felt-tip fine-line marker**

Romare Bearden's collage **(Figure 6.30)** seems deceptively simple. If you look closely, however, you will see an unusual mixture of media and color. Bearden's art was influenced by his experience as an African-American, but his goal was to create a universal art.

Figure 6.30 is one of Bearden's many collages. In this work, he combined many different pieces to complete the picture. To compose the figures and background, he used photographs of textiles, water, cloth, wood, leaves, grass, metal, and people. He made the faces by cutting details from pictures of African masks, marbles, animal eyes, and mossy vegetation. Then he enlarged his small, original works photographically. Finally, he added paint to complete the colorful collage.

What You Will Learn

In this project, you will create a composition in the style of Bearden. Choose a theme that interests you. Cut out objects and shapes from magazine and newspaper photographs. On a small background approximately 6 × 9 inches, arrange the shapes and recut them as necessary to create a composition similar to Bearden's. Using a photocopy machine, enlarge your work as much as possible. Paint your enlarged work with a color scheme that best expresses the theme of your work. Use any combination of the following: crayons, oil pastels, colored pencils, and school acrylics.

158 | **CHAPTER 6** Color

MORE ABOUT... Romare Bearden

In 1936, Bearden enrolled at the Art Students League in New York City. There he met and studied under the German Expressionist George Grosz. Because Bearden wanted to make a social statement about his African-American heritage, Grosz introduced him to the work of Daumier, Goya, and Kollwitz and led him to study composition through the analysis of Brueghel and the great Dutch masters. Grosz also pushed Bearden to refine his draftsmanship by studying the work of Ingres, Dürer, and Holbein. In 1938, Bearden left the Art Students League, but he continued to paint while working at the New York City Department of Social Services.

Creating

Study Bearden's collage. Notice how the faces take on a masklike quality because they are made of parts that do not necessarily match. Notice how the entire space is filled. Select a theme related to people to use in your work.

Step 1 Collect magazines and newspapers. Cut small pieces from the photos that you might use. Remember that the first step of the finished product will be small, so keep your pieces small. Put the cut pieces into the envelope for storage. You may combine color with black and white, since the photocopy machine will produce a black-and-white image. However, you must consider how the values of the colors will reproduce in the photocopy.

Step 2 Arrange the cut pieces until you are pleased with your composition. Do not leave any negative space. Every area must be filled. When you are satisfied, glue it down.

Step 3 When your work is dry, enlarge it using the photocopy machine. Make more than one copy so that you can experiment.

Step 4 Choose a color scheme that is appropriate for your theme. Use crayons, oil pastels, colored pencils, school acrylics with gloss medium, and brushes, or any combination of the mentioned color media.

EVALUATING YOUR WORK

▶ **DESCRIBE** Tell the theme you chose and explain how you carried it out. Did you have to create most of the shapes you needed or were you able to find them in photographs?

▶ **ANALYZE** Did the shapes you arranged carry out the effect of your theme? What color scheme did you choose?

▶ **INTERPRET** Did your work express the mood of the theme you selected? Does your title enhance the expressive effect?

▶ **JUDGE** Is your work successful? Does it have the look of the Bearden collage style? Which aesthetic theory would be best to judge this work?

▲ **FIGURE 6.30A** Student work.

STUDIO PROJECT *Photo Collage and Mixed Media* | **159**

Cross-Curriculum: Music

Music, particularly jazz, has always been important to Bearden; the theme of music appears often in his artwork. Have students find examples of various forms of jazz and listen to the variations. Then find recordings of African music and find the essence of jazz in them.

ASSESS...........
Keeping a Portfolio

Remind students that the preliminary sketches and the final artworks for this Studio Project are likely candidates for their portfolios. Encourage them to label their work, evaluate the process, and make any notes that will help them make meaningful choices when they prepare a portfolio for evaluation.

Self-Assessment

Have students apply the steps of art criticism to their own artwork using the "Evaluating Your Work" questions on this page.

Enrichment

Have students create a collage in which they combine personal photos, drawings, magazine photos, and photocopies. Rather than enlarge the collage on a photocopy machine, reduce it and make several copies. Arrange the reduced copies onto the copy machine in a grid or pattern. Make a final copy of the repeated design and add color.

CLOSE............

Have each student explain how the color scheme of his or her finished artwork expresses its theme.

TECHNIQUE TIP ✓

Using Acrylics or Watercolors To help students complete this activity without complication, make these suggestions: Some copy machines will handle thicker drawing paper if it is hand fed. When using water-based colors, students may find it necessary to tape the edges of their paper to the table to help prevent rolling and wrinkles. Also, vary techniques when using acrylics or watercolors. Dampen areas of the paper to create a wash effect. Use a dry brush or dry paper for stipple and sharp-line effects. For watercolor techniques, which can be adapted for acrylics, see page 433 in the Handbook.

Photo Enlargement

Photo Enlargement

(pages 160–161)
(National Standards: 1a, 1b, 2b, 2c, 3b)

FOCUS............

Objective

After completing this lesson, students will be able to:

■ Enlarge a reproduction of a master artwork and create individual rectangles that stand alone as a nonobjective artwork.

Resources

📁 Enrichment 12, *A Close Examination of Style*

TEACH..........

Motivator

Encourage a class critique of Steir's *A Vanitas of Style* (Figure 6.31). Ask the students to study each panel as a separate piece. Magnifying glasses may be necessary for a true detailed search of the reproduction in the book. Ask students to list all of the various art styles that they can find in the painting. Remind them to use the vocabulary terms they have learned since Chapter 1, especially those associated with the elements and principles of art.

Vocabulary

Ask students to look up the definitions for the word *appropriation*. Have them explain how the word is an accurate description of Pat Steir's process.

Art History

Have students locate books on the Brueghels, Rembrandt, Bosch, and Rubens. Begin a session in which the students discuss similarities and differences in these artists' works.

160

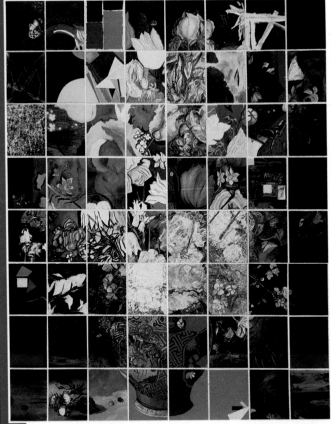

▲ **FIGURE 6.31**

Pat Steir. *The Bruegel Series (A Vanitas of Style)*. 1982–84. Oil on canvas. Sixty-four panels, each 72.4 × 57 cm (28½ × 22½"); total dimensions approximately 5.8 × 4.6 m (19 × 15'). Courtesy of Robert Miller Gallery, New York, New York.

SUPPLIES

■ **Reproduction of a masterpiece**
■ **Ruler, pencil, soft eraser, and scissors**
■ **Large rectangles of white paper**
■ **Sketchbook**
■ **Acrylic paints and assorted brushes**

Pat Steir was looking for a unique way to express her vision of the history of painting. She had studied art history, and as a painter she had practiced the styles of the masters. She explored the colors and brushwork of Rembrandt, Bosch, Rubens, and the Bruegels. To practice, she used what she called appropriation: following the themes and styles of the masters. The subject for her painting-about-painting was a reproduction of the sixteenth-century still life by Jan Bruegel (**broi-gul**) the Elder called Flower Piece in Blue Vase.

After laying grids over the reproduction to divide it evenly into rectangles, Steir painted each panel as an homage to one of the great artists in history.

What You Will Learn

You will study a work of art by *appropriating* it in the manner of Pat Steir. Working in a group, divide a reproduction of a masterpiece into rectangles using a grid. Distribute the pieces among the group members. Enlarge your individual rectangle using a grid. (See Technique Tip 8 on page 432 in the Handbook for instructions on how to enlarge a work using a grid.) Paint your individual rectangle using colors that are the complements of the original colors.

TEACHER TALK 📖

Classroom Management An alternate method of managing a studio project such as the Photo Enlargement, above, is to let the whole class work on one large reproduction, or set up smaller groups to work with smaller reproductions. To get the whole piece finished, one or two students may have to work on more than one rectangle. You might precut and number the rectangles so that the students do not know which reproduction is being used. Alternately, you may wish to decide the ratio of enlargement since the size of the finished work depends on the available space and available materials. Have the students place the works on the floor for viewing. They may be glued to a large paper background, then later cut up.

160

Creating

Study Steir's *The Bruegel Series (A Vanitas of Style)* **(Figure 6.31).** Notice how each rectangle is painted in a different style.

Step 1 Using a ruler and pencil, divide the back of the reproduction evenly into rectangles. Number them in order and then cut them apart.

Step 2 Follow the directions on page 432 to draw a grid on the face of your rectangle and a matching grid on your large sheet of white paper. Using the grids as a guide, enlarge your section of the reproduction onto the white paper. You do not have to erase the grid lines. They are part of your work.

Step 3 Paint your enlarged composition using complements of the original colors. For example, if one shape was red-orange in the reproduction, you will paint it blue-green. Keep the values the same. If the shape was a light red-orange, paint it a light blue-green.

Step 4 Join all the finished rectangles back together using the numbers as a guide.

EVALUATING YOUR WORK

▶ **DESCRIBE** What is the name of the artwork your group appropriated? Describe the look of your individual rectangle. Is it realistic or nonobjective? When you join your work with that of the rest of your group, can you recognize the original subject?

▶ **ANALYZE** Describe the lines, shapes, and colors in your individual panel. When you join the group's panels together, do they fit? Do the shapes and lines match? Have you all interpreted the color complements the same way? Do the colors match?

▶ **INTERPRET** Has changing the colors to their complements affected the expressive quality of the whole work? Do the individual styles affect the look of the work?

▶ **JUDGE** Which aesthetic theory would you use to judge your individual panel? Would you use the same theory to judge the whole group's work?

▲ **FIGURE 6.31A** Student work.

STUDIO PROJECT *Photo Enlargement* **161**

Keeping a Portfolio

Remind students that the preliminary sketches and the final artworks for this Studio Project are likely candidates for their portfolios. Encourage them to label their work, evaluate the process, and make any notes that will help them make meaningful choices when they prepare a portfolio for evaluation.

Self-Assessment

Have students apply the steps of art criticism to their own artwork using the "Evaluating Your Work" questions on this page. Allow each group to exhibit their finished artwork and explain how colors and styles work together to form a unified composition.

Enrichment

Students may be interested in doing a similar project in which only neutrals are used to create an array of values. Also, try this lesson with monochromatic or warm and cool color schemes.

Extension

Ask students to research various artists and the variety of jobs they held to support their creative efforts. For example, inform students that Pat Steir worked as a model and art director. Norman Rockwell worked as an extra at the Metropolitan Opera. Sculptor David Smith worked as a welder in an automobile factory and Robert Rauschenberg designed window displays.

TECHNIQUE TIP ✓

Photo Enlargement When cutting the individual rectangles of paper for the panels, make certain that each piece of paper is cut exactly the same size. Even a slight variance can affect the final assemblage of the whole work. In some cases it may be necessary to use the neutrals, black and white, when the values are adversely affected by a color's complement. As the students progress, you might advise them to paint beside those who are painting adjacent panels. By doing this, students can compare colors and placement of objects that cross from one panel to another. It will also be helpful to begin each class by putting the entire painting together for a brief critique of matching panels.

Using Color to Create an Expressive Statement

Studio Project

Using Color to Create an Expressive Statement

(pages 162–163)
(National Standards: 1a, 1b, 2b, 2c, 3b)

FOCUS...........

Objective

After completing this lesson, students will be able to:

■ Use color and symbols to create a drawing that expresses a personal concern and emphasizes the issue.

TEACH.........

Motivator

Ask students what values, beliefs, traditions, and other influences from their childhood molded and shaped their world today. Ask students to recall from memory a speech, poem, or song that made an impact on them in a similar way that Chief Seattle's television commercials concerning the environment made an impact on so many.

Promoting Discussion

Tell students to collect images and articles from magazines and newspapers concerning the environment. Generate a class discussion based on the subjects of these clippings. Ask students to discuss other issues that are important to them. The issues may be political, religious, environmental, educational, and so on. Ask them to explain why an artwork might be an appropriate vehicle for expressing their concerns.

▲ **FIGURE 6.32**

Jaune Quick-To-See Smith. *Spotted Owl*. 1990. Oil and beeswax on canvas, wood panels, and axes. 203 × 294.6 cm (80 × 116″). Courtesy of the Steinbaum-Krauss Gallery, New York, New York. Collection of the artist.

SUPPLIES

- Sketchbook and pencil
- Large sheet of white paper
- Crayons and chalk
- Acrylic paints and assorted brushes
- Scissors and nontoxic rubber cement
- Large sheets of colored poster board

Jaune Quick-To-See Smith was born in St. Ignatius, a small town on the Flathead reservation of the Confederated Salish and Kootenai peoples of southwestern Montana. Her Shoshone grandmother named her *Jaune,* French for "yellow." *Quick-To-See* was an insightful prediction of her life's work.

Drawing came easily to Smith, who wanted to be an artist from childhood. Her hunger for learning took her on a long journey out of the Flathead valley, but the things she learned there are still a part of everything she does. In 1980 she received a master's degree, and in her work she combines her university training with her heritage. She draws deeply from her own life experiences as well as from mainstream modern art to communicate her concern for the vanishing West.

In *Spotted Owl* **(Figure 6.32),** Smith focuses on the new West. This work symbolizes the concern over endangered species, and she uses neutral colors and visual symbols to convey her message that all living things must coexist. Her paintings are a plea to each of us to save the earth.

What You Will Learn

Jaune Quick-to-See Smith expresses her concerns in her paintings. In this project, you will choose an issue that is important to you. Create a shaped painting, without words, that expresses your concern. Use visual symbols and color contrast to emphasize your point.

162   **CHAPTER 6**   Color

MORE ABOUT...   Jaune Quick-to-See Smith

Although she lives in New Mexico, Smith still maintains close ties to the people and the landscape of the Flathead Reservation. She draws deeply from her own life experiences, traditional Indian heritage, historical western landscape, as well as the mainstream modern art to communicate her concern for the vanishing west. In her new body of work, she quotes from Chief Seattle's visionary speech given in 1854. The environmental concerns that he addressed are as relevant today as they were nearly 130 years ago. Her paintings insist that all living things must coexist and that no single life form controls another. Jaune Quick-to-See Smith's work is her plea to each of us to save the earth.

Creating

Select an issue. Discuss your concerns with your classmates. This may help you think of ways to express your ideas visually. Your subject may be about school issues. It could be a world issue concerning politics or the environment.

Write about your issue in your sketchbook. List words and concepts. Make several small sketches for your painting. Use crayons to plan your color scheme. The shape of your finished work does not have to be rectangular. You may choose a circle, a free-form shape, or the shape of an object that is part of your idea. Objects may protrude from the edges of the shape for emphasis.

Discuss your sketches with a small group of classmates and share composition ideas. For example, you might want to make the people larger, or the negative spaces larger than the positive shape to emphasize loneliness. Try painting everything in warm colors except a calm area. Express the calmness with a cool color.

Step 1 Draw your final idea on a large sheet of white paper with beige or yellow chalk. Paint with acrylics before you cut out the final outline. Remember to use color contrast for emphasis.

Step 2 Cut out your finished piece. Test your work on several different colors of poster board before you choose the final background color. Certain colors could change the message of your painting while others may enhance it. Mount your painting on the poster board. Give your work a title that incorporates a reference to the issue.

EVALUATING YOUR WORK

▶ **DESCRIBE** Name the issue that is the subject of your painting. Tell which visual symbols you selected to illustrate your idea and explain why you chose them.

▶ **ANALYZE** How did you use color contrast to make your point? Which other elements did you emphasize to express your ideas? Explain.

▶ **INTERPRET** Did your work convey your message without words? Were your classmates able to understand your visual symbols?

▶ **JUDGE** Which aesthetic theory would you use to judge this work? Was it successful? If you were to do it over, what would you change?

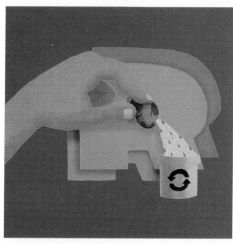

▲ **FIGURE 6.32A** Student work.

Expressive Portrait

TECHNOLOGY
Studio Project

Expressive Portrait

(pages 164–165)
(National Standards: 1a, 1b, 2b, 2c, 3b)

FOCUS...........

Objectives

After completing this lesson, students will be able to:

■ Select and alter a scanned portrait using a computer paint application.

■ Add text to the computer paint image and shape it to fit the composition.

■ Select appropriate music to match the expressive quality of the completed image.

Supplies

■ Photographs, sketchbook, magazine, or postcard

■ Scanner

■ Computer

■ Color editing and/or paint application

■ Printer

■ Sound capacity—computer CD player, cassette tape player, CD player; selected music

TEACH..........

Motivator

Ask the following question. Why do artists create portraits? Generate a list of reasons on the board. Show examples of portraits from one of the following: Matisse, van Gogh, Jawlensky, Warhol or Neel. Ask the following questions: What was the artist doing with color in these portraits? What seems to be the purpose of the portrait here? Briefly discuss how images and text can be manipulated by color, shape, and texture. Many artists choose to do this in creating their art.

▲ **FIGURE 6.33**

Henri Matisse. *Femme au Chapeau (Woman with the Hat)*. 1905. Oil on canvas. 80.6 × 59.7 cm (31¾ × 23½"). San Francisco Museum of Modern Art, San Francisco, California. Bequest of Elise S. Haas.

SUPPLIES

■ **Photograph, sketchbook, magazine, or postcard**

■ **Scanner**

■ **Computer**

■ **Color Editing and/or Paint application**

■ **Printer**

■ **Sound capacity: computer, tape or CD player**

In 1905, Henri Matisse and a group of his friends presented an exhibit of brightly–colored paintings that were more daring than those of van Gogh in their use of color and bolder than Gauguin's in their use of flat shapes. The style enraged one art critic who called the group *Fauves* (wild beasts). Matisse had no complicated theories to explain his artworks. He claimed they had only one purpose: to give pleasure.

In *Femme au Chapeau (Woman with the Hat)* **(Figure 6.33)** you see every loose brushstroke, and the colors used are not related to the shapes they cover. Notice the blue-green line describing the edge of the woman's nose, the green shadow on her forehead, and the red-orange shadow on her neck.

What You Will Learn

You will select a portrait of yourself, a friend, or a celebrity and scan it into your computer. Then, you will alter the image using color and line to create a new mood or emotion that you wish to express. Include text, such as a poem or a phrase, that fits the idea you are trying to express. Arrange the text into a shape that acts as an area of texture in the composition.

Creating

Capture a portrait using a digital camera or scan a color photograph, sketch, or magazine clipping of yourself, a friend, relative, or celebrity. Scan in 256 colors unless your computer has adequate memory for a higher resolution.

TEACHER TALK

Classroom Management Techniques This lesson could be completed without the computer application by completing the portraits using traditional tools—crayons, markers, scissors, glue. Portraits could be drawn in charcoal or pencil or cut from magazines. These images would then be copied. Students could then manipulate the images to emphasize color, shape, and texture. The music would support the images.

Step 1 Follow the procedures for your scanner software. Crop, adjust the color, brightness, and size of the image and then scan it. Save and title the image to your hard drive, a disk, or a file. Use a file format that can be read by the software you will use to manipulate the image. If uncertain, pict is a good choice because it is read by most applications. Other common choices include tiff, eps, and jpeg or gif for Web pages. Quit the scanner software application.

Step 2 Launch the paint application to turn your scanned portrait into a work where color is the most important expressive element. Go to the File menu, choose Open, and select the saved scanned file. Begin by further cropping and adjusting the image. Next, explore menus and settings to change color contrast/brightness, lines and edges, hue/saturation, and balance. These options alone can produce intriguing results.

Investigate other options. Use the Undo command immediately after each attempt until you discover an effect you want to keep. Select the Save As command to retitle and save.

Step 3 Decide on a quote, poem, or short verse that corresponds with the mood of the portrait. Pick the Text tool and select a font, style, color, and size. Letters and words can be manipulated to emphasize their meaning. Arrange the text in a shape that acts as an area of colored texture in your total design.

Remember to credit the source for the photograph and text even if they are your own original creations. List these sources on the back of your work.

EVALUATING YOUR WORK

▶ **DESCRIBE** Who is the subject of the portrait? Tell what color changes and effects you have used including the menus, options, and tools that produced these results. Identify the source of the photograph and text.

▶ **ANALYZE** Describe the colors you used. Have these colors created surprising results? Did you arrange the text into a shape that acts as an area of colored texture? How have you altered the lines and edges using different brushstrokes? Did you distort any areas to make the work more expressive?

▶ **INTERPRET** What mood or emotion does your altered portrait express? What special effects support this mood or emotion? Does the text you added enhance the mood you were trying to achieve? Give your work a title that sums up your feelings about it.

▶ **JUDGE** Did you achieve the expressive quality you were trying to convey? Would you make any changes to make your work more successful? Which aesthetic theory would you use to defend your judgment of your work?

▲ **FIGURE 6.33A** Student work.

TECHNOLOGY STUDIO PROJECT *Expressive Portrait* **165**

Aesthetics

Conduct a discussion on how color, texture and shape influences our interpretation of images. Use the completed portraits with selected music by the students as a common point of reference. Ask: Why do certain colors make us feel a certain way? Why can different artists use similar colors in portraits, but the images evoke completely different feelings? How is texture used? In which image is shape emphasized? Why? Does the selected music match the use of color, shape, and texture in the image?

ASSESS..........
Portfolio

Remind students that the final artworks for this Studio Lesson are likely candidates for their portfolios.

Self Assessment

Have students apply the steps of art criticism to their own artwork.

Reteaching

Have the students review their work and indicate what they might change or do differently the next time. They may want to use a computer paint application that makes this possibility very easy.

Enrichment

Have students do this lesson focusing on self-portraits and how they feel about a particular issue—such as peace, the environment, animal rights, war, global warming. The emphasis on themselves and an issue will provide a rich bank of ideas for color, text, and composing the portrait.

CLOSE............

Have students prepare a class display of the completed portraits.

Critiquing the Work

▶ Describe
What do you see?

- There are two adults sitting on a yellow bench. The woman is holding an infant in her arms. To the right there are two people standing: a young man and a young woman. The man seated next to the woman is wearing a suit the same color as the woman's dress. His skin is the same as the woman's face, but his nose and mouth are pink. The young man is standing close to the side of the man and has one arm around the man's shoulders.

- The young woman is wearing a wide-brimmed yellow hat decorated with red cloth to protect her neck. There is a yellow textured bench on which the adults are sitting.

▶ Analyze
How is this work organized?

- The hues are red, orange, yellow, and green. Blue, green, and yellow are in the background.

- The neutral colors are gray, white, and black. The bottom of the painting is a tint of gray. The bench has tints and shades of yellow. The area above the people is a tint of yellow.

- He has used all the spectral colors except violet, plus neutral black, white, and gray. This does not fit any of the color schemes in the book.

166

ART CRITICISM IN ACTION

▲ **FIGURE 6.34**

Romare Bearden. *Family.* 1988. Collage on wood. 71.1 × 50.8 cm (28 × 20"). National Museum of American Art, Smithsonian Institution, Washington, D.C. © Romare Bearden Foundation/Licensed by VAGA, New York, New York.

MORE ABOUT... Bearden's Collages

Bearden's first collages were made in 1964 in response to meetings held in his studio with other African-American artists to discuss the position of black artists in society. Bearden suggested that they work together on a joint collage, and although this idea did not come to fruition, Bearden himself got seriously involved with the medium. He began by combining magazine photographs with pieces of painted paper to create unusual juxtapositions of size, color, and spatial relationships. He chose subjects from his own observations of African Americans. For Bearden, making collages was like jazz improvization in that he gathered various elements and "played" with them until he hit upon the right composition.

1 DESCRIBE What do you see?

During this step, you will collect facts about the artwork. List all of the information found in the credit line. Use your perception skills to study the objects you see in the work.

- Describe the people you see. Include details about their clothing, their features, and their hair.
- Describe the objects in the work. Remember not to make guesses.

2 ANALYSIS How is this work organized?

This is the step in art criticism that deals with the composition of the work. This is a clue-collecting step. Remember not to make guesses.

- What hues do you see? Where are they? Which are used the most?
- Do you see any neutral colors? Where? Can you find any tints or shades?
- Has the artist used one of the color schemes you studied to organize this work?

3 INTERPRET What is the artist trying to communicate?

During this step, you will combine the clues you have collected with your personal feelings and experiences to guess what this work is about.

- What family relationship does this artwork express?
- How has the artist organized color to give you hints as to the relationship of the people to each other and to their environment?
- Create a new title for this work based on your personal interpretation.

4 JUDGE What do you think of the work?

Now it is time to decide if this is a successful work of art. You may make a personal opinion; however, it is important to make an objective judgment based on aesthetic theories.

- Do you find this work interesting? Did it make you think?
- Did the artist use the element of color to convey his message well?
- Do you think this is a successful work of art? Why or why not? Use one or more of the aesthetic theories described in Chapter 2 to defend your judgment.

MEET THE ARTIST
ROMARE BEARDEN

American, 1914–1989

Romare Bearden was born in rural Charlotte, North Carolina. Although he spent his summer vacations with his grandparents in Charlotte, he spent most of his youth in Harlem. Bearden grew up in the 1930s, when many of the talented members of the Harlem Renaissance still lived in Harlem. This influenced his artistic development and his awareness of his heritage. After World War II, Bearden attended the Sorbonne in Paris.

Today his work doesn't fit into any neat category. In his collages he tied together his personal experiences as an African-American, his knowledge of his African heritage, and his understanding of art history and techniques.

▶ Interpret
What is the artist trying to communicate?

- Answers will vary. Some may say that the boy is an outsider because his skin color is different from the others, who are all the same. He is a close member of the unit, however, because he has one arm around the man and one around the girl. The hair color of the adults indicate age, so they may be the grandparents of the baby, the girl may be their daughter, and the young man may be her husband.
- Answers will vary. The following are just some possible answers. The adults are wearing the same color, which may indicate a strong bond. The blues and green of the environment match the people's clothes. That might indicate a close relationship to this environment.
- Responses will vary.

▶ Judge
What do you think of the work?

- Answers will vary.
- Answers will vary.
- Answers will vary. Most will probably choose Formalism or Emotionalism.

Art Criticism in Action **167**

Time & Place   Late Twentieth Century

Romare Bearden made the collage *Family* in 1988. Some other events that happened the same year:

- **Social Studies:** George Bush won a landslide presidential election over Michael Dukakis, carrying 40 of the 50 states.
- **Social Studies:** A 6.9 earthquake in Soviet Armenia killed an estimated 25,000 people.
- **Art:** Romare Bearden died in New York at age 75.

CONNECTIONS
SCIENCE

Where Do Paint Pigments Come From?

(National Standards: 6a, 6b)

Objectives

After completing this feature, students will be able to:

■ Define pigment.

■ Discuss different minerals used in pigments.

Teaching the Connection

Have students read the feature on this page. Ask students to describe what is being portrayed in this work. Tell them that Aafenmut is a scribe or secretary in the Pharaoh's treasury. In the painting Aafenmut is making a food offering to Horus, the falcon-headed deity believed to be the god of the sky. The Sun appears twice: once on the head of Horus, and again in a barque, or vessel, at the top of the painting. At least six different pigments have been used in this work. Although the painting may have faded since it was originally created, these pigments have endured for almost 3,000 years.

Review with students the basic ingredients of paint. Tell students that pigments must be mixed with a binder that will dry out. When Jan van Eyck began to use oil as a binder in the fourteenth century, he set the standard for pigment mixing still followed today. To make a glossy paint, first linseed oil and resin are blended. A solvent is added, then the impurities are removed. After a period of settling, the pigments and more solvent are added. Finally, the paint is thoroughly mixed in a ball mill then tested for consistency.

Where Do Paint Pigments Come From?

▲ **FIGURE 6.35**

Funerary Stela of Aafenmut. *Aafenmut Offering Before Horus, Above Sun's Barque.* Thebes, Khokha, Third Intermediate Period, Dynasty 22, ca 924–715 B.C. Painted wood. 23 × 18.2 × 3.5 cm (9 × 7¼ × 1³/₈"). The Metropolitan Museum of Art, New York, New York. Rogers Fund, 1928.

About 20,000 years ago, Stone Age people made paint from plant matter and animal parts to decorate their caves, clothing, and bodies. The human desire for variety led to the discovery of minerals that, when ground into powders and mixed with liquids, formed a range of brilliant colors. Ultramarine, crimson, and cerulean blue are just a few of the colors of pigments that derive from minerals.

Different shades of green and blue come from minerals that contain large amounts of copper, such as azurite and malachite. Reddish pigments derive from cinnabar, a mineral containing sulfur and mercury. Yellow pigments can be made from ochre, an iron-rich clay that turns red when heated. Precious minerals such as gold and silver can be pulverized to make glittery pigments.

In addition to mineral-based pigments, many vibrant colors come from plants and animals. For example, saffron yellow comes from the root of the rubia plant. Today, many paint pigments are synthetically produced from coal tars and petrochemicals. The bright and often longer-lasting colors of modern synthetic pigments are achieved through chemical reactions.

Making the Connection

1. What mineral-based pigments do you think were used to decorate the painting in **Figure 6.35**?
2. What are the effects of the artist's use of color in this painting?
3. Look at a good reproduction of one of your favorite older paintings. Make a list of the colors you think the artist used and blended to create the work. Then, approximate as best you can the different minerals that appear on the canvas. Write down your answers.

Answers to Making the Connection

1. The colors range from white, black, and brownish-gray to pale green, golden yellow, and rusty red. The pigments might be derived from carbon (black), zinc, lead, or calcium (white), ochre (yellow), copper (green), and sulfur and mercury (red). The brownish gray is probably a clay-based pigment.

2. The colors in this painting are mostly warm. Since Horus is a god associated with the sun and sky, the warm, analogous hues convey a mood of warmth appropriate to the subject. Color is also used repeatedly and evenly to convey a sense of balance and unity.

3. Answers will vary.

Building Vocabulary

On a separate sheet of paper, write the term that best matches each definition given below.

1. An element of art that is derived from reflected light.
2. Produced when light passes through a wedge-shaped glass, called a prism, and is bent and separated into bands of color.
3. The name of a color in the color spectrum.
4. A light value of a hue.
5. A dark value of a hue.
6. The brightness or dullness of a hue.
7. The colors opposite each other on the color wheel.
8. A color scheme that uses only one hue and the tints and shades of that hue.
9. Colors that sit side by side on the color wheel and have a common hue.
10. Finely–ground, colored powders that form paint when mixed with a binder.
11. A material that holds together the grains of pigment.
12. The liquid that controls the thickness or thinness of the paint.

Reviewing Art Facts

Answer the following questions using complete sentences.

1. Explain how the eye sees color.
2. What is an afterimage? How is it produced?
3. Name the three components of color.
4. What is color value?
5. Name the seven different kinds of color schemes.
6. What are complementary colors? How do complementary colors affect each other?
7. What are synthetic pigments? How do they differ from natural pigments?
8. What is arbitrary color?

Thinking Critically About Art

1. **Synthesize.** Figure 6.20 on page 148 and Figure 6.21 on page 149 use very different color schemes. Compare the two works. List the similarities and differences in their style and use of color.
2. **Interpret.** Look at Figure 6.9 on page 141. The artist has used a color scheme of dark values to create a specific mood. Study the lines and shapes in this work. How do they affect the feeling of the painting? Notice the areas of bright, intense color. How does this add drama? Does the title add to the mood?

Read how Joanna Featherstone paints a picture with words as a professional storyteller in the Performing Arts Handbook on page 418. Like a painter, Joanna uses tonality, contrast, intensity, and movement to tap into the emotions that each color evokes.

Explore the use of color in the expressive works of Monet, Morisot, Gauguin, and Kandinsky on the Internet. Find additional information about color theory and the use of color during specific historical periods. Visit us at **www.glencoe.com/sec/art**

Answers to Building Vocabulary

1. color
2. color spectrum
3. hue
4. tint
5. shade
6. intensity
7. complementary colors
8. monochromatic
9. analogous colors
10. pigments
11. binder
12. solvent

Answers to Reviewing Art Facts

1. Light waves are reflected from objects to your eyes. The light hits the retina, where cells receive the color images.
2. An opposite color image that remains after viewing a shape or object. Your brain creates the afterimage as a reaction to the color you stared at originally.
3. Hue, value, intensity.
4. A value is related to the amount of light a color reflects.
5. Monochromatic, analogous, complementary, triad, split-complementary, warm, and cool.
6. Colors located opposite each other on the color wheel. When placed side by side they seem to vibrate.
7. Artificially made pigments. They are brighter and more permanent.
8. When the artist uses color to express feelings and ignores optical color.

ASSESSMENT ✓

Evaluate

- Have students complete the *Chapter 6 Test* in the TCR. 📁
- Alternative Assessment teaching strategies are provided below or in the *Testing Program and Alternative Assessment* booklet. 📁

Extension

Have each student select one artwork that he or she created while studying this chapter. Ask them to write critiques of their artworks using the four steps of art criticism, paying particular attention to their use of color. Then ask them to form small groups and present their artworks and discuss their critiques.

Texture
(page 170–195)

Resources

While studying this chapter, use Performing Arts Handbook page 419 to help students discover how Paul Winter captures the texture of the sounds of nature through his music.

▲ **FIGURE 7.1** The artist has used a variety of beads to create different textures. Which area of the throne looks smooth? Which looks rough?

Bamileke. *Throne.* African, nineteenth century. Wood and beads. Height: 47 cm (18½″). The Detroit Institute of Arts, Detroit, Michigan. Founders Society Purchase, Eleanor Clay Ford Fund for African Art.

FEATURED ARTISTS

Ivan Albright
Bamileke
Edgar Degas

Max Ernst
Janet Fish
Audrey Flack
James Hampton
John Hoover
Joan Mitchell

Pierre Auguste Renoir
Miriam Schapiro
Robert Silvers
Vincent van Gogh
Frank Lloyd Wright

Texture

E very surface has a texture. **Texture** is *the element of art that refers to how things feel, or look as if they might feel if touched.* Texture includes the slick, smooth surface of ice, the bumpy, rough surface of a brick, and the prickly surface of a scrub brush.

A nineteenth–century African artist created the ceremonial throne shown in **Figure 7.1.** Notice the animal figure that supports the seat. What might be symbolic about the use of an animal as an important part of the throne? Notice how the artist has used different shapes, sizes, and colors of beads to create texture. The areas where he has used many small, white beads look rough. The lines he has created using long blue beads look smooth and slick. Notice the cowry shells around the edges of the seat and the base. What kind of texture do they suggest?

This artwork almost asks to be touched. You can easily imagine what the beads and shells would feel like if you touched them. Do you think the artist meant for the artwork to be inviting in this way? Why or why not? In this chapter, you will learn how artists use texture to convey ideas and feelings through their art.

OBJECTIVES

After completing this chapter, you will be able to:

- Understand how texture is perceived through the senses.
- Describe various textures.
- Reproduce textures by changing values.
- Use texture as the expressive element in creating two- and three-dimensional works of art.
- Understand how artists use texture.

WORDS TO KNOW

texture
visual texture
matte surface
collage
frottage
grattage
decalcomania

Developing Your PORTFOLIO

Collect small samples of various textures, such as a scrap of sandpaper or a swatch of fabric. You can also use magazine illustrations that show texture. Mount these samples on a piece of posterboard. Under each sample, write two words that describe the texture, such as "slick, smooth" or "bumpy, rough." Then write a short paragraph describing how you could use various textures (or the appearance of texture) in your art. Include your texture board and paragraph in your portfolio.

Chapter Overview

Texture is an element of art that refers to how things feel, or look as though they might feel, if touched. The viewer perceives this element of art with two senses—both sight and touch.

Examining the Artwork

Point out to the students that the throne (Figure 7.1) is made with real texture, but the photograph of it in this book is visual texture, a picture of texture, which they will study in this chapter. In Africa, beads were valuable objects imported from Europe. Lavish beaded objects and clothing showed rank and wealth. Beaded stools were prestigious furniture used by royalty in the Cameroon Highlands. Beads were reserved for use in the palace only. They decorated many objects belonging to the royal family, including masks, thrones, and pipe stems.

The leopard motif is derived from the king's association with the most powerful animals in African wildlife. Sitting on top of a leopard enhanced a king's image. Ask students: What do you think would indicate power in your society? What kind of a special stool would be made for a person of high rank such as a state governor, a city mayor, or the president of this country? Would the designer choose an animal as a symbol or something else?

National Standards

This chapter addresses the following National Standards for the Visual Arts:

1. (a, b)	**4.** (b, c)
2. (a, b, c)	**5.** (a, c)
3. (a, b)	**6.** (a, b)

DEVELOPING A PORTFOLIO

Self-Reflection The success of a portfolio as a indication of a student's artistic competency is enhanced by the continual awareness of the process of personal development. Students who are encouraged to reflect often on the stages of growth of their work are less mystified by the process of learning. Their education, then, is not limited to the class period; they become active participants in their growth. Ask them frequently to evaluate their personal development. For example: How do you measure the success of your artwork? What have you learned about art that helps your talent grow? What have you learned about yourself as an artist? What new areas do you wish to explore?

Texture in Your Life
(pages 172–176)
(National Standards: 2b, 3a)

FOCUS............

Objectives

After completing this lesson, students will be able to:

- Understand how texture is perceived through the senses.
- Describe various textures.
- Reproduce the appearance of texture by changing values.

Supplies

- Bags containing various textured objects
- Photographs of the same textures
- Crayons, paper
- Magnifying glasses
- Tag board
- Construction paper or cardboard
- Tempera, acrylic, and watercolor paints

Resources

📁 Application Activity 13, *Best-Loved Textures*
📁 Concept Map 7, *Textures and Value*
📁 Cooperative Learning Activity 13, *What a Relief!*
📁 *National Gallery of Art Bar Code Correlation Guide*

TEACH..........

Motivator

Have students work with partners. Give each pair of students a bag containing scraps of material such as rock, bark, cotton, silk, feather, marbles, staples, keys, and so forth. Ask the partners to take turns feeling the material inside the bag, describing it as fully as possible, and then trying to identify it.

172

Texture in Your Life

Textures play a role in decisions you make every day. Think about how fabric textures have influenced your clothing choices. Would you wear a shirt made of rough burlap against your bare skin? Probably not. Clothing manufacturers consider this when they decide what fabrics to use and how to make their clothes. They may use warm, heavy wool for a coat, but then line the coat with silky material so that it feels comfortable.

Think about the textures of food. Imagine the smoothness of ice cream, and consider how different it is from the angular roughness of potato chips. Would grilled steak taste the same if it were ground up in a blender? Textures are important to us in a variety of ways.

How You Perceive Texture

You perceive texture with two of your senses: touch and vision. Infants learn about things by touching them and by putting them into their mouths. Toddlers are attracted to all objects that are within their reach. When you look at surfaces, you are able to guess their textures because you have learned how textures feel. Your eyes tell you what something would feel like if you were to touch it **(Figure 7.2).**

▲ **FIGURE 7.2** What textures are represented in these photographs?

172   **CHAPTER 7**   Texture

TECHNOLOGY OPTIONS

National Gallery of Art Videodisc Use the following to show how artists use texture.

Peter Paul Rubens
Daniel in the Lions' Den

Search Frame 776

Eugène Delacroix
The Edge of a Wood at Nohant

Search Frame 2916

Mary Cassatt
The Boating Party

Search Frame 2016

Use Glencoe *National Gallery of Art Correlation Bar Code Guide* to locate more artworks.

When you actually touch something to determine its texture, you experience real texture. When you look at a photograph of a texture, such as velvet, leather, concrete, or ice, you see surface patterns of light and dark that bring back memories of how those objects actually feel. When this happens, you are experiencing **visual texture,** *the illusion of a three-dimensional surface.* If you touch visual textures, you do not feel what your eyes told you to expect.

There are two kinds of visual texture: *simulated* and *invented.* Simulated textures imitate real textures. Plastic tabletops can be made to look like wood. Vinyl flooring can be made to look like ceramic tile or stone. Manufactured fabrics imitate natural leather and fur.

Artists can do the same. For example, painter Peggy Flora Zalucha simulates textures in her paintings so accurately that you think you might be looking at a photograph **(Figure 7.3).**

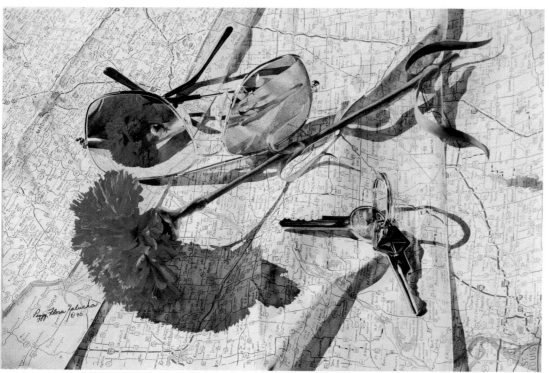

▲ **FIGURE 7.3** At first you might think you are looking at a photograph because the artist has simulated the textures of objects so realistically. This is actually a still-life painting of items associated with taking a road trip. The details of the map are so clear that if you recognized the area of the country, you could read the map. Zalucha has used white highlights to represent the brilliant reflections of light off the shiny surfaces of the glasses and keys, and more subtle changes of value to represent the textures found in non-reflective surfaces, such as the wrinkles on the map.

Peggy Flora Zalucha. *Map Still Life with Carnations, Keys, and Glasses.* 1989. Mixed watermedia. 76 × 111.8 cm (30 × 44"). Private collection.

LESSON 1   *Texture in Your Life* | **173**

Vocabulary

If possible, devote a large section of classroom wall space to a "Wall of Words." On the wall, list the elements and principles of art. As students study each chapter, put up the specific vocabulary terms listed on the chapter opening page. Especially in Chapter 7, students will encounter several unusual words that need to be reinforced as they progress through the lessons. As students discuss and critique artworks, remind them to look at the "Wall of Words" and use the terms properly in their discussions.

Critical Thinking

One interesting way to help students see the relationship between real and visual textures is to show them a collection of interesting surfaces, such as shells, carpeting, burlap, denim, a slice of bread, and so forth. Find photographs of the same textures and ask students to match the real and visual surfaces and explain their decisions. (The photos do not have to match the real objects in size, shape, or color.)

Aesthetics

To help students understand simulated texture, ask them to think of things in the classroom or at home that are made of manufactured material that imitates a natural material, such as wood. Point out that many synthetic fabrics imitate natural fibers such as linen and silk. Then look at Figures 7.3 and 7.4 on pages 173 and 174 and ask students to determine how the textures in each work were created. Point out that there are similarities among the works. Both stimulate the viewer's sense of touch.

MEETING INDIVIDUAL NEEDS

Visually Impaired Students who are blind enjoy feeling textures and telling what it reminds them of. In addition to the usual visual stimulation material brought to the lesson by the art teacher, tactile motivational materials can supplement each lesson. For example, still-life materials need not just be looked at, they can be passed around, handled, and discussed. Also, when germane to the topic, materials that can be smelled, such as cinnamon, charred wood, and perfume, enrich lesson motivations as do audiocassettes. Multisensory materials are especially helpful for students who learn through sharing their personal responses and who learn through their senses.

Art on a Shoestring

Ask students to bring in textured materials from home to complete the exercises in this chapter. You might prepare a list of suggested materials, which could include the following: aluminum foil, plastic wrap, wrapping paper, ribbons, wax paper, paper napkins, paper towels, tree bark, sandpaper, screening, foam plates, paper plates, loose sand (in a bag), scrap fabrics, gum wrappers, grasses, pine straw, and so on.

Activity

Creating Textures

Applying Your Skills. This activity involves rubbings and designs. Most students rub the crayon back and forth across the surface of the paper, and sometimes this succeeds. More often, rubbing back and forth moves the paper and ruins the rubbing. Students do not need any special dexterity, so they should not be afraid to change hands during the procedure.

This activity also requires drawing skills. It may seem to be too demanding for some students, but it is not. Ask the students to study the rubbings for repetition of lines, dots, or small shapes. A magnifying glass can help them analyze the rubbings more easily. When the activity is finished, display the rubbings and the drawings made from them in a random manner, and then ask the students to match the drawings to the rubbings. Of course a student may not choose his or her own to match.

FIGURE 7.4 In this painting, the artist has used a number of techniques to suggest texture. A variety of line types and shading techniques have been used. Can you identify the textures? Do they represent real textures or are they invented? The artwork clearly depicts two people and an elephant, but would you call it realistic? Why or why not?

Artist Unknown. *Stalling Elephant With Two Riders.* Deccan, Bijapur. 1590-95. Ink, gold, and watercolor on paper. Brooklyn Museum of Art, Brooklyn, New York.

Invented textures are two-dimensional patterns created by the repetition of lines or shapes. These patterns do not represent real surface qualities, but the patterns of light and dark suggest real texture. The purpose of invented texture is to create decorated surfaces that evoke memories of unusual textures **(Figure 7.4)**.

Activity — Creating Textures

Applying Your Skills. Make a collection of texture rubbings. To make a rubbing, place a sheet of thin paper against a rough object or surface. Hold the paper in place with one hand. Use the flat side of an unwrapped crayon or the side of a pencil lead to rub over the paper. Rub in one direction—away from the hand holding the paper. Rubbing back and forth can cause the paper or object to slip. Examine the rubbings closely, paying special attention to the lines, dots, shapes, and values.

Computer Option. Explore the textures on your computer application as well as those you can create. Begin with a Pencil, Brush, or Shape tool. Draw objects or shapes. Fill each shape with a different texture from available menus. Make some new textures by editing or adding textures. Use a variety of available tools and paper textures. Experiment with a blending tool to soften surfaces. Identify which objects look rough and which look smooth.

COOPERATIVE LEARNING

Identifying Textures Divide the class into two groups. Have one group work together to identify objects around their classroom and school that effectively represent textures with a matte texture. Ask them to identify words that describe the texture. Ask the other group to locate objects that effectively represent a shiny texture. Have them also develop a list of terms that describe the shiny texture. Ask students to compare their lists of adjectives and find works of art in this text that use the different types of textures.

Texture and Value

The appearance of a surface depends on how it reflects light. Every surface displays a pattern of light and dark values. From the pattern of light and dark values, we can make a judgment about the texture of a surface or an object even if we cannot touch it.

Rough and Smooth Textures

The roughness or smoothness of a texture can be determined by looking at its light and dark values. A rough surface reflects light unevenly. It shows irregular patterns of light and shadow. Look at a shag rug, an orange, tree bark, or a patch of bare ground. Notice how the high places catch the light, casting shadows of different sizes and shapes.

A smooth texture reflects light evenly. Look at a sheet of paper, an apple, or a new, unmarked desktop. Your eyes glide across these objects, uninterrupted by shadows, just as your fingers would glide across them, uninterrupted by bumps and dents.

Matte and Shiny Textures

In addition to rough and smooth, textures can be matte or shiny. A **matte surface** is *a surface that reflects a soft, dull light*. It absorbs some light and reflects the rest. Matte surfaces, such as paper, denim, unfinished wood, and your skin, have a soft, dull look.

A shiny surface is the opposite of a matte surface. A shiny surface is a surface that reflects so much bright light that it seems to glow. Shiny surfaces also have highlights. Some surfaces reflect bright sunlight with such intensity that you have to squint your eyes to protect them from the glare. Window glass, a new car, a polished brass candlestick, and the surface of a calm pool of water are all examples of shiny surfaces.

Matte and shiny surfaces can be rough or smooth. Sandpaper is matte rough, and a freshly–ironed pillowcase is matte smooth. Aluminum foil is shiny and smooth until it gets crumpled up; then it becomes shiny and rough. In **Figure 7.5** on page 176, Janet Fish has illustrated all of these texture variations.

Activity — Creating Contrasting Textures

Applying Your Skills. Make a series of small drawings and paintings of objects that have different textures. Try to reproduce both smooth and rough textures. You may use a different medium for each drawing, but study the lights and shadows on each object before you choose the medium. For example, you might examine a hairbrush, an old work shoe, weathered wood, a wig, a fuzzy slipper, or a satin slip, then select a medium that would work best for each texture.

Computer Option. Make a series of small drawings and paintings of objects that have different textures, as in the preceding activity. Use the Pencil or Brush tool on the computer. First, sketch your shapes. Then reproduce the texture of each shape using dots, lines, and value blending. Concentrate on the shadows, lights, and highlights of each different texture.

Activity — Creating Contrasting Textures

Applying Your Skills. This activity is a perception drawing problem and does not require students to focus on the composition. Instead, students can concentrate on rendering various textured surfaces one at a time.

Computer Option. Students who wish to continue this activity at another level might try this: Choose the Rectangular shape tool and a Fill pattern you have altered, created, or have available to you. Use one color and a variety of invented patterns. Print several sheets. More textured papers can be created as needed, either printing from the computer or making additional copies on a copy machine. On a stiff piece of construction paper or cardboard, sketch a simple still life, landscape, or imaginary animal. Cut out the shapes from your textured papers and glue them onto the sketch using a glue stick or other adhesive that won't stretch and wrinkle the computer paper. After all the shapes have been collaged with texture, use colored pens, pencils, or inks to add shadows, shading, and highlights.

THE NATIONAL GALLERY OF ART This Web site features a comprehensive tour of The National Gallery of Art in Washington, DC. After you preview what is available, invite students to tour selected areas of Collections, Exhibits, and Highlights to view art of many genres. The site also includes a search area where more than 100,000 items can be accessed.

Visit the museum corner at **www.glencoe.com/sec/art** There, you will also find a rich array of teacher resources waiting for you. Check the *Internet Activity Booklet* included with the *ArtTalk* program for more information.

Promoting Discussion

It is important to help students realize that textures may have more than one characteristic. For example, rough and smooth can be either matte or shiny. Sandpaper and aluminum foil are good examples. Pull a piece of foil out of a box. It is smooth. Crinkle it up. It is still shiny, but it is no longer smooth.

Studio Skills

Have students bring to class various small objects with different textures. Have them glue these objects to a large sheet of tag board. After you and your students have assembled a wide range of objects, shine a light on the anchored objects and have students draw the different textures. Move the source of light and repeat the activity as many times as you can.

ASSESS...........

Self-Assessment

Have students complete the lesson review questions. Answers are provided below.

Reteaching

Have students photograph, sketch, or write notes about different types of textures, both natural and manufactured.

CLOSE............

Have students volunteer responses to this question: How is texture used in art?

176

 LOOKING CLOSELY   Visual Texture Combinations

Janet Fish has used pastels to create the visual textures in this work. The diagram points out some areas where she has combined different kinds of visual texture such as shiny-rough, shiny-smooth, and matte-smooth. Can you find more areas where she has created combinations of visual texture?

shiny–smooth   matte–smooth   matte–rough

shiny–rough

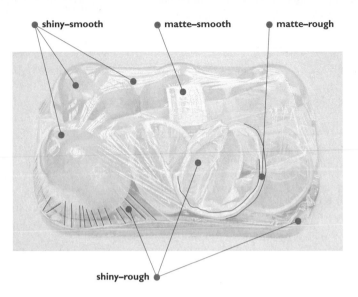

◄ **FIGURE 7.5**

Janet Fish. *Oranges*. 1973. Pastel on sandpaper. 55.5 × 96.5 cm (21⅞ × 38"). Allen Memorial Art Museum, Oberlin College, Oberlin, Ohio. Fund for Contemporary Art, 1974.

 Check Your Understanding

1. Define visual texture.
2. Describe, in detail, the two types of visual texture.

3. Compare how rough and smooth textures reflect light.
4. What is the difference between a matte and a shiny surface?

✓ *Answers to Check Your Understanding*

1. Visual texture is the illusion of a three-dimensional surface.
2. Simulated visual texture is deliberately designed to give the appearance of a specific texture, such as vinyl floors that appear to be tile. An invented visual texture is a pattern created by line and shape that doesn't represent a real surface.
3. Rough textures reflect light unevenly. A smooth texture reflects light evenly.
4. A matte surface reflects a soft, dull light. A shiny surface reflects a bright light so that the object seems to glow.

How Artists Use Texture

The texture of surfaces is important in every form of visual art. Our minds are full of texture memories. Artists use both visual and real textures to make you remember those texture experiences.

Ivan Albright was a painter who loved to depict decaying, aging objects with meticulous precision. He painted the skin of the old farm woman in **Figure 7.6** to accent and exaggerate every tiny wrinkle. Look at the painting. How many different kinds of textures can you identify?

In contrast, Pierre Auguste Renoir (ren-**wahr**) painted young people with healthy, glowing complexions **(Figure 7.7)**. He preferred to focus on beautiful

▶ **FIGURE 7.7** Renoir started his career as an artist in a porcelain factory. He copied famous portraits of beautiful women onto the porcelain plates. Renoir spent the rest of his life painting beautiful people. Notice how he uses his brushstrokes to create texture.

Pierre Auguste Renoir. *Madame Henriot*. 1876. Oil on canvas. 66 × 50 cm (26 × 19⅞"). National Gallery of Art, Washington, D.C. Gift of Adele R. Levy Fund, Inc.

◀ **FIGURE 7.6** Albright worked on this painting for two years creating the painstaking details of the surface textures shown in the work.

Ivan Albright. *The Farmer's Kitchen*. 1933–34. Oil on canvas. 91.5 × 76.5 cm (36 × 30"). National Museum of American Art, Smithsonian Insititution, Washington, D.C.

MORE ABOUT... Pierre Auguste Renoir

Pierre Auguste Renoir was born in 1841. His artistic talents became apparent early. By the age of 13, he was already making a living as an artist in a porcelain factory. His job was painting scenes on pieces of china. His earnings helped pay for his education at a Paris art school, the École des Beau-Arts. It was at school that Renoir met two other young artists, Claude Monet and Alfred Sisley. The three soon became friends and began experimenting together by making paintings outdoors in natural sunlight. Their goal was to give objects a shimmering, sunlit quality. At first, their works were scorned by critics. Today they are among the most admired in the history of art.

How Artists Use Texture

(pages 177–183)
(National Standards: 2b, 3a)

FOCUS..........

Objectives

After completing this lesson, students will be able to:

■ Use texture as the expressive element in creating two- and three-dimensional works of art.

■ Understand how artists communicate through texture.

Supplies

■ Acrylic paints
■ Magnifying glasses

Resources

📁 Application Activity 14, *Sharpening Your Skills*
📁 Cooperative Learning Activity 14, *Texture Bingo*
📁 Enrichment Activity 13, *Is It the Real Thing?*
📁 Enrichment Activity 14, *Creating Texture with Macrame*
📁 Studio Lesson 10, *Textured-Clay Wind Chimes*
📁 Studio Lesson 11, *Texture Stitchery*
📁 Studio Lesson 12, *Weaving with Texture*
📁 *National Gallery of Art Bar Code Correlation Guide*

TEACH..........

Motivator

Ask students to brainstorm a list of adjectives that can be used to describe texture; record their adjectives on the board. Finally, ask students to suggest specific objects with textures that might be described by the listed adjectives.

Aesthetics

Have students compare the works by Albright (Figure 7.6) and Renoir (Figure 7.7, on page 177). Ask students to describe the different painting styles and techniques that were used to render the subjects' complexions. Additionally, have them study Vermeer's *Girl with the Red Hat* (Figure 13.13 on page 362) and find other artworks that show subjects' faces. Have students speculate about the techniques used to show skin quality in the artworks they find.

Art History

Remind students that as an Impressionist, Renoir was fascinated by the way light reflected off his subjects. Ask students to look at Figure 7.7 on page 177 and identify the way color is broken up by light. Ask them how this technique affects the texture of the painting. Ask them to describe the kind of mood they sense in this work. How does color and texture influence the mood?

Aesthetics

Remind students that when looking at the works of Albright and van Gogh, they should remember that photographs and reproductions can never duplicate the experience of seeing the originals. The aesthetic quality of these works is largely dependent on the thick, rich textures of paint that can never be fully appreciated until seen in the original.

◀ **FIGURE 7.8** At times, van Gogh became so impatient with the progress of his work that he squeezed the paint directly from the tube onto the canvas. Then he used anything that was handy, including his fingers, to move and swirl the globs of paint around.

Vincent van Gogh. *Sunflowers.* 1888. Oil on canvas. 92 × 73 cm (36¼ × 28¼"). National Gallery, London, England.

and pleasing subjects. How many different textures can you identify in this painting? Notice that both Albright and Renoir have imitated the texture of human skin. In each case, the artist has used texture to convey a feeling about the subject. In one painting the skin is appealing, in the other it is almost repulsive. Both artists have tried to control your reaction to the subject of the paintings through their use of visual texture.

Many painters use color and value patterns to produce the illusion of textures. Look, for instance, at the painting by Judith Leyster (Figure 10.4, page 257) or Rembrandt van Rijn (ryne) (Figure 11.5, page 290). These artists were experts at suggesting textures such as soft velvet, shiny satin, delicate lace, and fluffy feathers. When you look closely at their paintings, you discover that these artists do not paint every texture in photographic detail. They use a few brushstrokes to suggest the texture from a certain distance.

Instead of relying only on visual texture, many painters add real textures to their paintings. Vincent van Gogh (vahn **goh**) used such thick paint on his canvas that his swirling brushstrokes created a rough surface **(Figure 7.8)**. The surface ridges of the thick paint actually make the paint look brighter. The ridges catch more light and reflect brighter colors to the viewer. If you were to touch a van Gogh painting you would feel the texture you see. Even today, artists feel that such textural qualities enhance their work. Joan Mitchell is one contemporary painter who brushes on paint and does not try to smooth out the brushstrokes **(Figure 7.9).**

Some painters add real textures to their work by attaching various materials to the work's surface. Some artists add sand and other materials to the paint. In some cases, artists create what is called a **collage** (kul-**lahzh**), or *an artwork onto which materials such as textured paper and fabric have been attached.* Although folk artists have used this technique for centuries, fine artists only

Studio Skills

If cost is not a problem, give students some thick acrylic paints to manipulate. There is a satisfaction in working with thick paints that cannot be realized just by looking at two-dimensional reproductions.

Cross-Curriculum: Language Arts

Have students imagine that they have just become best friends with someone who has been blind since birth, and they want to share their visual world with this person. To do so they must talk about how things feel, their textures, and describe how the objects look. Have them describe clouds, blue sky, the first light of dawn, or the glow of sunset.

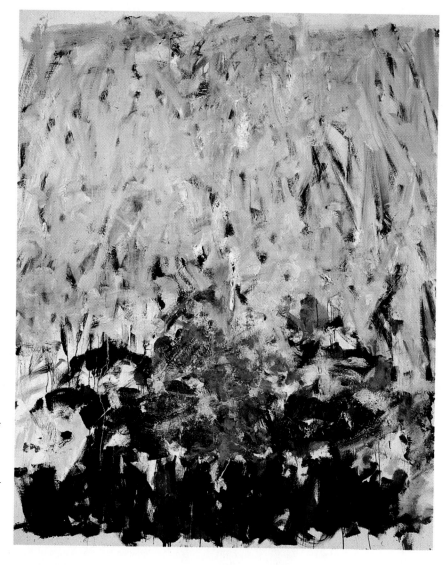

▶ **FIGURE 7.9** Joan Mitchell remained an Abstract Expressionist throughout her entire painting career. This work refers to the snow and cold of her Chicago childhood. Notice how she has used the brushstrokes to show the excitement and tension of a snowy day in the city. What kinds of lines do you find in the brushstrokes?

Joan Mitchell. *Dirty Snow.* 1980. Oil on canvas. 220 × 180 cm (86¼ × 70⅞″). National Museum of Women in the Arts, Washington, D.C. Gift of Wallace and Wilhelmina Holladay.

LESSON 2 *How Artists Use Texture* | **179**

Critical Thinking

Call students' attention to the caption of Figure 7.10 that explains the origins of Schapiro's invented word *Femmage*. Ask them to think about a new word that would describe their personal interests. Additionally, what would they include to add real texture to a collage designed to call attention to their interests in the way Schapiro uses fabrics created by women?

Promoting Discussion

Have students read the credit line for Figure 7.10. Have volunteers mark off the size of the canvas so that students will have a better sense of the painting's dimensions. Ask them to guess the sizes of some of the textured fabric in the artwork.

Promoting Discussion

Have students form small discussion groups and consider this issue: What techniques have the artists used to emphasize texture in the two artworks shown on these two pages? Since both are three-dimensional works, what special considerations, if any, should critics and art collectors make regarding the success of the artworks?

Cross-Curriculum: Language Arts

Allow students to work in pairs or small groups and write an imaginative history of the wood carving shown in Figure 7.11. Encourage them to use any literary form they wish: prose, poetry, or drama.

◄ **FIGURE 7.10** Schapiro invented the word *Femmage* to describe her collages. Rather than scraps of discarded paper, she used pieces of embroidered, appliquéd, and crocheted fabrics that were created by women to add real textures to her work. In this way, she connected her work to the traditional women's arts of the past.

Miriam Schapiro. *Yard Sale*. 1993. Acrylic and fabric on canvas. 208 × 228 cm (82 × 90″). Courtesy of the Steinbaum Krauss Gallery, New York, New York.

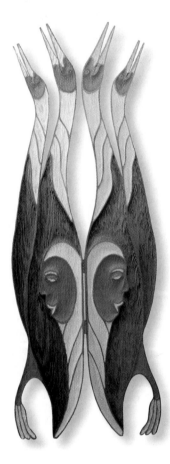

began using collage in the last century. (The word wasn't even invented until 1919.) Miriam Schapiro, an artist who uses collage, added bits of fabric, lace, and thread to her paintings to enrich the surface and to convey a message **(Figure 7.10)**.

Sculptors must also be aware of texture because the texture of each surface must fit the whole. Some sculptors imitate the real texture of skin, hair, and cloth, while others create new textures to fit new forms. In **Figure 7.11**, the artist lets the texture of the cedar wood show through the paint. In contrast, the sculptor of **Figure 7.12**, Edgar Degas, imitated real textures. He even added materials (a cotton skirt and a satin ribbon) to the figure to make it more realistic.

◄ **FIGURE 7.11** John Hoover is an Aleut sculptor. He uses the folklore of his people as subject matter, but he has developed a style that is not traditional. Notice how he lets the texture of the wood show through the paint. He uses only natural pigments. Can you identify the colors?

John Hoover. *Loon Song*. 1990. Cedar and natural pigments. 152 × 61 cm (60 × 24″). Glenn Green Galleries, Scottsdale, Arizona.

Curriculum Connection

Geography On a geographic or topographical map of Asia and North America, have students locate the Aleutian Islands. Ask them to trace the most logical path early migrating tribes would have taken across the Bering Strait into present-day Alaska. Ask them to speculate about what cultural influences would have remained, especially in the arts. After studying John Hoover's work, above, do they see any familiar use of the elements of art that might suggest an ancient influence? Encourage them to learn more about the geographical conditions of the Northwest Coast region that have an impact on daily life in this area.

French, 1834–1917

Edgar Degas. *Self-Portrait.* 1855. Oil on canvas. 81 × 64.5 cm (32⅕ × 25⅞"). Musee d'Orsay, Paris, France.

Edgar Degas (day-**gah**) was born in Paris in 1834. His family, wealthy bankers, supported his ambition to become an artist. He was educated at the École des Beaux-Arts by a French Classicist who trained him in classical drafting. This expertise in drawing is a main element in Degas' work.

Around 1865, Degas fell under the influence of the Impressionist movement and abandoned academic, classical subject matter and began painting contemporary subjects such as music halls, theatres, and cafés. Unlike the Impressionists with whom he is often associated, however, Degas was not interested in the use of light or in depicting nature on canvas. He worked in a studio and tried to capture his models in natural and spontaneous movements. He preferred women as his subjects and is best known for his studies of ballet dancers, although he also painted milliners (hat makers) and laundresses.

In the 1860s, he began experimenting with unusual methods of composition, such as alternate perspectives, odd visual angles, asymmetrical balance, and accidental cut-offs. These methods of composition would inspire many modern artists. As he grew older, his eyesight began to fail and he turned to a new media: sculpture. In his sculpture, as in his painting, he tried to capture spontaneous movement and realistic poses.

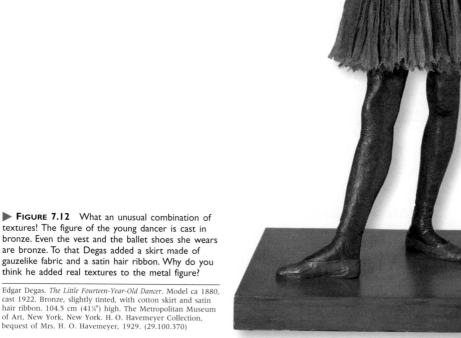

▶ **FIGURE 7.12** What an unusual combination of textures! The figure of the young dancer is cast in bronze. Even the vest and the ballet shoes she wears are bronze. To that Degas added a skirt made of gauzelike fabric and a satin hair ribbon. Why do you think he added real textures to the metal figure?

Edgar Degas. *The Little Fourteen-Year-Old Dancer.* Model ca 1880, cast 1922. Bronze, slightly tinted, with cotton skirt and satin hair ribbon. 104.5 cm (41¼") high. The Metropolitan Museum of Art, New York, New York. H. O. Havemeyer Collection, bequest of Mrs. H. O. Havemeyer, 1929. (29.100.370)

Art History

Have students research what subject matter Degas typically painted. List the results on the board. Then discuss how an art historian might use this information.

Art in Everyday Life

To foster students' awareness of the texture of sculpting media, suggest this: Textures in sculpture come from the medium and the tools the sculptor uses. Stone is chipped off and leaves a rough granular surface that can be polished smooth. Because wood is cut with gouges, a sculptor often will leave a surface of smooth grooves. Clay is shaped with fingers or tools and will take any shape that is pressed into it. Ancient Sumerians wrote in soft slabs of clay, pressing their cuneiform shapes into it with small wedges. Copper sheets can be hammered into three-dimensional forms with every hammer stroke making a texture. Bronze sculptures are cast from molds made of clay or wax. Compare examples of sculpture materials that you find in your environment.

LESSON 2   *How Artists Use Texture*   **181**

CULTURAL DIVERSITY

Real Texture Invite students to explore the ways texture is used by artists from different cultures. They can accomplish this task by researching the following topics: Native American pottery and blankets, Spanish lace, African sculpture, and Japanese woodcuts. Have them compare the similarities and differences and the effects that texture has on artworks from different cultures. Encourage students to record their findings, along with original pencil illustrations, in an art journal or sketchbook.

Art History

Tell students that the following quotation is credited to Frank Lloyd Wright: "No house should ever be *on* any hill or *on* anything. It should be *of* the hill, belonging to it, so hill and house could live together, each one happier for the other." Ask students to volunteer their evaluation of his quotation and the building they see in Figure 7.13. Ask: In your opinion, has Wright designed *Taliesin West* to be *of* the hill? In what way(s) are the hill and house interrelated?

Encourage students to find other examples of Wright's architecture and apply the same questions to them. To start, have them look again at *The David Wright House* (Figure 13.30 on page 377) then look ahead to *Fallingwater House. Bear Run, Pennsylvania* in Figure 11.20 on page 301.

Architects are also aware of the importance of texture. They use stucco, brick, wood, stone, concrete, metal, and glass to create texture. Frank Lloyd Wright, one of the most influential architects of the twentieth century, believed that a building should develop out of its natural surroundings **(Figure 7.13)**. Because of this, he selected textures that seemed natural. Interior designers select textures for rugs, drapes, furniture, and artwork that complement different wall surfaces. This gives a sense of cohesiveness, or unity, to a design.

In crafts, textures are essential. Potters manipulate textures by pressing different objects into wet clay. They can also change surfaces by applying glazes. Some glazes are shiny, while others are matte. Some glazes result in a crackle finish that gives a rough texture to a piece of pottery. Weavers control texture through the use of fibers and weaving techniques. For example, rough wool fibers have a different texture than smooth cotton fibers. In addition, weavers use different techniques to create texture. By twisting fibers as they weave, they can create a rough texture. Other artisans also use texture. Jewelry makers work with different kinds of metal to create various textures. They might emboss or press a raised design into metal or facet a stone to give its surfaces a smooth, shiny appearance. Feathers, river rocks,

▲ **FIGURE 7.13** The colors, forms, and textures of this building were planned so that Taliesin West would blend into the colors, forms, and textures of its desert setting. Wright believed that a building should be in harmony with its environment.

Frank Lloyd Wright. *Taliesin West.* Near Phoenix, Arizona.

MORE ABOUT... Trompe-l'oeil

Skilled artists can create the illusion of realistic texture through the technique of trompe-l'oeil. This technique can make a viewer believe that a two-dimensional object is real, such as a painting of a brick wall that to the eye appears textured and three-dimensional when, in fact, it is a flat surface. During the Classical age in Greece, famous painters amused themselves, and others, with the technique. According to legend, Giotto di Bondone (c. 1267–1337) slyly painted a fly on the nose of a subject in a painting that his master, Cimabue, was working on. The image was so real that Cimabue tried several times to brush the fly away from the painting, not realizing he was the victim of a practical joke.

seashells, seeds, bones, and teeth have been used to make jewelry and hair ornaments **(Figure 7.14).**

Artists also invent textures to enrich their works. Max Ernst used three unusual techniques—*frottage, grattage,* and *decalcomania*—to create his Surrealist fantasy paintings (Figure 7.16 on page 184). In **frottage** (froh-**tahzh**), *a freshly-painted canvas is placed right-side-up over a raised texture and scraped across the surface of the paint.* The paint that remains on the canvas creates a pattern that reflects the texture. The texture rubbings you made earlier in this chapter are another form of frottage. To create **grattage** (grah-**tahzh**) effects, *wet paint is scratched with a variety of tools, such as forks, razors, and combs.* In **decalcomania,** *paint is forced into random textured patterns* **(Figure 7.15).** Paint is placed between two canvas surfaces. The canvases are then pulled apart.

▲ **FIGURE 7.14** The native people of Ecuador used brilliant, tropical bird feathers to create ornaments. The ornaments pictured were created to decorate ears and hair.

Native people of South America. *Featherwork Ornaments.* Collected in 1938 by E. Erskine. National Museum of the American Indian, Smithsonian Institution, Heye Foundation, New York, New York.

Activity — **Inventing Textures**

Applying Your Skills. On a small piece of white paper, draw nine shapes of different sizes with a pencil or felt-tip pen. Some shapes should touch the edges of the paper. Fill each shape with sketches of a different texture. The textures should be invented. For instance, you could put lines of writing close together in one shape, or you could try repeating small shapes in another. Try line patterns, stippling, or smooth shadow.

Computer Option. Explore textures and effects that can be made with the Brush tool or other tools on the computer. Menus provide choices from thick, opaque oils to wet, transparent paint. Experiment. Save your results by applying your discoveries to objects, shapes, or scenes.

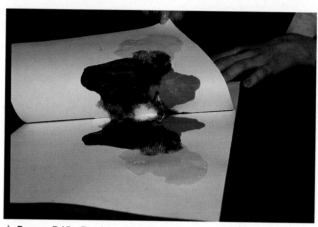

▲ **FIGURE 7.15** Decalcomania technique.

 Check Your Understanding

1. Define *collage.*
2. Describe a form of frottage.
3. How does an artist create a grattage effect?
4. In what technique is paint forced into random textured patterns?

Activity

Inventing Textures

Applying Your Skills. Words written in cursive and repeated over and over, line after line, make very interesting invented textures.

🖥 **Computer Option.** As an alternative activity, use these instructions: Explore the tools and menus on your software program to create visual textures or patterns. Use a gradient or pattern as the Brush to draw images with varying textures or values. Select Shape tools, automatically filled with pattern. Create your own patterns and use them. Draw empty shapes and fill them using the Bucket Flood-fill tool. Explore the Spray Can or Airbrush tool; if available, alter the settings. Add shading, shadows, and highlights. If your application allows, create your own gradients. Flood-fill large portions of the screen with pattern and then draw into the area with an eraser, changing size if possible. Save your results for future reference or collages.

ASSESS..........

Self-Assessment

Have students complete the lesson review questions. Answers appear below.

Reteaching

Have students work in pairs, each student taking a turn describing a specific texture while the other person sketches an object that exhibits the texture identified.

Enrichment

■ Assign Enrichment Activities 13 and 14 in the TCR. 📁

CLOSE.............

Ask students to summarize what they learned about texture.

 Answers to Check Your Understanding

1. Collage is an artwork onto which materials such as textured paper and fabric have been attached.
2. One form of frottage is created by placing a freshly painted canvas right-side up over a textured surface and then rubbing or scraping the painting.
3. Grattage is done by scratching a painted canvas with a variety of tools, such as forks or combs.
4. In decalcomania, paint is forced into random textured patterns.

Studio Project

Fantasy Landscape

(pages 184–185)

(National Standards: 1a, 1b, 2b, 2c, 3b)

FOCUS...........

Objective

After completing this lesson, students will be able to:

■ Create a fantasy painting using Max Ernst's techniques to produce textured areas.

TEACH..........

Motivator

Have students offer suggestions of various objects that might be included in a fantasy landscape. If possible, ask them to identify sketches in their sketchbook that might be used in this activity. Students may enjoy practicing the three techniques of frottage, grattage, and decalcomania. Set up three stations in the room, one for each technique. Allow students to move from station to station to practice each technique. Students should carry the same piece of paper from each station to the next so they will have a sample of each technique.

Studio Skills

It is important to stress skill in cutting if cut-outs are to be added to the collage. Also indicate to students that the shape of the object must fit into the work. Students should not cut out a rough shape and glue it down without considering the area on which it is to be placed. Any details being painted or glued onto the textured background must be planned so that the shapes relate to the background. If needed, students could blend the shapes into the background by painting over the edges.

Fantasy Landscape

▲ **FIGURE 7.16**

Max Ernst. *The Eye of Silence.* 1943–44. Oil on canvas. 108 × 141 cm (42½ × 55½"). Washington University Gallery of Art, St. Louis, Missouri.

SUPPLIES

■ **Acrylic paints and assorted brushes**

■ **One sheet of heavy paper or canvas**

■ **Scratch paper for practice**

■ **Wax paper**

■ **Scratching and rubbing tools such as combs or rulers**

■ **Magazine clippings**

■ **Scissors and white glue**

Max Ernst was among the artists, philosophers, and writers who formed the Surrealist movement in the mid-1920s. Surrealists searched for a new reality—one that rejected the long-established rules of composition and logic. They believed that this reality could be found in the subconscious mind, and they created paintings that took on the look of dreams or nightmares. Salvador Dali (Figure 13.28, page 375) and René Magritte (Figure 5.37, page 126) were members of this movement.

Ernst used three unusual techniques—*frottage, grattage,* and *decalcomania*—to bring his fantasies to life. Ernst then elaborated on the design. Sometimes he cut the textured pieces into forms with which he created collages. Sometimes he painted over areas such as the sky in *The Eye of Silence* **(Figure 7.16).**

What You Will Learn

You will create a fantasy painting using Max Ernst's techniques to produce textured areas. You may cut and rearrange the textured area to make new shapes. Add details and contrasting shapes using paint, oil pastels, markers, and collage. The work should be unified. One object must blend into the next without empty spaces separating them. When you are finished, the work must look like a Surrealist's dream.

Creating

Study Ernst's painting (Figure 7.16). Notice that the woman's face has been cut from another picture and pasted on. Notice also how the realistic sky has been painted up to the edges of the textured areas. Can you guess which shapes have

184 | **CHAPTER 7** Texture

MORE ABOUT... **Dada**

After World War I, Max Ernst joined with several other artists and writers to form the Dada movement. This group was angry about the terrible destruction that the war had brought, and they believed that the civilized world was destroying itself. Writers created nonsense poetry by cutting individual words from printed pages and dropping the words onto a sheet of paper. The Dadaists tried to shock the public into awareness. The word *Dada* is the French word meaning "hobby horse." It was chosen as the name of the group because it made no sense. Because of the rebellious nature of this group, the movement did not last long.

been cut and attached to the surface of the canvas? Can you tell where he has brushed on paint and where he has used decalcomania, frottage, or grattage?

Using scratch paper, experiment with Ernst's three techniques. For decalcomania, try placing translucent wax paper over the blobs of paint so that you can see the way the paint moves as you gently push the colors around. With a little practice you can control the shapes and the blending of colors. Don't let the paint dry before you separate the sheets of paper. You will need a partner to hold the bottom paper down while you quickly pull the top paper off the surface.

Step 1 Apply blobs of color to your large sheet of paper. Place the second painting surface over the first and use gentle pressure to push the paint around. Then pull the surfaces apart quickly. Rub or scratch the wet surfaces if you wish. Allow the paint to dry. Save both surfaces.

Step 2 Study the textured shapes you have made and let them give you ideas for your fantasy picture. Do you see land or animal forms among the shapes and textures? Do you want to cut up one of the surfaces and glue it on the other? Do you need to paint out some parts?

Step 3 Release your imagination. Add details using paint, oil pastels, markers, and collage. If you glue on shapes cut from magazine pictures, you may need to paint over the edges of the added shapes with a color that unifies them with the background.

Step 4 Mount or mat your finished work for display.

EVALUATING YOUR WORK

▶ **DESCRIBE** Identify the subjects of the fantasy scene you created. List and explain the techniques you used to create visual textures in your fantasy scene.

▶ **ANALYZE** How did the visual textures affect the look of your work? Did you attach any textured shapes or magazine cutouts? What color scheme did you use? How did it affect the work? Are the shapes predominantly geometric or free-form? How does that affect the look of the work?

▶ **INTERPRET** What kind of mood does your work express? Give it a title that sums up your feelings about the meaning of this work.

▶ **JUDGE** Which aesthetic theories would be the most important in judging this work? Do you think your work is successful? If you were to do it over, is there anything you would change to improve it?

▲ **FIGURE 7.16A** Student work.

STUDIO PROJECT *Fantasy Landscape* **185**

Assemblage
(pages 186–187)
(National Standards: 1a, 1b, 2b, 2c, 3b)

FOCUS............
Objectives

After completing this lesson, students will:

■ Design and create a throne with a theme by assembling and joining found objects.

■ Create texture with found objects.

TEACH ....
Motivator

Ask students to bring in examples of art and craft objects made by friends and family members. Ask them to find out if there are any artists in their family's history.

Art History

Some visionary artists claim to have visions that tell them what and why to create. For example, in North Georgia, the Rev. Howard Finster has created a beautiful and fantastic garden composed of what most people would call junk. He also paints visions and messages from God. Eddie Martin built and painted colorful walls, sculptures, and architectural pieces in his yard. Italian tile setter Simon Rodia used ceramic tile, broken glass, dishes, and other found objects to create the Watts Towers in Los Angeles. Students may want to research and study other visionary artists. Ask students to speculate about the sources of inspiration for these artists. Are they driven by an inner purpose?

Assemblage

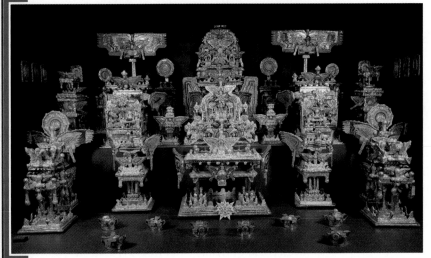

▲ FIGURE 7.17

James Hampton. *The Throne of the Third Heaven of the Nations Millennium General Assembly.* c. 1950-64. Gold and silver aluminum foil, colored Kraft paper, and plastic sheets over wood, paperboard, and glass. 180 pieces. 3.2 × 8.2 × 4.4 m (10 ½ × 27 × 14.5'). National Museum of American Art, Smithsonian Institution, Washington, D.C.

SUPPLIES

■ **Sketchbook and pencils**

■ **Materials that will serve as a base for the throne**

■ **Found objects such as boxes, tubes, lightbulbs, and small spice jars**

■ **White glue, nontoxic rubber cement, masking tape, duct tape**

■ **String, rope, wire**

■ **Scissors and utility knife**

■ **Aluminum foil, foil wrapping paper, sequins**

James Hampton, a soft-spoken African-American, was born in 1909 in a small South Carolina community. Around 1950, he rented an unheated, poorly–lit garage near the boarding house where he lived. By November 4, 1964, the day he died, he had built in that garage an astonishing artwork called *The Throne of the Third Heaven of the Nations Millennium General Assembly,* a collection of 180 glittering objects **(Figure 7.17).**

Although Hampton never studied art, he had a natural sense of design. Notice how the throne at the rear serves as the heart of the assemblage. Bordering both sides of the throne are matching pairs of objects. Hampton used old furniture and discarded objects, such as cardboard tubes and insulation board, to construct the major pieces. He joined the pieces with strips of cardboard or metal cut from coffee cans. Glass vases, light-bulbs, and jelly glasses completed the tops and

corners of objects. Upholstery tacks, small nails, and straight pins held everything together. Finally, all of the objects were covered with recycled foil of various colors. Some of his foil came from store displays, some from gift wrap, and some was ordinary aluminum foil.

After Hampton's death, the massive construction was moved to the National Museum of American Art in Washington, D. C., where it can be viewed today.

What You Will Learn

You will design and create a small throne with a theme by assembling and joining found materials. Working individually or in small groups, symmetrically join the found materials to make a chairlike structure. Then, as James Hampton did, alter the surface texture by covering the entire structure with foil and foil wrapping paper.

186   CHAPTER 7   Texture

MORE ABOUT...   The Throne

James Hampton used his imagination to collect and transform the discarded materials he used to construct *The Throne.* All of the objects in the throne are covered with different kinds of gold and aluminum foils. In addition to wooden furniture, Hampton used layers of insulation board and hollow cardboard tubes from rolls of carpeting, jelly glasses

and light bulbs covered with foil, while construction paper and cardboard are the foundations for decorative forms such as stars and wings. The edges of tables are sometimes trimmed with tubes of electrical cable camouflaged with gold foil. Rows of small knobs are made of balls of crumpled foil or newspaper covered with foil.

Creating

Brainstorm with classmates for themes for your throne. Think of school subjects such as math, science, or history. Think of activities you do after school. Consider outer-space themes, underwater themes, or time-period themes. Choose a theme.

Step 1 Working in a small group, design a chair-shaped object that will serve as the base for your throne. Collect small discarded objects and pieces of heavy cardboard that can be used to construct and decorate the throne.

Step 2 Each person should look at the collected objects and make sketches of his or her ideas for the throne structure and the decorations that will go on it. Then, as a group, study all the sketches and select the best ideas. Each member of the group should make one final drawing of the combined ideas.

Step 3 Join your found objects, organizing them symmetrically. If necessary, cut shapes out of heavy cardboard. Before you cover the finished work with foil, decorate the surfaces with rope and wire, buttons, and layers of cardboard to create raised surfaces and interesting textures. You may even add words or phrases with raised block letters or rope that imitates cursive writing. Be sure everything is joined securely.

Step 4 Change the surface by covering everything with shiny foil. You may glue paper-backed foil to smooth surfaces, or press aluminum foil tightly to irregular surfaces. Some aluminum foil may be left smooth, and some may be crumpled up. Sequins and other shiny objects can be attached with pins or glue. Give your throne a poetic title.

EVALUATING YOUR WORK

▶ **DESCRIBE** Describe the way you constructed the basic form of the throne. Name the theme. Identify the objects and shapes you attached to the main form and explain how they represented the theme.

▶ **ANALYZE** What kinds of materials did you use to create your throne? Did you use symmetry to organize your decorative objects? How did the addition of shiny foil change the surface quality of the structure?

▶ **INTERPRET** Can your classmates recognize the theme? Did your group find a poetic title that reflects the theme?

▶ **JUDGE** Which aesthetic theories would you use to judge this work? Do you think your throne is successful? If you were going to do it over, what would you change?

▲ **FIGURE 7.17A** Student work.

Studio Skills

Some places to look for old or damaged chairs are behind furniture stores, trash piles on the streets, at garage sales, junk stores, surplus warehouses, attics, and junk yards. Decorating materials can be found in home and school kitchens or trash piles. Grocery stores or department stores are often willing to donate materials to schools. When assembling the throne, a hot glue gun may be helpful in speeding up the gluing process.

Studio Skills

Have students create assemblages that use as the theme one of the elements of art studied thus far in the course (line, shape, form, space, color, value, and texture).

ASSESS..........
Keeping a Portfolio

Remind students that the preliminary sketches and the final artwork for this Studio Project are likely candidates for their portfolio.

Self-Assessment

Have students apply the steps of art criticism to their own artwork using the "Evaluating Your Work" questions on this page. In addition, ask the following: Where did the idea or theme for the throne originate? Where were most of the added materials found? Why were certain ones chosen over others?

CLOSE............

Go around the classroom and ask each student to name something he or she learned about how artists use texture when creating assemblages.

MORE ABOUT... Assemblage Art

The roots of assemblage art were established during the first decade of the twentieth century. Dadaists and Cubists had profound effects on assemblage art fifty years later when it was defined and recognized as its own genre. While it may at first seem nonsensical, assemblage sculpture is a natural medium for affecting an audience. Using common objects that have not been designed for artistic purposes, the artist effectively bridges the gap between the viewer's world and the artistic world. When the viewer sees an everyday object in the context of art, he or she is forced to consider its place in the artwork and in society.

Paper Sculpture Creature

Studio Project

Paper Sculpture Creature

(pages 188–189)
(National Standards: 1a, 1b, 2b, 2c, 3b)

FOCUS...........
Objectives

After completing this lesson, students will be able to:

- Design and create a three-dimensional, freestanding, imaginary paper creature using a variety of strong papers.
- Experiment with alternative media such as feathers, foil paper, ribbons, yarn, sequins, glitter, mylar, or papers with contrasting colors on each side.

TEACH..........
Motivator

Distribute photos and prints of various animals and creatures for students to study. Ask students to choose a creature, then describe it to the class without revealing its identity. They should describe both its behavioral and physical characteristics. The rest of the class should try to guess what type of creature is being described.

▲ FIGURE 7.18

Artist unknown. Mexico. *Bird.* 1988. Tin and gold paint. 28 × 22 × 17.8 cm (11 × 8½ × 7″). Private collection.

SUPPLIES

- **Sketchbook and pencil**
- **Colored construction paper**
- **Variety of other papers to decorate the surface, such as wallpaper samples, shiny wrapping papers, and paper ribbons**
- **Scissors, ruler, and sharp knife**
- **Pointed tool for piercing, such as a compass point**
- **Transparent tape, white glue, straight pins**
- **Cardboard tubes and containers for internal support**

188   CHAPTER 7   Texture

In Mexico, artists create beautiful traditional tinwork pieces such as frames, candleholders, chandeliers, crosses, and trinket boxes. Using flat sheets of tin, craftspeople cut, score, and pierce the tin to form three-dimensional works of art that are used to decorate their homes and churches.

The bird in **Figure 7.18** was made by a craftsperson in Mexico. The techniques used by the artist have been used in Mexico for more than 200 years. These decorative processes are part of a long tradition of surface decoration developed in Spain and brought to Mexico by the Spaniards.

Such surface decorations, which produce highly–textured real and visual effects, are made by cutting, piercing, stamping, scoring, and soldering. Another method of joining, tab-and-slot construction, is also used.

As you study the tin bird in Figure 7.18, you can see how the artist used these processes to create a three-dimensional form. The back has been scored and is bent into a curve. The textural effects of the feathers have been created by layers of fringe that have been curled. Notice the contrast obtained by using fringes of different lengths. The ones on the head and around the eyes are very short. The wing areas have short and long fringes. The longest fringes are shaped into a spiral to create the round tail. The breast of the bird is decorated with oval shapes that have been applied to the form in a repeated, overlapping pattern.

These same techniques can be used to create paper sculpture. Try to use many

---

TECHNOLOGY OPTIONS

Developing Computer Skills If computers are available to your students, suggest this activity: Use paper sculpture techniques to create a three-dimensional box using sturdy paper or cardboard. Each of the six sides should measure 6 × 6″ (15.2 × 15.2 cm).

Next, you will create a square motif on the computer that can be printed six times and applied to the cube to observe the changes in a design motif when it is transferred from a two-dimensional to a three-dimensional form.

forms of decoration to give your paper sculpture varied textures. Design a creature that is interesting from every point of view.

What You Will Learn

After studying the Mexican bird and practicing paper sculpture techniques, you will design and create a three-dimensional, freestanding, imaginary paper creature using a variety of strong papers. You will cover the surface with a variety of interesting textures using fringing, cutting, curling, and scoring. This sculpture should look interesting from every point of view.

Creating

Study the paper sculpture techniques on page 436 in the Handbook. Practice them using construction paper. Study the tin bird to see what techniques you think were used to construct it.

Step 1 Make several sketches in your sketchbook to plan your sculpture. Select your best design. Make some sketches showing different views of the sculpture. List the materials and techniques you will use to construct your three-dimensional creature and those you will use to create surface textures.

Step 2 Collect the materials you will need. Construct your sculpture based on the drawings you have made. You may change your plan as you go along. If your creature is too heavy to stand, support it on the inside with cardboard tubes and containers.

Step 3 Place the finished sculpture on a firm base for display. Glue or pin it to the base.

EVALUATING YOUR WORK

▶ **DESCRIBE** List the materials and paper-sculpture techniques you used to create your artwork. Did the practice session with paper-sculpture techniques help you in planning your final project? How did you prepare it for display?

▶ **ANALYZE** What form did you create for your sculpture? Describe the different textures you created. Is the work interesting from every point of view?

▶ **INTERPRET** What kind of mood or idea does your finished sculpture express? Give your work a title that expresses the mood.

▶ **JUDGE** Have you created a freestanding, three-dimensional, fantasy creature? Is your work successful? Is there anything you would change to make the work more successful? Which aesthetic theory would be best to judge this work?

▲ **FIGURE 7.18A** Student work.

Aesthetics

Remind students that many Mexican towns are famous for producing a certain type of art or craft, such as pottery, jewelry, glassware, hand-woven clothing, or handbags. Also, Mexico is famous for the magnificent murals that adorn its city's buildings. Mexican painters often express the pride of the Mexican people by rendering images of traditional folklore, daily life, and political history. Encourage students to study other arts and crafts of Mexico as well as other artists, such as Frida Kahlo, Diego Rivera, and José Clemente Orozco.

ASSESS..........
Keeping a Portfolio

Remind students that the preliminary sketches and the final artworks for this Studio Lesson are likely candidates for their portfolios.

Self-Assessment

Have students apply the steps of art criticism to their own artwork using the "Evaluating Your Work" questions on this page. In addition, ask the following: What types of papers and materials were used? Were various textures and patterns created? How?

CLOSE............

Have each student display his or her paper sculpture creature from all sides.

CULTURAL DIVERSITY

Mexican Sculpture The ancient cultures in West Mexico did not demonstrate the trademark architectural achievements or stone sculpting skills of the Aztecs. However, they established a remarkable artistic culture that shows its influence on Mexico's contemporary art, such as the tin bird shown in Figure 7.18. Ancient artists presented humans and animals in typical situations, not as gods or supreme spiritual powers as the Maya often did. These animals sing, hug, and play instruments and are most often found depicted in a natural, plump state.

TECHNOLOGY
Studio Project

Still-Life Collage

(pages 190–191)
(National Standards: 1a, 1b, 2b, 2c, 3b)

Still-Life Collage

FOCUS...........

Objectives

After completing this lesson, students will be able to:

■ Select and sketch five or more objects into one still-life image.

■ Render the image or scan and alter the image on the computer. Manipulate the still-life collage by applying different colors, textures, and contrasts so that one object becomes the center of interest.

Supplies

■ Sketchbook
■ Computer
■ Paint or draw application
■ Printer

TEACH.........

Motivator

Refer students to Figure 7.19, one of Robert Silver's photomosaics. Ask students to identify the overall image that they see. Introduce the term *photomosaic.* Tell students about Robert Silvers and how he developed a computer program that sorts thousands of digitized photographic images based on color, density, internal shapes, and light. Have students scrutinize the work and note the range of small photographs within the overall image. Color, shape, and texture makes our eyes see the small photographs as one huge image.

▲ FIGURE 7.19

Robert Silvers. Based on van Gogh's *Self-Portrait*, 1889, in the collection of Musee d'Orsay, Paris. Photomosaic™. 1997.

SUPPLIES

■ **Sketchbook**
■ **Computer**
■ **Paint or Draw application**
■ **Printer**
Optional
■ **Scanner**
■ **Digital camera**
■ **CD–ROM with textures**
■ **Real textures and photographs of textures**

Robert Silvers has used an exciting merger of art, photography, and computer graphics to create his unique photomosaics. The inspiration for his high-tech art came from a very low-tech idea. He saw a portrait made of seashells and realized that he could create a similar effect digitally. As a photographer and a student of computer science at the Massachusetts Institute of Technology, he tried to find a way to unite the two. He wrote and refined a computer program that sorted thousands of digitized photographic images by color, density, internal shapes, and light. This program enabled him to create his first photomosaics. The Internet was also important as it gave him access to hundreds of thousands of digitized images he needed for his palette.

When you first look at **Figure 7.19,** you may be tricked because it closely resembles van Gogh's original work. When you look closely, however, you will see that this is a mosaic. Instead of using traditional mosaic materials, such as small cubes of colored marble or glass, Silvers has created a mosaic using individual, rectangular photographs as his "tiles."

What You Will Learn

You will select five or more objects for a still life, arrange them into an interesting composition, and make several sketches from different points of view in your sketchbook. Choose your best idea and draw or scan it into your computer. Then apply different textures and colors to the objects and the background so that the entire image has texture and color. Use color contrast to make one object or area the center of interest.

TEACHER TALK

Studio Option Students can complete their still-life collage sketch as indicated in the lesson, but instead of using the computer paint application, they can use old magazines for collecting textured images. They should go through the magazines looking for images that have a range of colors and visual texture. Cut them out and sort them accordingly. Use glue to apply them to the sketch.

Creating

Explore the textures your application provides. Locate textures that simulate real surfaces. Discover if your application allows you to edit existing textures or create new textures using the paint tools that you can add to the menu.

Step 1 Use a variety of tools on your palette to create surfaces that represent cloth, wood grain, reflective, and transparent surfaces. For example, the air brush can spray a coarse or fine mist by changing the settings. Other menus allow you to choose colors for a gradient fill as well as selecting the direction and shape of the fill. These can result in reflective textures. Research other sources of textures such as CD–ROMs. If available, use a scanner or digital camera to capture textures from real objects or from photographs.

Step 2 Combine these textures and produce a simple still life with four or five objects, all made from different textures. Look at the textures you have collected and decide what objects you will create. Then make several sketches for your composition. Choose the one you like best.

Step 3 Use your choice of tools to draw these objects and arrange them. Consider a center of interest or focal point that can be emphasized by size, color, shape, or texture.

Step 4 Place the objects in a setting. Are they indoors or outside? What surface are they sitting on? Add details and texture to the background. Include texture on every surface you can—table, cloth, floor, and wall. Remember to save your work. Use the Save As command to retitle and save in editions. Print and display your final textured still life.

EVALUATING YOUR WORK

▶ **DESCRIBE** What objects have you included in your still life? Describe the setting in which you placed the objects.

▶ **ANALYZE** List the textures you selected for each area of your image. Did you repeat any of the textures? What colors did you choose? How did you use color to emphasize one object or area of your work?

▶ **INTERPRET** How has the application of textures to your image affected the mood, feeling, or idea of your still life? Give your work a title that sums up your feelings about it.

▶ **JUDGE** Do you think the textured surfaces create a satisfying still life? Is there anything you would change? What aesthetic theory would you use to evaluate this work?

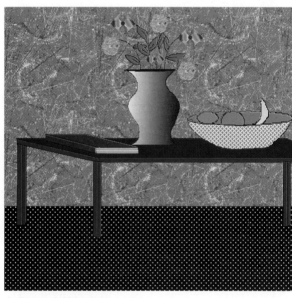

▲ **FIGURE 7.19A** Student work.

Using the Internet and search engines, have students research how photomosaics are actually made using technology. Have them compile their information, including web sites that provide examples of images.

Art History

Review with students the work of Impressionist painters, especially Georges Seurat who featured the use of pointillism in his work. Instead of thousands of digitized photographs, he used thousand of dots of colors to build up one overall image. Using the computer paint application, have students develop a pointillism painting featuring color, shape, and texture.

ASSESS..........
Portfolio

Remind students that the final artwork for this Studio Project is a likely candidate for their portfolios.

Self-Assessment

Have students apply the steps of art criticism to their artwork.

Enrichment

Have students take their completed computer paint image and alter it so that a different object within it becomes the center of interest. Have them give this new image a different title and save it. Ask: Which is more appealing to you? Why?

CLOSE............

Have a class display of the completed still-life collages. In pairs, students can view the completed work of classmates and note their three favorite still-life collages based on the use of color, texture, and center of interest.

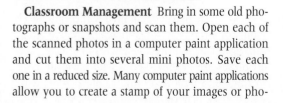

TEACHER TALK

Classroom Management Bring in some old photographs or snapshots and scan them. Open each of the scanned photos in a computer paint application and cut them into several mini photos. Save each one in a reduced size. Many computer paint applications allow you to create a stamp of your images or photos. You can then use your own bank of small photo images to create your own photo mosaic by copying the mini photo you want to use and pasting it or stamping it several times to create the color or texture you need in a certain area.

(pages 192–193)
(National Standards: 2b, 4c, 5a, 5c)

Critiquing the Work

▶ Describe
What do you see?

- On the left from top to bottom is a woven orange and black ribbon with little light blue and pink flowers in the center of the designs. At the top is a gold, glass bottle. Below that is a pink rose in full bloom and a rosebud with two leaves. Below that is an open compact with a powder puff, and you can see a reflection of a porcelain figure and the pocket watch in the mirror.

▶ Analyze
How is this work organized?

- Lines are on the ribbon, and all the edges of the objects are clearly defined. Free-form shapes are the ribbon; the rose, bud, and leaves; the pear; the cherub, and the lady in the book. The rest of the shapes are geometric.

- The colors are optical colors. You see all the hues of the spectrum. There are tints of red, blue, and violet. The painting of the woman in the book is in tints and shades of brown, which is a low-intensity of orange.

- The artist has used simulated texture.

- Rough is the ribbon; smooth is the table top; matte is the portrait of the lady. Shiny is on the glass, the silver container, the two gold, glass bottles, and the broach.

192

ART CRITICISM IN ACTION

▲ **FIGURE 7.20**

Audrey Flack. *Leonardo's Lady.* 1974. Oil over synthetic polymer paint on canvas. 188 × 203.2 cm (6'2" × 6'8"). The Museum of Modern Art, New York, New York. Purchased with the aid of funds from the National Endowment for the Arts and an anonymous donor.

MORE ABOUT... Audrey Flack

In the early 1980s Audrey Flack shifted her focus from Photorealist paintings to sculpture. Her involvement in sculpture combines her interests in anatomy and in nineteenth-century painting and sculpture. She has dedicated herself to inventing a series of female deities, some from classical mythology and others of her own imagination. Done in a highly realistic style, her goddess figures incorporate elements of various cultures including Native American, Egyptian, and Greek references. For Flack, these goddesses are healing figures who have the power to transcend time and bring comfort to all, a role which Flack believes also belongs to artists.

1 DESCRIBE What do you see?

List all of the information found in the credit line. Use your perception skills to study the things you see in the work.

- What materials were used to create the artwork? What is the size? Measure it on a wall or the floor to see how big it is.
- This painting has many objects. Organize a system for listing the objects. For example, you may start at one edge and work your way through the painting until you reach the other edge. List reflections of objects wherever you find them.

2 ANALYSIS How is this work organized?

This step deals with the composition of the work. You will collect information about all the elements of art.

- Where do you find lines in this work? Are they static or active?
- Can you find free-form and geometric shapes? Where?
- What hues, values, and intensities of color do you see?
- What kinds of visual texture has the artist used?
- Can you find rough, smooth, matte, and shiny textures in this work? Where?

3 INTERPRET What is the artist trying to communicate?

Now you will combine the clues you have collected with your personal experiences to decide what the artist is saying.

- How has the artist's unique use of texture affected the look of this work?
- Do you recognize the painting of the lady in the center of the work? Check it to be sure.
- How does this work make you feel?
- Give this work a new title based upon your interpretation.

4 JUDGE What do you think of the work?

Decide if this is a successful work of art.

- Did the artist use the element of texture successfully?
- Do you think this is a successful work of art? Why or why not? Use one or more of the aesthetic theories described in Chapter 2 to defend your judgment.

Art Criticism in Action | **193**

MEET THE ARTIST
AUDREY FLACK

American, 1931–

Audrey Flack. *Self-Portrait*. 1974. Acrylic on linen. 203.2 × 162.6 cm (80 × 64"). Private collection.

Audrey Flack grew up in Manhattan and attended the High School of Music and Art in New York City. Later she won a scholarship to Yale to study art with Josef Albers. He stressed the importance of color relationships and a pared down, minimal use of the other art elements.

Flack is perhaps best known for her Super-realistic paintings. In her art, Flack focuses on the surface qualities of objects. She alerts us through vibrant color, texture, and a unique use of space to the immediate, but often timeless, images of our world.

Interpret
What is the artist trying to communicate?

- The artist has simulated the surfaces of the objects so carefully that this looks like a photograph.
- Answers will vary. Some may recognize the style of the painting and relate the title to Leonardo da Vinci. The image in the painting definitely looks like it was by Leonardo da Vinci, but it is not *Mona Lisa*, or *Ginevra dé Benci*. It is a painting in the Louvre, *La Belle Ferronniere*. The authentication of this work is disputed. If the students know this fact, does that change their impression of the whole painting? Some may say that objects such as the watch, the rose, the fruit, and the beautiful young woman are symbols of time passing because the fruit will rot, the rose will wither, and the young woman will age.
- Answers will vary.

Judge
What do you think of the work?

- Answers will vary
- Answers will vary, but most will say yes, because she has simulated all the textures perfectly.
- Answers will vary. Most students will choose the theory of Imitationalism; some may say that plus Formalism. Those who understand the symbolism of the time passing might also mention Emotionalism.

Time & Place Twentieth Century

Audrey Flack painted *Leonardo's Lady* in 1974. Some other events that happened the same year:

Social Studies: Faced with impeachment over the Watergate scandal, Richard Nixon resigned his presidency.

Language Arts: Nobel Prize-winner Alexander Solzhenitsyn was expelled from the Soviet Union after the publication of his book on the prison system, *The Gulag Archipelago*.

**CONNECTIONS
HISTORY**

The Secret of Silk

(National Standards: 6a, 6b)

Objectives

After completing this feature, students will be able to:

■ Explain why silk remained a valuable trade item for centuries.

■ Describe how the secret of silk production spread throughout the world.

Teaching the Connection

Have students read the feature on this page.

Ask volunteers to share what they know about silk. What are examples of products made from silk? *(Examples include clothing, accessories, linens.)* What are other examples of fine fabrics? *(Examples include velvet, satin, angora.)* Why do you think the artist who created this temple hanging chose to use silk? *(Silk gives the piece an elegant look. It was created for special religious celebrations.)*

Tell students that the silk panel contains appliquè and brocade work. The temple hanging shows several Buddhas surrounded by lotus blossoms and other Buddhist symbols.

The Secret of Silk

◄ **FIGURE 7.21**

Central Tibet. Temple Hanging. Detail. 1940. Appliqué with cut silk, brocade, and pearls. 1.2 × 13.1 m (4 × 43'). Los Angeles County Museum of Art, Los Angeles, California. Gift of Mr. and Mrs. James Coburn.

Have you ever heard the expression "as smooth as silk?" Silk is a valuable fiber used to make fine fabrics. It is produced by the silkworm. Silk is also used in decorative textiles, such as the Tibetan Temple Hanging in **Figure 7.21.**

The origin of silk dates back to the twenty-seventh century B.C. The silkworm moth was originally found only in China. For thousands of years, the people of China kept the silk-producing process a secret. Because silk was difficult to obtain, it became a valuable trade item.

Although silk fabric was traded to other countries, it was produced only in China. In about A.D. 300, however, a group of people from Japan smuggled silkworms out of China. They brought the silkworms and four young Chinese women back to Japan to teach them how to produce silk.

About 200 years later, a Roman emperor sent two monks to China to smuggle silkworm eggs. The monks hid the eggs in their hollow walking canes. With the secret revealed, silk production spread throughout Asia and the West.

Making the Connection

1. How do you think silk fabric enhances this textile art?
2. Explain why silk was a valuable trade item.
3. How did the people of Japan learn the Chinese secret of silk production?

Answers to Making the Connection

1. Silk is a fine fabric that gives a rich, lustrous look to the textile art.
2. Because silk was produced only in China, it was difficult to obtain and became a valuable trade item.
3. They smuggled silkworms and four Chinese girls out of China. The girls taught them how to produce silk.

Building Vocabulary

On a separate sheet of paper, write the term that best matches each definition given below.

1. The element of art that refers to how things feel, or look as if they might feel if touched.
2. The illusion of a three-dimensional surface.
3. A surface that reflects a soft, dull light.
4. An artwork onto which materials such as textured paper and fabric have been attached.
5. A method of producing textures by placing a freshly-painted canvas right side up over a raised texture and scraping it across the surface of the paint.
6. The technique of scratching into wet paint with a variety of tools to create texture.
7. A technique of creating random texture patterns by applying thick paint to two surfaces, pressing them together, and then pulling them apart.

Reviewing Art Facts

Answer the following questions using complete sentences.

1. With what senses is texture perceived?
2. What is the difference between real and visual texture?
3. What is the difference between simulated and invented texture?
4. Name the four types of textures.
5. Name two ways in which painters may add real textures to their paintings.
6. In what ways do sculptors create texture in their works?
7. Describe the similarities and differences between frottage, grattage, and decalcomania.

Thinking Critically About Art

1. **Describe.** Look at the photographs in Figure 7.2 on page 172. Describe them without naming any of the objects shown. Describe only the lines, shapes, spaces, values, and textures in the photographs. From your description, have classmates guess which photograph you are describing.
2. **Compare and contrast.** Compare the ways Albright (Figure 7.6, page 177), and Renoir (Figure 7.7, page 177), have used texture in the representation of women's clothes.

Use the Performing Arts Handbook on page 419 to find out how Paul Winter captures the texture of the sounds of nature through his music.

inter NET CONNECTION Find out how textures are used in creating two- and three-dimensional works of art. Explore the Glencoe Fine Arts Site at **www.glencoe.com/sec/art** To begin your search, find the chapter you are studying in the Table of Contents and click on one of the "hot links."

Answers to Building Vocabulary
1. texture
2. visual texture
3. matte surface
4. collage
5. frottage
6. grattage
7. decalcomania

Answers to Reviewing Art Facts
1. Touch and vision.
2. When you actually touch something you are experiencing real texture. When you look at a photograph of textures and remember how they feel, you are experiencing visual texture.
3. Simulated textures imitate real textures. Invented textures do not represent any real surface qualities but stimulate memories of real textures.
4. Rough, smooth, matte, and shiny.
5. By using collage, frottage, grattage, or decalcomonia.
6. Sculptures add texture to their works by leaving tool marks on the surfaces.
7. Similarities: In frottage and grattage the surface of the paint is altered with tools or rubbing.
Differences: In frottage, paint is scraped off; in frottage, paint is etched with a tool; in decalcomania, paint is forced into random textured pattern by pressing tow surfaces together.

Evaluate
- Have students complete the *Chapter 7 Test* in the TCR. 📁
- Alternative Assessment teaching strategies are provided below or in the *Testing Program and Alternative Assessment* booklet. 📁

Extension
In Chapter 7, students learned that many artists used the collage technique to create exciting and innovative textures in their artworks. Have students research the use of collage and write three paragraphs about the technique. Instruct them to include an analysis of one unfamiliar collage they discovered in their research.

UNIT 3

(page 196–197)

THE PRINCIPLES OF ART

Unit Overview

Unit 3 focuses on the principles of art. These principles are guidelines by which artists organize the elements for specific effects.

CHAPTER 8—Rhythm and Movement

Chapter 8 introduces students to the five types of rhythms and how they are used to add a sense of movement to artworks.

CHAPTER 9—Balance

In Chapter 9, students learn why balance is important in art and how visual weight is created.

CHAPTER 10—Proportion

Chapter 11 focuses on the principle of proportion. Students learn about the Golden Mean, the two kinds of visual scale, and human proportions.

CHAPTER 11—Variety, Emphasis, Harmony, and Unity

Chapter 12 explains how artists use variety, emphasis, and harmony to express ideas and feelings. Also in this chapter, students appreciate that the elements and principles are not isolated characteristics that exist in an artistic vacuum. Rather, it is the interplay between the elements of art and the principles of art that makes an artwork unified.

Unit Resources

📕 Print 17, Frederick S. Remington. *A Dash for the Timber*

📁 Unit 3 Test

📁 Portfolio and Assessment Techniques

196

196

MORE ABOUT...   Ogata Korin

Japanese artist, Ogata Korin (1659–1716) was born into a family of painters. He was known for his paintings of landscapes, animals, and flowers, which exhibited an elegance and stylized grace unsurpassed in Japanese art. Korin's ink strokes and lines were simple, but the color displayed in his artworks was highly complex. He often mixed ink and gouache directly on the paper to create spontaneous and unexpected effects. Korin's most famous piece, the pair of twofold screens, *White and Red Prunus in the Spring,* is housed in the National Museum in Tokyo. It shows two stylized trees arching over a gracefully drawn stream. The swirling pattern of the stream inspired the famous "whiplash" line in late nineteenth-century art nouveau in Europe.

THE PRINCIPLES OF ART

“The lines employed in Korin's [painting] are very distinctive . . . but actually the manner of brushwork in it contains endless variations matching the different aspects of the motion of water, so that the depiction is very vivid and invigorating.”

Teiji Chizawa, *The Art of Korin*

◄

Ogata Korin. Detail from *Waves at Matsushima* (inset). Edo period, eighteenth century. Six-panel folding screen; ink, colors, and gold on paper. 155 × 370 cm (61 × 145⅛"). Fenollosa-Weld Collection. Courtesy, Museum of Fine Arts, Boston, Massachusetts.

197

Introducing the Unit

Ask students to imagine a world without any form of organization. Ask: What would this world be like? What would you miss? What would be improved? Would the improvements outweigh the losses? Tell them that in this unit they will learn how artists use the principles of art to organize the elements of art.

Unit Motivator

Have students volunteer what comes to mind when you say these words: *rhythm, movement, balance, proportion, variety, emphasis,* and *unity*. Ask them to give examples of how each word is a part of their life experiences.

Discussing the “ Quotation ”

Have students look carefully at the screen painting by Ogata Korin. What characteristics of his line quality would lead someone to describe it as "stylized?" (*Students should note the regularity and repetition of line, as well as the fact that ocean waves are not actually made up of lines.*) Ask students to indicate where they see variation? (*The artist brings in variation in the white caps.*) What do students think about the artist's use of line to create both waves and clouds?

National Museum of Women in the Arts

You may wish to use the National Museum of Women in the Arts videodisc and/or CD-ROM. The videodisc features a bar code guide, and the interactive CD-ROM provides stimulating activities.

 **GROUP PARTICIPATION** Guide students in sharing computers and working cooperatively to enhance their Internet experiences and make lessons more enjoyable. Arrange students in groups of 2, 3, 4 at each computer terminal so that everyone can view the monitor. Assign responsibilities among group members for use of the keyboard and the mouse. Have one member of the group read aloud from the computer screen. Have one student take notes as needed. Encourage students with experience to demonstrate for others. Be sure to provide each student an opportunity to practice using computer skills. Find us at **www.glencoe.com/sec/art**

Rhythm and Movement

(pages 198–225)

 While studying this chapter, use Performing Arts Handbook page 420 to help students discover how rhythm and movement are used in dance.

▲ **FIGURE 8.1** Shotgun houses are built with a hall in the center that runs from the front door to the back, with all of the rooms lined up on either side of the hall. A "ward" is a district in the city of Houston, Texas. Fourth ward was the oldest African-American community in the city and was originally called Freedmanstown.

John Biggers. *Shotguns, Fourth Ward.* 1987. Acrylic and oil on board. 106 × 81.3 cm (41¾ × 32″). Hampton University Museum, Hampton, Virginia.

FEATURED ARTISTS

Bernice Abbot
William van Alen
Giacomo Balla
George Bellows
John Biggers

Rosa Bonheur
Alexander Calder
Maurits Cornelis Escher
Chief Black Hawk
Allan Houser
Lucy Leuppe McKelvey
Louisa Keyser
Abd Allah Musawwir

Antonio M. Ruiz
Augusta Savage
Louis Sullivan
Annie M. Peachey
Andy Warhol
Hale Woodruff
Chaing Xiong

Rhythm and Movement

Life is full of rhythmic events. Each year, one season follows the next in a predictable order. Such rhythms are comforting. The rhythmic routines of daily living create a sense of stability and security.

In his painting *Shotguns, Fourth Ward* **(Figure 8.1),** John Biggers recalls the visual rhythms or repetitions in the comforting quilts of his childhood. In the painting, the roofs of the shotgun houses create a quiltlike pattern of diamond shapes. Standing on the front porches of the first row are three women, each holding a miniature shotgun house with a miniature figure standing on the tiny front porch. What other examples of repetition can you find in this work?

Biggers indicates the strength and importance of the women in the painting by placing each one in a spotlight, on the stage of the porch. Each woman holds her miniature house proudly, for she represents the keeper of African-American traditions. These traditions, like the rhythms and repetitions in the painting, are comforting, giving a sense of stability, security, and order.

OBJECTIVES

After completing this chapter, you will be able to:

- Identify rhythms occurring in the world around you.
- Understand how rhythm adds a sense of movement to a work of art.
- Identify and explain motif and pattern.
- Name and identify the types of rhythm.
- Use the principle of rhythm to create your own works.

WORDS TO KNOW

rhythm
visual rhythm
motif
module
pattern
visual movement
kinetic

Developing Your
PORTFOLIO

Rhythm can be comforting and predictable. Make a list of several events and activities that you enjoy that happen in a predictable way. For example, you might list your birthday or track meets each Saturday. Using magazines and newspapers, find images that symbolize the events. A cake could stand for your birthday and a pair of running shoes could stand for the track meet. If you are unable to find appropriate symbols, sketch your own. Then write a brief paragraph about why the rhythm of these events is meaningful. Place the pictures and the paragraph in your portfolio.

199

CHAPTER 8

Chapter Overview

Chapter 8 calls students' attention to the presence of rhythm around them. It helps them see that visual rhythm is a part of their environment. They learn that rhythm and repetition are interrelated and that there are five different types of rhythm. Finally, they learn that artists use rhythm to create a sensation of movement in artworks.

Examining the Artwork

Have students examine Figure 8.1 and point out some of the repetitions they see. *(The wooden railroad ties; the sets of steps in front of the houses; the white pickets of the fence between the houses.)* Point out the women's clothes: all three skirts are patterned with squares divided into triangles, but each design is different. At the top of the painting you can see repeated triangles of white.

Tell students that Biggers shows pride in his African-American culture through symbols in this painting. The wash pots on the front porches stand for the many tasks that his mother and other women of her time did. They represent preparing soap, cooking meals, and bathing babies. The washboard symbolizes the laundry that females did to support their families. Have students share their personal interpretations of the symbols in the painting.

National Standards

This chapter addresses the following National Standards for the Visual Arts:

1.	(a, b)	**4.**	(c)
2.	(b, c)	**5.**	(a, c)
3.	(b, c)	**6.**	(a)

DEVELOPING A PORTFOLIO

Personal Style The success of a portfolio is somewhat based on the ability of the student to impress evaluators with his or her style. Personal talents are showcased in the portfolio but can only be effective when students learn to set long-term aims and sustain projects that eventually meet those goals. Ask them to regularly evaluate their constructive efforts toward the complete portfolio. How aware is each student of his or her style? What do they know about their style that will help them strengthen the portfolio's presentation? Have they chosen pieces that emphasize their style?

Rhythm and Repetition

(pages 200–204)
(National Standards: 2b, 3c)

FOCUS...........
Objectives

After completing this lesson, students will be able to:

■ Identify rhythms occurring in the world around them.

■ Understand how rhythm adds a sense of movement to a work of art.

Supplies

■ Natural objects such as: leaves, acorns, pebbles, and shells

■ A painting of a bouquet of flowers and a stop-action photo of an athlete

■ Fabric samples showing repeated motifs

■ A collection of buttons

Resources

📁 Artist's Profile 20, *Rosa Bonheur*

📁 Application Activity 15, *Rhythmic Word Search*

📁 Cooperative Learning Activity 15, *Advertising with Rhythm*

TEACH..........
Perceptual Skills

Ask students to look around and identify five visual rhythms that they see every day. Instruct students to list the rhythms and describe the images that create the positive beats. Then describe the negative space that acts as the rests between the beats. Discuss their findings.

200

Rhythm and Repetition

Rhythm is *the principle of art that indicates movement by the repetition of elements.* The principle of rhythm is found in all the arts: music, dance, poetry, and theatre. In music, rhythm is created by the measure of time between musical sounds. Beats are followed by rests. In poetry, the repetition of words, sounds, and phrases creates rhythm. The visual arts combine repetition and pauses to create rhythm.

Visual Rhythm

Visual rhythm is *rhythm you receive through your eyes rather than through your* ears. Visual rhythm is created by repeated positive shapes separated by negative spaces. Everywhere you look you can see visual rhythms. Books lined up in a bookcase and cars in a parking lot are examples of visual rhythms. A line of people in the cafeteria has visual rhythm. Each person is a positive shape, and the space between each person is a negative space.

In **Figure 8.2,** Chief Black Hawk has used visual rhythm to suggest the rhythms of a dance ceremony. The repeated images of the six Crow men are the major beats, or positive shapes, of the rhythm. The spaces between the men are the rests, or negative spaces, in the rhythm.

▶ **FIGURE 8.2** In the winter of 1880–81, Chief Black Hawk, a Lakota man, supported his family by selling drawings to a trader on the reservation. He was unknown until 1994, when a book of his drawings emerged on the auction market. Chief Black Hawk's book shows natural history drawings, hunting and ceremonial activities of the Lakota, and many pictures of Crow ceremonies.

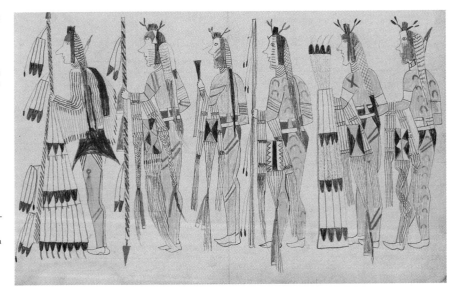

Chief Black Hawk. *Crow Men in Ceremonial Dress.* 1880–81. Ink and pencil on paper. 26 × 41.9 cm (10¼ × 16½"). Thaw Collection, Fenimore Art Museum, Cooperstown, New York.

200 | **CHAPTER 8** Rhythm and Movement

TECHNOLOGY OPTIONS

National Gallery of Art Videodisc Use the following to show examples of rhythm and movement in art.

Henri Matisse *Large Composition with Masks*	Edgar Degas *Ballet Dancers*	Honoré Daumier *The Young Courier*
Search Frame 2211	Search Frame 1344	Search Frame 2918

Use Glencoe's *National Gallery of Arts Correlation Bar Code Guide* to locate more artworks.

MEET THE ARTIST
ROSA BONHEUR

French, 1822–1899

Rosa Bonheur (**roh**-zah bah-**nur**) was born in Bordeaux, France in 1822. When she was seven years old, her family moved to Paris. Her father, Raymond Bonheur, was a landscape artist and painting teacher. He trained Rosa and her three siblings. As a member of the religious group called Saint-Simonians, he believed in the equality of women. This attitude allowed Rosa Bonheur to develop unrestrained by traditional women's roles.

When she was ten years old, she refused to be apprenticed to a dressmaker, preferring instead to sketch animals in nearby woods and to draw scenes from the balcony of the family apartment. This lifelong love of animals would inspire her later art. She painted huge compositions in which horses and other animals played a major role. She visited slaughterhouses to learn the anatomy of animals. She also traveled to livestock markets. *The Horse Fair* **(Figure 8.3)** is a painting that depicts one of these scenes. Bonheur became a famous, well-known artist. In 1865, she became the first woman to be awarded the Grand Cross of the Legion of Honor.

▲ **FIGURE 8.3** Bonheur, a lifelong animal lover, often created large-scale artworks with horses and other animals as the subject matter. In this painting Bonheur has used the horses as a motif. The rhythm the horses create pulls your eyes through the painting. Where does the movement start? From which direction does the viewer get drawn through the art?

Rosa Bonheur. *The Horse Fair.* 1853–55. Oil on canvas. 244.5 × 506.7 cm (96¼ × 199½"). The Metropolitan Museum of Art, New York, New York. Gift of Cornelius Vanderbilt, 1887. (87.25)

Vocabulary

Have students look up definitions of the word *module*, as well as its variations. Ask students to practice using *module* or any other form of the word in sentences. As an alternative exercise, have them sketch a three-dimensional drawing of the word *module*, then decorate it with rhythmic designs.

Aesthetics

Ask students to think of implied lines when they look at *The Horse Fair* in Figure 8.3. Where do they see an implied line? How does Bonheur control the movement of the viewer's eyes in this work?

MORE ABOUT... *The Horse Fair*

Have students study Figure 8.3 and answer the questions in the caption. Help students to see that the horses are the beats of the rhythm. They are all horses, but they all move differently, and are different colors and sizes. We know by the way they are placed that there is space between them, but they all overlap so that we do not see any negative space between them. The movement starts in the center of the left side with the white horse that is pulling up. The artist pulls us from center left toward the foreground in the center and then back up to the right. The men make up the counterpoint of beats. The trees move along with a steady beat. They start out small in the distance on the left and get progressively larger as they move to the right.

Developing Perceptual Skills

Bring in some natural objects such as leaves, acorns, small round pebbles, or shells. Demonstrate the feeling of movement by asking students to arrange them in a row across a table top. Give different groups of objects to different groups of students and ask them to make patterns that move the viewers' eyes across the table. Some students may see that these regular rhythms are implied lines. Point out that the elements and principles of art are all interwoven and, in real life, it is hard to separate them.

Critical Thinking

In some complex patterns, finding motifs is hard to do, but if students study each other's clothes, it will be easy. Ask them to find the exact areas that are being repeated. It would be also helpful if you wore clothes with obvious motifs and brought fabric samples that showed motifs clearly.

Promoting Discussion

To emphasize how we perceive visual movement, bring to class a painting of flowers and a stop-action photograph of an athlete. Ask students to explain how the painting demonstrates visual movement while the photograph does not. (*The painting may cause your eyes to jump from one flower shape to the next, while the stop-action photograph may have frozen the movement in such a way that your eyes hardly move.*)

▲ **FIGURE 8.4** In this unusual night view of New York City, you can see examples of random rhythms made by the buildings. Each building shows a regular rhythm of windows, but the lit windows create a random rhythm. Notice how the change in value also creates a sense of rhythm.

Bernice Abbott. *The Night View*, 1936. Photograph. Museum of the City of New York, New York. Gift of Mr. Todd Watts.

In visual rhythm, a beat may be one element or a combination of elements. Look at the photograph in **Figure 8.4.** The strongest beats are the big, tall buildings. The lighted windows make a random rhythm. The streets and the spaces between the buildings create negative, empty space—the rest between the beats.

Visual rhythms create a sensation of movement. Rhythms cause the viewer's eyes to follow the visual beats through a work of art. Visual movement is different from real action, which involves a physical change in position. For example, a ball bouncing across a room is real action. Visual movement simply suggests movement. In an artwork, round shapes separated by negative spaces can create the visual sensation of the movement of a ball. Your eyes bounce from one round shape to the next. In **Figure 8.6** on page 203, the artist has used rhythm to pull your eyes through the work. Notice how the curved figures and the slanted hoes give a sensation of visual movement.

Repetition

Rhythm results from repetition. *Motif* and *pattern* are often used to talk about repetition in art. A **motif** is *a unit that is repeated in visual rhythm* (**Figure 8.5**). Sometimes every motif is an exact duplicate of the first unit, and sometimes the repetitions vary from the original.

Look around and you will find examples of motif and repetition. In a marching band, one band member is a motif, even though each band member carries

◄ **FIGURE 8.5** There are two major motifs in this design. One is a solid blue square set on its point. The alternating motif is bordered with a light blue band and divided in the center into four smaller squares.

Annie M. Peachey. *Four in Block Work Quilt*. 1925–35. Cotton, rayon, and synthetics. 216 × 184 cm (85 × 72½"). Collection of the Museum of American Folk Art, New York, New York. Gift of Mr. and Mrs. William B. Wigton.

Visual Rhythms Create Visual Movement

Woodruff has used many random visual rhythms in this work to create the feeling that the workers are singing and working to the rhythm of the song as they hoe the cotton. In the diagram you can see how he has used repeated shapes to move your eyes through the work. How many visual beats can you find in this painting?

◀ FIGURE 8.6

Hale Woodruff. *Poor Man's Cotton.* 1944. Watercolor on paper. 77.5 × 57.2 cm (30½ × 22½"). The Newark Museum, Newark, New Jersey.

Developing Perceptual Skills

Let students know that the difference between pattern and rhythm can be difficult to see clearly. In fact, artists do not always agree, and many use the terms interchangeably. Pattern is flat and decorative. Rhythm is a repetition that causes a viewer's eyes to move around a composition. Ask students to look through the textbook and find examples of patterns and rhythms.

Activity (on page 204)

Motifs and Patterns

Applying Your Skills. If magazines are scarce, you might photocopy patterns from books and let students color one motif.

💻 **Computer Option.** As an alternative activity, have students follow these directions: Select two of the geometric Shape tools: square, circle, triangle, hexagon, oval, diamond, and so on. Combine the two shapes. Add a straight, curved, or zigzag line. Select the motif and make copies using the Copy and Paste commands. As you paste each copy, arrange the motifs in a row. When the row is complete, it can be selected, copied, then pasted directly below or shifted a half space to the right. Fill the page. Use the Bucket-fill tool to add color and/or patterns.

MORE ABOUT... Louis Sullivan

Known for his motto "Form follows function," Louis Sullivan combined decorative elements of his work to create functional buildings that please the eye. After studying at the Massachusetts Institute of Technology, he trained in the United States and Paris until he found his own practice in Chicago. There he became one of the founders of the Chicago School of Architecture. The Chicago Fire of 1871 had created a need for many new buildings, and the price of land dictated the need for taller buildings. At the same time, steel frames and electric elevators became practical. Sullivan's work in designing functional, yet aesthetic, skyscrapers has influenced the work of modern architects.

Art History

If you have students who are interested in architecture, suggest that they find out more about Louis Sullivan. Ask them to make a presentation to the class that includes biographical information, as well as a description of his style and examples of his work.

ASSESS..........

Self-Assessment

Have students complete the lesson review questions. Answers appear below.

Reteaching

Let students work in pairs to arrange buttons or other small objects into various patterns. Ask students to describe the rhythm each pattern creates. How does it create rhythm?

Enrichment

Have students make a design using shapes and lines to illustrate the difference between a 3/4-time waltz rhythm and a 4/4-time march rhythm. As an alternative exercise, have students listen to various types of music: rock, waltzes, marches, or music from other cultures. After each listening session, they should create designs using lines that visually match the beat of the music.

CLOSE............

Allow time for students to share and discuss what they learned about the principle of rhythm.

a different instrument. On a grocery store shelf full of canned goods, one can is a motif. In a herd of cattle, one cow is a motif.

In sculpture and architecture *a three-dimensional motif* is sometimes called a **module.** Modular furniture is composed of standard matching units.

 FIGURE 8.7
This elevator grille is a delicate pattern of lines and round forms. It was once part of a large bank of elevators in the 1893 Chicago Stock Exchange. The building was torn down in 1972, but parts of it, such as this grille, have been saved and housed in various museums.

Louis Sullivan. *Elevator Grille.* 1893–94. Bronze-plated cast iron. 185.4 × 78.7 cm (73 × 31"). High Museum of Art, Atlanta, Georgia. Virginia Carroll Crawford Collection, 1982. 291.

Pattern is a word used to describe a decorative surface design. **Pattern** is *a two-dimensional decorative visual repetition.*

A pattern of lines can decorate a piece of fabric or wallpaper. **Figure 8.7** shows a pattern decorating an elevator grille. These are decorative patterns meant to be visually appealing. Other patterns are functional. A bricklayer places bricks in a certain pattern in order to build a sturdy, durable wall. The bricklayer may make the pattern more complex in order to create a finished work that is very decorative, but the main purpose is still functional.

 Activity — Motifs and Patterns

Applying Your Skills. Make a collection of decorative patterns. You may use photographs, clippings from magazines, and scraps of fabric. Identify the motif in each pattern by drawing a circle around one. Organize your pattern collection into a poster, a bulletin board, a booklet, or some other type of presentation.

Computer Option. Start with a rectangle and design a simple motif. Use three colors or three original textures in black and white. Create a variety of patterns with that motif. Print your patterns. If your printer is black and white, you can add color with other media such as colored pencil after the design is printed out.

☑ **Check Your Understanding**

1. Define *rhythm.*
2. What is *visual rhythm*?
3. What is a pattern?

☑ ## Answers to Check Your Understanding

1. Rythm is the principle of art that indicates movement by the repetition of elements.
2. Visual rythm is rhythm that you receive through your eyes rather than through your ears.
3. A pattern is a two-dimensional decorative visual repetition.

Types of Rhythm

Arranging motifs and space in different ways creates different visual rhythms. There are many ways to combine motifs and space. Each combination gives a different character to the rhythm depicted.

Random

A motif repeated in no apparent order, with no regular spaces in between, creates a random rhythm. One example is autumn leaves that cover the ground. Cracks in mud and splashes of paint are also examples of random rhythm.

Crowds of people often create random rhythms —think of holiday shoppers, rush-hour commuters, and students in the halls between classes. A large group of people pushing onto a bus is full of rhythm. The motif is one person. Every person is different, and the space between and around them is slightly different.

The Sundi woman who created the bowl shown in **Figure 8.8** deliberately splashed the bowl with vegetable juices while it was still hot from the fire. This created the random pattern of round shapes that decorate the surface. If she had dipped the bowl into the liquid, it would have resulted in an even, brown hue. Applying the vegetable liquid to the hot clay allows the bowl to withstand the heat of the cooking fire. The bowl can be used over an open fire without shattering. In some parts of Africa, the marks left by vegetable juices are interpreted as proof of the thermal strength of the vessel.

▲ **Figure 8.8** The potter who created this bowl made an aesthetic decision to splash the ware with vegetable juices to create a random pattern of round shapes and lines.

Bowl. Kongo peoples, Congo and Democratic Republic of the Congo. Before 1910. Ceramic, vegetable dye. 11.3 × 15.6 cm (4⁷⁄₁₆ × 6⅛"). National Museum of African Art, Smithsonian Institution, Washington, D.C. Purchased with funds provided by the Smithsonian Collections Acquisition Program, 89-13-31.

| **Activity** | **Using Random Rhythm** |

Applying Your Skills. Choose one letter of the alphabet. Look through newspapers and magazines for large examples of that letter. Cut out about 20 letters. Arrange them on a piece of colored paper in a random pattern. If you have trouble finding large letters, draw letters of your own on your design.

Computer Option. Choose one letter of the alphabet. Using different fonts, create about 20 different examples of the letter. You can use Flip, Rotate, Size Change, and Color options if your program has them. Then arrange the letters in a random pattern.

Types of Rhythm
(pages 205–210)
(National Standards: 2b, 3c)

FOCUS...........
Objectives
After completing this lesson, students will be able to:

■ Identify and explain motif and pattern.

■ Name and identify the types of rhythm.

Supplies
■ Newsprint

■ Banner paper

■ White paper

■ Rulers

■ Chinese scroll painting

■ White glue

■ Small found objects

Resources

📁 Application Activity 16, *Sharpening Your Skills*
📁 Concept Map 8, *Types of Rhythm*
📁 Studio Lesson 13, *Modular Sculpture*

TEACH..........
Motivator
Have students place a leaf or a paper cutout under a sheet of newsprint and make a series of rubbings in a random manner. They may form teams at different tables, cut out all of their leaves, and make the rubbings using a variety of leaf shapes. They might also form teams at different tables, cut out all of their leaves, and arrange them into a specific kind of rhythm on a large sheet of colored banner paper.

MEETING INDIVIDUAL NEEDS

Learning Disabled Students with disabilities may enjoy cutting out a collection of patterns, large letters, or examples of different types of rhythm. They can find these patterns in magazines and then put them into envelopes or paste them into a notebook. All students will enjoy exercising their perceptive skills by looking around the room to locate examples of patterns of repetitive rhythm (in ceiling tiles, air conditioner grids, chairs in a row) and alternating rhythms (perhaps in designs on sweaters or other clothing). Students can become attuned to the idea of flowing rhythm by moving their arms or bodies to a flowing musical selection.

Activity (on page 205)

Using Random Rhythm

Applying Your Skills. Ask each student to bring in something with which to make a stamp. As an alternative to finding letters, enlarge some letters using the photocopy machine. Emphasize that students must cut out the letters slowly, exactly on the outline.

Computer Option. As an alternative activity, have students follow these directions: Choose the Brush, Pencil, Line, or Shape tools to create a motif reflecting a personal interest. Make copies by using a Selection tool and the Copy and Paste commands. Arrange the motifs randomly on the screen. Experiment.

Art in Everyday Life

To foster students' awareness of rhythm and sound in everyday life, suggest this: Russian composer Modest Mussorgsky wrote *Pictures at an Exhibition* to capture the rhythm of his visit to a museum. In "Promenade," you hear the rhythm of his heavy footstep (he was a very big man). "Gnome" picks up the spry, jerky movements and dragging steps of the gnome. In "Tuileries" you can hear the beat of chattering children and anxious nurses against the soft rustle of the park trees. "Ballad of the Unhatched Chicks" is a lively musical sketch of chicks chirping, bouncing, and pecking inside their shells.

▲ **FIGURE 8.9** This building was the first office building to rise above 1,000 feet. Notice how the pairs of windows form a regular beat both vertically and horizontally. The negative spaces between them are the rests between the beats.

William van Alen. *Chrysler Building*, New York, New York. Completed in 1930.

Regular

Regular rhythm has identical motifs and equal amounts of space between them **(Figure 8.9)**. Regular rhythm has a steady beat. Regular repetitions are used to organize objects. Parking spaces are laid out with regular rhythm. Stores organize merchandise into regular stacks and rows. This makes it easier for you to find things, and it also makes the displays more attractive than if items were arranged in a random fashion.

A grid is based on regular rhythm. It is a regular arrangement of parallel lines. A football field is laid out in a grid, as is a checkerboard. Windows form a grid pattern on the side of a building. The artist who created the cloth in **Figure 8.10** had a grid pattern in mind when he wove the long, narrow strips of cloth. Later the artist cut and sewed the strips together to make the wide cloth you see. Notice the regular repetition of the various motifs.

Regular rhythm can be boring if it is overdone. It is like playing one note on a piano over and over again. Pop artist Andy Warhol used regular rhythm to make a social-protest statement **(Figure 8.11)**. How would you describe the effect of this regular rhythm? What do you suppose Warhol intended to convey with this repeated motif?

TEACHER TALK

Technology in the Classroom The use of digital technology can be particularly instructive in helping students appreciate and analyze works of art. If your classroom contains a computer with a CD-ROM drive and/or laserdisc player, you may want to investigate some of the art-based packages on the market. Such programs add immediacy to the study of art by displaying works as they were meant to be seen (i.e., from various angles and, in the case of outdoor sculptures and works of architecture, in the context of their natural surroundings). You might also ask your students if any are proficient with art-based programs. If so, arrange a classroom demonstration by the student.

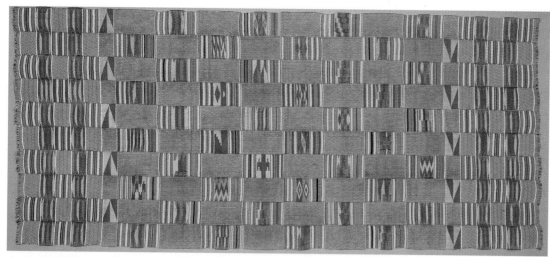

▲ **FIGURE 8.10** This elaborate grid pattern fits together perfectly because the weaver has memorized the whole plan through many years of practice.

Wrapper. Asante peoples, Ghana. Date unknown. Cotton, rayon. 190.2 × 83.2 cm (74⅞ × 32¼"). National Museum of African Art and National Museum of Natural History, Washington, D.C. Purchased with funds provided by the Smithsonian Collections Acquisition Program, 1983–85, Lamb EJ10554.

▲ **FIGURE 8.11** One pair of lips on the face of Marilyn Monroe would be beautiful and appealing. What has Andy Warhol done to them by repeating them in a regular rhythm?

Andy Warhol. *Marilyn Monroe's Lips.* 1962. Diptych. Synthetic polymer, enamel, and pencil on canvas. Left: 210.7 × 204.9 cm (82¼ × 80⅛"). Right: 210.7 × 209.7 cm (82¼ × 82⅜"). Hirshhorn Museum and Sculpture Garden, Smithsonian Institution, Washington, D.C. Gift of Joseph H. Hirshhorn, 1972.

Art History

Inform students that Andy Warhol, like other Pop artists, turned to mass media for subject matter. (See Chapter 13, pages 378 and 379 for a review of Pop art.) In typical Pop art fashion, he made people take a new look at everyday objects. In repeating Marilyn Monroe's lips many times, Warhol makes us take a new and somewhat negative look at a familiar image from the film medium and popular magazines. Ask students to discover more about Warhol's art and speculate about what accounted for its popularity.

Critical Thinking

Have each student create a grid with the types of rhythm listed down the left column. List music, literature, math, language arts, and so on, across the top. Have them work in groups to complete the grid, showing how each area of study demonstrates characteristics of rhythm.

CULTURAL DIVERSITY

African Textiles Tell your students about the rich, indigenous textile tradition that exists in West Africa. Adire cloths are indigo home-dyed "country cloths" and are impressive because of their large number and variety. They are created in what is present-day Nigeria. Every individual pattern has a name. Traditional designs are used in village ceremonies.

Many motifs are governed by Yoruba (located in the western part of Nigeria) mythology and folklore. Stylized designs on a variety of themes such as lizards, turtles, snakes, birds, trees, and even human beings can be found. These designs are created in praise of Oduduwa—the creator of the world.

Cross-Curriculum: Science

Call students' attention to the date in the credit line of Figure 8.12. Point out that prior to this date, the world of art was in great transition, beginning in 1500. At the same time, the field of science was undergoing an unprecedented revolution. Divide the class into research teams and have each team investigate the theories of one of the following: Nicolaus Copernicus, Galileo, Johannes Kepler, Andreas Vesalius, Sir Francis Bacon, or Sir Isaac Newton.

Aesthetics

After students have studied the arrangement of motifs in Figure 8.13, ask them to use their knowledge about the elements of art to describe how the elements are used in the bag. For example, what types of lines are evident? What are the color schemes? What type of balance is used? How is shape, space, and form used?

Activity

Alternating Rhythm

Applying Your Skills. This would be a good opportunity to have students practice measuring and using a ruler correctly.

💻 **Computer Option.** As an alternative activity, have students follow any of these directions: Design two geometric motifs, similar in size, using a minimum of two shapes and one line. If available, use the Grids and Rulers option to help measure size and align motifs. Save and title "Geometric Motifs." Make copies by using a Selection tool and the Copy and Paste commands. Arrange both motifs in an alternating pattern. Fill the page. Use the Save As command and retitle the work.

▶ **FIGURE 8.12**
The artist who painted this dish used an alternating pattern of sets of blue curved lines to symbolize waves of water.

Footed Dish, Japanese. 1700–50. Nabeshima ware (porcelain with underglaze enamel decoration). 5.3 × 20.2 cm (2⅛ × 7⅞"). The Nelson-Atkins Museum of Art, Kansas City, Missouri. Purchase: Nelson Trust.

◀ **FIGURE 8.13** How many sets of motifs can you find embroidered on this Creek shoulder bag? How many different ways has the artist alternated the motifs?

Shoulder Bag. Creek. Georgia or Alabama. 1810–30. Wool fabric, cotton fabric and thread, silk ribbon, glass beads. Strap: 135 × 18.7 cm (53¼ × 7⅜"). Bag: 19.4 × 10 cm (7⅝ × 4"). The Detroit Institute of Arts, Detroit, Michigan. Founders Society Purchase with funds from Flint Ink Corporation.

Alternating

Alternating rhythm can occur in several ways. One way is to introduce a second motif. Another way is to make a change in the placement or content of the original motif. A third way is to change the spaces between the motifs. Sometimes alternation is created simply by changing the position of the motif. For example, the motif may be turned upside down. The Japanese artist who painted the wave design on the bowl shown in **Figure 8.12** created the feeling of movement by alternating the placement of the wave shapes. The Native American who embroidered the shoulder bag in **Figure 8.13** made the design interesting by changing the sets of motifs several times.

Bricks are often laid in an alternating pattern. As a child, did you ever play with interlocking blocks? You had to use an alternating pattern to join the blocks.

An alternating rhythm using two motifs can still be very repetitive. Your eyes keep returning to the first motif even after the second motif joins the design, but the alternation does create interest and relieve monotony.

Flowing

Flowing rhythm is created by repeating wavy lines. Curved shapes, such as rolling hills or ocean waves, create

Activity

Alternating Rhythm

Applying Your Skills. Draw a checkerboard grid on a sheet of white paper. Create an alternating rhythm using one motif. Turn the motif upside down in every other box. Next, draw a checkerboard grid and create an alternating rhythm using two motifs.

Computer Option. Design two motifs using the tools of your choice. Use the Selecttool and the Copy and Paste options to create an alternating rhythm using both motifs. On a new screen, create an alternating rhythm using only one motif. In this design, you can change the placement of the motif. Label and save both designs.

MORE ABOUT... Andy Warhol

Probably the best-known American Pop artist, Andy Warhol (1928–1987) was trained at the Carnegie Institute of Technology. During the 1950s he worked as an advertising illustrator. In 1960 he created his first enlarged comic strip figures to be used in window displays. During the next decade he used innovative silk screening techniques to create images of such subjects as Campbell's soup cans, Coca-Cola bottles, and the faces of Hollywood celebrities. Warhol mass-produced representations of mass-produced consumer goods. He defended his creations by pointing out that mechanical reproduction was an important part of American society and a legitimate means of creating art.

flowing rhythms. In **Figure 8.14,** the artist was able to capture the flowing movement of the waterfall as it rolled over the rocks. Your eyes follow the curving path as it changes direction gradually. There are no sudden breaks in the line. In **Figure 8.15,** the artist has used flowing rhythm to arrange the heads of the singers to create the mood of the flowing melody coming from the harp.

Flowing rhythm is created using upward swells and downward slides. You might think of the upward moves as the beats and the downward moves as the rests. Allan Houser has used flowing rhythms symbolically in his sculpture, *Coming of Age* **(Figure 8.16).** The work expresses the symbolic union of nature and femininity. The thick, rhythmically flowing strands of her hair suggest motion and the act of running. They also suggest the movement of the wind, of water, or even the blazing motion of flames.

◀ **FIGURE 8.14** Borsky captured the white flow of this waterfall in his photograph by increasing the amount of time he exposed the film to light.

David Borsky. *Waterfall.* Photograph. Courtesy of the artist.

▶ **FIGURE 8.16** This sculpture, with its upturned head and flowing hair, was created to celebrate feminine youth and beauty. The upturned head symbolizes the girl's desire to run to the four directions of the earth. The small shape above her forehead represents an abalone shell, a fertility symbol. The feather in her hair signifies a long life.

Allan Houser. *Coming of Age.* 1977. Bronze, edition of 12. 19 × 39.4 × 17.8 cm (7½ × 15½ × 7"). Denver Art Museum, Denver, Colorado.

▲ **FIGURE 8.15** This sculpture was inspired by the song *Lift Every Voice and Sing,* which was a popular song among African-Americans in the 1930s. The sculpture was a towering, 16-foot plaster work commissioned for the 1939 World's Fair. There were not enough funds to cast it in metal, so the original was destroyed along with all of the other temporary structures after the Fair ended. All that is left are a few small souvenirs that were sold at the Fair.

Augusta Savage. *Lift Every Voice and Sing.* 1939. Cast iron. 27.6 x 23.5 x 11.4 cm (10⅞ x 9¼ x 4½"). Countee Cullen Collection, Hampton University Museum, Hampton, Virginia.

LESSON 2   *Types of Rhythm* | **209**

Aesthetics

Point out that often, bronze sculptures such as Allan Houser's *Coming of Age* (Figure 8.16) are parts of a series of castings with between five and seven "editions." Arrange a debate in which students argue the relative value of sculptures that have been reproduced in multiples. Ask: Is it important to destroy a mold after a certain number of reproductions have been made? Is the aesthetic value of a work diminished if that piece is reproduced?

Aesthetics

Have students study Houser's sculpture in Figure 8.16. Encourage them to visualize the work from all sides. Ask: Can you see how the artist introduced a sense of action? How did he achieve this sense of action?

Aesthetics

Have students discuss the painting shown in Figure 8.17 on page 210. Direct them to consider how line, color, texture, shape, form, and space are used. What principles of art emphasize those elements? What message or idea do they think Balla was trying to convey in this painting?

MORE ABOUT... Allan Houser

Chiricahua Apache sculptor Allan Houser (1914–1994) is credited with developing the modern style of Native American sculpture almost single-handedly. Raised on a farm near Fort Sill, Oklahoma, Houser could not afford formal art training and worked in a rubber plant and on a farm to support himself. By 1948 he was seriously thinking of becoming a house painter, when his design for a statue commemorating Native American servicemen killed in World War II was selected by the Haskell Institute in Lawrence, Kansas. After creating this monument, he was determined to pursue a career as a professional artist.

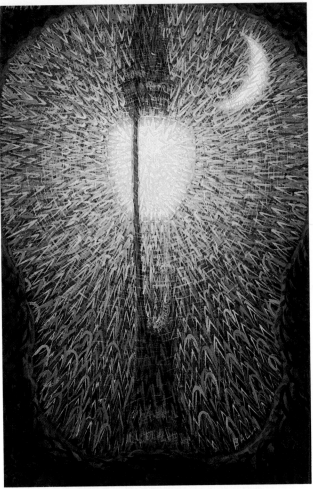

▲ **FIGURE 8.17** The light glowing from the street lamp is represented by a progressive rhythm of both line and color. Notice how the light close to the lamp is white and yellow in color and is created with thin, small V-shaped lines. Why do you think the artist has used the V lines to represent the movement of light from the lamp out into the darkness?

Giacomo Balla. *Street Light.* 1909. Oil on canvas. 174.7 × 114.7 cm (68¾ × 45¼"). Collection, The Museum of Modern Art, New York, New York. Hillman Periodicals Fund.

Progressive

In *progressive* rhythm there is a change in the motif each time the motif is repeated. The change is a steady one. Each time the motif appears, it is slightly different **(Figure 8.17)**. A progressive rhythm may start with a square as its motif. The size of the square may be changed by making it slightly smaller

each time it is repeated, or each square may be made a different color of the spectrum or a different step on the value scale each time it is repeated. Shapes can be progressively changed. The sides of a square can be gradually rounded until the square becomes a circle.

Activity Progressive Rhythm

Applying Your Skills. Start with a simple geometric shape, such as a square, for your motif. Create a progressive rhythm by gradually changing the square into a free-form shape. Next, draw a picture using simple shapes. Change the shapes gradually, using progressive rhythm, to tell a visual story.

Computer Option. Look around the room and select a simple hand-made object such as a stapler, a chair, or a faucet. Use the tools of your choice to draw the outline of this shape, adding details. Consider what shapes can be used to simplify and represent the object—circles, squares, rectangles, or triangles. Gradually change the image using a minimum of six or seven steps so that the transition appears smooth. Begin in black and white but later you may explore changes in size, value, or color to enhance the progression. Tip: After completing each step, make a copy of it and place it next to the one you are about to alter, or use the tracing paper option, if available, to guide your changes.

✓ Check Your Understanding

1. Give one example each of random rhythm and regular rhythm.
2. In what ways can an alternating rhythm occur?
3. Describe a progressive rhythm.

✓ Answers to Check Your Understanding

1. Random rhythm is created when a motif is repeated in no apparent order, with no regular spaces in between (such as raindrops on pavement). Regular rhythm occurs when objects are repeated systematically (such as railroad ties).
2. An alternating rhythm can occur by introducing a second motif, changing the space between the motifs, and changing the position, placement, and content of the original motif.
3. A progressive rhythm changes the motif each time the motif is repeated.

How Artists Use Rhythm to Create Movement

Artists use rhythm in a work of art just as they use the elements and other principles of art—to convey feelings and ideas. Rhythm, which can be comforting and predictable, can also be monotonous, symbolic, or graceful, depending on the artist's goals. Rhythm can also create visual movement.

Visual Movement

Visual movement is *the principle of art used to create the look and feeling of action and to guide the viewer's eyes throughout the work of art.* In **Figure 8.18,** the artist has used visual movement to tell her story. Xiong has arranged the figures and objects in her art using visual rhythm to

▲ **FIGURE 8.18** This story cloth tells the story of the artist's flight from Laos, across the Mekong River, to an American refugee camp in Thailand. The story starts in the upper right corner. Can you follow the family as they move toward safety?

Chaing Xiong. *Hmong Story Cloth.* 1987. Pieced and embroidered polyester, cotton blend. 140.3 × 145.4 cm (55¼ × 57¼"). Wadsworth Atheneum, Hartford, Connecticut. Florence Paull Berger Fund.

FOCUS...........
Objective
After completing this lesson, students will be able to:
- Use the principle of rhythm to create their own artworks.

Resources

- 📁 Artist's Profile 26, *Alexander Calder*
- 📁 Application Activity 16, *Sharpening Your Skills*
- 📁 Cooperative Learning Activity 16, *Modular Sculpture Using Boxes*
- 📁 Enrichment Activity 15, *Some Basics of Animation*
- 📁 Enrichment Activity 16, *Patterns in Quilts*
- 📁 Studio Lesson 14, *Printing a Rhythmic Fabric Design*
- 📁 Studio Lesson 15, *Clay Coil Pot*

TEACH..........
Art History
Although the Futurist movement lasted only a short time, the artists were important because they tried to express movement on nonmoving surfaces using rhythmic effects. They took the philosophy of Cubism a step farther. Figure 8.19 is an example of visual rhythm used to create the effect of movement. Ask students to analyze how Giacomo Balla created this illusion.

COOPERATIVE LEARNING

Moving Sculpture Tell students that *mobile* is a fairly new term invented to describe sculptures that move. The work for which Calder is most noted is wind mobiles. These mobiles were made from rods, wires, and delicate shapes made of sheet metal and wire hung from a single point.

Many of Calder's mobiles are based on natural forms—animals, birds, fish, or plants—and the motions were carefully planned to imitate the movement of the subject. His later works show that he became more interested in shapes and movements that had little to do with natural objects. Have students work in small groups to create a freestanding mobile based on natural forms.

Developing Perceptual Skills

Find copies of Marcel Duchamp's *Nude Descending a Staircase* and Umberto Boccioni's *Dynamism of a Cyclist.* Ask students to compare these two reproductions with Balla's work in Figure 8.19. Help students to analyze the movement in each painting.

Sparking CREATIVITY

Want students to think creatively about movement? Suggest this: Have someone pose for you in an action position and cut a silhouette of his or her figure. Then move your figure around on a large sheet of paper and plan a continuous action for it. Start tracing the figure into a strobe light of pattern, either in contour, drawing the whole figure every time, or overlapping, drawing figures behind other figures. Glue your model figure into the design when you are finished. Watch a person move in a dark room with a strobe light flashing on him or her. It will look just like your design.

▲ **FIGURE 8.19** The many repetitions of the legs, feet, tail, and chain in this work give it the appearance of actual movement.

Giacomo Balla. *Dynamism of a Dog on a Leash.* 1912. Oil on canvas. 89.9 × 109.9 cm (35½ × 43"). Albright-Knox Art Gallery, Buffalo, New York. Bequest of A. Conger Goodyear and Gift of George F. Goodyear, 1964.

◄ **FIGURE 8.20** McKelvey's repetition of lines and forms that swirl out from the neck of her pot create the illusion of movement. The intricate sandpainting design along the graceful curve of the vessel is the hallmark of a McKelvey pot.

Lucy Leuppe McKelvey. *Whirling Rainbow Goddesses.* Ceramic container. 18 × 30 cm (6¼ × 12"). Keams Canyon Arts and Crafts, Keams Canyon, Arizona.

create the sense of movement. The main motif is Xiong's family. Notice how they change slightly from one appearance to the next. Is the rhythm random, alternating, or progressive?

One group of artists tried to do more than control the way in which viewers looked at works of art. This group of artists, called the *Futurists,* used rhythm to capture the idea of movement itself. They used the word *dynamism* to refer to the forces of movement. They believed that nothing was solid or stable. They also believed that art should show such dynamism. They showed forms changing into energy by slanting and overlapping surfaces, which made the surfaces seem to move. In **Figure 8.19,** notice how the dog and its leash practically vibrate off the page. What kind of rhythm did the artist use to suggest this frenetic movement?

When you look at the modern Navajo pottery by Native American artist Lucy McKelvey **(Figure 8.20),** you will also find rhythmic repetitions of shapes and lines that seem to move across the surface. The designs are inspired by traditional Navajo sandpaintings. McKelvey says that her grandfather, who was a medicine man, told her she could use the designs as long as she didn't reproduce one of the sacred sandpainting figures exactly as it was depicted in a ritual ceremony. She always changes the original and adds something different.

You can also see movement in the visual art of Alexander Calder. He was a

---

MORE ABOUT... Alexander Calder

Perhaps the most famous American sculptor of this century, Alexander Calder's fanciful, witty, and ingenious work reflects his training as an engineer and illustrator. Born into a family of artists, Calder began sculpting at the age of five with bits of wire and wood. In 1924 he landed his first job as an artist, illustrating for the *National Police Gazette.* After spending several years in Paris creating miniature circus figures, he began working on mobiles in 1931. During his lifetime he played a significant role in defining contemporary art and culture. Two of his more widely known ventures included a campaign poster for George McGovern and a design that appeared on Braniff jets in the mid-1970s.

▲ **FIGURE 8.21** Look closely at the places where the rods are joined by a carefully planned set of loops. Calder's works are so carefully balanced that the slightest movement of air will set the sculpture in motion. Watching a Calder sculpture is like watching a graceful dancer.

Alexander Calder. *Lobster Trap and Fish Tail.* 1939. Hanging mobile. Painted steel wire and sheet aluminum. About 2.6 × 2.9 m (8'6" × 9'6"). Collection, The Museum of Modern Art, New York, New York. Commissioned by the Advisory Committee for the stairwell of the museum.

mechanical engineer who believed in what the Futurists were doing. In his work he repeated abstract shapes and put them into real motion. He did this using the real forces of air currents and gravity. Calder's creations were dubbed **kinetic** sculpture, because they *actually move in space* (**Figure 8.21**). Artist Marcel Duchamp gave Calder's moving sculptures another name, *mobiles.* Moving sculptures of this kind have been called mobiles ever since.

 Check Your Understanding

1. Define *visual movement.*
2. Which group of artists used rhythm to capture the idea of movement itself?
3. Describe a kinetic sculpture. By what other name are these sculptures often referred to?

Cross-Curriculum: Engineering

Remind students that Calder was an innovator. His mobiles seem to float in the air like dancing forms. Most students have made imitations of mobiles by tying strings to rods. Ask them to study the engineered joints of *Lobster Trap and Fish Tail* closely to see how Calder made them move so gracefully. If possible, ask a professional engineer to come to class and discuss the engineering problems an artist might face when designing a mobile.

ASSESS..........

Self-Assessment

Have students complete the lesson review questions. Answers appear below.

Reteaching

■ Have students work with partners to review how artists use rhythm in their works to create visual movement. Provide each pair with an example. Have students ask the partner how rhythm has been used in the piece.

Enrichment

■ Assign Enrichment Activities 15 and 16 in the TCR. 📂

CLOSE.............

Have students explain how they will create rhythm and movement in future artworks.

 Answers to Check Your Understanding

1. Visual movement is the principle of art used to create the look and feeling of action and to guide the viewer's eyes throughout the work of art.
2. Futurists tried to capture the idea of movement itself.
3. Kinetic sculptures, also called mobiles, are created by assembling mechanical parts that can be moved.

Painting With a Rhythmic Activity

Painting With a Rhythmic Activity

(pages 214–215)

(National Standards: 1a, 1b, 2b, 2c, 3b)

FOCUS...........

Objective

After completing this lesson, students will be able to:

■ Create a painting expressing rhythmic movement.

TEACH..........

Motivator

Involve students in some type of rhythmic activity such as dancing, clapping, or drumming. Ask them to share their own interpretations of rhythm.

Promoting Discussion

Encourage students to select an activity they like, then think about the movements inherent in that activity. Are the movements light and bouncy as in soccer, or are they the heavy, thudding movements of football? Take time to discuss the different movements and how they can be expressed in rhythms.

▲ **FIGURE 8.22**

Antonio M. Ruiz. *School Children on Parade.* 1936. Oil on canvas. 24 × 33.8 cm (9½ × 13¼"). The Metropolitan Museum of Art, New York, New York. © Antonio M. Ruiz/SOMAAP MÉXICO, 1999.

SUPPLIES

■ **Sketchbook and pencils**
■ **Large white paper**
■ **Yellow chalk**
■ **Acrylic paints and a variety of brushes**

Antonio Ruiz painted *School Children on Parade* (**Figure 8.22**) as a depiction of Independence Day in Mexico. Notice how the artist has used several motifs: the children in their white uniforms and yellow hats is one motif; the tricolor flags they carry is another. Repetition is also shown in the group of adults, dressed in black, who are watching the parade. If you look closely, you will be able to spot other rhythms in the painting.

Ruiz has used repeated colors, sizes, and shapes to create the rhythm of the marching students. The contrast between the light and dark colors adds interest. The painting evokes a serious, dignified mood by its use of repetition.

What You Will Learn

In this project, you will create a painting expressing rhythmic movement. Show one or more groups of people or objects involved in rhythmic activity. Base the figures in your work on your own sketches of people or objects in action. As in Ruiz's *School Children on Parade,* use more than one motif. Strengthen the rhythmic quality of your work by using four of the five kinds of visual rhythm described in this chapter. Use repetition to accent the visual rhythms. Choose a color scheme that will help to express the mood of the rhythms in your work.

MORE ABOUT... Antonio Ruiz

Antonia Ruiz was born in 1897 in the small town of Texcoco, Mexico. It was here that the gifted artist began focusing his paintings on simple scenes of every day life. At the age of 17, Ruiz entered the Academy of San Carlos in Mexico City to study painting and drawing. A few years later, Ruiz became actively interested in the field of architecture. With the skills he had developed at the academy, Ruiz began his career of teaching. In 1942, Ruiz founded the Escuela de Pintura y Escultura (School of Painting and Sculpture), where other artists such as Diego Rivera and Frido Kahlo also taught. One of Ruiz's most accomplished pieces, *The Bicycle Race,* reveals a dynamic sense of composition as well as features a variety of bright and bold colors.

Creating

Brainstorm with your classmates for ideas of rhythmic activities. Think of marching bands, sporting events, cheerleaders, dancers, joggers, or children on a playground.

Select the rhythmic activities you will use in your painting. Do visual research by making gesture sketches in your sketchbook of people or objects involved in the activities.

Step 1 Select your best gesture drawings. In your sketchbook, plan how to organize the figures into a composition. Remember to emphasize rhythmic movement that will pull the viewer's eye through the painting. As in Figure 8.22, you may create several different rhythms by using more than one motif. Be sure to use rhythmic repetition.

Step 2 Choose your best rhythmic composition and sketch it on a large sheet of white paper using yellow chalk. Press lightly with the chalk so that it will not show when you paint over it. Before you start painting, plan how you will repeat the elements of line, shape, space, and color to accent the visual rhythms in your painting. Also plan a color scheme that will express the mood of the rhythms in your work. Make notes with crayons or colored pencils in your sketchbook.

Step 3 Paint your work, covering the entire surface of the paper. Mount or mat your work for display.

EVALUATING YOUR WORK

▶ **DESCRIBE** Tell which rhythmic activities you chose. Describe how you did your visual research. How many motifs did you use?

▶ **ANALYZE** Explain how and where you repeated the elements of line, shape, space, and color. What color scheme did you choose? Which kinds of rhythm did you use? Explain how and where you used them.

▶ **INTERPRET** What is the expressive mood of your work? Which elements helped to create that mood? Give your work a title.

▶ **JUDGE** Which aesthetic theories would you use to judge this work? Were you satisfied with the finished work? If you were to do it over, what, if anything, would you change to improve it?

▲ **FIGURE 8.22A** Student work.

Studio Skills

Spend time practicing gesture drawing. Timed sessions set to music will help motivate students. Ask volunteers to take turns posing. If any are willing, they might dance or march to music in front of the class while the gesture drawings are being made. Students could freeze in mid-action and the rest of the class could begin drawing their pose.

Studio Skills

If it is desirable for lines to show through the painting, instruct students to sketch with a soft pencil such as an 8B instead of the yellow chalk. Heavy graphite lines will show through transparent acrylic colors. Tell students to notice how Ruiz has used bold colors to create a festive mood. If they use repeated colors, this effect will add another element to the rhythm of the painting.

ASSESS..........
Keeping a Portfolio

Remind students that the preliminary sketches and the final artwork for this Studio Project are likely candidates for their portfolios.

Self-Assessment

Have students apply the steps of art criticism to their own artwork using the "Evaluating Your Work" questions on this page.

CLOSE............

Ask each student to describe the kinds of visual rhythm used in his or her painting.

TECHNIQUE TIP ✓

Gesture Drawing Remind students that gesture drawing is a way of capturing movement in a sketch; there are no outlines or details. Suggest the following guidelines and see page 429 in the Handbook for more about gesture drawing:

■ Use the side of the drawing tool. Do not hold the medium as if writing.

■ Find the lines of movement that show the direction in which the figure is bending. Draw the main line showing this movement.

■ Use quickly drawn lines to build up the shape of the person.

A Pattern Collage

FOCUS...........
Objective

After completing this lesson, students will be able to:

■ Create a collage in the Persian style by presenting more than one point of view.

TEACH..........
Motivator

Display as many examples of Islamic art as possible, such as woven rugs and wall hangings, metalwork, and pottery. Wooden carvings, glassware, and architecture are important areas of the art of Islam. Ask students to bring to school any Middle Eastern artifacts that they may have at home and share any information that they may have about the objects.

Art History

Students may be interested in knowing why the teachings of Mohammed prohibited the production of images of living things. It was believed that the people might regard these images as idols or objects of worship. Artists who produced such images were condemned in the afterlife. Consequently, floral images and geometric patterns were widely produced. As mentioned in the text, calligraphy was used, primarily for copying the Koran. Two types of Arabic calligraphy are Kufic and Neskhi. Kufic, a more geometric style, was first used for copying the Koran. Later, Neskhi was used for writing text, and Kufic was used to title chapters in the Koran.

216

▲ **FIGURE 8.23**

Abd Allah Musawwir. *The Meeting of the Theologians*. c. 1540-50, Uzbek Shaybanid dynasty. Watercolors on paper. 28.9 × 19.1 cm (11⅜ × 7½"). The Nelson-Atkins Museum of Art, Kansas City, Missouri. Purchase: Nelson Trust.

SUPPLIES

■ Sketchbook and pencils
■ Ruler, scissors, and white glue
■ One large sheet of paper or poster board
■ A variety of patterned fabrics and papers
■ Colored pencils, watercolors, or acrylics
■ Assorted brushes
■ Small pieces of white paper for figures

216   **CHAPTER 8**   Rhythm and Movement

Persian miniature paintings such as the one shown in **Figure 8.23** were made to illustrate book manuscripts. The primary purpose of these illustrations is to tell stories about sacred religious events and to depict the exploits of heroes who accomplished superhuman feats.

Persian painters filled every available space with a rhythmic pattern. Notice how each pattern is filled with intense colors. This emphasis on pattern compresses space. Everything seems to lie flat against the picture plane.

The style of Persian art is not like Western Realism. More than one point of view appears in the composition, allowing the artist to portray several events in the same picture.

The Meeting of the Theologians (Figure 8.23) takes place in a religious school, where a young man is seated with a teacher and seven other bearded men. In the doorway a theologian approaches while two beggars hold out their hands begging. This artwork was one page of an illustrated book. Look at it closely and see how the colors, patterns, and calligraphy have been merged to make the story easy to read and visually interesting.

What You Will Learn

You will create a collage in the Persian style by presenting more than one point of view. In this way you can show different aspects of one event in the picture. Organize your work so every shape and space is filled with brightly–colored patterns. Create the background shapes using patterned fabrics and papers. People and other objects can be made by drawing and painting them on white paper and cutting them out. The

MORE ABOUT... **Islamic Style**

Because early Islamic artists could not depict the figures of humans or animals, they developed a style of flat, abstract designs to be used in a variety of works. Best known is the arabesque, which comes from the Italian word meaning "Arablike." These swirling, interlaced designs are apparently based on plant shapes, but the forms of leaves, branches, and vines have been transformed into scrolls, spirals, and curves. Such arabesque designs were first used during the 900s in all Muslim countries. Arabesques and other geometric designs have been used to decorate the walls of buildings, tiles, miniature paintings, rugs, metalware, and other craft objects.

finished composition should look flat. It should not have any feeling of three-dimensional form or space.

Creating

Brainstorm with classmates about complex events that would be appropriate for this project. Think of an event that can be best explained by showing several scenes. For example, a play involves tryouts, rehearsals, costume fittings, and performing.

After the group discussion, choose a situation from your personal experience to illustrate. In your sketchbook, list the different scenes that make up the event. Make some rough sketches. Choose the scenes that you would like to illustrate.

Step 1 Now sketch a plan for dividing your composition into shapes of different sizes and decide where to place your figures. Using the ruler and pencil, lightly draw the dividing lines on a large sheet of paper.

Step 2 Before you add figures, fill all the rectangles with patterns. Measure each shape and cut out patterned fabrics and papers to fit. As you select each pattern for the background, consider how one will look next to another. Use contrasting patterns so you can see the distinction between each shape. If you wish, you may draw and color patterns in some of the spaces. Glue the fabrics and papers to the background.

Step 3 On the small pieces of white paper, draw and paint figures and objects. Consider the pattern you will place each figure against. Make sure the figure will contrast. Cut out the drawn figures and objects and glue them onto the design. Mount or mat your finished work for display.

EVALUATING YOUR WORK

▶ **DESCRIBE** Identify the event you chose to illustrate. Describe the different scenes. What kinds of patterned materials did you use for your background spaces?

▶ **ANALYZE** How did you organize your background spaces? How did you arrange the figures? Did you fill the background with patterns? Is there contrast between patterns and between the figures and the background? Does everything look flat?

▶ **INTERPRET** What mood does your artwork express? Give your work an expressive title.

▶ **JUDGE** Which aesthetic theories would you use to judge this work? Is it successful? If you were going to do it over, what would you change?

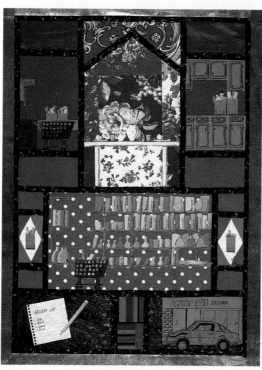

▲ **FIGURE 8.23A** Student work.

Studio Skills

Before dividing the paper into rectangles, talk to students about methods of creating visual balance. If you wish to preview balance, refer to Chapter 9. Also, be aware that white glue will work in this activity, but stitchery tape or a hot glue gun may be desirable for attaching fabric to the paper.

ASSESS..........
Keeping a Portfolio

Remind students that the preliminary sketches and the final artwork for this Studio Project are likely candidates for their portfolios.

Self-Assessment

Have students apply the steps of art criticism to their own artwork using the "Evaluating Your Work" questions on this page. In addition, ask the following: What events were portrayed in the collage? Was every space and shape filled? How? What colors and patterns were chosen to fill the background? What types of people and objects were put into the composition?

CLOSE............

Allow time for students to walk around the room and survey the finished designs. If time allows, have volunteers show their collages while other students critique them using the four-step process.

▶ COOPERATIVE LEARNING

Miniature-Style Painting Persian miniature paintings are richly colored illustrations. To keep the flat effect that works well with Islamic calligraphy, these artists used several composition devices. One was to build upward in the picture plane instead of using perspective to move back into space. The figures in the back are the same size as those in the foreground but are placed higher in the picture. Another device is the combination of several planes into one—outside and inside spaces. Study Figure 8.23.

Work in small groups to plan a miniature-style painting of the inside and outside of a home, placing people in both spaces.

Studio Project

Coil Baskets

FOCUS...........

Objective

After completing this lesson, students will be able to:

■ Design and create a coil basket form that has a functional or decorative purpose.

TEACH.........

Motivator

Ask students to bring baskets from home. Display as many sizes and varieties as possible.

Promoting Discussion

Generate discussion about the purposes of baskets. Discuss how some baskets are designed for specific purposes. Start some friendly competition by dividing the class into research teams. Tell them to search for books and magazines on basketry. Reward the group or groups who find the following: the oldest basket in existence; the biggest variety of basketry techniques; and the most unusual baskets.

Studio Skills

To make this studio experience more satisfying, students may need to know the following: When cutting the coiling core by using the taper method mentioned in the directions, the cut should be made at an extreme angle. Whenever beginning, ending, or joining cords in the basket, use the taper method. For a tightly stitched basket, wrap around the previous coil every third or fourth stitch. If a looser design is desired, do not stitch as often.

▲ **FIGURE 8.24**

Louisa Keyser (Dat So La Lee). *Basket.* c. 1917–18. Willow, redbud, braken fern. 30 × 41.2 cm (12 × 16¼"). Philbrook Art Center, Tulsa, Oklahoma. Clark Field Collection.

SUPPLIES

■ **Core material for the warp**
■ **Fibers for the weft: colored yarns, raffia, or natural fibers**
■ **Tapestry needle**
■ **Sharp scissors**
■ **Masking tape**
■ **Sketchbook, pencil, and crayons**

The basket shown in **Figure 8.24** was created by Louisa Keyser (Dat So La Lee). She belonged to a small Native American group known as the Washoe. They were hunters and gatherers who ranged through the territory around Lake Tahoe, California. The Washoe women made many types of baskets for carrying possessions as they moved between the lakes, mountains, hills, and valley floors in their yearly gathering circuit. Washoe basketry is woven primarily from willow, which was found in the valleys. The Washoe used the coiling technique to make large storage baskets, watertight cooking baskets, and *degikups,* which were small spherical baskets for ceremonial use.

This basket is one of Keyser's variations of the *degikup* form. It rises gradually from a narrow base until it reaches a maximum width at three-quarters of its height. This design is called the scatter pattern. It consists of a series of stepped triangles arranged vertically. In this basket, the artist has increased the size of the triangles to match the form of the basket. Then she has diminished the design as the form curves inward. She has used the progressive rhythm of the design to emphasize the form of the basket. She created an illusion of perspective in which the exaggerated curve of the design mirrors the form of the basket, unifying the basket with its design.

What You Will Learn

In this project, you will plan your own coil basket. To prepare, study Louisa Keyser's basket to see how she

---

MORE ABOUT... Louisa Keyser

Louisa Keyser was free to experiment with aesthetic concerns because she had a patron, Abe Cohn. He provided Louisa and her husband Charlie with food, clothing, and medical care. He even built them a house next to his own home. Secure from economic concerns, Louisa was free to develop her art. Louisa designed larger baskets and developed finer stitching. She created a new color scheme based on the contrasting colors of black (mud-dyed, bracken-fern root) and red (redbud branch). The result was her variation of the *degicup,* a fabric sculpture without utilitarian function and without precedent in traditional Washoe basket-weaving.

used rhythm in her design. Then practice the coil method of basket making until you have satisfactorily started and completed a simple flat coaster using the "lazy squaw" stitch in a regular rhythm. When you have mastered the technique, design and create a unique coil basket form that has either a functional or decorative purpose. Organize arrangement of the colors of the weft into a random, regular, alternating, or progressive rhythm.

Creating

Study the directions for the coil method of basket making in Technique Tip 24 in the Handbook, on page 440. Following those directions, use about 2 feet of core material to make a small coaster using the "lazy squaw" stitch. If the center of your coaster does not look right the first time, undo it and start over. This is the most difficult part of making the basket. Finish the coaster using the taper method.

Step 1 Draw several plans in your sketchbook and select your best plan. Choose your color scheme and note the materials and colors you will use to make the weft. Decide whether you will use regular, alternating, or progressive rhythm to organize your colors. Note your decision in your sketchbook and color the design to indicate how you will use the colors.

Step 2 Construct the basket based on your design. Control the position of the warp coils by holding them in position as you sew the stitches that connect the coils. You can position them to go up vertically or to slant in or out. Finish your basket using the taper method.

EVALUATING YOUR WORK

▶ **DESCRIBE** Explain the procedures you followed to create your basket, including the practice coaster.

▶ **ANALYZE** Describe the form of your basket. Tell what color scheme you used and explain which type of rhythm you used to organize your colors.

▶ **INTERPRET** Is your basket functional or decorative? Explain. How did your use of color and pattern affect the feeling of your basket?

▶ **JUDGE** Which aesthetic theories would you use to judge this work? If you were to make another basket, what, if anything, would you change? Explain your answer.

▲ **FIGURE 8.24A** Student work.

ASSESS...........
Keeping a Portfolio

Remind students that the preliminary sketches and the final artwork for this Studio Project are likely candidates for their portfolios. Encourage them to label their work, evaluate the process, and make any notes that will help them make meaningful choices when they prepare a portfolio for evaluation.

Extension

Gather grape vines, willow branches, wisteria vines, or any nontoxic pliable vines that grow locally. Remember, the vines must be gathered during late spring through early fall when the sap is still in the vine, making it more flexible. If it is difficult to locate vines, ask a local florist or nursery owner for information. Allow students to create their own baskets with the vines you have gathered.

Self-Assessment

Have students apply the steps of art criticism to their own artwork using the "Evaluating Your Work" questions on this page. In addition, ask the following: What influenced the design of the basket? What is its function? Will it serve its function well? What makes the basket different from those of other students?

CLOSE............
Display the finished baskets. Ask students to tell what they learned while making this artwork.

TECHNIQUE TIP ✓

Working with Clay If students have not worked with clay recently, they may need to feel the way the clay works before they can plan how to use it. Students might begin by squeezing and shaping the clay into forms from their own imagination. Have a variety of clay tools available for them to experiment with modeling techniques. Remind them of the following guidelines or see page 434 in the Handbook:

- Dip one or two fingers in water.
- Spread the moisture from their fingers over their palms.
- Never completely dip their hands in water as too much moisture turns clay to mud.

TECHNOLOGY
Studio Project

Progressive Rhythm

(pages 220–221)
(National Standards: 1a, 1b, 2b, 2c, 3b)

Progressive Rhythm

▲ **FIGURE 8.25**

M. C. Escher. *Day and Night.* 1938. Woodcut in black and gray, printed from two blocks. 39.1 × 67.7 cm (15⅜ × 26⅝"). © 1996. Cordon Art-Baarn-Holland. All rights reserved.

SUPPLIES

■ Sketchbook
■ Computer
■ Paint or Draw application
■ Printer

FOCUS...........
Objectives

After completing this lesson, students will be able to:

■ Sketch several images of a living creature in their sketchbooks and select one for further development.

■ Recreate their selected images of living creatures using a computer paint application.

■ Manipulate the creature image by copying, pasting and rotating it to create a progressive rhythm motif that features positive and negative space.

Supplies

Sketchbook
Computer
Paint or draw application
Printer

TEACH.........
Motivator

Show several examples of M.C. Escher's works featuring progressive rhythm. Ask students to identify the basic images that they see within the overall image. Introduce the terms *motif, positive space*, and *negative space.* Have students identify examples of these terms in Escher's work. Discuss how one image can be repeated, rotated, and revised to create a powerful graphic image. Introduce the term *tessellation* and explain how it is based in both art and mathematics. Students will have the opportunity to develop a motif and put it into a progressive rhythm pattern for themselves.

220

Mauritius Cornelius Escher (1898–1972) was a Dutch artist and brilliant mathematician. As a child Escher struggled in school, but his tremendous art ability helped him to graduate and later major in graphic arts. Following his studies, Escher traveled through Europe. He was intrigued by the intricate patterns on the Moorish mosaics he saw while in southern Spain. These tiles inspired him to research geometric shapes that could be altered to make recognizable organic forms such as birds, animals, fish, or people. These he used to make mathematical patterns or rhythmic repetitions.

Escher is known for his carefully drawn shapes that undergo a metamorphosis into new shapes. Carefully study *Day and Night* **(Figure 8.25).** Look closely at the white bird on the right and notice all the details. Now notice the negative space between it and the two birds to its left. As you move your eyes from right to left, the white birds lose their details and gradually become the background negative space. The birds in the third column become rectangular fields on the ground as they progress downward. They become open sky as they progress upward. Now notice how the black negative space on the right has changed into sharply–defined bird shapes on the left.

What You Will Learn

Create a complex motif of a living creature and use it to create a regular rhythm. You will change the motif gradually three or more times to develop a design illustrating the changes of progressive rhythm in the manner of M.C. Escher. You will also change any negative spaces created in your motif so that they progressively become positive spaces as Escher does in *Day and Night.*

TEACHER TALK 📖

Studio Options Many computer paint programs have an animation option for artists. Have students try making a simple animation. They should begin with a simple line or shape and plan a series of actions or changes to that line or shape that demonstrate progressive rhythm. Have them decide the direction of the action or movement and investigate the tools and menus to make these changes. Encourage them to try to achieve smooth transitions in movements. Have them make a minimum of nine slides, cards or cels in their animation and save this file. Then, they should replay the animation and watch the animation for progressive rhythm.

Creating

Choose a favorite mammal, bird, reptile, insect, or sea-life creature. Draw several versions of it in your sketchbook. Give it an irregular outline, including wings, beaks, limbs, feathers, or tails that break out of the main shape into negative space.

Step 1 Choose your best drawing. Using the computer tools of your choice, re-create it on the computer. This is your motif. Title and save your work.

Step 2 Choose the Lasso selection tool and the Copy then Paste option to make several identical copies of the form. Choose the Grids and Rulers option to arrange your motif in a horizontal row of three or more motifs. Explore different placements of the motif so that the negative space between them has interesting possibilities. Retitle this and later editions by adding a different number to the title to indicate the sequence of production.

Step 3 Place an extra copy of the original shape in an area where you can make changes without affecting the original row of motifs. Simplify the shape by eliminating some of the details. Create a second horizontal row of the new motif and place it beneath the row of original motifs. Add some details to the negative spaces between the rows. Continue using the Save As command to retitle and save each new step.

Step 4 Continue modifying the motif, creating new horizontal rows and adding to the negative spaces as often as you can. Print your final work.

EVALUATING YOUR WORK

▶ **DESCRIBE** Tell what creature you used to create your motif. Explain, in detail, how you modified the motif and the negative spaces as you constructed your progressive rhythms. What tools and menu items did you use? How many times did you change the original motif?

▶ **ANALYZE** Did you change your motif, the horizontal rows of motifs, and the negative spaces to create progressive rhythm?

▶ **INTERPRET** What mood or idea does your work express? Give your work a descriptive title that sums up how you feel about it.

▶ **JUDGE** Were you successful in creating a progressive rhythm in the manner of Escher? What, if anything, would you change to improve your work? Which aesthetic theories would you use to judge your work?

▲ **FIGURE 8.25A** Student work.

Cross-Curriculum: Math

There are several techniques based on symmetry and rotation for generating tessellations. Have students research tessellations and find a technique they would like to try. Have them develop a progressive rhythm pattern based on the technique they have selected. Have them share their results with the class.

ASSESS..........
Portfolio

Remind students that the final artwork for this Studio Lesson is a likely candidate for their portfolios.

Self Assessment

Have students apply the steps of art criticism to their artwork.

Enrichment

Have students try this lesson a second time, but develop a completely different living creature motif. Suggest they focus on the irregular outline of the motif more than they did in their first image. Tell them that by breaking out of the main shape in their initial sketches they will have more variation in their positive and negative space relationships. This will make the image more visually striking.

CLOSE............

Have students print copies of their completed progressive rhythm images and mat them in a consistent manner. Then have them display the images for viewing. Ask students to look at each image and identify the living creature motif that was used to create the progressive rhythm image. Have them identify and discuss the different ways students manipulated their motifs to create positive and negative space.

TECHNOLOGY OPTIONS

Computers Many computer paint applications have a slide show option that will allow you to show a series of images if they are housed within a single folder. Collect all the completed progressive rhythm images done by the class and save them in one folder. Some applications require that the images be in PICT format while others use the JPEG format. Check to see what your application specifies. Give a class presentation of all the student work. You can set the images to change automatically after so many seconds and you can have the images show in a continuous loop. If you prefer, you can set it to advance and then click the mouse.

(National Standards: 2b, 4c, 5a, 5c)

Critiquing the Work

▶ Describe
What do you see?

- The largest crowd of people are on the sidewalk. Many people are looking out of windows, and many are outside on their fire escapes. In the foreground children are playing on the sidewalk. The clothes are mostly simple. Three tall buildings close in the space.

▶ Analyze
How is this work organized?

- **Line:** the curved clothes lines, the vertical and horizontal lines on the fire escapes. **Shape:** The people are free-form, organic shapes; the buildings are geometric with rectangular windows. **Space:** The space looks very closed in and crowded. **Depth:** The lines of the windows on the two side buildings slant back toward different vanishing points. **Color:** Most of the colors in this work are dull. **Texture:** All the textures are the texture of paint strokes.

- The brightest, lightest area is in the center, near the viewer, where the women and children in the sun are wearing white.

- Random rhythm is seen in the repetition of people. Regular rhythm is seen in the patterns of rectangular windows. An alternating rhythm can be seen in the bricks on the far right of the work.

ART CRITICISM IN ACTION

▲ **FIGURE 8.26**

George Bellows. *Cliff Dwellers.* 1913. Oil on canvas. 102 × 106.8 cm (40⅛ × 42⅛"). Los Angeles County Museum of Art, Los Angeles, California. Los Angeles County Fund.

MORE ABOUT... George Bellows

In New York, Bellows studied with the American realist painter, Robert Henri (1865–1929), who advocated the depiction of contemporary, urban subjects. Henri was influential to a whole group of young artists who had started as newspaper illustrators and were skilled at capturing the vitality of city life. In 1908, the group exhibited together under the name "The Eight." Because these artists used sketchy strokes to paint gritty urban scenes, they became known as the Ashcan School. Although not officially part of the group, Bellows is associated with them because of his bold, vibrant style and his interest in subjects like the city's streets, the boxing ring, the piers and the bars.

1 DESCRIBE What do you see?

List all of the information found in the credit line. This will give you an idea about when this was painted, but you really need to study the work carefully to get everything the artist is trying to say.

■ Study the people. Where are they? Describe their activities. What are they wearing?

■ Now look at the objects in this work. What do you see on the ground? Does this give you an indication of the location of this painting? Do not make guesses. Use only what you observe.

2 ANALYSIS How is this work organized?

During this step you will collect information about the way the elements of art are organized using the principle of rhythm. This is still a clue-collecting step, so do not make guesses.

■ List outstanding things you notice about the elements of line, shape, space, color and texture.

■ How does the artist use value to focus your attention? Where are the lightest areas? Where are the darkest areas?

■ Find examples of random, regular, alternating, progressive, and flowing rhythms. Explain the locations of the rhythms you observe.

3 INTERPRET What is the artist trying to communicate?

Combine the clues that you have collected with your own personal experiences to tell what message the artist is sending to you through this painting.

■ How does the artist's use of elements and different rhythms affect the mood of the work?

■ Were you able to tell the time, place, and season of this work? What do you think about these people and this place?

■ Based on your interpretations, explain what the artist is communicating to you. Give the work a more descriptive title.

4 JUDGE What do you think of the work?

Now you will decide if this is a successful work of art or not.

■ Is this work interesting? Did it make you think?

■ Did the artist use the elements of art and the principle of rhythm successfully?

■ Do you think this is a successful work of art? Use one or more of the aesthetic theories described in Chapter 2 to defend your

Art Criticism in Action | **223**

➡ Interpret
What is the artist trying to communicate?

■ The closed in space and the dull colors create a depressing mood. The random repetition of crowded people also add to this mood. The regular rhythm of windows, randomly filled with people also add to this mood. The bright colors in the center of the work seem to contradict this mood.

■ Answers may vary. Most should recognize that this is a turn-of-the-century tenement district in a city, probably the lower east side of New York City. The state of dress and undress of the people, and all the people on the fire escapes tell us it is a hot summer day. Most will guess that these are recent immigrants to New York, others may just think these are poor people who cannot afford to get away from the city heat. The clotheslines tell us that this was before city pollution because all the clothes are white.

■ Answers will vary.

➡ Judge
What do you think of this work?

■ Answers will vary.

■ Answers will vary.

■ Answers will vary. Most will choose the theory of Emotionalism. A few may use Imitationalism. Some may use Formalism because the use of the elements and the principle of rhythm affect the expressive quality of the work.

Time & Place   Early Twentieth Century

George Bellows painted *Cliff Dwellers* in 1913. Some other events that happened the same year:

Fine Art: Cubism and post-impressionism were introduced to American audiences at the Armory Show in New York.

Social Studies: New York's Grand Central Terminal, the largest railway station in the world, opened.

Science: Niels Bohr formulated his theory of atomic structure.

Rhythm in Design
(National Standards: 6a)

Objectives

After completing this feature, students will be able to:

- Make comparisons between rhythm in visual designs and dances.
- Discuss the concept of a motif in fine art and dance.

Teaching the Connection

Have students read the feature on this page.

Ask students to look closely at the meticulously embroidered floral design. Does the regularity of the design detract from its naturalistic style? (Not necessarily. We find regularity and even symmetry in nature, too.) Encourage students to think about regular patterns and rhythms as they occur in nature. Compare the beaded flowers and leaves to those found in nature as you discuss the concept of motif.

Tell students that articles of formal regalia such as this one helped to preserve and celebrate traditional Native American values. These leggings were worn during social dances and religious ceremonies. Throughout the late nineteenth century, Native American artisans (mainly women) preserved what they could of their culture through artistic craft, such as beadwork and embroidery. Ojibwa women originally learned the floral motif from the missionaries. They adapted these designs to enhance their own tradition of decorating regalia.

Rhythm in Design

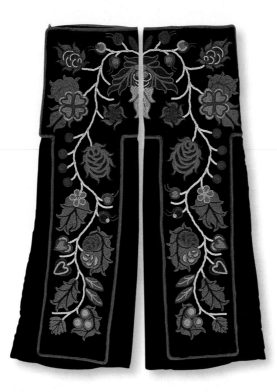

▲ **FIGURE 8.27**

Chippewa Man's Leggings. Minnesota. c. 1890. Cotton velveteen, polished cotton, glass beads, wool twill. 74.6 × 28 cm (29⅜ × 11"). The Detroit Institute of Arts, Detroit, Michigan. Founders Society purchase.

The leggings shown in **Figure 8.27** were designed to be used in Native American dances. For many native peoples, dancing plays an important role in religious, agricultural, hunting, and curing ceremonies. Often the purpose of a dance is to give thanks to the gods, animals, and plants for their generosity. In these ceremonies, dancers represent the harvest or imitate sacred animals. Drumming, chanting, and singing almost always accompany the dancing. Both the music and the movement tend to be highly rhythmic and repetitive.

The most basic element of all dance is design—the organization or pattern of movement in space and over time. In dance, the pattern in time is provided by the rhythm of beats and movements. Similar patterns can also be found in painting, sculpture, and even the intricate beadwork of these leggings. If you look closely at the embroidered design, you will find that, like a dance, it appeals to your sense of rhythm and your awareness of motion. Do these leggings have a rhythm? In fact, they do.

In art, rhythm is produced by the repetition of motifs. Even a static object, such as a painting or a sculpture, can give us a sense of motion. The different arrangements of motif and space allow for variations in rhythm.

Making the Connection

1. How many different motifs can you find embroidered on the leggings in Figure 8.27? How many different ways has the artist alternated the motifs?
2. How would you describe the rhythm of this design?
3. Suppose you wanted to paint a picture of some of your friends in the act of dancing. What techniques would you use in your painting to convey their motion and rhythm?

Answers to Making the Connection

1. Students should have little difficulty describing the identical patterns on each leg. They should be able to make a list of the quantities of each type of flower, bud, or fruit represented. A very close inspection of this garment will reveal that each floral motif is identical down to the quantity of beads.

2. The rhythm is regular since it is based on identical motifs and a symmetrical organization of space. The floral design is continuous rather than broken, which conveys a sense of flowing rhythm, as well.

3. Answers will vary.

Building Vocabulary

On a separate sheet of paper, write the term that best matches each definition given below.

1. The principle of art that indicates movement by the repetition of elements.
2. Rhythm you receive through your eyes rather than through your ears.
3. A unit that is repeated in visual rhythm.
4. A three-dimensional motif.
5. A two-dimensional decorative visual repetition.
6. The principle of art used to create the look and feeling of action and to guide the viewer's eyes throughout the work of art.
7. A work of art that actually moves in space.

Reviewing Art Facts

Answer the following questions using complete sentences.

1. In general, how is visual rhythm created?
2. How does rhythm add a sense of movement to a work of art?
3. How are different rhythms created?
4. What is the difference between a module and a pattern?
5. Name and describe four types of rhythm.
6. What is *dynamism* and with what group is it associated?

Thinking Critically About Art

1. **Compare and contrast.** Study the subject matter of the *Hmong Story Cloth* (Figure 8.18 on page 211) and *School Children on Parade* (Figure 8.22 on page 214). List the similarities and differences you find. Are the themes of the two works similar or different? Explain your answer.
2. **Extend.** The *Elevator Grille* in Figure 8.7, page 204, was designed by the architect Louis Sullivan for a building he designed. Find information about Louis Sullivan in the library. Discover what contributions he made to the field of architecture in the late nineteenth and early twentieth centuries. Give a brief report to the class about the importance of Louis Sullivan in the history of American architecture.

 Explore rhythm and movement with Chuck Davis and the African American Dance Ensemble in the Performing Arts Handbook on page 420.

inter NET CONNECTION Explore *Studio Cyberspace* on the Glencoe Fine Arts Site at www.glencoe.com/sec/art. You will find links to art museums, artists at work, and other exciting art adventures that will show how artists use the principles of rhythm and movement.

Chapter 8 Review **225**

Answers to Building Vocabulary
1. rhythm
2. visual rhythm
3. motif
4. module
5. pattern
6. movement
7. kinetic

Answers to Reviewing Art Facts
1. By repeated positive shapes separated by negative spaces.
2. The viewer's eye follows the visual beats through a work of art.
3. With different arrangements of motifs and space.
4. A module is a three-dimensional motif. A pattern is a two-dimensional decorative visual repetition.
5. **Random:** a motif is repeated in no apparent order, with no regular spaces. **Regular:** by using identical motifs and equal amounts of space between the motifs. **Alternating:** a second motif is used, the placement or content of the original motif is changed, or the spaces between the motifs are changed. **Flowing:** repeating wavy lines are used. **Progressive:** a steady change is made in the motif each time it is repeated.
6. Dynamism was a term coined by the Futurists to refer to the forces of movement.

Reteaching
- Bring to class some locking block toys and let students create three-dimensional rhythms with the blocks and modules.

ASSESSMENT ✓

Evaluate
- Have students complete the *Chapter 8 Test* in the TCR. 📁
- Alternative Assessment teaching strategies are provided below or in the *Testing Program and Alternative Assessment* booklet.

Extension
Ask students to work in pairs or small groups and design, create, then display an artwork that reflects what they have learned about rhythm and movement. Remind students that they will be evaluated on the material selected as well as the overall aesthetic value.

225

Balance
(pages 226–253)

Chapter Scan

Lessons

1 Visual Balance
2 Natural Balance
3 The Expressive Qualities of Balance

Studios

🎨 Formal Portrait

🎨 Informal Group Portrait

🎨 Linoleum Print Using Radial Balance

🖱 Invent an Inside View of a Machine

Resources

📁 Chapter 9 Study Guide

📁 Chapter 9 Test

📁 Computers in the Art Classroom

📁 Cultural Diversity in Art

📁 Portfolio and Assessment Techniques

📁 Reproducible Lesson Plan 9

🎞 Transparency CC-9, Katsushika Hokusai. *A Gust of Wind at Ejiri,* from the series *The Thirty-Six Views of Fuji*

🎞 Transparency 9, Ramon José Lopez. *Santa Maria y Jesus*

📕 Fine Art Print 19, John Sloan. *Red Kimono on the Roof*

📕 Fine Art Print 20, Milton Avery. *Seated Blonde*

While studying this chapter, use Performing Arts Handbook page 421 to help students discover how balance is used in the performing arts.

▲ **FIGURE 9.1** Hokusai has used solid white lines to represent falling water. Compare this woodblock print to the photograph of a waterfall in Figure 8.14 on page 209. What similarities and differences can you find in the two depictions of flowing water?

Katsushika Hokusai. *The Kirifuri Waterfall at Mt. Kurokami, Shimozuke Province.* ca. 1831. Color woodblock print. 37.2 × 24.5 cm (14⅝ × 9⅝″). The Nelson-Atkins Museum of Art, Kansas City, Missouri. Purchase: Nelson Trust.

FEATURED ARTISTS

Emily Carr
Mary Cassatt
Cram, Goodhue, and Ferguson
Beau Dick
Thomas Eakins

Jean-Honoré Fragonard
Giorgione
Ferdinand Hodler
Katsushika Hokusai
Edward Hopper
Frida Kahlo
Rie Muñoz

Gerald Murphy
Alice Neel
Georgia O'Keeffe
Diego Rivera
Dorothy Torivio
Jan van Eyck
Frank Lloyd Wright

Balance

Balance is a principle of life. Each day we balance work with play. We balance the pros and cons of a decision before we make it. We learn to take conflicting or opposing elements and make them work together. This is the essential purpose of balance. Artists use different kinds of balance to convey information in their work.

The woodblock print, *The Kirifuri Waterfall at Mt. Kurokami, Shimozuke Province* **(Figure 9.1)** by Hokusai shows an inventive, bold use of balance. His work, along with those of other famous Japanese printmakers, had a strong influence on the French Impressionists. His use of balance changed the way many artists organized their compositions, encouraging them to move away from traditional balance and experiment with new kinds of balance. Notice how the waterfall flows from the upper left corner to the water below, but stays primarily on one side of the work. He balanced this strong flowing rhythm of thick white lines with a small area of green grass and busy looking trees and men on the right. In this chapter, you will learn about different types of balance and how artists use them to convey ideas and feelings in their works.

OBJECTIVES

After completing this chapter, you will be able to:

- Understand why balance is important in a work of art.
- Explain how visual weight is created and produce it in your own work.
- Describe the types of balance and use them in your own work.
- Tell what different types of balance can mean in a work of art.

WORDS TO KNOW

balance
central axis
formal balance
symmetry
radial balance
informal balance

Developing Your
PORTFOLIO

Consider how you use balance in everyday life. Make a list of things you do in a normal week, placing them in broad categories. For instance, getting your hair cut, shopping for clothes, and getting dressed in the morning might all be under the heading "Taking Care of Myself." Then list the amount of time you spend on each category. Next, draw a big circle in your sketchbook and divide it into wedges based on how much time you spend on each category. For instance, sleeping probably takes about one-third of your time, so it should take up one-third of your circle. Look at the results. Do your activities seem well-balanced? Draw another circle that represents a better balance. Label each and keep both in your portfolio.

Chapter Overview

Chapter 9 examines balance as a principle of art as well as a principle of life, and it helps students understand the different types of balance. They expand their knowledge by exploring the expressive qualities of balance in art. Have students make a list of at least five objects they use or see every day that have balance. Ask them to imagine what the objects would be like if they did not have balance. Tell them that in this chapter they will learn about another principle of art—balance.

Examining the Artwork

Ask the students to point to the center of the top of Figure 9.1. Point out that the top part of the waterfall is on the left side of the print and that most of the rest of the waterfall is positioned on the left side. If students point to the bottom of the print they will see that the two standing figures are to the left of center and the one seated figure is to the right.

Ask them to notice that the lightest areas of the work and the thickest areas of white are left of center. Ask them to notice how the green area on the upper left compares to the green in the upper right. Point out that although all these areas are not even, they are balanced with a type of balance that they will study in this chapter. Ask them to compare this print to Borsky's photograph of a waterfall in Figure 8.14 on page 209.

DEVELOPING
A PORTFOLIO

Personal Style Encourage students to observe the evolution of individual pieces of art as a way of identifying their developing style. Remind them that creative people take risks and see failure as an indication of where the creative process needs modification. For example, if they are not happy with a sketch, instead of discarding, have them make notes about their displeasure with the design or make corrections without erasing the old. Their increased awareness of the process of artistic creation will help them recognize their choices about style. During private conferences, encourage students to articulate progress in the style of their work.

National Standards

This chapter addresses the following National Standards for the Visual Arts:

1. (a, b)	**4.** (c)
2. (b, c)	**5.** (a, c)
3. (b, c)	**6.** (a, b)

Visual Balance

Visual Balance

Visual
Balance
(pages 228–233)
(National Standards: 2b, 3c)

FOCUS...........
Objectives

After completing this lesson, students will be able to:

- Explain why balance is important in a work of art.
- List the different types of balance and what they can mean in a work of art.

Supplies

- Two-sided balance scale and weights
- Variety of objects to weigh
- Pencils, tempera paints, paper, and ruler
- Live flowers that show radial balance (daisies)
- Fruits such as apples, oranges, green peppers with radial balance when cut horizontally

Resources

- Artist's Profile 7, *Jan van Eyck*
- Enrichment Activity 17, *Radial Design for a Tempera Batik*
- *National Gallery of Art Correlation Bar Code Guide*

TEACH..........
Motivator

If you have or can borrow a two-sided balance scale, bring it to class. Another method that will achieve the same results is to balance a sturdy ruler or piece of board over a square block, flat cup, or even the palm of your hand. Challenge students to place small, unlike objects on the sides of the scale or on the ends of the ruler. Coach them in rearranging, adding, or subtracting objects to make the sides balance.

▲ **FIGURE 9.2** This building is known throughout the world, not because of its beauty or because the architect is well known, but because it leans. The many diagonal lines tell the viewer that this building must either straighten up or fall down. Because it remains off balance, defying gravity, it is famous.

Bell Tower of the Cathedral at Pisa (The Leaning Tower of Pisa). Begun in 1174.

A work of art must contain balance. **Balance** is *the principle of art concerned with equalizing visual forces, or elements, in a work of art.* Visual balance causes you to feel that the elements have been arranged well.

If visual balance creates a feeling that the elements have been arranged just right, visual imbalance creates the opposite feeling. It causes a feeling of uneasiness. It makes you feel that something is not quite right. The Leaning Tower of Pisa **(Figure 9.2)** attracts attention because it is out of balance. It has tilted into a danger zone. The top edge overhangs the base by about 17 feet. This imbalance makes the viewer feel uneasy.

In order to know whether two objects are of equal weight—that is, if they balance—a balance scale can be used. In the visual arts, however, balance must be *seen* rather than weighed. The art elements become the visual forces, or weights, in an art object. A **central axis** is *a dividing line that works like the point of balance in the balance scale.* Many works of art have a central vertical axis **(Figure 9.3)** with

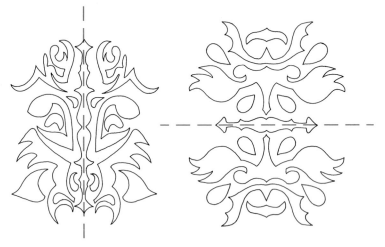

◀ **FIGURE 9.3** *(at left)* With a vertical axis, there is equal visual weight on both sides.

◀ **FIGURE 9.4** *(at right)* With a horizontal axis, there is equal visual weight above and below.

228 CHAPTER 9 Balance

TECHNOLOGY OPTIONS

National Gallery of Art Videodisc Use the following to show examples of balance in art.

Pierre Bonnard
The Artist's Sister and Her Children

Search Frame 2117

Botticelli
The Adoration of the Magi

Search Frame 152

Botticelli
The Adoration of the Magi

Search Frame 154

Use *Glencoe's National Gallery of Arts Correlation Bar Code Guide* to locate more artworks.

MEET THE ARTIST
DIEGO RIVERA

Mexican, 1886–1957

Diego Rivera. *Self-Portrait.* 1941. Oil on canvas. 61 × 43 cm (24 × 17″). Smith College Museum of Art, Northampton, Massachusetts.

Diego Rivera, the son of two teachers, was born in 1886 in the small town of Guanajuato, Mexico. As a young man, Rivera received a government grant to study art in Spain. He also studied with Picasso in France and traveled to Italy to study the works of Raphael and Michelangelo.

When he returned to Mexico, he decided to paint only Mexican subjects. He used the simplified forms of pre-Columbian art in his work. His concern for the workers, the poor, and the illiterate influenced all of his art. He painted many murals with political themes, considering them a way to teach people who could not read. In his art, he combined the techniques of European painters with the history of Mexico to create a new way to portray his ideas about the people and culture of Mexico.

▶ **FIGURE 9.5** Rivera used his art to show his serious concern for the Mexican working people. Many of his works depicted the labors of the Mexican peasants. His work reflects the style of the solid-looking, pre-Columbian artwork of the Mayans.

Diego Rivera. *Flower Day.* 1925. Oil on canvas. 142.3 × 120.6 cm (58 × 47½″). Los Angeles County Museum of Art, Los Angeles, California. Los Angeles County Fund. Reproducción autorizada por el Instituto Nacional de Bellas Artes y Literatura.

equal visual weight on both sides of the dividing line. Works of art can also have a horizontal axis. In this case, the visual weight is balanced between top and bottom **(Figure 9.4).**

Formal Balance

One type of balance is called formal balance. **Formal balance** occurs *when equal, or very similar, elements are placed on opposite sides of a central axis.* The axis can be vertical or horizontal. It may be a real part of the design, or it may be an imaginary line, as in Figures 9.3 and 9.4. Formal balance is the easiest type of balance to recognize and to create **(Figure 9.5).** After you find the axis, all you have to do is place similar objects on each side, equally distant from the center.

LESSON 1 *Visual Balance* **229**

Critical Thinking
Ask students to think about balance in sports. If possible, borrow a balance beam from the physical education teacher. Invite students to walk the beam, then ask them to describe how they felt trying to maintain their balance. Relate this to how a young child feels when learning to walk. Ask students to discuss specific events that require good balance in sports. If possible, have them demonstrate.

Cross-Curriculum: Dance
If you have ballet dancers in the class who can dance on point, ask them to discuss the training. Ask for a demonstration of the technique and discuss balance.

Developing Perceptual Skills
To help the students understand the concept of the axis that divides a work, first show them how the axis works in Figures 9.3 and 9.4 on page 228. Ask them to look through other chapters to find works where the axis is obvious and where the axis can only be sensed.

Studio Skills
Challenge students with this exercise: Using formal balance, create a composition that presents the image of something that you think is very important. Make several sketches with pencil and paper. Be sure that you have drawn the object you are presenting very accurately. Choose your best design. Draw it large and paint it with tempera paint.

MEETING INDIVIDUAL NEEDS

Physically Disabled Students with neurological or orthopedic disabilities may have physical problems with balance; some will use wheelchairs, canes, or walkers. Thus, in discussing balance, it may be sensitive to also discuss the occasional advantages of being a little off-balance, such as falling into new exciting circumstances and meeting new people. In as much as a study of symmetry (bilateral and quadrilateral) has analogies to orthopedic disabilities, some terminology may be helpful: paraplegia affects either both arms or both legs; hemiplegia affects the arm and leg on one side of the body; and quadriplegia affects all four limbs.

Cross-Curriculum: Physics

Borrow a balance scale with weights from the science department to help students grasp the concepts of balance and imbalance. Bring in an assortment of objects of varying densities, such as paper clips, foam forms, a baseball, a leather football, a foam football, a large feather, an acorn, a live plant in a pot of soil, an arrangement of silk flowers in a basket, pebbles, corks, a plastic cup, a stoneware mug, and so on. Try to find more objects that are the same size but different weights, such as the leather and foam balls. Allow students time to experiment with the scales to discover that size and weight are not always equal.

Use the scales to demonstrate the difference between formal and informal balance. With formal balance both size and weight must be equal. With informal balance the weights must remain equal, but the sizes may change. For example, a few small paper clips may balance a large styrofoam ball.

Cross-Curriculum: Mathematics

Explain to students that formal balance, as shown in Figures 9.6 and 9.7, is based on mathematics and that the field of geometry includes the methods for developing a great variety of designs. Have students find the formulas and tools necessary for making formally balanced designs. After they have tried the techniques, have them analyze examples of radial design and identify which formulas were used to make them.

▶ **FIGURE 9.6** This urn shows a young man wearing a headdress depicting his guardian spirit, the goddess Quetzal, an unforgettably beautiful bird. The artist who created this urn used symmetry to emphasize the seriousness of this work.

Mexican (Monte Alban; Zapotec). *Figural Urn.* A.D. 500–700. Painted earthenware. 63.5 × 63.5 × 31.7 cm (25 × 25 × 12½"). The Nelson-Atkins Museum of Art, Kansas City, Missouri. Purchase: Nelson Trust.

Symmetry

Symmetry is *a special type of formal balance in which two halves of a balanced composition are identical, mirror images of each other.* Another term for this is *bilateral* symmetry **(Figure 9.6)**.

Symmetry appeals strongly to us, probably because of the bilateral symmetry of the human body. Objects closely associated with our bodies, such as clothing and furniture, are usually symmetrical. Most traditional architecture, especially public architecture, is symmetrical **(Figure 9.7)**.

Symmetry can be very stiff and formal. Artists use it to express dignity, endurance, and stability. Because formal balance is so predictable, however, it can be dull. Many artists avoid boring the viewer by using approximate symmetry, which is *almost* symmetrical.

▲ **FIGURE 9.7** This entrance to the Federal Reserve Building in Washington, D.C. gives the building a dignified, important look. The symmetrical arrangement of vertical and horizontal shapes makes the building appear secure and stable.

Cram, Goodhue, and Ferguson. Federal Reserve Building. 1935. Washington, D.C. Façade. Photography by Sandak, Inc., Stamford, Connecticut.

COOPERATIVE LEARNING

Demonstrating Balance To help students remember the different types of balance, divide the class into small groups. Write the following terms on cards: *symmetry, approximate symmetry, radial balance,* and *informal balance.* Turn the cards over so the words are hidden; then have one student from each group choose a card. Each group is to pose in a tableau to illustrate the type of balance on the card. Give the groups about five minutes to plan their design. They may use props found in the classroom if they wish. For example, each member of one group may hold a book, but the way that the book is held may add to the pose. When they are ready, have them act out the scenes.

Approximate symmetry has the stability of formal balance (Figure 9.8). Some small differences make it more interesting than perfect symmetry. If you look carefully in a mirror, you may discover that your face has approximate symmetry. The two sides do not match perfectly.

Activity   Using Symmetry

Applying Your Skills. Arrange a symmetrical still life. Make a pencil drawing of the arrangement on a small sheet of paper. Then rearrange or change the objects slightly to create approximate symmetry. Make a drawing of the second arrangement. Mount the drawings side by side on a sheet of construction paper and label each drawing. Which one do you prefer? Survey your friends to find out their preferences.

Computer Option. If available, use the Symmetry menu and Brush or Pencil tool to create a symmetrical landscape. Vary the Brush shape, thickness, pattern, and color. If the Symmetry menu is not available, determine the central axis or line of symmetry. Draw half of the scene. Use the Select tool and Copy, Paste, and Flip commands to make the matching second half. Title and save the work. Try rearranging the shapes in your scene so that it is not perfectly symmetrical. Compare the two drawings. Which do you prefer?

▲ **FIGURE 9.8** Van Eyck used approximate symmetry to depict this wedding portrait. The halves of the picture are not quite the same. However, the work still has the dignity of perfect symmetry, only the composition is more interesting and less monotonous than if he had used perfect symmetry.

Jan van Eyck. *The Arnolfini Wedding.* 1434. Oil on panel. 83.8 × 57.2 cm (33 × 22.5″). National Gallery, London, England.

Promoting Discussion

After students have examined the balance of Figure 9.7 on page 230, challenge them to think creatively about balance in architectural design. Suggest this: Use structural elements such as domes, columns, doors, windows, turrets, or pediments (the triangular or curved sections over columns or doors) to design a symmetrical building. Start with the door and build out. Decide if your building is to be a home, church, theater, or store. Look for examples of symmetrical structures in your neighborhood. The Greek temple is a perfect example of symmetry.

Activity

Using Symmetry

Applying Your Skills. This activity requires some time and perception. Therefore, it might be a good homework assignment. It will be impossible for you to set up one still life in the classroom for all of the students. If each student is to view a symmetrical arrangement properly, each one must set up his or her own arrangement. If you wish to do this in school, you might ask each student to use a few small objects, such as erasers, scissors, pencils, paper clips, and so on.

▶ COOPERATIVE LEARNING

Illumination Jan van Eyck's painting of Giovanni Arnolfini and his bride was one of the first examples in art of the effects of atmospheric diffusion of light. Have students form small groups and designate one person in each group to trace the effects of light in the painting, beginning at the light source (i.e., the window on the left), continuing with the soft illumination of the back wall, and noting finally the way light is used to accentuate the bride. Then have another group member record the group's answers to the following questions: What is the quality and diffusion of light in van Eyck's painting? Is it artificial or natural? Have groups share their observations with the class.

Studio Skills

Bring in live flowers so that everyone in the room can hold one. Have each student imagine that he or she is studying the blossom analytically so that it can be reconstructed artificially. Have them look at it from every angle, make rough pencil sketches of the blossom from different points of view, and analyze the patterns of the seeds or miniature blossoms in the center of the flower. Does the center have a definite structure?

The blossom may not display perfect symmetry, but even if the blossom has five petals, it is still organized so that the petals radiate out from the center.

Art in Everyday Life

To foster students' awareness of visual balance in everyday life, suggest this: Study the balance in a Japanese garden, floral arrangement, or a bonsai tree. To the Asian, symmetrical balance symbolizes death. Consequently, you will find asymmetry in most Asian artworks. The Japanese garden accents space, flowing movement, and textures of rocks and foliage organized to create a balance that is both calm and alive. The Japanese art of flower arrangement, called Ikebana, follows complex rules of placement, all based on symbolism. Arrangements are always asymmetrical. Tiny bonsai trees are carefully cultivated into an often twisted, but always asymmetrical, shape having the character of full-sized ancient trees.

▲ **FIGURE 9.9** The use of radial balance adds to the decorative quality of this design. This print is based on the stained-glass dome found in the main synagogue of Szeged, Hungary.

N. Anderson, Israel. *Blue Dome - House Blessing.* 1995. Etching. 43.2 x 43.2 cm (17 × 17″). Private collection.

Radial Balance

Radial balance occurs *when the forces or elements of a design come out (radiate) from a central point.* The axis in a radial design is the center point. In almost all cases, the elements are spaced evenly around the axis to form circular patterns **(Figure 9.9).**

Radial balance is a complex variation of symmetry. While symmetry requires only two matching units, designs with radial balance usually involve four or more matching units. In **Figure 9.10,** notice that the center of the design is a red circle. Flower petals radiate out from that central point. Each flower petal points to the head of a figure, and the body of each figure acts as a continuation of the ray coming from the center point. Each set of matching shapes form a circular ring around the center point.

Radial balance occurs frequently in nature. Most flower petals are arranged around a central axis and radiate out-

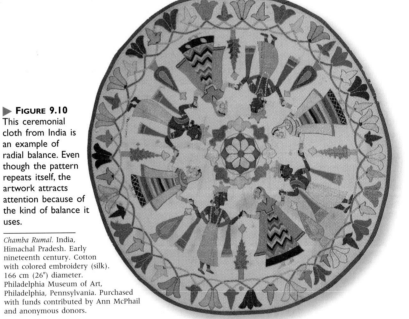

▶ **FIGURE 9.10** This ceremonial cloth from India is an example of radial balance. Even though the pattern repeats itself, the artwork attracts attention because of the kind of balance it uses.

Chamba Rumal. India, Himachal Pradesh. Early nineteenth century. Cotton with colored embroidery (silk). 166 cm (26″) diameter. Philadelphia Museum of Art, Philadelphia, Pennsylvania. Purchased with funds contributed by Ann McPhail and anonymous donors.

*inter*NET
CONNECTION

ART ON THE WEB
Radial balance occurs when objects are positioned around a central point. There are many different objects surrounding us every day that exhibit this degree of equilibrium and stability. Flowers, quilts, and paintings are all examples of radial balance.

Check out Glencoe's art site to see other examples of radial balance and to learn more about the techniques artists use to create their designs and arrangements. Visit us at **www.glencoe.com/sec/art**

ward. Many plants follow radial patterns of growth. For instance, if you cut an apple in half horizontally, you will see a radial star design. Cut an orange the same way and you will notice the radial pattern of segments.

You can find many examples of radial balance in architecture. Domes are designed on the principle of radial balance. Manufactured items such as gears, wheels, tires, dials, and clocks are also radial in structure. Radial designs are used by many potters to decorate the surfaces of their work because they adapt well to the rounded forms of pottery **(Figure 9.11)**.

◄ FIGURE 9.11 Torivio, a Native American potter, has developed her own style for decorating her pots. She repeats the designs in radial patterns. The motif starts out small at the top rim and then expands to the widest part of the vessel.

Dorothy Torivio. *Vase.* c. 1984. Clay. Height about 20 cm (8"). Heard Museum Collection, Phoenix, Arizona.

Activity — Creating Radial Balance

Applying Your Skills. Make a series of drawings of five natural or manufactured objects that have a radial structure. Emphasize the radial quality of each object.

Computer Option. Choose from a variety of Shape tools. Determine the center of the computer page. Use a dot, an "X," an addition sign (+), or other shape to mark this spot. Copy and Paste a shape four times around the center point. Continue to add and arrange shapes to maintain radial balance. Try a variety of sizes to add interest but make sure each set of four shapes is identical. Title and save your work. Now explore a more complex radial design. Combine lines and shapes and use more than four repeated combinations to complete the design.

Check Your Understanding

1. What is a central axis?
2. What is the easiest type of balance to recognize and create?
3. Which type of balance can be found frequently in nature and in architecture?

Activity

Creating Radial Balance

Applying Your Skills. This activity requires perception drawing. You might arrange a still life using objects that have radial balance, such as clocks, wheels, baskets, round toys, round pillows, some kitchen utensils, pumpkins, and cantaloupes. If you want to use smaller objects, place some of the following on each table: an apple cut horizontally; half of an orange, lemon, or grapefruit; green pepper cut crosswise; cut cucumber; onion; or individual flowers such as daisies.

ASSESS...........

Self-Assessment

Have students complete the lesson review questions. Answers are provided below.

Reteaching

Ask students to find and sketch examples of formal or radial balance in their homes or in such public areas as malls or parks.

Enrichment

Have students work in small groups to brainstorm lists of objects, both natural and manufactured, that exemplify radial balance. *(wheels, flowers, jewelry)*

CLOSE.............

Have students give one example of formal balance.

 ### Answers to Check Your Understanding

1. A central axis is a dividing line that works like the point of balance in the balance scale.
2. Formal balance is the easiest type of balance to recognize and create.
3. Radial balance can be found frequently in nature and in architecture.

Natural Balance
(pages 234–238)
(National Standards: 2b, 3c)

FOCUS...........
Objectives
After completing this lesson, students will be able to:
- Define informal balance.
- Describe how to achieve informal balance in artworks.

Supplies
- Wire clothes hanger
- Found objects
- Pencil and paper
- Architectural magazines
- City maps such as Washington, D.C. and Paris

Resources
- Application Activity 17, *A Balancing Act*
- Artist's Profile 32, *Frank Lloyd Wright*
- Cooperative Learning Activity 17, *Maintain Your Balance*
- Enrichment Activity 18
- Artist's Profile 35, *Edward Hopper*
- Artist's Profile 19, *Katsushika Hokusai*
- *National Gallery of Art Correlation Bar Code Guide*

TEACH..........
Motivator
Write the word *asymmetrical* on the board. Ask students to speculate on the meaning of the word. Tell them that in this lesson, they will learn the meaning.

Natural Balance

Natural balance gives the viewer the same comfortable feeling as formal balance, but in a much more subtle way. While natural balance can express dignity, endurance, and stability, these qualities are less pronounced. Natural balance seems more realistic because it is closer to what appears in nature. It does not consist of two equal or nearly equal halves or sides. Instead, it relies on the artistic arrangement of objects to *appear* balanced. Natural balance is used in Figure 9.1 on page 226.

Informal Balance

Informal balance, or asymmetry, involves *a balance of unlike objects.* Informal balance creates a casual effect **(Figure 9.12).** Although it seems less planned than formal balance, it is not. What appears to be an accidental arrangement of elements can be quite complicated. Symmetry merely requires that elements be repeated in a mirror image. Informal balance is more complex. Artists must consider all the visual

▲ **FIGURE 9.12** The complex shapes of the wagon and the child are informally balanced by the potted plant and the foliage in this casual scene. Informal balance gives this composition the look of a snapshot.

Thomas Eakins. *Baby at Play.* 1876. Oil on canvas. 81.9 × 122.8 cm (32¼ × 48⅛"). National Gallery of Art, Washington, D.C. © 1998 Board of Trustees. John Hay Whitney Collection.

TECHNOLOGY OPTIONS

National Gallery of Art Videodisc Use the following to show examples of balance in art.

Meindert Hobbema *A View on a High Road*	Jean-Baptiste-Camille Corot *River Scene with Bridge*	Gustave Courbet *Beach in Normandy*
Search Frame 934	Search Frame 1138	Search Frame 1220

Use *Glencoe's National Gallery of Art Correlation Bar Code Guide* to locate more artworks.

Edward Hopper. *First Row Orchestra.* 1951. Oil on canvas. 79 × 101.9 cm (31⅛ × 40⅛"). Hirshhorn Museum and Sculpture Garden, Smithsonian Institution, Washington, D.C. Gift of the Joseph H. Hirshhorn Foundation, 1966.

weight factors and put them together correctly. Many factors influence the visual weight, or the attraction, that elements in a work of art have to the viewer's eyes.

Size and Contour

A large shape or form appears to be heavier than a small shape. Several small shapes or forms can balance one large shape **(Figure 9.13).**

An object with a complicated contour is more interesting and appears to be heavier than one with a simple contour. A small, complex object can balance a large, simple object.

Color

A high-intensity color has more visual weight than a low-intensity color. The viewer's eyes are drawn to the area of bright color. What does this mean in terms of balance? It means that a small area of bright color is able to balance a larger area of a dull, neutral color **(Figure 9.14).**

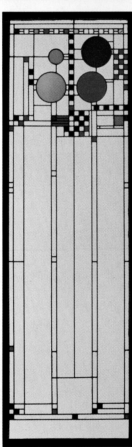

◀ **FIGURE 9.14** In this stained-glass window designed by Frank Lloyd Wright, the bright colors at the top balance the large area of clear glass.

Designed by Frank Lloyd Wright. American stained-glass window, one of a triptych. Twentieth century. Glass, lead, wood. 219 × 71 × 5 cm (86¼ × 28 × 2"). The Metropolitan Museum of Art, New York, New York. Purchase. Edward C. Moore, Jr., gift and Edgar J. Kaufmann Charitable Foundation gift, 1967.

CHAPTER 9 LESSON 2

Art History

Remind students that Edward Hopper was strongly influenced by Robert Henri and the Armory Show of 1913, which Hopper took part in. Encourage students to research more about this artist and this important event. Have them share their findings with the class.

Promoting Discussion

Have students carefully study Hopper's painting—Figure 9.13. Then ask them to suggest words that describe the mood and the scene of the painting. Using their knowledge of the elements and principles of art, they should explain how the painting evokes their responses.

Aesthetics

Direct students' attention to the stained-glass window on this page. Ask them to consider these questions: Would an aesthetician of the emotionalist school find this design appealing? Why or why not? What would a formalist find most successful? Encourage thorough responses and remind students to use the terms that relate to the elements and principles of art.

Show them other examples of stained glass. Ask if the mood or feeling they have when viewing the new examples is similar to, or different from, the mood or feeling they have from viewing Figure 9.14.

Aesthetics

Remind students that some artworks that were created as applied arts are now considered examples of fine art, for example, the stained-glass window in Figure 9.14. Have students work in small groups to discuss this question: How is a work of applied art similar to, and different from, a common useful object?

TEACHER TALK

Resources Beyond the Classroom One way of adding immediacy to the art experience for students is to arrange for them to meet and speak with local artists and craftspeople. To find out who lives and works in your area, begin by getting in touch with local art gallery dealers and curators in the education departments of local museums. It is also helpful to read reviews of art shows in your area. Even though a given artist may not live in your city, he or she will very likely be in town for the opening of the show and might be willing to visit your class. Finally, art supply stores are another source of information on local artists.

235

Art History

Tell students that Jean-Honoré Fragonard was a court painter in France during the years prior to the French Revolution. Like his contemporary Antoine Watteau, Fragonard's paintings were intended to be displayed in the palaces and elegant homes of the French upper class. His themes reflected the carefree, idle lives of the aristocracy, which would soon be altered by the revolution. Ask students to examine Figure 9.15 and identify symbols of the French upper class.

Cross-Curriculum: Language Arts

Ask volunteers to research examples of poetry written in the eighteenth century. Then have them select a poem that is similar in tone to Fragonard's painting. Ask the volunteers to lead a class discussion where they read the poem aloud, then discuss what both the painting and the poem suggest about the Rococo era.

Warm colors carry more visual weight than cool colors. Red appears heavier than blue, and orange appears heavier than green **(Figure 9.15).**

Value

The stronger the contrast in value between an object and the background, the more visual weight the object has **(Figure 9.16).** Black against white has more weight than gray against white. Dark values appear heavier than light values. A dark red seems heavier than a light red.

Texture

A rough texture, with its uneven pattern of light highlights and dark, irregular shadows, attracts the viewer's eye more easily than a smooth, even surface does. This means that a small, rough-textured area can balance a large, smooth surface. In a poster or advertisement, a block of printed words has the quality of rough texture because of the irregular pattern of light and dark. Graphic designers must keep this in mind when balancing words with other visual elements.

▶ **FIGURE 9.15** In this Rococo painting, Fragonard balances all the cool, low-intensity colors with the warm, bright red on the dress in the foreground.

Jean-Honoré Fragonard. *A Game of Hot Cockles.* 1767–73. Oil on canvas. 115.5 × 91.4 cm (45½ × 36"). National Gallery of Art, Washington, D.C. © 1998 Board of Trustees. Samuel H. Kress Collection.

COOPERATIVE LEARNING

Searching for Facts Explain to students that while viewing artworks such as *A Game of Hot Cockles* in Figure 9.15, they are given clues to the lifestyles of the subjects through their clothing. From those clues, students can research further into the histori-cal, social, and economic status of the persons wearing them. By working in collaborative groups, students can divide the areas of research, share their findings when finished, and create artworks or reports that are more comprehensive than if done individually.

▲ **FIGURE 9.16** The face and head scarf of the Virgin are no lighter in value than the infant on his blanket or the shepherd's white skirt. Her face stands out so much more because it is placed against the dark value of the cave's interior, while the infant and the shepherd are placed against the midvalue tan of the ground.

Giorgione. *The Adoration of the Shepherds.* c. 1505–10. Oil on panel. 91 × 111 cm (35¾ × 43½"). National Gallery of Art, Washington, D.C. © 1998 Board of Trustees. Samuel H. Kress Collection.

Position

Children playing on a seesaw quickly discover that two friends of unequal weight can balance the seesaw by adjusting their positions. The heavier child moves toward the center; the lighter child slides toward the end. The board is then in balance **(Figure 9.17).**

In visual art, a large object close to the dominant area of the work can be

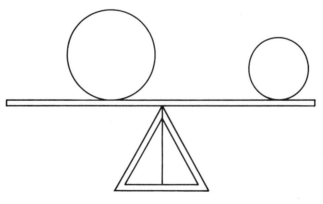

▲ **FIGURE 9.17** Does the seesaw look balanced?

LESSON 2 *Natural Balance* | **237**

Art History

Have students study Figure 9.16 and consider how the artist uses color. Point out to students that although this event took place in the town of Bethlehem, the scenery depicted by Giorgione looks like European farmland, and the buildings are reminiscent of those built during the sixteenth century.

Art Criticism

Have students study Figure 9.18, on page 238, then answer the questions in the caption. Remind them to notice that the shape of the negative space looks similar to the water except it is upside down. It is the visual balance of the positive. How does it help to balance the positive shape of the wave? The two boats with the most detail are on the right side; the boat that shows the least is on the left with the wave.

The men sit low so as not to tip the boat. Their position brings their weight closer to the base to maintain balance, to make the boat more stable. The small curved shapes are decorative, and they seem to diminish the seriousness of the situation.

237

▲ **FIGURE 9.18** Notice the large wave on the left. It is balanced informally by the small triangular shape of Mount Fuji in the distance. Notice the shape of the negative space of the yellow sky. How does it help to balance the positive shape of the wave? How do the three small fishing boats affect the balance of the work?

Katsushika Hokusai. *The Great Wave at Kanagawa* (from the series "The Thirty-Six Views of Mount Fuji"). c. 1823–29. Polychrome woodblock print. 25.7 × 36 cm (10⅛ × 14⁵/₁₆"). The Metropolitan Museum of Art, New York, New York. H. O. Havemeyer, 1929. (JP1847)

Activity

Using Informal Balance

Applying Your Skills. This activity requires perception, but it also calls for drawing skills. Before students try these activities, be sure that they review the factors that influence visual weight and discuss Figures 9.12–9.18 with you.

 Computer Option. As an alternative activity, have students follow these directions: Experiment with the elements used to create informal balance: size and contour, intensity of color, contrasting value, texture, position, and relationship of positive and negative space. Then create an example of each type of informal balance by using your choice of Drawing and Shape tools, colors, and textures. Each example can be an entirely different design or begin with elements of size and contour to create a series of variations emphasizing the other elements listed above.

ASSESS...........

Self-Assessment

Have students complete the lesson review questions. Answers appear below.

Reteaching

Have students review the visual weight factors that affect informal balance: size and contour, color, value, texture, and position.

Enrichment

Let students use the media of their choice to illustrate an example of informal balance using one of the factors. Then arrange a display of the best examples.

CLOSE.............

Call on students to summarize how they achieved informal balance in their examples.

Activity — Using Informal Balance

Applying Your Skills. Create small designs using cut paper and/or fabric shapes to illustrate five weight arrangements that create informal balance. In each design keep all of the elements as alike as possible. Vary only the weight factors. For example, to illustrate differences in size, a large red circle could be balanced by several small red circles.

Computer Option. Use the drawing tools of your choice to make a series of small compositions that show informal balance. Use both lines and shapes. Explore changes in size, color, texture, value, contour, and position to create these asymmetrical compositions. Make several of each kind. Title, save, and print your best examples. Display them and compare with your classmates.

balanced by a smaller object placed farther away from the dominant area **(Figure 9.18).** In this way, a large, positive shape and a small, negative space can be balanced against a small, positive shape and a large, negative space.

 ### Check Your Understanding

1. What is the effect of informal balance?
2. Name the six factors that influence the visual weight of an object.
3. Which has a heavier visual weight, an object with a simple contour or one with a complicated contour?

Answers to Check Your Understanding

1. Informal balance creates a casual effect.
2. Size, contour, color, value, texture, and position are the six factors that influence the visual weight of an object.
3. An object with a complicated contour has a heavier visual weight.

The Expressive Qualities of Balance

The type of balance an artist uses to organize a work of art affects the feeling expressed by that work. Artists choose balance based on the feeling they wish to convey. An artist who wants to present a calm arrangement will use formal balance. Formal balance can be used to present a person in a dignified portrait **(Figure 9.19)**.

LOOKING CLOSELY

Using Formal Balance To Organize A Composition

Frida Kahlo has used formal balance to organize this painting to give it a sense of dignity and importance. In the diagram you can see that if the painting were folded in half along the vertical axis the shapes would match. Notice, however, that there are a few small variations. They would not match perfectly because she has used approximate symmetry. Can you find any matching shapes that were not included in the diagram?

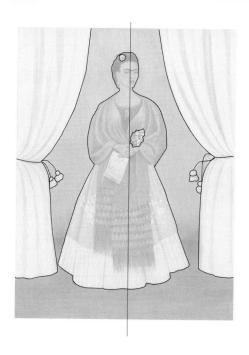

◄ **FIGURE 9.19**

Frida Kahlo. *Self Portrait Dedicated to Leon Trotsky.* 1937. Oil on masonite. 76.2 × 61 cm (30 × 24"). National Museum of Women in the Arts, Washington, D.C. Gift of the Honorable Clare Boothe Luce.

MORE ABOUT... Frida Kahlo

The life and work of Mexican artist Frida Kahlo (1907–1954) was filled with pain. Born in Mexico City, Kahlo had hoped to pursue a career in medicine. A serious traffic accident during her teenage years fractured her spine and crushed her pelvis. Kahlo survived, but endured thirty-five operations and spent much of her life in pain. While convalescing, Kahlo taught herself to paint. She showed her work to the famous Mexican muralist Diego Rivera, whom she eventually married. It was a difficult union and became one of the three main themes that Kahlo painted. Physical pain and frustration over her inability to bear a child were the other two subjects that obsessed Kahlo.

The Expressive Qualities of Balance

(pages 239–241)
(National Standards: 2b, 3c)

FOCUS

Objectives

After completing this lesson, students will be able to:

- Describe the expressive qualities of balance.
- Identify types of balance.

Supplies

- Large sheet of white paper; found objects; pencil and paper; architectural magazines

Resources

- 📁 Application Activity 18, *Sharpening Your Skills*
- 📁 Artist's Profile 36, *Georgia O'Keeffe*
- 📁 Artist's Profile 40, *Frida Kahlo*
- 📁 Cooperative Learning Activity 18, *Scrambled Rhythm*
- 📁 Studio Lesson 16, *Formal and Informal Group Portraits*
- 📁 Studio Lesson 17, *Fabric Medallion in Radial Balance*
- 📁 Studio Lesson 18, *Round Plaster Relief in Radial Balance*

TEACH

Motivator

Show students an arrangement of black squares on the overhead projector. Ask them to move or add shapes and lines and try to arrange the items to create balance. Tell students they will learn about various types of balance in this lesson.

239

Art Criticism

Have students choose an artwork from this chapter and write a brief description of the elements they find in the composition. Then have them analyze, interpret, and judge the artwork. Finally, ask them to describe how the principle of balance influenced their evaluations and judgments. You might also have them study artworks from other chapters and describe how balance is used.

Developing Perceptual Skills

In this section it is important that you discuss the reproductions and their expressive effects with students. Figure 9.19 on page 239 is an excellent example of the dignity and regal quality of formal balance. Figures 9.20 and 9.21 on page 240 are examples of the Minimalist's use of formal balance for simplicity. Figure 9.22 on page 241 is an excellent example of how informal balance contributes to the expressive qualities.

Studio Skills

Georgia O'Keeffe is famous for her paintings of parched bones and flowers. She forced viewers to take a new and different look at everyday objects. Have students experiment with O'Keeffe's style by choosing an object that is ordinary. Examine the lines, shapes, and details of the object. Have them use pencils to make sketches of the object so that it fills the paper. Instruct them to pay particular attention to the elements of line, space, texture, and shape. Also, remind them to consider how they will arrange the shape to create a pleasing balance.

◄ **FIGURE 9.20** Ferdinand Hodler used formal balance to create a stiff, stable portrait of his friend. The line from the sculptor's nose through the line in his shirt divides the portrait vertically into almost perfectly matching halves.

Ferdinand Hodler. *James Vibert, Sculptor.* 1907. Oil on canvas. 65.4 × 66.4 cm (25¾ × 26⅛"). The Art Institute of Chicago, Chicago, Illinois. Helen Birch Bartlett Memorial Collection, 1926.212

Formal balance can also be used in religious paintings to evoke feelings of dignity and endurance. In the past, paintings used as altarpieces in churches were designed to fit in with the formal balance of the church altar. The artist Ferdinand Hodler developed a personal aesthetic theory called Parallelism that relied on symmetry and repetition to create images that expressed stability **(Figure 9.20)**.

Many government buildings, hospitals, and office buildings are designed using formal balance. One purpose of this type of balance is to imply that the business conducted in these buildings is serious and solemn.

With approximate symmetry, artists express the same sense of calm stability, but they avoid the rigid formality of pure symmetry. Georgia O'Keeffe used approximate symmetry in her paintings of large close-ups of flowers. This impresses the viewer with feelings about the importance of the natural world. The use of approximate symmetry lends dignity to the flowing curves and alternating pastel colors of her painting, *White Rose with Larkspur, No. 2* **(Figure 9.21)**.

Radial design, on the other hand, is almost purely decorative. It appears in architecture, jewelry, pottery, weaving,

◄ **FIGURE 9.21** How has O'Keeffe arranged the shapes in this painting to create approximate, not absolute, symmetry? Would you like the painting more if it were perfectly symmetrical? Why or why not?

Georgia O'Keeffe. *White Rose With Larkspur, No. 2.* 1927. Oil on canvas. 101.6 × 76.2 cm (40 × 30"). Courtesy, Museum of Fine Arts, Boston, Massachusetts. Henry H. and Zoë Oliver Sherman Fund.

240 | **CHAPTER 9** Balance

MORE ABOUT... Georgia O'Keeffe

Georgia O'Keeffe (1887–1986), American abstract painter, is best known for her close-up views of desert flowers, sun-bleached animal skulls, and New Mexico landscapes. Most of O'Keeffe's flower paintings have an abstracted effect and are created using single blossoms. O'Keeffe studied at the school of the Art Institute of Chicago and at the Art Students League of New York City. In 1997 the Georgia O'Keeffe Museum opened in Santa Fe, New Mexico, and features the largest public collection of works by O'Keeffe.

FIGURE 9.22 Notice how Carr has used informal balance by placing most of the raven to the right of center in this landscape. She made many trips to the Northwest Coast of Alaska to record images of the Native American villages. This work was made in her studio based on sketches she had done on her trip to Queen Charlotte Island. The Haida village had been deserted and the large carving of the raven remained. She has balanced the raven, flowers, and trees near the foreground against the blue mountain in the distance.

Emily Carr. *Cumshewa.* c. 1912. Watercolor over graphite on wove paper. 52 × 75.5 cm (20½ × 29⅝"). National Gallery of Canada, Ottawa, Ontario, Canada.

Aesthetics

Direct students to look at Emily Carr's painting in Figure 9.22. Have them work in pairs or small groups to discuss how Carr uses the elements of art and the principles of art. Ask: What mood or feeling do you have when looking at Figure 9.22? How do the elements and principles achieve that mood?

Activity

Identifying Balance

Applying Your Skills. If students are not able to complete this activity at home, bring in architectural magazines and let them sketch from photographs.

ASSESS..........

Self-Assessment

Have students complete the lesson review questions. Answers are provided below.

Reteaching

Review with students the kinds of balance and how they can be used to affect the expressive qualities of a work of art.

CLOSE............

Have students select one of their artworks created before they read this chapter and write an evaluation of their use of balance.

---

and textile design. It is not often used by painters in its pure form. You can, however, find loose arrangements of radiating lines in many paintings. Artists use this technique to focus attention on an important part of an artwork.

Informal balance has a more natural look. When you look around your natural environment, you seldom find objects arranged with formal balance. To capture this natural quality in their works, artists use informal balance in arranging landscapes or groups of people **(Figure 9.22).**

Architects are using informal balance in many modern structures (see Figure 14.21, page 401). Single-family suburban homes have become the symbol of casual living. These houses are often designed using informal balance.

 Check Your Understanding

1. What feeling does formal balance convey?
2. What kind of buildings use formal balance? Why?
3. Why might an artist prefer approximate symmetry over pure symmetry?

Activity — Identifying Balance

Applying Your Skills. Look around your neighborhood for buildings that have been constructed using formal or informal balance. Make a rough sketch of one building and describe the feeling it gives you. If you live in a city and the buildings are too tall to sketch, look at the entrances to the buildings and sketch one of them. The entrance includes the door and all the decorative shapes around the doorway.

Computer Option. Use the tools of your choice to create a complex design illustrating one of the following: formal balance, informal balance, symmetry, approximate symmetry, radial balance. Save your work and then print it. If your printer is black and white, use colored pencils to add color. Evaluate your design. Does it meet the criteria for the kind of balance you chose to illustrate?

 Answers to Check Your Understanding

1. Formal balance conveys a calm feeling.
2. Churches, government buildings, and office buildings often use formal balance because it suggests that the business conducted in these buildings is serious and solemn.
3. Approximate symmetry expresses the same calm stability as perfect symmetry but it is less rigid.

Formal Portrait

Formal Portrait

(National Standards: 1a, 1b, 2b, 2c, 3b)

FOCUS...........

Objective

After completing this lesson, students will be able to:

■ Design and create a formal portrait of a person from history or current events.

TEACH..........

Motivator

Talk to teachers in the areas of social studies, literature, science, and math to find out what famous people are being studied during the school year. Ask students to share what they have learned about those people. Then ask about movie, television, or music stars. Students should enjoy sharing information about these figures.

Studio Skills

If your students feel they are unable to make sketches that resemble the person, you might permit them to make photocopies of the person's face from a book, magazine, or a newspaper. The photocopy can be enlarged or reduced on the machine until it fits the proportions of the figure in the portrait.

▲ FIGURE 9.23

Artist unknown. *Winxiang, Prince Yi.* Qing dynasty. 1644-1911. Ink and color on silk. 186.7 × 121.9 cm (73½ × 48"). Arthur M. Sackler Gallery, Smithsonian Institution, Washington, D.C. Gift of Richard G. Pritzlaff.

SUPPLIES

■ **Sketchbook and pencil**

■ **Large sheet of white paper**

■ **Yellow chalk**

■ **Black fine-line marker**

■ **Acrylic paints and brushes**

242 | **CHAPTER 9**   Balance

T his portrait of a Chinese prince **(Figure 9.23)** is very different from the Chinese landscape paintings that one often sees. The pose is dictated by tradition.

Notice the details in this formal portrait and think about how you can use them in your portrait.

What You Will Learn

You will design and create a formal portrait of a person from history or from current events. Arrange the person in a symmetrical pose in the center of the composition. The figure should fill the page. Use approximate symmetry to place objects that symbolize important events in that person's life on and around the figure. Choose a color scheme that expresses a specific mood you are trying to convey.

Creating

Choose a person you have studied in history or in current events that you admire. Research information about this person. If this person is from past history, you will find information in encyclopedias or in biographies. If your subject is involved in current events, look through newspapers and the *Readers' Guide to Periodicals* for magazines that will provide information about your subject. The Internet may also be a valuable source of information on your subject. Make visual and verbal notes about your subject in your sketchbook.

TECHNIQUE TIP ✔

Some students are intimidated by the idea of creating a portrait. The following is a list of a few helpful ideas worth reviewing:

■ The human face is three nose lengths.

■ The eyes are one eye-width apart. A third eye would fit perfectly between the two.

■ The eyes are aligned with the top of the ears.

■ The tip of the nose is aligned with the ear lobe.

■ The distance from the tip of the nose to the end of an outstretched finger extended at arm's length is 36 inches (91 cm).

■ The length of an individual's forearm from the inside fold of the wrist to the inside fold of the elbow is the length of the individual's foot.

Step 1 Make rough sketches for your composition. Remember that the figure must be organized in a symmetrical pose and that it must fill most of the paper. Make some accurate sketches of details needed for the portrait such as clothing of the historical period, furniture, symbols that will surround or cover the figure, and an appropriate background setting. Choose your best design and sketch it lightly with yellow chalk on the large white paper.

Step 2 Choose a color scheme that expresses the appropriate mood. Paint your composition. Use large brushes to fill in the largest shapes. Use small brushes to paint the symbols and clothing details. If necessary, use a fine-line black marker to define some of your details and labels.

Step 3 Write a paragraph about your subject. Mount or mat your portrait for display. Integrate the written paragraph into your display.

EVALUATING YOUR WORK

▶ **DESCRIBE** Name the subject of your portrait. What symbols did you select to represent the events in that person's life? How did you do visual and verbal research? Where did you look and what kind of information did you find? How did you prepare your work for display? Did you include a paragraph about the subject? How did you incorporate it into the display?

▶ **ANALYZE** What kinds of balance did you use in your composition? Explain. Describe the color scheme you selected for this work and explain why you chose it.

▶ **INTERPRET** What does your painting express about the subject of your portrait? Did the kinds of balance and the color scheme affect the mood? Give this work a poetic title.

▶ **JUDGE** Which aesthetic theories would you use to judge this work? If you were to do this over, what would you do to improve it?

▲ **FIGURE 9.23A** Student work.

STUDIO PROJECT   *Formal Portrait*   **243**

Make a frame by drawing several objects that symbolize the character in your portrait. Use the Pencil or Brush tools to draw these symbols. Make them small enough and consistent in size so you can use them to create a repeated pattern for the picture frame. Use the Selection tool and the Grids and Rulers option, if available, for alignment. Select, copy, and arrange the shapes around the outside edge of the page. Lines may be added with the Pencil, Brush, Straight Line or Rectangle tool. Save and retile the drawing. Color before or after printing.

ASSESS..........
Keeping a Portfolio
Remind students that the preliminary sketches and the final artwork for this Studio Project are likely candidates for their portfolios.

Self-Assessment
Have students apply the steps of art criticism to their own artwork using the "Evaluating Your Work" questions on this page.

Enrichment
By making several photocopies of a full-length photograph of the person, and by reducing and enlarging various parts of the photographed person's body on the machine, students could create a collage by reassembling the differently sized parts of the figure on their paper.

CLOSE............
Have each student read his or her paragraph while displaying the portrait.

MEETING INDIVIDUAL NEEDS

Building Self-Esteem Students with some types of disabilities may be unable to sketch or copy from a reproduction. One alternative for students with severe disabilities is to photocopy artworks that the student might then paint or color with markers, following the directions in the Studio Project above. Even more exciting is to transfer the design onto hooked rug mesh. The enlarged reproduction can be placed behind the mesh and the outlines of shapes drawn onto it. Then students can hook the design according to the chosen color scheme. The repetitive movements found in hooking a rug can be very satisfying.

Studio Project

Informal Group Picture

(National Standards: 1a, 1b, 2b, 2c, 3b)

FOCUS...........
Objective

After completing this lesson, students will be able to:

■ Design and create a painting in the Impressionist style.

TEACH..........
Motivator

If possible, have students practice some initial paintings outside, taking turns posing and painting. Encourage students to notice how the sunlight changes the surface of objects within just a one-hour period. This lesson would be most effective if taught during the early morning or late in the afternoon when the sun is at an angle, and changes in light and shadows are more noticeable.

Studio Skills

If possible, students should make the snapshot as well as the painting. If the students themselves do not have access to a camera, obtain a school camera and a roll of film for the project. Recording the order in which they shoot, allow each student to take one unposed snapshot of other students in the class. Another option is to bring in old snapshots made for the school yearbook and allow each student to select one.

Informal Group Portrait

SUPPLIES

■ **Sketchbook and pencil**
■ **Snapshots you have taken**
■ **Large sheet of white paper**
■ **Acrylic paints and an assortment of brushes**

▲ **FIGURE 9.24**

Mary Cassatt. *The Tea*. About 1880. Oil on canvas. 64.8 × 92.1 cm (25½ × 36¼"). Courtesy, Museum of Fine Arts, Boston, Massachusetts. M. Theresa B. Hopkins Fund.

Many late-nineteenth-century American artists painted in the Impressionist style, but Mary Cassatt was the only one who actually joined the radical French artists and showed her artwork in their independent exhibitions in Paris. She followed their practice of capturing a moment of everyday life as it would look in a snapshot—one single moment in time. Like snapshots, her compositions were asymmetrical and closely–cropped **(Figure 9.24).**

The Japanese woodblock print, which had arrived in Paris in the late 1800s, was one source of inspiration for the Impressionists' asymmetrical compositions. The Japanese printmakers were not afraid to cut off part of a figure. European artists, who had never done this in the past, began to imitate this technique.

The new art of photography also influenced the compositions of the Impressionists. The camera presented them with candid, or unposed, views of people. Snapshots showed familiar subjects from new and unusual points of view. Look at Cassatt's painting. Observe how she used balance, cropped figures, and color.

What You Will Learn

In this project, you will plan and create a painting in the Impressionist style. Use asymmetrical balance, a close-cropped composition, loose brushstrokes that resemble the dabs and dashes of the Impressionists, and the colors of the Impressionists. This painting must be based on an unposed photograph you have taken. It must include at least two people.

244 **CHAPTER 9** Balance

MORE ABOUT... **Photography**

Tell students that by 1855, photography was included in the Paris World's Fair exhibition. The Royal Academy of France accepted photographs into their salon in 1859. Artists led by Jean-Auguste-Dominique Ingres formed a League of Artists Against Photography, but despite their protests, the French government officially declared photography to be art in 1862. Early photographers took the camera where the easel could not go. Paul Nada went up in a hot air balloon in the 1840s and photographed Paris from above. The ordinary person was now able to see all parts of the world through photographs.

Creating

Collect photographs you have taken of your family or friends. Select one that you think will make an interesting painting. Remember that it must show asymmetrical balance, two or more people must be visible, and part of each figure must be cropped off, as in *The Tea*.

Step 1 Make a large, rough sketch in your sketchbook based on the photograph. Work on your first sketch to improve the composition as needed. Do not worry about whether the faces in the sketch and the painting look like the real people.

Step 2 Practice using the colors of the Impressionists in your sketchbook. Use only spectral colors and white. Blues and violets replace grays, browns, and blacks even in the shadows. Make grays by placing complements side by side. Use white side by side with your colors and add white to some of your colors to create light values. Apply the colors using loose brushstrokes and short dabs and dashes of paint.

Step 3 Using a brush and a very light value of yellow, sketch the final composition onto the large sheet of white paper. Use what you have learned during practice in your sketchbook to paint your composition. Create an expressive title for your work.

Step 4 Mount or mat your work for display.

EVALUATING YOUR WORK

▶ **DESCRIBE** What is the subject matter of your work? How many people have you used? What other objects are important in the composition?

▶ **ANALYZE** Did you use asymmetry? Which kind of informal balance did you use? Did you keep the effect of a photograph by cropping off parts of the figures? Did you use Impressionists' colors? How many ways did you use white?

▶ **INTERPRET** Describe the difference between the look of the photograph and the look of your finished painting. How did style affect the look of your work? Give your work a title that expresses the mood of your work.

▶ **JUDGE** Which aesthetic theories would you use to judge this work? If you were to do this over, what, if anything, would you do differently?

▲ **FIGURE 9.24A** Student work.

STUDIO PROJECT *Informal Group Portrait* | **245**

Studio Project

Linoleum Print Using Radial Balance

(National Standards: 1a, 1b, 2b, 2c, 3b)

FOCUS............

Objective

After completing this lesson, students will be able to:

■ Create a relief print that features symbols of family heritage.

TEACH..........

Motivator

Display and have students examine prints of Rembrandt, Dürer, and other printmakers. Students would benefit by learning about other printmaking processes such as intaglio, lithography, serigraphy, and the process they are about to experience, relief printing. Students should be given the opportunity to experiment with these techniques as well as more simplified techniques that will be described in the Enrichment activity in this lesson.

Aesthetics

Some students are disturbed when they see the lines in the negative areas. It is important that they understand that this is a special quality unique to linoleum and woodcuts.

Art History

Ask students to research the cultural traditions of the Native Americans of the Northwest coast, including information on the various arts and crafts of that area. Sources of information might include *National Geographic, Smithsonian,* encyclopedias, and books on Native Americans.

246

Linoleum Print Using Radial Balance

▲ **FIGURE 9.25**

Beau Dick. *Sacred Circles.* 1991. Serigraph 98/155. 50 × 50 cm (19³/₄ × 19³/₄"). Private collection.

SUPPLIES

■ **Sketchbook and pencil**
■ **Ruler, compass, and scissors**
■ **Tracing paper and carbon paper**
■ **Linoleum and dark marker**
■ **Linoleum cutting tools**
■ **Bench hook or C clamp**
■ **Water-base printing ink**
■ **Brayer and inking plate**
■ **Printmaking paper**

The making of *serigraphs* (limited-edition silk-screen prints) is a relatively new art form for the Northwest Coast artists. These artists started making serigraphs around 1970. *Sacred Circles* **(Figure 9.25)** was originally designed for a drum. Beau Dick's daughter, who is a teacher in Queen Charlotte, British Columbia, asked him to design something for her students for Rediscovery Week. The Rediscovery program in Canada was begun to teach young Native Americans to rediscover their heritage as a source of self-esteem.

This design shows a group of young people sitting in a circle, holding hands to show unity and friendship. The dark round shapes in the center are stones, inside of which a bonfire is to be built. This symbolizes the artist's belief that children are the ones who will carry on Native American traditions.

What You Will Learn

You will select symbols from your cultural heritage to create one or more motifs for a relief print. Produce an edition of five relief prints. Sign, date, and number your prints.

Creating

Brainstorm with your classmates about well-known symbols for different cultures. Then discuss your cultural heritage with members of your immediate family. Select symbols you prefer and make some rough sketches for arranging them into a radial design.

MEETING INDIVIDUAL NEEDS

Learning Disabilities For students with mental disabilities, the abstract quality of this lesson may pose difficulties. Having several suitable cultural symbols displayed on a poster to use as models can help them acquire concrete ideas. These might include symbols such as the peace sign, a heart, a cross, a Star of David, the recycling symbol, a stop sign, the Olympic symbol, and an American flag, as well as symbols of students' personal interests, perhaps in sports, art, or music.

Step 1 Trace the shape of your piece of linoleum onto a page in your sketchbook. Using the ruler, connect the opposite corners of the rectangle to find the center of the shape. Place the point of the compass on that center and draw the largest circle possible within the shape. Select your best design and draw it in the circle.

Step 2 Trace your finished design onto the tracing paper. Use a piece of carbon paper to transfer the design from the tracing paper to the piece of linoleum.

Step 3 Use a dark marker to color the lines and shapes on the areas of linoleum that will not be cut away.

Step 4 Use a bench hook to hold your linoleum safely in place. You have left the linoleum in the shape of a rectangle so that it can be held in place by the bench hook. Do not cut it into a circle until all your linoleum cuts are finished. Use the narrow V-gouge to outline the shapes. Always move the cutting tool in an outward motion away from your body. Use wider U-gouges to cut away the negative areas. The pattern of your cuts will show in the final print. Plan the direction of the cuts as carefully as you plan the positive shapes in your design. Finally, use the V-gouges to cut the fine lines on the positive shapes.

Step 5 Select your paper to make an edition of five prints. Locate your drying place. Squeeze out an inch of ink onto the inking plate. Roll the brayer in both directions until it is loaded with ink. Ink the linoleum. Make five prints. When they are dry, sign each one in pencil at the bottom of the print. Write the title on the left, the number in the center, and your name and date on the right. The number should include the number of the print and the total number of prints in the edition.

EVALUATING YOUR WORK

▶ **DESCRIBE** List and describe the symbols you used to create the motifs for your radial design.

▶ **ANALYZE** Did you use radial balance to organize the motifs? Did you use size to indicate the dominant motif? Did you use radial lines to help organize the motifs?

▶ **INTERPRET** What is the expressive quality of your personal print? Does it represent your cultural heritage?

▶ **JUDGE** Which aesthetic theories would you use to judge this work? If you were going to do this again, what, if anything, would you change?

▲ **FIGURE 9.25A** Student work.

STUDIO PROJECT *Linoleum Print Using Radial Balance* | **247**

When researching their family heritage, students may wish to tape record family stories told by relatives. They may also be interested in writing the family history in biographical form. They could use a print as the cover for their report.

ASSESS..........
Keeping a Portfolio
Remind students that the preliminary sketches and the final artwork for this Studio Project are likely candidates for their portfolios.

Self-Assessment
Have students apply the steps of art criticism to their own artwork using the "Evaluating Your Work" questions on this page. In addition, ask the following: How did you choose a motif for the print? How was this information translated into a visual image? Do the prints adequately reflect your feelings about your heritage?

Enrichment
Involve the students in various printmaking activities. The range of involvement could extend from simple vegetable prints to the more complicated processes of intaglio and lithography. To challenge the relief printers, allow them to use the subtractive method of making multicolored prints. It is recommended that the teacher and students refer to a printmaking manual for instructions for these more complicated processes.

CLOSE.............
Ask students to write personal reflections about their designs and their cultural heritage.

TECHNIQUE TIP ✓

To help students enjoy this lesson, consider the following:
- Linoleum can be ordered in rolls or various sized pieces and mounted on wood blocks.
- Linoleum cutting tools can be purchased through art supply catalogs.
- The use of a bench hook is a safe method for holding the linoleum in place.
- Linoleum becomes softer if it is heated. A heating pad or the classroom heater are adequate sources of heat.
- Remind students that their prints will be mirror images of their carvings. Therefore, all letters and images will be reversed.

Invent an Inside View of a Machine

FOCUS...........
Objectives:

After completing this lesson, students will be able to

■ Sketch several ideas for an inside view of a machine emphasizing formal balance.

■ Construct their selected sketch for an inside view of a machine emphasizing formal balance.

■ Feature overlapping shapes, lines, and a limited color scheme in their inside view of a machine image using a computer paint application.

TEACH..........
Motivator

Share actual examples of small machines with students. Have them look closely at the working parts. Watches, telephones, cameras, and computers are common and easy to access. Other machines will provide a range of shapes and design ideas. Have students generate a list of shapes that they see in the machines and what they think they would find inside these machines. Post the noted shapes on the board for all to see. Discuss formal balance. Show students examples of symmetry and approximate symmetry on the machines they have been viewing. Provide definitions and examples of overlapping, hard-edge, and limited color schemes.

▲ FIGURE 9.26

Gerald Murphy. *Watch.* 1925. Oil on canvas. 199.4 × 199.4 cm (78½ × 78½"). Dallas Museum of Art, Dallas, Texas. Foundation for the Arts Collection. Gift of the artist.

SUPPLIES

■ **Sketchbook**

■ **Computer**

■ **Paint or Draw application**

■ **Printer**

Optional

■ **Scanner or digital camera**

The influences of abstract artists mingled with Gerald Murphy's early training as an architect to create a very precise, hard-edged style. Murphy chose everyday, common objects such as a watch, razor, or pen as the subjects for his compositions.

Notice in **Figure 9.26** how Murphy painted many circular shapes in a variety of sizes. These are carefully arranged to create a composition that not only is formally balanced, but also has a center of interest. All of the watch parts look as if they belong together even though a few of the shapes may have been invented and others appear to be exterior mechanisms. Observe the unusual shapes Murphy has used in the four corners of the painting to quickly lead your eye back to the center.

What You Will Learn

Design an inside view of a machine using one type of formal balance. Use rhythm by repeating similar shapes and related shapes in a variety of sizes. You may repeat the shape using a variety of sizes and use parts of the original shape as Murphy has done. To give your design a strong sense of unity, use overlapping shapes and connect shapes with lines.

Creating

Brainstorm and list different moving, mechanical parts such as cogs, springs, dials, and gears. Consider other modern advances found in today's technology. Decide what kind of formal balance you will use.

248   CHAPTER 9   Balance

Creating Art with Formal Balance Collect old pieces of machines, wire, and cardboard. Construct machines that can be hung on the wall for display. These are machines that are viewed from the outside. What do they do? Where would they be found? Who would use them? Think about repeated shapes, overlapping lines, and shapes that connect the parts. Paint the machines with no more than three colors.

Step 1 Choose from the shape tools, such as the Round or Rectangular tool, to begin the inside view of a machine. Be inventive. Make three or four sketches on the computer to help you decide.

Step 2 Select your best idea. Begin with your choice of shape tools to create an interior view. Use the Selection tools and Copy, Paste, and Scale Selection menus to repeat similar, simple shapes in a variety of sizes. Arrange the shapes to match the kind of balance you have chosen.

Step 3 Continue to add interest by representing many different kinds of mechanical parts. Show not only different sizes of similar shapes, but also change line thickness and add details to many of the surfaces. Add a few contrasting shapes.

Step 4 Unify your design. Overlap shapes. If available, use the Arc and Line tools to connect and draw portions of handles, cogs, gears, or dials. Cover every available space with a mechanical part. Title and save your drawing as you work.

Step 5 When your drawing is complete, title, save, and display your work.

EVALUATING YOUR WORK

▶ **DESCRIBE** What kind of machine did you choose for your design? List the different machine parts you drew and the tools you used to create them. How many times have you repeated the same shape? Do the shapes vary?

▶ **ANALYZE** What kind of balance did you use? Did you use repetition to create rhythm? Explain. Have you used overlapping? Do the shapes of the parts of your design look like they belong together? How did you achieve this effect?

▶ **INTERPRET** What mood, feeling, or idea does your machine convey? Identify the elements or principles of art you applied to support this emotion. Does the artwork suggest any other ideas to the viewer? Do you think if you created this design in another medium you could achieve the same effect?

▶ **JUDGE** Were you successful in arranging the parts of your design to create formal balance? Do you think this design would look the same created in another medium? Which aesthetic theory would you use to decide on the success of this work?

▲ **FIGURE 9.26A** Student work.

ASSESS..........
Keeping a Portfolio
Remind students that the preliminary sketches and the final artwork for this Studio Project are likely candidates for their portfolios.

Self-Assessment
Have students apply the steps of art criticism to their own artwork using the "Evaluating Your Work" questions on this page. Have each student read his or her paragraph while displaying their machine.

Reteach
Try this lesson a second time but take the viewpoint of being outside the machine instead of inside the machine. Ask students to think about what would make them want to investigate a machine more closely. What would catch their eye? A sleek design? Buttons and lights? Colorful wires?

Enrichment
Have students take their completed image and import different textures for the shapes. Give their new version a different title and save it. Print out copies of both versions and write a brief critique of what you think the strengths and weaknesses are of both versions. Have students put copies of the images and their summary critique in their portfolios.

CLOSE............
Have students form small groups and critique their completed inside views of machines. Criteria for discussion should include identification of type of symmetry used, instances of overlapping, use of hard-edge lines, lines connecting shapes, and the limited color scheme. Further discussion should focus upon the entire composition of the image and the computer tools the students used to achieve their specific results.

249

MORE ABOUT... Symmetry

The artwork of Gerald Murphy features hard-edge lines and symmetry. Computer paint programs make it easier for the artist to draw and paint hard-edge lines and to place objects in the painting for precise symmetry. Have students sketch a machine with a variety of overlapping shapes that has formal balance. Then paint the hard edges using a small flat brush. This is a studio skill that requires patience and practice. Students may want to consider a series of small machines to sketch and paint.

➤ Describe

What do you see?

- Once students understand that this painting is over 4-feet tall, ask them to estimate the size of the woman's and child's heads and the height of the woman if she stood up. (The woman's head is over one foot in height, and the child's head is just slightly smaller.)

- We see an adult woman and a young girl sitting closely together on a sofa. The woman is holding her right arm around the child and her other arm is stretched out and resting on the arm of the sofa. There is a large blue and violet ring on the left hand. The girl's right hand is resting on her knee and her left arm echoes the position of the woman. The woman is wearing khaki slacks, a bright yellow shirt under a violet long-sleeved blouse, and plain khaki shoes. She is sitting so that her torso leans slightly toward the child. Her legs are crossed with her right leg over the thigh of her left leg. The young girl is wearing a long-sleeved, light blue jacket and matching slacks.

- They are both sitting on a shiny, light-green sofa that has a wood frame. The shadows on the fabric under the woman are bright green, but the shadow under the girl's right arm is a very dull green.

ART CRITICISM IN ACTION

▲ **FIGURE 9.27**

Alice Neel. *Linda Nochlin and Daisy*. 1973. Oil on canvas. 141.9 × 111.8 cm (55⅞ × 44″). The Hayden Collection. Courtesy, Museum of Fine Arts, Boston, Massachusetts.

250 | **CHAPTER 9** Balance

MORE ABOUT... Alice Neel

Alice Neel stubbornly went against the trend of abstract art popular in the 1940s and 1950s by pursuing her career as a figurative painter. Because her portraits were not commissions requested by the sitters, Neel was free to characterize them as she wished, rather than as they wished to be seen. Although she began to receive wider recognition in the 1960s, she never sold many of her paintings. Most of her sitters could not afford to buy them, and collectors generally did not want to purchase pictures of unknown people done in her strong, idiosyncratic style. When Neel died, most of her work was still in her own collection.

1 ▶ DESCRIBE What do you see?

Do not be fooled by the limited number of objects in this work. You must use your perceptive skills with care to uncover the message being sent in this painting.

■ Find out the size of this oil painting from the credit line and measure it out somewhere so that you can understand how big it is.

■ Describe the two people including their features, hair, hands, skin, clothing, positions, and body size.

■ List the other objects you see in this work.

2 ▶ ANALYZE How is this work organized?

The elements and principles are very important in this work. The way the artist has used them will give you clues for understanding the work.

■ Where can you find rhythmic repetitions? Use your perceptive skills carefully to notice all the repetitions.

■ What kind of balance has the artist used to arrange this work? How are things positioned in relation to the vertical axis? Explain.

3 ▶ INTERPRET What is the artist trying to communicate?

Now you will combine the clues you have collected along with your own personal reactions to them to discover the meaning of this work.

■ How has the artist's use of balance affected the feeling of this work?

■ What is relationship between these two people? Explain.

■ Give this work a new title that sums up your interpretation of it.

4 ▶ JUDGE What do you think of the work?

Decide if this is a successful work of art. You may make a personal opinion, but it is also important to make an objective judgment based on aesthetic theories.

■ Is this work interesting? Did it make you think?

■ Did the artist use the elements and the principles of rhythm and balance to send a clear message to you, the viewer?

■ Do you think this is a successful work of art? Why or why not? Use one or more of the aesthetic theories described in Chapter 2 to defend your judgment.

MEET THE ARTIST
ALICE NEEL

American, 1900–1984

Alice Neel attended the Philadelphia School of Design for Women (now called Moore College of Art), where she was exposed to the ideas of the Expressionists. After graduating she moved to New York City, where she found the inspiration for her work: in people's faces. Her works convey a lively sense of vibrancy and character. She found subjects everywhere, especially in the neighborhoods of Greenwich Village and Spanish Harlem.

Neel "collected" subjects by painting portraits of people and even stopped strangers in the street to ask them to pose for her. Her paintings reflect the personalities of her subjects. Some seem carefully and precisely done, while others are more casual and less formal.

▶ Analyze
How is this work organized?

■ The body positions create a feeling of repetition: the position of the arms, the verticality of the heads and the torsos, the feet all pointing to the left of the painting. The legs of the sofa repeat the direction of the outstretched arms. The fabric has a repetitive design.

■ This work has been organized using informal balance. The vertical axis of the work crosses through the woman's left eye and the child's right eye. The large shape of the woman close to the center of the work is balanced by the busy little shape of the girl.

▶ Interpret
What is the artist trying to communicate?

■ Some may say it is a visual trick. It looks like it should have formal balance, but it does not.

■ Answers will vary. Most will say they are mother and daughter. Even though the woman has a fierce, piercing gaze, her body language suggests protection of the eager, innocent child. The complementary colors might suggest that both figures are strong, outspoken, and bold.

■ Answers will vary.

▶ Judge
What do you think of the work?

■ Answers will vary.

■ Answers will vary.

■ Answers will vary. Most will use the theory of Emotionalism. Some might include Imitationalism since the work is representational. Others will use Formalism because the arrangement of the figures is very important.

Time & Place Late Twentieth Century

Alice Neel painted *Linda Nochlin and Daisy* in 1973. Some other events that happened the same year:

Social Studies: The official cease-fire agreement was signed in Paris that ended the involvement of United States ground troops in the war in Viet Nam.
Art: Pablo Picasso died in southern France at the age of 92.
Science: Skylab III astronauts spent a record 59.5 days in space.

CONNECTIONS
LANGUAGE
ARTS

What Is Symbolism?

(National Standards: 6a, 6b)

Objectives

After completing this lesson, students will be able to:

- Define and offer examples of symbolism.
- Discuss relationships between design principles and symbolism or meaning.

Teaching the Connection

1. Have students read the feature on this page.
2. Ask students to discuss familiar poems or works of literature containing symbols. Introduce emotions or concepts and ask students to envision ways to symbolize them. For example, ask students to imagine symbols for "sadness" or "generosity," "manhood" or "womanhood," and so forth. Then, discuss whether the symbols they imagine are conventional or unique.
3. Tell students that the interpretation of symbols in literature and art is not an exact science. In other words, there is not necessarily a right or wrong way to interpret the meaning of a particular image. However, there are stronger and weaker interpretations. A strong interpretation is persuasive; it considers all of the factors and conditions under which an image is presented. Strong interpretations look for connections between the different images or elements in a work and are based on informed judgment rather than personal opinion.

252

What Is Symbolism?

◀ **FIGURE 9.28**

Rie Muñoz. *Both the Sun and Moon Belong to Women.* 1990. Watercolor. 48.2 × 55.9 cm (19 × 22"). Rie Muñoz Ltd., Juneau, Alaska.

A symbol is something that stands for or represents something else. In this sense, all words are symbols. In literature a symbol is an object, image, event, or even a person which suggests an important meaning beyond itself. For example, in Virginia Woolf's novel *Mrs. Dalloway,* the husband expresses his love for his wife by giving her a bouquet of roses, a conventional symbol for love. Many literary symbols are not so obvious, however.

Artists use symbols in much the same way writers do. In **Figure 9.28,** there are two Inuit women in similar positions. Notice the stylized use of shape and high-intensity color. Smooth curves contrasted with sharp points establish a motif in the work. The painting uses balance for the purpose of visual pleasure; however, it may contribute to the painting's symbolic meaning as well.

The gestures of the women indicate that they are celebrating, but the artist has chosen to express this idea symbolically rather than literally or realistically. The sun, moon, and stars may symbolize the universal nature of artistic expression. However, the painting's title, along with the two women in the painting, suggest something more specific. What symbolic connection do you think the artist is attempting to make between women, the sun, and the moon?

Making the Connection

1. How has the artist symbolized day and night in the painting?
2. What type of balance has the artist achieved in this painting?
3. Interpret the painting as though it were a short story or poem. Describe what you think the women represent. Write your response in the form of a short essay.

Answers to Making the Connection

1. Day and night are symbolized as two halves of a whole. The moon and stars in the dark portion of the painting represent night, while the sun in the brighter portion represents day. The women's bodies conform to the curve of both the sun and moon. They provide a sense of continuity or unification.

2. Informal balance is used in this work. The painting is divided in half diagonally. Each part contains similar, rather than identical, elements.

3. Responses will vary. Encourage students to explain their interpretation in terms of the painting's design elements.

Building Vocabulary

On a separate sheet of paper, write the term that best matches each definition given below.

1. The principle of art concerned with equalizing visual forces, or elements, in a work of art.
2. A dividing line that works like the point of balance in the balance scale.
3. The type of balance that results when equal, or very similar, elements are placed on opposite sides of a central axis.
4. A special type of formal balance in which two halves of a balanced composition are identical, mirror images of each other.
5. When the forces or elements of a design come out (*radiate*) from a central point.
6. A balance of unlike objects.

Reviewing Art Facts

Answer the following questions using complete sentences.

1. Why is balance important to a work of art?
2. What are the visual forces, or weights, in art?
3. What is the difference between symmetry and approximate symmetry?
4. What factors in a work of art influence the visual weight of the art elements?
5. Which carry more weight, warm or cool colors?
6. How can value affect visual weight?
7. What does a formally balanced building express?

Thinking Critically About Art

1. **Research.** The Leaning Tower of Pisa (Figure 9.2, page 228) is in serious trouble. It is about to collapse. Search the *Readers' Guide to Periodicals* for recent articles about the tower. Find out what, if anything, is being done to keep it from falling.

2. **Analyze.** Edward Hopper, who painted *First Row Orchestra* (Figure 9.13, page 235), was not considered a member of the Regionalist school of painting. Find a book about him at the library, and look at his paintings. In what way does his subject matter and themes differ from those of the Regionalists? Explain your findings to the class using visual examples to illustrate your conclusions.

Turn to the Performing Arts Handbook on page 421 to learn how Eth-Noh-Tec uses a balance of music, movement, and words to present their unique style of theatre and storytelling.

inter NET CONNECTION Learn more about why balance is so important in a work of art by exploring the Glencoe Fine Arts Site at **www.glencoe.com/sec/art** . You can also discover your own techniques for creating balance in your art by finding the chapter you are studying in the Table of Contents and clicking on one of the "hot links."

Chapter 9 Review | **253**

Answers to Building Vocabulary
1. balance
2. central axis
3. formal balance
4. symmetry
5. radial balance
6. informal balance

Answers to Reviewing Art Facts
1. Artists use this feeling to communicate with us. An unbalanced work gives us an uneasy feeling.
2. Balance.
3. In bilateral symmetry the two halves of a composition are identical. In approximate symmetry, the two halves are almost identical (in other words, almost symmetrical).
4. Size and contour, color, value, texture, and position.
5. Warm colors.
6. The stronger the contrast in value between an object and the background, the more visual weight the object has. Also, dark values are heavier than light values.
7. Dignity, stability, calm.

Reteaching
■ Have students complete Concept Map 9 in the Reteaching booklet. 📁
■ Ask each student to randomly pick out five artworks from other chapters and identify the types of balance used.

CLOSE............
Instruct students to loosely sketch one design for each type of balance discussed in the chapter.

ASSESSMENT ✓

Evaluate
■ Have students complete the *Chapter 9 Test* in the TCR. 📁
■ Alternative Assessment teaching strategies are provided in the *Testing Program and Alternative Assessment* booklet. 📁

Extension
Have students work in groups to write and produce a five-minute documentary on the life and work of either Frida Kahlo or Georgia O'Keeffe. The profile should include information about the artist's career and examples of her work. Students should create visuals, such as montages of important paintings and drawings.

Proportion

(pages 254–285)

Resources

📁 Chapter 10 Study Guide

📁 Chapter 10 Test

📁 Computers in the Art Classroom

📁 Cultural Diversity in Art

📁 Portfolio and Assessment Techniques

📁 Reproducible Lesson Plan 10

🖋 CC-10, James C. Christensen. *Vanity*

🖋 Transparency 10, Miriam Schapiro. *Anna and David*

📕 Fine Art Print 21, Beau Dick (Kwakiatl). *Bookwus Mask*

📕 Fine Art Print 22, Thomas Eakins. *Baby at Play*

While studying this chapter, use Performing Arts Handbook page 422 to help students discover how proportion is used in Eugene Friesen's performances that combine stories, songs, masks and music of the cello.

▲ **FIGURE 10.1** This statue represents Guanyin, a Chinese Bodhisattva. In Buddhism, a Bodhisattva is an advanced spiritual being who has chosen to delay nirvana, the state of complete enlightenment, in order to bring salvation to the people. Guanyin, the most popular of the Bodhisattvas, appears to people in 108 different human forms.

Chinese. *The Water and Moon Guanyin Bodhisattva.* Eleventh/twelfth century. Northern Song (960–1127) or Liao Dynasty (907–1125). Wood with paint. 241.3 × 165.1 cm (95 × 65″). The Nelson-Atkins Museum of Art, Kansas City, Missouri. (Purchase: Nelson Trust)

FEATURED ARTISTS

George Bellows
Isabel Bishop
Pierre Bonnard
Marc Chagall
John Singleton Copley
Le Corbusier

Salvador Dali
Giotto
Paul Gauguin
Henry Hunt
Gaston Lachaise
Judith Leyster
Annie Liebovitz
Marisol
Michelangelo

Claes Oldenburg
Napachie Pootoogook
Pablo Picasso
Faith Ringgold
Annette Romero
David Alfaro Siqueiros
Leo Twiggs
George Walkus

Proportion

"You put too much salt in the soup!"
"This desk is too small for me!"

These statements present problems of proportion. **Proportion** is *the principle of art concerned with the size relationship of one part to another.* When you shop for clothes, for example, you look for sizes designed to fit the proportions of your body. The size of a chair for a kindergarten classroom must fit the proportions of small children, while the size of a chair for your classroom must fit your proportions.

The figure of the Bodhisattva, Guanyin **(Figure 10.1),** was created using human proportions. Notice how realistic and lifelike the sculpture appears. Although the Bodhisattva exudes dignity and calm, his proportions make him appear natural and human. In Buddhism, the worshiper is encouraged to feel that this compassionate saint is accessible to ordinary people. Anyone can pray to him for help. If the proportions had been different—for instance, if the statue were monumental, several times the size of a human—the saint would not appear so approachable. The proportions of the figure make the sculpture universally appealing to viewers.

OBJECTIVES

After completing this chapter, you will be able to:

- Explain and recognize the Golden Mean.
- Understand how we perceive proportion and scale.
- Measure and draw human faces and bodies with correct proportions.
- Understand how artists use proportion and distortion to create meaning.

WORDS TO KNOW

proportion
Golden Mean
scale
hierarchical proportion
foreshortening
exaggeration
distortion

Chapter Overview

In Chapter 10, students learn about the relationship between mathematics and visual art, evident from the Golden Mean. They understand how scale can affect the expressive qualities of a work of art.

Examining the Artwork

The sculpture in Figure 10.1 represents a Buddhist Bodhisattva, a being of enlightenment, a being who has reached a state of nirvana in which the evils of greed, hatred, and ignorance have been conquered.

The Bodhisattvas are considered personifications of the virtues of the Buddha. One represents his wisdom, another his happiness. Guanyin represents the compassion of Buddha. The central core of the figure is carved from a single piece of wood. He sits in a royal pose with his right arm resting on an upraised right knee. His costume is elaborate and in the style worn by princes of India. His body is adorned with knotted veils and drapery that seem to be flowing in a breeze. Tell students that in this chapter they will learn about the principle of proportion.

Developing Your
PORTFOLIO

Caricatures (**car**-ik-ah-choors) are drawings that use exaggeration and distortion of distinctive physical features for the purpose of comic satire and ridicule. Today caricatures are seen frequently in newspaper and magazine editorial cartoons. Search the editorial pages of newspapers for caricatures of politicians or celebrities. Then look for realistic photographs of the same person. Mount each caricature and photograph of the person side by side. Then, for each set of images, write a brief paragraph about the difference between the photograph and the caricature, explaining what the artist has exaggerated and/or distorted and what expressive effect the artist created.

National Standards

This chapter addresses the following National Standards for the Visual Arts:

1. (a, b)	**4.** (c)
2. (b, c)	**5.** (a, c)
3. (b)	**6.** (a, b)

255

DEVELOPING
A PORTFOLIO

Assessment To help students form opinions and develop awareness of critical standards, remind them that assessment is a process of thoughtful, informed engagement of a viewer with a piece of art. Questions designed to generate critical thinking about the relative values of artwork will help them make better judgments about the work they intend to include in a portfolio. Examples are: How does the artwork demonstrate successful use of the elements of art? How are principles of art used to organize the elements? How are media used to enhance the subject of the piece? Does the artwork suggest an innovative use of form, media, or technique?

The Golden Mean

FOCUS...........
Objective

After completing this lesson, students will be able to:

■ Explain and recognize the Golden Mean.

Supplies

■ Desks, tables, and chairs, from kindergarten and third grade

■ Measuring tapes or yard sticks

■ Mirror

■ Photograph of pyramids including people

Resources

📁 Application Activity 19, *A Study in Proportion*
📁 Cooperative Learning Activity 19, *Environmental Sculpture*
📁 Enrichment Activity 19, *The Golden Rectangle*

TEACH..........
Motivator

Borrow a desk, table, and chair from a kindergarten classroom and the same objects from a third-grade room. Have students measure the desks, tables, and chairs and compare the differences in size and proportion between the furniture from the lower grades, then between the third-grade items and students' own classroom furniture. Ask them to speculate how designers know what measurements are appropriate for each grade level.

Through the ages, people have sought an ideal of harmony and beauty. One way they have tried to capture this ideal is through correct proportion. Artists and architects have looked for a ratio (a mathematical comparison of sizes) that would produce an ideal form for figures and structures.

The ancient Greek philosopher Pythagoras found that he could apply mathematical equations to both geometric shapes and musical tones. If this was so, he thought, there must also be a way to explain other things—even the universe—in mathematical terms.

Euclid, a Greek mathematician, discovered what he considered a perfect ratio, or relationship of one part to another. He called this ratio the Golden Section, or **Golden Mean,** *a line divided into two parts so that the smaller line has the same proportion, or ratio, to the larger line as the larger line has to the whole line* **(Figure 10.2).** With this ratio, the ancient Greeks felt they had found the ideal proportion. It was used to control the relationship of parts in their sculpture, architecture, and pottery. In math, this ratio is written 1 to 1.6 or 1:1.6.

The Golden Rectangle **(Figure 10.3)** had sides that matched this ratio. The longer sides were a little more than one and a half times as long as the shorter sides. This ratio was thought to be the most pleasing to the eye. If you look closely at Leyster's *The Concert* **(Figure 10.4),** you can see that the wall and the two figures on the right side of the work is a square, while the wall and the single figure on the left is the smaller section of the Golden Rectangle.

One of the many fascinating facts about the Golden Mean is its relationship to the human figure. If you divide the average adult male body horizontally at the navel, the two body measurements that result (head to navel = a and navel to toes = b) have a ratio of 1 to 1.6 **(Figure 10.5).**

The secret of the Golden Mean was forgotten with the fall of Ancient Greece. The ratio was rediscovered, however, during the Renaissance, and a book was written about it. This time the ratio was called the Divine Proportion, and it was thought to have magical qualities.

▲ **FIGURE 10.2** The ratio of the Golden Mean is 1 to 1.6.

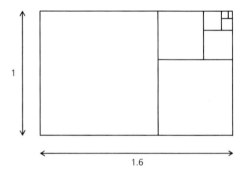

▲ **FIGURE 10.3** The Golden Rectangle is interesting to study. If you divide it into two shapes, one of which is a square, the remaining shape will always be a smaller Golden Rectangle. This new Golden Rectangle can be divided again and again.

MORE ABOUT... Greek Aesthetics

The Greek artist was also a mathematician and philosopher. From the earliest times, in Greek sculpture, pottery, and architecture, proportion was central to the design; the philosophical concept of the human being as the highest form of creation led artists to devise the classical—or perfectly proportioned—human figure.

Logic and order were central to Greek thinking and art. The Greeks devised the Golden Rectangle—the perfect mathematical proportion—and applied it to architecture as well as sculpture. Rather than copying from a model to carve human figure sculptures, they proportioned features mathematically.

▲ **FIGURE 10.4** Judith Leyster has used the proportions of the Golden Mean to organize this painting. Look at the line dividing the back wall. The section on the right forms a perfect square. The section on the left is a Golden Rectangle. It can be divided just like the smaller section of the diagram in Figure 10.3.

Judith Leyster. *The Concert.* ca 1633. Oil on canvas. 109.2 × 167.6 cm (43 × 66″). The National Museum of Women in the Arts, Washington, D.C. On loan from Wallace and Wilhelmina Holladay.

Since that time, some artists have chosen to use the Golden Mean as the basis for their compositions. Others, unaware of the mathematical ratio, used the Golden Mean just because that arrangement of parts looked good. Most artists now reject the idea that only this one rule can define the "correct" proportions for all works of art. The ratio, however, is found in visual art so often that it is hard to ignore its importance (**Figure 10.6,** on page 258).

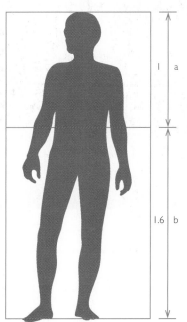

◄ **FIGURE 10.5** The relationship of the Golden Mean to the human body. Section a extends from head to navel and section b extends from navel to toes.

LESSON 1 *The Golden Mean* **257**

Promoting Discussion

Although most students are too self-conscious to discuss their own body proportions, probably everyone in class wishes that some of his or her proportions were different. Since this subject may be sensitive for a class discussion, encourage students to talk about the popularity of cosmetic (plastic) surgery. Have students discuss bodybuilding, weight training, and cosmetic (plastic) surgery as techniques people use to change their body proportions. How do attitudes toward "ideal" body proportions change among generations and cultures?

Aesthetics

Have students take a survey to learn if people really prefer the Golden Rectangle over other rectangles. They could make up a chart showing five rectangles, one of which would have the proportions of the Golden Rectangle. This chart could be drawn on a sheet of notebook paper and the rectangles numbered. Each student would show the chart of shapes to different people and ask each person which shape he or she prefers. Encourage students to compile and discuss their findings.

Critical Thinking

Encourage students to become aware of how often proportion is present in their environment. For example, give this assignment to students: Notice the rectangles in your home. List and describe five that use proportions close to those of the Golden Rectangle. Instruct students to sketch the rectangles in their sketchbooks and identify the function of the object or space. Ask students to discuss the examples they observed.

Curriculum Connection

Humanities Music in ancient Greece was a combination of poetry, dance, drama, and tonal art. Most Greek festivals honored gods, and music was thought to be a kind of charm connecting humans with the gods. As in all other arts, mathematics and proportion were central to Greek music. Pythagoras, a famous Greek mathematician, formulated the ratios that gave us the octave, a precursor to the scale that we use today. Our science of acoustics is based on the theories of Pythagoras and other mathematicians over the centuries. Mathematical discoveries such as periodic functions are basic to today's electronic music and voice-activated computers.

Looking Closely: Bellows

Point out to the students that the large rectangle of the painting fits the proportions of the golden rectangle. Tell students that the vertical line that runs through the standing boxer divides the work into a perfect square and a smaller rectangle. In the left corner of the painting they can find another square which is defined by the vertical line of the boxer and the horizontal line of the rope that is closest to the viewer. Then, point out that the rectangle below the square also has the proportions of the golden rectangle.

Developing Perceptual Skills

Another important topic involving scale is the misrepresentation of scale in advertisements, such as those for jewelry. If possible, bring in jewelry shown in advertisements and let students see how small the objects really are. Caution them to read carefully to see if objects are photographed life-size or are made to appear larger.

Students also need to be conscious of scale during grocery shopping. Labels should always be studied for weights and sizes. If students help with grocery shopping, ask them to look at sizes of boxes and the weights of the contents to see if they can find examples of deceptive packaging.

Cross-Curriculum: Math

Challenge students to look for other interesting proportional ratios in paintings and three-dimensional works and share their findings with the class.

LOOKING CLOSELY   Using the Golden Mean to Organize an Active Painting

Notice how Bellows has used the Golden Rectangle and the diagonal of the square in the rectangle to give this action painting stability. He has used the vertical line for his standing figure and the diagonal line to help him place the leaning figure. Can you find the square in the small rectangle? Can you find any other artworks that use the Golden Mean? Many of them are very subtle and hard to notice.

◀ **FIGURE 10.6**

George Bellows. *Both Members of This Club.* 1909. Oil on canvas. 1.150 × 1.605 cm (45¼ × 63⅛"). National Gallery of Art, Washington, D.C. © 1998 Board of Trustees. Chester Dale Collection.

MORE ABOUT...   *Both Members of This Club*

Critics call this painting the best boxing painting Bellows produced, because it captures the energy of the boxers and the frenzied delight of the spectators enjoying this battle between two men.

The title of this work highlights the irony that this fight is taking place in a private club. Public boxing was banned from 1900 to 1910 and could only be witnessed in private clubs for members only. Everyone in the painting is a member of this private club. The patrons were permanent members and the boxers were members for only this night. Ask the students to discuss the irony of a black man being admitted to Tom Starkey's athletic club just for the fight.

▲ **FIGURE 10.7** Le Corbusier has been called the poet of the apartment house. This building has many of the features of a resort, such as a kindergarten and nursery, a roof garden, children's swimming pool, gymnasium, and snack bar. Lead sheets were placed between the walls to soundproof the apartments.

Le Corbusier. *Unite d'Habitation.* Marseille, France. 1947–52.

ASSESS..........

Self-Assessment

Have students complete the lesson review questions. Answers appear below.

Reteaching

Work with small groups of students to review the principle of proportion. Display a collection of reproductions, or make several art books available. Let each group member select one reproduction; help the group identify the way proportion is used in the artwork.

Enrichment

Some students might wish to study the proportions of other everyday objects, such as stairs, doors, and hand tools. Have students think of a unique item that is encountered frequently but often overlooked.

CLOSE............

Have students write short statements about their own ideas about the importance of proportion.

Many people looked to the human body as a source for perfect proportions. Artists during the Golden Age of Greece believed that the human body was the true expression of order. Statues created during that time were not realistic portraits of real people. The artists of the period showed the ideal form rather than the real form (see Figure 13.3, page 353).

In the first century B.C., Vitruvius, a Roman writer, determined typical ratios for human proportion. These were later used by Leonardo da Vinci and other Renaissance artists. The twentieth-century architect Le Corbusier applied human dimensions to architecture and city planning **(Figure 10.7)**.

✓ Check Your Understanding

1. What is the Golden Mean?
2. Describe the Golden Rectangle.
3. What is the ratio of the Golden Mean?
4. How does the Golden Mean apply to the body?

✓ Answers to Check Your Understanding

1. The Golden Mean is a line divided into two parts so that the smaller line has the same proportion, or ratio, to the larger line as the larger line has to the whole line.
2. The Golden Rectangle had sides that matched the ratio of the Golden Mean. The longer sides were a little more than one and a half times as long as the shorter sides.
3. The ratio of the Golden Mean is written 1 to 1.6 or 1:1.6.
4. If you divide a typical adult's body horizontally at the navel, the two body measurements that result (head to navel = a and navel to toes = b) have a ratio of 1 to 1.6.

Scale

FOCUS............
Objectives
After completing this lesson, students will be able to:

■ Understand how we perceive proportion and scale.

■ Measure and draw human faces and bodies with correct proportions.

Supplies
■ Ad showing jewelry

■ Video digitizing equipment

■ Photos of TV and movie stars

■ Tape measures

■ Drawing paper

■ White glue

Resources
📁 Cooperative Learning Activity 20, *Don't Be Puzzled by Proportion*

📁 Enrichment Activity 20, *Drawing Floor Plans*

📁 Studio Lesson 19, *Life-Size Papier-Mâché Figure*

TEACH..........
Motivator
Find a photograph of the pyramids that has people in it so that the students can comprehend the immensity of the pyramids. Then ask students if they have heard of someone creating a work of art on the head of a pin, or at least in miniature. Drawing on the two examples that represent extremes of proportion, encourage a discussion of how artists approach such projects.

Scale is much like proportion, but there is a difference. Proportion refers to the relationship of one part to another. **Scale,** on the other hand, refers to *size as measured against a standard reference,* such as the human body. A 7-foot basketball player may not look tall next to other basketball players. The player will look tall, however, when you see him in scale—that is, compared with a crowd of people of average height.

In art there are two kinds of scale to consider. One is the scale of the work itself. The other is the scale of objects or elements within the design.

▲ **FIGURE 10.8** The servants in this painting are not all the same size. Two figures are as large as the priest and his wife, some are half their size, and some are even smaller. The painting uses hierarchical proportion. The more important figures are larger than the less important figures.

Nakht and Wife. Copy of a wall painting from the Tomb of Nakht. c. 1425 B.C. 2 × 1.53 m (6.5 × 5'). Egyptian Expedition of The Metropolitan Museum of Art, New York, New York. Rogers Fund, 1915 (15.5.19 e).

The pyramids of Egypt are of such large scale that people are overwhelmed by their size. These pyramids were designed to be large to express the eternal strength of Egypt.

Wall paintings inside a pyramid depict important people in a larger scale than less important people. The tomb painting *Nakht and Wife* (**Figure 10.8**) depicts stories about the priest and his wife. They watch their busy servants hunting, fishing, and farming on the priest's land. In the painting, the figures of the priest and his wife are much larger than the servants. *When figures are arranged in a work of art so that scale indicates importance,* the artist is using **hierarchical proportion.** This arrangement disregards the actual size of figures and objects in order to indicate rank in a society. Use of scale to emphasize rank appears in the art of many cultures (Figure 5.36, page 124).

Actual works of art are usually much larger or much smaller than they appear to be when you look at photographs of them. You may have seen photos with a human hand or a human figure added for the purpose of showing the size of the objects in relation to human scale. Without some sort of measure, no illustration in any book can convey the effect of the scale of a work of art.

Some works that seem monumental are really quite small in size. This is why the dimensions are always listed in the credit line of the work. Try to visualize the size of a work in relation to your size. Imagine how it would look if it were in the room with you.

MORE ABOUT...   Proportion and Scale

To foster students' awareness of proportion and scale in everyday life, suggest this: If you have a camera or a video recorder, take a walk to record examples of good and bad proportion in buildings. Feel the scale of the interior of a home and the interior of a public building or an amphitheater. Find churches that are designed as intimate communal space and others that seem to soar. Look for the space around buildings and see if it is in proportion to the building. Many large buildings have plazas proportioned both for movement of people and for flow of oxygen.

▶ **FIGURE 10.9** An ordinary clothespin takes on a whole new meaning when it is 45 feet tall and installed in a plaza in front of the Philadelphia City Hall.

Claes Oldenburg. *Clothespin.* 1976. Cor-Ten Steel. Height: 13.7 m (45′). Centre Square, Philadelphia, Pennsylvania.

Claes Oldenburg often uses scale to make you look at ordinary objects with a new perspective. He created a 45-foot tall pair of binoculars, a soft saxophone that is 69 inches tall, and a 45-foot tall clothespin **(Figure 10.9).** Can you imagine what it would feel like to stand in front of a clothespin that is over eight times taller than you?

Variations in scale within a work can change the work's total impact. For example, interior designers are concerned with the scale of the furniture that is to be placed in a room. The designer considers the scale of the space into which the furniture will be placed. The needs of the people who will use the space must also be considered. An oversized, overstuffed sofa would crowd a small room with a low ceiling. However, the same sofa would fit comfortably in a large hotel lobby with a four-story ceiling. The large scale of the lobby would make the size of the sofa look right.

Activity

Experimenting with Scale

Applying Your Skills. This activity can be achieved successfully by all students. Before starting this activity, review perspective techniques in Chapter 5 on pages 113 to 116. Students will need to use these techniques to make the objects seem to fit together.

💻 **Computer Option.** If available, use video digitizing equipment to capture the portraits of students in your classroom or use different figures from other sources such as a videodisc or CD-ROM. Import the images into a drawing program. Alter the images by changing colors or using special effects such as Water Color, Oil Pastel, Smudging, and so on. Experiment using the Selection tools and Copy and Paste commands. Explore exchanging heads, bodies, or features. Use drawing tools to blend cut-and-pasted areas. With practice, it becomes difficult to tell where alterations have occurred. Challenge students to explore what they, or their friends, would look like with a body or head of a famous person, or the eyes of a cat or other animal. Tell students that sensationalist tabloids use this technique to attract consumers' attention and sell papers.

Activity **Experimenting with Scale**

Applying Your Skills. Create a small collage scene using magazine cutouts of people, furniture, and hand-held objects such as books, combs, pencils, hair dryers, and dishes. Arrange the cutouts on a small sheet of paper using realistic, accurate scale. All of the objects in the scene should be in scale with the people, and all of the people should be in correct proportion to each other. Use perspective techniques and arrange things in depth to create an accurate scale. Draw a background environment for the scene using water-base markers, colored pencils, or crayons.

Computer Option. Use digital hardware such as a camera, scanner, or video camera and accompanying software to capture a variety of photographs of people and objects. Use the Selection tool and Copy and Paste commands to assemble a computer collage that shows unrealistic scale. Apply the tools of your choice to manipulate the images. Images can be selected from many other sources such as laser disc, CD–ROM, or the Internet. If you do not have these capabilities, use the drawing and painting tools of your choice to create a surrealistic scene.

Art History

Tell students that Claes Oldenburg created other works that are much larger in scale than normal, including a 9-foot soft sculpture titled, *Shoestring Potatoes Spilling from a Bag.* The french fries appear about as tall as a person and the bag is another 3 feet taller. Ask the students why they think Oldenburg takes ordinary objects and makes them larger than life.

Curriculum Connection

Science Until the present, the relationship between human proportions and architectural forms has been studied purely for aesthetic reasons. Today there is a discipline of science called *ergonomics* that is concerned with the relationship between people and the environment. It started during World War II with the design of efficient aircraft cockpits, and it is now concerned with all areas of interface between a user and a designed interior environment. This applies to comfort and safety in the everyday environment. Kitchen counters, classroom desks, auditorium seats, shelves in stores, automobiles, and many other objects are designed for comfort and maximum efficiency.

Aesthetics

Use large photos of individual television or movie stars to discuss beauty in facial proportions. More than likely, the conclusion will be that even idolized stars will have features that vary greatly from the ideal. This awareness will help students whose own features vary from the ideal to respect themselves.

Art History

Vitruvius (see bottom column on page 262) wrote about how the Greeks used human proportions as the basis for architectural construction: the inch came from one joint of a finger, the palm of the hand and the foot were measures, and the cubit was the length of the forearm from the tip of the middle finger to the elbow.

Critical Thinking

Discuss how industrial designers must consider human proportions. Look around the classroom at tables, counters, sinks, scissors, pencils, brushes, paper, and windows. Think about objects at home, in factories, and examples farther from the local environment, such as space vehicles and space stations. Each time the student mentions an object, make sure that he or she explains how proportion affects the size and shape of the final product.

Critical Thinking

One proportional problem that every student can relate to is the proportion of ingredients used in cooking. Ask what would happen to a chocolate cake if the cook added one teaspoon of sugar instead of one cup. What would happen to a pot of homemade vegetable soup if the cook added one cup of salt instead of one teaspoon?

▲ **FIGURE 10.10** In the art of the Benin people, symbolic proportions were used. Notice how large the head of the Oba (in the center of the work) is in proportion to the rest of his body.

Warrior Chief, Warriors, and Attendants. Plaque. Nigeria, Edo. Court of Benin. Sixteenth to seventeenth centuries. Brass. Height: 48 cm (18⅞″). The Metropolitan Museum of Art, New York. Gift of Mr. and Mrs. Klaus G. Peris, 1990.

▲ **FIGURE 10.11** Wilt Chamberlain, an NBA star, was a seven-time consecutive winner of the NBA scoring title from 1960 to 1966. He retired in 1974. Willie Shoemaker, an American jockey, won 8,833 races in his career and is considered the best rider in thoroughbred racing history. Chamberlain is over seven feet tall, while Shoemaker is approximately five feet tall.

Annie Liebovitz. *Wilt Chamberlain and Willie Shoemaker.* Photograph.

Drawing Human Proportions

In Western art, realistic representation of people has been the dominant style from the Renaissance to this century. However, many artists around the world use symbolic proportions rather than representational accuracy. To the Benin people of West Africa, the head represented life and intelligence. The prosperity of the Benin people depended on the head of the Oba, the divine ruler. In **Figure 10.10** the head of the Oba is one third of the whole body. This demonstrates its symbolic importance.

Figures

People come in a variety of sizes and shapes. Categories for clothes sizes—husky, petite, tall—are just one indication of the many different shapes and sizes of people.

Although they vary in height and width, most people do not vary with regard to proportion. Many basketball players, such as Wilt Chamberlain, are tall. Jockeys, such as Willie Shoemaker, are usually small and light. In **Figure 10.11,** notice that Chamberlain's arms, legs, and torso have the same proportions as those of Shoemaker. Body proportions cannot be defined in inches or

MORE ABOUT... Vitruvius

A Roman who lived in the first century B.C., Vitruvius noted that the height of a person from the soles of the feet to the top of the head equals the width of the outstretched arms from finger tip to finger tip. He also recorded that if a person lies flat and extends the arms above the head, the navel becomes the center of the body's total length.

According to Vitruvian proportions, if the navel is used as a center, both the tips of the fingers and the toes will touch the circumference of a circle drawn around the person. Leonardo da Vinci's famous drawing of the human male within a circle and a square is based on the Vitruvian norm.

centimeters. They can only be defined in ratios of one part of the body to another.

The unit usually used to define the proportions of an individual figure is the length of the head from the chin to the top of the skull. The average adult is seven and one-half heads tall **(Figure 10.12);** a young child is five or six heads tall; and an infant is only three heads long. Many artists use adult proportions when drawing an infant, and the painting looks strange because the head is small in relation to the rest of the body. In Giotto's painting *Madonna and Child* **(Figure 10.13),** the child looks like a miniature adult because of proportion.

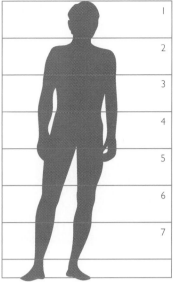

◀ **FIGURE 10.12**
Average body proportions.

◀ **FIGURE 10.13** Giotto was the first artist to make a flat surface appear three-dimensional by using shading. He was the first to attempt realism. The child in this painting looks awkward, like a little adult. This is because Giotto used incorrect proportions to depict the child. However, when you compare this work to the *Madonna and Child on Curved Throne* (Figure 13.5, page 354), a work by an earlier artist, you realize how much more lifelike Giotto's work appears.

Giotto. *Madonna and Child*. 1320–30. Paint on wood. 85.5 × 62 cm (33⅝ × 24⅜"). National Gallery of Art, Washington, D.C. © 1998 Board of Trustees. Samuel H. Kress Collection.

LESSON 2 *Scale* | **263**

Promoting Discussion

Ask the students to measure the height of the infant's head, and then use it to see how many heads tall Giotto has painted the child. They will discover it is about 6 heads tall, almost adult in proportion. Have them notice how the Madonna's head and hands, and the body of the child, have been shaded to create the illusion of form. They should notice that, although the bodies have the illusion of form, the background is flat like the gold leaf background in figure 13.5. Ask them to compare the treatment of the folds of drapery in the Giotto work to those in figure 13.5. They will notice some shading in the Byzantine art, but most of the folds are represented by a pattern of gold lines. They should also notice that there is an attempt to add shading to the Byzantine Madonna, but the face proportions are not accurate. They should also notice that the halos in the Byzantine work are prominent and look like crowns, while the halos in the Giotto are more subtle.

Art History

The subtitle of Siqueiros's work in Figure 10.14 is *El Coronelazo* (Self-Portrait), an affectionate title given to the artist by his friends. This painting is meant to be confrontational against his political and artistic opponents. It was painted after his return to Mexico from Chile in 1942 where he had been in exile following his participation in the 1940 attempted assassination of communist Leon Trotsky. This event had put him at odds with Rivera and other intellectuals who had supported Trotsky's break with Stalin.

Activity

Human Proportions

Applying Your Skills. You might team the students up in groups of two or three to record measurements. Team girls with girls and boys with boys to avoid embarrassing moments. You might assign this activity as homework, or you might ask for a few volunteers to do the measuring for the entire class. The important point is for students to understand that proportions are not just numbers created out of thin air—they are accurate.

■ **Computer Option.** Have students follow these directions: Use a live model and the drawing tools of your choice to make several body sketches. Have the model change positions so you can try foreshortening of the arms or legs. Save and title. Then, use the Grids and Rulers option and a Selection tool to select the head on one of your drawings. Move the head down the body counting how many "heads" tall the figure is. Select the one that best represents ideal proportions. Experiment with the Scale Selection or Resizing tool. Create some figures that are tall and thin or short and fat, but maintain the average 7½-heads proportion.

◄ **FIGURE 10.14** Siqueiros used foreshortening in this painting to dramatically exaggerate his reach. It is as if the artist wants to grab everything he can. His hand becomes a burst of superhuman energy.

David Alfaro Siqueiros. *Self-Portrait (El Coronelazo).* 1945. Pyroxylin on Masonite. 91 × 121 cm (35⅞ × 47⅛"). Museo de Arte Moderno, Mexico City, Mexico.

Sometimes an artist may purposely distort proportion to make a drawing look more realistic. If a person is pointing at you, the arm from the fingertips to the shoulder will look shorter than it actually is. In a painting, an artist will use a technique to visually shorten the arm. **Foreshortening** is *to shorten an object to make it look as if it extends backward into space* **(Figure 10.14).**

Activity | Human Proportions

Applying Your Skills. Use the length of your head (from the top of your skull to the bottom of your chin) as a unit against which to measure the rest of your body. In this way you can calculate the relationship, or ratio, of all parts of your body to your head. You may need a friend to help you obtain accurate measurements. Determine the number of head lengths that each of the following represents: total height, chin to waist, waist to hip, knee to ankle, ankle to bottom of bare heel, underarm to elbow, elbow to wrist, wrist to tip of finger, and shoulder to tip of finger. Record the ratios and create a diagram or chart to show your findings. Compare your findings with those of your classmates. Find averages for the class, because the ratios will not be exactly alike.

Computer Option. Use video digitizing software and a video camera or a scanner to capture a variety of photographs of people and objects. Clip art and videodiscs can also be used. If you do not have these capabilities, use the drawing tools of your choice to create your images. Use the Selection tool and the Copy and Paste options to assemble a computer collage using unrealistic scale. Use the tools of your choice, such as Resize, to manipulate the images. Create a surrealistic scene.

Heads and Faces

As you read this section, look in a mirror or at a classmate to check the examples discussed.

The front of the head is approximately oval. No one has a head that is perfectly oval—some people have narrow chins, and some have square jaws.

A face is approximately symmetrical. It has a central vertical axis when viewed from the front **(Figure 10.15)**. If the face turns away from you, the axis curves over the surface of the head. You can divide the head into four sections along the central axis. This is done by drawing three horizontal lines that divide the axis into four equal parts, as shown in Figure 10.15.

The top fourth of the head is usually full of hair. The hair may start above the

---

MORE ABOUT... The Language of Design

The way we use the elements and principles of art comes largely from the ideas developed in a German school of design known as the Bauhaus. By 1926 it had secured a worldwide reputation for design research and education. Master craftspeople were hired to teach there and students participated in an introductory program of creative experiments that stressed free manipulation, originality, and sensitivity to the individual qualities of different materials.

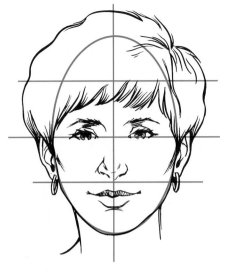

▲ **FIGURE 10.15** Facial proportions.

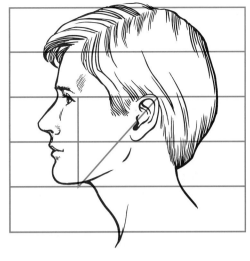

▲ **FIGURE 10.16** Profile proportions.

top horizontal line, or it may fall below it if the person wears bangs.

The eyes usually appear on the central horizontal line. They are at the center of a person's head. Notice the width of the space between the eyes. How does it relate to the width of one eye? The bottom of the nose rests on the lowest horizontal line, and the mouth is closer to the nose than to the chin. Use the sighting technique to determine other relationships, such as nose width, mouth width, and ear placement.

When you view a head in complete profile, or from the side, all of the vertical proportions remain the same as in the front view. However, both shape and contour change. Try to discover the new ratios **(Figure 10.16).** Notice the relationship between the distance from the chin to the hairline and the distance from the front of the forehead to the back of the head. Can you find a ratio to help you locate the ear in profile? Study the contour of the front of the face. Which part protrudes the most? Notice the jawline from the chin to the ear and the relationship of the neck to the head. In **Figure 10.17,** the artist has drawn

▲ **FIGURE 10.17** The center face in this drawing is a young woman whom Gauguin painted on his first visit to Tahiti. These serene faces with blank eyes look like ancient stone heads sculpted in Egypt or Mexico. The Maori people were the inspiration for many of Gauguin's paintings.

Paul Gauguin. *Tahitians.* c. 1891–93. Charcoal on laid paper. 41 × 31 cm (16⅛ × 12¼"). The Metropolitan Museum of Art, New York, New York. #1996.418.

Promoting Discussion

Tell students that in Figure 10.15, on page 264, Siqueiros has portrayed himself reaching out to grab something, and has used foreshortening to express the power of his reach. Have the students measure the size of his fist from the top thumb joint to the bottom of his little finger and compare that to the size of his head. They will discover that the fist is larger than the head. Ask them to make fists and compare the size of their own fist to their own head. They will discover that their fist is half the size of their own head. Also have them notice the difference between the smooth application of paint to the skin of the artist and the rough surrounding textures. Notice that this material is sliding off his fingernails as if he has scraped through the rough matter to reach out. What do they think he is reaching through? Why do they think he has used foreshortening and the contrast of texture in this work.

Studio Skills

When drawing heads and faces, people tend to pay attention to the parts that identify the model: the distinctive features. The features are often drawn accurately, but the areas we do not use for identification, such as the top of the head and back of the skull, are often drawn too small. Have students measure the different lengths in Figure 10.16 to be sure that they understand how much width they must allow from the eyes to the back of the skull.

MORE ABOUT... **Facial Proportions**

Ask the students to compare Gauguin's drawing to the diagrams in figures 10.15 and 10.16. They will discover that the frontal view is exactly correct. They may discover that the bottom profile is a little short. Ask them to notice the shading of the lips. The upper lip is in shadow because it is slanting inward, while the bottom lip has highlights because it protrudes and catches the light. Also have them notice the front view of the nose. Blended shading has been used rather than a line to indicate the side of the nose. If you have students look in a mirror, they will discover that the nose is a form that blends into the cheek. Explain that there is no line they can use to define an edge when the head is facing forward. They can only see a line on the edge of the nose if the head is turned in a three-quarter view.

Art Criticism

Discuss the three different heads in this print. Point out how the father's head is presented in profile. Explain that from the bottom of his chin to the top of his hair, his proportions are accurate. The artist has been able to indicate the tilt of the woman's head with two lines. A few dots of color have been used to indicate her eye and a small cured line to represent her ear. There is no shading anywhere in the print. This is most obvious in the child's head: We sense the form of the skull through the placement of a few lines that depict the infant's features.

Activity

Drawing the Head

Applying Your Skills. Help students understand where the central axis can be found on a three-quarter view by showing an example. *Parents* magazine would be a good one in which to find the faces of children and infants.

ASSESS..........

Self-Assessment

Have students complete the lesson review questions. Answers appear below.

Reteaching

Have students work in pairs to identify artworks in this lesson that exemplify use of scale, hierarchical proportion, and foreshortening.

Enrichment

Have students take photos of buildings in the community that display exemplary proportions and then make a bulletin board display.

CLOSE............

Ask students to review what they learned in this lesson about scale, hierarchical proportion, and foreshortening.

both the front and two profile views of a woman's head.

Notice that the facial proportions of infants are different, as shown in the print by Bonnard **(Figure 10.18).**

Activity — Drawing the Head

Applying Your Skills. Look through magazines for large photographs of heads. Look for adults, children, and babies. Remember that a head is not flat, and when it is turned, the central axis moves and curves around the shape of the head. You can always find the axis because it goes through the center of the nose, lips, and between the eyes. Draw the central axis and the three horizontal dividing lines on each face you have selected. What are the proportional differences among the faces of adults, children, and infants?

Computer Option. Gather some pictures of the faces of babies, young children, and adults. Notice that facial proportions change with age. Use the drawing tools of your choice to draw a human face using average facial proportions. Save your work. Use the Selection tool and the Copy and Paste options to duplicate the first face you drew. To experiment with the size of facial features, use the Selection tool to select the features of the face but not the outline of the head itself. Use the Resize option to create the correct feature size for a young child. Save your work. Reduce the size even more to create the correct feature size for an infant. The features need to be small and in the lower third of its face. Save your work. If possible, save all three faces on the same screen. Finally, compare the three faces you have created.

▲ **FIGURE 10.18** Even though Bonnard has flattened and simplified this work, the differences in the proportions between the profile of the father and the infant are easily measured. The skull of the infant is very large, and the baby's features seem to be squeezed down into the lower part of the head.

Pierre Bonnard. *Family Scene.* 1893. Color lithograph from "L'Estampe originale." 31 × 17.8 cm (12¼ × 7″). The Metropolitan Museum of Art, New York, New York.

Check Your Understanding

1. What is scale?
2. What are the two kinds of scale present in a work of art?
3. Describe hierarchical proportion.
4. How does the credit line help you understand the scale of an artwork?
5. Explain foreshortening.

 ### Answers to Check Your Understanding

1. Scale refers to size as measured against a standard reference, such as a human body.
2. Scale of the work itself and the scale of objects or elements in the composition.
3. This occurs when figures are arranged in art so that the scale indicates their importance.
4. It indicates the dimensions of a work.
5. Used to reduce the size of an object so that it appears to extend backward into space, allowing for a more realistic representation.

How Artists Use Proportion and Distortion

Many artists use correct proportions in their work. They want every viewer to recognize the person, place, or thing being shown. These artists use correct proportion to create illusions of reality. This ability to show objects as though they were real seems magical to many viewers. Other artists choose exaggeration and distortion to create works with unusual expressive qualities.

Realistic Proportion

During the Renaissance in Italy there was a renewed interest in art and literature. Ancient Greek and Roman sculptures were discovered, and artists were inspired to create work with the realistic proportions of the ancient masters. To better understand the human body, the artists Leonardo da Vinci and Michelangelo Buonarroti dissected cadavers in secret because dissection was illegal at that time.

Michelangelo's statue of *David* is an outstanding example of Renaissance proportional accuracy. The artist was asked to create a bigger than life size figure of *David* **(Figure 10.19)** for the façade of the Cathedral in Florence. When it was finished, the people decided that it was too important to be placed high up on the cathedral. Instead, it was placed in the main square and became a symbol of the city of Florence.

Early American artists were hired to paint portraits to record accurate

▲ **FIGURE 10.19** One unusual feature of Michelangelo's *David* is the fiery intensity of the young man's facial expression. He is staring at an enemy, the giant Goliath. What do you think David is thinking?

Michelangelo. *David (detail)*. 1501-1504. Marble. Galleria dell' Accademia, Florence, Italy.

CHAPTER 10
LESSON 3

How Artists Use Proportion and Distortion
(pages 267–273)
(National Standards: 2b, 3c)

FOCUS...........
Objective
After completing this lesson, students will be able to:

- Understand how artists use proportion and distortion to create meaning.

Supplies
- Magazines
- Construction paper
- Scissors

Resources
📁 Application 20, *Sharpening Your Skills*
📁 Studio Lesson 20, *Modern Spirit Mask*

TEACH..........
Motivator
Have students form small groups. Let the members of each group draw quick sketches of the other members in a chosen pose.

Ask students if they drew accurate proportions of their models. Tell students they will learn how proportion and distortion are used in art.

MORE ABOUT... *David*

Michelangelo imagined the statue *David* already existing within the marble, and that his job was to set it free. *David* was carved from an 18-foot-high marble block that had already been carved by another sculptor during the 1460s. Michelangelo studied the block and decided that it could be used. First, Michelangelo made a small model in wax. Then, he sketched the contours of the figure on only one side of the marble. According to his biographer and friend, Vasari, Michelangelo carved in from the one, already sketched, surface as if he was creating a high relief. Then he worked his way around the whole figure.

Developing Studio Skills

Make a series of figure drawings using a live model. Remind students to use the sighting technique to help see proportions. Also remind them that as their model's poses change, the proportions will look different. They should keep in mind that they will measure what they see, not what they think they should see. If the model is sitting facing students, the length from hip to knee may be foreshortened. Refer back to Figure 10.14 on page 264 to reinforce the concept of foreshortening, if necessary.

Art Criticism

After students have had a chance to study John Singleton Copley's painting in Figure 10.20, ask these questions: What do you see in this painting? What lines, shapes, spaces, colors, and textures can you identify?

Developing Perceptual Skills

Marisol combined painted images on flat surfaces with carved three-dimensional parts. Ask the students to study the work to see which parts are painted and which are three-dimensional. *(The boy is entirely painted. The girl on the far left is painted except for her feet, which are carved. The girl next to the mother has a painted body, but her legs and shoes are three-dimensional. The mother has three-dimensional hands, legs, and feet. The baby's head and feet are three-dimensional, but there is something unusual about her lap—it also appears to be painted on a three-dimensional form.)*

▲ **FIGURE 10.20** In this painting, Copley not only tells us what Paul Revere looked like, but he also tells us the man's profession. Revere was a silversmith, and the artist shows Revere holding a finished piece of work. The tools on the table were those used by Revere to engrave designs on the surface of his finished forms.

John Singleton Copley. *Paul Revere.* c. 1768–70. Oil on canvas. 88.9 × 72.3 cm (35 × 28½"). Museum of Fine Arts, Boston, Massachusetts. Gift of Joseph W., William B., and Edward H. R. Revere.

▲ **FIGURE 10.21** This mixed media work is based on a photograph that Marisol found among waste papers near her studio. She uses realistic painting on the flat surfaces of rectangular solids and recycled doors, and combines it with carved wooden forms to create a realistic portrait of the unknown family. Notice the different accurate proportions in this work. Use a ruler and you will see that the head-to-body ratio is appropriate for each figure.

Marisol. *The Family.* 1962. Painted wood and other materials in three sections. 209.8 × 166.3 × 39.3 cm (82½ × 65½ × 15½"). Collection, The Museum of Modern Art, New York, New York. Advisory Committee Fund. © Marisol/Licensed by VAGA, New York, New York.

information about real people **(Figure 10.20).** A contemporary American artist, Marisol, painted in the Pop style in the 1960s. In **Figure 10.21,** she has used an unusual combination of materials, yet she still uses accurate proportions for all of the figures.

Exaggeration and Distortion

Some artists use exaggeration and distortion rather than realistic proportion to convey their ideas and feelings. **Exaggeration** and **distortion** are *deviations from expected, normal proportions.* They are powerful means of expression. Artists can lengthen, enlarge, bend, warp, twist, or deform parts or all of the human body. By making these changes, they can show moods and feelings that are easily understood by viewers. The exaggeration used by the artist in

Curriculum Connection

Media By the turn of this century, motion pictures had become a popular attraction in amusement arcades, music halls, and vaudeville theaters. However, until the advent of the "talkies" in the 1920s, movies were silent and had to rely on the skill of actors to convey a story. Actors used exaggerated facial features and gestures to replace what their dialogue would otherwise relate. While the silent movies played, often a piano or organ player would provide live accompaniment to the action on the screen. This musician had the added responsibility of creating mood, tempo, and tone with music.

Napachie Pootoogook. *My Daughter's First Steps.* 1990. Lithograph. 55.8 × 85.8 cm (22 × 33¼"). Permission courtesy of the West Baffin Eskimo Co-operative Limited.

Art History

Caricature is another powerfully expressive technique. Artists have used it since the days of ancient Egypt and Babylon, and it is still a powerful political weapon. Editorial cartoonists can sway public opinion. If you have students who are interested in this field, suggest that they research Honoré Daumier or Thomas Nast. Both of these artists were successful with the technique of caricature. Nast, an illustrator, was able to turn people against the infamous Tammany Hall political machine in New York City. His work appeared in newspapers and magazines.

Developing Perceptual Skills

Point out to the students that the distortions in this work are for expressive effect. The artist stretches out the length of the torso as if it were putty to exaggerate the emotional stretching out toward the daughter. The mother's back and arms form a sweeping horizontal curve toward the child. Help students notice that the sleeves of the child's parka are the proper length, yet the toddler's arms are depicted as very small in proportion to her body. This is to show her fear of falling, her weakness, and her need for the mother's support.

Figure 10.22 lets us know how the woman feels.

In the past, movie stars of the silent screen had to exaggerate facial expressions and body language to convey meaning without words. If you have ever seen an old silent movie, you have probably laughed at the exaggerated eyelid movements used to express meaning.

It takes study and skill to use exaggeration and distortion effectively. Before an artist can distort a person or an object, he or she must study perception drawing and anatomy of the human figure. It takes knowledge to know what to exaggerate and how to distort images effectively.

In *Single Family Blues* **(Figure 10.23),** Twiggs has used exaggeration to express the feeling of "the blues" that engulf this family. Notice that the hand is twice the size of the child's blue head or the mother's navy blue face. This distortion allows the viewer to see how dominant "the blues" are in this family.

▲ **FIGURE 10.23** Twiggs uses exaggeration to emphasize the hand playing the blues for this family.

Leo Twiggs. *Single Family Blues.* 1996. Batik on cotton. 26.7 × 34.3 cm (10½ × 13½"). Courtesy of the artist.

MORE ABOUT... *Single Family Blues*

This painting was made with unusual materials. Twiggs paints using batik dyes and waxes on untreated, cotton cloth. Have the students notice the white lines in the man's shirt. Notice how they start with little round shapes and then thin out. Twiggs creates this effect using a tjantig tool, which holds hot wax. He places the tool where he wants to make a white line, uncovers the spout, and allows the hot wax to pour out and make a line on the white fabric. When the work is complete, all the wax is removed with heat.

Point out how Twiggs uses color to show relationships. The blue of the child's head matches the man's hat. Ask the students why the warmest colors, yellow and orange, are coming out between the man's fingers. Ask them what the white dots stand for. Could they represent sounds?

Art History

Figure 10.24 is from what is now called Picasso's "Blue Period." During this time he lived in poverty in Paris, and was not yet famous. The most emotional work he created, *Guernica,* was painted for the Spanish exhibit at the 1937 World's Fair. Guernica was a town in Spain chosen by the Germans to test the ability of their air force to destroy towns and cities. The test was successful. The painting is a timeless expression of anguish and pain.

Developing Perceptual Skills

Direct students' attention to Figure 10.24. Help students notice that Picasso has used the proportions of the golden rectangle to control this composition. The bottom of the gray rectangles in the upper left corner divides the composition. Below those, the background is a square of darkness. Point out that the rest of that area on the right is another square. Ask the students if they think Picasso planned this, or do they think it just happened because it was a comfortable division of space?

Ask the students why the head of the old man is placed against the only light area of the background. Is it to emphasize the head? What are the lightest areas in the work? *(The white hair and the highlights on the arm strumming the guitar.)* Why was this done? *(For emphasis.)* Help students understand that everything has been exaggerated for expressive effect in this painting. Try to bring in some sorrowful Spanish guitar music. How does that relate to the look of this painting?

MEET THE ARTIST
PABLO PICASSO

Spanish 1881–1973

Pablo Picasso (**pah**-blow pee-**cah**-so) was born in Malaga, Spain in 1881. One day his father, a painter and teacher, came home to a surprise. His son had finished a portrait. After examining the work, Pablo's father gave the boy all his art materials. So great was Picasso's work that his father vowed never to paint again. Picasso was just eight years old.

He went to Paris in 1904. There he met other artists and writers. The creative climate encouraged him to develop a new style, which he called Cubism. Combining his appreciation of African art with his interest in geometrical forms, he created a unique and innovative form. His aim was to shock viewers into visual awareness. His intensity drove him to experiment with all media, discovering new forms and new ideas. He painted Cubist works as well as realistic representations of people. He also created prints and collages throughout his long and full life.

▶ **FIGURE 10.24** Picasso exaggerates the thinness of this old man, elongates his limbs, and places him in an impossibly angular position to create a painting that expresses sympathy for his condition. How does the contrast between the thin, angular man painted in blue and the warm brown, rounded guitar affect the meaning of this work?

Pablo Picasso. *The Old Guitarist.* 1903. Oil on panel. 122.9 × 82.6 cm (48⅛ × 32½"). The Art Institute of Chicago, Chicago, Illinois. Helen Birch Bartlett Memorial Collection.

Picasso was also a master of distorting proportion to express an idea or feeling. The first years of the twentieth century were called Picasso's "Blue Period." During this time he painted poor and tragic people. Despite the sorrowful condition of the figures, there seems to be a sense of optimism in the works. In *The Old Guitarist* **(Figure 10.24),** the grotesquely thin old man seems unaware of his condition. His head is bent toward the instrument as if nothing matters but the beautiful sound of his music.

ART ON THE WEB Discover how artists use the elements of art to create different kinds of proportion in their works by visiting the Glencoe Fine Arts Site at **www.glencoe.com/sec/art.**

You can also explore through the *Glencoe Student Galleria* to see examples of how other students used proportion and distortion in their two- and three-dimensional art.

▲ **FIGURE 10.25** Chagall's painting shows a childlike belief in love's power to conquer all. He often created distorted fantasies full of bright colors that looked like joyful dreams.

Marc Chagall. *Birthday.* 1915. Oil on cardboard. 80.6 × 99.7 cm (31¼ × 39¼"). Collection, The Museum of Modern Art, New York, New York. Acquired through the Lillie P. Bliss bequest.

Chagall uses distortion to present a happy theme in his painting *Birthday* **(Figure 10.25).** The subjects of this work are the artist himself and Bella, his fiancée. The birthday is the artist's. Instead of simply showing himself leaning over to kiss Bella, Chagall used distortion. In the painting he appears to leap backward, stretch his neck like a swan, curve it around, and give Bella a kiss as he floats by. It is as if Chagall might have been thinking, "I'm so happy, I'm floating on air," when he created this work.

Artists can create feelings of great stability and calm by placing a small head on a large body. A monumental, or large and imposing, quality results. The monumental quality of Gaston Lachaise's

LESSON 3   *How Artists Use Proportion and Distortion*   **271**

Aesthetics

Have students compare Chagall's painting in Figure 10.25 to Thomas Hart Benton's *The Sources of Country Music* (Figure 13.29 on page 376). Encourage them to describe the similarities and the differences.

Art History

Marc Chagall was influenced by the works of such artists as van Gogh, Gauguin, and Matisse while he studied in St. Petersburg, Russia. From there he went to Paris, France, where he was further influenced by the artistic innovations of the Cubists as well as the theories of Sigmund Freud. His own style is marked by brightly colored fantasies that draw little distinction between dreams and actual objects.

Critical Thinking

Both Figures 10.24 and 10.25 depict distortion and exaggeration. However, Chagall and Picasso have created quite different tones to their respective works that cause the reader to react in different ways. Tell students that writers accomplish the same distinction through language. To illustrate this point, ask students to begin two letters responding to either of the subjects in the two artworks. Each letter should express the person's feeling toward the other person in the same painting at the exact moment of the painting. Ask volunteers to read their two letters. Then compare the variations of tone in the letters.

Art Criticism

After students have had a chance to study Lachaise's sculpture in Figure 10.26, ask these questions: What is your opinion of the work? Do you like it? Why or why not? Does it make you think? If so, what does it make you think of? If not, why not? Does it express an emotional effect? How would you describe the effect?

Remind students to rely on the theories of art criticism when defending an opinion about a work of art.

Developing Studio Skills

Have students examine the bronze sculpture in Figure 10.26. Ask a volunteer to read aloud the analysis of the work beginning at the top of page 272. Then, using markers, bits of colored paper, and glue, students are to construct plaques on paper plates celebrating themselves as individuals. Each student's plaque is to show him- or herself; symbolic representations of personal skills, character traits, and other features of self-identity. Like the Lachaise sculpture, the plaques should reveal an interesting sense of proportion.

Aesthetics

Ask students to explain how the medium used in Figure 10.26 affects the feeling of the work. Does the title help a viewer to interpret the image? Why or why not?

▲ **FIGURE 10.26** This sculpture is only 19¼ inches (48.8 cm) high and yet it has a monumental quality because Lachaise has made the head small in comparison to the body.

Gaston Lachaise. *Walking Woman.* 1922. Bronze. 48.8 × 26.9 × 18.9 cm (19¼ × 10⅝ × 7½″). Hirshhorn Museum and Sculpture Garden, Smithsonian Institution, Washington, D.C. Gift of Joseph H. Hirshhorn, 1966.

Walking Woman **(Figure 10.26)** is created through exaggerated proportions and spacing rather than through large scale.

Another use of exaggeration can be seen in the features of a mask. Masks have been used in all societies, from early primitive tribes to our modern computer age **(Figure 10.27).** A mask allows a person to hide his or her real self and become someone, or something, else.

Masks are used in many cultures as part of religious ceremonies and rituals. In many cases the features of the mask are exaggerated for expressive purposes. Each culture has specific traditions and procedures that are followed for making and using masks. Sometimes the mask appears to the person in a dream. Sometimes the mask is part of a cultural tradition. In most cases the mask is intended to aid efforts to communicate with the spirit world.

Cartoons are another way in which exaggeration can be used. Editorial cartoonists use this technique to make caricatures of famous people. The caricatures emphasize unusual facial features. Similarly, characters in comic strips are often made by using proportions that are larger than life. The most distorted comic-strip characters are often the funniest ones.

MEETING INDIVIDUAL NEEDS

Building Self-Esteem While masks can hide our real selves, they can also reveal aspects about us that we wish to share with others but are uncomfortable expressing under normal circumstances. The mask allows us to adopt any persona and act out repressed emotions. Good mental health is usually facilitated through expressing one's feelings clearly. Despite the fact that bad things do sometimes happen to a good person, making art can help that person deal with bothersome feelings and help one to feel good about one's self.

▶ **FIGURE 10.27** Imagine sitting in the dark around a fire when a mysterious figure jumps out of the dark into the dim flickering light wearing one of these masks. How would you feel? How does exaggeration and distortion affect the expressive qualities of these masks?

(bottom right) *Mask.* New Ireland. c. 1920. Wood, paint, fiber, seashells. Height: 38 cm (15″). Milwaukee Public Museum, Milwaukee, Wisconsin.

(right) George Walkus. *Secret Society Mask.* (Four Headed Cannibal Spirit) 1938. Wood; cedar bark, shredded; string. 53.34 × 129.54 cm (21 × 51″). Denver Art Museum, Denver, Colorado.

Activity — Distorting Proportions

Applying Your Skills. Cut two ovals about 9 inches long from any color of construction paper. Using parts cut from magazines, create one face using accurate proportions. On the second oval, create a distorted face.

Computer Option. Use the drawing tools of your choice to draw a human face using average facial proportions. Use the Select tool and the Copy and Paste options to make four or five copies of the head and face on the same screen. Use the Select tool to experiment with the whole head and with individual facial features. Resize, Distort, Rotate, and Bend are some options that may prove useful to you. If your software does not have these options, draw the changes with the drawing tools of your choice. Save your work. Compare the faces you have distorted and changed. How does the distortion affect the way you would use each face in a piece of artwork?

 ### Check Your Understanding

1. How do exaggeration and distortion affect proportion?
2. What distorting effects can an artist use?
3. Why do artists use distortion?
4. How can artists create monumental qualities without using a large scale?

LESSON 3   *How Artists Use Proportion and Distortion*   **273**

 ## Answers to Check Your Understanding

1. Exaggeration and distortion deviate from expected, normal proportions.
2. An artist can lengthen, enlarge, bend, wrap, twist or deform parts or all of the human body to distort proportion.
3. Artists use distortion to communicate moods, ideas, and feelings to the viewers.
4. Artists can create monumental qualities by exaggerating proportions and spacing rather than through using large scale.

CHAPTER 10 LESSON 3

Activity — Distorting Proportions

Applying Your Skills. To keep this activity fun, tell students they may not use features from a photo to create the realistic proportions. The distorted face will be more fun if the students look for hats, glasses, and other accessories, as well as eyes, nose, mouth, and hair, from different faces.

💻 **Computer Option.** As an alternative activity, have students follow these directions: Use the Brush Symmetry tool to create a symmetrical portrait. Select vertical symmetry and a brush thickness of your choice. Experiment with colors, patterns, and brush thickness to draw a fanciful human or animal mask design. Now, experiment with distortion by using the Selection tool and Scale Selection or Resizing tool to change the proportion of the whole head or individual features by shrinking or exaggerating. Other manipulation tools such as Rotate, Flip, and Distort can be used.

ASSESS..........

Self-Assessment

Have student complete the lesson review questions. Answers appear below.

Enrichment

Have students collect comic strips and classify them according to whether they use accurate proportions or distortions. Have students analyze the distorted comics. Then discuss how the artist uses the distortion to express meaning.

CLOSE.............

Ask students to review what they learned in this lesson about exaggeration and distortion.

273

Storyteller Figure
(National Standards: 1a, 1b, 2b, 2c, 3b)

FOCUS...........
Objective
After completing this lesson, students will be able to:

■ Create a clay storyteller sculpture involving one adult interacting with many children.

Supplies
■ Several children's books that feature animals

TEACH..........
Motivator
Bring several children's books to class that feature animals. Ask students to read the stories aloud in class. Then discuss the human characteristics exhibited by each animal. Discuss why certain animals were given specific human characteristics or personalities. Encourage students to read the stories to younger siblings or neighborhood children so that they might get an inspiration for their clay figure.

Art History
About 5,000 years ago the ancient Pueblos, called the Anasazi by the Navajo and archaeologists (the Pueblos do not like this name), began to spread throughout the Southwest. This migration was a result of overpopulation and a lengthy drought. Nearly 3,000 years ago, the ancient Pueblos began a slow transition from hunters to agriculturalists. They began growing corn, squash, and other vegetables. They lived in multistoried dwellings called pueblos and created baskets and pottery. To avoid raiders, the Pueblos built homes atop high cliffs.

Storyteller Figure

▲ **FIGURE 10.28**

Annette Romero of the Cochiti Pueblo. *Storyteller Doll.* 1993. Clay and earth pigments. 20 × 10 × 17.7 cm (8 × 4 × 7"). Private collection.

SUPPLIES

■ **Sketchbook and pencil**

■ **Clay**

■ **Clay modeling tools**

■ **Slip and brush**

■ **Plastic bag**

■ **Tray or board**

■ **Acrylic paints and assorted brushes**

■ **Fine-line black markers**

When Helen Cordero of the Cochiti Pueblo shaped the first Storyteller doll in 1964, she brought the Singing Mother, one of the oldest forms of Native American self-portraiture, into the twentieth century. In doing so, she reinvented a dying Cochiti tradition of figurative pottery **(Figure 10.28).**

The first time Helen exhibited her work, a folk art collector named Girard bought all of her little people. He asked her to make an even larger seated figure with children, and Helen thought about her grandfather, who had been a very good storyteller.

It is impossible to determine how many Storytellers Helen Cordero has shaped since 1964. It is also impossible to measure the influence of her invention, which began a revival of figurative pottery in both her own and other New Mexico pueblos. All sorts of variations have appeared.

What You Will Learn

You will create a clay Storyteller sculpture involving one adult interacting with many children, using proper clay construction techniques. After firing, add color.

Creating

Brainstorm with your classmates to think up variations for the Storyteller project. You may depict a male or female person or an animal as the adult. The children must match the adult; for example, if you choose a bear as the adult, the children must be bear cubs. Use exaggerated scale to illustrate how an adult can enthrall children with storytelling.

MEETING INDIVIDUAL NEEDS

Physically Disabled For some students with disabilities, it may be more appropriate to do a collage variation of the Storyteller figure. If possible, allow these students to use a glue stick to paste tiny magazine pictures of figures onto a large cut-out magazine figure. Using this method, students learn about how changes in scale can create dramatic visual effects. You could use examples of each medium (clay and paper collage) to discuss the way media influences aesthetic appeal.

Step 1 When you have selected the subject of your sculpture, make several sketches of the adult. Draw different views of your adult. Then make some rough sketches to help you think through how you will arrange the children on the adult.

Step 2 Review clay construction procedures by reading Technique Tip 15 on page 434 in the Handbook. Decide which process you will use to build the adult figure. Remember that it needs to be hollow, and it needs an opening to allow air to get inside. The Storyteller's mouth would be appropriate for the opening. Decide which process you will use to create the smaller figures. Make notes about your construction plans in your sketchbook.

Step 3 Collect your construction materials. Build the adult first, adding all three-dimensional details. Keep the adult stored tightly in the plastic bag while you construct the children. When you have attached all the children using scoring and slip, cover the sculpture loosely and let it dry. Check it every day to be sure that the little people are not drying too fast. They might shrink faster than the adult and crack off. When the sculpture is bone dry, fire it in the kiln.

Step 4 After firing, paint the sculpture with acrylic paints. Use small brushes or fine-line markers to add linear details. You do not have to cover all of the clay. Use the color of the clay as one of the predominant colors in your sculpture.

Step 5 Write the story that your Storyteller is narrating. Record it on tape. Arrange the Storyteller sculpture in a display. Use a tape player to tell the story to your viewers.

EVALUATING YOUR WORK

▶ **DESCRIBE** Explain the subject of your Storyteller sculpture. How many children did you make? Which clay construction processes did you use?

▶ **ANALYZE** How much did you exaggerate scale in your sculpture? Did you use accurate or distorted proportions? How did you incorporate the color of the fired clay into the color scheme?

▶ **INTERPRET** What is the theme of your story? Does it match the mood of the sculpture?

▶ **JUDGE** Which aesthetic theories would you use to judge this work? If you were to do it one more time, what, if anything, would you change?

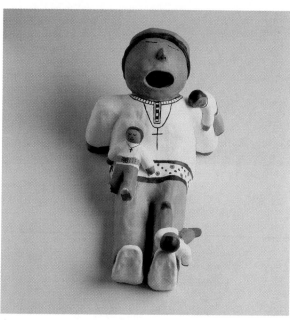

▲ **FIGURE 10.28A** Student work.

Studio Skills
To help students be successful with this activity, offer these suggestions:

■ Use a stiff piece of clay to support any children that project too far from the adult body of the sculpture. Place the support under the protrusion until dry.

■ Engobes, underglazes, and glazes may be substituted for acrylic paint.

ASSESS..........
Keeping a Portfolio
Remind students that the preliminary sketches and the final artwork for this Studio Project are likely candidates for their portfolios.

Self-Assessment
Have students apply the steps of art criticism to their own artwork using the "Evaluating Your Work" questions on this page. In addition, ask the following: How was scale exaggerated to emphasize the Storyteller? What animal or human characteristics were chosen for the sculpture?

Enrichment
Students can create a fantasy environment for the Storyteller figure based on images from its story. As an alternative idea, students could draw or paint a fantasy figure that has supernatural powers closely related to animal characteristics.

CLOSE............
Allow students to make a display of their Storyteller figures.

MORE ABOUT... Helen Cordero

Helen Cordero was 45 years old when she began doing beadwork with her husband's cousin, Juanita Arquero, to make a little extra money. At first, most of the profits were used to buy more materials. Grandma Juana suggested that they go back to pottery. "You don't have to buy anything; Mother Earth gives it all to you." Juanita, who had learned to make pottery as a child, renewed her interest in this medium. Helen spent six months as Juanita's apprentice, learning the ancient art. However, Helen's bowls and jars never looked quite right; they kept coming out crooked. The day Juanita suggested that Helen try making figures was the day Helen's success began.

Studio Project

Papier-Mâché Mask

(National Standards: 1a, 1b, 2b, 2c, 3b)

FOCUS...........

Supplies

- Slides, pictures of masks, actual masks
- Hot glue gun

Objective

After completing this project, students will be able to:

- Design and create a high-relief papier-mâché mask using distortion and exaggeration.

Motivator

Show slides, reproductions, and if available, actual masks. Discuss the similarities and differences in masks from various cultures. Notice how some masks are symmetrical and others are not. Discuss possible reasons why masks were made or worn. (Death masks were worn to give immortality; hunting masks were worn during rituals to give power.)

TEACH..........

Understanding Art History

Ask students to research other cultures known for their masks. Students should study the various nations of Africa, Native American tribes, cultures of Central and South America, and the people of Asia. Three common purposes for masks are adornment, concealment, and ritual.

Papier Mâché Mask

▲ **FIGURE 10.29**

Henry Hunt, Southern Kwakiutl. *K'umugwe' (Komokwa) Mask.* 1970. Wood, copper, paint. 31.6 × 28.7 × 20.7 cm (12⅖ × 11⅓ × 8"). Royal British Columbia Museum, Victoria, British Columbia, Canada. #13215.

SUPPLIES

- **Sketchbook and pencil**
- **Newspaper and paper towels**
- **Nontoxic papier-mâché paste**
- **Acrylic paints and a variety of brushes**
- **Scissors and white glue**
- **Found material for decorations such as yarn and foil**

The mask shown in **Figure 10.29** represents the chief of the undersea world, K'umugwe' (Komokwa). The copper teeth, eyes, and eyebrows on this mask are indications of great wealth. This creature, whose dance is part of the Red Cedar Bark dance series, is a monster who causes trouble in the waters. He can stop rivers, create great waves on bodies of water, and swallow or overturn canoes. This mask was designed to be viewed on the head of a costumed figure dancing around a flickering firelight. The movements used in the dance of the K'umugwe' imitate those of a sea mammal in water, including surfacing to breathe. Notice how the wood has been carved into high relief. This is done so that the viewer will see changing shadows alternating with bright light.

Just as the K'umugwe' was used to explain things that happened in the water, you will create a myth that explains something about modern technology. Each member of the team will be an actor in the drama. Each will design and create a high-relief papier-mâché mask using distortion and exaggeration to make the mask expressive. Choose a color scheme that matches the character of the mask. Paint and decorate the mask.

What You Will Learn

Brainstorm with your classmates to list mysteries of modern technology. Make a list of possible themes that could be explained in a storytelling dance drama.

Divide into work teams for a planning conference. Have one group member keep notes from the conference.

Curriculum Connection

Language Arts Poetry expresses emotional, aesthetic, and self-fulfilling needs. Have students choose one poem by an American and one by a poet of another culture. Have them analyze the emotions expressed in the poems' words and symbols. "Lost" by Carl Sandburg is a good example.

Have students express themselves by writing a short poem. Encourage them to use any of the following poet's tools: imagery, simile, metaphor, personification, onomatopoeia, alliteration, rhyme, symbols, rhythm, or free verse.

Select a specific theme or topic. Choose music. Name and define the character of each participant. Write the story. Decide how you will communicate with the audience. Will you all speak lines, will a narrator tell the story, or will you act it out in pantomime? List the props and setting you will need. Plan body movements to match the music.

Creating

Draw several ideas for your mask. Plan the side view as well as the front view. Use exaggeration and distortion to create the mood you wish your character to express.

Meet with the team to make final decisions about the masks. At this time decide on colors and the extra materials you will need for decorations. Decide if you need costumes.

Step 1 Draw the final plan for your mask in your sketchbook. List the colors and special decorations you plan to add. Collect the extra materials such as yarn, costume jewelry, and fabrics.

Step 2 Construct your mask. See the different directions for papier-mâché construction in Technique Tip 19 on page 435 in the Handbook. Use high relief. Make some ridges rise 2 inches from the surface of the mask. Plan how you will hold the mask on your head. You must be able to see through it when you are wearing it. The holes for your eyes do not have to be the eyes of the mask.

Step 3 When the papier-mâché is dry, paint your mask with acrylic paints. Glue on the additional decorations.

Step 4 Rehearse with your group using all the props you will need for the performance, including special lighting. Perform your dance drama for the class.

EVALUATING YOUR WORK

▶ **DESCRIBE** Explain the theme and story of your dance drama. Describe the music you used and explain why you chose it. List and explain all the characters in your drama. Describe your mask.

▶ **ANALYZE** Did you use high relief? Explain the shadows and highlights that resulted. Explain your color scheme. Which parts of the mask did you exaggerate and distort? Did the body movements you used match the character of the mask and the music?

▶ **INTERPRET** What was the message of your production? Did the audience understand the message?

▶ **JUDGE** Which aesthetic theories would you use to judge the entire production? Are they different from the theories you would use to judge the mask? Why?

▲ **FIGURE 10.29A** Student work.

STUDIO PROJECT *Papier Mâché Mask* **277**

Developing Studio Skills

Suggest that various media might be applied to the surface of the mask including copper, wire, aluminum foil, metallic and neon paint, window screen nails and screws, sequins, glitter, costume jewelry, and small mirrors.

Developing Studio Skills

To help students be successful with this activity, suggest the following:

- An alternative medium is plaster of paris gauze. Cut the gauze into small strips, dip in water, and apply to a mold.
- A hot glue gun is necessary when attaching various media to the outside of the mask.
- Attach a wooden dowel to the bottom of the mask to serve as a handle. A string attached to the back of the mask might work, but may be uncomfortable.

ASSESS..........
Keeping a Portfolio

Remind students that the preliminary sketches and the final artwork for this Studio Project are likely candidates for their portfolios.

Enrichment

Students may want to combine their group's performances into a school production. A narrator could introduce and explain each dance drama.

Self-Assessment

Have students apply the steps of art criticism to their own artwork using the "Evaluating Your Work" questions on this page.

CLOSE...........

Have the groups write an assessment of their performances.

Soft Sculpture

Soft Sculpture

(National Standards: 1a, 1b, 2b, 2c, 3b)

FOCUS...........
Objective

After completing this project, students will be able to:

■ Design and construct a soft sculpture symbolizing a person from history, art history, literature, or current events.

TEACH..........
Motivator

The text says that Faith Ringgold blended her African heritage, her Europeanized education, and her African-American culture to create her art. Discuss the blending of various cultures and how it influences who we are. Ask students to think about and discuss how their backgrounds and heritage have influenced their lives.

Art History

Tell students that Faith Ringgold is a link between the women in her family. She connects the craftswomen and storytellers of the past with her daughters, Michelle and Barbara, and the grandchildren who follow in her creative footsteps. Michelle writes fiction and teaches African-American literature, women's studies, and creative writing at the University of Oklahoma. Barbara, a mother of three, is a third grade teacher in Harlem, working toward a doctorate degree focusing on linguistic characteristics of African-American women who were raised in Harlem.

▲ FIGURE 10.30

Faith Ringgold. *Mrs. Jones and Family*. 1973. Mixed media. Mrs. Jones: 152 × 30 × 41 cm (60 × 12 × 16"). Andrew: 122 × 30 × 30 cm (48 × 12 × 12"). Barbara: 58 × 16 × 28 cm (23 × 6½ × 11"). Faye: 63 × 14 × 30 cm (25 × 5½ × 12"). Faith Ringgold, Inc.

SUPPLIES

■ **Sketchbook and pencil**
■ **Paper for patterns**
■ **Scissors and pins**
■ **Sewing and embroidery threads**
■ **Variety of sewing needles**
■ **Assorted fabrics**
■ **Stuffing material such as fiberfill**
■ **Yarns and other trims**
■ **Sewing machine (optional)**

278 | **CHAPTER 10** Proportion

Faith Ringgold, an African-American artist, is a painter and soft sculptor as well as a performance artist. *Mrs. Jones and Family* **(Figure 10.30)** represents Ringgold's family. Mrs. Jones is her mother, and Andrew is her father.

Ringgold started as a traditional painter. Her education, like that of any other art student in the 1950s, was in the European tradition. In the late 1960s, during a period when she was incorporating African designs and motifs into her painted canvases, Ringgold began to experiment first with masks and later with soft sculpture. These media enabled her to work in the center of her family. The interaction of the people in her family nourished her spirit. Notice in the sculpture *Mrs. Jones and Family* that all the dolls have their mouths open. They are all talking at once!

Look closely at the figures in Ringgold's work to see how she used media, distortion, and exaggeration to create her sculpture. Think about the techniques you can use to create yours.

What You Will Learn

Design and construct a soft sculpture symbolizing a person from history, art history, literature, or current events. Ringgold made the faces large according to African traditions. She made all the mouths open to indicate that her family is very talkative. Use distortion and exaggeration to emphasize the most important attributes of the person you have chosen. Select colors and fabrics to fit the personality of your sculpture, and add details using stitchery and/or appliqué.

TEACHER TALK 📖

Classroom Management Encourage local craftspeople to demonstrate and display their work. Invite a craftsperson to visit the class or arrange to take the class on a field trip to a craftsperson's studio. Help students prepare by learning about the person, the craft he or she practices, and the specific works he or she has created. If possible, have students try to create an artwork with the techniques or tools of the craftsperson. Even though your students may not be proficient at the craft, they will be in a better position to ask meaningful questions.

Creating

Brainstorm with classmates about subjects to consider for your soft sculpture. Select the person you will symbolize. Do some research about this person. Make visual and written notes in your sketchbook. What is your person famous for? What kind of clothing is appropriate? Which features will you exaggerate? For example, if you are doing a track star, you may make the feet oversized; if you are representing a rock star, you may wish to exaggerate the mouth.

Step 1 Draw a plan for constructing your sculpture in your sketchbook. Draw your sculpture from the front, back, and sides. On a sheet of paper, make a pattern for cutting the body fabric. Cut out fabric and pin the pieces, right sides together. Sew the body together on the inside, leaving a small opening. Then turn it inside out and stuff it. You may shape a three-dimensional face, or you may use stitches and appliqué as Ringgold did. Use yarn or other material to make hair. Make clothes to fit your sculpture, or use doll clothes. Add details with stitchery. See Technique Tip 22 on page 437 of the Handbook.

Step 2 Arrange your soft sculpture for display. You may add props and a setting if desired. Write a few paragraphs about your sculpture and include it in your display.

EVALUATING YOUR WORK

▶ **DESCRIBE** Name the subject of your soft sculpture and explain why you selected that person. Describe the procedures you followed to construct this sculpture. List the attributes of your subject that you chose to emphasize and explain why.

▶ **ANALYZE** Explain how, where, and why you used distortion and exaggeration. Which colors did you select for your sculpture?

▶ **INTERPRET** What kind of a mood does your sculpture express? Give it a title that symbolizes the character of your subject. Do not use the subject's name.

▶ **JUDGE** Which aesthetic theories would you use to judge this work? If you were to do it over, what would you change?

▲ **FIGURE 10.30A** Student work.

ASSESS..........
Keeping a Portfolio
Remind students that the preliminary sketches and the final artwork for this Studio Project are likely candidates for their portfolios.

Self-Assessment
Have students apply the steps of art criticism to their own artwork using the "Evaluating Your Work" questions on this page. In addition, ask the following: What processes were used to create the work? How is exaggeration and distortion used to emphasize the most important aspects of the person? What type of materials were used to create the sculpture?

Enrichment
Encourage students to design a stage for their artworks, then write a script for a puppet performance of the soft sculptures. Performances could be held in class.

CLOSE.............
Allow time for each student to describe the person who was the inspiration for his or her sculpture.

MORE ABOUT... Faith Ringgold

When asked about her different media, Faith explained that they all grew out of each other. They overlap, and she moves through the media backward and forward. Before 1970 she just painted on canvas in oils. The first dolls she created were for a lecture. At that time, she painted gourds for heads. Later, coconuts took the place of gourds. Next she made soft, realistic faces using foam rubber features that represented famous people, such as her *Martin Luther King* life-size portrait mask. The soft masks evolved into soft sculptures. Faith believes that the soft sculptures were really the people coming out of her paintings, and then as the quilts evolved, the dolls went back into the quilts.

TECHNOLOGY
Studio Project

Hybrid Creature

(National Standards: 1a, 1b, 2b, 2c, 3b)
[Figure 10.31]

FOCUS............
Objectives

After completing this lesson, students will be able to:

- Use a computer paint program to construct an imaginary creature using distortion, exaggeration, and illogical combinations of body parts from several animals.

- Use a computer paint program to construct an illogical setting with contrasting colors for the imaginary creature.

Supplies

- Sketchbook
- Computer
- Paint or Draw application
- Printer

Optional

- Scanner or digital camera, Clip Art,

TEACH..........
Motivator

Conduct a brainstorming session with the class. Generate a list of animals—large and small, meek and ferocious, wild and domestic. Try to get as many as you can. The list exchange features next to the brainstorming list. The exchange features would include: head, neck, legs, wings, tail, ears, texture or animal skin. Think of others to add. As a group, construct an imaginary creature by combining assorted features. What is the creature's name? Where does it exist? Introduce the vocabulary words.

Hybrid Creature

▲ **FIGURE 10.31**

Salvador Dali. *The Elephants (Design for the Opera La Dama Spagnola e il Cavaliere Romano)*. 1961. Pencil, watercolor, gouache. 69.9 × 69.9 cm (27½ × 27½"). Indianapolis Museum of Art, Indianapolis, Indiana. Gift of Mr. and Mrs. Lorenzo Alvary, photograph ©1987 Indianapolis Museum of Art.

SUPPLIES

- **Sketchbook**
- **Computer**
- **Paint or Draw application**
- **Printer**
- *Optional*
- **Scanner or digital camera**

Salvador Dali was a Spanish Surrealist painter and printmaker. Surrealist artists and writers emphasized the role of the subconscious or dreamlike state in their art. Dali's works depict dreamlike images that are painted in a very precise, realistic manner. Commonplace objects, people, and animals are distorted and often changed into bizarre and irrational creations. He placed unrelated objects together in strange, barren landscapes.

In *The Elephants* **(Figure 10.31),** Dali has rendered the bodies of the elephants in a realistic manner and then placed them on thin, birdlike legs with bird claws for feet. You will see that the giraffe is not distorted but some of the trees in the distance seem to be levitating. Also, notice the red curtain in the right corner. It does not seem to belong in this landscape.

What You Will Learn

You will create an imaginary creature using distortion, exaggeration, and illogical combinations of body parts from several animals. After completing the new creature, you will place it in an equally illogical setting using colors that contrast with the creature. Print your final work.

Creating

Begin with a favorite animal. Make several sketches of possible combinations that exchange features such as the head, neck, legs, wings, tail, ears, texture, or animal skin with other animals. Remember that your creature can be based on scientific fact, fiction, or fantasy. Like Dali's *The Elephants,* some-

TECHNOLOGY OPTIONS

Scanning Tell students to scan photographs of animals that they have taken or drawings of animals that they have done and save them in a folder. Using the computer paint program have them select parts from each of the files, lasso them, and paste them to a new page. Tell students they are basically creating their own clip art file of animal parts from their own photographs and drawings. Have them try creating an imaginary animal using a combination of photograph parts and drawn parts.

times pairing the most dissimilar features helps to exaggerate and emphasize an idea or tone. However, different moods from magical to ferocious can be achieved by using unique combinations. Choose the idea and mood you find most appealing.

Step 1 Use your choice of art applications and tools to draw your imaginary creature. If you use photographs or scanned images, make significant changes to include your own drawing and alterations. Choose from the Selection tools to move, delete, or add features. Use the Copy and Paste commands to arrange duplicate parts. While a body part is selected, explore how you might stretch, shrink, or distort proportions. Be adventurous.

Step 2 Use tools, such as Zoom In, or menus to smooth lines, match colors, and clean up leftover pixels. Retitle and save frequently as you work. This records the history of your production so you can return to an earlier point and try another solution.

Step 3 Consider adding duplicates of the creature on the page. While the image is selected, you can arrange it. Try overlapping or choose options to Flip, Rotate, and change sizes or Scale. Consider colors or surface textures to enhance the new creature. These may include scanned textures, menu choices, or invented textures. Apply with a Brush, Bucket, or Selection tool.

Step 4 Select from the tools to add an illogical background with contrasting colors. When you are satisfied, print, view, and make any changes. Display your final copy. Include the source of any photographs or scanned images.

EVALUATING YOUR WORK

▶ **DESCRIBE** What parts have you used to create your imaginary creature? Identify the features you have distorted and exaggerated. Describe the things you have added to create an illogical background. List, in order, the specific software, tools, and menus you used. Name any sources you have used.

▶ **ANALYZE** Explain how you used distortion and exaggeration to create your creature. Describe the colors and textures you used for the creature and the background.

▶ **INTERPRET** Describe the mood, theme, or idea you have created. Explain how combining various body parts, changing proportion, and applying color and texture affect the mood of your work. Give your work a descriptive title that sums up your feelings about it.

▶ **JUDGE** Have you successfully combined, distorted, and exaggerated the features of your animal to emphasize an idea or mood? Is there anything you would change? What aesthetic theory would you use to judge this artwork?

▲ **FIGURE 10.31A** Student work.

Cross-Curriculum: English

Write a short, descriptive story about your new hybrid creature to accompany the artwork. Explain the significance and purpose of the features you have chosen to explain.

ASSESS..........
Portfolio

Remind students that the final artwork for this Studio Lesson is a likely candidate for their portfolio.

Self Assessment

Have students apply the steps of art criticism to their own artwork.

Enrichment

Have the students take their completed image and import different textures for the shapes. Have them give their new version a different title and save it. Then have the students print out copies of both versions and write a brief critique of what they think the strengths and weaknesses are of both versions. Remind the students to put copies of the images and their summary critique in their portfolio.

CLOSE............

Ask students to explain how the use of distortion and exaggeration can affect an artwork.

Curriculum Connection

History The Surrealism movement, which flourished in Europe between World War I and World War II, represented a reaction against what its members saw as the destruction wrought by the "rationalism" that had guided European culture and politics in the past, including the horrors of World War I. Conduct an Internet search using at least three different search engines to find out more about Surrealism. List the web pages where you find your information and the date you visited site. Share your findings with the class.

(National Standards: 2b, 4c, 5a, 5c)

Critiquing the Work

▶ Describe
What do you see?

Ask students to notice unusual combination of media. First Bishop laid down an undercoat of tempera. We see the white horizontal lines of tempera peeking through the oils because she used thin, translucent glazes of oil over the tempera.

■ The painting shows a seated woman and a child who was sitting next to her but has fallen over onto her lap. The woman is sitting straight even though her arms look relaxed. The woman has a plain face, and her hair looks brunette with blond highlights. She is wearing a dress with green, flaring, pleated sleeves. The child seems to be wearing a dress. The woman's body looks solid and muscular. The child looks healthy.

■ They are sitting on a plain wooden bench. The rest of the scene is vague and fuzzy

▶ Analyze
How is this work organized?

Point out how the artist has created the illusion of form. The figures look very solid, even thought the paint style is light and airy. Also note how color affects the mood of the work. All the colors are low intensity, dull colors.

■ The proportions of the figures are accurate.

■ The bench on which they are sitting shows that they are in scale to the environment.

▲ **FIGURE 10.32**

Isabel Bishop. *Waiting.* 1938. Oil and tempera on gesso panel. 73.6 × 56.5 cm (29 × 22¼"). Collection of the Newark Museum, Newark, New Jersey. Purchase, 1944. Arthur F. Egner Memorial Fund.

MORE ABOUT... Isabel Bishop

Isabelle Bishop (1902–1988) was the youngest of five children. She began her art studies at an art school in Detroit, but when she graduated from high school in 1918, she moved to New York to study commercial illustration at the New York School of Applied Design for Women. The artistic life style in New York pulled at her. She decided to become a painter.

The subjects of her paintings were the working girls she saw in the trains, and from her studio apartment window in Manhattan. Her concern was composition; the subjects were a means to attack the abstract problem of time and space. She tried to express the possibility of momentary change. To her, the working girls did not belong to a specific class. They could move in any direction at any moment.

1 DESCRIBE What do you see?

List all of the information found in the credit line. Next, make a list of all of the objects in the work. Remember not to make guesses.

- Describe the people and their clothing.
- Describe the setting.

2 ANALYZE How is this work organized?

During this step, you will discover clues that will help you find the message the artist is trying to send.

- What unusual rhythms has the artist created using line?
- Are the proportions of the figures accurate? Are the proportions of the woman the same as those of the child?
- Is there anything in the work to indicate scale?

3 INTERPRET What is the artist trying to communicate?

During this step, you will express your ideas about the work and decipher the message the artist is sending.

- What is the relationship between these two people? What do you think are they waiting for?
- How has the artist's style affected the mood of the work?
- Create a new title that sums up your interpretation of the work.

4 JUDGE What do you think of the work?

Now it is time to make a decision about the quality of this work. You may make a personal opinion, but it is also important to make an objective judgment based on aesthetic theories.

- Do you think this is a successful work of art? Use one or more of the aesthetic theories explained in Chapter 2 to defend your decision.

MEET THE ARTIST

ISABEL BISHOP

American, 1902–1988

Isabel Bishop. *Self-Portrait.* 1927. Oil on canvas. 36 × 33 cm (14⅛ × 13"). Wichita Art Museum, Wichita, Kansas. Gift of the Friends of the Wichita Art Museum, Inc.

In 1920, with financial support from an inheritance, Isabel Bishop enrolled at the Art Students' League in New York City. She made the daily trip to Grand Central Station by train and then transferred to the subway, which took her to the studio. During the trips she sketched.

The subjects of her paintings were the working women she saw on the trains and from her studio window. She tried to express the possibility of momentary change. To her, the young women did not belong to a specific class.

➤ Interpretation

What is the artist trying to communicate?

- Answers will vary. Some will notice the clothing is old fashioned. Probably from the forties. The woman's hairdo is definitely WWII style. The child's shoes are also old fashioned. Most will see a close relationship because of the pose, probably mother and child. The stern look on the woman's face may lead others to guess otherwise, as if the woman found this whole task annoying. The bench tells us they are in a public waiting room. They may be waiting to go somewhere, or waiting for someone to arrive. Possibly a father coming home from war. Many different moods can be read into the facial expression of the woman, but her body language is calm and at rest.
- Answers will vary. Some may say that the hazy style of the work creates a sense of a place out of time. The solid triangular shape the figures create gives a sense of strength. They seem isolated from the rest of the people around them. Are they alone? Will the waiting be over soon?
- Answers will vary.

➤ Judge

What do you think of the work?

- Answers will vary. Most will choose emotionalism because of the mood of the work. Some may include realism, since everything is accurate, even though it is vague. Some may choose composition because the figures create a strong, solid based triangle with their bodies.

Time & Place Early Twentieth Century

Isabel Bishop painted *Waiting* in 1938. Some other events that occurred that same year:

Art: In June *Action Comics* No. 1 introduces Superman, the amazing super-power hero, created by Jerry Siegel and Joe Shuster.

Music: American jazz musician Benny Goodman and his orchestra hold the first swing concert in Carnegie Hall, New York City.

Technology: The largest airship, *The Graf Zeppelin,* was built.

Proportion and Scale

Proportion and Scale

(National Standards: 6a, 6b)

Objectives

After completing this feature, students will be able to:

- Determine the approximate proportions of different body parts of the original statue of Constantine the Great.
- Discuss mathematical methods for calculating proportion and scale.

Teaching the Connections

Have students read the feature on this page. Remind students that ratios are also expressed as fractions, such as: a/b. Ask students to imagine how they use proportion to create smaller rather than larger figures. For example, how would they use math to determine the proportions of a statue of a standing human that was only two foot high? (To create a two-feet tall human figure to scale, students would need first to use the scale provided in figure 10.12 to determine the ratios for each section or part, then divide the length of the smaller figure by the second part of the ratio. For example, the ratio of head to total body length is about 1:7.5.)

Tell students that the head, arms, hands, legs, and feet of the original statue were marble. The drapery of the emperor's clothing was probably made out of bronze plates over a brick or stone frame. The head and neck of the statue's remains are realistically modeled, but the eyes appear too large. Exaggerated eyes are common in the art of the early Christian period.

▲ **FIGURE 10.33**

Colossal Head, Constantine the Great. Fourth century. Marble. Head about 8¼′ (2.5 m) high; original seated figure 30′ (9.2 m) high. Palace of the Conservatory, Rome, Italy.

Suppose you wanted to reconstruct the colossal monument of *Constantine the Great*. How would you determine how to accurately re-create his larger-than-life proportions? In art, proportion has to do with the relationship of the size of one part to another. In mathematics, this relationship (proportion) is described in ratios. For example, 4:2 = 6:3 because 4 is twice the amount of 2, just as 6 is twice the amount of 3. This is determined by dividing 4 by 2 and 6 by 3.

Scale refers to size as measured against a standard reference. You have probably seen a scale used on a map. If 1 inch on the scale equals 10 miles, and the distance between two cities is 3 inches, you can multiply to determine that the actual distance is 30 miles. Artists can use scale to create figures with proportions that are larger or smaller than real-life people. If we know the standard height of the average human is 5 feet 6 inches, then we can either multiply the measurements for a larger-than-life artwork or divide them for a smaller depiction.

Making the Connection

1. Using the scale provided in Figure 10.5 on page 257, compute the approximate size of the hands, torso, and shins of the original statue of *Constantine the Great*.
2. Using Euclid's Golden Mean, on page 256, compute the length of the top portion of the body (head to navel) as well as the length of the lower portion (navel to feet). Then calculate approximately how high this statue would be if the figure of Constantine were standing.
3. What other mathematical processes do you think the original creator(s) of *Constantine the Great* used in building this monument?

Answers to Making the Connection

1. The approximate measurements of the statue are: hands = 4 feet 1 inch each; torso = 16 feet; shins = 12 feet 5 inches each.
2. The top half of the statue would be about 33 feet long. Multiplying this measurement by 1.6 results in 52.8 feet for the length of the lower portion of the body. The statue, if standing, would reach nearly 86 feet.
3. Answers may vary.

Building Vocabulary

On a separate sheet of paper, write the term or terms that best matches each definition given below.

1. The principle of art concerned with the size relationship of one part to another.
2. A line divided into two parts so that the smaller line has the same proportion, or ratio, to the larger line as the larger line has to the whole line.
3. Size as measured against a standard reference.
4. Figures arranged in a work of art so that scale indicates importance.
5. To shorten an object to make it look as if it extends backward into space.
6. Deviations from expected, normal proportions.

Reviewing Art Facts

Answer the following questions using complete sentences.

1. What is the Golden Mean ratio?
2. Explain the difference between scale and proportion.
3. What was the name for the geometric form that had sides matching the ratio of the Golden Mean?
4. What are the two kinds of scale in art?
5. What unit is usually used to define the proportions of any individual figure?

Thinking Critically About Art

1. **Extend.** Do some library research to determine how hierarchical proportions have been used in the art of different cultures. Photocopy examples to show and report your findings to the class.
2. **Compare and contrast.** Siqueiros's painting, *Self-Portrait* (Figure 10.14, page 264) uses a distortion called foreshortening to create a symbolic proportion. The Oba figure (Figure 10.10, page 262) also uses symbolic proportion. Compare the two works. List the similarities and differences. Explain what the distortion conveys in each artwork.
3. **Analyze.** Study the illustration of the Golden Rectangle in Figure 10.3, page 256. Look through this book to find works of art that have been organized using those proportions. Choose at least one to diagram.

Use the Performing Arts Handbook on page 422 to discover how Eugene Friesen explores the elements of exaggeration and distortion of human proportions through the use of masks in his performance of **Cello Man**.

Discover how artists use the elements of art to create different kinds of proportion in their works by visiting the Glencoe Fine Arts Site at **www.glencoe.com/sec/art**. You can also explore the Glencoe *Student Galleria* to see how other students have used proportion and distortion in their two- and three-dimensional art.

Answers To Building Vocabulary

1. proportion
2. Golden Mean
3. scale
4. hierarchical proportion
5. foreshortening
5. distortion or exaggeration

Answers To Reviewing Art Facts

1. 1 to 1.6 (or 1:1.6).
2. Proportion is the relationship of one part to another; scale refers to size as measured against a standard reference.
3. Golden Rectangle.
4. The scale of the work itself and the scale of objects or elements within the design.
5. Length of the head from the chin to the top of the skull.

Reteaching

- Have students complete Concept Map 10 in the Reteaching booklet.
- Look through the illustrations in the other chapters of *ArtTalk* to find and list reproductions of paintings and sculptures that fit the following categories: 1) works showing realistic, accurate use of proportion; 2) works in which human proportions are exaggerated or distorted to create special effects.

CLOSE

Have each student select one work from each of the categories above. Ask them to write a brief statement to explain how the artist has used proportion or scale to enhance the meaning of the work.

ASSESSMENT ✓

Evaluate

- Have students complete the *Chapter 10 Test* in the TCR.
- Alternative Assessment teaching strategies are provided in the *Testing Program and Alternative Assessment* booklet.

Alternative Assessment

Instruct students to create two self-portraits in a medium of their choice. In the first work they will use accurate proportions; in the second, they will use exaggeration and distortion. When the artworks are completed, have students explain how the altered proportions affect the expressive quality of the second portrait.

Variety, Emphasis, Harmony, and Unity

(pages 286–315)

▲ **FIGURE 11.1** This building was designed to look like a ship with its sails full in the wind. It sits on Bennelong Point which is named after the first Aborigine born on the site who learned to speak English.

Joern Utzon. Sydney Opera House, Australia. 1959–72. Reinforced concrete. Height of highest shell: 5.1 m (200″).

FEATURED ARTISTS

Marie Bashkirtseff
Florence Bayless
Cecilia Beaux
Emily Carr
Lois Dvorak
Allan Houser
Georgia Mills Jessup

Jasper Johns
Lee Krasner
Berthe Morisot
Alice Neel
Louise Nevelson
Claes Oldenburg
Irene Rice Pereira
Robert Rauschenberg
Rembrandt van Rijn

Auguste Rodin
Henri Rousseau
Peter Paul Rubens
Sean Scully
Joern Utzon
Vincent van Gogh
Jane Wilson
Frank Lloyd Wright
John Yancy

CHAPTER 11

Variety, Emphasis, Harmony, and Unity

The principles of art help artists organize artworks. They use these principles to express their feelings and ideas. You have already learned about the principles of rhythm, balance, and proportion. In this chapter you will learn about three additional principles: *variety, emphasis,* and *harmony.* Finally, you will learn about the most important principle, *unity.* Unity occurs when all the elements and principles of art work together. A unified work is the goal of every artist.

The Sydney Opera House **(Figure 11.1)** is unified with its setting. It looks like it belongs in the harbor because the shells that make up its walls and roof look like the sails of a clipper ship, which you would expect to see in a harbor. Although it is called an "Opera House," the term does not describe the full purpose of the building. It is really a performance arts complex that houses 1,000 rooms including a concert hall, an opera theater, a drama theater, and a playhouse. It also includes a reception hall and four restaurants.

Developing Your
PORTFOLIO

Artists usually want their artworks to appear as if everything is in the right place. Sometimes they will deliberately place something unusual or unexpected in an artwork in order to make a statement. Look through magazines and find several pictures or advertisements that show an object that seems to be out of place. Write a sentence or two ~~ose to make a statement,~~ ~~gazine pictures and your~~

OBJECTIVES

After completing this chapter, you will be able to:

- Identify and describe variety, emphasis, harmony, and unity in your environment and in a work of art.
- Understand how artists use variety and emphasis to express their ideas and feelings.
- Understand how artists use the elements and principles of art to create unified works of art.
- Use variety, emphasis, and harmony to create your own unified works of art.

WORDS TO KNOW

variety
emphasis
focal point
harmony
unity

287

Chapter Overview

In Chapter 11 students learn that unity is the ultimate principle of art and that when all of the elements and principles work properly, the result is a unified work of art. Artists achieve the expressive qualities of unity through harmony, simplicity, proximity, repetition, and continuation.

Examining the Artwork

Direct students' attention to Figure 11.1. Tell them this building was planned as a symbol of the port city of Sydney, Australia. The effect of a clipper ship at full sail is created with three sets of pointed shells, each set facing a different direction. This transforms the entire building into a giant sculpture, where the walls and roof are unified. The repetition of the shell forms creates harmony. The different directions add variety.

Tell students that the building took over fourteen years to construct. The original design by the Danish architect Joern Utzon was beautiful, but so daring that technology had to be invented as the project went along.

 While studying this chapter, use Performing Arts Handbook page 423 to hear how musicians use harmony and unity.

National Standards

This chapter addresses the following National Standards for the Visual Arts:

1. (a, b)	**4.** (c)
2. (b, c)	**5.** (a, c)
3. (b)	**6.** (a, b)

DEVELOPING A PORTFOLIO

Assessment A successful portfolio requires attention to organization. One that is carelessly put together reflects poorly on students, therefore encourage them to stay focused on their goals and objectives. Assessment will include an evaluation across time, materials, and artistic contents. Importantly, it will demonstrate that students take their work seriously. Remind them to give deliberate consideration to each piece of art they include, as well as to the relative merit of each piece in context with the entire portfolio. With ample assignments and opportunities to undertake projects on their own, portfolio pieces can be selected from a larger pool of works, allowing for greater variety.

Variety, Emphasis, and Harmony

FOCUS...........
Objectives

After completing this lesson, students will be able to:

■ Identify and describe variety, emphasis and harmony in works of art.

■ Explain how artists use variety and emphasis in their artworks.

■ Use variety, emphasis, and harmony to create their own unified works of art.

Supplies

■ Book of typefaces
■ Magazines
■ Paper and scissors
■ Variety of media
■ Found objects

Resources

📁 Artist's Profile 12, *Rembrandt*

📁 Artist's Profile 8, *Peter Paul Rubens*

📁 Artist's Profile 28, *Vincent van Gogh*

📁 Enrichment Activity 21, *Creating Emphasis with Chiaroscuro*

📁 Enrichment Activity 22, *Contemporary Totem*

📁 *National Gallery of Art Bar Code Correlation Guide*

Variety, Emphasis, and Harmony

Variety is a principle of art that adds interest to an artwork. Emphasis is a principle of art that enhances variety because it creates areas that draw your attention. The eye-catching, or dominant, area is usually a focal point that first attracts the attention of the viewer. The viewer then looks at the less dominant, or subordinate, areas. Harmony makes variety and emphasis work together in a piece of art. Variety and harmony complement one another in the same way that positive and negative spaces complement each other. Variety adds interest to an artwork while harmony prevents variety from causing chaos.

Variety

People need variety in all areas of their lives. Imagine how boring it would be if daily routines were exactly the same every day of the week for a whole year. Imagine how visually boring the world would be if everything in it—everything—were the same color.

People put a great deal of time and effort into creating variety in their environment. They may buy new furniture or paint the walls, not because the furniture is old or the paint is peeling, but simply because they need a change. They add variety to other aspects of their lives as well. New clothes, new foods, new friends—people make endless changes to relieve the sameness or boredom in life.

Just as people must add variety to their lives to keep it interesting, so must artists add variety to their works. **Variety** is *the principle of art concerned with difference or contrast.*

◄ **FIGURE 11.2** The artist has used only one shape (an equilateral triangle) and two colors to create this print. How has he used variety to change two elements of art into an interesting design that has the illusion of three dimensions?

Miroslav Sutej. *Ultra AB.* 1966. Color silkscreen. 49.2 × 45 cm (19⅜ × 17¾"). Library of Congress, Washington, D.C. Pennell Fund, 1970.

288 | **CHAPTER 11** Variety, Emphasis, Harmony, and Unity

TECHNOLOGY OPTIONS

National Gallery of Art Videodisc Use the following to show examples of variety, emphasis, harmony, and unity in art.

Henri Matisse	Auguste Renoir	Claude Monet
Large Composition with Masks	*Young Spanish Woman with a Guitar*	*The Artist's Garden at Vétheuil*
Search Frame 2213	Search Frame 1328	Search Frame 1388

Use Glencoe's *National Gallery of Art Correlation Bar Code Guide* to locate more artwork.

A work that is too much the same can become dull and monotonous. For example, a work composed of just one shape may be unified, but it will not hold your attention. Variety, or contrast, is achieved by adding something different to a design to provide a break in the repetition **(Figure 11.2)**. When different art elements are placed next to each other in a work of art, they are in contrast **(Figure 11.3)**. This type of contrast, or variety, adds interest to the work of art and gives it a lively quality.

Almost every artist uses contrasting elements to balance unifying elements. Wide, bold lines complement thin, delicate lines. Straight lines contrast with curves. Free-form shapes differ from geometric shapes. Rough textures add interest to a smooth surface. Colors can contrast in limitless ways. The degree of contrast may range from bold to subtle. The amount of difference between the elements depends on the artist's purpose.

Activity | Variety and Contrast

Applying Your Skills. Look through *ArtTalk* and find works of art that show bold contrast of line, shape, color, value, and texture. List one work for each kind of contrast. Explain how the contrast was created.

Computer Option. Make a simple design using five or six shapes. Overlap some shapes. Choose the Selection tool and Copy and Paste commands to make five copies of the design on the same page. Leave the original design unchanged but alter the rest to show a type of variety. Change color schemes, contrasts, and value as well as line thickness and textures. Use the Bucket fill or Selection tool to make changes quickly.

▲ **FIGURE 11.3** Which elements of art has Pereira used to create variety in this painting? Which element do you think shows the strongest contrast?

Irene Rice Pereira. *Untitled.* 1951. Oil on board. 101.6 × 61 cm (40 × 24″). The Solomon R. Guggenheim Museum, New York, New York. Gift, Jerome B. Lurie, 1981.

Emphasis

Have you ever underlined an important word or phrase several times in a letter? Have you ever raised the volume of your voice to make sure the person you were talking to understood a key point? These are just two ways that people use emphasis to focus attention on the main points in a message.

CHAPTER 11
LESSON 1

TEACH..........
Motivator

Ask students to discuss what they do to relieve boredom. Help them to see that they are introducing variety or contrast into an otherwise dull situation. Tell them that in this lesson they will learn how artists introduce variety, emphasis, and harmony into their art.

Activity

Variety and Contrast

Applying Your Skills. This activity requires perception of the bold contrast of the elements of art in this text.

💻 **Computer Option.** Create a simple design unit using several geometric shapes and lines. Save and title "Basic Unit." Now, explore ways the unit can be changed using color, line, and/or patterns to add emphasis, variety, and contrast. See *Computers in the Art Classroom.* 📁

LESSON 1 *Variety, Emphasis, and Harmony* | **289**

Developing Perceptual Skills

It is important that students see the difference between the dominance of one element, as in Figure 11.4, and the dominance of an area, or focal point, as in Figures 11.5, on this page, 11.7 on page 291, and 11.8 and 11.9 on page 292.

It is also important to point out that every work of art does not need to have one focal point. Some have several with different degrees of importance, as in Figure 11.26 on page 308, and some, as in 11.4 on page 290 and Figure 11.6 on page 291, have no focal point at all.

Art Criticism

Have students study Robert Rauschenberg's painting in Figure 11.4, which illustrates the principle of emphasis. Ask students to describe how the artist used the element of color to achieve emphasis. Which colors blend well with other colors in the work? What color schemes has he used? Which other elements besides color have been organized in the artwork?

Developing Perceptual Skills

Arrange a display of student works that are all the same size. Add interest to the display by varying the size of the negative areas. Ask groups of students to take turns rearranging the display to show different ways to create aesthetically pleasing results.

▶ **FIGURE 11.4** Many different values of red are present in this work. In this way, the artist has created variety and added interest to a painting that might otherwise be boring. Locate areas of the painting that use different values of red.

Robert Rauschenberg. *Red Painting.* 1953. Oil, cloth, and newsprint on canvas with wood. 200.6 × 84.1 cm (79 × 33⅛"). The Solomon R. Guggenheim Museum, New York, New York. Gift, Walter K. Gutman, 1963.

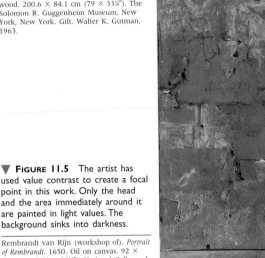

▼ **FIGURE 11.5** The artist has used value contrast to create a focal point in this work. Only the head and the area immediately around it are painted in light values. The background sinks into darkness.

Rembrandt van Rijn (workshop of). *Portrait of Rembrandt.* 1650. Oil on canvas. 92 × 75.5 cm (36¼ × 29¾"). National Gallery of Art, Washington, D.C. © 1998 Board of Trustees. Widener Collection.

In advertisements, music, news stories, your lessons at school, and your day-to-day communications, you see and hear certain ideas and feelings being emphasized over others.

Emphasis is *the principle of art that makes one part of a work dominant over the other parts.* Artists use emphasis to unify a work of art. Emphasis controls the sequence in which the parts are noticed. It also controls the amount of attention a viewer gives to each part.

There are two major types of visual emphasis. In one type, an *element of art* dominates the entire work. In the other type of emphasis, an *area* of the work is dominant over all the other areas.

Emphasizing an Element

If the artist chooses to emphasize one element, all the other elements of the work are made *subordinate,* or less important. The *dominant,* or most important, element affects the viewer's perception of the total work. This element also affects the way in which all the separate items and elements in the work are perceived.

Sometimes the dominant element is so strong that the whole work seems to be drenched in that element. Rauschenberg's *Red Painting* **(Figure 11.4)** is saturated with the color red. Even though he has used a variety of textures to create different areas, the redness takes on a meaning all its own. It affects the viewer's perception of the painting as a whole. It also affects the viewer's perception of the separate parts of the work.

Emphasizing an Area

Sometimes a specific area in a work of art is emphasized. This area, called the **focal point,** is *the first part of a work to attract the attention of the viewer.* The other areas are subordinate to the focal point. Rembrandt used value like a spotlight to emphasize one important area—a focal point—in his paintings **(Figure 11.5).**

It is possible for a work of art to have

290 | **CHAPTER 11** Variety, Emphasis, Harmony, and Unity

▶ FIGURE 11.6 In this painting the artist used three different greens, three values of brown, and white to make a net of colors. She used thick and thin brushstrokes as well as curves, lines, and dots squeezed straight from the tube. No one color or line advances toward the viewer. All are equal in importance.

Lee Krasner. *The Springs*. 1964. Oil on canvas. 109.2 × 167.6 cm (43 × 66"). The National Museum of Women in the Arts, Washington, D.C. Gift of Wallace and Wilhelmina Holladay.

more than one focal point. Artists must be careful about this, however. Too many focal points cause the eye to jump around and will confuse the viewer. Artists must also determine the degree of emphasis needed to create a focal point. This usually depends on the purpose of the work.

Of course, a focal point is not necessary. Many artists don't create a focal point in their works **(Figure 11.6).** When artists do create focal points, they are usually careful not to over-emphasize it. They make certain that the focal point is unified with the rest of the design.

Artists use several techniques to create a focal point in a work of art. Following are some examples of these techniques.

Contrast. One way to create a focal point is to place an element that contrasts with the rest of the work in that area. One large shape, for example, will stand out among small ones. One angular, geometric shape will be noticed first among rounded, free-form shapes. A bright color will dominate low-intensity colors, while a light area will dominate a dark design **(Figure 11.7).** An object with a smooth texture becomes a focal point in a design filled with rough textures.

Aesthetics

Allow students to work in pairs or small groups to study Figure 11.5, on page 290, and respond to the following questions: Which elements are used to create emphasis in the painting? How does the artist achieve a sense of excitement through emphasis? What feeling(s) do you have when looking at the artwork? Ask students to read the size of the artwork in the credit line. Have them draw a square the same size on the board and try to sketch the portrait in the chalk frame. Ask: How does the size of Rembrandt's portrait affect the impact it has on viewers?

Sparking ▲▲▶
CREATIVITY

Want students to think creatively about variety? Suggest this: Look at the many typefaces available for graphic art today. Design an alphabet of your own, working toward repetition of design elements, balance, proportion, variety, emphasis, contrast, and harmony, all working toward unity. You could cut the letters directly from printed material or draw them. Try working on a theme to unify the design, perhaps a quality like bold, graceful, nervous, rigid, happy, or a central idea such as ecology, food, fitness, architecture, and so on. Arrange the letters of the alphabet on a background that will best accent them.

▶ FIGURE 11.7 Rubens has created contrast between the light, smooth skin of Daniel against the dark rocks and the rough fur of the lions. Daniel sits in a closed position while the lions growl and stretch in active poses.

Peter Paul Rubens. *Daniel in the Lions' Den.* c. 1615. Oil on linen. 224.3 × 330.4 cm (88¼ × 130⅛"). National Gallery of Art, Washington, D.C. © 1998 Board of Trustees. Ailsa Mellon Bruce Fund.

LESSON 1 *Variety, Emphasis, and Harmony* | **291**

Curriculum Connection

Humanities Emphasize the comparison in the text between Rauschenberg's use of simplicity and a writer's use of simple language and syntax to strip a work of literature down to its bare essentials. Have groups of students research the power of simplicity as a statement in other movements in twentieth-century art, literature, and music. One group might concentrate on the deceptively simple sentences in works by Ernest Hemingway (e.g., *The Old Man and the Sea*), another on the minimalist compositions of contemporary composer Philip Glass, still another on the minimalist paintings of Barnett Newman. Have groups note similarities in each of these approaches to artistic expression.

CHAPTER 11
LESSON 1

Art History

Alice Neel was not recognized by the art establishment until she was in her mid-seventies. She found the strength to keep going because she believed in her work. Never doubting the quality of her own work, she knew that she was doing the right thing by remaining true to her style. Time was on her side and she lived to enjoy acclaim and financial success.

Figure 11.8 is a departure from Neel's more common subject—people. She painted only people in whom she was interested. Her brush was not for hire. Most of her subjects did not buy the finished paintings because she revealed, in harsh terms, what the world had done to them. She called her works "paintings of people" and did not like them to be called portraits. She thought that portraits had to be flattering, and Alice Neel did not want to lie. She had to paint the scars left by the psychological and emotional battles her sitters had endured.

Art History

Tell students of the difficulty Berthe Morisot had in achieving recognition for her art in the nineteenth century. Then have students research whether the situation for women artists has improved much during the intervening century since Morisot's time. The resource *Making Their Mark: Women Artists Move into the Mainstream, 1970–1985* contains excellent material on this subject, including statistics that compare the funding and exhibition of works by male and female artists.

▲ **FIGURE 11.8** Neel has isolated the red chair to make it the focal point in this painting. How do the elements of color and line create the feeling of isolation?

Alice Neel. *Loneliness.* 1970. Oil on canvas. 203.2 × 96.5 cm (80 × 38"). National Gallery of Art, Washington, D.C. © 1998 Board of Trustees. Gift of Walter M. Bullowa, in honor of the 50th Anniversary of the National Gallery of Art.

▶ **FIGURE 11.9** The young woman appears to be in the center of this painting. If you measure, however, you will see that her head is to the left of the vertical axis and far above the horizontal axis. What devices has Morisot used to make the woman's face the center of interest?

Berthe Morisot. *In the Dining Room.* 1886. Oil on canvas. 61.3 × 50 cm (24⅛ × 19¾"). National Gallery of Art, Washington, D.C. © 1998 Board of Trustees. Chester Dale Collection.

Isolation. Artists sometimes use isolation to create a focal point and thereby emphasize one part of their work. They do this by putting one object alone, apart from all the other objects **(Figure 11.8)**. This draws the viewer's eye to the isolated object.

Location. Location is another method used to create a focal point for emphasis. A viewer's eye is normally drawn toward the center of a visual area. Thus, something near this center will probably be noticed first. Because the exact center is a predictable location, most artists place the objects they wish to emphasize a bit off center. They select a location a little to the left or right of center and a little above center **(Figure 11.9)**.

292   CHAPTER 11   Variety, Emphasis, Harmony, and Unity

292

MORE ABOUT... Berthe Morisot

Direct students' attention to Berthe Morisot's *In the Dining Room.* Berthe Morisot was a French Impressionist painter in the nineteenth century. In her time it was unusual for a woman to train as a painter. However, Berthe Morisot was the daughter of wealthy and prominent parents who astonished their society by encouraging their daughter's painting.

Dedicated to Impressionism, Morisot produced Impressionist still lifes, landscapes, and scenes of women in various settings. Morisot used loose, undisguised brushstrokes in her work and her models were primarily close family members and friends.

Convergence. When many elements in a work seem to point to one item, that item becomes the focal point. This technique, called convergence, can be created with a very obvious radial arrangement of lines. It can also be achieved through a more subtle arrangement of elements **(Figure 11.10)**.

Creating a Focal Point

Many lines lead your eyes toward the brightly-lit, yellow area of the café. Notice the ruts in the cobble stones, the edge of the awning, and the top of the blue door frame all point to the yellow area. How many more objects can you find that point to that area?

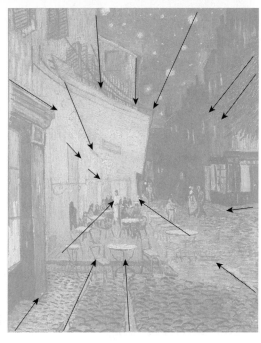

◄ **FIGURE 11.10**

Vincent van Gogh. *Café Terrace at Night.* 1888. Oil on canvas. 81 × 65.5 cm (31⅞ × 25¾"). Rijksmuseum Kroller-Muller, Otterlo, the Netherlands.

Looking Closely

Have students look at *Café Terrace at Night.* Ask if they think van Gogh captured a particular mood (*the excitement of a popular café at night*). How did he use color to emphasize the outdoor eating area? (*He used warm colors and light values to focus attention on the outdoor diners.*) What are the weather conditions? (*Judging by the reflections of the light on the cobblestone street, it had probably rained recently.*) Ask if van Gogh made this place look inviting.

Keeping a Sketchbook

Have students use the media of their choice to make a set of small designs showing strong focal point using one of the following elements: line, shape and form, space, color, value, and texture.

LESSON 1 *Variety, Emphasis, and Harmony* | **293**

MORE ABOUT... Vincent van Gogh

Vincent van Gogh was not content simply to capture a scene. Instead, he needed to express his deep feelings about it. These feelings come through in short brushstrokes of bright, intense color. An example of his unique style may be found in *Café Terrace at Night.* "Instead of trying to reproduce exactly what I have before my eyes," he wrote, "I use color more arbitrarily so as to express myself more forcibly."

Having created more than 1600 pieces of artwork, van Gogh sold only one painting during his entire lifetime. It was only after his death in 1890, that van Gogh became considered one of the most influential artists of modern times. Van Gogh's work had significant impact on Expressionism and Fauvism throughout much of the 20th century.

Using Emphasis

Applying Your Skills. Allow students to choose the medium they prefer if possible. Some students may wish to use paint, some a collage of magazine pictures, others a collage using found materials. Any medium is acceptable for this activity.

If you have some students who need an extra challenge, let them make clay relief tiles to illustrate the types of focal point. If you don't have colored glazes, the tiles can be painted with acrylics after they have been bisque-fired.

Computer Option. Using the drawing tools of your choice, create a series of designs that emphasize dominance. Experiment. Examples could begin with one of the design units drawn earlier and enlarged to fill the page. See *Computers in the Art Classroom* for suggestions.

▲ **FIGURE 11.11** In this painting the artist has chosen a point of view that is at the eye level of the child. We see only the skirt and the hand of Ernesta's nurse. Why is this unusual?

Cecilia Beaux. *Ernesta (Child with Nurse)*. 1894. Oil on canvas. 128.3 × 96.8 cm (50½ × 38½"). The Metropolitan Museum of Art, New York, New York. Maria DeWitt Jesup Fund, 1965. (65.49)

294   **CHAPTER 11**   Variety, Emphasis, Harmony, and Unity

COOPERATIVE LEARNING

Art Principles Consider dividing the class into two groups and assigning one group the principle of harmony and one the principle of variety. Each group is to browse through the book and write down the name and page number of ten works—besides those in Chapter 11—that exhibit the principle they have been assigned. The groups are then to trade lists and analyze the works named in an effort to find evidence of their own principle in a work that was singled out as containing an "opposite" principle. Allow time for a discussion of the reciprocal relationship between harmony and variety.

The Unusual. In a work of art, an object that is out of the ordinary can become the focal point **(Figure 11.11)**. In a row of soldiers standing at attention, the one standing on his head will be noticed first. The unexpected will always draw the viewer's attention.

 Activity Using Emphasis

Applying Your Skills. Make a series of small designs with strong focal points, using each of the following: contrast of shape, contrast of color, contrast of value, contrast of texture, isolation, location, convergence, and the unusual.

Computer Option. Use the drawing tools of your choice to create a series of small designs with strong focal points, using each of the following: contrast of shape, contrast of color, contrast of value, contrast of texture, isolation, location, convergence, and the unusual.

One advantage in using computers to create art is the ease with which images can be manipulated. You will be able to transform some designs to others by using the Fill Bucket tool. Others can be changed by using the Selection tool and rearranging the shapes. See if you can create all seven designs by starting with only three designs and making alterations to them. Save your work.

Harmony

Harmony is *the principle of art that creates unity by stressing the similarities of separate but related parts.* In musical harmony, related tones are combined into blended sounds. Harmony is pleasing because the tones complement each other. In visual harmony, related art elements are combined. The result looks pleasing because the elements complement each other.

Used in certain ways, color can produce harmony in a work of art. Repeti-

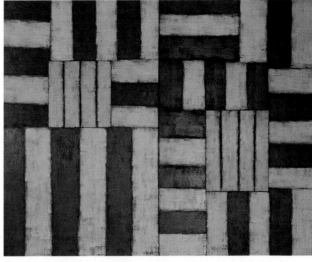

▲ **FIGURE 11.12** Scully has used related shapes and colors to create harmony in this work. What has he done to introduce variety?

Sean Scully. *White Robe.* 1990. Oil on linen. 243.8 × 304.8 cm (96 × 120″). High Museum of Art, Atlanta, Georgia. Purchase in honor of Richard A. Denny, Jr., President of the Board of Directors, 1991–94, with funds from Alfred Austell Thornton Sr. in memory of Leila Austell Thornton and Albert Edward Thornton Sr. and Sarah Miller Venable and William Hoyt Venable, 1992.5 a-b.

tion of shapes that are related, such as rectangles with different proportions, produces harmony **(Figure 11.12)**. A design that uses only geometric shapes appears more harmonious than a design using both geometric and free-form shapes. Even space used in a certain way can produce harmony. If all the parts in a work of art are different sizes, shapes, colors, and textures, the space between the parts can be made uniform to give the work a sense of order.

 Check Your Understanding

1. Describe the principle of *variety*.
2. What is a focal point?
3. Name the five ways *emphasis* can be created.
4. What is *harmony?*

ASSESS...........
Self-Assessment
Have students complete the lesson review questions. Answers are provided below.

Reteaching
Write the following statement on the board: *The work uses variety to achieve a sense of harmony.* Have students examine a painting in the chapter and then discuss how the statement on the board might apply to the work. Remind students to pay careful attention to all the elements.

Enrichment
Have students form groups and have each group choose an illustration from the text. Have them list the elements they find in the composition and explain how the principles are used. Ask each group to choose which of the elements has the strongest effect on the mood and organization of the work. Have them identify the focus of the composition and explain how the artist creates a center of interest and leads the viewer's eyes to it. Ask them to decide whether the artist was successful in establishing and supporting the center of interest. Then have each group share their findings with the class.

CLOSE............
Review with students art principle terms and definitions.

Answers to Check Your Understanding

1. Variety is the principle of art concerned with difference or contrast.
2. A focal point is the first part of a work to attract the attention of the viewer.
3. Emphasis can be created through contrast, isolation, location, convergence, and the unusual.
4. Harmony is the principle of art that creates unity by stressing the similarities of separate but related parts.

Unity

Unity
(pages 296–303)
(National Standards: 2b, 3c)

FOCUS...........
Objective
After completing this lesson, students will be able to:
- Identify and describe the principle of unity in artworks.

Supplies
- Tape; pencils and paper
- Found objects, yarn, thin sticks
- Squares and circles cut from magazines; note cards; poster board

Resources
- 📁 Application 21, *The Principles in Everyday Life*
- 📁 Application Activity 22, *Sharpening Your Skills*
- 📁 Artist's Profile 32, *Frank Lloyd Wright*
- 📁 Cooperative Learning Activity 21, *Lights, Camera, Action!*
- 📁 Cooperative Learning Activity 22, *The Body Language of Art*
- 📁 Studio Lesson 22, *Tissue and Found-Paper Collage*
- 📁 Studio Lesson 23, *Mixed-Media Collage, Combining Visual and Verbal Symbols*
- 📁 National Gallery of Art Correlation Bar Code Guide

Unity is oneness. It brings order to the world. Without it, the world would be chaotic.

Countries made up of smaller parts are political unities: the United States is such a country. Its 50 states are joined by a single federal government. As a unit, the United States is a world power far stronger than the combined power of the separate states **(Figure 11.13)**.

A tree is an example of unity in nature. It is composed of roots, trunk, bark, branches, twigs, and leaves. Each part has a purpose that contributes to the living, growing tree. An electric lamp is a manufactured unit composed of a base, electric wire, sockets, bulbs, shades, and so on. The parts of the lamp work together as a unified whole to provide light. If any part does not work, the unity of the lamp is impaired.

Creating Visual Unity

In art, **unity** is *the quality of wholeness or oneness that is achieved through the effective use of the elements and principles of art.* Unity is like an invisible glue. It joins all the separate parts so that they look as if they belong together.

Unity is difficult to understand at first because it is not easily defined. It is a quality that you feel as you view a work of art **(Figure 11.14)**. As you study an artwork, you may think that you would not change one element or object. You are receiving an impression that the work is a unified whole.

Unity helps you concentrate on a visual image. You cannot realize how important this is until you study a work that lacks unity. Looking at a work that lacks unity is like trying to carry on a serious discussion while your little sister

◄ **FIGURE 11.13** Johns combines the loose brushwork of Abstract Expressionism with the commonplace objects of American Realism. His map of the United States could be pulled apart by the wild action painting, but it is unified by the harmonious, limited color scheme of a primary triad.

Jasper Johns. *Map.* 1961. Oil on canvas. 198.2 × 312.7 cm (78 × 123⅛"). Collection, Museum of Modern Art, New York, New York. Gift of Mr. and Mrs. Robert C. Scull. © Jasper Johns/VAGA, New York 1994.

TECHNOLOGY OPTIONS

National Gallery of Art Videodisc Use the following to show examples of unity in art.

Vincent van Gogh
Farmhouse in Provence, Arles

Search Frame 1524

Grant Wood
New Road

Search Frame 2104

Winslow Homer
Key West: Hauling Anchor

Search Frame 3001

Use Glencoe's *National Gallery of Art Correlation Bar Code Guide* to locate more artwork.

▲ FIGURE 11.14 Rodin created this monument to honor six citizens who gave their lives in 1347 to save the city of Calais, France. Rodin showed the six men getting ready to see the king, who was laying siege to the city. He spent two years modeling faces and bodies to express the men's tension and pain. Each figure would be successful as an individual statue, but Rodin has placed them so that unity results. The work was designed to be placed at street level, not on a pedestal above the heads of the people.

Auguste Rodin. *The Burghers of Calais.* 1886, cast 1930s. Bronze. 2 × 2 × 1.9 m (79⅜ × 80⅞ × 77⅛"). Hirshhorn Museum and Sculpture Garden, Smithsonian Institution, Washington, D.C. Gift of Joseph H. Hirshhorn, 1966.

TEACH.........
Motivator

To illustrate how space can help create harmony, gather together ten totally unrelated objects. Using tape, mark off ten rectangular shapes of equal size on the top of a table or on the floor. Be sure the shapes are large enough to contain the objects. Place one object directly in the center of each rectangle. Such an organization has more unity than if the objects were arranged haphazardly.

Aesthetics

Ask students to recall what they learned in Chapter 9 about balance. Ask students to identify the types of balance used in Figure 11.15, *Snuff Containers.* Have them also discuss the way the artists used shapes and space to create a unique design on each one. How do the designs complement the shape of the containers? What makes the designs unified?

is practicing the violin, your brother is listening to the stereo, and your mother is running the vacuum cleaner. It would be difficult to concentrate on your conversation with all these distractions. It is the same with a work of art that lacks unity. You can't concentrate on the work as a whole, because all the parts demand separate attention.

To create unity, an artist adjusts the parts of a work so they relate to each other and to the whole work. A potter adjusts decorations on a bowl to complement the bowl's shape, size, and purpose. The artist who decorated the containers in **Figure 11.15** carefully planned where the holes would be

▲ FIGURE 11.15 The decorations on these containers were created by drilling small holes into which short lengths of wire were inserted to form the various designs. The polished surface is the result of frequent handling and an occasional application of oil.

Used by the Zulu peoples, South Africa; the Tsonga or the Shona peoples, Mozambique and Zimbabwe. *Snuff Containers.* Hard fruit shell with copper, brass, and iron wire. Largest: 6 × 7.6 cm (2⅜ × 3"). National Museum of African Art, Smithsonian Institution, Washington, D.C. Acquisition grant from the James Smithsonian Society. 89-8-27, 28, 29, 30.

▶ COOPERATIVE LEARNING

Unity in Everyday Life Have students list five different kinds of unified objects that they might find in their environment. Ask them to name the whole unit, describe its various parts, and explain how and why the separate parts are joined into a unified whole. Small discussion groups might be set up so that every student has some input into the discussion. To make the small groups meet a greater challenge, you might prepare several slips of paper on which the term *natural* or *manufactured* is written. Each discussion group must draw one slip from a bowl and then think of unities on that topic.

If students have trouble coming up with ideas, suggest any of the following: *natural unities,* such as animals, countries or flowers; *manufactured unities,* such as buildings, cities, and machines.

Cross-Curriculum: Language Arts

One of early America's outspoken literary voices was that of Henry David Thoreau, who once stated that people should "Simplify. Simplify." He practiced this philosophy by living an austere, reclusive life that consisted of the barest of essentials. Ask students to consider how they would simplify their lives. Does it seem easy? How would they learn to adjust to a minimalist's lifestyle? Encourage students to read Thoreau's writings.

Studio Skills

Divide the class into small working groups of two or three students. Assign each group the project of developing a composition that illustrates one of the principles of art. Include both two- and three-dimensional projects in the assignment. If the class is small, each group might be assigned several of the projects so that all of the principles are covered. Have the groups make their compositions on sheets of paper and provide them with yarn, thin sticks, found objects, and squares and circles cut from magazines.

Encourage the groups to experiment with a number of arrangements to find one that uses the space effectively and best illustrates the assigned principle. When the students have determined the best layout, they should glue the pieces into place.

▶ **FIGURE 11.16** The designer of this coat travels around the world looking for fabrics with unusual colors and textures. She then designs and creates unique patterns for her wearable art.

Florence Bayless. *Haori Coat.* 1992. Silk peau de soir, Thai silk, and silk lamé. Private collection.

drilled so that the design would complement the shape of the container. Clothing designers choose fabrics that complement the design and purpose of each outfit **(Figure 11.16).** Artists adjust the elements in a work to each other. A "busy" work with a variety of shapes and textures can be unified with a limited color scheme, for example.

Simplicity

Another way to create unity is through *simplicity.* Simplicity is not easy to achieve. An artist must plan carefully to create a good, simple design. This is done by limiting the number of variations of an element. The fewer variations the artist uses, the more unified the design will seem **(Figure 11.17).**

A painting in which the entire surface is covered with a single, even layer of one hue will appear strongly unified. A sculpture of a single person expresses a simple unity **(Figure 11.18).**

◀ **FIGURE 11.17** Carr has used simplification to eliminate the details of bark, grass, and leaves. The foliage seems to be solidified into diagonally–flowing living forms.

Emily Carr. *Forest, British Columbia*, VAG 42.3.9. 1931–32. Oil on canvas. 130 × 86.8 cm (51⅛ × 34⅛"). Vancouver Art Gallery, Vancouver, British Columbia, Canada.

MORE ABOUT... Emily Carr

Modern Canadian art can trace its origins to 1920 and a small group of landscape painters working in Toronto. These painters eventually came to be known as the Group of Seven. Their style was uniquely Canadian.

The work of the Group of Seven played an important role in the career of Emily Carr, who was to become Canada's best-known early modern artist. Like the painters in the Group of Seven, she was greatly impressed by the expressive qualities of the Fauves' works and adapted their qualities to her own painting style. Emily Carr's art heralded a period of artistic activity in Canada that continues to grow in diversity and quality.

MEET THE ARTIST
ALLAN HOUSER

Native American,
1914–1994

Allan Houser created contemporary Apache sculpture. As a child, he listened to his father's stories about the adventures of Chief Geronimo. This gave him a deep attachment to his ancestral background, an attachment that is shown in his artwork. Houser studied at the Indian School in Sante Fe, New Mexico, and then remained in Sante Fe, where he worked as a free-lance artist. During World War II, he traveled to California, where he became interested in the media of sculpture. He created works in a variety of styles and mastered bronze, metal, and stone sculpture. Houser's designs are modern, yet firmly rooted in the special tradition of his Native American forefathers. He drew inspiration from both past and present, but like all successful artists, his sculpture transcends race and language. The sculpture *Reverie* (Figure 11.18) shows a distinct Native American influence, but it can be appreciated by anyone, regardless of his or her background.

▶ **FIGURE 11.18** Notice how the artist has used simple lines and few details to create this artwork. The simplicity serves to emphasize the faces of the mother and child, which become focal points. The unity of the design shows the connection between mother and child. What feeling does this piece evoke?

Allan Houser. *Reverie*. 1981. Bronze, edition of 10. 63.5 × 58.4 × 33 cm (25 × 23 × 13"). Collection of the Duke and Duchess of Bedford. The Glen Green Galleries, Santa Fe, New Mexico. Copyright Allan Houser Inc.

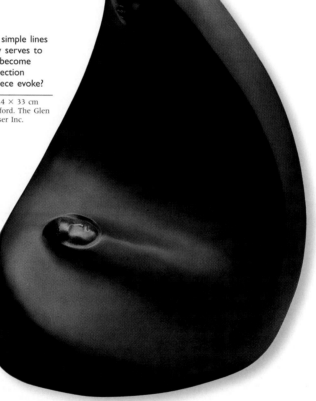

Art in Everyday Life

To foster students' awareness of art in everyday life, suggest this: Cut a 1 × 1½ inch (2.5 × 3.8 cm) rectangle out of the center of a note card and use the card as a view finder, just as you use a camera lens. Look through the finder at your world, finding examples of all of the principles of art. Look for the rhythm of repeated rows of windows, the variety in the directions of tree branches, the contrast in light and shadow on a sunny day, or the formal and informal balance in furniture arranged in a room. Start to see your world with the eyes of an artist.

LESSON 2 *Unity* | **299**

CULTURAL DIVERSITY

Unity in Art Across Cultures Divide students into small groups and give each group a post card of an artwork from another culture. Have them identify the following unifying devices: simplicity, harmony of color, harmony of shape, harmony through space, proximity, and continuation. Have each group show the image to the class and point out the major unifying devices. Encourage them to make a unified display of the post cards, emphasizing the cultural influences present in the cards.

Art History

Dawn was originally part of an installation called *Dawn's Wedding Feast*. This installation consisted of 85 separate pieces, including reliefs, columns, and boxes. The Museum of Modern Art displayed it as part of the exhibition, *Sixteen Americans*. This was to be Nevelson's first exhibition in a major museum.

At the time of the exhibition, Nevelson was known for her all-black wooden constructions. She painted her works totally black to emphasize the shape of the work instead of the colors of the found pieces. When Dorothy Miller, then curator of The Museum of Modern Art, invited Nevelson to participate in this exhibit, Nevelson decided to fill one gallery with one installation. She also decided that this environment would be all white. This was the first monochrome environment that she did in a color besides black. She was very interested in the surprise value that such a change would have. She even secretly rented a second studio solely to produce her new "white work."

After the exhibition closed, *Dawn's Wedding Feast* was dismantled, and many of the parts were sold to collectors.

Repetition

The repetition of objects and elements can be an effective way to unify a work of art. Louise Nevelson's assemblages are good examples. She collects objects that are not alike. This presents a problem of unity, which she solves in one or more ways. Often, she places the objects in a series of boxlike containers **(Figure 11.19)**. The boxes help to unify the work. She sometimes paints the entire structure the same color. Sometimes she repeats both container shape and color to unify her assemblages.

Most architects are concerned with unity. Their goal is to design structures

▲ **FIGURE 11.19** The artist has collected different found objects and assembled them together. What has the artist done to unify this work and make the objects look like they belong together? Can you identify any of the found objects?

Louise Nevelson. *Dawn*. 1962. Wood painted gold. 323 × 240 × 19 cm (127 × 94½ × 7½"). The Pace Gallery, New York, New York.

MORE ABOUT...   Louise Nevelson

Showing concern for artistic unity in all her works, Louise Nevelson was one of the best-known sculptors of her time. Her assemblages of wooden forms, created from posts, balustrades, blocks, and slats, range in size from small box-like shapes to full walls. In spite of the large variety involved, each work is balanced and unified.

Nevelson sprayed most of her sculptures a single color. At first, almost all her work was black. Later in her career, she sometimes used white or gold. She used this single-color technique as a symbol for unity. Black means everything, she explained; black encompasses all and makes it one.

that blend with the surroundings **(Figure 11.20).** They may use materials that repeat the colors and textures found in the structure's environment. They may also use materials that reflect the surroundings. For instance, mirrored outside walls have been used on skyscrapers. The mirrors reflect the shapes and colors of the clouds and sky, and the buildings seem to blend with their surroundings and the atmosphere.

Proximity

Proximity, or closeness, is another way of unifying very different shapes in a work **(Figures 11.21** and **11.22,** page 302). This is achieved by limiting the negative space between the shapes. Clustering the shapes in this way suggests unity and coherence. The sense of unity can be made even stronger if the cluster of unlike items is surrounded by an area of negative space.

▲ **FIGURE 11.20** Wright was a genius who dared to be different. In 1936 he was asked to design a house close to this waterfall. Instead, he placed the house right over the falls. Terraces hang suspended over the running water. Even though they are made of reinforced concrete, the terraces repeat the shapes of the natural stone terraces below. The stones that make up the walls come from the building site, which ties the house more closely to its surroundings.

Frank Lloyd Wright. *Fallingwater House. Bear Run, Pennsylvania.* 1936. Photography by Sandak, Inc., Stamford, Connecticut.

◄ **FIGURE 11.21** The artist has used proximity by grouping the children close together. What do the children appear to be doing? What kind of meeting are they having?

Marie Bashkirtseff. *A Meeting.* 1884. Oil on canvas. 190.5 × 172.2 cm (74¹⁵/₁₆ × 68¹⁵/₁₆″). Musée d'Orsay, Paris, France. Art Resource, New York, New York.

LESSON 2   *Unity*   **301**

Developing Perceptual Skills

Tell students that not all of Frank Lloyd Wright's designs met with the public's approval. If possible, show a reproduction of the Solomon R. Guggenheim Museum in New York City. Inform students that many people thought it looked like a giant cupcake and did not consider it an appropriate design for a museum. Ask: Why would Wright have considered it a unified design?

Art History

To help students further appreciate the life and times of Frank Lloyd Wright, assign *Artist's Profile 32* in the TCR. 📁

Art on a Shoestring

As the end of a term approaches, you might be faced with a dilemma about too many odds and ends of supplies in the classroom. On the other hand, you may need supplies to finish term projects but have no budget left with which to purchase them. In either case, Louise Nevelson's assemblage provides inspiration. If you have on hand an assortment of unrelated supplies, challenge students to work in groups to create a unified assemblage. If you are low on supplies and even lower on budget, ask students each to bring ten items from home that are unneeded. Proceed with the same activity.

► COOPERATIVE LEARNING

Understanding the Elements of Art Divide the class into eight groups and explain that they are about to become a group of experts. Assign to each group a different principle of art. Explain that the group's task is to analyze every artwork reproduced in Chapter 11 and show how that principle was used to organize the elements of art.

301

Aesthetics

Have students form small groups and ask each group to create a list of ten qualities that they feel are essential for a work to be considered "art." Then have each group choose one work from the chapter that they feel is art and one they feel is not art. Each group should make a presentation and be prepared to discuss and defend their list using the information they have learned about the language of art, the elements and principles, the media, and the work of art itself.

Art Criticism

Have students study Figure 11.22, which illustrates the principle of emphasis. Ask students whether the work also makes use of the principle of harmony. Which colors blend well (i.e., "harmonize") with other colors in the work? Which elements besides color have been organized in a harmonic fashion?

▶ **FIGURE 11.22** Jessup has created a unified composition using many techniques. What has she simplified to unify the work? What has been repeated?

Georgia Mills Jessup. *Rainy Night, Downtown.* 1967. Oil on canvas. 112 × 122 cm (44 × 48″). National Museum of Women in the Arts, Washington, D.C.

How Artists Use Variety, Emphasis, and Harmony to Enhance Unity

As you know, artists use variety, emphasis, and harmony to make their works more interesting and appealing. If carried to extremes, however, these principles can destroy the unity of a visual work. This means that artists must be careful to balance the contrasting qualities of variety and emphasis with harmonizing and unifying techniques to create a unified work.

Jane Wilson has successfully balanced the harmonizing and varying devices in *Solstice* **(Figure 11.23).** She has divided the work into two contrasting rectangles. The sky in the upper rectangle is painted with both light and dark values. The focal point of the work is the bright yellow glow of sunlight peeking through the dark clouds.

Teacher Notes

_____

_____

_____

_____

_____

▲ **FIGURE 11.23** Explain how the artist has balanced harmony with variety in this painting.

Jane Wilson. *Solstice.* 1991. Oil on linen. 152.4 × 178 cm (60 × 70"). Fischbach Gallery, New York, New York.

You cannot see any specific shapes in the water, shown in the lower rectangle, yet the sky is full of loose triangular shapes. These contrasting factors would pull the work apart if the artist had not used a harmonious color scheme. The entire work is composed of various values of blue, green, and yellow. The artist has simplified this work, showing nothing but clouds, sky, and water. She has tied the work together using repetition. The clear triangle of sky repeats the color of the water. The bright yellow of the sun is reflected along the edge of the clouds and in the water below. The active clouds are repetitions of loose triangular shapes. Without the repetitions and simple color scheme, this work might not be the unified composition that it is.

Check Your Understanding

1. Define *unity*.
2. What is simplicity?
3. How is proximity used to create unity?
4. What can happen if variety, emphasis, or harmony is carried to an extreme?

ASSESS..........

Self-Assessment

Have students complete the lesson review questions. Answers are provided below.

Reteaching

■ On pairs of index cards write the name and definition of each art principle covered in the section. Then have pairs of students play "concentration" by matching a principle with its definition. A student who makes a successful match draws two more cards. The student who collects the most matches wins.

Enrichment

■ Have students take photographs of six examples of visual unity in their neighborhoods. After their photographs are developed, have students mount or frame them, then arrange their photographs in a display. Encourage them to arrange the display in different ways to achieve unity.

■ Have the students select work that was done early in the course. As a class effort, you could put these works on the bulletin board and let classmates offer positive suggestions on how the work might be improved.

CLOSE............

Have students open their textbooks and randomly select an artwork. Invite students to discuss how the elements and principles have been used to achieve unity.

 ### Answers to Check Your Understanding

1. Unity is the quality of wholeness that is achieved through the effective use of the elements and principles of art.
2. A way to achieve unity in an artwork by limiting the number of variations of any element.
3. Proximity is used to create harmony by limiting the negative space between shapes or by clustering shapes together, which suggests unity and coherence.
4. Carrying variety, emphasis, or harmony to an extreme can destroy unity in an artwork.

303

Assemblage with Handmade Paper

Assemblage with Handmade Paper

(National Standards: 1a, 1b, 2b, 2c, 3b)

FOCUS...........

Objectives

After completing this lesson, students will be able to:

■ Create a relief assemblage that contains symbols of each student's life.

■ Use found materials that can be incorporated into the relief assemblages including yarn, leaves, old photos, twigs, shells, sand, colored clay, feathers, costume jewelry, seeds, grasses, weeds, and dried bones.

TEACH.........

Motivator

Bring an abandoned wasp's or hornet's nest to class. Ask students to compare its strength and texture to that of various manufactured sheets of paper. Show examples of handmade paper. If none are available, show slides or pictures from the text. If there are any paper-making artists in the area, invite one to class to demonstrate techniques.

Studio Skills

Be sure that students experiment with the handmade paper before they work on their finished compositions. They need to understand how the materials behave before they use them in a finished work.

▲ **FIGURE 11.24**

Lois Dvorak. *Spirit Boxes I.* 1985. Assemblage with handmade paper, construction paper, tree bark, colored pencils, pastels, and embroidery thread. 51 × 76.2 × 5.1 cm (20 × 30 × 2"). Private collection.

SUPPLIES

- ■ **Sketchbook and pencils**
- ■ **Large strong sheet of paper for background**
- ■ **Your own handmade paper**
- ■ **Variety of other paper and fabric**
- ■ **Found materials**
- ■ **White glue**
- ■ **Scissors**
- ■ **Pencils, markers, and/or crayons**

*S*pirit Boxes I is a mixed-media assemblage **(Figure 11.24).** The background is a sheet of paper Lois Dvorak made from cotton pulp. The swirling pattern was drawn with colored pencils and pastels. The dark tree shape was made from construction paper with pastel shading that continues the movement of the design in the background. The boxes were made from bark that was soaked and beaten into a very strong, thin paper, which was then glued and sewn together. Inside the boxes are bits of bark paper embroidered with colored threads. Notice that in some places the details in the boxes are unified with the background. Across the front of the boxes you can see very thin, transparent paper that has bits of homemade and construction paper glued in strategic places to unite the rhythmic repetition of the boxes.

Dvorak is always searching for little treasures in the environment to put in her spirit boxes, such as bits of bird eggshells, locust wings, and dried-out lizards. Begin to think about how you can adapt Dvorak's techniques to your own assemblage.

What You Will Learn

Create a relief assemblage that contains symbols of your life. Each symbol should be protected in a handmade paper container just as Dvorak has protected each symbol in a spirit box. Use the principle of harmony to join the various symbols and containers into a unified composition. Use handmade papers, other papers, fabrics, fibers, and small found objects to construct the relief. Like Dvorak, add details using pencil, crayon, markers, and/or fibers.

MEETING INDIVIDUAL NEEDS

Mentally Disabled Students with mental disabilities may especially enjoy the making of paper pulp into paper. They usually enjoy the kinesthetic sensation of handling the semi-liquid pulp. Creating a piece of paper from a mass of pulp is almost a feat of magic. The moral lesson of "strength through sticking together" (the lesson taught by a Native American chief who easily broke one stick but could not break a bundle of sticks), can be applied to the fibers coming together for strength. The experience of being in a group while working on this activity may benefit persons who tend to feel outcast or isolated.

Creating

Study Dvorak's assemblage, *Spirit Boxes I*. She has used several different techniques to unify her work. Notice how the forms of the spirit boxes are related. Observe how the paths that weave over and under each other in the background are alike, and most of the shapes between the paths are covered with an invented texture. The boxes are placed close to each other and are held together in the branches of the tree.

Brainstorm with your classmates about objects that can be used to symbolize aspects of your life.

Step 1 Working in groups, make handmade paper to use in this project. See the instructions for making paper in Technique Tip 21 on page 436 in the Handbook. Plan the colors you will use when making the paper, because they will be some of the colors in your final project. Collect other materials and symbolic objects you plan to use.

Step 2 Make plans for your relief assemblage in your sketchbook. List and sketch the symbolic objects you will use and explain what each represents. Design the forms of the containers. Draw each container from two or more views. List the ways that you will use harmony to unify your project.

Step 3 Draw several plans for your mixed-media relief. As you draw, think about the materials you will use for construction and how you will alter them using drawing or stitching materials. Choose the best design.

Step 4 Plan the procedures you need to follow to construct your work and follow your plan. Prepare your finished product for display.

EVALUATING YOUR WORK

▶ **DESCRIBE** Explain the process, step by step, that you used to make paper. Describe the three-dimensional containers you made to hold the symbolic objects and explain how you constructed them.

▶ **ANALYZE** Which elements did you emphasize in this project? List and describe the methods you used to create harmony. Does the work have visual rhythm? Describe.

▶ **INTERPRET** Do the symbols you used represent only one part of your life or all of it? Are the symbols obvious or are they personal?

▶ **JUDGE** Does your work have a strong sense of unity? Which of the aesthetic theories would you use to judge this work? What, if anything, would you change to give it more unity?

▲ **FIGURE 11.24A** Student work.

STUDIO PROJECT *Assemblage with Handmade Paper*   **305**

Studio Project

Clay Sculpture Unifying Two Ideas

(National Standards: 1a, 1b, 2b, 2c, 3b)

FOCUS...........

Objective

■ Create a clay sculpture that combines two unrelated objects

TEACH..........

Motivator

Ask students to locate two works of art in the text that represent different specific themes. Direct them to list on paper the similarities and differences of the two pieces.

Art History

Review the subtractive, additive, and casting processes used by sculptors. Remind students that most sculptors combine two or more of these methods. An example of the subtractive process is carving. The sculpture is created when the artist cuts away pieces of stone, clay, or wood. In the additive process, parts are attached to create a whole or finished sculpture. Casting involves pouring a liquid material into a mold to create a form. When the liquid dries or hardens, the mold is removed to reveal a positive shape of the mold's cavity.

Cross Curriculum: Music

Discuss harmony as it relates to art and other areas of life. Play tapes of musical groups known for using harmony in their songs. Discuss the techniques used to harmonize the instruments and/or voices. How are these methods similar to the challenge in this Studio Project?

306

Clay Sculpture Unifying Two Ideas

▲ **FIGURE 11.25**

Artist unknown. Folk art from the town of Acallan, State of Puebla, Mexico. *Fiesta Rodeo.* 1975. Ceramic with nichrome wire and acrylic paint. 55.8 × 33 × 33 cm (22 × 13 × 13"). Private collection.

SUPPLIES

■ **Sketchbook and pencil**
■ **Clay and clay tools**
■ **Slip and brush**
■ **Cloth-covered clay board**
■ **Plastic bags**
■ **Glaze or acrylic paint (optional)**

The piece shown in **Figure 11.25** comes from the town of Acallan in the State of Puebla in Mexico. What makes this particular work so unusual is that the artist has taken two themes that are not really related and tied them together by using a balance between harmony and variety. The artist took two different themes of celebration: the secular rodeo and the religious tree of life, and carefully organized the elements of art so that the two themes merged into a unified whole. The rodeo is a worldly event. The tree of life represents the tree in the Garden of Eden from which Adam and Eve gained knowledge.

Notice how the artist has used contrast. The negative spaces in the fence are small rectangles, but when your eyes move up to the tree, the lines explode into active, blossoming curves.

Observe the ways in which the two themes have been related in this sculpture and think about how you will relate two themes.

What You Will Learn

Like the Mexican folk artist who combined two different themes in the sculpture *Fiesta Rodeo*, you will create a clay sculpture that combines two unrelated objects. Create unity in your work by using a balance between variety and harmony. Use some of the following harmonizing techniques: simplification, repetition, and proximity. To help you tie the two parts together, use emphasis of an element and/or emphasis of an area.

TEACHER TALK

Classroom Management Occasionally, students struggle when faced with the task of originating ideas, such as in the Studio Project above. In these cases, a brainstorming session can help. To help them get started try the following: Give each student two slips of paper. Have each student write the name of an object on each slip of paper. Fold the papers and put them in a container. Have one person draw two slips of paper and write the names of the objects on the board. As a class, try to develop different ideas for creating a sculpture that unifies the two objects. Now encourage them to think of two separate themes or objects that they would like to unite into a unified sculpture.

Creating

Study *Fiesta Rodeo*. Notice how the artist has unified two different themes. In your sketchbook, describe how the artist has used a balance between variety and harmony to create unity. List the most important elements and explain why they are important. Discuss your findings with your classmates.

Brainstorm with your classmates about different themes or objects that could be unified in a sculpture as the artist has done with *Fiesta Rodeo*. Think of your favorite school subject, your favorite after-school activity, or a hobby. Write the two ideas in your sketchbook. Make verbal and visual notes about how you could create your sculpture. Make some sketches based on your ideas. Choose your best idea. List the harmonizing techniques you want to use and which elements you will use. Then list the way you will use emphasis.

Step 1 Construct your sculpture. For proper clay construction techniques see Technique Tip 16 on page 434. Between work sessions, cover your sculpture tightly with a plastic bag so the clay does not dry. When you are finished with construction, cover your work loosely so the clay does not dry too quickly. Remember that thin clay will dry and shrink more quickly than thick clay, so cover thin areas very carefully.

Step 2 When your work is bone dry, fire it in the kiln. After your sculpture is fired, you may decorate it by glazing and glaze firing the piece or painting it with acrylic paints. Prepare your work for display.

EVALUATING YOUR WORK

▶ **DESCRIBE** List the two different themes or objects you combined in your sculpture. Describe the clay-building techniques you used to construct your work. How did you prepare your work for display?

▶ **ANALYZE** Which harmonizing techniques did you use to unify your work? Describe how you used emphasis to pull the piece together visually. Does your finished product look unified?

▶ **INTERPRET** What is the expressive effect of your sculpture? Give your work an expressive title. Write a poem or a brief paragraph about your sculpture that expresses your feelings toward this work.

▶ **JUDGE** Which aesthetic theories would you use to judge this work? If you were to do this over, what would you change?

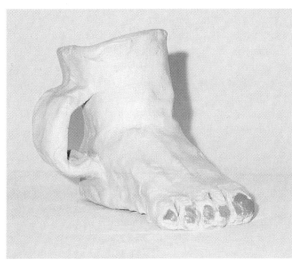

▲ **FIGURE 11.25A** Student work.

ASSESS..........
Keeping a Portfolio

Remind students that the preliminary sketches and the final artwork for this Studio Project are likely candidates for their portfolios.

Self-Assessment

Have students apply the steps of art criticism to their own artwork using the "Evaluating Your Work" questions on this page.

Enrichment

Students could play their own version of "Pictionary" in which each player, or teams of players, pulls to random nouns, written on slips of paper and placed in a hat. Students are challenged to combine the nouns into a unified drawing on the board. For example, *cup* and *tree* might look like a coffee mug with a hollow trunk as the cup and a curved branch as a handle.

CLOSE.............

Ask volunteers to read their paragraphs or poems aloud and name one concept about unity that they now understand better.

SAFETY NOTE

To help students enjoy this lesson, consider the following:

■ Most commercial glazes sold for school use are lead-free, but you should still read labels and check specifications before using ceramic materials or ordering supplies.

■ Remind students to wash their hands thoroughly after handling clay and glazes.

■ Place kilns in a separate room. If that is not possible, locate the kiln in an out-of-the-way part of the room where students are not likely to come into contact with it when it is in operation. In addition, all kilns should have local exhaust ventilation.

Designing a Mural

Studio Project

Designing a Mural

(National Standards: 1a, 1b, 2b, 2c, 3b)

FOCUS...........

Objective

After completing this lesson, students will be able to:

- Design and create a presentation painting of a mural for a specific site.

TEACH..........

Motivator

If there is a mural in your city, plan a field trip to study it. Discuss its theme, the site, and the surface on which it is painted. If the artist is available, have him or her discuss what is involved in planning and painting a mural.

Art History

The earliest known murals are cave paintings where hunting scenes were painted on the walls. It is theorized that the purposes for these images included rituals and storytelling. During the Renaissance, Giotto, Raphael, and Michelangelo painted large frescoes. Fresco is a method of painting in which water-based pigment is applied to freshly spread plaster. The plaster must be damp. As it dries, the plaster absorbs the paint. This technique is still used today by some muralists. Diego Rivera, a Mexican muralist, painted large frescoes. The messages in his art were often political in nature.

SUPPLIES

- **Sketchbook, pencil, and ruler**
- **Photograph of proposed site**
- **Enlarged photocopy of photograph**
- **Large sheet of white paper**
- **Tempera or acrylic paints**
- **Brushes**

▲ **FIGURE 11.26**

John Yancy. *Celebration of Arts: Vibrations of Life.* 1991. Permanent exterior mural, acrylic on panels. 2.4 × 9.7 m (8′ × 32′). Located at 1531 West 60th Street, Chicago, Illinois.

John Yancy received his first mural commission during his senior year in high school. He liked murals because of their scale and visibility. During his studies at The Art Institute of Chicago, he began to realize that murals inform, enlighten, and motivate people. His *Celebration of Arts* mural depicts the programs and contributions of the Boulevard Art Center and expresses the excitement and vitality of all the visual and performing arts **(Figure 11.26)**. The patterns on the mural portray textile designs that are seen in the masquerade ceremonies of the Yoruba people of Africa. The dancers in the mural function as dynamic, formal elements to increase movement and drama. The mural was completed with the help of a small crew of 16- to 20-year-old participants who had expressed interest in a career in the arts.

Yancy created the mural to let people know what was going on in the Center. Notice which elements he used to create variety and which ones he used to create harmony in the composition so that the mural became a unified whole.

What You Will Learn

Design and create a presentation painting of a mural for a specific site. Yancy used the events in the building as a theme for his mural. Choose a theme and design a mural using subject matter that is linked to the site. Use a balance between the principles of variety, emphasis, and harmony, to create a unified composition. Make your final painting to scale.

Creating

Brainstorm with classmates about sites and themes for your mural designs. Decide whether you all want to work on the same theme, such as the environment or the history of the community, or whether you all want to use independent themes. Then find an interesting site for your mural and choose your individual idea. Think of the subject matter you will use to express your theme.

MEETING INDIVIDUAL NEEDS

Advanced Learners Artistically gifted students can make models of their mural or of a sculpture, called a *maquette* (small model), about one foot (30.5 cm) in height. This model-making experience in high school can lay the groundwork for public art competitions in later years. Many cities have a percent of their budget allocated to public art for new construction. Proposals frequently require teamwork between sculptors, landscape designers, and architects.

Step 1 Photograph your site and enlarge the photograph using a photocopier. Measure the area of the photocopy on which you will place your mural. Make some rough sketches in your sketchbook. Create a unified composition by balancing the varying and unifying techniques. Because this is a plan for a large mural, you may not want to have a single focal point; you may decide to create several centers of interest. Plan your color scheme.

Step 2 Select your best idea and draw it carefully with pencil on the measured area of the photocopy. Enlarge your mural plan, to scale, onto a large sheet of white paper. See Technique Tip 8 on page 432 of the Handbook for directions on using a grid to enlarge a work to scale. Paint the enlarged presentation drawing.

Step 3 Arrange a display that includes the photograph, the enlarged photocopy with the drawing for the mural, the presentation painting, and a written statement that explains your theme, the subject matter, and why you selected them for that specific site.

EVALUATING YOUR WORK

▶ **DESCRIBE** Tell the theme, the subject matter, and the site you selected for your mural.

▶ **ANALYZE** Explain which principles of art you used to create a unified composition. Explain which color scheme you chose and why you chose it.

▶ **INTERPRET** What kind of a mood does your mural express? How do you think the mural would affect the site for which it was planned? Give your work an expressive title.

▶ **JUDGE** Which aesthetic theories would you use to judge this mural? What, if anything, would you change before you painted it on the site?

▲ **FIGURE 11.26A** Student work.

STUDIO PROJECT *Designing a Mural* **309**

TECHNIQUE TIP ✓

Painting a Mural Because this project involves public property, it might be better if you selected the sites for the murals. If the finished work can be displayed at the site, have the mural painted on plywood in the classroom and then mounted on the site when it is finished. Then you may obtain sites that are not on the school grounds, such as a shopping center or a store.

It is very difficult in many school districts to get any work done after school. It is also difficult to work in a heavy traffic area or in the lunchroom during the school day. If extra-curricular time is needed, it is wise to organize a weekend painting session, when everyone is fresh.

School Web Page Design

TECHNOLOGY
Studio Project

School Web Page Design

(National Standards: 1a, 1b, 2b, 2c, 3b)

FOCUS...........

Objectives

After completing this lesson, students will be able to:

■ Design a 9 × 12-inch web page that features the principles of variety, emphasis, harmony, and unity.

■ Create a web page for a specific department within a school.

Supplies

■ Sketchbook
■ Computer
■ Paint or draw application
■ Printer

TEACH.........

Motivator

Distribute several different copies of school Web pages printed from the Internet. In small groups, have students review the Web page designs for the principles of variety, emphasis, harmony, and unity. Have each group present their findings to the entire class. Conduct a class discussion that considers the following questions: What makes a Web page appealing? What similarities are there in the Web pages that the class likes? How is space used in the designs to unify the entire page?

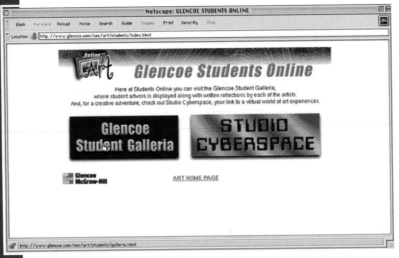

▲ FIGURE 11.27

SUPPLIES

■ Sketchbook
■ Computer
■ Paint or Draw application
■ Printer
Optional
■ Scanner or digital camera, clip art, photographs
■ Drawing/Graphics Tablet
■ Web Page software application

When you view a Web site, you encounter more than words and information. Web sites are designed to catch your eye and hold your attention, as well as to inform you. Web pages and art designed for them are recent developments. General use of the Internet by public schools began around 1993. The technology that artists use to make graphic images for the Internet has improved and changed so rapidly since then that there are literally hundreds of thousands of artists exploring the possibilities of art and Web page design. Artists and Web page designers have learned how to create Web pages that are interesting to view and use. There are as many different ways to design a Web page as there are ways to paint a picture. Like a good art gallery exhibition, good Web page designs keep you coming back to visit.

What You Will Learn

You will design and create a Web page for your school, or for a specific department in your school, using a computer paint program. Use the principles of variety, emphasis, harmony, and unity to organize your design. Include your school name, address, phone number, e-mail address, an introductory paragraph, one or more pieces of artwork and/or photos, and at least four buttons that link to specific information about your school or the department of your choice. Do not forget to credit any sources you use.

Creating

Determine the purpose of your Web page. Consider who the audience will be. Then, research and gather information about your school or the department you are featuring and related topics. What will be emphasized in your layout? How will you use harmony to tie it all together? What size will your artwork or photos be?

310 | CHAPTER 11 Variety, Emphasis, Harmony, and Unity

TEACHER TALK

Resources Beyond the Classroom If you have a Web page application, you can have students develop their Web page design within that program. They will be able to type text, import computer artwork, or digitize photos and move the layout around until the design suits them. Remind students to include **.html** at the end of each page they save.

Explain that planning a Web page or a complete Web site (many web pages linked together) requires many initial, off-computer tasks. Have them research the software and technical support they have available. Have them ask: Does the school or district have Internet software? Who can help or provide advice?

Step 1 In your sketchbook, organize your information using diagrams and sketches that show headings, sub-headings, and related information into ideas for your Web page. Create at least three different possibilities. Most computer screens are 9" wide by 12" high so your sketches should fit this format.

Step 2 Select your best design. Open your computer paint program and use the outline rectangle tool to map out the size of your Web page on the computer screen.

Step 3 Using the same computer paint tool or the oval outline tool, designate shapes within the Web page for your school name, address, and phone number; four buttons to links about specific school information; the space needed for an introductory paragraph about your school; artwork or photo.

Step 4 Add the details for each of the spaces you designated in your layout. Select a font that is easy to read. Type in the text that you will use to introduce your school. Consider your color scheme. Type in the actual titles that you will use on your buttons.

Step 5 For the artwork or photos, either use the computer paint tools to develop your artwork on your Web page design or open a new file in the computer paint program and work on your

EVALUATING YOUR WORK

▶ **DESCRIBE** Did you include the name of your school and/or the department, the address, phone number, e-mail address, introductory paragraph, artwork and/or photos, and four buttons that lead to specific information? Describe procedures you used to arrange and finish your Web page.

▶ **ANALYZE** Identify the techniques you used to create visual unity. Identify the area of emphasis. How did you create this emphasis? Describe how the components of your design demonstrate variety. How do they also create harmony?

▶ **INTERPRET** What is the feeling or mood of your Web page design? Is it playful or more formal? How do the colors you chose influence the feeling of the design? How does the artwork and/or photos you selected affect the mood?

▶ **JUDGE** Is your design well-planned, informative, and visually satisfying? Are text, graphics, and links logical and easy to view? Have you credited your sources? Would you change anything to make your work more successful?

artwork there. Once you have completed your artwork, save it as file. Then copy and paste it into your Web page design. If you have scanned a photo or taken one with a digital camera, import it into your Web page.

Step 6 Print your Web page design to visually check and proofread it. Make any necessary corrections and print out your final copy.

Cross Curriculum

Divide students into pairs to develop a Web page that features content for a specific subject or lesson that is being taught at your school. Have them consider the content, the images, the contact information, and the layout of their design. What links will provide further information about the specific subject or lesson?

Studio Skills

Have students design a Web page for the art class that features a specific studio skill or technique that they have learned in their art class. Consider background information, the specific steps needed to accomplish the technique, photos or drawings that will help to demonstrate the skill or technique, and the time it takes. Provide links for more in-depth information or related information. If several students select different studio skills and techniques, you could plan an Art Department Web site that features links to each of these.

ASSESS..........
Reteaching

Have students work in pairs to compare and contrast their completed Web page designs based on their use of the principles of variety, emphasis, harmony, and unity. Then challenge them to take the best of both of their completed Web page designs to come up with a new and different Web page design that features the same information.

CLOSE............

Completed Web page designs can be printed, matted, and displayed for the entire school to view.

Teacher Notes

ART CRITICISM IN ACTION

(National Standards: 2b, 4c, 5a, 5c)

Critiquing the Work

▶ Describe
What do you see?

- See the credit line.
- There are two people. Their faces, arms, and hands are dark black. You cannot tell if that is a shadow or skin color. The figure on the left is wearing a long, white, flared tunic with sleeves that flare out at the wrist. The white pants are also flared. The figure on the right is wearing a white skirt.
- The land is a wide horizontal band of black across the bottom of the work. The house is black, with indications of gray windows in which you see reflections of the trees. The trees are bare, and many limbs, branches, and twigs are silhouetted against the sky.

▶ Analyze
How is this artwork organized?

Before you ask the questions of this section, ask students to define the colors that dominate this work. The answer is neutral.

- **Rhythm:** There are random repetitions of vertical tree trunks and diagonal tree limbs. The clouds form a random horizontal rhythm of free-form, organic shapes. **Balance:** This artist has used informal balance. **Proportion:** The artist has used accurate proportions to represent the people.
- The focal point is the two figures in white costumes. The secondary point of interest would be the moon

312

▲ **FIGURE 11.28**

Henri Rousseau. *Carnival Evening.* 1886. Oil on canvas. 116.8 × 90.2 cm (46 × 35½"). Philadelphia Museum of Art, Philadelphia, Pennsylvania. Louis E. Stearn Collection.

MORE ABOUT... Henri Rousseau

Henri Rousseau is best known for his mysterious and colorful jungle scenes. It is uncertain how he got his ideas for these unusual images as shown in Figure 11.28. One legend has it that Rousseau traveled to the jungles of Mexico when he was fifteen with the French army. It is more likely that the mild-mannered artist probably made frequent trips to the zoo and botanical gardens of Paris and used these locales as the inspiration for his fantasy jungles. Among his fellow artists, Rousseau was known as Master of the Trees because of his sensitivity to trees, plants, and animals.

1 DESCRIBE What do you see?

Read the credit line for information about the artwork and then make a list of everything you see in this painting. Remember to be objective. Do not make guesses.

- List the size and media of this work.
- Describe the people and what they are wearing.
- Describe the land, the sky, the trees, and the house.

2 ANALYZE How is this work organized?

Now you will look at the elements of art and how they are organized by the principles of art. You will discover the clues that tell you what the artist is trying to convey.

- Describe the artist's use of the principles of rhythm, balance, and proportion.
- Where is the focal point in this work? Is there a secondary point of interest? How did the artist create these focal points?
- How does the artist use harmony? Explain. How has he unified this work? Which element has he used to create unity?

3 INTERPRET What is the artist trying to communicate?

Now you will combine the clues you have collected and your personal ideas to form a creative interpretation of this work.

- How does the element of color affect the mood? How does the strong focal point affect the way the work looks?
- What are the people doing? Where are they?
- Give this work a new title based on your interpretation.

4 JUDGE What do you think of the work?

Decide if this is a successful work of art. You may have a personal opinion, but it is also important to make an objective judgment based on aesthetic theories.

- Do you think the artist has successfully used the elements and principles of art to create an unusual mood ? Explain.
- Has the artist created an interesting work? Did it make you think?
- Is this a successful work of art? Use one or more of the aesthetic theories you learned in Chapter 2 to defend your decision.

MEET THE
ARTIST
HENRI ROUSSEAU

French, 1844–1910

Henri Rousseau. *Moi-Meme, Portrait-Paysage (I Myself, Portrait-Landscape).* 1890. Oil on canvas. 143 × 110 cm (57⅛ × 44″). Narodni Galerie, Prague, Czech Republic.

Henri Rousseau was born in Laval, France. He lacked formal training and was entirely self-taught. At first he painted mostly street scenes and portraits, but as he gained confidence, he became more adventuresome. He created fantastic landscapes and metaphorical works that used bold colors and flat designs. Rousseau influenced other European painters who attempted to imitate his so-called primitive or naïve style.

He exhibited with artists such as Paul Gauguin, Pablo Picasso, and Georges Seurat, winning their admiration and the acclaim of the art world.

Art Criticism in Action **313**

that is as white as the costumes. The artist used contrast of value to create the focal points.

- The artist has used repetition of trees and clouds to create harmony. He has also used a **limited,** neutral color scheme of black, white, and gray as the dominant colors.

▶ Interpret

What is the artist trying to communicate?

- Answers will vary. Most will say the colors make the work gloomy, or spooky. Some will say the strong focal point of the two light figures against the dull, dark background makes the figures look isolated, and possibly in trouble, in this dark, scary place.
- Answers will vary. Some will guess the figures are dressed up to go to a costume party. Some will say the people feel frightened. Some may say they are going to the house; others may think they are leaving. Some may say they are spirits of people from long ago.
- Answers will vary.

▶ Judge

What do you think of the work?

- Answers will vary.
- Answers will vary.
- Answers will vary. Most may choose Emotionalism because of the mood created by the colors. Some may add Formalism because the elements and principles are effectively organized. Many may use Imitationalism because, although very weird looking, everything is portrayed realistically.

Time & Place   Late Nineteenth Century

Henri Rousseau painted *Carnival Evening* in 1886. Some other events that happened the same year:

Social Studies: The Statue of Liberty was completed and dedicated by President Cleveland at the entrance to New York harbor. It became a symbol of freedom to immigrants from all over the world.

Art: The Impressionist Exhibition was held in Paris, featuring Georges Seurat's painting, *Sunday Afternoon on the Island of La Grand Jatte.*

Science: In Atlanta, pharmacist John S. Pemberton first produced a fizzy, non-alcoholic drink called Coca Cola.

CONNECTIONS
THEATRE

How Does Stage Lighting Create Drama?

(National Standards: 6a, 6b)

After completing this feature, students will be able to:

- Discuss the dramatic effects of lighting in painting and theatre.
- Describe different lighting techniques.
- Conceptualize lighting effects of their own.

Teaching the Connection

- Have students read the feature on this page.
- Ask students to look carefully at the painting and imagine what type of light source Rembrandt may have used with his models. Encourage students to describe the emotional effect of lighting in this painting.
- Tell students that theatrical lighting is a fairly modern art form. In Shakespeare's time, stage lighting was limited to candles, oil lamps, and torches. Today, computers are often used to control a lighting switchboard. Stage lights come in a wide variety of strengths and sizes, some having as much as 10,000 watts of power. Lenses can now be added to soften or sharpen light effects. Tinted filters may also be used to remove certain wavelengths of color from white light, or to combine wavelengths to create a third color.

How Does Stage Lighting Create Drama?

◀ **FIGURE 11.29**

Rembrandt. *The Night Watch (Group Portrait of the Amsterdam Watch Under Captain Frans Banning Cocq).* 1642. Oil on canvas. 3.7 × 4.4 m (12′2″ × 14′7″). Rijksmuseum, Amsterdam, Holland.

Stage lighting is as essential to the production of a play as characters and dialogue. The way a stage is lit conveys both setting and mood. A lighting director may use downlighting for a shadowy effect or uplighting to distort the features of the characters. General illumination of the stage combines lighting from all sides. Spotlights can also be used to light a specific area. Stage lighting helps us to feel like we are a part of the unfolding drama.

A painting can have a similar impact on viewers. One of Rembrandt's best–known paintings, *The Night Watch* **(Figure 11.29),** achieves an almost theatrical effect. Although there are many figures in this crowded scene, we can spot the main "characters" in part because they are more fully illuminated than the others. The light source emanates from the upper left. Notice how the shadow of the officer's hand falls across the aide's uniform. As the focal point of the painting, the officer's illuminated hand conveys authority. Like theatrical lighting, the painting's use of contrast, light, and shadow helps to convey the activity as well as the emotional intensity of the scene.

Making the Connection

1. Imagine that Rembrandt's painting is actually a moment in a play. What do you think is happening?
2. Study the shadowed figures in this painting. What do they have in common? Why do you think Rembrandt used such dark values to paint them?
3. Experiment with light by using several flashlights in a dark room. Then, pick a scene from a play you have read or seen and design the lighting for it. Write down your directions and explain the effects you desire.

Answers to Making the Connection

1. Answers will vary.
2. Answers will vary. A close inspection of the figures in the painting reveals that most of them are soldiers in the act of preparing for battle. Some seem to be performing maintenance on weapons. Others appear to be waiting for orders. The drummer on the far right may actually be drumming. Perhaps Rembrandt wanted to convey the anticipation of a waiting army while placing the authoritative figure of Captain Cocq in the foreground.
3. Responses will vary.

Building Vocabulary

On a separate sheet of paper, write the term that best matches each definition below.

1. The principle of art concerned with difference or contrast.
2. The principle of art that makes one part of a work dominant over the other parts.
3. The first part of a work to attract the attention of the viewer.
4. The principle of art that creates unity by stressing the similarities of separate but related parts.
5. The quality of wholeness or oneness that is achieved through the effective use of the elements and principles of art.

Reviewing Art Facts

Answer the following questions using complete sentences.

1. Why do artists use variety in artworks?
2. Name the two major types of visual emphasis.
3. What is the most important part of an artwork called?
4. Name and describe the five ways in which artists create a focal point.
5. Name and describe three techniques that artists use to create unity in a work of art.

Thinking Critically About Art

1. **Analyze.** Look at Figure 11.1, page 286 and Figure 11.20, page 301. How do these buildings fit into their surroundings? How was the principle of unity achieved?
2. **Compare and contrast.** Notice the variety used in Figure 11.2, page 288. Compare this with the variety used in Figure 11.3, page 289. Explain how each artist used variety and point out the similarities and differences between the two works.
3. **Analyze.** Look through the other chapters of this book to find three examples of works in which the artist has emphasized one element, making all the others subordinate to it. List the works and explain which element has been emphasized.

Read how the "Vocalworks Radio Hour" presents variety and harmony in the re-creation of a live radio broadcast from the 1930s era. Showcasing swing music, comedy, and drama programs, Vocalworks swings us back to the past in the Performing Arts Handbook on page 423.

interNET **CONNECTION** Learn more about how artists achieve unity through harmony, variety, and emphasis. Visit the Glencoe Fine Arts Site at **www.glencoe.com/sec/art.** To begin your search, find the chapter you are studying in the Table of Contents and click on one of the "hot links."

Answers to Building Vocabulary

1. variety
2. emphasis
3. focal point
4. harmony
5. unity

Answers to Reviewing Art Facts

1. To keep the artwork interesting.
2. (a) The type in which an element of art dominates the entire work and (b) the type in which one area of the work is dominant over all of the other areas.
3. The dominant element.
4. Contrast, isolation, location, convergence, and the unusual.
5. Simplicity, repetition, and proximity.

Reteaching

■ Have students complete Concept Map 11 in the Reteaching booklet. 📁

■ Instruct students to look at the illustrations in other chapters of the textbook and find examples of works that have been unified through each of the following techniques: simplicity, harmony of color, harmony of shape, repetition, proximity, and continuation.

ASSESSMENT ✓

Evaluate

■ Have students complete the *Chapter 11 Test* in the TCR. 📁

■ Alternative Assessment teaching strategies are provided in the *Testing Program and Alternative Assessment* booklet. 📁

Extension

Suggest that students pretend they have taken an assignment to write a book titled *Everything There Is To Know About My Favorite Artist.* Challenge students to conceive a method of making a unified study of an artwork or an artist. If students prefer to work in groups, allow them to do so but have each one submit an analysis of their methodology.

Unit Overview

Unit 4 focuses on the developments of art traditions and styles through the ages and around the world. Students are introduced to artists from many different cultural groups and art movements. Unit 4 also helps students explore ways they themselves can pursue a career in an art-related field.

CHAPTER 12—Art Traditions from Around the World

In chapter 12, students will explore the art traditions from non-Western cultures. They will briefly explore the origins or art in prehistoric times and in the ancient river valleys. Students will also read about art developments in India, Asia, the Middle East, Africa, and in the Americas.

CHAPTER 13—Western Traditions in Art

In Chapter 13, students explore the many different types of Western art, beginning with the art of Greece and Rome, and progressing to contemporary times.

CHAPTER 14—Careers in Art

In Chapter 14, students examine the career opportunities in art and art-related fields.

Unit Resources

- 📁 Artist's Profile 1, Pablo Picasso
- 📁 Unit 4 Test
- 📁 Portfolio and Assessment Techniques

316

316

MORE ABOUT... Pablo Picasso

Spanish painter and sculptor Pablo Ruiz y Picasso (1881–1973) is considered one of the greatest artists of the twentieth century. He was a unique innovator of styles and techniques and a master of various media. His art style went through several developmental stages referred to as the Blue Period (characterized by the use of various shades of blue and expressing human misery), The Rose Period (displaying an emphasis on pinks and reds), Cubism (depicting harsh, angular planes), and Realist and Surrealist works (possessing a surreal and disturbing quality).

Picasso was influenced early on by the French postimpressionist artist Paul Cézanne and French artist Georges Braque.

ART
THROUGH
THE AGES

"Painting is stronger than I am. It makes me do what it wants."

Pablo Picasso
1881–1973

◄

Pablo Picasso. *Still Life*. 1918. Oil on canvas. 97 × 130 cm (38¼ × 51¼"). National Gallery of Art, Washington, D.C. © 1998 Board of Trustees. Chester Dale Collection.

317

Introducing the Unit

Assign groups the task of developing a "Top Ten" list of the most famous artists who ever lived. Ask students if they have any artists on their lists that are not from Western cultures. Tell students that in this unit they will learn about art through the ages in both Western and non-Western cultures.

Unit Motivator

Review with students the characteristics of art produced by Picasso and other artists of the Cubism art style. Tell students that the cubist art movement was actually influenced by the art of Africa. Have students examine other artworks in this unit and discuss similarities and differences between Western and non-Western art styles.

Discussing the "Quotation"

Have students comment on *Still Life* in light of Picasso's statement. Have them look for some elements that seem very deliberate (for example, the repetition of shapes, colors, or textures) and others that seem accidental (places where colors change or forms overlap unexpectedly). Ask students: Do you feel that Picasso was more in control than he would have us believe?

National Museum of Women in the Arts

You may wish to use the National Museum of Women in the Arts videodisc and/or CD-ROM. The videodisc features a bar code guide, and interactive CD-ROM.

interNET CONNECTION

VIRTUAL FIELD TRIPS Your students can experience and appreciate the fine art collections of countless museums and art galleries in every part of the world represented on the World Wide Web. Have your students spend a class period roaming the collections of the M.H. de Young Museum in San Francisco, or check the current exhibits of the Solomon R. Guggenheim Museum in New York. Work on a longer-term project as students discover art of the masters at the National Gallery of Art in Washington D.C. Give students a close-up view of ethnic works and indigenous galleries. Locations of some sites are in the Curriculum Links or the Online and Multimedia Resources of the Teacher Resources. Find us at **www.glencoe.com/sec/art**

Art Traditions from Around the World

(pages 318–349)

Chapter Scan

Lessons

1 Art of Earliest Times
2 Art of Asia and the Middle East
3 The Art of Africa
4 Art of the Americas

Resources

📁 Chapter 12 Study Guide

📁 Chapter 12 Test

📁 Cultural Diversity in Art

📁 Portfolio and Assessment Techniques

📁 Reproducible Lesson Plan 12

🎦 Transparency CC-12, *Buddha*. Ling Yin Si Hangzhou Temple, China

🎦 Transparency 12, *Stone Lintel,* Mayan Stela Stone

 While studying this chapter, use Performing Arts Handbook page 424 to help students discover the Korean traditions in ancient formal court music and dance.

▲ **FIGURE 12.1** This Bella Coola Sun Mask was created by a member of a secret society that staged performance rituals on special occasions. During a ceremony, this mask was raised against the rear wall of the dance house and traveled across the ceiling by means of ropes and pulleys that were not revealed to the viewers. This movement represented the journey of the sun across the sky.

Sun Mask. Bella Coola, nineteenth century. Central British Columbia. Red cedar, alder; carved, painted. 108.5 × 106.9 cm (42¾ × 42⅛″). The Seattle Art Museum, Seattle, Washington. Gift of John Hauberg.

FEATURED ART

African Clay Sculpture
Altamira Cave Painting
Asante Gold Necklace
Benin Bronze Relief
Bwa Leaf Mask
Chinese Scroll

Egyptian Wall Painting
Great Stupa at Sanchi
Haida totem pole
Indian Hindu Sculpture
Japanese Pagoda
Japanese Woodblock Print
Inuit Wood Mask
Islamic Illustration
Kente Cloth

Machu-Picchu
Maya Great Plaza of Tikal
Mohenjo-Daro
Olmec Colossal Head
Stonehenge
Sumerian sculpture
Taj Mahal
Temple at Angkor Wat

Art Traditions from Around the World

Art from the past shows what the people who created it were like. The art reveals their feelings, their ideas, their actions, and their way of life. This combination of *behaviors and ideas of a group of people* is called **culture**.

The history of visual art is like the history of the world itself—broad and complex. This chapter—and the one that follows—offers just a peek into the world's artistic heritage.

As you look at the Bella Coola mask in **Figure 12.1,** you can see that it was created with great care. Even though you may not know the purpose of this work you can appreciate its colors, shapes, and forms. You can see that formal balance organizes the art elements. Using art criticism, you can try to understand the mask and guess its purpose. If you do art history research, you will learn that this mask represents the sun. By researching, you will learn the symbolic meanings of the objects and shapes painted on the mask.

OBJECTIVES

After completing this chapter, you will be able to:

- Briefly discuss art traditions from many cultures around the world.
- Understand how cultural traditions influence artists' works.

WORDS TO KNOW

culture
Paleolithic period
Neolithic period
megaliths
cuneiform
ziggurats
pharaohs
dynasty
stupas
scroll
pagoda
woodblock printing
mosques
griots
totem poles

Developing Your
PORTFOLIO

Art history is the record of art from past to present. Create a historical time line tracing the development of your own artwork. Consider the work that you have done in the past. Collect a representative sample of artwork you have created, going as far back into your past as you can. Write a brief description of several of these works. Then draw some conclusions about how your art skills have developed as you have grown as an artist. Keep your artwork samples and your written art history in your portfolio.

DEVELOPING A PORTFOLIO

Written Summaries Art assessment involves an evaluation technique that challenges students to think critically and to see and understand the range of possibilities. Students need to know how to support these possibilities through opinions, based on reasonable rationales. When giving students the opportunity to write about works of art, be sure to assess the quality of the responses not the quality of the written expression. You may want to develop a rubric, which is a guide for scoring or passing judgment on the art assignment. For more information for developing a rubric, refer to the separate booklet, *Portfolio and Assessment Techniques,* that accompanies the *Arttalk* program. 📁

Chapter Overview

In Chapter 12, students learn about the art traditions that flourished outside of Western Europe. They will briefly explore the origins of art and discover that art from the past reveals many things about the culture that created it.

Examining the Artwork

Direct students to Figure 12.1. Tell them this mask was created by the Bella Coola people who live on the Northwest Coast of British Columbia. They staged elaborate masked rituals during the winter feasts and potlatches. This mask represents the sun, which is Alquntam, the creator of all men and animals. He used his canoe to cross the sky, while wearing a cloak lined with salmon. It was believed that when he reversed his cloak the rivers would run full with salmon. The three-dimensional face in the sun may represent Alquntam being transported in his spirit canoe. The face is framed by two ravens, a killer whale, and painted wings. The oval and split-U shapes, as well as the shape of the eye, are typical of Northwest coast design. The separated, protruding lips, the bent eyebrows, and the dominant blue color are all characteristic of Bella Coola art. Tell students that in this chapter they will learn about other art traditions from around the world.

National Standards

This chapter addresses the following National Standards for the Visual Arts:

1. (a, b)   3. (a, b, c)
2. (a, b, c)   4. (a, b)

Art of Earliest Times

FOCUS...........

Objectives

After completing this lesson, students will be able to:

■ Describe life during ancient times.

■ Tell what kinds of art were created during ancient times.

Supplies

■ A collection of contemporary pictorial symbols or icons

■ Prints of images from various cultures studied thus far

■ World map

Resources

📁 Application Activity 23, *Art Treasures*

TEACH..........

Motivator

Explain to students that archaeologists use artifacts to gain information about early civilizations that kept no written records. Point out that the first three letters of artifact are ART. The art of prehistoric people is an important source of information about their daily lives.

Vocabulary

Write the word part *-lith* on the board and ask whether students can think of words they have seen that contain this stem. Explain that this word part means "stone." Challenge students to brainstorm definitions of the terms *megalith* and *Paleolithic period*.

The artworks produced many thousands of years ago tell us a great deal about the earliest cultures and civilizations of our world. These ancient people left no written records. What we know of them has been learned from the objects and the art that they left behind.

Prehistoric Art

Prehistoric means before history, or before written records were kept. The objects made by people during this period are all that remain to tell us about the people who lived long ago.

Figure 12.2 is one of many cave paintings left by cave dwellers in Europe during the Paleolithic period. The **Paleolithic** (pay-lee-u-**lith**-ik) **period,** or *Old Stone Age, began about two million years ago, and ended with the close of the last*

ice age about 13,000 B.C. It was a time when people began using stone tools. In these cave paintings, the colors are so bright and the animals so realistic that, for a long time, scholars refused to believe they had been created by prehistoric people.

To this day no one knows the purpose of the paintings. Found deep inside caves, far from the entrances and living areas, they probably were not created for decoration. Some scholars believe the paintings were part of a hunting ritual. A shaman, or medicine man, may have created the image of the animal, believing that it would help hunters capture the animal. The paintings may also have been visual prayers for animals to appear during the next hunt. According to another theory, cave dwellers created the paintings to celebrate a successful hunt.

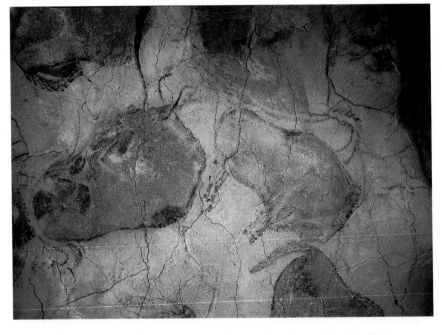

◄ **FIGURE 12.2** An amateur archaeologist excavated in this low-roofed cave for four years before his daughter, who was small enough to stand up straight in the cave and look up, discovered these paintings of sleeping, galloping, and crouching animals.

The Hall of the Bulls. c. 15,000 B.C. Altamira Caves, Spain.

MORE ABOUT... The Art of Writing

Humans produced their first pictures in cave paintings such as those shown in Figure 12.2. It was another seventeen millennia before the art of writing evolved, primarily out of a practical need. The population of Mesopotamia, now modern Iraq, was made up largely of shepherds and farmers, which explains

why the oldest writing samples are clay tablets that show agricultural accounts from the Sumerians. Other later tablets preserve information about Sumerian life—religion, interest on money-lending, even tablets that have a teacher's text on one side and the pupil's text on the other.

Prehistoric Builders

Eventually prehistoric people moved out of caves and began constructing their own shelters. Small communities developed and some hunters gave up their nomadic life and settled down, becoming farmers. After some time, small tribal groups grew into organized villages surrounded by cultivated fields and domesticated animals.

During the Neolithic period, people built structures of stone. The **Neolithic** (nee-uh-**lith**-ik) **period,** or *New Stone Age, is a prehistoric period stretching roughly from 7000 B.C. to 2000 B.C.* During this time, humans developed agriculture and stone tools were refined. Ancient structures from this period, called megaliths, have been found throughout Europe, Asia, and even North America. **Megaliths** (**meg**-uh-liths) are *large monuments created from huge stone slabs.* As early as 4000 B.C., circular arrangements of huge, rough-hewn stones were created in Western Europe. The most famous of these is Stonehenge in England (see Figure 12.35 on page 348). Built around 2000 B.C., it consists of a series of four concentric rings. Builders used an ancient building method that we now call *post-and-lintel construction.* Upright slabs, called posts, support horizontal slabs, called lintels. If you look at the photograph, you can see how the posts support the lintels. More than half of the original stones still stand. The tallest measures 17 feet and weighs more than 50 tons. Scholars are uncertain how prehistoric people, working with primitive tools, were able to cut these huge stones, transport them many miles, and then raise them into position. The purpose of Stonehenge has also baffled scholars for many centuries. In the past, people believed a great magician created it. Today, Stonehenge is thought to have served as a kind of observatory, enabling people to practice a type of astronomy and serve as an accurate calendar.

As prehistoric peoples learned to herd animals and grow crops, they also learned to live in harmony with their surroundings. This peaceful balance was upset by population growth. Small tribes began to fight over grazing land and soil suitable for growing crops. They were forced to band together into more organized groups for protection and also to be able to produce more food. By around 3000 B.C. four major civilizations had developed at different points on the globe. The ancient civilizations of Mesopotamia, Egypt, India, and China emerged at this time.

Ancient River Valleys

The ancient civilizations of Mesopotamia, Egypt, India, and China, are referred to as river valley civilizations. Each of these civilizations were ruled by a monarchy, practiced a religion based on nature, and achieved great skill in art and architecture.

Mesopotamia

The area of Mesopotamia included the cultures of many people within an extensive region. The region was the fertile crescent of land between the Tigris and Euphrates rivers in the Middle East. The people lived in city-states, and each city was ruled by a monarch. Today, this land is shared by Syria and Iraq.

The Sumerians were the first dominant group in the area. They were the first people to have a system of writing (using symbols to represent spoken language). **Cuneiform** (kyoo-**nee**-uh-form) was *the Sumerian writing system made up of wedge-shaped characters.* These characters stood for concepts and ideas. Because paper was not yet developed, clay tablets were used. Some of these still exist.

Studio Skills

The Altamira cave artists of Figure 12.2 on page 320 were of necessity limited to a narrow range of colors, but they made striking use of them. For students to experience a similar restraint, have them select an object and illustrate it with just one earth-tone color of paint plus black. They may use different values of the color.

Cross-Curriculum: Geography

Have students locate a map of the world. Have students work in pairs or small teams to identify and trace the location of the major river valleys discussed in this section. Then have them name the major cities found along the rivers' banks. Ask them to imagine they are traveling by boat on any one specific river from its source to its end. From the map, what land formations would they see? What do they speculate about the climatic conditions? What do they already know about each specific river and the country surrounding it?

CULTURAL DIVERSITY

Ancient Architecture The ziggurats were the Sumerians' most distinctive and monumental form of architecture, and they reflect the importance of religion in Mesopotamia. Explain to students that the larger and more developed buildings of other cultures also suggest the values of the people. Have students work in small groups to brainstorm the different concerns that are reflected when a society spends large sums of money to construct a pyramid, a cathedral, a grand opera house, a skyscraper, and a sports stadium. Have them present their findings to the class.

Aesthetics

Have students examine the artwork illustrated in Figure 12.3. Then have them find another reproduction of a figural sculpture. (See pages 327, 329, and 333.) Have them create a chart or diagram to compare how the artists depicted the facial features and other forms of the body.

Art History

The Sumerians have been credited with many "firsts." In addition to the ziggurat, they invented a system of writing. Cuneiform or wedge shaped script, was developed by wealthy temples to keep written business records. Cuneiform eventually evolved into arithmetic as well as language, which was very important for trade. The earliest preserved tablets from around 3100 B.C., were pictographs that represented a thing or a concept. A bull's head represented a bull. The pictograph evolved into phonograms which were representations of syllables in the Sumerian language. By 700 B.C., the writing had evolved into very abstract wedge-shaped symbols. This writing was very difficult to understand and only selected children were able to attend schools where the language was taught.

Art History

The ziggurat was a stepped pyramidal structure with a temple or shrine on the top. The first structures were the result of repeated rebuilding at a sacred site. The rubble from the first structure served as the foundation for the second. The elevation of shrines may also have come about to protect them from flooding.

▶ **FIGURE 12.3** This figure was placed in the temple to represent the worshiper. The wide eyes, hands folded in prayer, and attention to detail are typical of Sumerian sculpture.

Statua di Donna. c. 2700–2600 B.C. Marble. The Iraq Museum, Baghdad, Iraq.

Sumerian artists depicted figures in a lifelike and realistic way. Look at **Figure 12.3**. This small sculpture shows precise details of dress and facial features. Sumerians also constructed structures known as **ziggurats** (**zig**-uh-rats), or *stepped mountains made of brick-covered earth* (**Figure 12.4**). These temples had exterior staircases. A temple honoring the god of the city was placed at the top. Does it resemble other buildings that you have seen?

In time, the Sumerian civilization merged with that of Akkad, its northern neighbor, giving rise to the civilization of Babylonia (around 750 B.C.). Babylonian art and architecture resembled Sumerian to a great extent. Another Mesopotamian civilization, called Assyria, emerged after the decline of Babylonia. A distinct Assyrian artistic style began to emerge around 1500 B.C. Assyrian artists created precise, detailed stone reliefs, which they painted using many colors. They depicted royal events, hunts, wars, and animals, especially horses and lions. Human figures were given less emphasis, although they were still depicted in a realistic and detailed way.

◀ **FIGURE 12.4** A temple honoring the god of the city was placed at the top of the ziggurat. This structure was built in 2100 B.C. What other art and architecture was being created throughout the world at that time?

Ziggurat. Ur, Iraq. c. 2100 B.C.

MORE ABOUT... Sumerian Artwork

The Sumerians constructed ziggurats in the belief that mountaintops were the dwelling places of their gods. Lacking real mountains on the Mesopotamian plain, the Sumerians had to create their own artificial ones to provide a suitable home for their gods. The cult statues placed inside the ziggurat temple were believed to embody the deities that they depicted. Sumerians also made statues of worshipers to send prayers and messages to the gods in their places.

Egypt

The culture of ancient Egypt developed along the banks of the Nile River more than 3,000 years before the birth of Christ. Religion influenced every part of Egyptian life. The **pharaohs,** or *Egyptian rulers, were worshiped as gods and held complete authority over the kingdom.* Egyptians believed in life after death and preserved the bodies of the pharaohs in preparation for the afterlife. The famous pyramids were built as the tombs of the pharaohs.

Egyptian artists decorated temples and tombs according to very strict rules set forth by the priests. The rules required that each part of the body be shown from the most visible angle. Look at **Figure 12.5.** The heads, arms, legs, and feet are shown in profile. The shoulders and eyes, however, are shown from a frontal view.

The paintings found on the walls inside the tombs reveal a great deal about life in Egypt. Scenes from the life of the person buried in the tomb were intended to remind the spirit of life on earth.

India

In the Indus River Valley, the ancient civilization of India arose. Only in recent times have historians realized the age of Indian culture. For many centuries, no one knew that a civilization had flourished on the banks of the Indus River in northwest India. Then in 1865, railroad workers uncovered a hill of crumbling, fired-clay bricks near the city of Harappa (in present-day Pakistan). The bricks were found to be thousands of years old, dating back to 2500 B.C.

In 1922, a second city was discovered in the same area. Called Mohenjo-Daro (moh-hen-joh dahr-oh), meaning "Hill of the Dead" **(Figure 12.6),** the city was

◄ **FIGURE 12.5**
What symbols or features make these figures seem important? Observe the shapes in the boxes along the top border. These are hieroglyphs, an early form of picture writing. They give information about the painted scene.

Egyptian. *The Goddess Hathor Places the Magic Collar on Sethos I.* Thebes, Nineteenth Dynasty. c. 1303–1290 B.C. Painted bas-relief. 226.5 cm (89⅛"). The Louvre, Paris, France.

▲ **FIGURE 12.6** Experts believe the city of Mohenjo-Daro was abandoned because the climate changed. The ancient Indians built with fire-baked bricks, which meant they had ready access to timber. The area is a desert today.

Mohenjo-Daro, India. c. 2500 B.C.

Critical Thinking

Mohenjo-Daro was carefully planned to meet the needs of those that dwelled there. Have students draw a map of their neighborhood on the board. Ask whether the layout reflects any principles of urban planning and whether the ideas of Mohenjo-Daro still seem relevant today.

Art History

The Indus Valley civilization was the earliest civilization of South Asia. Today this area is in Pakistan and northwest India. This Harrapan civilization flourished from about 2700 to 1500 B.C. This was also the case for the Old Kingdom period in Egypt, the Minoan civilization of the Aegean, and the dynasties of Ur and Babylon in Mesopotamia. Evacuations beginning in the 1920s and continuing to present-day, have uncovered a number of urban areas including Harrapa and Chanhu-Daro. All of these cities are built with fired brick, while other civilizations of their time were using less durable, sun-dried bricks. Mohenjo-Daro, the best preserved of all the sites, consisted of an elevated area which probably contained important government structures. One building contained a watertight pool that may have been used for ritual purposes. Ask a volunteer to research more information about the types of structures that were discovered in these excavation sites. Have the volunteer share the findings with the class.

CULTURAL DIVERSITY

Egyptian Artists Discuss with students the team nature of Egyptian artistic production. Point out that Egyptian artists worked as members of a team of professional craftspeople that usually include an "outline scribe" who marked out the preliminary drawing, a person who chiseled the relief, and a third artist who added the paint. Artists in many other cultures have also worked in teams. Have students work in teams of three to plan and create a simple clay relief carving in the manner described. Discuss the advantages and the drawbacks of teamwork in creating art.

Studio Skills

Have students examine Figure 12.7. Ancient Indians used chiseled and drilled seals as amulets to stamp their agreements. Have students use utility knives to carve personal seals out of their rubber erasers. Then have them print the seals with ink or paint on plain paper to make "official" stationery.

Art History

Shang dynasty bronzes were embellished with a number of characteristics motifs, some of which were placed in a horizontal band, or covering the entire surface, as shown in Figure 12.8 on page 325. Among the most common decorative features were dragons, birds, the thunder scroll, the cloud scroll, a bowstring ornament, small circles, vertical ridges, and a variety of animals including the ox, the sheep, the goat, and the cock. Remind students as they create artworks in this class that there are many subjects that can be used as motifs, and they may wish to look back at these ancient works for examples.

once home to about 35,000 people. Architectural remains indicate that it served as a major commercial center. Wide, open streets divided the city into large blocks. The city featured multi-storied houses made from fired brick and wood, and elaborate, sophisticated drainage systems.

At this archeological site, workers discovered a number of small relief carvings in soapstone **(Figure 12.7).** These carvings are the earliest known examples of Indian art. As you can see, several unusual lines and shapes are incised above the animals. These are characters from the ancient Harappan system of writing.

Over 70 cities, towns, and villages have been discovered in the Indus valley, as well as evidence of an organized kingdom with a central government that existed about 4,500 years ago.

China

The Yellow River valley became the site of the ancient Chinese civilization, a civilization that retains many of its ancient traditions today. Beginning 4,000 years ago, it is the oldest continuous culture in the history of the world.

As their civilization developed, the Chinese gained skill and knowledge in many different areas. They invented paper, porcelain (a type of ceramic), and

▲ **FIGURE 12.7** The designs on these seals "belonged" to their owners. Seals were pressed into soft clay to secure a container or document.

Soapstone seals from Mohenjo-Daro (Indus Valley culture). Karachi Museum, Karachi, Pakistan.

324   CHAPTER 12   Art Traditions from Around the World

Curriculum Connection

Language Arts Scholars, able to trace how people learned to write cuneiform (see More About... on page 320), have identified hundreds of pictograms. These simple drawings were stylized representations of an object. By combining several pictograms, humans expressed a thought or idea in an ideogram.

Scribes wrote on clay slabs or tablets using a stylus, or special tool for writing. These forerunners of our quill pens and fountain pens were made out of perishable materials like river reeds or wood and were cut with a triangular tip. (The word cuneiform comes from the Latin word *cuneus* which means "wedge.")

woodblock printing as well as the compass and gunpowder. Until modern times, emperors ruled China. Its historical periods were divided into dynasties, which were named after ruling families. A **dynasty** is *a period of time during which a single family provided a succession of rulers.* Bronze vessels found in ancient graves reveal that Chinese artisans cast bronze as early as the first imperial Chinese dynasty, the Shang dynasty, which began in 1766 B.C. The ritual wine vessel shown in **Figure 12.8** is an example of the intricate work done at that time. Abstract motifs and spirals cover the vessel. Experts believe the spirals stand for clouds, rain, or water. Such images reveal an ancient Chinese regard for nature. Many early bronze vessels show extraordinary technical mastery—evidence of the centuries of development required before such artworks could be created.

 FIGURE 12.8 This vessel was used in a ceremony to ensure harmony with the spirits of deceased ancestors. Notice the large eyes and beak of an owl on the lower part of the vessel. Can you find other animals in the designs that cover this container?

Ancient China. *Ritual Wine Container.* Shang dynasty. Thirteenth century B.C. Bronze. 76.4 × 31 × 31.8 cm (30 × 12⅛ × 12½"). Arthur M. Sackler Gallery, Smithsonian Institution, Washington, D.C.

 Activity | **Creating a Writing System**

Applying Your Skills. Imagine that you are from a past civilization and have been called upon to create a new writing system. As you begin to work on this task, remember that you know nothing of modern alphabets. Think about what ideas you will need to express in your culture and create a shape for each idea. When your system is complete and you have created a key to your language, write a sentence using your symbols and see if anyone in your class can read it.

☑ **Check Your Understanding**

1. For what purpose might cave paintings have been created?
2. What is a ziggurat?
3. Why and for whom were the pyramids built?
4. Define the word *dynasty.*

ASSESS...........

Self-Assessment

Have students complete the lesson review questions. Answers appear below.

Reteaching

Present prints of images from all the cultures studied so far. Have students identify where each work was produced and explain what clues were used to identify the location.

Enrichment

Have students speculate on how archaeologists date cave paintings and other artifacts. Explain that while the technique of carbon-14 dating has been archaeology's most powerful tool for determining the age of prehistoric artifacts, it is not always as accurate as scientists would like. The best artifact dates come from combining data from carbon-14 analysis with information from ancient calendars, rock layers, geologic activity, and the annual growth rings in trees (dendrochronology).

 Answers to Check Your Understanding

1. Cave paintings might have been created as hunting rituals, in order for hunting to go well or as prayers for animals to appear during the next hunt, or to celebrate a successful hunt.
2. A ziggurat is a Sumerian building, a stepped mountain made from brick-covered earth with a temple on top.
3. The pyramids were built as tombs for Egyptian pharaohs.
4. A dynasty is a period of time during which a single family provides a succession of rulers to a country.

CLOSE.............

Hold up an object from your classroom and ask students to imagine what art historians could determine about our culture by studying the markings on it.

Art of Asia and the Middle East

Art of Asia and the Middle East

(pages 326–331)
(National Standards: 3b, 4a, 4b, 4c, 5a, 5b)

FOCUS...........
Objectives

After completing this lesson, students will be able to:

- Describe the role of religion in the art of India, China, Japan, and Middle Eastern art.
- Identify key developments in Indian, Chinese, Japanese, and Middle Eastern art.

Supplies

- World map
- Paper, ink, pens, brushes
- Time line, copy machine
- Paper, drawing media

Resources

📁 Cooperative Learning Activity 23, *Chinese Dynasties*

📁 Enrichment Activity 23, *Making Art Connections*

TEACH.........
Motivator

Turn students' attention to a world map and point out the lands of India, China, Japan, and the Middle East. Ask students to note the dates of artworks represented by each region and consider the distances on the map between each of the cultures represented. Do they imagine that the peoples of these ancient lands had contact with one another, or were they isolated from each other as their individual art styles developed?

326

The cultures of India, China, Japan, and the Middle East have all produced exciting art forms, some very different from European art. The art of Asia and the Middle East reflects different philosophies and religious beliefs from those in Western art.

India

The art of India has been strongly influenced by the Hindu and Buddhist religions. Hinduism is one of the world's oldest religions. It began in ancient India around 2000 B.C. It is not one religion but a group of many related sects. Buddhism began as a Hindu reform movement, and had a strong influence over the country from the third century B.C. to the sixth century A.D. Among the earliest, and most important, examples of modern Indian architecture are **stupas** (**stoop**-uhs), which are *beehive-shaped domed places of worship*. These were built by Buddhist architects to house relics of Buddha, their religion's founder. Each stupa was reached through four gates covered with relief sculptures **(Figure 12.9)**.

After the fifth century, Hinduism rose again in popularity because it was encouraged by the monarchs of the period. Hindu temples and sculptures of the Hindu gods were created. Hinduism combined several different beliefs and practices that developed over a long period of time. In Hinduism there are three primary processes in life and in the universe: creation, preservation, and destruction. The three main Hindu gods reflect this belief system. They are Brahma, the Creator; Vishnu, the

▶ **FIGURE 12.9**
Domes such as this were often erected over holy places, burial mounds, and holy relics. What is the purpose of preserving such things?

Great Stupa. Sanchi, Madhya Pradesh, India. c. first century B.C.

▶ COOPERATIVE LEARNING

Art History If you don't wish to spend a lot of time on art history, divide the class into groups of two or three and assign different time periods to each group. The groups then would study only that period in the text and report on it to the class. To make the reports more interesting, they can be spaced throughout the year. Suggest that they use large prints of artworks if they are available; the library is a good source of either prints or oversize art books. Slides ensure that everyone in the class can see the works being discussed. Encourage dressing up in costumes, role-playing, or presenting a dramatization.

Preserver; and Siva, the Destroyer **(Figure 12.10)**. In Hinduism, both humans and animals are believed to have souls which undergo reincarnation. Reincarnation is a purification process in which the soul lives in many bodies in many lifetimes until it becomes one with Brahma, the great soul.

India exported its religions to the rest of Asia. In Kampuchea (previously Cambodia) many temples were built of stone in the Indian style. The temple at Angkor Wat **(Figure 12.11)** was originally a Hindu temple built between A.D. 1113 and 1150. Dedicated to Vishnu by its builder, it represents the Hindu view of the universe.

China

China adopted Buddhism during the Han Dynasty, which lasted from 206 B.C. to A.D. 220. Buddhism was easily adopted in China because, like other Chinese religions, it stressed the harmony of human beings with nature. An important part of Buddhism is meditation, focusing one's thoughts on a single object or idea. Chinese artists found that long periods of meditation enabled them to perceive the beauty of an object or a scene with greater clarity. This enabled them to more effectively capture the beauty of the subject in their paintings. Chinese art of the last 2,000 years has been greatly influenced by Buddhism and meditation.

The Chinese were the first people to consider "picture painting" a valuable endeavor. This was because many artists were also scholars who wrote poems in beautiful writing (called calligraphy) using brushes that could make thick and thin lines. They used these same brushes and line techniques to paint pictures.

▶ **FIGURE 12.10** The Hindu god Siva is called the Destroyer. This sculpture is rich in symbolism. Notice what the figure is standing on. The objects he holds are a drum that symbolizes creation and a flame that symbolizes destruction. How is destruction related to creation?

Unknown, India, Tamil Nadu. *Siva as Lord of the Dance.* c. 950. Copper alloy. 76.2 × 57.1 × 17.8 cm (30 × 22½ × 7"). Los Angeles County Museum of Art, Los Angeles, California, given anonymously.

▲ **FIGURE 12.11** The layout of this temple was designed to create a solar calendar by which the summer and winter solstices and the spring and fall equinoxes could be fixed. Why was this important in an agricultural society?

Southeast Asia. Temple at Angkor Wat, Kampuchea (Cambodia). 1113–50.

Vocabulary

Discuss with students the *Yamato-e* painting style and point out that it contrasts with *Kara-e*, which means "pictures of Chinese themes." Ask how this new style was imported to the Japanese culture. Then discuss the *Ukiyo-e painting of the* "floating world." How is this style related to Japanese geography and how is it related to the subject of the artworks?

Art History

Have students consider the photograph of the Great Stupa at Sanchi in Figure 12.9. Then have students write a paragraph explaining what religious concept the circular shape of the dome calls to mind.

Aesthetics

Guide students in discussing the Great Stupa at Sanchi shown in Figure 12.9, on page 326, and the Temple at Angkor Wat in Figure 12.11. How do students respond to each work? What similarities between the two works can students identify? What are the most important differences? Explain that stupas were not houses of worship. Instead they housed a statue of the god, and worshipers gathered around the outside to offer prayers.

Aesthetics

Guide students in discussing the sculpture of Siva, the Destroyer in Figure 12.10. Ask: What message or mood do you think this sculpture was intended to communicate?

TEACHER TALK

Classroom Management If you have a copy machine with enlarging capability, make an enlargement of a major time line, laminate it, and display it in the room. Students can attach sketches of the masterpieces shown in the text in the proper spot on the time line. They might even add small prints of works that are not in the text or photocopy works from books. If there is not enough room for all of the pieces at one place in time, strings of yarn can be attached to the photocopy and pictures arranged above or below the proper place with yarn leading to the time line.

Studio Skills

Have students study the Chinese painting in Figure 12.12 to understand the artist's approach to space, giving a sense of distance with mountains, and moving into the middle ground and foreground detail. Point out the brush and ink technique often used in Chinese paintings. Tell students that every brushstroke counts and that the Chinese painters used long horizontal scrolls to represent a continuous viewing of a scene. Have students plan and execute a drawing like this to detail a nature scene.

Art History

Briefly introduce the use of perspective, directing students' attention to Chapter 5, page 113. Then have students view a Chinese landscape painting like that in Figure 12.12. Let students point out the various vanishing points of the Chinese work. Have them discuss the way that multiple perspectives affect their experience of looking at the art. Do students find the Chinese method confusing, or does it make the work interesting? Does it leave less or more to the viewer's imagination? Can one approach to art be considered more spiritual than another? Discuss how multiple-perspective art may reflect a view of life different from that depicted in art of the West.

▲ **FIGURE 12.12** Notice how small the people are in relation to the landscape. The hut blends in with the natural setting. The calligraphy bordering the drawing is an important part of the picture. Notice how it echoes the shapes of the leaves. How might the calligraphy be part of the "conversation"?

Hua Yen. *Conversation in Autumn*. 1762. Ink and color on paper. 115.3 × 39.7 cm (45⅜ × 15⅝"). The Cleveland Museum of Art, Cleveland, Ohio. The John L. Severance Fund.

They painted fans, pages of books, and scrolls **(Figure 12.12)**. A **scroll** is *a long roll of parchment or silk.* Some were hung on walls, while others were meant to be unrolled a little at a time and read like a book.

The earliest Chinese paintings were filled with images illustrating the beliefs that people should live together peacefully and be respectful of their elders. With the influence of a new religion, Buddhism, the focus of painting began to shift away from humans and toward nature. By around A.D. 1100, the landscape was the main theme of Chinese painting.

The Chinese also produced sculpture for religious purposes and to honor the dead (see Figure 10.1, page 254). During the Sung **(soong)** Dynasty (A.D. 960–1279), artists first produced ceramic objects of porcelain made from a fine-grained white clay called kaolin (**kay**-uh-luhn). Work in porcelain reached its highest point during the Ming Dynasty (A.D. 1368–1644). Today, collectors especially prize porcelain from this dynasty (see Figure 5.4, page 99).

Japan

In A.D. 552 the ruler of a kingdom in nearby Korea sent the Emperor of Japan a gift. The gift was a bronze figure of the Buddha, the founder of Buddhism. Along with the sculpture came priests to spread Buddhist teachings. Eventually many of the people of Japan accepted this new religion. They also learned about different ways of making art. For the next 250 years, Japanese art would show strong traces of Korean, Chinese, and other Asian styles.

The first important Japanese art objects of "modern times" were started in A.D. 594. These were magnificent Buddhist temples that were built throughout the country. Since the islands of Japan are made of volcanic rock, the Japanese could not use stone

---

MEETING INDIVIDUAL NEEDS

Logical/Math Learners Have students use a Venn diagram to compare and contrast the Hindu and Buddhist religions. Venn diagrams are constructed by using two or more overlapping geometrical figures, such as a circle, that share an area in common. Have students list characteristics and beliefs unique to each religion in the areas of the circle not shared, and elements that are common to both religions in the commonly shared area of the circle. This will give students an opportunity to focus on the contrasts and comparisons between the two religions.

Kinesthetic Learners Have students draw poster-size pictures of calligraphy, geometric shapes and patterns, or other objects used in Asian or Islamic art.

to build their temples. Instead, they made them from wood. In the process, they elevated the architecture of wooden structures to new levels.

Japanese temples are intricately assembled and richly decorated. They are carefully fitted together with special joints. Because Japan suffers frequent earthquakes and violent storms, the buildings had to be durable. One of the most interesting features of early Japanese temples was the **pagoda** (puh-**gohd**-uh). This is *a tower several stories high with roofs curving slightly upward at the edges* **(Figure 12.13).**

The Japanese also created monumental sculptures, often of the Buddha. Such a sculpture can be seen in **Figure 12.14,** the Great Buddha at Kamakura. It was cast in bronze in A.D. 1252. It is situated outdoors in a grove of trees, which seems an appropriate setting for this contemplative Buddha.

▲ **FIGURE 12.13** This pagoda stands as the oldest wooden structure in the world. Its purpose is to preserve relics.

Pagoda from the Temple Complex at Horyuji, near Nara, Japan. c. A.D. 616.

◄ **FIGURE 12.14** The Great Buddha was once housed in a temple but the temple was destroyed by a tidal wave. What effect does its current location have on this artwork?

Great Buddha. Kamakura, Japan. c. A.D. 1252.

LESSON 2 *Art of Asia and the Middle East* | **329**

Promoting Discussion

Ask students to suggest ways that culture can influence art. After studying Figures 12.13, 12.14, and 12.15 (on page 330), ask students to describe their impressions of Japanese art. Ask: What elements cause them to recognize a work as being Asian or Asianlike? Based on their answers, discuss the influence that a viewer's prejudices and preconceptions have on the way they view art. Is it ever possible for someone to judge a work from another culture without referencing their ideas and feelings about that culture? Why or why not?

Art in Everyday Life

To foster students' awareness of the heritage of art in everyday life, suggest this: Compare the works of art from past and present, from Western and Asian cultures, to see how artists saw (or see) the natural world. Look at a Chinese landscape and see how it invites you to sit quietly and meditate. Notice how the artist suggests mountains and trees with a few brushstrokes. Compare it to the art of American painter George Inness (see Figure 1.9 page 11). How do you see your landscape?

MORE ABOUT... Scrolls

Chinese artists intended scrolls to be viewed in portions. Unlike Western painters, who rely primarily on composition and subject matter to affect audiences, the Chinese scroll artists force viewers to study their works actively. As the scroll is slowly revealed to the viewer, the relationships of height, depth, and direction draw the audience's interaction. The scroll provides the artist with an excellent medium for presenting a panoramic view of nature. If any human elements are included, they are overwhelmed by the natural elements. Villages and boats are portrayed in a miniature scale to emphasize their insignificance in comparison to the huge landscapes.

Art in Everyday Life

Explain to students that every culture has its own art forms—designs, music, dance, and ritual—that express its lifestyle and values. Suggest to students the following: visit ethnic museums to enjoy the art forms of the Polish, Lithuanian, German, Greek, Mexican, Irish, Native American, African, and other countries. Find lists of ethnic museums in your town or city. Find out about seasonal festivities like the Chinese New Year with its Dragon Dance. Watch parades that celebrate ethnic heroes. The history of art reaches right into our homes. Learn the traditions of your culture from your own family.

Developing Perceptual Skills

As students study Figure 12.15, tell them that the artists of many cultures were less interested in exploring the psychological aspect of the subject and more interested in their symbolic, historical, or spiritual meanings. Ask them to find other artworks in the textbook that make use of stylized facial expressions instead of faces that describe the feelings of that person.

MEET THE
ARTIST
ANDŌ HIROSHIGE

Japanese, A.D. 1797–1858

Andō Hiroshige (hear-oh-shee-geh), a Japanese painter and printmaker, was born in Edo (now Tokyo) in 1797. Following in his father's footsteps, he became a fire warden. However, inspired by the work of Hokusai, he later decided to apprentice as a painter. He became an apprentice to Utagawa Toyohiro, a renowned artist, and graduated in 1812. At that time he took his teacher's name as a sign of respect and began signing his work "Utagawa Hiroshige."

Hiroshige worked in the Ukiyo-e tradition of printmaking, the last great artist to do so. Eventually he became even more successful than his role model, Hokusai. He depicted the experiences of ordinary people and places, capturing moods and changing times and seasons. For the first 15 years of his career, he created traditional prints of traditional subjects, such as women and the theatre. From 1830 to about 1845, he achieved fame as a landscape artist, creating poetic, lyrical works.

During the last part of his career, the quality of his work suffered as he apparently had difficulty keeping up with demand. A prolific artist, he made more than 5,400 prints. In 1858, he died of cholera in Edo.

▶ **FIGURE 12.15** The Japanese perfected the art of woodblock printing so that all people could afford art. This print depicts a famous pine tree as seen during a rainstorm. How is line used to convey the impression of rain? What is the main color? What effect does this have?

Andō Hiroshige. *Evening Rain on the Karasaki Pine* (from the series Eight Views of Omi Province). Nineteenth century. Woodblock print. 26 × 38.1 cm (10¼ × 15″). The Metropolitan Museum of Art, New York, New York. H. O. Havemeyer Collection. Bequest of Mrs. H. O. Havemeyer, 1929. (JP1874)

In A.D. 784, Japan entered its golden age of art. During this period, Japanese artists developed a painting called *Yamato-e* (yah-**mah**-toh-ay), or "pictures in the Japanese manner." Paintings done in this style were the first examples of pure Japanese art, meaning there was no influence of other Asian cultures in them. Yamato-e screen paintings were often made in sections and were used to brighten the dimly lit interiors of temples and homes as a temporary wall to divide a room.

Another new Japanese style of art was called Ukiyo-e (oo-**kee**-yoh-ay), meaning "pictures of the floating world," which depict different aspects of the pleasures of life. The demand for artworks in this new style was great. To meet this demand, artists turned to a new technique, **woodblock printing.** This is *making prints by carving images in blocks of wood.* Using this technique, artists could produce many inexpensive prints of one image **(Figure 12.15).**

MORE ABOUT... Mosques

The main religious building of Islam is the mosque. The word comes from the Arabic *masjid*, meaning "a place to kneel or prostrate oneself." Every mosque must be oriented toward Mecca, the birthplace of Muhammad. In addition, a mosque must have a courtyard, a mihrab, a gate, and at least one minaret. Statues or other visual depictions of human animal forms are not found within mosques. Most decoration takes the form of geometric and floral motifs on the walls of the mosque. The floor is usually covered with carpets or matting on which worshipers kneel and touch their foreheads to the ground in prayer.

Taj Mahal, garden and pools. 1632–43. Agra, India.

Art of Islam

In A.D. 570, an event took place that had a major effect on both the religious beliefs and the art of the Middle East and much of Asia. Muhammad was born in Mecca. He grew up and became a merchant, following the tradition of his family. However, he believed he received personal revelations that challenged him to change the religion of his people, the Arabs, who worshiped many idols. Muhammad taught that there was only one god, called Allah. After his death, his teachings were assembled into the Koran, a holy scripture. Islam was the name given to the religious faith of people who followed Muhammad. Worshipers are called Muslims.

Islamic art (art of the Muslim world) was characterized by the use of ornate line, shape, and pattern. The interior of **mosques,** *Muslim places of worship,* were decorated with calligraphy, geometric patterns, and stylized plants and flowers. Art depicting people or animals was not permitted in mosques. Such art was prohibited early in the history of the Islamic religion and was meant to prevent Muslims from worshiping images when they should

instead be worshiping the idea of Allah.

Book illustrators, however, were not limited by the same restrictions. They depicted people and animals in everyday scenes. They filled their illustrations with beautiful decorative patterns. The illustration shown in Figure 12.34, on page 346, depicts such a scene from a book about court life in Iran. The illustration was completed in A.D. 1525, just 25 years after Michelangelo created the *Pietà* (pee-ay-**tah**) (Figure 13.8, page 357).

The religion of Islam, and its influence on art, also spread to the East. Muslims conquered Delhi in India and converted many Indians to Islam. **Figure 12.16** shows a famous building, the Taj Mahal, which was built by an Indian Muslim leader as a memorial to his wife. The building is an outstanding example of Islamic architecture and is considered one of the most beautiful structures in the world. The building emphasizes formal balance and harmony with its surroundings. Its cool marble walls and placid lake evoke a response of serenity and tranquility in those who visit.

Check Your Understanding

1. What is a stupa?
2. What medium did the Chinese often paint on that could be hung on walls or read like a book?
3. What material did Japanese architects commonly use and why?

Art History

Inform students that because early Islamic artists could not depict the figures of humans or animals, they developed a style of flat, abstract designs to be used in a variety of works. The most familiar form is arabesque, which comes from the Italian word meaning "Arablike." These swirling, interlaced designs are apparently based on plant shapes, but the forms of leaves, branches, and vines have been transformed into scrolls, spirals, and curves. Such arabesque designs were first used during the 900s in all Muslim countries. Arabesques and other geometric designs have been used to decorate the walls of buildings, tiles, rugs, metalware, and other craft objects.

ASSESS..........

Self-Assessment

Have students complete the lesson review questions. Answers appear below.

Reteaching

On the board, write the terms *painting, sculpture,* and *architecture.* Have pairs of students each select one of these terms and discuss it as it applies to the ancient art of one of the cultures studied in this lesson.

Enrichment

Invite volunteers to learn more about the gods of Hinduism and their representation in sculpture and other art forms. Volunteers should present their findings jointly. If possible, the group should include slides or photographs in their presentation.

CLOSE............

Ask students to respond to this statement: The study of the art of Asia and the Middle East must ultimately be the study of the religion of each region.

Answers to Check Your Understanding

1. A stupa is a small, round burial shrine erected over a gravesite to hold relics.
2. The Chinese often painted on scrolls, or long rolls of parchment or silk.
3. Japanese architects commonly used wood. The Japanese islands are made of volcanic rock, so stone couldn't be used. No other material was as easy to find and use as wood.

The Art of Africa

FOCUS............

Objectives

After completing this lesson, students will be able to:

■ Discuss some of the purposes for which African art was created.

■ Describe the artworks produced by various African cultures.

■ Identify some of the common materials used by African cultures in the creation of their art.

Supplies

■ Cardboard

■ Construction paper, tempera paint, found objects

■ Papier-mâché or plaster gauze

■ World map or globe

■ Index cards

■ Recorded African music

Resources

📁 Enrichment Activity 24

TEACH..........

Motivator

Reveal that Africa was at one time mysterious and unfamiliar to the Western world. Help students identify and discuss words commonly used to describe African people and societies—such as *primitive, underdeveloped,* and so on. Explain that these terms reflect Western prejudices and ignorance regarding African culture and history.

Throughout Africa, in both the past and the present—even within the context of modern nation-states—the visual arts are well integrated with other art forms, including music, dance, and drama. The art of Africa was an integral part of the daily lives and religious rituals of the people.

The Role of Art in African Cultures

The huge continent of Africa has a population of millions that is subdivided into about 1,000 cultural groups. The peoples of Africa have long-established,

▶ **FIGURE 12.17** The vertical lines on the face of this figure probably represent ornamental scars made to indicate ancestry and to enhance physical beauty. How did the artist use the principles of art in creating this portrait of a king?

Portrait of a king. Ife, Nigeria. Copper alloy. Eleventh–fifteenth century. H: 36.2 cm (14¼"). Museum of Mankind, London, England.

highly-developed cultures that have been producing sophisticated art forms for centuries. The arts are as varied as the peoples.

Everything is made with great care, whether for rituals or everyday use (see Figure 11.15, page 297). Art addresses not only the concerns of the living, their ancestors, and those yet to be born, but also those of the spirits of nature. A great deal of African art emphasizes the important events of life and the forces of nature that influence the lives of individuals and communities.

Dominant themes in African art include birth and death; the roles of men, women, and children; coming of age; sickness and healing; the importance of food and water; and the human relationship with nature. Artworks are often linked to celebrations and rituals, both nonreligious and sacred. Westerners are fascinated with objects from these cultures and have put them in museums. It is important to understand the original context in which these objects were made and used.

Ancient Ife

For the Yoruba (**yaw**-ruh-buh)people of Nigeria, the city of Ife (**ee**-feh) is the place where life and civilization began. Yoruba cities developed between the years A.D. 800 and 1000. By A.D. 1100, artists of Ife had developed a highly–refined, lifelike sculptural style to create portraits of the first Yoruba kings and queens. The display of royal portraits, with their composed, balanced facial features, added a sense of stability in periods of political transition between rulers, or following the death of a ruler **(Figure 12.17)**.

MEETING INDIVIDUAL NEEDS

Auditory/Musical Learners Play excerpts of recorded African music. Ask students to listen to the music and identify the use of percussion instruments and repeated rhythms. Have students use both hands to play the rhythm patterns on their laps. Suggest that students can use these rhythm patterns to set a mood for their studio activities.

Kinesthetic Learners Challenge students to create a dance through which they can teach classmates about some aspect of African culture. Dancing groups may have a narrator who helps interpret the symbolic meaning of the dance steps. Encourage students to bring rhythm instruments, such as hand drums, bells, rattles, or maracas to play during the dance.

According to Yoruba beliefs, the world consists of two realms: the real world that can be seen and touched; and the supernatural world of ancestors, gods and goddesses, and spirits. Works of art created for the real, or visible, world tend to be realistic, whereas works of art created for the supernatural, or invisible, world tend to be more abstract.

As memorial portraits of Yoruba royalty, these sculptures celebrate the lives and accomplishments of individuals. Like Yoruba poems, which record family history and personal deeds, these refined works of art encourage living generations to strive for perfection. They encourage the living to match or surpass the cultural accomplishments of previous generations.

The Empire of Mali

Works of art made centuries ago in Ife and elsewhere in West Africa document the rise of city-states throughout the region. The terra-cotta sculptures of cavalrymen and foot soldiers from the Inland Niger Delta, near the ancient city of Jenne, date back to the early thirteenth century, when the empire of Mali was founded by a powerful military leader and king named Sundiata. These figures reveal proud profiles, with jutting chins and heads held high atop sturdy necks. Their bodies appear straight and tall whether shown standing or seated upright on stallions **(Figure 12.18).** The figures represent members of the well-outfitted and well-organized army described in an epic that recounts Sundiata's life history.

The strength of Sundiata's great cavalry and army of foot soldiers enabled him to gain political power. Under his leadership, the empire of Mali became one of the largest and wealthiest kingdoms the world has ever known. The epic story of the rise of Sundiata is passed on by **griots (gree**-oh), *oral historians who are also musicians and performers,* throughout West Africa to this day.

The city of Jenne is the oldest city in sub-Saharan Africa. In the art and architecture from this city there is an

▲ **FIGURE 12.18** Because wet clay is soft, artists can easily add texture to the overall forms of clay sculptures. How many different kinds of texture can you identify in this work?

Inland Delta Region, Mali. Equestrian figure. c. thirteenth century. Ceramic. 70.5 cm (27¾"). National Museum of African Art, Smithsonian Institution, Washington, D.C. Museum purchase, 86–12–2.

Promoting Discussion

African artists, as well as other artists throughout history, have used proportion to emphasize importance. For example, the Egyptian artists enlarged the proportions of pharaohs in tomb paintings as a way to emphasize their importance as kings and gods. More recently, artists have used exaggeration or enlargement of figures or objects in their works to create certain feelings.

Aesthetics

Divide the class into three groups of aestheticians—Imitationalists, Formalists, and Emotionalists (see Chapter 2, page 31). Direct students' attention to Figure 12.18. Ask each group to brainstorm the strengths of the work in terms of its aesthetic theory.

Promoting Discussion

Help students study a world map or globe. Point out that Africa is more than three times the size of the United States. Explain that there are approximately as many nations in Africa as there are states in the United States. Describe the continent's enormous cultural diversity, with many different peoples (or ethnicities) living together within each nation. Tell students that there are more than 1,000 distinct languages spoken in Africa, and that most people speak at least several languages.

Cross Curriculum: Language Arts

In Yoruba society, *oriki*, or praise poems, are recited publicly to honor particularly accomplished members of the community. Ask students to write an oriki for someone they admire and to recite the praise poem for the rest of the class to hear.

MORE ABOUT... Griots

In Mali, griots, oral historians, use poetry, music, drama, and dance to recount the epic history of Sundiata, the first king of the medieval empire. They celebrate living individuals too, publicly reciting family histories and personal achievements. As the twentieth-century griot, Djeli Mamadou Kouyate describes his role in the book *Sundiata* by D.T. Niane, "Since time immemorial, my family has been in the service of the princes of Mali. I teach kings the history of their ancestors so that the lives of the ancients might serve them as an example, for the past is old, but the future springs from the past. Whoever knows the history of a country can read its future."

Art History

Explain that, as reflected in their forms, African figures and masks are generally created to serve life-sustaining purposes, to promote the well-being of both individuals and the larger society.

Ask students to survey briefly the artworks illustrated in this lesson. Instruct students to use their imaginations to write a detailed description of an African ceremony or ritual in which one of these objects might be used. In their descriptions, students could identify features of the art objects that would help young people learn the meaning of these rites. Have volunteers share their descriptions with the class.

Aesthetics

Introduce the following information to the class and ask for volunteers to learn more about these topics:

The colors most commonly used to paint African sculptures are red, black, and white. These colors generally have symbolic significance, though their precise meaning varies according to social context.

The color white is often associated with purity and coolness and with the ancestral and spiritual world. In many African societies, white bands are painted across the eyes to show that a person has special visionary power, able to communicate with the spiritual realm. One of the main sources for the color white is kaolin, a white clay also used to make porcelain dishes.

▶ **FIGURE 12.19** This solid iron figure shows the strong vertical lines that characterize Mali sculpture.

Bamana peoples, Mali. Bamana iron figure. Iron, string, cowrie shells. Indiana University Art Museum, Bloomington, Indiana. Gift of Ernst Anspach.

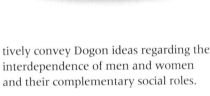

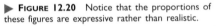

▶ **FIGURE 12.20** Notice that the proportions of these figures are expressive rather than realistic.

Seated Man and Woman. Dogon people, Mali. Wood. 76.2 cm (30″). Photograph © 1993 by the Barnes Foundation, Merion Station, Pennsylvania.

emphasis on vertical elements (**Figure 12.19**). This can be seen in the corner pinnacles of house façades, which are made tall and straight.

The sculpture shown in **Figure 12.20,** made by the Dogon (**doh**-gahn) people of Mali, conveys a sense of harmony and balance. As images of the first man and woman described in Dogon myths of creation, this sculpture serves as an inspiration to living generations. These figures are seated on a stool with a circular support that symbolizes the link between the earth below and the spirit world above. Carved from a single piece of wood, the interlocking forms effec-

tively convey Dogon ideas regarding the interdependence of men and women and their complementary social roles.

The Kingdom of Benin

The Benin (**buh**-neen) kingdom, situated in what is now southern Nigeria, was a society of many class levels, with an oral tradition that goes back seven or eight centuries. The kingdom reached the peak of its power in the sixteenth century. Like earlier artists in nearby Ife, Benin artists excelled in creating metal sculptures using a copper alloy possessing many of the same qualities as bronze.

334 CHAPTER 12 Art Traditions from Around the World

MORE ABOUT... Wooden Figures

Help students understand the creation of carved wooden figures by presenting this information: To fashion a sculpture's basic form, African sculptors use an adze, an axlike tool with an arched blade at right angles to the handle. A chisel or small knife is used for details. Rough leaves, or now, sandpaper, is used to create a smooth finish. Sculptures are generally oiled or painted with pigments made from natural ingredients or using Western paint. Colors are applied by the sculptor, or by someone else after it leaves the carver's hands, within the context of later use.

Among the most ambitious of the Benin castings are the high-relief sculptures that once covered the walls and pillars of the royal palace. One of these contains the figure of the *oba* (**oh**-bah), or king, flanked by two chiefs bearing shields, sword bearers, and palace attendants **(Figure 12.21)**.

Here four social ranks are depicted. The king, or *oba* is placed in the center and is the largest figure. The two chiefs are almost as large as the king. Two sword bearers, one a child, are even smaller. Three tiny figures, one supporting the king's foot and two in the top corners, represent the least powerful members of the court.

The *oba* wears a patterned wrapper, or waist cloth, a six-ringed coral necklace, and sits side-saddle on a horse. In Benin culture, horses are symbols of political power.

The Asante Kingdom

The Akan people lived in central and coastal Ghana. In the first half of the eighteenth century, these people joined together to form a powerful confederation of states that included many cultural groups. The largest of these groups was the Asante (ah-**sahn**-tee).

Gold was the measure of wealth for the Asante and their kings, who tightly controlled its use. Items fashioned from the precious metal were made to be worn by these kings as a sign of their divine authority and absolute power.

Cross Curriculum: History

Within the Kingdom of Benin, metal-casters, like ivory carvers and other groups of specialized artists, worked together in artistic guilds controlled by the king. Artworks made of enduring materials, such as copper alloy, document the history of the Kingdom of Benin and its encounters with foreign powers. Ask students to research this history. Then have students work in groups to plan and prepare timelines showing the major events in Benin's history.

Studio Skills

Discuss with students the various ways the artist emphasized the importance of the Oba in Figure 12.21. Have students complete a drawing in colored pencil that includes no less than five figures or objects. Tell them to emphasize one of these figures or objects using the same techniques observed in the Benin relief. Exhibit the completed drawings and discuss them in terms of their success in using the principle of emphasis.

◀ **FIGURE 12.21** In Benin art the most politically powerful person is represented as the largest figure. This representation reflects the central organization of the kingdom. Less powerful individuals are smaller.

Kingdom of Benin, Edo people, Nigeria. *Mounted King with Attendants.* c. sixteenth–seventeenth century. Bronze. 49.5 × 41.9 × 11.3 cm (19½ × 16½ × 4½"). The Metropolitan Museum of Art, New York, New York. The Michael C. Rockefeller Memorial Collection. Gift of Nelson A. Rockefeller, 1965. (1978.412.309)

LESSON 3   *The Art of Africa*   **335**

MORE ABOUT... Benin

Explain to students that the sculptures of the Benin Empire (such as the one shown in Figure 12.21) are among the most famous examples of African art. The sculptors of Benin, most of whose work was created between the sixteenth and nineteenth centuries, probably learned the techniques of casting from the sculptors of Ife. Ife is in southwestern Nigeria. From about the eleventh century until the seventeenth century, Ife was the seat of the Yoruba kindgom. Many art historians think that the sculptures of both Benin and Ife can be traced back to the Nok culture, centered in what is now northern Nigeria. Examples of Nok sculpture have been dated between the fifth century B.C. and second century A.D.

Art History

After students have reviewed Figure 12.23, tell them that many people in the United States first became aware of Kente cloth when it was worn by the first president of Ghana, Kwame Nkrumah, at meetings of the United Nations in New York City. During the 1960s, Kente cloth became closely associated with the black consciousness movement. Today the patterns of Kente cloth may be worn in the United States to make both political statements and fashion statements. Ask a small group of interested volunteers to learn more about the uses of Kente cloth in the United States and to share their findings with the rest of the class.

Art History

Tell students to study the gold necklace in Figure 12.22. Inform them that only a few gold pieces like this one have survived to recent times. Ask several volunteers to research reasons for this phenomenon. Ask students if they can recall reading about any other period in which works of art were melted down so that the metal could be used for other purposes (i.e., ancient Greek bronze sculptures).

Art History

Although Europeans regarded gold as a highly valued metal for centuries, this was not always true in Africa. Copper was thought to be more valuable by early Africans. It was not until the seventh century that Africans learned to appreciate the market value of gold.

▲ **FIGURE 12.22** Works of art made using the lost-wax casting technique often show finely textured details. What elements of art are especially important in this work?

Akan people, Asante Kingom, Ghana. *Necklace.* Nineteenth century. Gold. 2.5 × 40 cm(1 × 15¾″). Virginia Museum of Fine Arts, Richmond, Virginia. The Adolph D. and Wilkins C. Williams Fund.

Asante necklaces, bracelets, and anklets were crafted by stringing cast-gold beads with gold nuggets, glass and stone beads, and other items. In **Figure 12.22,** a pendant in the form of a land crab is used. This necklace was probably designed for a queen mother, because the land crab was widely recognized by the Asante as a symbol for a person of this rank.

The work of goldsmiths in Kumase, the Asante capital, was regulated by the king. He allowed people to commission works of art from these highly–skilled craftsmen. Items obtained through the king's court included gold ornaments, staffs, and swords.

The Asante king also controlled the use of special cloth. During the 1600s, weavers created the first *Kente* (**ken**-tee) *cloth,* a brilliantly colored and patterned fabric that became the royal cloth. Kente cloth is woven in narrow strips that are then stitched together to form large pieces with complex patterns **(Figure 12.23).** By the 1720s, Asante

▶ **FIGURE 12.23** Weavers of Kente cloth have invented many different patterns. These patterns often have names that are immediately recognized by members of Akan societies. What elements of art have been used to create the patterns on this cloth?

Asante people, Ghana. Man's cloth (Kente cloth). Rayon. L: 314 cm (123¾″), W: 217 cm (85⅜″). UCLA Fowler Museum of Cultural History, Los Angeles, California. Anonymous gift.

COOPERATIVE LEARNING

Myths and Legends The various cultures of Africa have a rich heritage of myths and legends that explain the mysteries of life and death. Ask teams of volunteers to research further the mythology of various African groups. Have each team choose one kingdom or group of people and use references from the library and/or Internet to find information on the mythological traditions. One excellent resource is *World Mythology* by Larousse. Teams may also find relevant information in collections of legends and stories from various cultures. After completing their research, have teams share their findings with the class in oral presentations.

weavers were unraveling imported silk fabrics and reweaving them into cloths featuring their own unique designs. Silk cloths woven with special symbolic patterns were reserved exclusively for kings.

The Bwa People

Although wood is the most common material used to carve face masks and headresses, African masks were constructed in different ways using a wide variety of materials. For example, the Bwa people of Burkina Faso made masks of leaves, plant fibers, porcupine quills, and feathers. Leaf masks were made at the end of the dry season, before the rains that marked the beginning of the next agricultural cycle. The Bwa people considered leaf masks the most ancient mask form and closely associated them with nature (**Figure 12.24**).

The Bwa people also produced wooden masks that were used during village ceremonies or harvest festivals. The music of flutes, drums, and gongs accompanied the dancers wearing these masks, which took different forms— animal, human, and abstract. All were painted with black, white, and red geometric patterns. Plank masks were among the most abstract of all mask forms made by the Bwa people (**Figure 12.25**).

▲ **FIGURE 12.24** African masks are generally more than just a face covering. Imagine wearing a leaf mask like this one. How would you feel?

Bwa people, Burkina Faso, village of Boni. Detail of a leaf mask. 1985.

Art Criticism

Discuss with students the plank masks (Figure 12.25 on page 338) created by the Bwa. Explain that the patterns painted on these tall, vertical masks function as a coded language. To the uninitiated, the checkerboard patterns painted on these masks might be interpreted using Western symbolic systems structured by corresponding sets of opposites: white and black, light and dark, good and evil, etc. However, for those initiated into Bwa masking traditions, the black squares of the checkerboard represent the dark, worn animal-hide mats used by knowledgeable elders as they sit watching the mask rituals. The white squares represent the fresh, new light-colored hides that more junior initiates sit on. Thus, the black squares symbolize wisdom, and the white squares symbolize ignorance, as darkness is associated with the deep knowledge of the elders. Through mask performances, initiates learn the rules of Bwa society.

After these explanations, have students meet in groups to discuss the use of the elements of art in these Bwa masks.

ASSESS...........

Self-Assessment

Have students complete the lesson review questions. Answers appear below.

Reteaching

On index cards, write the name of one of the following materials: wood, bronze, copper alloy, gold, terra-cotta, cloth. Permit small groups of students to select one card each. Groups are then to name an African culture that used the material indicated and tell what kinds of art objects the material was used to create.

Activity

Constructing a Mask

Applying Your Skills. For students using cardboard, instruct them to cut strips of the material and staple them into cones and cylinders large enough to fit over their heads. Have them cut holes or slits to see through. Suggest that they use construction paper, tempera paint, and found objects to create facial features and decorations. Instead of constructing masks out of cardboard or paper, you may find your students would like to use papier-mâché or plaster gauze to design and create masks molded of their own faces. Make this an after-school or extra-credit project.

Enrichment

Since metaphoric thought is the essence of creative thinking, all students, especially gifted ones, should be challenged to conceive and integrate symbols in their artwork. Ask them how they could symbolically show an idea, then use their original symbols in their artworks. Some students may have difficulty with symbolic thinking; instead, use real objects to convey ideas, and provide them with tangible examples from which to get ideas.

CLOSE.............

Ask each student to write a sentence identifying the most fascinating fact he or she learned in this lesson. Have students read their statements aloud and compare their responses. What fact was mentioned most often?

▲ **FIGURE 12.25** Though large and cumbersome, plank masks are made of lightweight wood. To help steady the mask, the performer holds a stick between his teeth. This stick projects through rim holes at the back of the mask. How does a person wearing a plank mask see?

Bwa people, Burkina Faso, village of Pa. Plank masks entering performance area, harvest celebration.

Activity — Constructing a Mask

Applying Your Skills. What happens when you cover your face with a mask? Can you hide your identity from others? Design your own mask using thin cardboard, construction paper, paint, or other materials. In choosing your design and materials, think about what you want your mask to represent.

✓ Check Your Understanding

1. What beliefs are reflected in the terra-cotta and bronze sculptures of the Yoruba people?
2. What are griots?
3. How do artists of the Benin kingdom signify the importance of figures in their artworks?
4. What is Kente cloth and what is it used for?

✓ Answers to Check Your Understanding

1. Art of the Yoruba culture reflects the values of inner calm, self-confidence, and dignity.
2. Griots are oral historians who are also musicians and performers.
3. Artists of the Benin kingdom signify the importance of figures in their artworks by size. The most politically powerful person is represented as the largest figure.
4. Kente cloth is brilliantly colored patterned fabric that became the royal cloth. This cloth was reserved for the exclusive use of Asante kings.

Art of the Americas

Archaeologists believe that the first visitors to North America were groups of Asian hunters who crossed an ancient land bridge across the Bering Strait. They began to arrive in what is now Alaska between 20,000 and 40,000 years ago. Gradually these people spread out to cover all parts of North and South America. In this lesson, you will study the contributions of Native peoples of the Americas.

Art of Mesoamerica and South America

The term *pre-Columbian* refers to the time period before the arrival of Christopher Columbus in the Americas in 1492. Art historians use the term to refer to the art of the Indian civilizations of early Mexico, Central America, and South America. However, archaeologists are discovering that many of these pre-Columbian civilizations were highly sophisticated and created magnificent works of art and architecture.

Olmec Culture

Olmec (**ol**-mek) culture is often called the "mother culture" of Mexico because the artifacts found in the region are the most ancient. The Olmec civilization dates from 1200 B.C. to A.D. 500. The artifacts left by the Olmec had an influence on all the civilizations that were to follow. They carved altars, pillars, sarcophagi (sahr-**kah**-fuh-guy) (stone coffins), and statues. Among the most interesting of the Olmec creations are four huge human heads carved from volcanic rock (**Figure 12.26**). These were discovered at La Venta, a center for religious ceremonies. These sculptures weigh up to 40 tons and stand 8 feet tall.

Notice the childlike features on this giant face. The full lips, which seem almost to be pouting, are typical of the Olmec style.

Mayan Culture

By around A.D. 800 the Mayan (**my**-uhn) empire covered the Yucatán peninsula, modern Belize, Guatemala, and Honduras. The Maya were gifted mathematicians. They had the most

▲ **FIGURE 12.26** This monumental sculpture depicts a simple, stylized face. The stone was quarried and transported over many miles of swampland before reaching its destination. What does this indicate about the technology of the Olmec people?

Olmec. Colossal Head. 1200 B.C.–A.D. 500. Basalt. 243.8 cm (8') high. Anthropology Museum, Veracruz, Mexico.

LESSON 4   *Art of the Americas*   **339**

FOCUS...........
Objectives

After completing this lesson, students will be able to:

■ Name and describe four major Pre-Columbian cultures.

■ Identify the contributions the various Pre-Columbian cultures made to the art world.

■ Name and describe five major groups of Native Americans.

■ Identify the contributions to art the different Native American cultures have made.

Supplies

■ Varied works of American/Native American art

■ Magazines

■ Photographs of Mayan, Aztec, and Egyptian pyramids

■ Brown butcher paper, watercolor markers

■ World map

■ Tagboard

■ Video cassette recorder

Resources

📁 Application Activity 24, *Sharpening Your Skills*
📁 Cooperative Learning Activity 24, *Aztec School Calendar*

MORE ABOUT... The Olmec

Little is known about the Olmec culture that carved the series of gigantic heads resting in La Venta, Mexico. The Olmec pantheon included gods with human and animal elements. The widespread appearances of half-human, half-jaguar figures indicates that reli-gion played a big role in the arts as well as other aspects of Olmec life. Because they flourished early, from about 1200 B.C. to 300 B.C., and shared many practices with future cultures, the Olmecs are considered to be a "mother culture" to the area.

TEACH..........

Motivator

Write the phrase *American art* on the board. Then arrange along the chalk rail numbered reproductions of unmistakably American paintings (e.g., by Winslow Homer), along with photographs of Mayan and Aztec temples, Native American headdresses, and other "American" works of art. Ask students: Is this an American work of art? Why or why not?

Promoting Discussion

Have students study the Olmec head sculpture in Figure 12.26 on page 339, noting its size. Ask: What does the capacity to produce larger-than-life works of art such as this reveal about people?

Art History

In addition to being advanced in mathematics and architecture, the Maya also developed a sophisticated religious world view. Like other cultural groups of North, Central, and South America, the Maya were governed by shamans, who served as mediums between the spiritual and physical worlds. Although the shamans were almost exclusively male, the Mayan religion emphasized the equal importance of the two genders. In the Mayan religious view, humans and animals were believed to share the surface of a world confined to a single branch of a ceiba tree.

accurate calendar of any people in history and had developed the most advanced hieroglyphic writing in Mesoamerica. They were also great builders. The Maya erected huge temples and cities with tools of wood, stone, and bone. In the late 1800s, scientists discovered an ancient city in northern Guatemala. This Mayan city, Tikal (tih-**kahl**), is known to have covered an area of 50 square miles. The city is thought to have been home to some 55,000 people **(Figure 12.27).**

The surviving works of Mayan civilization range from the smallest objects to great temples covered with relief carvings. Among the smallest artworks of the Maya are many beautifully–designed clay figures only a few inches high. However, most of the Mayan sculpture that has survived consists of relief carvings on buildings and monuments. In the early stages of the Mayan civilization, these carvings were mostly simple and realistic. In some later temples, a more complex, geometric style came to be the rule.

Aztec Culture

The largest of the cultures of ancient Mexico and Central America was the Aztec. This civilization emerged sometime between A.D 1200 and 1325. The Aztecs were a warlike people. Like other pre-Columbian peoples, they were very religious. When their god told them to leave their comfortable homeland and settle where they saw an eagle perched on a cactus, they obeyed. There, they built a magnificent city, which they called Tenochititlán (tay-noch-tee-**tlahn**). A collection of tiny islands, the Aztec city was connected by a network of canals. In the fifteenth century, the Aztecs embarked on an aggressive military campaign to force other groups in Mexico to pay them tribute. They reached the height of their power and domination less than a century before the arrival of the Spanish. By the time Spanish conquerors arrived in 1519, their island city covered over 25 square miles. Today we know the city, which is no longer surrounded by water, as Mexico City.

The Aztecs adopted many of the ways of making art used by the people they conquered. They created a type of painted book called a codex. Such painted books told the stories of mythological or historical events. Like Mayan art, Aztec art was greatly influenced by religion. The Aztecs also built temples

◄ **FIGURE 12.27** The Mayan city Tikal included temples and other stone and stucco structures. The pyramids here are 230 feet high.

Maya. Great Plaza of Tikal, general view. A.D. 150–700. Tikal, Guatemala. Vanni/Art Resource, New York.

COOPERATIVE LEARNING

Mayan and Aztec Culture Have students form six groups and ask each group to learn more about one of these topics: the Mayan writing system, the Mayan calendar, the Mayan religion, the Aztec writing system, the Aztec calendar, the Aztec religion. Have members of each group research their assigned topic; then have them discuss the effect on the works of art in that culture. Ask each group to prepare and present a visual display or video summarizing what they have learned.

◀ **FIGURE 12.28** Machu–Picchu was built on a mountainside to discourage would-be attackers The city has withstood five centuries of earthquakes.

Machu-Picchu, Peru.

Art History

Have students obtain photographs of Mayan and Aztec pyramids and compare these structures with those produced by the Egyptians. Then have them discuss the following questions: How did the three structures differ in function and purpose? Were the building techniques different, and if so, how? What was the unifying element among the various pyramid types? How do you explain the building of such similar structures on two different continents by peoples who clearly never met?

Critical Thinking

Have students write a paragraph in which they identify which accomplishment covered in this section they find to be the most compelling. Students may choose an artistic achievement of one of the civilizations they read about, or they may respond to some other facet of culture. Be sure students explain their choices.

Art History

Have students note the date when Machu–Picchu was completed. Point out that it was within a year of this date that the renowned Renaissance sculptor Michelangelo began work in Florence on his statue of David.

Promoting Discussion

Have students note the passage in the text describing the precision with which the Inca fitted together the huge stone blocks of Machu–Picchu. Ask what other ancient civilization students have read about that was similarly adept at fitting together stones. Do the structures of that culture resemble those of the Incas? Have they survived equally well?

and shrines, some carved directly into the mountains. Highly–stylized and elaborately–ornamented sculptures depicted gods and religious symbols in bold, dramatic style.

Inca Empire

The Inca civilization flourished between the thirteenth and fifteenth centuries, and their empire stretched more than 2,500 miles from north to south. It included present-day Peru plus parts of Ecuador, Chile, Argentina, and Bolivia. In acquiring such a large territory, the Inca Empire absorbed many cultural and religious influences from neighboring groups and from civilizations that had flourished before it. Although governing such an immense territory required a vast administration and bureaucracy, the Incas managed to govern without the benefit of a written language. They made calculations and kept records using pieces of knotted string of different colors, called *quipu* (**kee**-poo). The Incas' ability with numbers is reflected in their art. Inca artifacts were made with great mathematical precision.

The Incas were masters of shaping and fitting stone. They were also highly skilled urban planners. Proof of both talents can be found in the walled city of Machu–Picchu (**mahch**-oo **peek**-choo) **(Figure 12.28).** The stones of its buildings were so carefully matched that a knife blade cannot be slipped between any two.

Native American Art

When Christopher Columbus reached North America in 1492, he thought his ship had landed on the east coast of India. He referred to the natives he found living there as Indians. Today these first settlers are called Native Americans.

Some groups became hunters while others turned to growing crops as a way to survive. Artifacts found in these regions show that all of these people created art of some kind. These works have given us insight into the cultures of these peoples. Native American art and traditions are still being practiced today by these cultural groups.

MORE ABOUT... The Inca Empire

Two aspects of the Inca Empire should be noted when considering current ideas of civilization. First, the cities were not the usual settlement type; and second, the people had no written language. (Their spoken language, Quechua, it should be noted, was imposed upon all they conquered.) Their primary form of religion was a form of ancestor worship centering on the perpetual care of the mummies of their dead, which were brought to participate in major ceremonies. Contrary to the Aztecs, the Inca practiced little in the way of human sacrifice and, even then, primarily sacrificed animals. Because the Inca Empire was designed to be ruled by a small, elite group, Francisco Pizarro was able to overtake them with 168 soldiers.

Promoting Discussion

Prepare and distribute copies of a *true-false* questionnaire about Native American peoples. Among the statements that might be included are the following: Some Native American cultures produced totem poles; all art produced by Native Americans is applied art; no Native American artists are at work today. Discuss student responses and correct any misconceptions.

Art Criticism

Point out that Native American artists have historically used whatever materials happened to be at hand to create their art. Have students create a chart listing some of these materials, the area of Native American art in which they have been most used, and the types of objects or artworks they have most often been used to create. Ask students to compare these materials and techniques with those used by the artists of Europe during the same periods.

Curriculum Connections: Geography

Provide students with a list of questions about the traditional Inuit lifestyle, such as the following: Where and how do the Inuit live? What kinds of work do men and women do? How many individuals today still maintain traditional lifestyles? Have volunteers select and research one of the above questions.

Aesthetics

Direct students' attention to the mask illustrated in Figure 12.29. Ask a group of volunteers to research in what ways these masks are similar to ceremonial masks of Africa. What common function do the masks of the two different cultures serve?

The Arctic Region

The Inuit (**in**-yuh-wuht) people inhabited present-day Canada and Alaska from the earliest times. Although they are often called Eskimos, they refer to themselves as the Inuit.

Inuit society is loosely organized into family groups that rely on hunting and fishing for survival. The images created by Inuit artists reveal the importance attached to the animals they relied on for food—seal, walrus, fish, whale, and caribou. Other animals such as the fox, wolf, and bear were also represented in their art. The human figure was shown in the masks and dolls that they created.

Figures are also found on the engravings done on walrus ivory. In these engravings, Inuit artists used a kind of pictorial writing that described various activities and events associated with

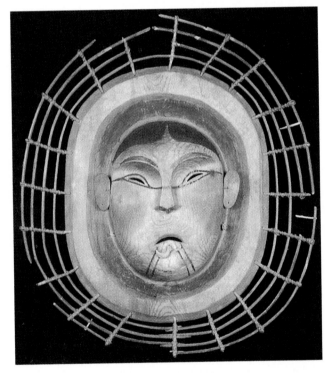

everyday life. In one such engraving on an ivory pipestem, a series of lively drawings record the activities associated with the daily quest for food. Since the surface of this pipestem is less than one inch wide, the engraving takes the form of tiny, decorative circles and miniature figures. Despite their small size, the artist still managed to present an easy-to-read account of the hunt. To accent the engraved lines used in works like this, artists filled them in with color or made them dark with soot.

Frequently, Inuit art was created to serve the religious needs of the people. The mask representing a moon goddess in **Figure 12.29** is an example. An Inuit shaman, or medicine man, wore such a mask during ceremonial dances. While dancing, he would go into a trance and act as a messenger between the world of the living and the mysterious world of spirits.

The Northwest Coast Region

The Northwest Coast Region refers to an area rich in natural resources that runs from southern Alaska to northern California. Native cultural groups in this region, including the Haida (**high**-duh), Tlingit, and the Kwakiutl (kwa-kee-**yoo**-tul), developed a complex culture in which art played a prominent role.

Like other people, the Kwakiutl held annual rituals to initiate new members, reinforce the status of old members, and

◀ **FIGURE 12.29** A mask of this kind was worn only by a shaman during ceremonial dances. How do you think the purpose of this mask is reflected in its design? What feelings do you think the mask evoked in viewers?

Inuit. Mask of Moon Goddess. Lower Yukon or Northwest Bering Sea. Before 1900. 63.5 cm (25¼") high. Hearst Museum of Anthropology, The University of California at Berkeley, Berkeley, California.

TEACHER TALK

Technology in the Classroom One way of enhancing students' appreciation of contemporary Native American art is by creating a well-stocked classroom library of Native American audiovisual and print resources. If you have a video cassette recorder at your disposal, you might purchase one or more of the several available outstanding videotapes about Native American artists, such as *Daughters of the Anasazi*, which traces the life and work of potter Lucy Lewis, and *Maria*, which deals in like fashion with artist Maria Martinez. You might also consider subscribing to Native American periodicals.

demonstrate their magical powers. Ceremonial masks and dramatic costumes were created for these rituals. Look at the Secret Society Mask pictured in Figure 10.27 on page 273. It is composed of several hinged pieces that moved. This movement was intended to add surprise and drama to the ritual. Often after a Kwakiutl ceremony, or to celebrate another important event, people gathered to enjoy a *potlatch*. This event enabled the members of one clan to honor those of another, while adding to their own prestige.

Native Americans of the Northwest Coast lived in large family groups. Each family group traced descent from a mythological animal or human-animal, from which they took their name. In order to symbolize their association with this mythic ancestor, they carved totem poles. **Totem poles** are *tall posts carved and painted with a series of animal symbols associated with a particular family or clan* **(Figure 12.30).**

The Southwest Region

The Native American groups of the southwestern United States include the Pueblo (**pweb**-loh) and the Navajo (**nav**-uh-hoh). Early Spanish explorers used the term *pueblo,* meaning village, to describe groups of people living in large, highly–organized settlements. Ancient Pueblo dwellings were built with adobe, or sun-dried clay, walls.

The Pueblo were especially skillful in creating painted pottery. Each community developed its own distinctive shapes and painted designs. In the Rio Grande Valley of New Mexico, for example, Pueblo potters used black outlines and geometric shapes to create bold designs over a cream-colored base **(Figure 12.31).**

◄ **FIGURE 12.30** Totem poles are similar to a European family's coat of arms and were erected in front of a dwelling as a means of identification and a sign of prestige.

Haida totem pole. Prince of Wales Island. c. 1870. Originally 16.2 m (53′) high. Taylor Museum of the Colorado Springs Fine Arts Center, Colorado Springs, Colorado.

▼ **FIGURE 12.31** The materials and techniques used in this water jar identify it as a Pueblo work. What elements of art can you identify in this design?

Water jar. Santo Domingo Pueblo, New Mexico. 1910. Ceramic. 24.13 cm (9½″) high × 24.45 cm (9⅝″) diameter. Denver Art Museum, Denver, Colorado.

Art Criticism

Totem poles like the one in Figure 12.30 rank among the world's largest wood carvings. The amount of effort spent creating these poles can be more fully appreciated when you discover that in one village every house had a totem pole, each measuring from 30 to 50 feet (9 to 15 m) high. Exceptional examples have been measured to stand as high as 80 feet (24 m) above the ground. To help students fully understand the dimensions of such works, as well as the planning and dedication that must have gone into each, have students pace off 50 feet on the school grounds. Have students imagine the path they have just paced off to be occupied by a large fallen tree, perhaps an oak. Ask: How would you go about preparing the tree for use as a totem pole? How would you arrange for the work of individual artists to form a unified whole? How long would you allow for the task of converting the raw tree into a finished work of art?

Critical Thinking

Have students examine the water jar in Figure 12.31. In what way is this object similar in shape and design to the water jars created by the ancient Greeks? Are the two objects similar in function? Can both of them be considered as examples of applied art and fine art?

Curriculum Connection

Geography The Four Corners region of the United States is located where the boundaries of Utah, Colorado, New Mexico, and Arizona come together. The Native Americans who settled in this region are thought to be Asians who traveled across the Asian continents to the Bering Sea. They crossed into what is now Alaska and made their way south along the West Coast and then inland. Have students find a map of the world and estimate the number of miles these people traveled before settling in the Southwest United States. Let students reflect on the fortitude these early settlers must have had in order to travel thousands of miles on foot, carrying their belongings with them.

Art History

Have students compare and contrast the cultures of the Pueblo and Great Plains Native Americans. Ask: What were the most important differences between the lives of people in the two groups? How was the architecture of the two groups different? How do the crafts of the two groups differ? What factors may explain some of these differences, as well as any similarities that exist?

Curriculum Connections: History

One of the largest of the Woodlands cultures was the Iroquois. The word *Iroquois* was coined inadvertently by French explorers, who heard the exclamation "Hiroquoue!" (spoken by tribal chieftains at the end of speeches) as "Iroquois" and associated it with the people who used it. Eventually all European settlers used Iroquois as the name for this Woodlands Region culture.

Activity

Sketching an Event

Applying Your Skills. When the Plains Indians painted tales of their battles on skins, they often used a birds-eye view in telling the tale. Before beginning this activity, have students crinkle sheets of brown butcher paper and then flatten. Tearing the edges will give the paper a more aged, natural look. Direct students to carefully outline each object in their design and color the work using watercolor markers.

The Navajo, another Southwestern cultural group, learned the art of weaving from the Pueblo. Male Pueblo weavers taught the Navajo weavers, who were women, to make cloth with looms at the beginning of the eighteenth century. As Spanish and Mexican settlers moved into the Southwest, they introduced new designs and patterns which the Navajo adopted. By the first half of the nineteenth century, the Navajo were using European dyes and Spanish wool to create weavings that matched the work produced by the best looms in Europe. A blanket once owned by the Civil War general Philip Sheridan **(Figure 12.32)** exhibits many of the qualities associated with the finest Navajo weavings. These include the closeness of the weave, rich, vibrant colors, and bold design.

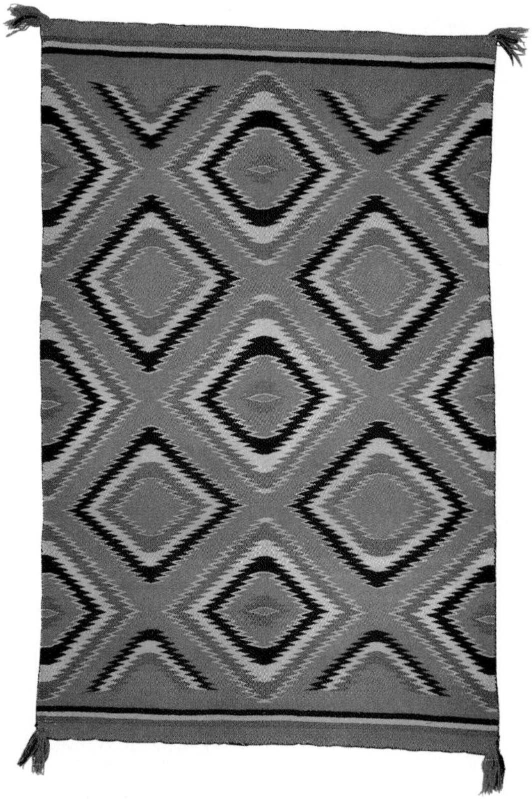

◀ **FIGURE 12.32** This saddle blanket, created for everyday use, is now on display in a museum. How are the principles of harmony and variety used in this design? How is rhythm suggested?

Saddle blanket. Navajo weaving. c. 1890. Wool. 129.5 × 83.8 cm (51 × 33″). Denver Art Museum, Denver, Colorado.

Great Plains Region

The Native Americans of the Great Plains followed the huge herds of bison that roamed the broad grasslands of central North America. The different cultural groups of the Plains—including Blackfeet, Crow, Cheyenne (shy-**ann**), and Sioux (soo)—were highly skilled in the preparation of skins used for clothing, footwear, shields, and various kinds of containers. These were then painted or embroidered with porcupine quills and, later, glass beads.

Because they were nomadic hunters, they created the *tepee* (**tee**-pee). This was a portable shelter made of buffalo hide stretched over poles that were lashed together in an upright position. The hides were covered with designs symbolizing the forces of nature and telling stories of heroic events. At its base, a tepee could range anywhere from 12 to 30 feet in diameter. A large tepee contained about as much space as a standard living room of today.

These artisans also created ceremonial headdresses for chieftains, which were worn during ritual dances. The elaborate headdress shown in **Figure 12.33** was created with natural materials found in the surrounding environment.

MORE ABOUT... Tepees

Most of the Plains people lived in tepees, houses of hide that provided several important advantages: (1) They were easy to erect—at least for experts; even large tepees could be assembled or disassembled in minutes: (2) They were easily transported; a dog or horse could pull the tepee poles attached to a drag frame, and the hides could be loaded onto the poles; (3) They afforded temperature control; the top could be opened, providing an escape route for smoke from the central fire, or firmly shut to keep out wind and rain. Plains people were not the only Native Americans to build tepees. Natives in Canada and along the northeast coast built tepees covered with birch bark.

Northwestern Plains people. *Feather Bonnet.* c. 1890. Rooster hackles, wood rods, porcupine hair, ermine skins, horsehair, buckskin, glass beads. 84 × 68.6 cm (33 × 27″). Buffalo Bill Historical Center, Cody, Wyoming. Chandler-Pohrt Collection.

ASSESS...........

Self-Assessment

Have students complete the lesson review questions. Answers are provided below.

Reteaching

Work with small groups of students to review the four Pre-Columbian cultures and the five Native American cultures. Ask each to imagine herself or himself as a member of one of these cultures and describe what life would be like. Remind students to refer to the text and reproductions of artworks to develop and add detail to their descriptions.

Enrichment

Ask students to imagine themselves as the archaeologists who first found and explored the hidden city of Machu–Picchu. To stimulate their thinking, ask questions such as these: Why were you exploring that area? What had you expected to find? How did you feel when you first saw the ruins of Machu–Picchu? What did you imagine about the lives of the people who built and lived in the city? Then ask students to write journal entries recording the events and their reactions on the day of the discovery.

CLOSE............

Guide the class in discussing the Pre-columbian and Native American cultures described in this lesson and the artworks they created. How are the artworks of these cultures alike or different? What is unique about the art created by each culture?

Woodlands Region

The Woodlands made up the largest cultural group of Native Americans east of the Mississippi River. The Woodlands people combined hunting and gathering with simple farming. The Iroquois (**ear**-uh-kwoi), made up of six different Woodlands groups, combined to form the highly organized Iroquois nation.

Expert wood carvers, the Iroquois created wooden masks that were usually painted and decorated with horse hair. The best known masks were created for a society of healers known as the False Faces because of the masks they wore. These False Face masks were thought to be sacred and represented the spirits who gave healers the magic they needed to treat illnesses. Because they were considered to be so powerful, these masks were hidden away when not in use so they would not cause accidental injuries. The masks were considered sacred and were not intended to be seen by nonbelievers.

Activity	Sketching an Event

Applying Your Skills. Native Americans of the Great Plains painted tales of their battles on skins. Look through a newspaper or magazine for coverage of an important event in your city or in the world. On a sheet of paper, sketch the story behind the event.

 Check Your Understanding

1. What does the term pre-Columbian refer to?
2. Which culture created huge heads carved from volcanic rock?
3. Which culture created the walled city of Machu–Picchu?
4. What were totem poles used for?

 Answers to Check Your Understanding

1. The term pre-Columbian refers to the time period before the arrival of Christopher Columbus in the Americas in 1492.
2. The Olmec created huge heads carved from volcanic rock.
3. The Incas created the walled city of Machu–Picchu.
4. Totem poles were used to symbolize a particular family or class of Native American cultures of the Northwest Coast Region.

ART CRITICISM IN ACTION

Critiquing the Work

▶ Describe
What do you see?

- First we see a blue tile floor with a fountain pool in the center. Above that is a wall decorated with a pattern of gold circles. Then we see four, thin, blue columns that support the roof of the pavilion. The sandalwood floor of the pavilion is covered with a diamond pattern. In the center of the floor is a black rug with a pattern of lines and flowers. The walls are orange with a pattern of black circles. The edge of the roof is represented by a brown band covered with a pattern of black dots and lines.

- In the lower left there is a group of three people. Two are sitting. The third is standing and covering the eyes of the center figure with its hands.

▶ Analyze
How is this work organized?

Ask the students to notice the lines and shapes in this work. The dominant lines are static verticals and horizontals. The architectural shapes and decorations are geometric.

- **Rhythm.** The work is filled with rhythmic repetitions. The people create a random rhythm. The dots on the orange walls and the designs on the roof are regular rhythms. The blue tiles are an alternating rhythm. The designs on the people's clothing seem to be flowing rhythms.

▲ **FIGURE 12.34**

Unknown. *Khamseh: Bahram Gur and the Chinese Princess in the Sandalwood Pavilion on Thursday.* 1524–25. Colors and gilt on paper. 32.4 × 22.2 cm (12¾ × 8¾"). The Metropolitan Museum of Art, New York, New York. Gift of Alexander Smith Cochran, 1913.

MORE ABOUT... Calligraphy in Islamic Art

One of the most dominant features of Islamic art and architecture is the use of calligraphic decoration. The prohibition of figures in Islamic religious art forced artists to turn their talents to developing elaborate decorative patterns that combined Arabic script, geometric forms, and leaf shapes. Furthermore, the rich linguistic and poetic traditions of the Arabs contributed to a deep respect for the Koran, the Islamic holy book. This respect, coupled with the gracefulness of Arabic letters led to the use of the written word, especially passages from the Koran, on many Islamic art forms including everything from pottery to mosques (Islamic places of worship).

1 ▶ DESCRIBE What do you see?

Read the credit line for information about the size and media. List all of the structures, objects, and people you see.

- Start with the architecture. Working from the bottom of the painting up to the top, list all of the structures you find.
- Describe the people, their clothing, and then tell where they are located in the work.

2 ▶ ANALYZE How is this work organized?

During this step, you will study the elements and principles of art to discover clues that will help you discover the message the artist is trying to send. Remember not to make guesses during this step.

- How is this artist's use of space different from that you have found in Western art? Is there any negative space?
- What rhythms do you find? Describe them. What kind of balance has been used to organize this work?
- Are the proportions of the figures accurate?
- Can you find an area of the work that is a focal point? What has the artist done to unify this work?

3 ▶ INTERPRET What is the artist trying to communicate?

Now you will decipher the message the artist is sending to you. Remember to combine the clues you have collected with your personal experiences to form your own interpretation of this work.

- Are all of the people in this work equal in importance? Explain.
- What do you think is happening in this scene? Explain.
- Based on your ideas, give the work a new title.

4 ▶ JUDGE What do you think of the work?

Decide if this is a successful work of art. You may make a personal opinion, but it is also important to make an objective judgment based on aesthetic theories.

- Do you think the artist has used the elements and principles of art effectively?
- Do you think this is a successful work of art? Use one or more of the three aesthetic theories to defend your decision.

Art Criticism in Action | **347**

▶ Interpret
What is the artist trying to communicate?

- There are levels of importance of people in this work. The elaborateness of clothing and the placement of the main figures at the center of the work show rank.
- Answers will vary. One possibility comes from the title: Bahram Gur is a man of royalty and is distinguished by his turban. He is entertaining the Chinese Princess, the other person seated on the black rug. The people beside them are waiting on them. The people on the blue tile may be courtiers and servants who are entertaining themselves while the main characters converse. Everything looks very formal and planned. The use of formal balance creates that effect.
- Answers will vary.

▶ Judge
What do you think of the work?

- Answers will vary.
- Answers will vary. Most will probably use the theory of Formalism since the elements and their arrangement by the principles control the look of the work.

Extension Activities

Language Art Ask the students to use their imaginations to create a story about this event. Describe the leading players' personalities. Tell what led up to this scene, what the people are saying, and what will happen next. Each student may choose a different character in the scene and write the thoughts of that person at the moment of this painting.

Time & Place Sixteenth-Century Islamic Art

This scene from an Islamic manuscript was made in 1524–25. Some other events that happened in 1524:

Politics: Persia's Shah Ismail died and was succeeded by his ten-year-old son Tahmasp.

Social Studies: Chile peppers and cayenne from the Americas were introduced to India by the Portuguese and became staple ingredients in curry.

Social Studies: In 1525, Spaniard Francisco Pizarro explored Peru in search of gold, and artist Albrect Dürer compiled the first German manual on geometry.

347

CONNECTIONS SOCIAL STUDIES

The Meaning of Stone Circles
(National Standards: 6a, 6b)

Objectives
After completing this feature, students will be able to:
- Describe the stages and components of Stone-henge.
- Discuss the possible meanings of stone circles.

Teaching the Connection
Have students read the feature on this page.

Ask students to think about the relationship between a circle and the concept of a calendar. Help them make comparisons between Stonehenge and the circular Aztec calendar. Encourage them to imagine life without a fixed calendar based on twelve months of roughly equal lengths. Discuss the human dependence on calendars, during the time Stonehenge was built and now.

Tell students that in addition to Stonehenge, there are several hundred other sites containing the ruins of stone circles in Britain. Like Stonehenge, many of these circles have alignments that point to the positions of sunrises and sunsets at the solstices. Other alignments point to the moon's northern and southern setting points. Studies of these stone circles conclude that their builders may have divided the year into 16 rather than 12 equal parts. There is also evidence of a standard unit of measurement, called a megalithic yard (2.7 feet).

The Meaning of Stone Circles

▲ **FIGURE 12.35**

Stonehenge. Wiltshire, Great Britain. c. 2000 B.C.

The English once believed that Merlin, legendary magician of King Arthur's time, created Stonehenge **(Figure 12.35)**. Later, scholars thought the structure was the remains of a Druid temple built around the time of the Roman invasion of Britain in A.D. 43. We now know that Stonehenge is even older, and that it was built in three stages by different peoples.

The first stage was built by the Neolithic people of the late Stone Age (c. 2800 B.C.). The second stage was built several centuries later by people of the Bronze age. They erected a double circle of 38 bluestones each. The bluestones (named for their bluish color) came from mountains 135 miles away. The remains of the third stage, built around 2100 B.C., are what we see today. These megaliths, called sarsens, came from about 20 miles away and weigh as much as 56 tons.

What does Stonehenge mean? It may have been a temple for worshiping a sun god or an observatory for studying the movements of the sun and moon. A line that runs through the center aligns with a point on the horizon where the sun rises on the day of the summer solstice (June 21). It is also possible that the circles and holes were used as a calendar. Just how this huge structure was built without the benefit of modern tools is uncertain, however, and its exact meaning remains a mystery.

Making the Connection
1. How do you think the builders of Stone-henge were able to carve and transport stones of such magnitude?
2. Why do you think prehistoric people were interested in seasons and the movements of the sun and moon?

Answers to Making the Connection
1. Answers will vary. Students may speculate that the builders of Stonehenge used technology similar to that which was used to build the pyramids.
2. Knowledge of when the summer and winter solstices occurred would have helped early farmers to fix dates for plowing, planting, and harvesting. The people who built and used Stonehenge may also have been interested in astronomy.

Building Vocabulary

On a separate sheet of paper, write the term that best matches each definition given below.

1. Large monuments created from huge stone slabs.
2. The Sumerian writing system made up of wedge-shaped characters.
3. Stepped mountains made of brick-covered earth.
4. Egyptian rulers who were worshiped as gods and held complete authority over the kingdom.
5. A period of time during which a single family provided a succession of rulers.
6. Beehive-shaped domed places of worship.
7. A tower several stories high with roofs curving slightly upward at the edges.
8. Muslim places of worship.
9. Tall posts carved and painted with a series of animal symbols associated with a particular family or clan.

Reviewing Art Facts

Answer the following questions using complete sentences.

1. During what time period did people begin to build structures of stone?
2. Describe the rules that Egyptian artists were required to follow when painting or sculpting a relief figure.
3. What influenced the style of Chinese "picture painting"?
4. What art technique did Japanese artists perfect to meet the demand for artworks?
5. Describe the differences between the art used in Islamic mosques and the art used in Islamic book illustration.
6. Which culture is often called the "mother culture" and why?
7. What do the images created by Inuit artists reveal about what they valued as a culture?

Thinking Critically about Art

1. **Explain.** For what reasons did people of African and Native American cultures create art? How does this differ from more recent European or American art that you find in a museum?
2. **Compare and contrast.** You can look at visual images from the past to learn what the people who lived before us were like. Compare two of the ceremonial masks in this chapter and explain how they are similar and how they are different.

Explore ancient folk traditions of music and dance in Asia on page 424 of the Performing Arts Handbook.

Travel through an illustrated art time line that will take you from the beginning of art history up to the twentieth century. Begin your journey on the Glencoe Fine Arts Site at **www.glencoe.com/sec/art**.

Answers to Building Vocabulary

1. megaliths
2. cuneiform
3. ziggurats
4. pharaohs
5. dynasty
6. stupas
7. pagoda
8. mosques
9. totem poles

Answers to Reviewing Art Facts

1. The Neolithic period.
2. Heads, arms, legs, and feet were shown in profile; eyes and shoulders were shown in frontal view. All body parts were depicted from the most visual angle.
3. Many Chinese artists were scholars who wrote with brushes that could make thick and thin lines.
4. The Japanese perfected the Chinese invention of woodblock printing in order to meet the demand for artworks.
5. Mosques were decorated with calligraphy, geometric patterns, and stylized plants and flowers. Book illustrations included people and animals, subjects not allowed in mosque art.
6. The Olmec culture, because the artifacts found in the region are the most ancient.
7. The Inuit attached great importance to the animals they relied on for food—seal, walrus, fish, whale, and caribou.

Reteaching

■ Have students complete Concept Map 12 in the Reteaching booklet. 📁

ASSESSMENT ✓

Evaluate

■ Have students complete the *Chapter 12 Test* in the TCR. 📁
■ Alternative Assessment teaching strategies are provided in the *Testing Program and Alternative Assessment* booklet. 📁

Extension

Ask students to investigate how the artworks created by the cultures discussed in this chapter influenced the art created by Western artists in later time periods. Students may want to focus on one particular culture and provide examples of how the art style of this culture can be seen in works of Western artists.

Western Traditions in Art

(pages 350–387)

Resources

📁 Chapter 13 Study Guide

📁 Chapter 13 Test

📁 Computers in the Art Classroom

📁 Cultural Diversity in Art

📁 Portfolio and Assessment Techniques

📁 Reproducible Lesson Plan 13

🖱 Transparency CC-13, Allan Rohan Crite. *School's Out*

🖱 Transparency 13, Kay Sage. *Danger, Construction Ahead*

Read about the compelling dance drama "The Green Table" on page 425 of the Performing Arts Handbook. Created by choreographer, Kurt Jooss, it is one of the most performed of all dance works created in the twentieth century.

▲ **FIGURE 13.1** Cassatt produced this print, one of a series of ten color aquatint prints, in 1891. When she created the series, the artist said she intended to imitate the Japanese printmaking methods. She combined her domestic themes with the decorative quality and grace of a Japanese print. To simulate the look of a color woodblock, she used several etching plates for each print.

Mary Cassatt. *The Letter*. 1891. Drypoint, soft-ground etching and aquatint; printed in color. Third state. From a series of ten. 4.2 × 3 m (13⅝ × 9'). The Metropolitan Museum of Art, New York, New York. Gift of Paul J. Sachs, 1916. (16.2.9)

FEATURED ARTISTS

Sofonisba Anguissola
Caravaggio
Mary Cassatt
Paul Cézanne
Jacques-Louis David
Eugène Delacroix

Richard Estes
Thomas Gainsborough
Francisco Goya
El Greco
Duane Hanson
Hans Hofmann
Lois Mailou Jones
Käthe Kollwitz
Leonardo da Vinci

Roy Lichtenstein
Édouard Manet
Michelangelo
Myron
Mark Rothko
Frank Stella
Joseph M.W. Turner
Rogier van der Weyden
Antoine Watteau

Western Traditions in Art

This chapter traces the development of Western art. It is called *Western* art because the culture of Western Europe produced it. Later, Western culture—and along with it, Western art—crossed the Atlantic with Europeans who settled in the Americas.

As you read this chapter you will see that developments and changes in Western art were often built on previous works. The print in **Figure 13.1** marks a major turning point in Western art. It is an example of Western art clearly influenced by outside sources. *The Letter* was created at the end of the nineteenth century by Mary Cassatt, the first famous American woman to join the French Impressionists. At this time, the United States and Europe began importing goods from Japan. French collectors acquired Japanese art objects. In 1890, a collection of Japanese woodblock prints was exhibited in Paris. Many Impressionists saw the exhibition and took away new ideas. Cassatt herself was impressed by the Japanese prints. Notice how she has flattened space, and used rhythmic patterns and contours in the manner of the Japanese printmakers (see Figure 12.15 on page 330).

OBJECTIVES

After completing this chapter, you will be able to:

- Identify how historical and cultural events shape art styles.
- Name the major Western art styles and movements.
- Identify major modern artists such as Monet, Cézanne, and Picasso.
- Briefly discuss modern art movements.

WORDS TO KNOW

Byzantine art
Romanesque
Gothic
Renaissance
Mannerism
Baroque
Rococo
Neoclassicism
Romanticism
Impressionism
Post-Impressionism
Expressionism
Cubism
Surrealism
Regionalists
Abstract Expressionism
Minimalism
Super-Realism
Post-Modernism

Developing Your
PORTFOLIO

Take an opinion poll about modern art. Ask family members and friends what they think about modern art and why they feel the way they do. Show them some artworks from this chapter to help them understand what you are referring to. When you have interviewed five to ten people, compile the results of your poll. Write a few paragraphs describing people's responses. Are the responses mostly positive or negative? Do you agree with the responses? Why or why not? Include your poll results and summary in your portfolio.

351

Chapter Overview

In Chapter 13 students will study the developments of Western art from its beginnings in Greece and Rome up through modern times. They will learn about the major art movements of Western Europe and the cultures and events that influenced these changing art styles. Students will also learn about the major artists that helped introduce and develop these Western art movements.

Examining the Artwork

Mary Cassatt, the first famous American woman artist, is best known for her oil paintings and pastel drawings depicting women and children. Her models were usually members of her family and the families of friends. Her themes were the everyday rituals of women. She spent her creative years working in Paris and was a member of the Impressionists.

Influenced in 1890 by an exhibit of Japanese prints in Paris, Cassatt created an innovative series of ten color prints on the same theme as her paintings. Her etchings combined aquatint, dry point, and soft-ground techniques. In these prints her emphasis shifted from the element of form to the element of line, and she filled her works with decorative patterns.

National Standards

This chapter addresses the following National Standards for the Visual Arts:

1. (a, b)	**4.** (a, b, c)
2. (a, b, c)	**5.** (a, b, c)
3. (a, b, c)	**6.** (a, b)

DEVELOPING A PORTFOLIO

Presentation Inform students that the purpose of a portfolio is to exhibit their competence as artists. It is most effective when it showcases their strengths while minimizing their weaknesses; thus, they will need to pay close attention to the selection and order of the pieces they include. When assembling the contents, students should keep in mind that the portfolio reflects pride in their work. It should never be incomplete, presented late, or carelessly put together. A student's sincere concern with the formalities of presentation and attention to detail could influence the overall impact of his or her portfolio on evaluators.

The Beginnings of Western Art Traditions

(pages 352–355)
(National Standards: 3a, 3c, 4a, 4b, 4c, 5b)

FOCUS............
Objectives

After completing this lesson, students will be able to:

- Briefly describe the beginnings of Western art traditions.
- Identify the Greek and Roman styles of art.
- Describe the Byzantine, Romanesque, and Gothic styles of art.

Supplies

- Wall map of Mediterranean countries
- Pencils and sketchbooks
- Computer art program
- Recording of canticles
- Chart showing cross section of a Gothic cathedral
- Colored markers
- Tempera paints and white paper
- Gold leaf and glitter
- Photo or painting of a cathedral

Resources

- Artist's Profile 6, Greek Art (Nike of Samothrace)
- Application 25, *Time Line Statements*
- Cooperative Learning 25, *A Picture is Worth a Thousand Words*

The Beginnings of Western Art Traditions

Greece was the birthplace of Western civilization. The influence of ancient Greek culture can still be seen today. Almost every city in our country has at least one building with features that resemble the architecture of the classic Greek temple.

The Art of Greece and Rome

The Greeks built temples in honor of their gods. The most outstanding example is the Parthenon in Athens **(Figure 13.2)**. The columns slant slightly inward to prevent a top-heavy look. Inside was a huge statue of the goddess Athena created of ivory and gold. The relief sculpture that covered the area under the roof is missing. Many of the missing pieces are in foreign museums. The Greeks worked to create a logical, harmonious world. They sought perfect proportions in buildings, sculpture, and music by following the guidelines of mathematical proportion. Their artists produced statues that represented the Greek ideal of the perfect body. According to one story, athletes used these

▲ **FIGURE 13.2** Although partially destroyed, you can see that the Parthenon was designed to look harmonious. Architects used mathematical formulas to make the temple look balanced and beautiful.

Parthenon. Temple of Athena. Fifth century B.C. Acropolis, Athens, Greece.

TECHNOLOGY OPTIONS

National Gallery of Art Videodisc Use the following to show examples of artists from the different art movements detailed in this lesson.

XIII century Byzantine School, *Enthroned Madonna and Child*	Giovanni Bellini, *Madonna and Child*	XV Century, Florentine School, *Madonna and Child*
Search Frame 18	Search Frame 347	Search Frame 2352

Use Glencoe's *National Gallery of Art Correlation Bar Code Guide* to locate more artworks.

statues, like the one shown in **Figure 13.3,** as inspiration for building up their own muscle structure.

When they were new, Greek temples and statues were not the pure white we see today. The Greeks loved color, and they painted their buildings and sculptures various hues. Time has since worn the paint away.

Even though the Romans conquered Greece in 146 B.C., they did not conquer Greek culture. Instead, the Romans adopted Greek culture, modifying it to suit their own needs. Greek sculptors, painters, architects, philosophers, and teachers exerted a great influence on the culture of the Roman Empire.

Earlier, the Romans had absorbed the culture of the Etruscans in Italy. Two outstanding Etruscan developments that the Romans adopted included a system of drainage and an improved use of the arch in the construction of buildings. What we call Roman art is a blend of the ideal Greek and the practical Etruscan arts.

The Romans added much to what they adopted. They used the arch and concrete to build large-scale structures, including huge vaulted and domed inner spaces. Engineers constructed a network of roads to connect all parts of the Roman Empire. The Romans also developed beautiful interior decoration and created realistic rather than idealized portrait sculpture **(Figure 13.4).**

◀ **FIGURE 13.3** Look at the proportions and detail of this athlete. Notice the idealized muscles and facial features. What does such a sculpture reveal about Greek culture? What features of the human body were admired by them and important to them?

Myron. *Discobolus (Discus Thrower).* c. 450 B.C. Roman copy of a bronze original. Life-size. Italy. Palazzo Vecchio, Florence, Italy.

◀ **FIGURE 13.4** Unlike the Greeks, the Romans did not seek to depict idealized human forms. Notice the attention to detail on this sculpture. The sculpture seems quite lifelike. How would you characterize the man depicted?

Graeco-Roman, from neighborhood of Cumae. *Man of the Republic.* Late first century B.C. Terra–cotta. 35.7 m (14′) high, face. 18 cm (7″) long. Courtesy of the Museum of Fine Arts, Boston, Massachusetts. Purchased by contribution. Purchase of E. P. Warren Collection.

Activity — Analyzing Architecture

Applying Your Skills. Find a building in your community in the Greek or Roman style. Write the location, the culture from which the style was adopted, the purpose of the building, and anything else you can find out about it. Make a sketch of the building in your sketchbook. Name the ancient culture and describe the features that match the style of the ancient culture.

TEACH..........
Motivator

Ask students to look at a wall map of the Mediterranean countries. Have volunteers point out the areas they think of when they study ancient Greece and the Roman Empire. Ask students if they can identify contributions made by these two great ancient civilizations. Explain that much of what we know of these cultures is derived from the art and architecture they left behind.

Vocabulary

Ask students to think about the word suffix *–esque.* What does this stem mean? Write the word *statuesque* on the board and ask students to explain what it means to be statuesque. Next write the word *Romanesque.* Ask students to write a paragraph indicating what features or characteristics the art of this period would possess. After reading this lesson, discuss whether their initial impressions were consistent with the facts.

Activity

Analyzing Architecture

Applying Your Skills. As an alternative activity, have students work in small groups to prepare a class presentation about architectural styles. Students might also enjoy sketching the building in a completely different style. If they find that idea too complex, ask them to work in groups to brainstorm new designs for famous buildings.

▶ COOPERATIVE LEARNING

Ancient Philosophies Explain that people living in the Roman Empire subscribed to numerous philosophies and world views. Divide the class into small groups and let each research one of the many philosophies popular from the second through the fourth centuries. Possible targets of research include the Stoics, who believed that the universe could be explained in purely rational terms, and the Epicureans, who rejected the idea that gods punish and reward and believed consciousness ended at death. Allow time for groups to share and compare their findings.

Aesthetics

Help students discuss the portrait sculpture shown in Figure 13.4 on page 353. Ask: What do you see when you look at this Roman sculpture? Who is the subject of the work? How does this subject compare with the athlete shown in the Greek sculpture in Figure 13.3 on page 353? What mood or message does the Roman portrait sculpture communicate to you? How is that mood or message different from the one communicated by the Greek sculpture?

Cross-Curriculum: Music

Play a recording of canticles used in the Orthodox church for your students. Although relatively little is known about Byzantine music, many of the ancient hymns are known to have survived in altered form into the present, and even the modern versions can be helpful in creating an atmosphere in which to appreciate Byzantine art.

Cross-Curriculum: Geography

Remind students that, in many parts of Europe, buildings from the Middle Ages are still standing—and in use. Ask students to work with partners or in small groups to explore European cities where Romanesque castles, churches, and walls can be seen. Suggest that they use travel books as well as art books and history books in their research. Then have each pair or group describe a short tour through Romanesque Europe.

354

▶ **FIGURE 13.5** This painting is a good example of the Byzantine blending of Western realism and Asian decorative patterns. The heads and graceful hands are shaded to give the illusion of roundness. The Asian influence is seen in the flat bodies and the patterns of gold lines.

Byzantine. *Madonna and Child on a Curved Throne.* Thirteenth century. Tempera on panel. 81.5 × 49 cm (32⅛ × 19⅜"). National Gallery of Art, Washington, D.C. © 1998 Board of Trustees. Andrew W. Mellon Collection.

▲ **FIGURE 13.6** This church was built in the Romanesque style. Identify the rounded arches.

Church of San Clemente. Tahull, Spain.

The Art of the Middle Ages

The Middle Ages began with the conquest of Rome in A.D. 476 by invaders from the north and lasted about 1,000 years. This period of time was also called the *Age of Faith* because the Christian religion exerted such an important influence. Monasteries, or buildings that housed people who had made religious vows, grew in number. The monks who lived in them created finely–decorated religious manuscripts. Churches grew in size, number, and political importance, reflecting the prominence of the Christian religion during this period.

Byzantine Art

In the eastern part of the former Roman Empire, a new style of art developed during the Middle Ages. This style thrived around the city of Constantinople (now Istanbul, Turkey) and spread to towns such as Ravenna in Italy. Constantinople, built on the site of the ancient city of Byzantium, served as the capital of the Byzantine Empire. **Byzantine art** featured *very rich colors and heavily outlined figures that appeared flat and stiff* **(Figure 13.5).** Constantinople was close to Asia as well as to Greece, and because of this proximity, Greek, Roman, and Asian art and culture all influenced Byzantine artists.

Romanesque Style

At the beginning of the Middle Ages, many new churches were built in Western Europe in a style of architecture similar to Roman buildings. It was called **Romanesque** and *featured buildings of massive size; solid, heavy walls; wide use of the rounded Roman arch; and many sculptural decorations.*

Churches, castles, and monasteries were all built in the Romanesque style **(Figure 13.6).** Architects building

---

MORE ABOUT...   **Romanesque Art**

The Romanesque interest in ancient Roman culture ultimately led to a revival of carved stone architectural ornamentation. Italian and French sculptors of the Early Medieval period studied local examples of ancient sculpture to develop their technique. The large numbers of churches built in the eleventh century provided masons with the first lucrative and steady labor they had since antiquity. Gradually specialties developed, and the more experienced masons ceased to cut pillars and stones in favor of constructing friezes, tympana, corbels, arcades, and capitals.

Romanesque structures could not include many windows because they weakened the structure of the walls and could cause the heavy stone roofs to collapse. As a result, Romanesque buildings were dark and somber inside.

Gothic Style

In Europe in the twelfth century, increasing numbers of people moved from the countryside into towns. Workers such as stone carvers and carpenters organized into craft guilds (or unions), and apprentices learned their crafts from the masters in these guilds. A wealthy new merchant class, pride in their growing cities, and religious faith led to the building of huge cathedrals. Two developments in architecture—the pointed arch and the flying buttress—brought about changes in how buildings were built, and how they looked. The flying buttress removed the weight of the roof from the walls, allowing for higher walls and many more windows than had been possible in Romanesque structures. This new style, called **Gothic,** *featured churches that seemed to soar upward, used pointed arches, and stained-glass windows,* like the cathedral shown in **Figure 13.7.**

By using stained-glass windows, Gothic builders changed the light that entered the churches into rich, glowing color. Gothic sculptors and painters sought more realistic ways to depict subject matter. Religious scenes were painted on church altarpieces with egg tempera paint and gold leaf.

▲ **FIGURE 13.7** This cathedral was built in the Gothic style. Notice the pointed arches and stained-glass windows. Compare this to Figure 13.6. Describe the similarities and differences between the two churches.

Reims Cathedral. Reims, France. 1225–99.

 Check Your Understanding

1. Name the characteristics of Byzantine art.
2. Describe Romanesque buildings.
3. What two developments of the Gothic period allowed builders to place many openings in walls and build churches taller?

Activity	**The Gothic Style**

Applying Your Skills. Research cathedrals built in the Gothic style. List the names of three of the cathedrals in your sketchbook and tell where and when they were built.

Activity

The Gothic Style

Applying Your Skills. Two excellent references for information about Cathedrals in the Gothic style are *The Horizon Book of Great Cathedrals* published by the American Heritage Publishing Company and *Cathedral: The Story of Its Construction* by David Macaulay.

ASSESS...........
Self-Assessment

Have students complete the lesson review questions. Answers appear below.

Reteaching

Have students write a paragraph describing the differences between the art styles discussed in this lesson.

Enrichment

Have students design a group mural in the manner of Figure 13.5 on page 354. First they will need to decide on a subject. Have students study the stylistic features and use tempera on a sheet of white paper. Colors should typify those of the Byzantine palette. Students can use metallic pigments to imitate gold leaf and apply glitter to the background.

CLOSE............

Provide students with a photograph of a cathedral or painting depicting one of the art styles discussed in this lesson. Use a photograph of art that was not included in this lesson. Ask students to identify the key features of the structure, as well as the principles and elements of art emphasized in it.

 Answers to Check Your Understanding

1. Byzantine art features very rich colors and heavily outlined figures that appear flat and stiff.
2. Romanesque buildings are of massive size with solid, heavy walls. They use the rounded Roman arch and have many sculptural decorations.
3. The two developments of the Gothic period that allowed builders to place windows in walls and to build churches taller were the flying buttress and the pointed arch.

The Beginnings of Modern Art Traditions

FOCUS............

Objectives

After completing this lesson, students will be able to:

- Identify artists of the Renaissance and describe their contributions.
- Explain how linear perspective is used to create depth and space.
- Discuss the reasons why there were few artworks by women artists before the Renaissance.
- Identify features of the Baroque style and name important artists who practiced it.
- Describe features of the Rococo style and identify important artists of the period.

Supplies

- Paper and pencils

Resources

📁 Artist's Profile 15, El Greco

📁 Cooperative Learning 26, The Restoration Dilemma

TEACH..........

Motivator

Ask students to compose a short poem that describes the coming of spring. Point out that human culture has experienced a number of rebirths. Tell students they will read about an important period of rebirth and the artistic legacy it produced.

356

At the beginning of the fifteenth century, the Middle Ages began drawing to a close. The invention of the printing press and the European exploration of the Americas and the Pacific Ocean expanded knowledge and contributed to a sense of the dawn of a new era. As the culture changed, so did the art. During the Middle Ages, most art had been made for religious reasons. Even artworks made for wealthy people, such as illuminated books, most often depicted religious subject matter. During the next period, artists continued to paint religious subjects but also expanded their repertoire to include mythological and secular themes.

Renaissance

Renaissance (**ren**-uh-sahns) is a French word for "rebirth." **Renaissance** is *the name given to the period at the end of the Middle Ages when artists, writers, and philosophers were "re-awakened" to art forms and ideas from ancient Greece and Rome.* The Renaissance did not happen all at once, nor did it spread to all parts of Europe at the same time. Rather, it dawned gradually, first in Italy, then spreading through northern Europe, finally reaching France and England. Along with a new appreciation of classical antiquity, social structures also changed. Kings and popes, who had always been extremely powerful, had competition from bankers and merchants, whose wealth also equaled political power. People challenged the authority of the Catholic Church.

Italian Renaissance

An architect named Filippo Brunelleschi (fee-**leep**-poh brew-**nell**-**less**-key) developed linear perspective, a graphic system that creates the illusion of depth and volume on a flat surface. Linear perspective provided a set of guidelines that allowed artists to depict figures and objects in space on a two-dimensional surface. This system made the placement of objects, and the depiction of their volume or form, measurable and exact, which gave an exciting illusion of reality to works of art. Italian artists sought to create realistic and life-like works. They studied the classical art of Greece and Rome and meticulously observed and recorded the world around them.

Michelangelo Buonarroti (my-kel-**an**-jay-loh bwon-nar-**roh**-tee), an Italian artist, was a master of poetry, painting, sculpture, and architecture. However, he always thought of himself primarily as a sculptor. One of his most famous works is **Figure 13.8,** *Pietà*. A pietà is a work showing Mary mourning over the body of Christ.

Like Michelangelo, Leonardo da Vinci (lay-oh-**nar**-doh da **vin**-chee) studied and mastered a broad range of disciplines, including mathematics, physics, geography, and painting. Although he had many ideas, Leonardo often left paintings and sculptures unfinished because he was not happy with them. One of his famous paintings is Figure 13.41 on page 384.

MORE ABOUT... Modern Drawing

Modern drawing techniques have their roots in the Italian Renaissance. The media of choice during that period included silverpoint (the forerunner of the lead pencil), pen, charcoal, and chalk. The common pencil is still the most often used medium for drawing. Drawing pencils come in seventeen degrees of hardness; they are made of graphite, carbon, or charcoal. Colored pencils are also widely used. Wax crayons are another popular choice for students and amateur artists. They come in a wide variety of colors and sizes and can be used the way paints are used.

MEET THE ARTIST
MICHELANGELO BUONARROTI

Italian, 1475–1564

Marcello Venusti. *Portrait of Michelangelo.* Casa Buonarroti, Florence, Italy.

Born in a small village near Florence, Italy in 1475, Michelangelo was apprenticed to a painter when he was 13. While still a teen, he joined the Medici household, a powerful ruling family. There he met many prominent Florentine citizens, artists, and philosophers. In 1494, the Medici family was overthrown and Michelangelo was forced to flee. He traveled to Rome, where many classical statues and buildings were being discovered. He eagerly studied their formal qualities and proportions.

Michelangelo created many masterpieces, mostly on a grand scale. When Pope Julius II asked Michelangelo to design a tomb for him, Michelangelo devised a design calling for 40 sculptures, only a few of which were completed before Pope Julius decided not to spend any more money. Instead, he asked Michelangelo to paint the ceiling of the Sistine Chapel in the Vatican. The chapel had a rounded ceiling high above the floor. Michelangelo was insulted at being asked to paint a ceiling, which was not considered a very prestigious assignment. He also did not know how he could paint a ceiling so far off the ground. However, the pope insisted and Michelangelo gave in. He built a high scaffold and lay on it to paint the wet ceiling plaster. He created nine different sections on the ceiling, each telling a Biblical story, from the creation of the world to the flood.

▶ **FIGURE 13.8** Notice the proportions of the two figures in this sculpture. Mary is much larger than her son. Michelangelo did this on purpose so that she would not seem overwhelmed by her son's body. What feeling does this proportion convey?

Michelangelo. *Pietà.* c. 1500. Marble. 174 cm (5'8½") high; base 195 cm (6'4⅝") high. Vatican, St. Peter's Basilica, Rome, Italy.

LESSON 2 *The Beginnings of Modern Art Traditions* | **357**

Promoting Discussion

Review with students the characteristics of art produced during the Gothic period. List these properties in a column headed *Gothic Art* on one side of the board. Head a second column with *Renaissance Art.* Ask students to brainstorm possible characteristics of this "new art."

Developing Perceptual Skills

Explain to students that various techniques can be used to achieve the gradual shifts from light to shadow that characterize works of the Renaissance and later. Illustrate the point by drawing a variety of geometric solids on the board and challenging students to create the illusion of three dimensions by using the techniques of hatching, cross-hatching, blending, and stippling.

Cross-Curriculum: Language Arts

Remind students that the Renaissance was a period of intellectual rebirth not only in the visual arts, but in literature as well. Writers of the Renaissance movement include Francesco Petrarch, Boccaccio, and Dante Alighieri. During this time, the sonnet form was created, although most students are inclined to credit William Shakespeare with its origin. Ask students to find out more about the history of literature during the Renaissance movement.

TECHNOLOGY OPTIONS

National Gallery of Art Videodisc Use the following to show examples of art from the Renaissance, Baroque, and Rococo styles. You might want to display some examples and have the students identify which art style is being shown.

Use Glencoe's *National Gallery of Art Correlation Bar Code Guide* to locate more artworks.

Jan van Eyck
The Annunciation

Search Frame 577

Francisco Goya
The Bookseller's Wife

Search Frame 565

Art History

This painting of three sisters is unique because it shows the girls enjoying themselves and laughing. Individual and group portraits of the sixteenth century were formal and emotionless. The sister on the right, Minerva, raises her hand to admit defeat to her sister Lucia. Europa is in the center and laughing with delight. Only the servant on the far right has a serious expression.

As a young girl, Sofonisba was trained in the needle arts, and her knowledge of fabrics and embroidery are obvious in the way she has painted the details of her sisters' dresses.

In keeping with the casual mood of the work, the artist has organized the composition using informal balance. Lucia and Europa are close to the central axis which starts at the fingertips of Minerva's left hand and passes by the left side of Europa's face. Minerva and the servant are farther from the axis.

Sparking CREATIVITY

Want students to think creatively about art history? Suggest this: The artist has his or her finger on the pulse of time. As you survey all these art forms, think about the kind of world in which each artist lived. Many new buildings have cornerstones containing objects representing the time of construction and are intended to be opened in the future. What would you want to put into one today?

Women first achieved fame as artists during the Renaissance. They had to overcome political, social, and economic obstacles to achieve artistic success. One of them, Sofonisba Anguissola, was the first Italian woman to gain wide recognition as an artist. The oldest of seven children, her father encouraged her to pursue art and allowed her to study with local artists. He even wrote to Michelangelo to tell him about Sofonisba's skills. Michelangelo responded with kind words of encouragement and a drawing for her to copy and study as part of her training. Much of her early work consisted of portraits of her family and herself **(Figure 13.9).** She also painted religious subjects. As her fame spread, the king of Spain asked her to join his court, where she painted many portraits and enjoyed respect and admiration as a court painter.

Northern Renaissance

The changes that took place during the Renaissance in Italy later filtered into northern European countries such as Flanders (a region in Belgium) and Germany. Flemish artists (those from Flanders) began to use oil rather than egg to bind their pigments. This new medium allowed artists more versatility than ever before.

Northern artists had little interest in recreating the classical art of Greece and Rome. They placed greater emphasis on depicting the accurate and precise details such as an intricate design on clothing or the details of the environment. Symbolism became even more important. Images in art conveyed more than just one meaning.

The art of Jan van Eyck (**yahn** van **eyek**) and his successors made Flanders the center of the Northern art world.

▲ **FIGURE 13.9** Notice the dramatic use of color in this painting. Observe the detail of the dresses the sisters are wearing. What does this tell you about them and their social status?

Sofonisba Anguissola. *A game of chess, involving the painter's three sisters and a servant.* 1555. Oil on canvas. 72 × 97 cm (28½ × 38⅕"). Muzeum Narodove, Poznan, Poland.

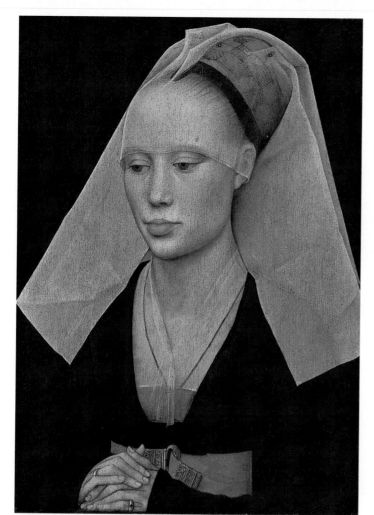

◄ **FIGURE 13.10** At first, this portrait of a well-to-do woman appears to be a realistic portrayal. If you look closely, however, you will see that her waist, as indicated by the red band, is about the same size as her head. Her head is elongated, which is emphasized by the severely pulled back hair. Do you think these odd proportions are natural? Why would the artist paint her this way if she did not look like this?

Rogier van der Weyden. *Portrait of a Lady.* c. 1460. Oil on panel, painted surface. 34 × 25.5 cm (13⅜ × 10¹/₁₆″). National Gallery of Art, Washington, D.C. © 1998 Board of Trustees. Andrew W. Mellon Collection.

Promoting Discussion

Ask whether any students in the class have ever participated in a protest (e.g., an effort to get city officials to clean up a dump site). Ask: What were some of the feelings that go along with a movement protesting the status quo? What are some ways of expressing these feelings so as to appeal to (and involve) a larger audience? Explain to students that Mannerism was a form of protest against the Church during the sixteenth century. Ask students to describe what kinds of changes this protest brought about in art of that period.

Aesthetics

Have students more closely examine Figure 9.8 on page 231. Ask students to describe what art historians mean when they call van Eyck's style highly realistic. Is there more than one type of realism in art? Have students look through the text and other art resources to identify as many forms of realism as possible. What in Figure 9.8 might be considered romanticized, idealized, prearranged, or otherwise lacking in realism?

Like other Northern painters, Jan van Eyck emphasized precision and accuracy. Look at Figure 9.8 on page 231. Notice the attention to detail, such as the lace on the woman's headcovering and the carpet under the bed. The picture includes many symbols. For example, the wedding couple is shown barefoot to symbolize that they are standing on holy ground. The burning candle indicates the presence of God. The little dog stands for loyalty.

The work of Jan van Eyck influenced another important Northern Renaissance painter, Rogier van der Weyden (roh-**jehr** van duhr **vy**-duhn). Like van Eyck, he paid meticulous attention to detail. Look at **Figure 13.10.** Notice the pins in her veil and the intricate design on her belt buckle.

As is often the case, changes in society brought about changes in artistic expression. In the mid-sixteenth century, religious reformers challenged the authority of the Catholic Church, causing conflict and turmoil. Great artists like Leonardo and Michelangelo had died, leaving behind a vacuum in artistic inspiration

MEETING INDIVIDUAL NEEDS

Auditory/Musical Learners Have students collect and present examples of court, church, and popular music that were common in Europe during the Renaissance period. Suggest they locate recordings by musicians such as Guillaume Dufay, Johannes Ockeghem, Jacob Obrecht, Heinrich Isaac, William Byrd, Thomas Morley, or Thomas Campion.

Visual/Spatial Learners Have students design a bulletin board display that contains a time line and identifies important renaissance paintings, sculptures, and buildings. Encourage students to use resources from history books and encyclopedias as well as information from this text.

Art Criticism

Reveal to students that it was once believed that El Greco's elongation of human figures in his paintings was an unintentional distortion caused by defective vision. To enable students to appreciate that this was not the case, have them try the following simple experiment. Instruct them to look at any horizontal line or shape in the painting by El Greco in Figure 13.11 (page 360). Ask students to tell what they find (i.e., that the artist did not stretch these lines or shapes vertically). Conclude the discussion of why El Greco elongated his figures (i.e., to give them a supernatural grace).

Art History

This is a story about a saint who lived during the reign of Constantine the Great. The saint was a member of the Imperial Cavalry stationed near Amiens, in what was then known as Gaul, which is now France. The saint saw a shivering beggar near the city gates on a cold winter day. The young soldier used his sword to cut his cape in half, and shared it with the beggar. It is said that Christ later appeared to St. Martin in a dream saying, "What thou hast done for that poor man, thou hast done for me."

El Greco has dressed the soldier in the costume of a nobleman of the Spanish Court, and set him on a white Arabian horse. Notice the difference between the natural proportions of the soldier, and the elongated proportions of the nearly nude beggar. How does the distortion of the beggar's body fit with the legend?

▲ **FIGURE 13.11** Notice the dreamlike quality of the background. It causes the viewer to focus on the two figures in the foreground. What appears to be happening in this painting?

El Greco. *Saint Martin and the Beggar.* 1597/1599. Oil on canvas; wooden strip added at bottom. 193.5 × 103 cm (76⅛ × 40½"). National Gallery of Art, Washington, D.C. © 1998 Board of Trustees. Widener Collection.

and innovation. Artists began showing the tension and struggle they experienced during this period of crisis in their art. The result was an artistic style called **Mannerism,** which *featured highly emotional scenes and elongated figures.* The style was developed by certain artists to be a deliberate shift away from the ideals and perfect forms of Renaissance art. If Renaissance artists preferred balance and harmony, Mannerists preferred imbalance and dynamic movement.

One of the most famous Mannerist artists was El Greco (el **greh**-koh). His name means "the Greek," for his birthplace on the Greek island of Crete. Because of his unusual style, El Greco found it difficult to secure patronage. In 1577, he traveled to Toledo, Spain, where he spent the rest of his life. There he gained a reputation as a superior artist. **Figure 13.11** shows the intense emotionalism and strong sense of movement characteristic of El Greco's work.

The Seventeenth and Eighteenth Centuries

A reform movement known as the Protestant Reformation, which began in the sixteenth century, caused many people to depart from the teachings of the Catholic Church. In order to gain them back, the Church started its own reform movement, known as the Counter-Reformation, in the seventeenth century. Art was an important part of this movement. Catholic Church authorities called upon artists to create works that would inspire renewed religious feeling in viewers.

Baroque Art in Italy

A new art style developed as a result of the Counter-Reformation. **Baroque** (buh-**rohk**) is *an art style emphasizing dramatic lighting, movement, and emotional*

CULTURAL DIVERSITY

Life in Europe Divide students into groups and have each group select and research one of the European cities mentioned in this section. Each group should determine: what life was like in the city of their choice during the sixteenth century; what other famous artists (if any) came from this area; in what ways the country pays homage to the artists it was

home to; other reasons for notoriety; and how it has changed in the intervening centuries. Groups can consult books and travel agents to obtain information, as well as photographs of their city in its present-day state. Set aside class time for students to share their findings in the form of informative travelogues.

intensity. The leader of the Baroque style in Italy, a young painter named Michelangelo Merisi da Caravaggio (my-kel-**an**-jay-loh mah-**ree**-see-dah kar-uh-**vah**-jyoh), depicted light in a daring new way. *The Conversion of St. Paul* **(Figure 13.12),** shows only St. Paul, his horse, and an attendant. The figures fill the canvas. Nothing distracts the viewer from the scene. Although the religious meaning may not be apparent at first, Caravaggio's mysterious use of light dramatizes the scene. This dramatic use of light and dark is also evident in the art of one of his followers, Artemisia Gentileschi (see Figure 5.17 on page 111).

Dutch Art

Dutch Protestants did not want religious paintings and sculptures in their churches. Dutch artists had to turn to ordinary people and places for their subject matter. The demand for landscapes, portraits, and still lifes grew as wealthy merchants surrounded themselves with art that depicted scenes of everyday life.

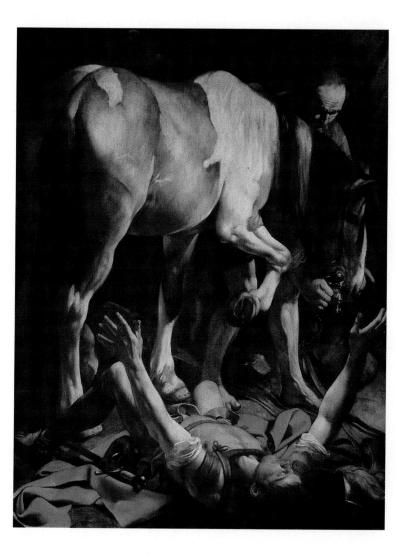

◀ **FIGURE 13.12** Notice the use of light in this picture. It is not a natural light. Where does it come from? What mood is created by it?

Caravaggio. *The Conversion of St. Paul.* c. 1601. Oil on canvas. Approx. 228.6 × 175.3 cm (90 × 69"). Santa Maria del Popolo, Rome, Italy.

Cross-Curriculum: Language Arts

After students have studied the art and artists of the Baroque period, ask them to find a picture of a Baroque sculpture and write a brief paragraph describing the emotions they think the artist has portrayed.

Art History

This does not look like a religious painting from the early seventeenth century because Caravaggio did not paint like other artists. Caravaggio was a rebel. He used ordinary people to depict religious subjects. This painting shows the moment when Saul the tax collector (who persecuted Christians) hears God's voice saying, "Saul, why do you persecute me?" The artist uses the light to represent the voice of God. This is the moment when he is converted to Christianity, yet there are no halos, no noble costume, and no elongated supernatural look to the figure. Caravaggio painted him in the costume of a peasant, lying on his back as if the sound of God's voice knocked him over with its magnitude.

Caravaggio's use of dramatic light and dark chiaroscuro, changed the course of seventeenth century European painting and influenced Rembrandt, Rubens, and many others who followed him.

MORE ABOUT...   Caravaggio

Michelangelo Merisi was born in 1573 in the Lombardy hill town of Caravaggio, Italy. Religious scenes were often depicted in the subject matter of Caravaggio's paintings. This style appealed to the Counter Reformation taste of realism, simplicity, and piety in art. Caravaggio was also well-known for his use of dramatic light-and-dark effects. This technique is more commonly referred to as *chiaroscuro*. Although chiaroscuro originated in northern Italian art in the sixteenth century, Caravaggio transformed this aspect of painting. Caravaggio's work reflected and incorporated the styles of other Renaissance masters such as Michelangelo, Simone Peterzano, and Giuseppe Cesari.

Art History

Point out to students the visual textures Vermeer portrays. Ask them to use adjectives to describe different textures in this painting: the red hat (fuzzy and furry), the girl's skin (matte and smooth), the blue dress or shawl (smooth, shiny, and soft because the folds in the fabric are gently rounded and don't show sharp creases), the chair (wooden, shiny, bumpy, rounded, and hard).

Ask them to compare Vermeer's use of chiaroscuro to Caravaggio's in figure 13.12 on page 361. Ask them to describe similarities and differences. In Caravaggio's piece the light is mysterious and from an unknown source. In Vermeer's work the light looks natural, as if it is coming through a window to the right of the painting. The light is above her head because her hat hides part of her face.

Critical Thinking

Share with students the view held by Madame du Châtelet, a product of the eighteenth-century high style of living. "We must begin," the Madame wrote, "by saying to ourselves that we have nothing else to do in the world but seek pleasant sensations and feelings." Discuss how this philosophy of life relates to Rococo art. Then ask students to write a page that compares Madame du Châtelet's point of view with the aesthetic philosophy of any other artist of an art period covered thus far in the text.

The greatest Dutch artist of this period was Rembrandt van Rijn (**rem**-brant van **reyn**). Like other Dutch artists, he painted ordinary people and everyday events. He was somewhat unusual, however, in that he also continued painting religious subjects as well. He was especially interested in the psychological character of the people he portrayed, suggested by his use of light and shadow to create atmosphere. *The Night Watch* (Figure 11.29, page 314), one of Rembrandt's best-known paintings, shows this use of light. Some figures are clearly illuminated while others remain in shadow, creating a dramatic effect.

Jan Vermeer (yahn vair-**meer**) is another important Dutch artist. For several hundred years, his artwork remained unappreciated, but in the second half of the nineteenth century critics recognized his artistic genius. Vermeer is best known for his use of light and texture. **Figure 13.13** shows his talent in using dark and light values to express a feeling or evoke a mood.

◀ **FIGURE 13.13**
This portrait depicts an ordinary woman engaged in an everyday activity. How does Vermeer add interest to the painting? What mood or feeling does it evoke?

Jan Vermeer. *Girl with the Red Hat.* c. 1665/1666. Oil on panel. 23.1 × 18.1 cm (9⅛ × 7⅛"). National Gallery of Art, Washington, D.C. © 1998 Board of Trustees. Andrew W. Mellon Collection.

MORE ABOUT... Rococo Style

In the eighteenth century, the French court at Versailles dictated the fashions of European footwear. Women were taught to lift their skirts to show off dainty shoes and ankles. Shoes had a curved heel and were frequently embellished with jewelry and embroidery. Buckles and ties over their instep were also typical. One of the most characteristic Rococo shoes was the backless silk and lace women's dress shoe. During the peak of the Rococo era, from 1740 to 1770, fashionable men wore heeled shoes with large silver or diamond buckles that complemented their colorful garments. By the 1780s footwear became more informal and facilitated a greater freedom of movement.

Rococo Style

As the seventeenth century ended and the eighteenth century began, France emerged as the strongest, wealthiest nation in Europe. Paris, its capital, became the center of the art world. When pleasure-loving King Louis XIV assumed the throne, a new style of art influenced by his lighthearted personality arose. Called **Rococo** (ruh-**koh**-koh), it is *an art style that expresses free, graceful movement, playful use of line, and delicate colors.*

One of the first painters working in the Rococo style was Antoine Watteau (an-**twahn** wah-**toh**). His paintings depict an idealized world filled with happy, carefree people **(Figure 13.14).**

In England, artists modified the Rococo style. They used its delicate, light-washed techniques but rejected artificial subject matter. One of the most famous English painters of this period, Thomas Gainsborough (**gainz**-bur-roh), began his artistic career as a landscape painter but later became a famous portrait painter for members of English high society.

▲ **FIGURE 13.14** Describe the dress and manners of these people. Notice how the colors and shapes blend together for a dreamlike, misty quality. Is this a happy occasion? How do you know?

Antoine Watteau. *Embarkment for Cythera.* 1717–19. Oil on canvas. 1.3 × 1.9 m (4′ 3″ × 6′ 4½″). The Louvre, Paris, France.

Aesthetics

Tell students that the great majority of eighteenth-century intellectuals strongly objected to Rococo art on the grounds that it was frivolous and lacking in serious moral purpose. Divide students into three debating teams. One should defend paintings such as those by Goya, highlighting the work's artistic merits. The second should say why such works are morally harmful. The third team should make a case for supporting all art, whether it entertains a serious theme (e.g., Baroque art) or dwells on more pleasurable moments.

Art History

Watteau is best known for his pictures showing the French Aristocracy at play. This painting is based on a play about the Island of Cythera, the legendary island of romance. However, this painting has been known by the wrong name. These people are not going *to* the island, but departing *from* the island! Notice how the woman near the center looks backwards as if she does not want to leave this wonderful place.

Watteau has used curves to indicate luxury and grace in this work. Notice the arrangement of the people. They form a flowing rhythm, repeating the curve of the land below them and the land across the river. The curve starts on the viewer's right at the statue of Venus, and flows across the painting until it ends gradually in the group of cupids.

Do the beautiful people in this work look like they are about to begin an adventure, or does their pleasure seem to be coming to an end?

▶ COOPERATIVE LEARNING

Period Clothing Have students discuss the clothing and hair styles they see in *Embarkment for Cythera,* by Antoine Watteau. Point out to student's that women's clothing styles during this period was very similar to that of men's fashion. Note that hairdos, for example, grew taller and taller until they made a woman's face appear to be located in the middle of her person. Have a group of volunteers consult an encyclopedia of fashion and obtain illustrations of a variety of clothing styles of the period. Instruct the group to include these illustrations in a presentation to the class, in which they discuss materials most commonly used, how long a given costume took to create and who were the foremost designers of the day.

Art History

Display a variety of portraits of children from different periods of art, and have students compare these with Figure 13.15. Possibilities include the Dutch Baroque artist Gabriel Metsu's *The Sick Child*, Mary Cassatt's *Maternal Caress*, and *Seed for Sowing Shall Not Be Ground* by Käthe Kollwitz.

Studio Skills

Have students use oil pastels to create portraits of themselves as younger children. Encourage students to consider how a childhood portrait can sum up many experiences, emphasize a particular personality trait, or show a child as a member of a larger family structure. Invite students to share their self-portraits with classmates.

Art History

Sir Joshua Reynolds, a rival of Gainsborough, said in a lecture that blue should always be used in the background of a painting, never in the focal point of an artwork. Gainsborough had a blue outfit made, and then set out to find a model to fit the outfit. This turned out to be his delivery boy.

Look closely at this work. What kind of expression does the boy have on his face? What do you think is going through his mind? Do you think Gainsborough was successful using blue in the foreground? How has he shown contrast between the boy and the background? (*Everything around the boy is painted with low-intensity, warm colors.*)

Ask the students to remember movies or TV shows about the late eighteenth century. Think about the story of Oliver Twist. Were delivery boys educated? Were they clean? How did they live?

◀ **FIGURE 13.15** The most striking element of this painting is the use of color. What does the background depict? Do you think it is important to the painting?

Thomas Gainsborough. *The Blue Boy.* c. 1770. Oil on canvas. 177.8 × 121.9 cm (70 × 48″). The Huntington Library, Art Collections, and Botanical Gardens, San Marino, California.

Figure 13.15, Gainsborough's most famous painting, resulted from a professional rivalry. A rival painter gave a lecture at the Royal Academy of Art and stated that blue, a cool color, should always be used in the background, never in the main part of a picture. When Gainsborough heard this, he considered it a challenge and painted a portrait of a boy dressed entirely in blue.

In Spain, Francisco Goya (frahn-**seese**-koh **goh**-ya) transformed Rococo art. Early in his career, Goya achieved considerable fame and fortune painting in the Rococo style. However, this changed after he suffered a serious illness and, later, a grave accident. He lost his hearing and endured other physical setbacks. A war in Spain made him aware of the suffering of others. He found he was no longer comfortable painting in the decorative Rococo fashion.

Goya's art reflected his bitterness and disillusionment. One of his most famous paintings shows the ugliness and brutality of war **(Figure 13.16).**

MORE ABOUT...   Thomas Gainsborough

Thomas Gainsborough (1727–1788), English painter, executed more that 500 paintings in his career. More than 200 are portraits that emphasize the refined beauty and grace of his subjects. He uses primarily cool, fresh colors, such as blues and greens. In 1774 Gainsborough was asked to paint portraits of King George III and the queen consort, Charlotte Sophia. He quickly became a favored painter in the British aristocracy and very wealthy with the commissions he earned.

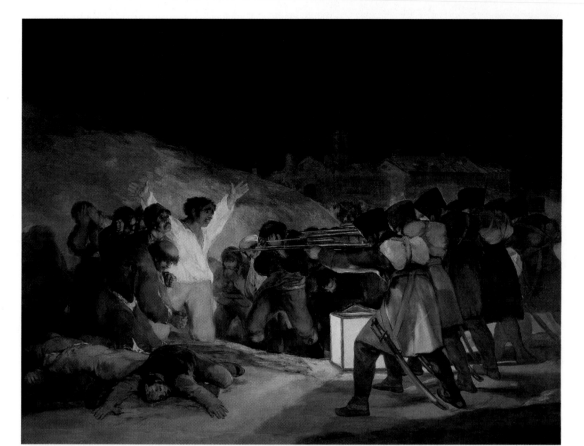

 FIGURE 13.16 The figures are arranged in this painting so that they seem in opposition to each other. Which is the most important figure in this composition? How has the figure been made to stand out? What is the feeling or mood of the piece?

Francisco Goya. *The Third of May, 1808.* 1814. Oil on canvas. Approx. 2.64 × 3.43 m (8'8" × 11'3"). Museo del Prado, Madrid, Spain.

Activity **Analyzing a Work**

Applying Your Skills. Select one work of art from the Renaissance or Baroque period. Use the four steps of the art history method discussed in Chapter 2 to discuss or write about the work. You may need to research the work of art and the artist in an encyclopedia, a book about the artist, or on the Internet. Write your findings in your sketchbook.

Check Your Understanding

1. What is linear perspective?
2. What medium used by Flemish artists revolutionized painting in the Renaissance?
3. Describe Mannerism.
4. What style of painting is characterized by contrast and variety?
5. Name the characteristics of Rococo art.

Activity

Analyzing a Work

Applying Your Skills. Students who prefer to select works from the Mannerism or Rococo art style should be encouraged to do so. Since students might be yet uncomfortable with the steps of art criticism, you might divide the class into four discussion groups and assign each group to choose one artwork from each area studied in this section and apply only one of the steps of art criticism to the works. Groups can present their findings to the class.

ASSESS..........
Self-Assessment
Have students complete the lesson review questions. Answers appear below.

Reteaching
Have students compare Figure 13.8, on page 357, with paintings in the Mannerism, Baroque, and Rococo art styles. List on the board the differences and similarities in the settings, gestures, garments, moods, and use of symbols. Ask: Do paintings from various times seem to express different ideas and feelings about what is important to the people of that period?

CLOSE.......
Ask students to describe the difference between linear and aerial perspective. Have them identify ways in which art of the Renaissance was different from the art of earlier periods, especially Gothic art.

Answers to Check Your Understanding

1. Linear perspective is a graphic system that creates the illusion of depth and volume on a flat surface.
2. The Flemish use of oil painting revolutionized painting in the Renaissance.
3. Mannerism is an art style featuring highly emotional scenes and distorted figures.
4. Baroque painting is characterized by contrast and variety.
5. Rococo art is characterized by free, graceful movement; playful use of line; and delicate colors.

The Nineteenth Century

(pages 366–373)
(National Standards: 3a, 3c, 4a, 4b, 4c, 5b)

FOCUS...........
Objectives

After completing this lesson, students will be able to:

- Identify the main features of Neoclassicism.
- Understand the attitudes and themes associated with the Romantic movement.
- Identify the objectives of the Impressionists and describe the painting technique they developed to achieve those objectives.
- Describe the Post-Impressionist style.
- Name major artists of the Neoclassic, Romantic, Impressionist, and Post-Impressionist styles.

Supplies

- Paper and media of choice
- Recording of Igor Stravinsky's *Rite of Spring*.
- Photograph of front of school building or tree
- Sketchbooks and pencils
- Charcoal pencils

Resources

📁 Artist's Profile 5, Jacques-Louis David

📁 Artist's Profile 23, Claude Monet

📁 Artist's Profile 27, Paul Gaugin

📁 Application Activity 26, *Sharpening Your Skills*

The Nineteenth Century

In the late eighteenth century, disruption in European society, including the French Revolution, caused artists to abandon the Rococo and Baroque styles, which mirrored the life of the aristocracy. In the nineteenth century, many artists wanted to create art that reflected the world they saw.

Neoclassicism

At the end of the eighteenth century, some European artists developed a new kind of art called **Neoclassicism** ("new classicism"), *an approach to art that borrowed subject matter and formal design qualities from the art of Greece and Rome.* Neoclassicism emphasized realism, minimized emotionalism, and featured epic or heroic events. The French artist Jacques–Louis David (**zjahk** loo-**ee** dah-**veed**) was the major artist working in this style. His work *The Death of Socrates* **(Figure 13.17)** depicts the last moments of the life of the great philosopher, who was tried for religious

▲ **FIGURE 13.17** This painting has a formal, dignified feeling to it. Even if you did not know the title, you would realize that the artist has depicted a serious and solemn occasion. What in the artwork tells you this? What do the different figures appear to be doing?

Jacques-Louis David. *The Death of Socrates*. 1787. Oil on canvas. 129.5 × 196.2 cm (51 × 77¼"). The Metropolitan Museum of Art, New York, New York. Catharine Lorillard Wolfe Collection, Wolfe Fund, 1931. (31.45)

MORE ABOUT... New Styles

Explain that Neoclassicism was the official style of the French Academy throughout the nineteenth century, particularly during the first half. This style made use of ancient Greek and Roman sculptures as models. It stressed the importance of balanced compositions, flowing contour lines, figures modeled in light and dark, subdued colors, and noble gestures and expressions. Romanticism was the style that developed and flourished during the first half of the century. It favored the use of rich, dramatic color and a sense of movement rather than balance. Paintings done in this style did not begin with contour lines but with patterns of color, which were used to create shapes and figures.

◄ **FIGURE 13.18** This painting is a romantic depiction of action and adventure in a distant land. Although the painting shows a battle scene, the battle seems more dreamlike than realistic. What gives the work this quality? Why is it called Romantic rather than Realistic?

Eugene Délacroix. *Arabs Skirmishing in the Mountains.* 1863. Oil on linen. 92.5 × 74.6 cm (36⅜ × 29⅜"). National Gallery of Art, Washington, D.C. © 1998 Board of Trustees. Chester Dale Fund.

heresy and sentenced to death. Although his friends and students appealed to the authorities to prevent the sentence from being carried out, Socrates willingly drank the cup of poison hemlock given to him.

Romanticism

At the dawn of the nineteenth century, the struggle to impose a new democratic political and social order continued. People grew anxious in response to ongoing political turmoil and uncertainty. Many did not want to be reminded of the events surrounding them, but instead wanted to be distracted. A new art style evolved as a reaction to contemporary events. **Romanticism,** as it was called, is *a style of art that found its subjects in the world of the dramatic and in cultures foreign to Europe. It emphasized rich color and high emotion.* Romantic artists disliked the cool colors, linearity, and subdued emotion in Neoclassicism.

Eugène Délacroix (oo-**zhen** del-uh-**kwah**) demonstrated a mastery for capturing action in foreign locales. **Figure 13.18** shows one of his famous works.

MORE ABOUT... Délacroix

Eugène Délacroix believed that art should electrify the viewer. He chose subjects filled with action, showing men and animals caught up in a conflict with nature or each other. The Romanticists were striving to show optical truth as well as things as they were in reality. Délacroix reflected the influence of David and Gericault. In addition, he chose to portray spectacular drama that would fire the imagination and appeal to a wide audience. He also realized that content was not the only concern. Of technique he said, "It is advisable not to fuse brushstrokes, as they will [appear to] fuse naturally at [a] . . . distance." In this respect, he anticipated the Impressionists' experiments with light and color.

CHAPTER 13
LESSON 3

TEACH.........
Motivator
Display slides or photographs of Baroque buildings that focus on Rococo details. Let students identify and describe what they see. Then ask: What style of art and architecture seems most different from the Baroque style? Let several students respond and encourage them to give specific reasons to support their ideas. Then show slides or photographs of ancient Greek temples and have students describe the differences. Artists reacted against the Baroque style and began working in a style called Neoclassicism, which was intended to echo the works of ancient Greece and Rome.

Vocabulary
Write the words *Impressionist, Neoclassicist, Realist,* and *Romanticist* on the board. Ask students to speculate on the kinds of artworks an artist fitting each of these descriptions might create. As students read, encourage them to check their hunches.

Art History
The works of artist in France reflected the impact of the French Revolution. Ask several students to read about the life and works of Jacques-Louis David. How did the French Revolution affect his life? How did it affect his works? Ask these students to share these findings with the rest of the class.

Art Criticism
Help students discuss and compare Jacques-Louis David's *The Death of Socrates,* Figure 13.17, and Eugène Delacroix's *Arabs Skirmishing in the Mountains,* Figure 13.18: How do these two works reflect the interests and concerns of the Neoclassic art movement and the Romantic art movement?

Promoting Discussion

Have students work in two groups. Ask one group to find reproductions of Romantic landscape paintings. Ask the other group to find reproductions of Japanese landscape prints and paintings. Then have the two groups share and discuss the artworks they have chosen: How are they alike? What are the most important differences?

Studio Skills

Have the class develop a group composition centering on a modern-day event or scene that expresses dramatic emotions. The class should begin by selecting a current event as the theme of the picture and then work out the most dramatic arrangement of the figures. Have students compare the spirit of the finished result with that of *Snowstorm: Steamboat Off a Harbor's Mouth*, Figure 13.19. Could the joint effort be fairly described as a Romantic painting? Have students defend their answers.

Cross-Curriculum: Music

After reinforcing the unkindness of critics' reception of Turner's *Snowstorm*, ask a volunteer to investigate parallels from the work of music. One possibility is the 1913 Paris debut of Igor Stravinsky's *The Rite of Spring*, which nearly incited a riot and led to characterizations of the avant-garde composer as "a monster." If possible, the volunteer should obtain and play a recording of the first movement of the composition for the class.

▲ **FIGURE 13.19** This painting is very different from traditional pictures of ships at sea. Describe the mood created by the swirling colors. What feeling do you experience when viewing this artwork?

Joseph M.W. Turner. *Snowstorm: Steamboat off a Harbours Mouth.* 1842. Oil on canvas. 92 × 122 cm (36 × 48"). Clore Collection, Tate Gallery, London, Great Britain.

Joseph M.W. Turner emerged as England's most dramatic Romantic painter. Turner expected his viewers to use their imaginations. For him, the depiction of light and atmosphere was the most important part of a painting. In **Figure 13.19,** he portrayed nature at its most violent. Instead of using precise detail, he suggests this violence by using loose brushwork to apply bright color and light values in swirling patterns.

Realism

One group of artists grew dissatisfied with both Neoclassicism and Romanticism. They felt that artists should portray political, social, and moral issues, but without glorifying the past or presenting romantic views of the present. Their art movement, called Realism, presented familiar scenes as they actually appeared. Édouard Manet (ay-doo-**ahr** mah-**nay**), an artist who participated in the Realist movement, discovered that the new style of art required new techniques. Therefore, he became more interested in *how* to paint rather than *what* to paint.

In *The Railway* **(Figure 13.20),** Manet painted a simple, common scene. A woman sits with a puppy in her lap. She is reading and has glanced up. A young girl faces away, watching the steam from a train. Manet avoided painting precise detail because he wanted to capture what a person would see with a

TEACHER TALK 📖

Classroom Management A way to help students become more familiar with artists is to set aside one small bulletin board as an "Artist of the Week" board. At first, you can provide the display. Later, responsibility for the bulletin board might be assigned to one student or a team of students. There are several ways to plan displays. You might decide which artists you want to feature and assign the artist as you assign the group. Or you might have a list of artists you wish to include during the year and allow each student or group to select one from your list. A third method might be to allow each student or group to freely choose an artist with your approval.

Aesthetics

Have students pretend that they are collectors with a taste for realist art. Their budget permits them to purchase any three paintings reproduced in this lesson. Which ones would they choose? Compare student's lists of choices. Did any students include Neoclassical or Romantic works? Use this exercise to introduce a discussion of the many different interpretations of "realism" and to clarify exactly what the Realists meant by this word.

Cross-Curriculum: Science

Part of the cultural background that influenced Realist artists was the development of science as a logical inquiry. There was an excitement revolving around the belief that virtually everything could in time be known through scientific means. In many fields, people sought to emulate the virtues of scientific discipline and the scientist's agenda to impartially collect the raw facts, reject metaphysical prejudices, and closely observe empirical phenomena. The Realist artists were also inspired by these goals. In the spirit of scientific fair-mindedness, they criticized traditional distinctions between beauty and ugliness and regarded truth as the highest criterion of beauty.

▶ **FIGURE 13.21** This photo depicts a civil war battle. The photographer was a journalist who reported on the war. Do you think this photograph is art? Why or why not? On what criteria do you base your judgment?

Mathew Brady. *Civil War.* c. 1865. Photograph. National Archives, Washington, D.C.

quick glance. Rosa Bonheur, a very successful artist of the time, combined the drama of Romanticism with the accuracy of Realism (see Figure 8.3, page 201).

Photography

In the mid-nineteenth century, photography was invented as a method for recording people and events on film. It was exciting for artists interested in realism. Early versions of the photographic process were very expensive and time-consuming, but by the 1850s, several new methods were introduced that made the process easier and less expensive. Because of this, artists could record news events in the second half of the nineteenth century. A famous Civil War photographer, Mathew Brady, documented a battle that took place around 1865 **(Figure 13.21).** Photography introduced a new kind of realism to art.

TECHNOLOGY OPTIONS

National Gallery of Art Videodisc Use the following to show examples of nineteenth-century artists.

Jacques-Louis David
Napoleon in His Study

Edouard Manet
Gare Saint-Lazare

Search Frame 1103

Search Frame 1246

Use Glencoe's *National Gallery of Art Correlation Bar Code Guide* to locate more artworks.

Art History

To help students further appreciate the life and times of Claude Monet, whose work is shown in Figure 13.22, assign *Artist's Profile 23* in the TCR. 📁

Critical Thinking

Emphasize that critics of the period were less than encouraging to Monet. Ask: If you had been the artist, would you have been more inclined to heed the allegedly expert opinions of the critics or pursue your own ideas? What characteristics of the individual does each decision reveal? What role may the support of fellow artists have played? To help students answer these questions, have volunteers role-play Monet discussing one of his paintings with both a critic and a supportive fellow artist.

Aesthetics

Remind students that Monet and the other Impressionists did not have all of the same media that are available to artists today. Black-and-white photography was in its infancy in the nineteenth century and color photography was nonexistent. Have students consider Monet's artistic goals and then write a page on whether they believe Monet would have been happier working in color photography if it had been a possibility in the late nineteenth century. Invite students to read their essays aloud.

Art History

Remind students that Impressionist painters favored casual, everyday themes for their subjects. Ask students to identify any time in art history when such subjects were not favored.

▲ **FIGURE 13.22** Notice the muted colors of this artwork. How does the artist indicate the time of day?

Claude Monet. *Palazzo da Mula, Venice.* 1908. Oil on canvas. 62 × 81.1 cm (24½ × 31⅞″). National Gallery of Art, Washington, D.C. © 1998 Board of Trustees. Chester Dale Collection.

Photographs were more realistic than drawings could be. They preserved a visual record of an event in a single moment in time with more detail and precision than a painter ever could. Photography influenced the development of painting for many years to come.

Impressionism

The Realists had taken a hard look at the real world. This interest in the world outside the studio influenced another group of artists who did much of their painting outdoors. Their style, which came to be known as **Impressionism,** *featured everyday subjects and emphasized the momentary effects of light on color.* Impressionist painters concentrated on the play of light over objects rather than on the shape of objects themselves. These artists broke up solid shapes and blurred the edges of objects by applying paint to the canvas in small dabs of pure color. When viewed from a distance, the dabs blend together visually. If you stand too close to an Impressionist painting, all you will see are colorful brushstrokes of paint. You have to step back to allow your eyes to perform the work of blending the colors.

One of the first artists working in the Impressionist style, Claude Monet (**klohd** moh-**nay**), painted many different series of landscapes, seascapes, and cityscapes that depicted the quality of light at various times of day, and in different seasons of the year (see Figures 6.24 and 6.25 on page 153). In **Figure 13.22,** all the edges and lines of the work have been blurred. The gently moving water distorts the reflection of the building, an effect created by the use of fragmented brushstrokes.

► COOPERATIVE LEARNING

Critiquing Impressionism Have students work in groups to examine and discuss the Impressionist paintings in Figures 13.22 and Figures 6.24 and 6.25 on page 153. Let the member of each group begin by selecting one of the works. Then have the group members work together to describe, analyze, interpret, and judge the work. Finally, have the group members prepare a short interpretation of the painting, explaining the meaning or mood of the work.

Post-Impressionism

Eventually, some artists felt that Impressionism was not suited to the way they wished to depict the world. These artists began working in a variety of styles that came to be called **Post-Impressionism,** *a more individual approach to painting, unique to each artist working at this time.* The term for this period is Post-Impressionism because these works appeared after Impressionism. The word *post* means *after.* Some of the most outstanding Post-Impressionist artists were Paul Cézanne (say-**zahn**), Paul Gauguin (goh-**gan**) and Vincent van Gogh (van **goh**).

Paul Cézanne, who had originally painted in the Impressionist style, felt that the blurred shapes of Impressionism did not depict the solidity of the world. He wanted to create an art that emphasized form more than light. Cézanne did this by laying down interlocking blocks of color rather than dots and dabs of paint. He joined these patches of color together as if they were pieces of a puzzle. In this way, Cézanne strengthened the underlying structure in his compositions, giving the images a feeling of permanence and solidity. In **Figure 13.23,** he used richly–colored patches to create the geometric shapes of the building, trees,

▲ **FIGURE 13.23** Cézanne was interested in the structure of objects. He used small brushstrokes like little building blocks to make forms look like geometric solids. Notice how the foliage looks as solid as the rocks. What does Cézanne's technique do to the appearance of this scene? Does he evoke any particular feeling?

Paul Cézanne. *Le Chateau Noir.* 1900–04. Oil on canvas. 73.7 × 96.6 cm (29 × 38″). National Gallery of Art, Washington, D.C. © 1998 Board of Trustees. Gift of Eugene and Agnes E. Meyer.

Art History

To help students further appreciate the life and times of Paul Cézanne, whose work is shown in Figure 13.23, assign *Artist's Profile 22* in the TCR. 📁

Art Criticism

Point out that the invention of the tin paint tube around 1840 opened up new possibilities for artists by permitting them to work outdoors for long periods of time. Have students appreciate the advantages of painting "at the source" by displaying a photograph of a familiar nearby subject (e.g., the front of the school building, a tree on the school grounds). Escort the class outdoors to the location in the photo. Have them record in their sketchbooks brief descriptions of the way sunlight, shadow, and other aspects of atmosphere play on the subject. Ask how many of these details are present in the photo. Conclude with a discussion of how being outdoors influenced the style of Impressionist works such as those shown in this lesson.

MORE ABOUT... Post-Impressionism

The term *Post-Impressionism* was first used in 1910 when Roger Fry arranged a London exhibit entitled "Manet and the Post-Impressionists." Some of the artists represented, such as Paul Cézanne, Paul Gauguin, and Vincent van Gogh, were dead and still unknown. The exhibition caused laughter among members of the public and anger among serious crit-

ics. All the works in the exhibit seem to attack traditional ideas of good art. The impact of Post-Impressionism influenced twentieth-century art movements such as Fauvism, Cubism, and the Nabis. Nonrepresentational artists, such as Wassily Kandinsky, and almost all modern graphic artists also developed largely from Post-Impressionism.

Art History

Have students work in small groups to develop a conversation between Cézanne, van Gogh, and Gauguin. Have students pretend that the three artists are taking a trip together to paint. Ask: Can the artists agree on where to go? Would they get along? If you wish, ask some students to research the actual friendship between van Gogh and Gauguin and see what they thought of each other and one another's art.

Art History

Gauguin used the brilliant colors of tropical Tahiti in his paintings. Ask the students to study his uses of color in this work. How many different colors has he used to depict her skin? (*Her face is golden orange and the shadows are low-intensity grays of orange. Her right hand is darker than her face. Her left hand seems to glow with warm yellow-orange. Her exposed foot is the color of her right hand, but the shadows look blue-black.*) She is wearing a red robe with a lavender collar. How many tints and shades of red can the students find in the dress? What other hue has the artist used in the shadows of the robe? *(violet)* How many greens can they find inside the picture frame? *(four)* Ask them to notice the variations of blue in the wall and browns in the rocking chair. In the floor they will find dull yellows, blacks, violets, light reds, and greens. He even used light violets and yellows to enhance the white handkerchief.

and even the sky, which of course, is not a solid object.

Paul Gauguin turned to the use of color and shape to create daring, unconventional works depicting far-off lands and people. Giving up his job as a stockbroker, he traveled around the world to learn about art and experience different artistic traditions. He finally settled in Tahiti, where he produced most of his famous works. Notice the simple shapes and brilliant colors in **Figure 13.24.** Gauguin used arbitrary color in most of his paintings.

Vincent van Gogh, like the other Post-Impressionists, was initially dazzled by Impressionist works but later felt that Impressionism was limited in what it could express. Van Gogh was not interested in achieving visual accuracy. Instead, he explored ways to convey his feelings about a subject. To do so, he used expressive elements in his paintings such as twisting lines, rich colors, and complex textures.

Van Gogh's art was rejected and he only sold one painting during his lifetime. His brother supported him

◄ **FIGURE 13.24**
Notice how color is the dominant element in this painting. Shape and form are also important. How do the elements create a dreamy quality?

Paul Gauguin. *Faaturuma (Melancholic).* 1891. Oil on canvas. 93.9 × 68.2 cm (37 × 26⁷/₈"). Nelson-Atkins Museum of Art, Kansas City, Missouri. Purchase: Nelson Trust.

TEACHER TALK

Improving Studio Skills Review the reproductions of Gauguin's paintings, emphasizing his ability to transform three-dimensional objects into relatively flat, decorative patterns. Then ask students to keep simple sketchbooks in their journals. The sketchbooks should include two parts. First, students should use watercolor markers to practice rendering a wide variety of objects as flat patterns. Second, students should observe as many two-dimensional patterns as they can find in their daily life, such as textile and packaging designs, and copy them into their journals. Invite students to share their sketches with the class and discuss the many decorative patterns they found.

▲ **Figure 13.25** Notice van Gogh's unusual use of color, texture, and line to depict rhythm and movement. He uses the elements to make the stars swirl and the trees dance as if all of nature was alive.

Vincent van Gogh. *The Starry Night.* 1889. Oil on canvas. 73.7 × 92.1 cm (29 × 36¼"). The Museum of Modern Art, New York, New York. Acquired through the Lillie P. Bliss Bequest.

financially. Toward the end of his life, he painted *The Starry Night* **(Figure 13.25).** He executed it using quick brushstrokes to create the dark trees that resemble flames. The stars in the sky seem to be alive with movement. He expressed the violent energy and creative force of nature in this painting. Today, we regard this artwork as one of van Gogh's greatest because it reflects his passion and originality in creating an energetic and forceful image.

Activity

Analyzing a Style

Applying Your Skills. Have students form small groups and find an example of each style discussed in this section. An alternative approach is to have each group find multiple examples of one specific style. Just be sure that each style is chosen by a group. If sending students to the library for research is not practical or if there is not enough time for them to adequately complete the activity, you might bring books to the classroom and allow students to use them in class.

ASSESS..........

Self-Assessment

Have students complete the review questions on this page. Answers are provided below.

Reteaching

Work with small groups of students to review the differences between Neoclassicism and Romanticism. How do the two art movements differ in subject and style?

Enrichment

Have the class visit an art museum. Let students choose a painting that they will closely observe and draw. Provide students with charcoal pencils and a sketchbook or sketch paper clipped to a firm backing. After this exercise, have students discuss their experience.

CLOSE............

Have several volunteers pretend to be posing either for a Neoclassic-style painting or a Baroque-style painting. Challenge the remainder of the class to guess the style of work for which the subject is posing.

Activity | **Analyzing a Style**

Applying Your Skills. Find a book about Impressionism in the library or read about it on the Internet. List at least four Impressionist works of art, each one painted by a different artist. Select one of the four works. Use the four steps of art history to write about the work. Include your paper in your portfolio.

 Check Your Understanding

1. Describe Neoclassicism.
2. What was Realism a reaction to?
3. What was emphasized in Impressionist painting?

 Answers to Check Your Understanding

1. Neoclassicism was an art style inspired by the art and culture of the early classical period of Greece and Rome. Neoclassicism emphasized realism, minimized emotionalism, and featured epic or heroic events.
2. Realism rejected the idealized depiction of places foreign to Europe and events that characterized Romanticism.
3. Impressionist paintings emphasize everyday subjects and the momentary effects of light. They feature dots or dabs of color.

Early Twentieth Century
(pages 374–377)
(National Standards: 3a, 3c, 4a, 4b, 4c, 5b)

FOCUS...........
Objectives
After completing this lesson, students will be able to:

- Discuss the objectives of the Expressionists and name some of the artists associated with this art movement.
- Understand the roots of Cubist and Surrealist art and describe the characteristic of these styles.
- Describe the Regionalist styles in which North American artists worked in the first half of the twentieth century.

Supplies
- Stiff white paper
- Tape
- Scissors

Resources
📁 Artist's Profile 1, Pablo Picasso

📁 Artist's Profile 32, Frank Lloyd Wright

📁 Enrichment Activity 25, *The Armory Show*

TEACH..........
Motivator
Explain to students that many works of modern art focus on expressing feelings. Ask students to try creating their own drawings that express feelings. Remind them to depict the emotion itself, not a person causing or feeling that emotion.

Early Twentieth Century

During the first half of the twentieth century, artists responded to rapid changes in technology, world politics, and culture by creating a variety of approaches in artistic expression. One style replaced another with bewildering speed. With the invention and spread of photography, artists no longer functioned as recorders of the visible world. They launched a quest to redefine the characteristics of art. Soon it became impossible to separate artists into neat categories or to group their works under clear art styles.

Trends in the arts changed rapidly because increased travel and new ways of communication helped artists to compare ideas. One individual or group could easily influence another. It no longer took years for one art movement or style of art to catch on in other areas. In fact, some artists who lived long lives, such as Matisse and Picasso, changed their own styles several times during their careers.

European Art

In general, European artists assumed one of three different directions in artistic expression: self-expression, composition, or imagination. Each direction emphasized a different aspect of art.

In Germany, artists began working in a style later called **Expressionism,** *a style that emphasized the expression of innermost feelings.* The German Expressionists did not think the purpose of art was to make pretty pictures. Instead, because they experienced the terrible economic and social conditions in Germany before and after World War I, they wanted to express their feelings about these conditions. Their emotional subjects ranged from fear and anger to a preoccupation with death. Käthe Kollwitz (**kah**-teh **kohl**-vits), an Expressionist concerned with poverty and war, created many moving images of mothers grieving for dead children. She based her work on personal experience: she lost her eldest son during the first weeks of World War I **(Figure 13.26).**

In France, a group of artists created works that focused on the qualities of design. Some of these artists created **Cubism,** *a style that emphasizes structure and design.* Three main concepts influenced the Cubists. The first concept was that shapes in nature are based on geometric forms. The second concept, based on a scientific discovery, showed that all

◀ **FIGURE 13.26** Describe the person that you see here. Identify the elements of art that the artist used. How does Kollwitz view herself? Is this a person you would be interested in meeting? Why or why not?

Käthe Kollwitz. *Self-Portrait.* 1921. Etching. 21.6 × 26.7 cm (8½ × 10½"). The National Museum of Women in the Arts, Washington, D.C. Museum Purchase: The Member's Acquisition Fund.

TECHNOLOGY OPTIONS

National Gallery of Art Videodisc Use the following to show examples of early twentieth century artists.

Käthe Kollwitz
In God's Hands

Search Frame 2567

Pablo Picasso
Juggler with Still Life

Search Frame 2281

Henri Matisse
Large Composition with Masks

Search Frame 2213

Use Glencoe *National Gallery of Art Correlation Bar Code Guide* to locate more artworks.

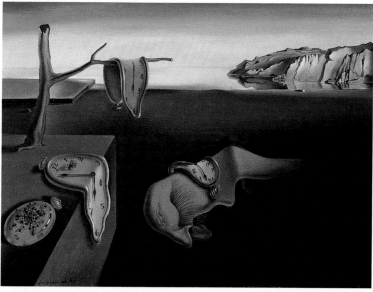

▲ **FIGURE 13.28** Dali has created a strange world in which metal objects that should be firm seem to melt. Realistic details, such as the ants, add to the nightmare quality of the scene. What might the clocks symbolize? Can you recognize the object lying on the ground in the center of the picture?

Salvador Dali. *The Persistence of Memory.* 1931. Oil on canvas. 24.1 × 33 cm (9½ × 13"). Collection, The Museum of Modern Art, New York, New York. Given anonymously.

matter is made up of atoms that are constantly in motion. The third concept, based on art from other cultures (African sculpture had recently been displayed in Paris), revealed that shape and form could be simplified and rearranged to increase the expressive qualities of an artwork. Pablo Picasso and Georges Braque pioneered the movement. In **Figure 13.27,** you can see how Picasso visually translated the human body into geometric shapes. He tried to paint three-dimensional objects as if they could be seen from many different points of view at the same time.

A third group of artists relied on fantasy to create art that expressed personal feelings. They explored the psychology of the mind as subject matter in their work. **Surrealism** emphasized *art in which dreams, fantasy, and the subconscious served as inspiration for artists.* Surrealists painted very realistic, almost photographic, images but combined objects that didn't belong together. The work of the Surrealists appears strange and dreamlike. Surrealist paintings can be funny or mysterious and frightening. **Figure 13.28** depicts a landscape with a cliff, lake, and tree painted in a realistic manner, but the landscape contains strange objects that don't seem to belong there and don't behave as one might expect.

MORE ABOUT... Cubism

Cubism is the first truly twentieth-century artistic style. Heralded by Picasso's 1907 work *Demoiselles d'Avignon,* Cubism involved entirely new approaches to the treatment of pictorial space and to the representation of emotions and states of mind. Cubists broke away from the two major features of Western art since the Renaissance: the classical model of rendering the human figure, and the spatial illusionism of one-point perspective. The result was not only the reduction of body parts to geometrical forms and the loss of a normal scale of human proportion, but also a means of suggesting three-dimensional relationships that did not hinge on the convention of illusionistic, one-point perspective.

Critical Thinking

Share with students the views of French poet and modern art critic Guillaume Appollinaire, who once attempted to explain the purpose of Expressionism to a skeptical fellow critic by commenting that "Exactitude is not truth." Have students analyze his statement and then apply it to the Expressionist artwork in this lesson. Ask: What truth is expressed in the work?

Studio Skills

Have students create a variety of geometric forms such as a cube, a cone, or a cylinder, using stiff white paper, scissors and transparent tape. Have students work in groups and agree on a still-life arrangement of these objects. Then, working individually, have students make drawings of the arrangement as seen simultaneously from various perspectives.

Aesthetics

Explain to students that the modern notion that art should be original began with the Dadaists and the Surrealists. Then divide the students into debating teams. One side should defend the proposition that originality in art is important. The other side must provide counter-arguments that great art can be produced without necessarily being entirely new or a unique act of self-expression. Encourage students to refer to specific works that have been discussed in class to support their conclusions.

Art Criticism

Have students imagine they are art critics assigned to write a review of Dali's painting in Figure 13.28. Ask them to begin writing notes that would eventually become their published review. Remind them to incorporate information from the four steps of art criticism.

Studio Skills

Remind students that the Armory Show of 1913 played a significant part in the introduction of European art to Americans. Tell students that the class will produce a similar show for other teachers, parents, and interested students. To begin, have students create a piece of art or select samples of original works with which they are pleased. Have them arrange the works in a way that showcases their creative efforts. On a given date, allow visitors to attend the show and have students take turns acting as docents. Tell students that they should be prepared to answer any questions that viewers might ask about their artworks or their training.

Critical Thinking

When discussing Regionalist art, ask students to share their travel experiences. Ask: What subject matter did they choose to photograph while on vacation? Why? If they were painters, would they want to paint the same subjects they photographed? If so, what choices about media and processes would they make in order to paint the subject in the style of the Regionalists? If they chose not to paint the same subjects, why not?

Aesthetics

Tell students that Thomas Benton studied traditional painting techniques and usually worked in egg tempera, which he finished in glazes that brought out the depth of his colors. Using the four steps of art criticism, have students evaluate Benton's painting in Figure 13.29.

North American Art

In the United States in the beginning of the twentieth century, a group of young artists turned to the harsh realities of the city for subject matter. They called themselves The Eight and organized an exhibition in 1908. Their original name was soon forgotten when critics immediately labeled them the Ashcan School. Critics expressed displeasure at the subject matter of their work: stark tenement buildings, crowded city streets, poor working people, and ragged children.

Although this realism shocked unwary viewers, the Armory Show of 1913 exerted an even greater impact on the American art world. This show introduced Americans to the work of European artists. Most Americans felt confused by what they saw. The art on display did not fit into their traditional understanding of the nature and purpose of art. However, the show energized many American artists, who responded to the challenge posed by the daring exhibition and took their first steps toward making modern art in the United States.

Alexander Calder, a sculptor, ranks among these twentieth–century innovators. Most sculptors at this time worked with traditional materials and methods. A few experimented with the new materials of modern industry. Calder created a new form of sculpture by arranging wire and sheet metal into balanced arrangements that stayed in motion (Figure 8.21 on page 213). He called these moving sculptures mobiles (**moh**-beels).

As a reaction against the infusion of European styles into American art, some artists decided to focus on strictly American themes. Called **Regionalists,** these artists *painted the farmlands and cities of the United States in an optimistic way.* Each artist had a slightly different style, but all of them portrayed upbeat messages in their work. They focused on the vast expanse, beauty, productivity, and abundance of the United States and depicted happy, hardworking people. **Figure 13.29** is an example of Regionalism. In

▲ **FIGURE 13.29** Notice the curving lines and simple, pure colors in this painting. Benton has used repetition to add interest, variety, and movement to the work. Identify the different figures and objects that are repeated throughout the painting.

Thomas Hart Benton. *The Sources of Country Music.* 1975. Acrylic on canvas. 1.8 × 3 m (6 × 10′). The Country Music Hall of Fame and Museum, Nashville, Tennessee. © T.H. Benton and R. P. Benton, Testamentary Trusts/VAGA, New York 1994.

MORE ABOUT...   Thomas Hart Benton

Benton (1889–1975) was born in Neosho, Missouri, and based his most popular paintings on familiar Midwestern life. Benton briefly studied with avant-garde artists in Paris, but he abandoned modernism around 1920 and began creating pictures that satirized city life and glorified rural life in the Midwest and the South. Benton was a member of the Regionalist painters' movement and became its spokesperson, speaking out against urban industrial civilization and what he called the sickly nature of modernist art. He continued to defend Regionalism and became one of its only remaining advocates in the 1940s, when abstract painting gained prominence.

▲ FIGURE 13.30 Wright designed this house to be functional as well as to blend in with the environment. What materials did he use to create this natural effect? What elements and principles of art did he use to unify the building with its setting?

Frank Lloyd Wright. *The David Wright House*. Scottsdale, Arizona. 1951.

Art History

Explain to students that Mexican murals are part of a long tradition of narrative art. Ask students to brainstorm a list of other artists who, like the Mexican muralists, were preoccupied with war and the suffering that goes along with it. Encourage students to find examples of such works, both within the text and in other resources. Then have individual students compose short essays in which they note common threads running through works that make anti-war statements.

ASSESS..........
Self-Assessment

Have students complete the review questions on this page. Answers are provided below.

Reteaching

Have small groups of students browse through art books. Let each student select and share reproductions of two Cubist paintings or sculptures. Ask: Why did you choose this work of art? What made you identify it as an example of Cubism? Which art elements did you find most interesting in this work?

CLOSE.............

Ask each student to state whether he or she would have preferred to paint in a Surrealist or Regionalist style during the first half of the twentieth century, and why.

this mural, Thomas Hart Benton portrayed a group of larger-than-life Americans who display the restlessness of energetic people. He included symbols of industrialization and historical events.

Another American artist working at the same time showed a different side of the American experience. African–American artist Jacob Lawrence used bright, flat areas of color in a geometric style to create his art (see Figure 4.19 on page 80). His series paintings tell the stories of historical African–American figures, as well as describe the struggles of African–Americans moving from the South to the North in the early twentieth century.

The twentieth century also saw vast changes in architecture. New materials and technology and new demands for commercial space led to the development of skyscrapers. Architects designed functional structures with steel frames that emphasized simplicity of form to replace heavy, decorated structures. One famous modern architect, Frank Lloyd Wright, believed that form should follow function, meaning that the look of a building should be based on its use. He designed buildings that blended harmoniously with the landscape around them **(Figure 13.30).**

Like France in the late eighteenth century, Mexico at the beginning of the twentieth century experienced deep social and political unrest. The tension erupted into the Mexican Revolution. Just as European artists groped for a new style of art to depict their response to war and unrest, some Mexican artists also felt the need to develop new approaches to art that would express their feelings about the plight of the people. These Mexican artists were referred to as the Mexican muralists, because they covered walls and ceilings with murals about Mexican history, the suffering of the peasants, and the immoral behavior of the ruling class. Artists such as Diego Rivera (Figure 9.5, page 229) and David Alfaro Siqueiros (Figure 10.14, page 264) combined the solid forms of ancient, pre-Columbian Mexican art with the powerful colors and bold lines of Cubism and Expressionism.

✓ Check Your Understanding

1. Define Expressionism.
2. Name the three main influences on Cubism.
3. Explain Surrealism.
4. What are mobiles?

✓ Answers to Check Your Understanding

1. Expressionism was a style that emphasized the expression of innermost feelings.
2. The realization that all shapes in nature are based on geometric forms, the scientific discovery that all matter is made up of atoms that are constantly in motion, and the introduction of African sculpture to Europe.
3. Surrealism was an art movement in which dreams, fantasy, and the subconscious served as inspiration for artists.
4. Mobiles are moving sculptures.

Art After 1945

Art After 1945

(pages 378–383)
(National Standards: 3a, 3c, 4a, 4b, 4c, 5b)

FOCUS...........
Objectives

After completing this lesson, students will be able to:

■ Explain the goals of Abstract Expressionism.

■ Explain what is meant by Op and Pop art and name some artists who employed these styles in their work.

■ Describe some innovations in architecture made during this period.

Supplies

■ Examples of Op art

Resources

📁 Enrichment Activity 26, *Becoming an Art Expert*

TEACH.........
Motivator

Point out to students that each of the artists in this lesson was working at a time when artists developed very unique and individual styles. Have students compare the experiences of these artists with that of Italian Renaissance artists, whose artistic styles were much more consistent. Is it harder for artists to develop a style of their own than to work in the same style as others?

After World War II ended in 1945, the European art world was in disarray. Paris was no longer the center of artistic creativity. The war displaced many people. A number of artists who had fled Nazi Germany settled in New York City. They began teaching there and by the 1950s, they and their students established a new center for the arts. New York City became the new capital of the art world.

In the years since World War II, artists have created many changes in artistic approaches, styles, and techniques. A variety of art forms once considered minor, such as printmaking, weaving, ceramics, and jewelry making, have come to be considered art forms equal to painting and sculpture. New kinds of art, such as computer animation, have also gained prominence.

Abstract Expressionism

Abstract Expressionism, the first new style to arrive on the scene in New York in the years following World War II, *emphasized abstract elements of art rather than recognizable subject matter, and also stressed feelings and emotions.* Following in the tradition of German Expressionism, Abstract Expressionist artists believed that art should function as a spontaneous expression of emotion, and they did not necessarily rely on planned structure to organize the design of their paintings. Look at **Figure 13.31.** It is called *Flowering Swamp,* but you cannot see any realistically–depicted flowers or swamps. If you use your imagination, however, you can see how the two rectangles seem to float over a background that suggests water and flowers.

Pop and Op Art

During the early 1960s, artists turned to the mass media, and especially to advertising, for subject matter. Pop art portrayed images of popular culture, such as soda bottles, soup cans, soap

▲ **FIGURE 13.31** Hofmann, who was inspirational to the Abstract Expressionist style that grew in New York, is best known for his use of brilliant colors. What does the artist appear to be expressing here? What is the mood or feeling of this work?

Hans Hofmann. *Flowering Swamp.* 1957. Oil on wood. 122 × 91.5 cm (48⅛ × 36⅛"). Hirshhorn Museum and Sculpture Garden, Smithsonian Institution, Washington, D.C. Gift of the Joseph H. Hirshhorn Foundation, 1966.

MORE ABOUT... **Hans Hofmann**

Hofmann explained his theory about the use of space in his paintings as a "push-pull" theory of movement. He said that Italian perspective was all wrong. He felt that the illusion had only one direction in depth, and that nothing came back. However, he said that in his paintings space goes in and it comes back. The tensions he creates show shapes that are constantly moving in and out. In his paintings we can see the hints of many art styles: Abstract Expressionism, Cubism, Color-Field, and Op art.

Roy Lichtenstein. *Blam*. 1962. Oil on canvas. 172.7 × 203.2 cm. (68 × 80"). Yale University Art Gallery, New Haven, Connecticut. Richard Brown Baker Collection.

Vocabulary

Explain to students that Op art sought to create a sense of movement on the picture surface by means of optical illusion. Have students examine Figure 13.33 and show other examples of Op art. Ask them how Op art's optical illusionism differs from that of other artworks in this text.

Art History

Tell students that Abstract Expressionists have been labeled "action painters." This name came from the tendency of Abstract Expressionists to concentrate more on the act of painting than on the subject matter. Ask students to find out more about other artists associated with this movement, such as Jackson Pollack, Arshile Gorky, James Brooks, and Helen Frankenthaler.

Art History

Op art developed in the United States after 1960. This nonobjective art movement had parallels in several European countries, including Germany and Italy. Op artists sought to create an impression of movement on the picture surface by means of optical illusion. In traditional paintings, the aim was to draw the viewer into the work. In contrast, Op pictures seem to vibrate and reach out to the spectator. Victor Vasarely is generally regarded as the founder of this movement. He used dazzling colors and precise geometric shapes to create surfaces that appear to move. They seem to project forward in some places and to recede in others. Op art extended illusionism into the realm of nonrepresentational art.

boxes, giant hamburgers, and comic strips, in a variety of art forms. Pop artists made people take a new look at everyday objects. They often used bright colors and cartoonish graphics to depict their subject matter. **Figure 13.32** is an example of Pop art. Artist Roy Lichtenstein (**lick**-ten-steyn) used a strong sense of design, a limited color scheme, and bold shapes to create a painting that was based on a comic strip.

Another style of art popular in this period took advantage of people's fascination with visual illusions. Op art, or optical art, uses scientific knowledge about vision to create optical illusions of movement. Op art relies on the special arrangement of the art elements such as the precise arrangement of lines, or the placement of complementary colors next to each other to create the illusion of movement. If you look at **Figure 13.33,** you will notice the unusual orange color of the background. The blue-green dots seem to be placed in no

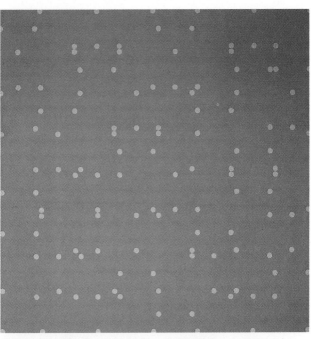

▲ **FIGURE 13.33** This piece of Op art is intended to cause a visual effect. Do you think the artwork has another purpose or meaning? Why or why not?

Larry Poons. *Orange Crush*. 1963. Acrylic on canvas. 203.2 × 203.2 cm (80 × 80"). Albright-Knox Art Gallery, Buffalo, New York. Gift of Seymour H. Knox, 1964. ©Larry Poons/VAGA, New York 1994.

LESSON 5 *Art After 1945* **379**

MORE ABOUT... **Abstract Expressionism**

Not all critics championed Abstract Expressionism. Harold Rosenberg, for example, felt that Abstract Expressionist painters were incredibly narcissistic, and his writings reflect his bitterly sarcastic attitude. In the article, "The American Action Painters," Rosenberg states: "[The artist] gesticulated upon the canvas and watched for what each novelty would declare him and his art to be." Rosenberg accused Abstract Expressionist painters of releasing themselves from any obligation to promote political, moral, or aesthetic values. He said that such artworks had no real audience—they were just objects used by the powerful and "accepted" by the public as "phenomena of The Age of Queer Things."

Art Criticism

Reveal to students that the rise of a new art movement often changes the way in which an earlier style or set of artworks is viewed. Explain that, until the advent of Color-Field painting (a movement closely related to Abstract Expressionism), Monet's water lily paintings were regarded as evidence of his decline. These paintings were done late in Monet's life, and their blurriness reflects the fact that his eyesight was very poor. As Color-Field paintings such as those by Mark Rothko gained favor, critics began to appreciate anew Monet's paintings of water lilies. People viewed them not as messy illustrations of lilies, but as extraordinary fields of color.

Art History

Stella's earliest works were black canvasses enhanced by a minimum of thin white lines. The thin white lines that separate the colors are actually the unpainted white of the canvas. By 1968 he was painting on shaped canvasses. This one is part of his protractor series. Looking back toward minimalism, he applies his colors flatly, and his shapes have hard, sharp edges.

Ask the students to compare this early work to his work of the 1980s (Figure 13.40 on page 383). Have them list similarities and differences. *(Some similarities include: hard edges between colors, geometric shapes, and the large size of both works. The most outstanding difference is that the 1984 piece is a three-dimensional painting using new media such as aluminum, and fiberglass honeycomb.)* The 1980s piece uses a variety of shapes. Negative spaces are also important to the look of the piece. In the 1960s piece the only negative space is that surrounding the outline.

▲ **FIGURE 13.34** Rothko limited the colors in this painting to an analogous scheme of yellow and orange. He blended the edges to blur the line between the two colors. Standing in front of the painting, which is almost 8 feet (2.4 m) tall, a viewer has an intense visual experience. What might the purpose of creating such an experience be?

Mark Rothko. *Orange and Yellow.* 1956. Oil on canvas. 231.1 × 180.3 cm (91 × 71"). Albright-Knox Art Gallery, Buffalo, New York. Gift of Seymour H. Knox, 1956.

▼ **FIGURE 13.35** Notice the outlines of this painting. It is not a traditional rectangular shape. Observe how the red border ties the work together. How has Stella used repetition and contrast to further unify the painting?

Frank Stella. *Agbatana III.* 1968. Acrylic on canvas. 304.8 × 457.2 cm (120 × 180"). Allen Memorial Art Museum, Oberlin College, Oberlin, Ohio. Ruth C. Roush Fund for Contemporary Art and National Foundation for the Arts and Humanities Grant, 1968.

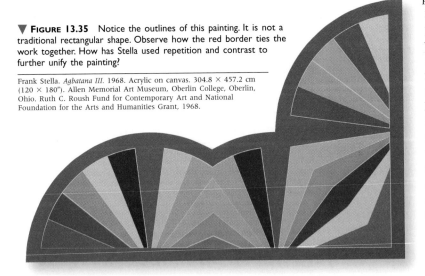

apparent order, but in fact the artist carefully planned their arrangement. If you look at the dots for a few moments, they appear to vibrate because the afterimage causes a visual response that creates the illusion of movement.

Color-Field Painting

As artists experimented with a variety of new styles, they occasionally selected just one element of art to focus on in their work. An example, Color-Field painting, is art created using only flat fields of color. It is created without the precision of Op art and also without its interest in illusion. It is color for the pure sensation of color. Look at the example by Mark Rothko in **Figure 13.34.** His color areas have hazy edges that seem to float in space.

Minimalism

Some artists sought absolute simplicity in their art. This focus came to be known as **Minimalism,** or *art that uses a minimum of art elements.* Minimalists emphasized either color or shape as the dominant element in painting. In sculpture, they used the fewest possible geometric forms. They depicted art at its most austere, arranging only the simplest art elements. Minimalist painters who placed importance on the crisp, precise edges of the shapes in their paintings came to be known as Hard-edge painters. Frank Stella **(Figure 13.35),** used different canvas shapes for his works and created art on a large scale. He relied on thin white lines to set off colors, define shapes, and unify the work.

CULTURAL DIVERSITY

Two-dimensional Art Around the World After examining the work by Frank Stella in Figure 13.35, groups of students may wish to investigate the use of boldly-colored, two-dimensional design by cultures outside of the United States. Some possibilities are the beadwork of the Pacific Northwest Coast Athapaskans, patchwork textiles by the Maroons in the Suriname rain forest of South America, Guatemalan woven textiles, woven telephone-wire baskets made by the Zulus in South Africa, and the traditional mud wall paintings that are repainted every year in Ghana after the rainy season. Groups should gather information and reproductions of the works of their culture for a round-table discussion.

New Forms of Realism

Although modern American artists have created many abstract and nonobjective artworks, Americans harbor a love for realism. Many American artists continue to portray subjects in a realistic style. Sculpture made by Duane Hanson **(Figure 13.36)** appears so lifelike that it once fooled a gallery security guard. The guard thought that one of Hanson's motionless, seated figures looked ill and called for an ambulance. The painting in **Figure 13.37** looks so accurate in visual detail that a casual observer could easily mistake it for a photograph. This is how the style earned one of its names: Photo-Realism. It is also called Hyper-Realism and Super-Realism. **Super-Realism** is *art that depicts objects as precisely and accurately as they actually appear.*

Activity	Applying the Steps

Applying Your Skills. Look through this book to find five paintings that were created after 1950. For each, list the name of the artist, the title of the work, and the style in which the work was painted.

Architecture

After World War II, architects developed the International Style of architecture, a plain, austere building style. Its origins could be traced back to the work of Frank Lloyd Wright and Louis Sullivan, who both designed buildings before World War II. In their Seagram Building, the architects Ludwig Mies van der Rohe (ludd-**vig** meez van der **row**) and Philip Johnson created a simple geometric glass box that exemplifies van der

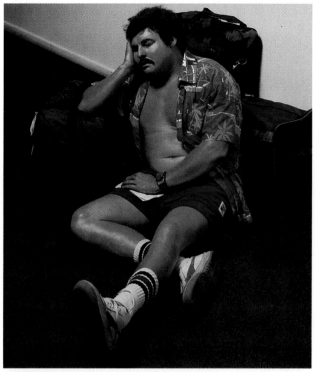

▲ **Figure 13.36**   This figure is an example of Super-Realism. If you observed this figure at an airport or in a hotel lobby, could you mistake him for a real person? Why or why not?

Duane Hanson. *Traveler with Sunburn.* 1986. Bronze, oil paint, and mixed media. Life-size. Private collection.

▲ **Figure 13.37**   This street scene seems almost like a photograph although it is a painting. How does the artist create this illusion? What is the purpose of painting such an illusion when one could simply take a photograph?

Richard Estes. *Paris Street Scene.* 1972. Oil on canvas. 101.6 × 152.4 cm (40 × 60″). Virginia Museum of Fine Arts, Richmond, Virginia. Gift of Sydney and Frances Lewis. © Richard Estes/Licensed by VAGA, New York, New York/Courtesy Marlborough Gallery, New York.

LESSON 5   *Art After 1945*   **381**

CHAPTER 13 LESSON 5

Critical Thinking

Using Duane Hanson's sculpture as a source of inspiration, have students suggest ideas for a sculptural group that represents the student population of their school. Ask: How would the design be arranged? How would models be chosen? Describe their appearance. What objects or props do you feel are essential?

Activity

Applying the Steps

Applying Your Skills. At this point students should be able to complete this activity without difficulty. However, if you feel it is necessary, have them work in pairs or small groups or assign the activity as homework.

💻 **Computer Option.** Look through magazines, the rest of this book, and other sources and find five examples of technology-generated art such as holographs, CAD designs, computer graphics, and so on. Research the history of the artist or work.

► COOPERATIVE LEARNING

Researching Modern Architecture Point out that new materials and technologies, including the development of reinforced concrete in the late nineteenth century, have greatly expanded the possibilities for architects. Have pairs of students research modern structures built from reinforced concrete, such as the Opera House in Sydney, Australia. Work should be guided by the following questions: When and where was the building constructed? What purpose is it intended to serve? How has it been accepted by the public and by critics? Why was reinforced concrete chosen for this building? What materials were used to reinforce the concrete? Then ask pairs to make brief oral presentations to the class.

381

Studio Skills

Have students select a collage, sculpture, or example of architecture from this chapter that interests them and create a painting or drawing inspired by that artwork.

Art History

Habitat was built to show what future housing could be like. It was built for Expo 67, the Montreal World's Fair. It is made of 354 prefabricated concrete boxes. They have been joined to form 158 apartments. All the boxes are the same size, but they were designed for a variety of uses and floor plans. One box could be a living-dining area with a kitchen and another could have two bedrooms and a bath. Some boxes are like efficiency apartments and contain a living room, kitchen, bedroom, and bath. Each apartment has a separate entrance, windows on all sides, and a terrace. The flat roof on one unit provides the garden terrace for another. At first people thought the structure looked too sterile. However, it has been inhabited since its construction, and residents have modified their boxes with sun porches, skylights, fireplaces, and chimneys. Everywhere you look, you will find plants and trees.

Ask the students how they would feel living in a modular building. What would they do to make the cement boxes more comfortable?

▶ **FIGURE 13.38**
This simple design, called International Style, appealed to architects as a reaction to the highly ornate Art Deco style that was popular in the 1920s and 1930s. Can you easily identify the purpose of the building? What is its purpose?

Ludwig Mies van der Rohe and Philip Johnson. *Seagram Building.* New York, 1958.

Rohe's favorite saying, "Less is more" **(Figure 13.38).**

Architects of the 1960s looked to the future as well as to the past. **Figure 13.39** shows an apartment complex that looks futuristic in its design but actually echoes the Pueblo apartment complexes built by Native Americans hundreds of years ago. The interlocking apartment units are designed to give occupants a sense of openness and space. Because the units are not lined up next to each other as in traditional apartment complexes, each apartment has plenty of windows that allow sunlight to enter and give the illusion that each apartment is a separate house.

Post-Modern Art

We are currently in a period of art that is rapidly evolving. Some say we are at the end of the modern era. Others insist that we have already entered the post-modern era. The subject is being hotly debated in artistic circles, but the answer is something that only time can judge.

▶ **FIGURE 13.39**
This apartment complex uses space efficiently. Do you find the complex attractive? Why or why not? What are some of the personal touches the residents have added?

Moshe Safdie. *Habitat.* Montreal, 1967.

382 | **CHAPTER 13** Western Traditions in Art

COOPERATIVE LEARNING

Researching Architects Have students form small groups and choose one of the following architects to research their pursuits and accomplishments: Pier Luigi Nervi, Buckminster Fuller, Walter Gropius, Moshe Safdie, Ludwig Mies van der Rohe, Frei Otto, Louis Sullivan, Frank Lloyd Wright, Helmut Jahn, Frank Gehry, Michael Graves, and I.M. Pei. Encourage students to bring in pictures of their chosen architect's work, if possible, and share their findings with the class.

The term post-modernism first appeared in reference to architecture. **Post-Modernism** is *an approach to art that incorporates traditional elements and techniques while retaining some characteristics of modern art styles or movements.* Post-Modern architecture was a reaction to the plain glass boxes of the International Style. It incorporates decorative elements from the past and takes advantage of the flexibility of new materials.

The Rock-and-Roll Hall of Fame and Museum (Figure 14.21 on page 401), designed by I. M. Pei, is an example of architecture's break from the modern glass box. The museum contains a concert hall, a film and video display center, several sound chambers, and a party area as well as the usual glass display cases for showing off costumes, instruments, sheet music, and the personal belongings of famous musicians. The architect designed a building that reflects the freedom of rock-and-roll, but also functions as a museum to house its memorabilia.

Other Post-Modern artists are breaking traditional restrictions. Painters are creating three-dimensional paintings and sculptors are adding paint to their works. **Figure 13.40** is an example of a Post-Modern work with some identifiable subject matter. Is it a painted sculpture or a three-dimensional painting?

No one knows what will happen next in the art world. The acquisition of images from the past, and the incorporation of them into new works with new meanings, is only one facet of this new era. We have entered a time in art in which the diversity of ideas reflects the diversity of contemporary life.

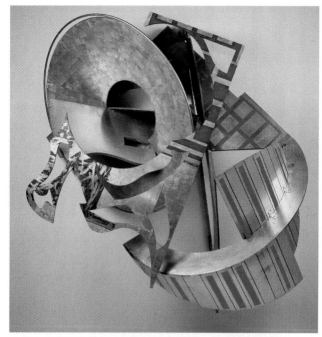

▲ **FIGURE 13.40** This sculpture represents several musical instruments. Can you identify what these instruments are? Notice how big the sculpture is. Why do you suppose the artist chose to make it so large?

Frank Stella. *St. Michael's Counterguard (Malta Series).* 1984. Mixed media on aluminum and fiberglass honeycomb. 396.2 × 342.9 × 274.3 cm (156 × 135 × 108″). Los Angeles County Museum of Art, Los Angeles, California. Gift of Anna Bing Arnold.

 Check Your Understanding

1. What is the subject matter of Pop Art?
2. How is Color-Field painting different from Op art?
3. Why is Super-Realism sometimes called Photo-Realism?
4. Describe Post-Modern architecture.

ASSESS..........
Self-Assessment
Have students complete the review questions on this page. Answers are provided below.

Reteaching
Have pairs of students show Figure 13.31, on page 378, to at least three people who are unfamiliar with Abstract Expressionist art and ask for their interpretation. Students should compare the various responses and categorize them according to the three main aesthetic theories. Conclude with a discussion of whether people's opinions correlated with their age, gender, or personality.

Enrichment
Have students choose a style of art that interests them and find an artwork in that particular style. Instruct them to tell what they see in the artwork and explain what characteristics of the work identify it as an example of that specific style.

CLOSE............
Have each student state which artist's work illustrated in this chapter seems the most "modern" and explain his or her choice.

 Answers to Check Your Understanding

1. Mass media and advertising provide the subject matter for Pop art.
2. Color-Field painting is concerned only with flat fields of color. It is created without the precision of Op art and also without its interest in illusion.
3. Super-Realism is sometimes called Photo-Realism because it is so realistic that a casual observer could easily mistake it for a photograph.
4. Post-Modern architecture incorporates decorative elements, exaggerates details, and uses traditional art elements and principles of design.

Critiquing the Work

➡ Describe
What do you see?

- We see a three-quarter view of the head and shoulders of a woman. Her skin is pale and smooth. It is shaded delicately. Her eyelids are half closed. They look unusual because they have no lashes. The hair framing her face falls in ringlets that are similar to the lines Leonardo used to depict water. Her hair is red-brown with highlights of golden yellow. She is wearing a low-intensity red velvet dress that is edged with a ribbon trimmed with gold embroidery.

- Directly behind her head is a juniper bush. On the right side of the painting we see a typical Renaissance landscape. Farther in the distance we see objects that fade to blue. This is Leonardo's invention called *ariel perspective*, because the colors in the distance fade as the air gets between them and the viewer. In that faded area you can see a church with two spires.

➡ Analyze
How is this work organized?

- The proportions are accurate. The students may feel like something is wrong because the subject's forehead is so high, but in those days ladies plucked their hair to give themselves a higher forehead because it was the fashion.

- We see random rhythm in the ringlets, in the leaves

384

ART CRITICISM IN ACTION

▲ **FIGURE 13.41**

Leonardo da Vinci. *Ginevra de' Benci.* c. 1474. Oil on panel, with addition at bottom edge. 42.7 × 37.0 cm (16¹³⁄₁₆ × 14⁹⁄₁₆″). National Gallery of Art, Washington, D.C. © 1998 Board of Trustees. Ailsa Mellon Bruce Fund.

MORE ABOUT... Leonardo da Vinci

In terms of his scientific ideas, Leonardo stood above all the contemporaries. He realized the importance of precise scientific observation and documentation. If his notebooks had been easier to decipher, his findings in anatomy, geology, meteorology, and hydraulics would have revolutionized the world at that time. He understood the circulation of the blood and how the eye worked. He determined that the moon had an effect on the tides, theorized correctly about continent formation, and surmised the significance of fossils. He invented a large number of ingenious machines including a hydrometer and an underwater diving suit. His flying devices, though not feasible, were based on sound theories of aerodynamics.

1   **DESCRIBE**   **What do you see?**

List all of the information found in the credit line. Describe the objects you see in the visual image. Use your perception skills.

- Describe the woman, including her clothing, her hair, and the features of her face.
- Describe the background of the work.

2   **ANALYZE**   **How is this work organized?**

During this step you will collect information about all the elements and principles of art.

- Did the artist use accurate proportions?
- What kind of rhythm, balance, and proportion has he used to organize the work?
- Which area of the work is emphasized? What techniques did the artist use to create a focal point? What techniques did he use to unify the work?

3   **INTERPRET**   **What is the artist trying to communicate?**

Now it is time to combine the clues you have collected with your personal experiences to guess what the artist is saying about this woman. You will solve the mystery of the work during this step.

- What is unusual about the woman's eyes and mouth? What feelings does her face express?
- Which elements and principles affect the mood of the work?
- What message do you get from this work? Based on your interpretation, give this work a new title.

4   **JUDGE**   **What do you think of the work?**

Now you will decide if this is a successful work of art or not. You may make a personal opinion, but the one that is important for now is the objective judgment based on aesthetic theories.

- Did Leonardo da Vinci use the elements and principles successfully?
- Do you think this is a successful work of art? Why or why not? Use one or more of the aesthetic theories described in Chapter 2 to defend your judgment.

MEET THE ARTIST

LEONARDO DA VINCI

Italian, 1452–1519

Leonardo da Vinci. *Self-portrait.*

Leonardo da Vinci was proficient in just about everything intellectual and cultural—mathematics, physics, anatomy, geology, botany, geography, music, sculpture, architecture, and, of course, painting.

He was constantly experimenting with new media and although he had many ideas, he did not complete that many works. Perhaps Leonardo da Vinci is most highly regarded today for a mind that was constantly inventing, searching, and trying new ideas. His notebooks fascinate us with ideas for ways to fly, a printing press improvement on Gutenberg's, war machines, plans for domes, anatomical studies, and details of flowers.

of the bush, and the areas of land and the trees in the distance. The balance is informal. The vertical axis goes through her neck and through the pupil of her eye on the left, but there is more face on the viewer's right, which is balanced by the hair on the viewer's left.

- The woman's face is emphasized. The artist used contrast of light against dark to create the focal point. He used harmony of color and simplification to unify this work.

Interpret
What is the artist trying to communicate?

- Her eyes have no shadows. The dark brown color is the darkest area on the face. Her mouth is closed and looks soft. If it were firmly closed, the line would be tighter. There is a slight downturn in the center. Her face looks sad. This is the first psychological portrait ever painted.
- Color value is an important element because the face is shaded to reveal her emotions. The texture of her skin and hair are also important. The isolation and simplification place strong emphasis on her face so that we can see her emotions.
- Answers will vary.

Judge
What do you think of the artwork?

- Answers will vary. Most will say yes.
- Answers will vary. Most will choose all three theories because of realism, composition, and emotion.

Time & Place   **Renaissance**

Leonardo da Vinci painted the portrait of *Ginevra de' Benci* in about 1474. Some other events that occurred around that time:

Social Studies: In 1470 the Incas rose to power in Peru.
Art: In 1475 Michelangelo was born in the small village of Caprese, not far from Florence.
Technology: In 1477 Johannes Gutenberg's movable type became widely used for bibles, sheet music, maps, and posters.

CONNECTIONS LANGUAGE ARTS

The Harlem Renaissance
(National Standards: 6a, 6b)

Objectives

After completing this feature, students will be able to:

■ Explain the art of the Harlem Renaissance.

■ Discuss subjects common to writers and artists of the movement.

Teaching the Connection

Have students read the feature on this page.

Ask students to think about the social and historical forces affecting African-Americans at the beginning of the twentieth century. The migration of African-Americans from the South to the northern cities at the turn of the century resulted in concentrated urban communities of black people for the first time in this country. The economic boom of the twenties resulted in greater opportunities and social mobility for many people. Racism and social inequality persisted, but social change was taking place. How does the art of the Harlem Renaissance reflect or respond to these changes?

Tell students that Harlem occupies approximately two square miles of northern Manhattan. The Harlem Renaissance flourished from the early 1920s to the onset of the Depression. African-American writing existed prior to this movement, of course, but not as an organized, self-conscious, and often avante-garde movement. The Harlem Renaissance embraced more than art, music, and literature—it also included progressive politics, racial integration, and the pursuit of hedonism.

386

The Harlem Renaissance

◀ **FIGURE 13.42**

Lois Mailou Jones. *The Ascent of Ethiopia.* 1932. Oil on canvas. 59.7 × 43.8 cm (23¹/₂ × 17¹/₄"). Milwaukee Art Museum, Milwaukee, Wisconsin. Purchase, African-American Art Acquisition Fund, matching funds from Suzanne and Richard Pieper, with additional support from Arthur and Dorothy Nelle Sanders.

The Harlem Renaissance refers to an explosion of creativity focused in the work of African–American artists and writers during the 1920s. The participants in this movement shared a deep sense of racial pride and a desire to represent faithfully the experiences and feelings of African–Americans. Many artists looked to African cultural traditions for inspiration, while others found their subjects in folk traditions. Topics of interest to both writers and fine artists included: life in the South, as well as the experience of migration to Northern cities; racial prejudice and the desire for social equality; images of Africa; and music, such as the blues and jazz.

Lois Mailou Jones's painting, *The Ascent of Ethiopia* **(Figure 13.42)**, captures the essence of the Harlem Renaissance. Behind the foreground figure of an ancient Egyptian royal (possibly King Tut) we see a procession of figures ascending a stairway. Their destination appears to be a modern, urbanized culture of artists represented by musicians, actors, and a painter. Symbolically, the painting depicts the descendants of Ethiopia, or Africa as a whole, rising from adversity and struggle.

Making the Connection

1. What symbols or images can you find in this painting? How would you interpret them in light of the Harlem Renaissance movement?

2. Why do you think artists and writers of the movement wanted to portray African–American history in their works?

3. Read a work of literature by a Harlem Renaissance writer, then write an essay in which you discuss the work's themes and ideas.

Answers to Making the Connection

1. Students should note the black star in the upper left-hand corner. The light emanating from this star shines upon and clings to the figures ascending to Harlem, suggesting an experience of cultural enlightenment. Other answers are possible.

2. Answers will vary. Students may speculate that artists and writers wanted to root their works in the experiences and traditions of African-Americans as a way of building a lasting cultural movement and/or as a means of authenticating and preserving African-American history.

3. Responses will vary.

Building Vocabulary

On a separate sheet of paper, write the term that best matches each definition given below.

1. A style of architecture in which churches soared upward, used pointed arches, and had stained-glass windows.
2. The period at the end of the Middle Ages when artists, writers, and philosophers were "re-awakened" to art forms and ideas from ancient Greece and Rome.
3. An art style that borrowed subject matter and formal design qualities from the art of Greece and Rome.
4. A style of art that found its subjects in the world of the dramatic and in cultures foreign to Europe. It emphasized rich colors and high emotion.
5. An art style that featured everyday subjects and emphasized the momentary effects of light on color.
6. An art style that emphasized the expression of innermost feelings.
7. A style of art in which dreams, fantasy, and the subconscious served as inspiration for artists.
8. Artists who painted the farmlands and cities of the United States in an optimistic way.

Reviewing Art Facts

Answer the following questions using complete sentences.

1. Why was the Middle Ages also called the *Age of Faith*?
2. What social changes was Mannerism a response to?
3. Identify the characteristics of Romanticism.
4. Name one similarity and one difference between the artworks created by the Realists and the Impressionists.
5. Describe the subject matter chosen by the Mexican muralists.
6. Explain the difference between Expressionism and Cubism.
7. Define Op art.

Thinking Critically About Art

1. **Explain.** In this chapter, you learned how political and social events can shape art movements. You also learned how advances in technology can influence art styles. What social and political events, along with technological advances, paved the way for the Renaissance movement?
2. **Compare and Contrast.** Figure 13.18, page 367, and Figure 13.21, page 369, are both artworks that capture battles, yet they are very different. Compare the two. Explain their differences as well as their similarities, taking into account the media used and the style of art of each work.

Read about one of the most performed dance works created in the twentieth century. The classic *The Green Table*, presented by choreographer Kurt Jooss, is featured on page 425 of the Performing Arts Handbook.

Explore museums and art galleries without leaving your classroom. Visit the Glencoe Fine Arts Site (**www.glencoe.com/sec/art**) and roam through the collections of famous art museums. Or, take a close-up view of folk art and ethnic works at regional galleries.

ASSESSMENT ✓

Evaluate

- Have students complete the *Chapter 13 Test* in the TCR. 🗀
- Alternative Assessment teaching strategies are provided below or in the *Testing Program and Alternative Assessment* booklet. 🗀

Extension

Instruct students to select a realistic artwork from the text that they like. Have them consider how they would alter the realistic qualities of the subject to make them surreal. Then have them make several sketches of the object or area to show an evolution from Realism to Surrealism.

Answers to Building Vocabulary

1. Gothic
2. Renaissance
3. Neoclassicism
4. Romanticism
5. Impressionism
6. Expressionism
7. Surrealism
8. Regionalists

Answers to Reviewing Art Facts

1. The Middle Ages was also called the *Age of Faith* because the Christian religion exerted such important influence during that period.
2. Mannerism responded to the challenge to the authority of the Christian church and a vacuum in artistic inspiration and innovation.
3. It emphasized rich color and high emotion.
4. Both were similar because they painted familiar subjects. They were different because the style of Realists was realistic; Impressionists broke up solid forms and blurred edges to show the effect of sunlight on their subjects.
5. Mexican muralists used the suffering of the peasants and the immoral behavior of the ruling class as their subject matter.
6. Expressionism is an art style in which artists tried to communicate their innermost feelings. Cubism is a style that emphasizes structure and design.
7. Op art, or optical art, uses scientific knowledge about vision to create optical illusions of movement.

Reteaching

- Have students complete Concept Map 13 in the Reteaching booklet. 🗀

Careers in Art

(pages 388-409)

Resources

📁 Chapter 14 Study Guide

📁 Chapter 14 Test

📁 Computers in the Art Classroom

📁 Cultural Diversity in Art

📁 Portfolio and Assessment Techniques

📁 Reproducible Lesson Plan 14

🕹 Transparency CC-14, Maria Martinez and Popove Da. *Plate*

🕹 Transparency 14, Palmer Hayden. *The Janitor Who Paints*

While studying this chapter, use Performing Arts Handbook page 426 to learn how artists collaborate with other professionals to achieve success in their careers.

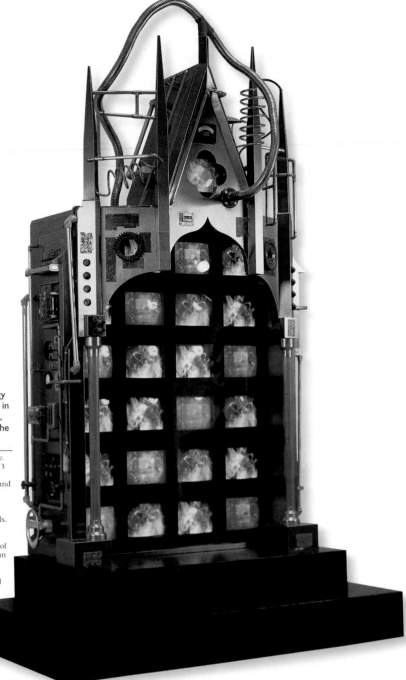

▶ **FIGURE 14.1**
Advances in technology help artists create art in new ways. In this case, technology becomes the artwork itself!

Nam June Paik. *Technology.* 1991. 25 video monitors, 3 laser disc players with unique 3 discs in a steel and plywood cabinet with aluminum sheeting and details of copper, bronze, plastic, and other materials. Approx. 332.6 × 192.1 × 131.7 cm (127 × 75⅝ × 51⅞″). National Museum of American Art, Smithsonian Institution, Washington, D.C. Museum purchase through the Lusita L. and Franz H. Denghausen Endowment.

FEATURED ARTISTS

Edward Harvey	Raymond Loewy	I.M. Pei
Liz Kingslien	Nam June Paik	Sandy Skoglund

Careers in Art

I n the distant past, a young person who wanted to be an artist would pay a master artist for permission to work as an *apprentice* in the master's studio. These apprentices learned as they observed and assisted the masters. Today students can develop their skills by taking courses in high school and post-secondary schools. Vocational schools and professional art schools provide the education for some art careers. Other careers may require a college degree. However, it's never too early to explore and prepare for a career in the arts.

The artist who created *Technology,* **Figure 14.1,** began his education in the arts at the age of 14 with piano and composition lessons. Nam June Paik's interest in contemporary music led him to performance art, which led him to use video and electronics in his art. He uses the video camera, the TV monitor, and the computer to create installation art and sculpture that has four dimensions: length, width, depth, and time.

Developing Your PORTFOLIO

Interview a person who is in an art-related career. Before you interview the person, brainstorm a list of questions to ask. Discover what education and work experience was necessary to obtain the position and find out what the job duties are. Then interview the artist and record the answers. Share the main points of the interview with your classmates and keep your interview notes in your portfolio.

OBJECTIVES

After completing this chapter, you will be able to:

- Discuss many fields in which one can pursue a career in art.
- Describe some of the skills artists need for various jobs.
- Determine your own interest in the field of art.

WORDS TO KNOW

graphic designer
logos
illustrator
package designer
photojournalists
animators
storyboards
architect
interior designer
museum curators

Chapter Overview

Chapter 14 introduces students to the opportunities for art careers in various fields. In particular, the areas of business and industry, environmental planning and development, entertainment, and education are examined.

Chapter Motivator

Instruct students to write down a career field that interests them. Ask volunteers to call out the identity of their selected fields. As each student responds, challenge the rest of the students to speculate how the training and knowledge they receive in an art class would be useful to people in the recognized profession.

Examining the Artwork

Although Paik claims to be a "clumsy guy" who can't drive a car or manage the complexities of a CD player, his antimachine mentality leads him to use machines in unique ways, creating machine-based art that is always on the cutting edge of technology.

His invention of a video synthesizer in 1970 made it possible for him to manipulate colors, shapes, and movement sequences on videotapes. Today his media are consumer electronics: the video camera, the TV set, and all the devices that he can use with a computer.

DEVELOPING A PORTFOLIO

Presentation When making decisions about the appearance of artworks in a portfolio, encourage students to pay attention to important concerns such as the mounting for paintings and protective jackets for pastels and chalk drawings. Remind them to label individual pieces sufficiently to avoid loss. Use slides for projects too large to include and show multiple viewpoints of three-dimensional artworks. When photographing a work of art, tell students that the investment in quality film and careful lighting is worthwhile, as it will enhance the finished slide. Use examples from the text to illustrate this point.

National Standards

This chapter addresses the following National Standards for the Visual Arts:
5. (a, b, c) **6.** (a, b)

Careers in Business and Industry

FOCUS...........

Objectives

After completing this lesson, students will be able to:

- Discuss many fields in which one can pursue a career in art.
- Describe some of the skills artists need for various jobs.
- Determine their own interests in the field of art.

Supplies

- Poster showing recognizable logos
- Magazines of various special interest areas (fashion, auto, current events, etc.)
- Sketching paper and pencils
- Computer
- Web page design software
- Magazines or newspapers with editorial cartoons
- Hair dryer or toothbrush
- Graph paper and colored pencils
- VCR and movie tape
- Clipping about technology

Resources

📁 Application Activity 27, *Help Wanted: Artists*

📁 Cooperative Learning Activity 27, *In Search of a Career*

📁 Enrichment Activity 25, *The Caldecott Medal*

Careers in Business and Industry

You are probably beginning to consider ideas about your future. If you have art abilities and you enjoy art, this chapter will introduce you to some exciting career possibilities. In addition to the major categories mentioned here, there are many careers within each field. Countless possibilities exist, so plan to explore art careers further. As you read, think about each career and keep those that interest you in mind. You will be surprised at how your skills might fit many different art-related jobs.

Today the business world needs art specialists in many areas. Trained artists design company reports, publications, and advertising. Company employees develop some of this design work. Other, more complex projects are assigned to outside designers or advertising firms with many different kinds of artists on staff. Plenty of opportunities are available for self-employed (or freelance) artists and salaried employees with art ability **(Figure 14.2).**

Technology and Careers in Art

In order to prepare for a career in an art-related field, you should become aware of the role technology plays in art and design. Most positions will require computer skills as well as artistic ability. Using computers, designers can create images that can be moved, changed, erased, duplicated, reduced, enlarged, colored, patterned, textured, and otherwise manipulated. Designers work with hardware tools, such as electric-light pens on electronic tablets, as shown in **Figure 14.3.** Designers also use software programs that enable them to design a page layout and insert artwork. Electronic equipment speeds up the design process. Some systems let the artist see the finished work in a variety of color and size arrangements. There are also computer-aided design programs to be used for other art tasks—

▲ **FIGURE 14.2** If you have art ability, there are many opportunities in art and art-related fields.

390 | **CHAPTER 14** Careers in Art

TECHNOLOGY OPTIONS

National Gallery Videodisc Use the following to show examples of how artists use art media and techniques.

Pieter Bruegel, the Elder
Landscape with the Penitance of Saint Jerome

George Bellows
Both Members of This Club

François Boucher
The Love Letter

Francisco Goya
The Disasters of War: Nada

Search Frame 2779

Search Frame 2064

Search Frame 1053

Search Frame 3256

Use the *National Gallery of Art Correlation Bar Code Guide* to locate more artworks.

such as planning a building (or drafting) or designing the interior of a room. Voice-activated software can be used by the physically-challenged to design images. With these tools, designers can create any type of artwork needed.

Once the artwork is completed, computers can also be used to send images by disk or e-mail to customers all over the world. These capabilities also allow collaborations among artists over distances. Technology has changed the way many artists work. In almost any area of art-related employment, artists use computers and other equipment to aid them in their jobs.

In the following pages, you will learn more about the many opportunities available in the art field.

Graphic Design

The early Christian monks who illustrated religious writings were artists **(Figure 14.4).** After the invention of the printing press in the fifteenth century, the craftspeople who arranged type and illustrations were what we now call graphic artists. They had to plan the *layout,* the way items are arranged on the page, before a page could be printed. It was slow work because it all had to be done by hand.

▲ **FIGURE 14.3** This designer uses an electric-light pen and electronic table to create his artwork. Computer technology is essential to many art-related careers.

▶ **FIGURE 14.4** Manuscript illuminators were fine artists. After the introduction of the printing press, craftspeople learned to create and arrange type and illustrations.

Artist unknown. *Missal.* 1389–1404. Tempera colors, gold leaf and gold paint on vellum in a medieval, blind-stamped binding. 33 × 24 cm (13 × 9⁷⁄₁₆″). The J. Paul Getty Museum, Los Angeles, California.

TEACH..........
Motivator
Ask students to list the qualifications they feel are necessary to pursue a career in an art field. Tell them in this chapter they will learn about art-related careers.

Aesthetics
Divide the class into groups and have each group choose one of the artists from the list of Featured Artists. Set aside one small bulletin board as an "Artist of the Week" board and assign each group the responsibility of featuring their artist for one week. Set up some guidelines for the student displays and share these with the class. Some criteria for the display could be:
- Catchy title and neat lettering
- Quantity and accuracy of information
- Creativity and aesthetic quality

The minimum information would include artist's name, country, dates of birth and death, style, and titles of works displayed, example of artists works, information about the artist, and portrayal of the artist's style or of the time and place in which the artist lived.

Critical Thinking
Ask students to imagine that suddenly the world was devoid of anything created by an artist. How would they describe the new condition of the world? What would be missing? What would they miss the most? If possible, have students work on this exercise in small groups. Challenge groups to compose the longest and most unique lists.

TEACHER TALK

Guest Speakers Bring in resource people during the time that you are presenting careers to make the material more meaningful to students. Students will be interested in learning from people who work directly in an art-related field. You may also invite the guidance counselor to discuss art-related careers and to talk about the various schools and colleges that prepare students for art-related careers. If you live in an urban area, it will not be difficult to find people who work at some of these careers. Even the smallest newspaper in a rural area needs a layout person. The local television station will also employ someone who fits one of the career categories mentioned in this section. Consider florists or window display people who can demonstrate how the elements and principles of art are used in their jobs.

Art Criticism

Remind students that every time they see letters and words on the television screen, a graphic designer had to plan them. Instruct students to watch television for a specific length of time (for example, one hour) looking for examples of graphic design. Have them record their observations in their sketchbooks using both visual and written descriptions.

Promoting Discussion

Ask students to bring to class a favorite magazine. Have them work in pairs or small groups to find the list of editorial personnel. (These names are usually listed on a page in the front of magazines.) Ask students to identify any people who have a position that directly involves the area of art, such as Art Director, Graphic Design Coordinator, and so on. Then, have them speculate about the responsibilities that person might have.

Art in Everyday Life

To foster students' awareness of aesthetic appeal in everyday life, suggest this: A well-tuned sense of art, design, and good taste reaches into many other careers. Marketing involves window displays, for example. Find store windows that attract your attention by their designs. Then find ones that are poorly designed. Take a walk in your business district to look at shop signs. Judge them for design, scale, aesthetic appeal, and relation to the products being sold.

▲ **FIGURE 14.5** Graphic designers plan every detail of a book or magazine page including the selection of the size and kind of typeface or font.

▲ **FIGURE 14.6** Kingslien used a computer drawing program to create these designs. Although the computer is a useful tool, the artist must still use her skill to design and compose a successful work.

Lis Kingslien. *The Seasons.* Macromedia Freehand vector images. Courtesy of the artist.

Graphic Designer

A **graphic designer** *translates ideas into images and arranges them in appealing and memorable ways.* He or she creates plans for visual presentations. Today graphic designers use computers, laser scanners, and other equipment that allows them to work much faster. Still, talented artists are required to use the technology to its greatest potential.

Newspaper, magazine, and book publishers employ graphic designers. A designer, sometimes called a publication or production designer, created the look of this book. The designer carefully planned the size of the type, the length of the lines, the layout of the text and artwork, and the length of the columns **(Figure 14.5).** The designer had to make sure the book was visually appealing while at the same time easy for students to use. Writers typed the manuscript into a computer, and the information was stored on a disk. An editor proofread the manuscript to ensure that the content was clear and concise. The manuscript was then given to the typesetting or printing company. The printer then followed the design plan provided by the book designer. Often the book designer and printer work together very closely.

Advertising Designer

Graphic artists also design promotional material for companies. They may be employed by outdoor advertising agencies to create billboards or by traditional advertising agencies to work on ad campaigns **(Figure 14.6).** When graphic artists apply their skills to promotional work, they are called advertising designers. Advertising designers create **logos,** or *symbols or trademarks that are immediately recognizable.*

Advertising agencies employ many kinds of artists. These artists work together as a team whose efforts are coordinated by an art director. They often work with copywriters and man-

---

MORE ABOUT... Careers in Advertising

Students interested in pursuing careers in advertising management should be encouraged to write to the following address for information on opportunities and job requirements:
American Advertising Federation
1101 Vermont Avenue NW
Washington, DC 20005-3521

Additional job resources may be identified throughout the Teacher's Wraparound Edition of this chapter. Encourage students to maintain any brochures or pamphlets received in an "Art Careers Job Bank" file. Part of this file might be devoted to newspaper articles or interviews of local artists that help students recognize the immediate role of artists in their community.

▲ **FIGURE 14.7** A career as an advertising artist usually requires a college education in art or design.

agers, all of whom may have different ideas and visions, so team-building skills are essential **(Figure 14.7).**

Web Artist

As the Internet continues to grow and expand as a center for information and commerce, businesses need to attract visitors to their Web sites (sometimes called Web pages). Web artists, who are often called Web masters, design Web pages, which may include text, photos, three-dimensional or moving graphics, sound, and interactive devices. The Web artist must make the page visually-appealing but easy to use. Because it can take a long time for the viewer's computer to process images, the Web artist must balance beauty with function. A confusing or poorly laid out Web page will cause Internet users to look elsewhere.

Web artists also organize Internet broadcasts of current affairs or events of special interest that television networks do not cover.

Illustration

Many businesses and industries require the work of an **illustrator** who can *create the visual images that complement written words.* Illustrations, or visual images that clarify or decorate a text, can be found in magazines, books, television, film, and elsewhere. Illustrations are used for advertising, editorial, institutional, and educational purposes.

Commercial Illustrator

In addition to the type and the paintings you see in this book, there are drawings by commercial illustrators. Some illustrators specialize in one area, such as fashion, medical, or technical illustration or they may work in several areas **(Figure 14.8).** Some commercial illustrators use computers to help them create maps or charts. They might also create drawings for a children's book by working with an author. Some illustrators work for one company while others prefer to freelance. Freelance artists are self-employed and do many different jobs for many different companies.

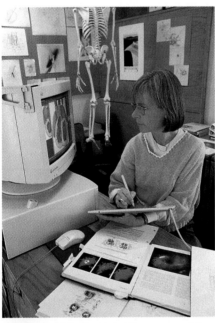

▲ **FIGURE 14.8** A technical illustrator specializes in drawing diagrams. A medical illustrator must study biology and medicine.

Studio Skills

Have students make rough sketches to design their own Web page. Instruct them to indicate lines of type with straight pencil lines. Then direct them to draw the large type and all the visual symbols they want to use. Have them detail what kind of Web site they would have and what type of information they would be exhibiting. Ask them why they feel certain graphics would be more effective on their Web site than others. If you have access to the Internet, preview some interesting Web sites and show these to your students; or you may want to print out some pages from Web sites. If you have access to Web page design software, provide your students with the opportunity to try their hand at actually creating their Web page on the computer.

Aesthetics

Provide students with photocopies of technical illustrations (e.g., architectural prints, street maps, computer circuitry, medical encyclopedias). Have them discuss the purpose for which each illustration was produced. How effectively does the illustration serve that purpose? Could the work be said to extend beyond the realm of applied art? Why or why not?

Computer Option

Acquaint students with the illustration program you will be using in the classroom. Have them experiment with the different tools and commands in order to become familiar and comfortable with them. If your application is mouse-driven, give students who have little or no familiarity with a mouse a chance to practice such techniques as "clicking" and "dragging."

Art Criticism

Distribute magazines that have a variety of editorial cartoons. Have students select their favorite cartoon and pair up with another student who selected the same cartoon. Direct students to analyze the style, content, and technique that the artist used in order to get the message across. Have students present their findings to the class and, if possible, provide background information about the artist who produced the editorial cartoon.

Critical Thinking

Bring to class a manufactured product you use everyday, such as a hair dryer or a toothbrush. Ask students to study the object, then think of one change in the product's design that would make it easier to use or more aesthetically pleasing.

Promoting Discussion

To make information on careers more meaningful to students, you may wish to arrange to have the school guidance counselor or career artists visit the class. For example, in most areas of the country you should find it relatively easy to contact a newspaper layout person or an individual who works in the display/design field. Before the speaker is scheduled to appear, have students brainstorm questions. As an alternative, individual students might interview career artists and write a summary of the interview for the "Art Careers Job Bank" file.

Cartoonist

Cartoonists produce distinctive, entertaining drawings meant to provoke thought and laughter. They submit their work for publication in magazines and newspapers. They may choose to draw single cartoons or comic strips. They usually try to make a humorous point about human nature. Editorial cartoonists, who are interested in politics and current events, present complex ideas in simple, humorous drawings. Editorial cartoonists try to make people think about current issues. They may also try to influence public opinion.

Cartoonists also create comic books and other publications. Several famous cartoonists have created comic books that deal with serious issues such as war and disease. They try to illuminate social problems for people to understand. Some cartoonists work in animation, creating moving cartoons such as those that entertain children (and adults) on Saturday mornings.

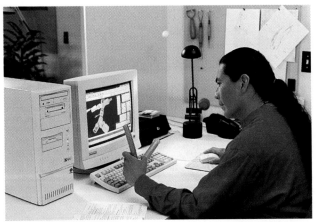

▲ **FIGURE 14.9** Industrial designers develop new products. They also make improvements to existing products, such as adding new features or changing the design of an automobile.

Industrial Design

Industrial design is the planning of the products of industry **(Figure 14.9)**. All objects, such as tools, home appliances, furniture, toys, and automobiles, must be carefully designed. These artists work closely with engineers who develop the products. Sometimes industrial designers are asked to work on things as simple as tamper-proof caps for medicines. At other times they are asked to work on projects as complicated as space vehicles. Before they begin work, industrial designers need to know how the product is to be used. Industrial designers plan products based on three requirements. First, it must do the job for which it was designed. Second, it must look like it can do the job. Third, it must be visually pleasing.

Product Designer

Product designers, or artists who plan the products of industry, usually specialize in one industry or product, such as machinery, furniture, medical equipment, or cars. Designers work in teams. For instance, planning a new automobile requires many different types of designers. Special designers plan the outer form or body of the car. Then fabric and plastic specialists create new interiors to go with the body. They must be certain that human needs are met, such as comfortable seats. Designers must make sure that controls are within reach of the driver, without the dash becoming crowded or confusing. Computers help ensure that all the parts fit together correctly. This way, potential problems are identified before the vehicle goes into production.

MORE ABOUT... **Careers in Industrial Design**

Information about careers in industrial design and academic programs in the field is available from the Industrial Designers Society of America. For price and ordering information, write:

Industrial Designers Society of America
1142 Walker Road
Great Falls, VA 22066

Raymond Loewy, a famous product designer, is best known for his automotive designs. The 1953 Starlight Coupe was chosen for exhibition at The Museum of Modern Art in New York because of its unique design quality. The Avanti **(Figure 14.10)** is a luxury sports car that was created in 1962. It has such an unusual design that it was produced and sold until 1992. The Smithsonian Institution has one on display as an outstanding example of industrial design.

With recent advances in technology, such as computer-simulated models and three-dimensional animation, designers can see what potential designs look like without having to produce physical models. This helps make product designers better able to meet the requirements of industrial design.

▲ **FIGURE 14.10** Look closely at this Avanti. Like many of today's aerodynamic cars, it has no grill. How do you think this design might affect the car's performance?

Raymond Loewy. Avanti. 1963.

Package Designer

A **package designer** *produces the containers that attract the attention of consumers.* They make boxes, tubes, bottles, shopping bags, and other kinds of containers. They use shape and color to make packages unique and appealing. Package designers must also consider package function. For example, when pill bottles first came on the market, the caps were so easy to remove that children were able to open them. Designers had to come up with a cap that was childproof but could be easily opened by an adult. It requires imagination and ingenuity to combine the visual, functional, and safety criteria needed to design for consumers.

Fashion Designer

Fashion designers plan and create clothing, hats, handbags, shoes, jewelry, and sportswear **(Figure 14.11).** They must know the appropriate materials to use for the articles being designed. They must also consider comfort and the way the human body moves when creating fashion designs. High-fashion designers create very expensive, one-of-a-kind

◄ **FIGURE 14.11** Fashion designers must come up with fresh, new ideas every season. Anyone considering a career in this area must be able to work under intense pressure to meet deadlines.

originals. Fashion designers also work for manufacturers who make clothes everyone can afford. A team of pattern makers, cutters, tailors, and factory workers who produce the clothes provide the necessary support for a fashion designer.

LESSON 1 *Careers in Business and Industry* **395**

CHAPTER 14
LESSON 1

Critical Thinking

Have students contact the following organization for a list of accredited schools of art and design:

National Association of Schools of Art and Design
11250 Roger Bacon Drive, Suite 21
Reston, VA 20190

Art History

If students are interested in the evolution of fashion design, suggest that they study at least three different historical periods that are widely separated. Encourage students to find any similarities among the three groups, using categories such as fabrics, accessories, and styles.

Sparking ▲▼
CREATIVITY

Want students to think creatively about art-related careers? Suggest this: Any career in the arts needs a person with *ideas.* Test and stretch your readiness to risk new ideas. Don't let the fear of failing hold you back. Often the best ideas grow from the wild ones that seem too far out to be practical. Think of ten ways to (1) design the letter "A;" (2) build a tree house; (3) use a pair of chopsticks; (4) take out the garbage; or (5) decorate your room.

TEACHER TALK ✎

A Success Story When Nelle Elam of Starksville, Mississippi, first began teaching art fifteen years ago, she wanted her students to have a vehicle for the community to see their accomplishments. She approached the local Kiwanis Club and asked them to support an art exhibition at a local bank, complete with reception, awards ceremony, and gift cer- tificates. To her delight the club members agreed and began a tradition that still supports the annual event. With an endowment that allows parents, faculty, and community to admire and appreciate the efforts of local youths, the school year culminates with an exhibition that gives students a profound sense of pride.

Promoting Discussion

Show several photographs to the class. Ask students to suggest how the elements and principles of art are important in photography. Encourage students to speculate about how photographers can be sure that their pictures contain these elements and principles.

Art Criticism

Present students with samples of work by foremost photojournalists, such as Mathew Brady or Dorothea Lange. Ask students to describe what they see in these works. Are the works typical of the newspaper photographs students encounter in their local daily papers? In what ways do works like these examples truly earn the photographer the title "artist?"

Studio Skills

Have students think about characteristics of video games with which they are familiar including the fantasy creatures featured in the games. Then have students invent a premise and cast of characters for a video game of their own. After noting details on a sheet of scratch paper, students should develop preliminary sketches of an action scene on graph paper. Final versions should be done using colored pencils.

Photography, Film, and Video

Artists and designers interested in the media of photography, film, and video can find employment in many fields, including publishing and entertainment. Although these fields are not always easy to break into, plenty of aspiring artists eventually achieve success in them. Hard work, persistence, talent, and some special training are all necessary.

Photographer

Photographers work in portrait studios or photograph illustrations for books and magazines. Fashion photography, product and food photography, architectural photography, and fine-art photography are all growing specialties **(Figure 14.12)**. Photographers also work for advertising agencies and corporations to create images that help sell products.

Digital cameras, which allow artists to record images digitally and then manipulate them using a computer, are becoming more and more important in the field. Digital cameras do not require special processing labs. The pictures can be viewed and printed immediately. They can also be manipulated and enhanced using computers.

Photographers also work in film and video. Moving picture photography for movies and television is one behind-the-scenes career many photographers find appealing **(Figure 14.13)**. Video photographers make documentaries, create visual presentations for companies to distribute to potential investors, and record celebrations, such as birthdays, weddings, and anniversaries, for clients.

◀ **FIGURE 14.12** Photographers are skilled artists who use their cameras to create artwork.

▶ **FIGURE 14.13** Cinematographers operate movie cameras. They are trained in using light and color.

TEACHER TALK

Class Discussions Many people associate art with relaxation and recreation. They think that artists live a carefree life and that anything associated with art is FUN. You, as an art teacher, know that this is far from the truth. There is joy in art, but it is no greater than the joy people get from creativity in other fields. While covering this chapter, it is important to emphasize that work in the area of art is really work, sometimes very demanding work. However, a job well done is rewarding in any field.

▲ **Figure 14.14** Photojournalists covering a game.

Photojournalist

Photojournalists are *visual reporters.* They work for newspapers and magazines and tell stories through their photographs. Photojournalists must understand design, know how to develop and print their own work, and have an eye for what is interesting to look at **(Figure 14.14).** Other photographers may be able to work in the comfort of a studio, but photojournalists must go where the news is happening.

Animator

Animators, or *artists who create moving cartoons,* use their skills in movies and television. The field of animation requires more visual artists than any other art–related field.

When artists create an animated film, they first select a story. They decide what styles of architecture and dress fit the story. Then they develop the story by drawing **storyboards,** *a series of still drawings that show a story's progress.* They draw approximately 60 sketches for each board. A short film needs three storyboards, and a full-length film may require more than 25. Storyboards look like comic strips. They provide the outline for the development of the film.

Layout artists are responsible for the overall look of the film. Background artists paint the settings from the layout artist's sketches. To create action, animators draw the major poses of each character, then other artists fill in the many drawings required to complete each movement. Each second of film requires 24 drawings to make the movement look smooth. As you can imagine, to create the more than 125,000 drawings required for a 90 minute movie is

Art History
Have students research the field of animation at the library. Direct them to find out when this art form began and who its pioneers were. What were the first forms of animation? Ask students to describe how this art form has been transformed over time and how technological advancements have influenced those transformations.

Studio Skills
Divide students into small groups and assign them to create their own storyboards depicting their own animated film. Limit students to 10 sketches for each storyboard. Students may also want to find out how to create a flip book. Have volunteers make a flip book and show their animated segment to the class.

Promoting Discussion
If you have access to a VCR, show the credit list that follows the end of a movie and instruct students to write a list of the categories that appear. (You can accomplish this by pausing the tape while the credits are running.) When they have listed all the categories, have them check off those that are related to art. Ask student volunteers to call out the categories that are checked and write them on the board. Use the list as a discussion of the many applications of art training in the movie production field.

LESSON 1   *Careers in Business and Industry*   **397**

Critical Thinking

Provide small groups of students with newspaper, magazine, and other media clippings that discuss recent developments in technology (e.g., medical scanning and imaging tools, virtual-reality machines). Have groups read about one of these technologies, then brainstorm possible implications it may have for art of the future. Have groups share and compare their speculations.

Aesthetics

Have students discuss outstanding examples of special effects they recall having seen in the movies. Have them consider what skills and decisions made these artistic efforts a success. Which of the aesthetic theories students learned about would be most applicable when assessing the merits of these special effects? Can students think of other criteria that could be used in evaluating special effects?

Activity

Critiquing Animation

Applying Your Skills. To assure that students will watch shows that offer quality material, you could preview several animated shows, then assign specific programs to be observed.

very expensive and time-consuming **(Figure 14.15).**

This has led to the creation of a new field, computer animation (optical electronic graphic arts), the art of making animated graphics by using the computer to fill in many of the images necessary to create the illusion of movement. An artist creates the main drawings and the important actions and scans these drawings into the computer. The artist may also do the drawings on the computer with the help of a special program. Then, using mathematical models, the computer determines how to make the drawings appear to move. The artist uses the computer to manipulate the images. This is a much less expensive and less time-consuming process than creating all the images by hand.

Special Effects Designer

Special effects designers plan the stunts and illusions in movies in order to make them look real. Training for this field may

▶ **FIGURE 14.15** Animator creating characters by hand.

Activity

Critiquing Animation

Applying Your Skills. Watch several animated programs on television. Notice the differences in quality. Then list the programs you watched in order, from best to worst. How did the backgrounds compare? Describe the quality of the movement. Did the programs with the best movement also have the best backgrounds?

require a college degree in art as well as film production and technology courses. Many large universities have cinema departments that offer courses in many aspects of film production.

Special effects artists require the skills of a painter, sculptor, and engineer. These artists have the ability to imagine and create fantasy scenes or imaginary creatures

---

MORE ABOUT... Motion Pictures

The first motion pictures truly seemed like magic. Pioneers such as George Melies experimented with the new technique. Melies accidentally invented the "jump cut" when his film suddenly jammed while he was filming a busy street in Paris. After developing the footage, he discovered that he had captured a bus suddenly turning into a hearse! In 1902 he made a five-minute film titled *A Trip to the Moon,* a fantasy that would later inspire *Star Wars.* In another piece, titled *The Man with the Rubber Head,* he combined forms into what he called "artificially arranged scenes."

▲ **FIGURE 14.16** Special effects artist.

that look real **(Figure 14.16).** They can make you believe you are watching a dinosaur driving a car or a battle scene in a galaxy light-years away. In their work they use papier-mâché, plaster, plastic molds, paint, makeup, trick photography, and computers.

Art Director

In film, as well as in theatre, an art director works with set, costume, and lighting directors, as well as makeup artists and hairstylists, to bring all the elements of the show together **(Figure 14.17).** Art directors need to know art history as well as the special techniques of their craft. If a film or play is set in the past, the setting, furniture, costumes, and hairstyles must correctly reflect that time period.

A set or stage designer is an artist who is responsible for planning the backdrops and many of the props for a production. He or she oversees a team of artists who prepare the stage or set itself for the production. The set designer works with the prop master, who supplies everything the actors use during the production. The costume designer is like a fashion designer, but he or she must create clothing that is appropriate to the time and setting of

◀ **FIGURE 14.17** An art director studies the information that needs to be presented. He or she must decide how that information can be shown in a visually–appealing way.

LESSON 1 *Careers in Business and Industry*   **399**

Field Trips

Field trips contribute greatly to a course. All trips will be more successful if guidelines are set up to help students understand the objectives. Research done prior to the trip and a follow-up evaluation will add to the value of the experience. Students should know what to look for and what to expect to gain from the experience. It might be pointed out that the business people they visit may be possible employers and that appropriate conduct and dress on a trip may make a future interview more likely. Students should know what kind of follow-up will be expected. For example, a written evaluation, a quiz, or participation in a class discussion might be required.

The instructor should make the necessary arrangements well in advance to ensure the students' welcome. A time schedule should be established and carefully followed. While museums, organizations, and industries are happy to conduct tours of their facilities, the staff members usually have other responsibilities, and group tours must be prearranged.

inter NET CONNECTION **BIOGRAPHY ON THE WEB** Visit the Glencoe Fine Arts Web site to read about such renowned artists as architect Frank Lloyd Wright, graphic artist M.C. Escher, and painter Käthe Kollwitz. Find out about their art backgrounds and how they got started. What influenced them to pursue a career in the world of art? What types of skills did they need to become successful? Read about many other professional artists that are highlighted on the Glencoe Web site: **www.glencoe.com/sec/art**

Art History

Today's advanced video games, with their reliance on realistic action and 16-bit color, are a far cry from the earliest works in this medium. As a case in point, consider that the video game *Pong*, which first appeared in the early 1970s, consisted of little more than a green blip bouncing around on a black screen.

ASSESS...........
Self-Assessment

Have students complete the lesson review questions. Answers are provided below.

Reteaching

Have students work in pairs. One partner is to call out a major heading from this section of the text (i.e., "Graphic Design," "Industrial Design," and so on). The other is to identify as many art-related careers that fall under this heading as he or she can. Partners then switch roles, selecting a different heading.

Enrichment

If your school has a computer specialist, ask him or her to speak to your students about the graphic capabilities of the computers in your school. Or, you can ask a local computer store to give your class a demonstration on the graphic possibilities of computers.

CLOSE............

Ask students to choose one of the art careers they have read about and write a paragraph explaining why they think this career might make an interesting vocation.

▲ **FIGURE 14.18** Costume designers must create clothing appropriate to the time and setting of a movie or play.

▲ **FIGURE 14.19** Game designers.

the production **(Figure 14.18).** For productions that travel, the work of the art director and set designer may include considerable technical problems. They may consult with engineers and archi-

tects, and work with property designers and location planners.

Computer, Arcade, and Video Game Designers

Game designers plan and create all aspects of computer, arcade, and video game design **(Figure 14.19).** They create the background renderings and the animated figures and objects. They work with computer programmers to design visually-appealing and exciting games. Because the game experience is a multimedia experience, the designer must have a special sensitivity to sound, story, and other aspects of game production.

Computer game designers also create virtual reality and three-dimensional worlds that gamers enjoy experiencing. As these technologies become more sophisticated, they will probably be used by more businesses, which means there may be many more opportunities in the field in the future.

Multimedia Designer

Multimedia designers combine text, graphics, sound, and interactive devices into a visually-appealing product. They create multimedia presentations using special hardware and software programs. These presentations are used by companies to acquire clients. Multimedia designers also create interactive CD-ROMs and software for business, education, and entertainment. This requires a team approach. One person is usually responsible for the overall concept, while others create the images and text and still others put everything together.

Check Your Understanding

1. What is a graphic designer?
2. What three requirements must a product of industrial design meet?
3. What are storyboards?
4. What types of designers do art directors work with?

400 | **CHAPTER 14** Careers in Art

Answers to Check Your Understanding

1. A graphic designer translates ideas into images and arranges them in appealing and memorable ways.
2. A product of industrial design must do the job for which it was designed, it must look like it can do the job for which it was designed, and it must be visually pleasing.
3. Storyboards are a series of still drawings that show a story's progress.
4. A performing arts art director works with set, costume, and lighting designers.

Environmental and Education Careers

Environmental Planning and Development

The first environmental designers were prehistoric cave dwellers who eventually moved out of their caves and into the countryside. They learned to build huts for protection and thus became the first architects. Today there are many kinds of designers who plan environmental space. Their jobs involve making homes, work-space, and the surrounding landscape attractive and functional.

Urban Planner

Urban planners are trained architects concerned with the care and improve-ment of city environments. Every major American city has an urban planner (sometimes called a city planner). This person helps control the growth and development of a city. Some of the responsibilities of the urban planner are land use, urban renewal, and the devel-opment of harbors, city parks, and shop-ping malls. A good urban planner meets the needs of the community while keeping it attractive and appealing (Fig-ure 14.20).

▶ FIGURE 14.20 Reston, Virginia is a planned community founded in 1962. About 40 percent of the total area is set aside for public use and as open space. Residents can work, shop, live, attend school, and enjoy many activities without leaving the community.

Aerial view of Reston, Virginia, a planned city. Courtesy of the Reston Land Corporation, Reston, Virginia.

Architect

An **architect** must *design buildings that are well-constructed, aesthetically-pleasing, and functional.* To function properly, a building must do what it was designed to do. Private houses and apartments must serve as comfortable homes for people. Office buildings, schools, and factories must also be comfortable, safe, efficient, and aesthetically-pleasing. The aesthetic

LESSON 2   *Environmental and Education Careers*   **401**

FOCUS...........
Objectives
After completing this lesson, students will be able to:
- Discuss many fields in which one can pursue a career in art.
- Describe some of the skills artists need for various jobs.
- Determine their own in-terests in the field of art.

Supplies
- Architectural magazines

Resources
- 📁 Application Activity 28, *Sharpening Your Skills*
- 📁 Cooperative Learning Activity 28, *The Contemporary Artist at Work*
- 📁 Enrichment Activity 26, *Dear Art School*

TEACH..........
Motivator
In small groups, have students study several examples of archi-tecture. Then ask: What exam-ples can you identify of buildings and materials intended to instruct or to communicate a specific message? What message or instruction is intended?

Vocabulary
Ask students to provide a def-inition for the term *Urban Plan-ner.* Students may either write their definition on a piece of paper, or ask volunteers to share their definition with the class. Discuss with students the types of situations that might arise that would require the skills of an urban planner.

MEETING INDIVIDUAL NEEDS

Building Self-Esteem While students read this chapter, encourage them to think about their future and imagine a profession they might enter. Ask what per-sonal qualities an individual in that profession might need in order to be successful. Do they have those qualities already? If not, what can they do to develop them? Ask them to imagine the tools, uniform or dress, place of work, and types of people found in their desired profession. How comfortably do they fit in this image of the profession? What is missing? What preparation or action is required of them to complete the picture? What do they speculate will be needed in order to keep the image a successful one?

Cross-Curriculum: Physical Science

Have students investigate city or state ordinances governing the design of buildings in areas subject to natural acts of destruction, such as earthquakes, typhoons, or hurricanes. How have these restrictions changed over the course of one hundred years? Ask students to speculate about how architects and city planners keep current with legal controls.

Critical Thinking

Have students work in small groups and brainstorm a planned urban or suburban community that could be built in your state and would specifically address the needs of the residents. Encourage students to submit a written summary of their planned community and, if possible, a visual map or a three-dimensional model.

Art History

Ask students to browse through the textbook, noting different examples of architecture from a variety of centuries and cultural boundaries. What changes are students able to discern among works of architecture from a particular culture? Do any structures remind them of buildings they have seen in their own community? What culture is responsible for examples of "imitated" works of architecture they may find? During what period of history were those structures built?

Developing Perceptual Skills

Have each student select a book, play, story, or poem that interests him or her and sketch a set design for an imaginary stage presentation of the piece of literature.

MEET THE ARTIST
I. M. PEI

Chinese-American, 1917–

If you have ever visited the Rock-and-Roll Hall of Fame in Cleveland, Ohio, or seen a picture of the pyramid entrance to the Louvre in Paris, you will be familiar with the work of the famous architect I.M Pei. Pei was born in Guangzhou (Canton), China, on April 26, 1917. When he was 18, he immigrated to the United States, where he studied architecture at the Massachusetts Institute of Technology and Harvard University. After World War II, he taught at Harvard for several years.

In 1956, he struck out on his own, creating his own company, I. M. Pei & Partners. Soon, he and his company were in great demand, not just in the United States, but all over the world. Pei has designed some of the largest constructions of the twentieth century.

Pei is known for approaching design problems with an innovative flair. Many of the buildings he is asked to design must meet multiple functions, such as the Rock-and-Roll Hall of Fame (Figure 14.21). This structure reflects the spirit of rock-and-roll while housing memorabilia, sound chambers, a concert hall, a film-and-video display center, a party room, and numerous other features.

◄ **FIGURE 14.21**
This building must hold an extensive collection of artifacts while expressing the spirit of rock-and-roll. Do you think it serves its purpose?

I. M. Pei. *Rock-and-Roll Hall of Fame and Museum*, Cleveland, Ohio. 1995.

effect of a building is extremely important. The structure must fit into its environment and enhance or complement the community. Because modern technology is so complex, architects usually specialize in particular types of buildings such as skyscrapers, shopping malls, or homes **(Figure 14.21).**

Architects must be knowledgeable about building materials, ventilation, heating and cooling systems, plumbing, stairways, and elevators. They must know basic engineering concepts so that they do not plan structures that are impossible to build. In addition, architects must be creative, be able to make accurate mechanical drawings, use a computer, have a strong background in mathematics and drafting, and be able to deal with customers.

COOPERATIVE LEARNING

Planning a City Present this challenge to students: Imagine that you have been hired as city planners to improve your town or community. Working in small groups, prepare a survey to ask people what they like the most and what they like least about the town or neighborhood. Find out which building is considered the most important and which is considered the most attractive. Ask about traffic flow, stores, recreation, entertainment, health services, police protection, and water and sewerage. Ask the students at your school and adults who live in the area to complete the survey. Compare adult and teen replies in graph or chart form. Do the two groups agree or disagree on each item?

▲ **FIGURE 14.22** Landscape architect.

Landscape Architect

Landscape architects design playgrounds, parks, and outdoor areas around buildings and along highways. They work closely with architects and urban planners to use and improve the natural setting so that it is easy to maintain and beautiful to look at. They create designs using flowers, plants, trees, shrubs, rivers, ponds, lakes, walks, benches, and signs, as shown in **Figure 14.22.** Landscape architects work with architectural firms, government agencies, individual homeowners, and facilities such as golf courses.

Interior Designer

An **interior designer** *plans the design and decoration of the interior spaces in homes and offices.* Successful designers use styles and materials that blend with the architecture and that please the client. They must understand decorating styles and materials **(Figure 14.23).** They must be able to look at an empty room and visualize the finished area.

Because interior designers spend as much time with clients as they do at the drawing board or computer, they must have patience and good communication skills. Some designers work for individual homeowners, while others plan and coordinate the interiors of department stores, offices, and hotels.

Exhibit and Display Designers

Exhibit designers plan presentations of collections, temporary exhibits, and traveling shows of all types. They work for trade shows, department stores, showrooms, art galleries, and museums. They decide how objects should be grouped and lit.

Display designers plan merchandise arrangements to attract customers and persuade them to buy products or services. A display designer is an important member of a sales team. The way a designer arranges merchandise in a store window helps draw customers into the store.

Activity — **Using Design for Display**

Applying Your Skills. Create a display of art objects for a display window in your school or one of flat artwork for a bulletin board display. Invent a title for your display, letter it neatly or use a computer application to print out the title. Include it with your arrangement.

▲ **FIGURE 14.23** Interior designer.

Developing Perceptual Skills

Have students find home designs in a magazine or architectural journal. Instruct them to look at lines, shapes, colors, values, and textures. Then, have students imagine they are landscape architects who have been asked to improve the appearance of the school campus. Direct them use their sketchbooks to illustrate their ideas.

Studio Skills

Instruct students to sketch an interesting building in their neighborhood. Give these instructions: Carry a drawing board for support. Tape your paper to the board. First plot the shape of the building to fit on your paper. Make light marks for walls, roof, a porch, and the like. Then start drawing one detail at a time.

Developing Perceptual Skills

Ask students to imagine they are interior designers who have been asked to plan a student lounge for the school. Before they make their individual designs, have them work in small groups to decide what areas will be needed. Encourage students to be creative and imaginative. Have them write descriptions of their plans as well as draw sketches.

Activity

Using Design for Display

Applying Your Skills. If possible, divide the class into small groups and give each group an area in which to create a display. Some groups could do three-dimensional displays and some could work on flat bulletin boards.

MORE ABOUT... Art-related Careers

For more information about careers in interior design, contact:

American Society of Interior Designers
200 Lexington Ave.
New York, NY 10016

Students interested in learning more about careers in museum science should be encouraged to write

to the following organization for information on opportunities and job requirements:

American Association of Museums
1225 I Street NW, Suite 200
Washington, DC 20005

Critical Thinking

Tell students that you will be setting aside a portion of class time to let them interview one member of the art professions mentioned on these pages. Then stand and introduce yourself, reminding students that your job title is "art teacher." Challenge pairs of students to brainstorm questions they might ask concerning art education as a career. Areas that students might explore include: details of your education (which schools you attended); degrees you hold; the parts of your education you found the most rewarding; and the influence of your own teachers on your decision to pursue a career in art education.

Art in Everyday Life

To foster students' awareness of the use of technology in art-related fields, suggest this: Today the artist's media include computers, lasers, video technology, chemicals, calculus, plastics, new metals, light, solar and artificial heat energy, and power machinery. Artists reshape acres of land, even wrap whole buildings and bridges with cloth. They also construct vast buildings on the screen of their computer, visualizing them in three dimensions, turning them around, shifting walls, enlarging, and reducing. A whole new world is open to the artist.

Art Education

Some art-related careers combine an interest in art with an interest in education. Teachers, art therapists, and museum curators and designers all use their training in different ways. Artistically-inclined people who want to help others may find careers in education rewarding and fulfilling.

Art Teacher

Art teachers share their artistic knowledge and skills with students. They work in elementary, middle, or high schools as well as colleges **(Figure 14.24).** Art teachers help students learn to make aesthetic judgments and to develop their artistic skills and talents. In order to be successful, they must have art abilities themselves, but they must also be able to nurture talent in others who might not be self-confident or who might be intimidated by the process of creating art. Some teachers specialize in art history and help students learn about art instead of teaching students to create art. Most art teachers combine both approaches.

▲ **FIGURE 14.24** Art teacher.

▲ **FIGURE 14.25** Museum curator.

Art Therapist

Art therapists use art to help people with emotional and physical problems. They help physically-challenged children and adults learn to explore the senses of vision and touch through artistic play and creation. Art therapists also help patients with mental and emotional problems change their behavior in a positive way. They show them how to express themselves in a constructive way – through art. Art therapy helps such patients talk about their problems and learn to handle them.

Art therapists may have training in physical therapy or psychology and usually work with members of these fields. They work in medical and psychiatric hospitals, community centers, physical rehabilitation programs, drug and alcohol treatment centers, and prisons.

Museum Curator and Designer

Museums house collections of paintings, sculpture, crafts, costumes, books, jewelry, and artifacts. **Museum curators,** who are usually trained in art history, *oversee the operations of museums.* They organize the collections and are responsible for recommending artworks that fit in with the theme or focus of the museum **(Figure 14.25).** Museum designers assemble and display these museum collections. Other artists might serve as tour guides, leading groups through the displays and providing information to the viewers. Some museums publish books that contain photographs of the objects in their collections, which requires the help of the curator and designers.

TEACHER TALK

Sources of Career Information Remember that teachers and school officials, especially guidance counselors, often receive catalogs from institutes of higher education that might be of interest to your students. If possible, arrange to get copies of these catalogs when discussing art-related careers. A map of the United States, even of the world, could be used to indicate the locations of colleges, universities, and schools that might be of interest to students interested in pursuing art careers. Students could be encouraged to research more about a specific institution and present the findings to the class, using the catalog, the map, and possibly interviews with alumni.

Fine Artists

Some artists choose to work independently as painters, sculptors, printmakers, weavers, or jewelers **(Figure 14.26)**. They create the art they want to create, not what an employer asks them to make. Such artists are committed to creating art on their own terms. Many need a second job to help pay their living expenses. In the visual arts, as in the performing arts, few opportunities for stardom and large incomes exist. Some fine artists work in commercial art fields to supplement their income. Many teach in schools and colleges. Some, like Jacob Lawrence (Figure 4.19 on page 80), continue teaching even after they have become financially successful, because they feel that the ongoing interaction with art students enhances their creative thinking.

▲ **FIGURE 14.26** The work of artists is usually classified as either fine art or applied art. Fine art, such as a painting, is created to be viewed and appreciated. Applied art, such as ceramics or other craft objects, is created to be used.

Thinking About an Art Career

Are you suited for a career in the art world? It may be too soon for you to make a final decision about your future. However, if you have art ability and art is something you enjoy, then an art career may be right for you.

If you decide you want a career in art, you should begin working toward that goal while in high school. In the meantime, practice your skills. Study the great artists. Learn how to use a computer to enhance your talent. Explore art-related careers. Talk with your art teacher or guidance counselor for advice. You can also write to art schools and college art departments for advice and information on art careers.

 Check Your Understanding

1. What is the difference between an architect and a landscape architect?
2. What type of artist or designer plans presentations of collections?
3. What do art therapists do?

Answers to Check Your Understanding

1. An architect designs buildings and a landscape architect designs outdoor areas such as parks and playgrounds.
2. An exhibit designer plans presentations of collections.
3. Art therapists use art to help people with emotional and physical problems.

Art History

Have students select contemporary artists that interest them and research their lives through biographies. In particular, ask students to look for information about how the artists make their livelihoods and how they promote their works. As a contrast, have students research the role that art patrons held when artists were once unable to make a living from their art. How does patronage differ from modern methods of support such as endowments and grants?

ASSESS..........
Self-Assessment

Have students complete the review questions on this page. Answers are provided below.

Reteaching

Have students create a simple chart with the names of the professions highlighted in this section listed in the left-hand column. In a second, right-hand column, direct students to jot down brief descriptions of the type of tasks performed and skills needed for each art profession.

Enrichment

■ Assign Enrichment Activity 26 in the TCR. 📁

■ Invite a personnel director to speak to the class about ways to prepare for job interviews.

CLOSE...........

Ask students to respond to the following question: If a person would like to pursue an art-related career, what types of skills or important qualities should that person possess, or attempt to develop?

405

ART CRITICISM IN ACTION

(National Standards: 5a, 5b, 5c)

Critiquing the Work

▶ Describe

What do you see?

- A man and woman are wearing green bathrobes. They both look relaxed and comfortable.

- There are over 30 animals, all dogs: bloodhounds, terriers, Chihuahuas, and a poodle.

- The setting is a living room.

▶ Analyze

How is this work organized?

- *Color:* Almost everything is green. Half of the dogs are blue. The only contrast is the warm, bright orange color of the people's skin. *Texture:* The use of rough, textured grass indoors is different. The forms are predominantly organic and free-form. Only the architectural forms are geometric.

- *Rhythm:* The strongest rhythm is the random repetition of the dogs. There is also a strong random rhythm of the orange arms, legs, and heads of the people. All of the proportions are accurate, and everything in the picture is in normal scale.

- *Harmony* is seen in the repetition of dogs, the repeated texture, and the use of blue-green. Variety is seen in the different kinds of dogs and their different states of alertness.

- *Emphasis* is created with the contrasting warm, orange skin of the people. That is the only warm color in the work.

▲ **FIGURE 14.27**

Sandy Skoglund. *The Green House.* 1990. Cibachrome photograph. 127 × 178 cm (50 × 70″). Skoglund Art Gallery, New York, New York.

MORE ABOUT...   Sandy Skoglund

Sandy Skoglund has occasionally used food and people in her installations and photographs. One piece, called the *Cocktail Party* (1992), involved eleven people situated as though they were conversing at a party. What is unusual about them is that they are completely covered with bright orange cheese puffs, as is the furniture and the floor and walls around them. After taking the photographs, Skoglund later made a permanent gallery installation of the piece using mannequins. Skoglund has also used meat, bacon, and raisins in her art. The use of foodstuffs which decay or attract insects adds to the fleeting quality of her work.

1 ▸ DESCRIBE What do you see?

List all the information found in the credit line. Next, list the objects that you recognize in the photograph. Remember that this is a clue-collecting step. If you are not sure of something, do not guess.

- Describe the people including their poses, clothing, and colors.
- Describe the animals including their poses, breeds, and colors.
- Describe the setting in which these people and animals are placed. Notice the colors and textures.

2 ▸ ANALYZE How is this work organized?

Now you will study how the artist has organized the elements of art using the principles that you have studied.

- How have color, texture, form, and space been used in this work?
- How has the artist used rhythm and proportion?
- Where do you see harmony, emphasis, and variety?

3 ▸ INTERPRET What is the artist trying to communicate?

During this step, you will make guesses about the meaning of the work. You do not need to know what the artist meant. Instead, you will decide what this image says to you.

- How do the poses of the people and the animals affect the look of this work?
- How do color and texture affect the mood of this work? How does the artist's use of the principles of art affect the expressive quality of this work?
- What does this artwork express to you? Give it a creative title that sums up the expressive quality of this work.

4 ▸ JUDGE What do you think of the work?

Now you will decide if this is a successful work of art or not.

- Is this work interesting? Did it make you think?
- Did the artist use the elements of art and the principle of rhythm successfully?
- Do you think this is a successful work of art? Why or why not? Use one or more of the aesthetic theories described in Chapter 2 to defend your judgment.

▸ Interpret
What is the artist trying to communicate?

- Answers will vary. Some may point out that the people seem to be unaware of the dogs that have filled the room. The people are self-absorbed. The dogs are active and dominating the room. One is even howling on the mantle of the fireplace.
- Answers will vary. Some may say the colors and textures create an unreal, weird look. The realistic proportions within the unreal colors and textures add to the strangeness. The random rhythm of the many strangely colored dogs is disturbing, almost frightening.
- Answers will vary. Some may see a message about the environmental, greenhouse effect. Others may talk about people carrying on their lives oblivious of their surroundings. Maybe the dogs represent family members or life situations that are being ignored.

▸ Judge
What do you think of the work?

- Answers will vary.
- Answers will vary. A few may cite Imitationalism because everything is realistic except the colors and textures. Some may choose Formalism because they like the way the artist has organized the elements using the principles. Most will choose Emotionalism because of the strange mood created by the work.

Art Criticism in Action | **407**

Time & Place Late Twentieth Century

Sandy Skoglund created the photograph *The Green House* in 1990. Some other events that happened in the same year:

History: Saddam Hussein invaded Kuwait.

Politics: Poland had its first free elections since before World War I. Solidarity leader Lech Walesa was voted president.

Social Studies: Nelson Mandela, leader of the African National Congress, was freed from a South African prison after twenty-seven years in jail.

How is 3-D Computer Art Created?

CONNECTIONS
TECHNOLOGY

How is 3-D Computer Art Created?

(National Standards: 6a, 6b)

Objectives

After completing this feature, students will be able to:

- Explain ray tracing as used to create a three-dimensional image.
- Identify the steps in rendering three-dimensional images.

Teaching the Connection

Have students read the feature on this page and study the illustrations. Ask volunteers to share what they know about computers and three-dimensional drawing. What kinds of software are used to create three-dimensional figures? *(Architects use CAD programs to render architectural drawings. The art on this page was done using 3-D Studio.)* What educational or entertainment computer games use three-dimensional images? *(Answers will vary.)* Why do the images in the illustrations appear to be 3-D? *(They appear to have form: height, width, and depth.)*

Tell students that creating 3-D images is also used to solve problems. Computers using X-ray data can create 3-D images of body parts such as the brain or spine, helping doctors identify disorders.

Checking Comprehension

- On a separate sheet of paper have students complete "Building Vocabulary" and "Reviewing Art Facts" on page 409.
- Assign Application 27 and 28 in the TCR to evaluate students' comprehension.

408

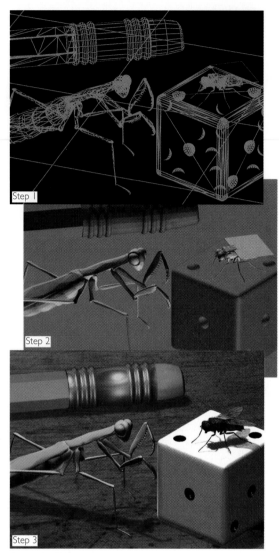

Step 1

Step 2

Step 3

▲ **FIGURE 14.28**

Edward Harvey. *Mantis and Fly.* 1996. Three-dimensional ray-traced image.

Light originates from a source, such as the sun or a light bulb, and bounces off objects. It is the light that is bounced off of objects that allows us to see them as three-dimensional (3-D) objects. Formulas for how light bounces off different types of objects are used by scientists when designing mirrors and lenses.

With the invention of modern computers and software, a tool became available to create images of objects that look three-dimensional. Recreating an image requires tracing many rays of light from their source to their destinations. This process is known as *ray tracing*. Only a computer can make the millions of calculations necessary to trace the path of all the rays of light in a scene.

Today, low-cost desktop computers are powerful enough to do ray tracing. Many artists have begun to use these formulas in their artwork. First, they use 3-D graphics design software to create "wire frames" of objects (see Step 1). Next, they create "skins" for the wire frames, identifying textures and the reflective qualities of the covering material (see Step 2). Then they set up the lights that they will use in the scene. Finally, they "render" the picture by directing the computer to compute the ray tracing. This provides a final picture that is photo-realistic (see Step 3).

Making the Connection

1. What does ray tracing mean and how does it help us see objects as three-dimensional?
2. Look at the illustration and use it to explain the steps involved in rendering three-dimensional images.
3. There are other types of animation used by artists, such as clay animation. Find out more about other techniques and how they are used.

Answers to Making the Connection

1. Ray tracing is the tracing of light from its source to its destination.
2. First "wire frames" are created; artists create "skins" for the wire frames; then the computer figures the ray tracing.
3. Responses will vary.

Building Vocabulary

On a separate sheet of paper, write the term that best matches the definition given below.

1. One who translates ideas into images and arranges them in appealing and memorable ways.
2. Symbols or trademarks that are immediately recognizable.
3. One who creates visual images that complement written words.
4. Designer who produces the containers that attract the attention of consumers.
5. Visual reporters.
6. Artists who create moving cartoons.
7. A series of still drawings that show a story's progress.
8. Designer of buildings that are well-constructed, aesthetically-pleasing, and functional.
9. One who plans the design and decoration of the interior spaces in homes and offices.
10. Oversee the operations of museums.

Reviewing Art Facts

Answer the following questions using complete sentences.

1. When did the field of graphic design begin? What invention made it possible?
2. What elements of art do package designers use to make packages unique and appealing?
3. How is a costume designer different from a fashion designer?
4. What training do special effects designers need?
5. Why is technology important in art-related fields?
6. For what purposes are illustrations used?
7. What three requirements must industrial designers plan for?
8. How does a photojournalist differ from other photographers?
9. What does an urban planner do?

Thinking Critically About Art

1. **Analyze.** Find a copy of a book you enjoyed reading, preferably one that has an interesting cover design. Look at the design and think about how it relates to the content of the book. Then write a few paragraphs describing the cover design, the meaning of any symbolism the designer used, and your opinion of whether the cover illustrates the story appropriately.

2. **Extend.** With the teacher's permission, show a group of younger students how to make an age–appropriate artwork (such as finger painting or clay modeling). Offer instruction, encouragement, and assistance as they create their own works. If possible, work with a team of other student teachers. Write a few paragraphs describing your experience.

Use the Performing Arts Handbook on page 426 to find out about storyboard artist John Ramirez.

Learn more about art-related careers, especially those in the growing field of Web design. Visit Glencoe's Fine Arts Site at **www.glencoe.com/sec/art**. Explore the site for information on educational requirements and salary ranges for various careers in art.

Answers to Building Vocabulary

1. graphic designer
2. logos
3. illustrator
4. package designer
5. photojournalist
6. animators
7. storyboards
8. architect
9. interior designer
10. curator

Answers to Reviewing Art Facts

1. In the fifteenth century; the printing press
2. See answer on page 395.
3. Costume designers create clothing appropriate to the time and setting of a movie or a play; fashion designers create clothing for everyday wear.
4. A college degree in art as well as film production and technology courses.
5. Because many kinds of art are being created on computers.
6. To complement written words, clarify text, and decorate the text.
7. See answer on page 394.
8. Photojournalists not only take photos, they tell stories through their photos.
9. Helps control the growth and development of a city.

Reteaching

- Have students complete *Concept Map 14* in the *Reteaching* booklet. 📁

CLOSE............

Have students write a paragraph to include in their portfolios in which they explain why achieving success in an art-related career requires more than just creative ability.

ASSESSMENT ✓

Evaluate
- Have students complete the *Chapter 14 Test* in the TCR. 📁
- Alternative Assessment teaching strategies are provided below or in the *Testing Program and Alternative Assessment* booklet.

Extension
Ask a local photographer to speak to the class about the various career applications of his or her profession. Have students plan their questions ahead of time with a focus on the photographer's education, training, experience, and areas of interest.

HANDBOOKS

Unit Overview

Unit 5 serves as a supplement to the core text and consists of the *Performing Arts Handbook* and the *Technique Tips Handbook*. The material in this unit can be used to enrich the information and activities in the student lessons, or can be used independently.

Performing Arts Handbook

The Artsource® *Performing Arts Handbook* features 14 artists or groups from three fields of performing arts—dance, music, and theatre. The artists and groups are specifically chosen to correlate to the chapters in the book. *ARTTALK* provides this handbook as an opportunity for students to recognize and appreciate the connections that exist between the four arts disciplines.

Technique Tips Handbook

The *Technique Tips Handbook* is a convenient reference section, which offers students step-by-step procedures and guidelines for working effectively on studio projects. The first section consists of **Drawing Tips** that include guidelines for basic drawing skills. **Painting Tips** include everything from mixing paints to cleaning brushes. **The Printmaking Tips** focus on stamp prints. **Sculpting Tips** helps students expand their familiarity with clay and paper. The Handbook also includes **Other Tips** and **Display Tips**. Finally, **Safety in the Art Room** reminds students of safety guidelines when working with specific media, tools, and potentially hazardous materials.

410

MORE ABOUT...   Minnie Evans

Minnie Evans was a descendant of a slave brought to the United States from Trinidad. She was born in a log cabin in North Carolina and attended school in Wilmington. By the mid-1940s, inspired by her dreams and visions, she was making colorful designs featuring exotic plant forms and faces.

Like *Design Made at Airlie Gardens*, the focus of Evan's works is the human face surrounded by graceful plant forms. The figures in her designs are the ancient, wise people she has encountered in her dreams. The plant forms were inspired by the natural beauty of Airlie Gardens, a botanical preserve near Wilmington. She worked there as a gatekeeper for more than 25 years.

HANDBOOKS

> **"** I never plan a drawing, they just happen. In a dream it was shown to me what I have to do, of paintings. **"**

Minnie Evans
1892–1987

◄

Minnie Evans. *Design Made at Airlie Gardens.* 1967. Oil and mixed media on canvas. 50.5 × 60.6 cm (19⅞ × 23⅞"). National Museum of American Art, Smithsonian Institution, Washington, D.C.

411

Introducing the Unit

Because this unit is primarily for reference and to supplement the chapters, the content will be referred to throughout the text. Remind students to review the technique tips on a regular basis so that their skills are routinely refreshed.

Unit Motivator

As a strategy for encouraging frequent self-evaluation, suggest that students set aside a section of their sketchbooks specifically for practicing and reflecting on techniques. This section could be invaluable for two reasons: When students struggle with a specific artwork, they can pull back from the piece itself and review a technique by writing about it. Secondly, when they are happy with the results of a particular piece, they can make notes that help them in the future.

Discussing the **"** Quotation **"**

Inform students that Minnie Evans began creating artworks using pen and ink in 1925, inspired by images from her dreams and other visions. Later, she experimented with wax crayons, oil paint, and watercolor. Have students list some of the aspects of her art that display a dreamlike quality.

National Museum of Women in the Arts

You may wish to use the National Museum of Women in the Arts videodisc and/or CD-ROM. The videodisc features a bar code guide, and the interactive CD-ROM provides stimulating activities.

PERFORMING ARTS HANDBOOK

(pages 412–426)

Purpose

The 14 features in the Performing Arts Handbook are designed to enrich students' learning by correlating what they learn about the visual arts to the performing arts—dance, music, and theatre. The featured performers and groups in this handbook were specifically chosen to supplement the chapters in the student text.

Using the Handbook

The following categories suggest ways to use the Performing Arts Handbook.

- **Mini-lessons** Use the features as stand-alone lessons about dance, music, and theatre.
- **Motivator** Use the features to introduce related chapters. Listed on each chapter opening page of your Teacher's Wraparound Edition is a segment that correlates each chapter to this section. As you plan lessons, consider how you might use the Performing Arts Handbook as a way of introducing the chapter's contents.
- **Extension** Refer to the recommended Artsource® feature found on the chapter opening page of the Teacher's Wraparound Edition, and use the appropriate feature to expand the study of that chapter.

412

PERFORMING ARTS HANDBOOK

TABLE OF CONTENTS

Performing Arts Handbook

The following pages were excerpted from Artsource: *The Music Center Study Guide to the Performing Arts,* developed by the Music Center Education Division, an award-winning arts education program of the Music Center of Los Angeles County.

The following artists and groups are featured in the *ARTTALK Performing Arts Handbook.*

MORE ABOUT... Artsource®

The materials provided in this Performing Arts Handbook are excerpted from *Artsource®: The Music Center Study Guide to the Performing Arts,* a project of the Music Center Education Division. The Music Center of Los Angeles County, the largest performing arts center in the western United States, established the Music Center Education Division in 1979 to provide opportunities for life-long learning in the arts, and especially to bring the performing and visual arts into the classroom. The Education Division believes the arts enhance the quality of life for all people, but are crucial to the development of every child.

Faustwork Mask Theater

Faustwork Mask Theater. "The Mask Man." Robert Faust, artistic director. Photo: Craig Schwartz, © 1993.

Robert Faust is an actor, athlete, dancer, choreographer, mask-maker, and the artistic director of his company, Faustwork Mask Theater. Born and raised in New Orleans, he experienced the color and pageantry of the Mardi Gras celebration throughout his youth and college years. Through his studies he came to realize that the carnival characters that annually paraded the streets of his hometown were actually works of art rooted in theatrical traditions. His one-man show, "The Mask Man," provides insights into the artistic, psychological, and historical aspects of masks. In his performance, Faust transforms himself into more than 20 different characters. Some characters speak, wearing *commedia dell'arte* style half-masks. Other characters are created with full masks worn on top of the head or on the back of the head. These masks can transform the performer into creatures on all fours or create distortions that baffle or surprise. Masks, found in many cultures throughout the world, are worn at festivals, celebrations, and rituals. In whatever ways they are used, masks have the power to transform an ordinary person into someone or something else.

■ Discussion Questions

1. The photo on this page shows Robert Faust with masks from "The Mask Man." Study the expression of the masks. What kinds of personalities are being shown? What can you tell about the character's age, culture, and personality traits from the mask alone?

2. The first Greek masks were used in plays to impersonate gods. What Greek gods and goddesses can you name? What were their attributes or symbols?

■ Creative Expression Activities

LANGUAGE ARTS. Read Greek myths such as "Theseus and the Minotaur" or "The Golden Fleece." How might masks be used in these works?

ART. Create a two-sided mask showing contrasting feelings on each side. You might choose happy and sad or good and evil. Think of movements to go with your mask to express each emotion.

Performing Arts Handbook | **413**

APPRECIATING THE PERFORMING ARTS

As a device for theatre, masks evolved from religious practices of ancient Greece. The masks depicting Tragedy and Comedy are derived from Greek theatrical traditions.

One advantage of using masks in a performance is that they can be seen from a distance; they are often larger than the human head. The mask elicits enchantment and fascination, and still retains a deep and complex meaning in many cultures. Masks are worn to evoke magic, to hide and deceive, to project humor, beauty, ugliness, and mystery, as protection, and as replicas of people who have died.

Faustwork Mask Theater

Optional Viewing Selection:
- Artsource® VHS tape, segment 1 *(playing time 5:13)*

Setting the Stage

Direct students to read the paragraph about Faustwork Mask Theater. Then have them view the Artsource® video, if available.

Connecting the Arts

Using the Discussion Questions on this page, help students recognize how masks have been used in many cultures throughout history. Possible responses:

1. Although masks at first look "blank," they show characters of various ages and outlooks—young, old, worried, etc.

2. Students might name, for example, Athena, warrior goddess, who carries a spear and shield; Zeus, father of the gods, who carries a thunderbolt and scepter; or Hermes, who wears winged sandals.

Extension

- After students have responded to the Discussion Questions and, if possible, viewed the Artsource® selection, have them complete the Creative Expression Activities.

- Have students research the traditional uses of masks in various cultures. Then encourage students to share their findings.

Use Artsource® Performing Arts Package, Lesson 1, for more about masks.

DANCE

Martha Graham

Martha Graham

Optional Viewing Selection:
- Artsource® VHS tape, segment 2 *(playing time 13:13)*

"Lamentation," 1930. Choreography and costume by Martha Graham. Performed by Janet Eilber. Photo: © Max Waldman. Max Waldman Archives.

"No matter what you say, you reveal yourself. Movement does not lie." These words, spoken to Martha Graham by her father when she was just a young girl, would hold great meaning for her later in life. Renowned for her contributions to the art of modern dance, Graham established a new way of communicating through the use of the body. Graham redefined the modern dance form by using movement to express emotion. She developed a vocabulary of movements to describe emotion in physical rather than verbal language. Exploring emotional moves that come from the center of the body, she based her movement system on the "contraction" or folding in of the torso that happens when you sob or laugh, and the "release" that happens when you inhale and unfold. "Lamentation" was created by Graham to represent the essence of grief and became her signature solo piece. Graham continued creating dances until her death, at the age of 96.

Setting the Stage

Direct students to read the paragraph about Martha Graham and view the Artsource® video, if available. Explain to students that by developing a "vocabulary of movements" Graham expressed various emotions and ideas through her dance creations.

Connecting the Arts

Using the Discussion Questions on this page, encourage students to think about how everyday body movements can be exaggerated into dance movements.

1. Body language refers to messages transmitted through body movements and gestures rather than words. Answers will vary. One example: to express a feeling of disappointment in a dance, a person may bow her head deeply.
2. Shyness might be communicated by averted eyes, etc.
3. Grief and sorrow are strong emotions that envelop our whole person, as the costume envelops the dancer.

Extension

- After students have examined the photograph and, if possible, viewed the video, have them complete the Creative Expression Activities.

  Use Artsource® Performing Arts Package, Lesson 2, for more about Martha Graham.

414

■ Discussion Questions

1. What is body language? How might body language be exaggerated and developed into a dance form?
2. Graham said that the movement of the torso called a contraction comes from where you laugh or cry. Think of other emotions that a person might feel. How are these emotions expressed by the body?
3. How do you think the costume in the picture could help in depicting movements that are the essence of grief or sorrow?

■ Creative Expression Activities

SCIENCE. Many of the movements in Graham's technique are based on contraction and release. The action that triggers or generates the contraction and release of muscles is breathing. Graham organized breathing for her stage purposes. Taking in the breath was a "release," pressing it out was a "contraction." Research the muscles involved in breathing and explore the action of your own breathing, trying to match it to the Graham idea of contraction and release.

APPRECIATING THE PERFORMING ARTS

Theatre or concert dance, which is done solely for the entertainment of the audience, is separate from social or folk dance, which is done for personal or cultural fulfillment. Ballet is concert dance for which the artists are trained in a technique geared toward certain dance aesthetics. The origins of classical ballet techniques date back to the days of the royal court in 1661. Modern dance developed in the twentieth century. It derived its form from the need to express human spirit and emotion. Ballet is performed upright and appears to defy gravity. Modern dance consciously works with gravity and includes movements in which the dancer repeatedly touches the floor and lifts off again. Martha Graham was one of the pioneers of modern dance and an extraordinary creator of her time.

DANCE

Merce Cunningham Dance Company

Members of the **Merce Cunningham Dance Company** in *CRWDSPCR* (Crowdspacer). Photo: Lois Greenfield.

Merce Cunningham recounts four events that have led to important discoveries in his work: 1) his initial collaboration with composer John Cage in the late 1940s, when they began to separate the music and the dance; 2) his use of chance operations in his choreography; 3) his use of video and film as a meduim to choreograph works specifically for the camera; 4) and his use of dance computer software in the 1990s. With the computer figure, the Sequence Editor, one can create movements, store them in the memory, and eventually have a phrase of movement. It is possible to vary the timing so that you can see the body change from one shape to another in slow motion. Even if the computer produces positions and transitions that are not possible for humans to perform, it opens up new possibilities to explore. The film *CRWDSPCR* (Crowdspacer) documents the choreographic process in which Cunningham and the dancers experiment and adapt the movement sequences derived from the computer.

■ Discussion Questions

1. Study the dancers' positions in the photograph. Discuss similarities or differences from partnering or "lifts" that you have seen in ballet, ice skating, or gymnastics.

2. Look at the group of dancers in the photograph. Can you visually pinpoint a "center of balance" within the group? Is it in the exact center of the group or not? Explain why or why not.

3. Describe how the costumes affect your impression of the dancers and the dance shown in this photograph.

■ Creative Expression Activities

TECHNOLOGY. Learn more about Merce Cunningham's ongoing creative work and the activities of the Cunningham Dance Company on the Internet. Research the company's touring schedules to countries and cities around the world.

SOCIAL STUDIES. Select one particular visual or performing artist from the 1950s and 1960s and find out what events during that period-might have influenced their work.

Performing Arts Handbook | **415**

APPRECIATING THE PERFORMING ARTS

Merce Cunningham began his long and distinguished career with Martha Graham in modern dance. As he developed his own work, Cunningham involved contemporary composers and visual artists. In his pieces he never sought to blend dance, music, and set design, but rather to allow a deliberate separateness. The continuity of his choreography relies on neither linear elements (narrative or psychological) nor movement toward and away from a theatrical climax. More like an abstract painting, it is assumed that an element (a movement, a sound, or a change of light) is in and of itself expressive. In this context, what a dance communicates has a lot to do with the interpretation of each individual viewer.

PERFORMING ARTS
DANCE

Merce Cunningham Dance Company

Optional Viewing Selection:
■ Artsource® VHS tape, segment 3 *(playing time 19:23)*

Setting the Stage

Direct students to read the paragraph about Merce Cunningham and view the Artsource® video, if available. Explain to students that a phrase of movement is a set of movements that together express an idea, or convey a complete thought, just as a phrase in text completes a thought.

Connecting the Arts

Possible responses to the Discussion Questions on this page are:

1. The partnering looks like ballet or classical dance. There is a formal quality about the figures.

2. There is a "center of balance," a point that the members of the group are leaning into or pulling away from. It is off center.

3. The costumes are like an abstract painting; they are designed as if they are patterns on a grid.

Extension

■ After students have examined the photograph and, if possible, viewed the video, have them complete the Creative Expression Activities.

Use Artsource® Performing Arts Package, Lesson 3, for more information about Merce Cunningham.

Ballet Folklorico de Mexico

Optional Viewing Selection:
- Artsource® VHS tape, segment 4 *(playing time 8:45)*

Setting the Stage

Direct students to read the paragraph about Amalia Hernández and her dance company, Ballet Folklorico de Mexico, and view the Artsource® video, if available.

Connecting the Arts

Using the Discussion Questions on this page, help students appreciate the blending of cultural influences in the traditions of Mexico. Possible responses are:

1. The man is wearing decorative riding pants, a kerchief, and a sombrero (Mexican hat). The woman is wearing a full, striped skirt and a blouse with puffy short sleeves. The man is demonstrating his skills and the woman is showing her admiration for him.
2. Answers will vary. Students may refer to Mexican dances performed at Cinco de Mayo celebrations.
3. Answers will vary.

Extension

- After students have examined the photograph and, if possible, viewed the video, have them complete the Creative Expression Activities.

Use Artsource® Performing Arts Package, Lesson 4, for more information about Ballet Folklorico de Mexico.

A R T S O U R C E ARTSOURCE

Ballet Folklorico de Mexico

Ballet Folklorico de Mexico, "Danza de la Reata." Amalia Hernández, artistic director. Courtesy of Ballet Folklorico de Mexico.

Amelia Hernández, director of Ballet Folklorico de Mexico, decided at the age of eight to make dance her life's work. Her parents made her dream possible, and her training and experiences inspired her artistic vision. For over 30 years she has researched the roots of Mexican folklore and traditions. Her intention has been to create a contemporary show based on Mexican themes, and to convey the heart and spirit of the Mexican people. From the time of the Olmec Indians to the birth of modern Mexico, more than thirty distinct cultures have influenced Mexican culture. The Spanish brought horses to Mexico and introduced the caballero, or rancher, lifestyle. The dance shown in this photo is called "Danza de la Reata" and celebrates the beauty and harmony of life on the ranchero, or Mexican ranch.

■ Discussion Questions

1. Look closely at the photo of the male and female dancers inside the lariat, or lasso. Describe the costumes and what you think the dance is about.
2. What do you know about Mexican culture and dance? Can you think of any other styles of Mexican dance? Describe the costumes and movements.
3. What dances, songs, or paintings can you think of that refer to the work of a group of people, or to a specific culture?

■ Creative Expression Activities

LANGUAGE ARTS. Look at the photo on this page and use your imagination to write a description about what is taking place. Describe the relationship between the two people and the types of movements that would be done.

SOCIAL STUDIES. The Spanish brought horses and the Catholic religion to the indigenous people of Mexico and taught them a new way of life. The word "Mestizo" is used to refer to the unique blend of European and native cultures and races that make up the majority of the Mexican people of today. Research what other European cultures influenced the people of Mexico.

APPRECIATING THE PERFORMING ARTS

Folk dance is the term given to dances that come specifically from a cultural group and are done in a traditional way, often at festivals and special events. Classical ballet is a style of dance that is very technical and requires a great deal of training to perfect. Amalia Hernández has done her research in the folk tradi-

tions of music, dance, costumes, and themes, but has trained her dancers in both the classical and folk styles. Like the Spanish and indigenous cultures combined, she has blended these two styles in order to present them in a professional, staged setting.

Lewitzky Dance Company

Lewitzky Dance Company. Bella Lewitzky, director. "Impressions #1 (Henry Moore)." Featured dancers: Jennifer Handel, Nancy Lanier, Laurie McWilliams, Theodora Fredericks, Deborah Collodel, Claudia Schneiderman. Photo: Vic Luke.

Bella Lewitzky has been a modern dance performer, choreographer, and dance educator for over 60 years. During her career, Bella realized that sculpture and other works of art could be used as a source of inspiration for dance movements. In particular, she focused on the work of sculptor Henry Moore. Since it was impossible to bring his sculptures into her studio, she and her dancers worked from photos found in books. They observed that his sculptures have massive physical weight and bulk and they also have two or three balance points, or places where the sculpture touches the ground. There are also holes, or negative spaces, that encourage the viewer to look through the sculptures, which alters the perspective. These observations and movement explorations evolved into a dance work called "Impressions #1 (Henry Moore)."

■ Discussion Questions

1. Look at the photo of the dancers on this page. Use the elements of line, shape, form, and texture to describe what you see.

2. Can you think of other artists who were inspired by an existing work of art and used it as a point of departure for a new work?

3. Use art books to locate a sculpture by Henry Moore. Observe it in terms of size, negative and positive space, form, and the number of balance points. Discuss how these concepts might be communicated through movement.

■ Creative Expression Activities

THEATRE/MOVEMENT. Working with partners, sketch out a few human *sculptures* of your own. Join with other pairs of students and position yourselves in relationship to each other to make more complex forms. Present your forms to the class.

DANCE. Dancers use the movements of their bodies to express action as it relates to weight, flow, space, and time. Explore ways to show the following eight actions using dance movements: press, flick, punch, float, slash, glide, wring, and dab.

SCIENCE. Select an object and answer the following questions: Is it light or heavy? How does it move or balance? How many points are touching the ground? What is the object's shape? Observe it from different perspectives (for example, upside down, and so on).

Performing Arts Handbook **417**

APPRECIATING THE PERFORMING ARTS

The art form of dance uses both sculptural designs and selected motion to achieve aesthetic expression.

Lewitzky has been a "visual collector" of Henry Moore's sculptures for many years. In her studio, she guided her company in experiencing the different aspects of his work. They explored how his pieces rested on the ground and "took off" from their resting places; how the feet, hands, and arms were carried; and how Moore's sculptures seemed to move with upright positions of the back. The dancers worked with interlocking shapes and have developed a "Moore movement vocabulary."

PERFORMING ARTS
DANCE

Lewitzky Dance Company

Optional Viewing Selection:
- Artsource® VHS tape, segment 5 *(playing time 3:36)*

Setting the Stage

Direct students to read about Bella Lewitzky and guide them in examining the photograph on this page. Have students view the Artsource® video, if available.

Connecting the Arts

Using the Discussion Questions on this page, help students recognize the inspiration Lewitzky found in works of visual art. Possible responses:

1. The dancers' bodies are aligned and parallel in groups of three vertically and three horizontally; shapes are repeated from one group to another; textures are smooth.

2. Students might mention Leonard Bernstein's *West Side Story,* inspired by Shakespeare's *Romeo and Juliet.*

3. Students might suggest large, sweeping movements, unusual balancing points, and formations such as that shown in the photograph.

Extension

- After students have responded to the Discussion Questions and, if possible, viewed the Artsource® selection, have them complete the Creative Expression Activities.

Use Artsource® Performing Arts Package, Lesson 5, for more information about Bella Lewitzky and "Impressions #1 (Henry Moore)."

PERFORMING ARTS
THEATRE

Joanna Featherstone

Optional Viewing Selection:
- Artsource® VHS tape, segment 6 *(playing time 3:50)*

Setting the Stage

Direct students to read the paragraph about Joanna Featherstone and view the Artsource® video, if available.

Connecting the Arts

Using the Discussion Questions on this page, help students understand that the expression of art is influenced by the artist's life and the times in which he or she lives.

1. A storyteller can move an audience by using words in a playful or emotional way. Tools a storyteller might need are gestures, facial expressions, emotional vocal tones, body language and movement skills.
2. Help students focus on the importance of reading as a tool that allows them to navigate through life.

Extension

- After students have completed the Discussion Questions and, if possible, viewed the selection, have them complete the Creative Expression Activities.
- Encourage students to recognize the importance of words as a tool for communication, for remembering, for expressing emotions, and for sharing lessons learned.

Use Artsource® Performing Arts Package, Lesson 6, for more information about Joanna Featherstone.

Joanna Featherstone

Joanna Featherstone. Photo: Craig Schwartz, © 1998.

Theatre artist and storyteller Joanna Featherstone has been "dancing with words" for as long as she can remember. A shy child who taught herself to read by studying cereal boxes, Featherstone read and memorized everything she could get her hands on, including boxes of baking soda, the Bible, and shopping catalogs. She discovered poetry at the age of 10 through a church reading of *Creation,* a work written by African American poet James Weldon Johnson (1871–1938). Featherstone memorized that poem too, although it wasn't until she was in college that she learned that it was the work of a writer of color, a man respected for his work in collecting and preserving much of the early poetry written by African Americans. An accomplished actress, Featherstone has performed on Broadway and off-Broadway stages, as well as for audiences in Europe and in West Africa. She has worked with award-winning string quartets, dancers, jazz musicians, and the New York Philharmonic. However, the performances in which she recites the work of early African American poets such as James Weldon Johnson, Paul Laurence Dunbar (1872–1906), and Phillis Wheatley (1753–1784) is where Featherstone finds her "dance of words" to be most fulfilling and complete.

■ Discussion Questions

1. Do you think it is possible for a solo storyteller or performer to move an audience by just using words? What other "tools" do they need to make an audience feel an emotion?
2. Featherstone taught herself to read by using cereal boxes. How did you learn to read? Have you ever helped someone else improve his or her reading skills? How many times each day do you use your reading skills?

■ Creative Expression Activities

LANGUAGE ARTS. Poetry is normal, everyday speech that has been "heightened" through the use of rhyming words, rhythmic patterns, and strong images. Think of a poem or song lyric that you know well and admire; write it down. Now translate it into normal speech, replacing or moving all rhyming words, changing rhythmic patterns, and turning the word images into less descriptive phrases. How does this "deconstruction" change the impact of the message the original writer tried to convey? Does the altered speech still contain as strong an emotional impact?

APPRECIATING THE PERFORMING ARTS

Storytellers use words, gestures, and emotions to paint pictures and trigger memories in the minds of their audience. However, storytelling has an even deeper purpose than just "entertainment." In many cultures, storytellers were the historians of their people—the ones who remembered important events and lessons. In such cultures, storytellers acted as a living library for their culture. People would come to them and hear stories about their origins, their culture, and their ancestors, and would use these stories to help guide their own lives. Using ancient or family stories as teaching tools is still common today among many families around the world. Remembering and learning from past events is a strong component of the storytelling art.

Paul Winter

Paul Winter. Photo courtesy of Paul Winter.

The music of Paul Winter includes the voices of animals from all around the world, including whales, wolves, elk, buffalo, eagles, tigers, and elephants. Paul listens to their songs, cries, and howls and adds melodies from his saxophone. In 1968, he heard the songs of the humpback whales, which strongly influenced his music and life. The humpback songs appear on some of his albums, which he considers a highlight in his musical career. The sounds of nature and animals help Paul create what he calls, "living music." Paul has recorded his music in the Grand Canyon, Yellowstone, and Glacier National Parks, and has visited the homes of many creatures throughout the world. These experiences are the foundation of his respect and concern for all living things. Paul views our planet as one big community and has received numerous awards in recognition of his musical efforts for endangered species and the environment, including two Grammy Awards. Paul lives in Connecticut and continues to pursue his love of music, nature, and community.

■ Discussion Questions

1. What is your favorite animal? What does this animal have in common with you?
2. What ecological or environmental issues are important to you, and how can they be reflected in your daily life?

■ Creative Expression Activities

SOCIAL STUDIES. Describe as many communities as you can—cultural, social, intellectual, spiritual, artistic, etc. Which communities are you a part of now or would like to be a part of in the future? How does nature and the environment fit within your definition of community?

LANGUAGE ARTS. Imagine human history with a greater understanding of nature and the environment. How would human progress be changed? What kinds of societies would be created and how would they coexist with nature? How would world relations be affected? Would we have a need for technology?

Performing Arts Handbook | **419**

PERFORMING ARTS
MUSIC

Paul Winter

Optional Listening Selection:

■ Artsource® audiocassette, segment 1 (*playing time 6:49*)

Setting the Stage

Direct students to read the paragraph about musician and composer Paul Winter and listen to the Artsource® audiocassette, if available.

Connecting the Arts

Using the Discussion Questions on this page, help students recognize the connection between man and nature. Possible responses are:

1. My favorite animal is the dog. Both the dog and I are very loyal creatures.
2. Protecting the ozone layer, cleaner air, saving the oceans, etc. Use less products that contain chlorofluorocarbons (CFCs), carpool or ride the bus, protect waterways that lead into the ocean, etc.

Extension

■ Research the animals on the current endangered species list. What factors put them on this list? How can we help them survive? Are any of them near your community?

■ Examine a few cultural ideas that have a strong connection to nature—Native American myths, Japanese gardens, Aztec calendars, etc. How do these cultures value their environment.

Use Artsource® Performing Arts Package, Lesson 7, for more information about Paul Winter.

APPRECIATING THE PERFORMING ARTS

In many ways, a musical ensemble is similar to a community, with many individuals making their own contributions, yet working together. For example, a conductor may direct an orchestra. However, it is up to each musician to deliver the correct notes.

The way the male humpback whale communicates is very similar to that of a musician. His songs have a wide variety of sounds, including the highest and lowest frequencies humans can hear. When Paul Winter adds the sound of his saxophone to these songs, he is creating new music with the humpbacks and performing an interesting duet. Artists like Paul Winter extend the concept of community to include the lyrical voices of humans and animals.

African American Dance Ensemble

Optional Viewing Selection:
■ Artsource® VHS tape, segment 7 (playing time 21:57)

Setting the Stage

Direct students to read the paragraph about Chuck Davis and the African American Dance Ensemble, and view the Artsource® video, if available.

Connecting the Arts

Using the Discussion Questions on this page, help students recognize the importance of dance and music in traditional African cultures. Possible responses are:

1. Mood, costumes, and actions suggest traditional African culture; they suggest that the dance echoes traditional African styles and that pride in African roots is being communicated.
2. Break dancing, swing, country music line dancing.

Extension

■ After students have responded to the Discussion Questions and, if possible, viewed the Artsource® selection, have them complete the Creative Expression Activities.
   Use Artsource® Performing Arts Package, Lesson 8, for more information about the African American Dance Ensemble and for additional related activities.

420

DANCE/MUSIC

African American Dance Ensemble

African American Dance Ensemble. Chuck Davis, founder and artistic director. *African Roots in American Soil.*

Chuck Davis, a towering African-American dancer and choreographer, came from a background that was poor financially but rich in love. His first dance break came when he substituted for an injured member of the Richardson Dancers in Washington, D.C. In 1959, he joined the Klara Harrington Dancers and studied and performed with a number of modern, jazz, Afro-Cuban, and African dance companies. With disdain for the way black people were being portrayed in the media, he set out to present the truth about black culture through dance. "I have gone to Africa and I have sat at the feet of elders and I have listened as their words poured like raindrops onto and into my being. I have danced on the dusty earth and the sound of my feet pounding against the earth brought the rhythms of life into my blood," states Davis. After two decades of building his company in New York, he returned to North Carolina to start a second company, the African-American Dance Ensemble, which he currently directs. Through dance, he works energetically to bring *all* people his message of "peace, love, and respect for everybody."

■ **Discussion Questions**

1. Look carefully at the photo on this page and describe the mood, costumes, and actions you observe. What clues do these give you about the style of dance and what is being communicated?
2. Study the clothing that Mr. Davis is wearing. Discuss how it is similar to or different from American outfits.

■ **Creative Expression Activities**

LANGUAGE ARTS. In many African ethnic groups, it is believed that wise people deliver proverbs. Read the following proverbs, then think of English equivalents: "Rain beats a leopard's skin, but it does not wash out the spots" (Asante); "When spider webs unite, they can tie up a lion" (Ethiopia); "Cross the river in a crowd and the crocodile won't eat you" (Kenya).

420 | *Performing Arts Handbook*

APPRECIATING THE PERFORMING ARTS

In the traditional societies of Africa, dance is an important medium of education. It helps African communities perpetuate themselves by assisting their members through rites of passage, teaching accepted behavior, identifying roles and rules, and assimilating their members into the prevailing attitudes, beliefs, and rituals of the group.

In African cultures, dance is an integral part of life.

For example, the Ibo of Nigeria teach about leadership through dance. A popular teenage dance among the Ubakala Clan is *Zik Meme Ka Odi Uma*. The name means "Zik tries to make things good." Zik is Nnamdi Azikiwewas, the president of Nigeria, who led his nation to independence. The dance emphasizes cooperation with a worthy leader.

Eth-Noh-Tec

Eth-Noh-Tec. Robert Kikuchi-Yngoyo and Nancy Wang, artistic co-directors. Photo: Allen Nomura.

Eth-Noh-Tec, an Asian American Company based in San Francisco, uses a synthesis of music, movement, and words to present their unique style of theatre and storytelling. Their work is characterized by rhythmic dialogue, tightly choreographed poses, comic facial expressions, extensive hand gestures, and body postures with low centers of gravity. The Eth-Noh-Tec performance style reflects ancient Asian theatre styles such as Chinese opera (highly moral stories about the lives of common people) and Japanese Kyogen (comic plays written in everyday language). Company founders Robert Kikuchi-Yngojo and Nancy Wang present stories drawn from centuries-old Asian legends and modern-day experiences of Asian-Americans. The musical sounds of *ditze* (Chinese flute) and *taiko* (Japanese drums) add excitement, color, and punctuation to their performance. The mission of Eth-Noh-Tec is to create a fusion of cultures with a weaving (tec) together of distinctive cultural elements (eth) to create new possibilities (noh).

■ Discussion Questions

1. Look at the photo and discuss the stylized posture, costumes, and facial expressions of these performers. How does this differ from other plays, dances, or films you have seen?

2. One of the stories presented by Eth-Noh-Tec, *The Long Haired Girl,* is about the heroic acts of a young woman who brings water to her village. This ancient story is still being lived out today. Describe some examples of courageous acts done by people who wanted to help others.

■ Creative Expression Activities

HISTORY/SOCIAL STUDIES. There are universal values shared by all cultures in the world. Values such as the importance of family and friendship, respect for bravery, helping others, protecting our homes, and sharing our experiences (storytelling) are common to most cultures. Make a list of other shared values that you think exist in many of our world's cultures.

Performing Arts Handbook | **421**

Optional Viewing Selection:
■ Artsource® VHS tape, segment 8 *(playing time 10:35)*

Setting the Stage

Direct students to read the paragraph about Eth-Noh-Tec and view the Artsource® video, if available.

Connecting the Arts

Using the Discussion Questions on this page, help students recognize that there are different styles of theatre and many different ways to tell a story. Possible responses are:

1. The actors look stiff, not natural, their faces are painted, they are wearing different clothes. Note: The actors are "presenting" characters (presentational theatre), as opposed to "representing" characters (representational theatre), or pretending to actually "be" those characters.

2. Answers may be drawn from current events, newspaper stories, etc., but some general answers may include: firemen who save people from burning structures, people who donate their time to serve meals to the homeless, etc.

Extension

■ After students have examined the photograph and, if possible, viewed the video, have them complete the Creative Expression Activities.

Use Artsource® Performing Arts Package, Lesson 9, for more information about Eth-Noh-Tec.

APPRECIATING THE PERFORMING ARTS

Eth-Noh-Tec combines three different types of performing arts. Theatre, dance/movement, and music can all be used separately to tell stories, but each uses a different primary method of expression. Dance tells a story primarily through movement, though it is often accompanied by music. Theatre tells a story through spoken words and staged images. Music tells a story through sound. Several performing art forms successfully unite all of these elements: opera, musical theatre, ballet, and even some rock concerts. By combining these elements of sound, word, and movement, artists are sure to reach their audience's ears, eyes, minds, and hearts.

PERFORMING ARTS
MUSIC

Eugene
Friesen

Eugene Friesen

Optional Viewing Selection:
■ Artsource® VHS tape, segment 9 *(playing time 13:41)*

Setting the Stage

Direct students to read the paragraph about Eugene Friesen and view the Artsource® video, if available.

Connecting the Arts

Using the Discussion Questions on this page, help students recognize the unique creative quality of "Cello Man," a performance that combines mask theatre and music. Possible responses are:

1. The mask seems to depict a squirrel. The music might be high-pitched; it might have short, quick musical phrases.
2. A cello rests on the floor between the player's legs; its strings may be bowed or plucked. It has a deep sound that is mellow and pleasing to the ear.
3. The violin, the viola, the double bass, and the harp.

Extension

■ After students have examined the photograph and, if possible, viewed the video, have them complete the Creative Expression Activities.

■ Encourage students to recognize that stringed instruments are found in cultures all over the world, from ancient to modern times.
Use Artsource® Performing Arts Package, Lesson 10, for more information about Eugene Friesen and his performance "Cello Man."

MUSIC

Eugene Friesen

Eugene Friesen. "Cello Man." Photo: Craig Schwartz, © 1998.

Eugene Friesen has created a unique voice among the cellists of the world. Drawing on a childhood filled with the great masterworks of Western music as well as the influences of hymn, ethnic, and popular music, Eugene uses cello and voice to create new music that is accessible and personal. At age eight Eugene began playing the cello, pulling it in a little red wagon to school for orchestra practice. In high school and college, Eugene played in school and community orchestras and began experimenting in rock and blues styles on an amplified cello. A graduate of the Yale School of Music, Eugene takes the cello out of its traditional classical realm, propelling it forward as an exciting instrument with immense powers of free expression. "Cello Man," featured in the photo, is a solo performance created in collaboration with Faustwork Mask Theater. In the show, Eugene weaves a spellbinding fabric with stories, songs, masks, and inventive techniques on cello and electric cello. The repertoire for "Cello Man" features Friesen's original music in a variety of styles: blues, contemporary, folk, electronic, and pop, and includes a duet with the recorded song of a humpback whale. The use of masks designed and created by director Robert Faust adds a dramatic element to the performance. During segments of the show, Eugene transforms himself with masks and costumes, integrating each character with the music he is playing.

■ Discussion Questions

1. Look at the photo and identify the animal depicted by the mask Eugene is wearing. Can you imagine the characteristics of the music Eugene might play based upon that animal?
2. Do you know how a cello is played? Can you describe the sound a cello makes?
3. Can you name any other instruments in the string family?

■ Creative Expression Activities

LANGUAGE ARTS. Write a story that has a musical instrument as a main character. The instrument's character may be personified, employing human traits and emotions, or it may appear as a key element in the story's plot. Think about the materials used in making the instrument you have selected to write about. Your story could begin with the tree from which a cello was made or the gourd from which a shakere was fashioned.

APPRECIATING THE PERFORMING ARTS

Stringed instruments are important in many of the world's musical cultures. In ancient Egyptian, Greek, and Hebrew cultures, plucked string instruments such as the lyre and the harp came before the introduction of the bow. An instrument played with a bow necessitated an arched bridge and allowed for greater musical expression. Ancient Oriental and Near Eastern cultures, however, enjoyed both bowed and plucked instruments. Stringed keyboard instruments, such as the clavichord, harpsichord, and piano, technically members of the percussion family of musical instruments, evolved later in European history.

Vocalworks

Vocalworks. Bruce Cooper, Michael Geiger, Timand Debbie Reeder, and Dave Eastly perform "Vocalworks Radio Hour."
Photo: Richard Hines, © 1998.

PERFORMING ARTS HANDBOOK

Since 1983, Bruce Cooper, Michael Geiger, Tim and Debbie Reeder, and Dave Eastly of Vocalworks have brought the music of the 1930s and 1940s to audiences throughout the United States and abroad. Singing the music of the swing era, they are proud to note that Vocalworks has lasted longer than the swing era itself. In the "Vocalworks Radio Hour," the group recreates a live radio broadcast from the period when home entertainment meant gathering around the radio in the living room to hear news, music, drama, or comedy programs. The Depression and World War II were very difficult times for the American people. They were concerned about their future and what would become of their country. Swing music was a wonderful escape that allowed people to lift their spirits and forget their troubles for awhile. Vocalworks shows the importance of music in that role and how it can still function in the same way today.

■ Discussion Questions

1. Improvisation is one of the characteristics of swing jazz. Look at the photo on this page. Identify the instruments. Which one is improvised?

2. Swing music was characterized by its positive message during the Depression in the 1930s and during World War II in the 1940s. Swing dance and music has had a resurgence today. How do you account for its renewed popularity?

■ Creative Expression Activities

LANGUAGE ARTS. Read about the Harlem Renaissance and its influence on jazz musicians and poets. Working in groups, present a choral verse reading of one of the following Langston Hughes poems to show how he was influenced by jazz: "The Weary Blues," "The Negro Speaks of Rivers," or "Afro-American Fragment."

SOCIAL STUDIES. Each of three groups will research one of the following periods: 1930–1935, 1936–1940, 1941–1945. Use the group period as a title and divide the paper into three sections: World, United States, and Swing Music. Group members should fill in the significant dates, people, and events during that time period.

Performing Arts Handbook **423**

PERFORMING ARTS
MUSIC

Vocalworks

Optional Listening Selection:
■ Artsource® audiocassette, segment 2 *(playing time 9:30)*

Setting the Stage

Direct students to read the paragraph about Vocalworks and listen to the Artsource® audiocassette, if available.

Connecting the Arts

Using the Discussion Questions on this page, guide students in developing an understanding of swing music.

1. A washboard is being used as an instrument.

2. In a world of increasing complexity dominated by technology, many people look to the past for inspiration, and swing's message of buoyant optimism is particularly appealing. Also, as the millennium approaches, people are taking a nostalgic look at the enduring qualities of the twentieth century.

Extension

■ After students have responded to the Discussion Questions and, if possible, viewed the Artsource® selection, have them complete the Creative Expression Activities.

■ One of the characteristics of swing jazz is scat singing, a series of vocal nonsense syllables created to express certain sounds. Encourage students to try using scat singing with a classmate.
Use Artsource® Performing Arts Package, Lesson 11, for more information about Vocalworks.

APPRECIATING THE PERFORMING ARTS

Swing is just one style in the continuum of jazz, which includes the blues, ragtime, Dixieland, boogie-woogie, and bebop. Many jazz specialists cite clarinetist and bandleader Benny Goodman's 1935 appearance at the Palomar Ballroom in Los Angeles as the opening of the swing era. Some who listen to swing today feel that all swing bands sound alike, but during the swing era there were so many bands that each one sought individuality by developing its own trademark sound. Swing band leaders wanted their fans to recognize their music after hearing just a few measures. Although not confined exclusively to swing, the following are characteristic of the style: scat singing, repetition, syncopation, and call and response.

Korean Classical Music and Dance Company

PERFORMING ARTS HANDBOOK

MUSIC/DANCE

Korean Classical Music and Dance Company

Korean Classical Music and Dance Company. Don Kim, artistic director. Photo: © Craig Schwartz.

Optional Viewing Selection:
■ Artsource® VHS tape, segment 10 *(playing time 5:30)*

Setting the Stage

Direct students to read the paragraph about the Korean Classical Music and Dance Company and view the Artsource® video, if available.

Connecting the Arts

Using the Discussion Questions on this page, help students recognize how music and dance are a long-standing expression of a culture. Possible responses are:

1. The costumes are brightly colored dresses with wide skirts. They seem to move with the dance and most likely accentuate those movements. The flowing skirts probably also give a fluid look to the performance.

2. Students may refer to Native American or African cultural groups.

Extension

■ After students have examined the photograph and, if possible, viewed the video, have them complete the Creative Expression Activities.

Use Artsource® Performing Arts Package, Lesson 12, for more information about the music and dance of Korea and for additional related activities.

Much of Korean folk music can be traced back more than 2,000 years. These rich traditions were passed down from person, rather than taught formally, and have remained a part of everyday village life. A childhood interest in Korean folk music developed into a rewarding career for Don Kim, director of the Korean Classical Music and Dance Company. At the age of twelve he began to study the music and dance of his birthplace, Korea. His studies eventually led him to a membership in a Korean government-sponsored troupe, which performed the music and dances of their country on a world tour. As part of the tour, Mr. Kim visited the United States and decided to make it his new home, eventually settling in southern California. In 1973, he founded a school for the study of Korean music and dance. The Korean Classical Music and Dance Company repertoire includes folk as well as the ancient formal court music and dance.

■ Discussion Questions

1. Look at the photo on this page and describe the details of the costumes the dancers are wearing. How might the costumes enhance the performance?

2. What other cultures can you think of that preserve their history, traditions, and dances by passing the knowledge from one generation to the next?

■ Creative Expression Activities

DANCE. Do some research on a traditional Korean folk dance and an ancient Korean formal court dance. Describe how these two styles of dance are similar or different from one another.

SOCIAL STUDIES. Both China and Japan have dominated Korea throughout its history. Do some research to find out how either China or Japan has contributed to Korean culture and traditions.

APPRECIATING THE PERFORMING ARTS

Music in Korea today divides itself into two categories: traditional music and music of the West. Traditional music includes court music and folk music. Court music and dance were created and performed for the royal household and upper class associated with the court. When Korea's last royal dynasty was abolished in 1910 under the Japanese occupation, traditional musical compositions and dances of the court became obsolete. The Korean Classical Music and Dance Company, under the leadership of Don Kim, has reconstructed and preserved both the folk and classical traditions in their repertoire, keeping the Korean cultural spirit alive.

THEATRE

Kurt Jooss

The Joffrey Ballet of Chicago performing "The Green Table," Kurt Jooss choreographer. Photo: © Herbert Migdoll, 1998.

The curtain rises on a rectangular green table with ten gentlemen in morning coats and spats. They posture and disagree until pistols emerge, a shot is fired, and war is declared. The scene goes black. Next we see the figure of Death. In the scenes that follow, soldiers are called to fight, battles rage, refugees comfort one another, a profit-maker preys on the miseries of his fellow man, and a lone soldier holds watch. Through every scene, Death stalks the stage, claiming victim after victim, warrior and citizen alike. In the end the scene returns to the table, where the Gentlemen in Black start it up all over again.

"The Green Table," created by choreographer Kurt Jooss in 1932, is a compassionate and humanistic dance drama about the horrors of war. The mysterious figure of Death is a constant companion, simultaneously strong and sensitive, sinister and soothing. Ultimately he comes to each character, slipping into their lives and claiming them. Some victims he takes swiftly and surely, others slowly and gently. Some resist, some welcome him. Through the movement vocabulary, we see each character meeting Death in their own way, just as we all will. Productions of "The Green Table" are given by dance companies almost every year all over the world, making it probably the most performed of all dance works created in the twentieth century.

■ Discussion Questions

1. What do you think a dance theatre or dance drama is? How might it be different from dance pieces you have seen before?

2. Why do you think the gentlemen at the table wear masks?

3. Ballet or dance is, for the most part, made familiar to audiences through the world of myths, fairies, and mechanical dolls. Should dance pieces confront disturbing issues? Can they do so successfully?

■ Creative Expression Activities

LANGUAGE ARTS. There is a theory that dance cannot compete with the complexity offered by the spoken word. Can dance works take on complex intellectual arguments? Discuss these ideas using "The Green Table" as an example. Write a play, a narrative, or a poem based on the characters in "The Green Table." Read or perform it. Compare it with the ballet/dance work you are familiar with.

Performing Arts Handbook   **425**

APPRECIATING THE PERFORMING ARTS

Born in this century in Germany, Kurt Jooss finished high school in 1919. He first studied music, voice, and drama. A chance meeting with Rudolf von Laban, a renowned dance innovator, changed the direction of his life. Laban was searching for contemporary forms of movement. Jooss became his dancer, assistant, and choreographer. Interested in finding and developing a new language of movement, Jooss sought a form of dance that would serve as a way to handle contemporary themes. "The Green Table" is a conjunction of classical and modern dance. The choreographer approached dance from the intellectual angle, as well as the physical. He brought about a revolution in attitudes to theatre dance that reverberates to the present day.

PERFORMING ARTS
THEATRE

Kurt Jooss

Optional Viewing Selection:
- Artsource® VHS tape, segment 11 *(playing time 7:30)*

Setting the Stage
Direct students to read the paragraph about Kurt Jooss and view the Artsource® video, if available.

Connecting the Arts
Using the Discussion Questions on this page, help students think about and explore the idea of dance drama. Tell students that abstract ballet concentrates on dance for dance's sake. Narrative ballets play on simple emotions rather than intellect. A dance drama such as "The Green Table" portrays a complex idea that involves emotion and intellect. Possible responses are:

1. Dance theatre incorporates music and dance with words to express a story. Students may have seen dance productions that did not include the spoken word.

2. The masks represent figures that the performers want to portray. The masks also signify that the characters are not presenting their true faces.

3. Answers will vary. Ask students to give reasons for their opinions.

Extension
- After students have examined the photograph and, if possible, viewed the video, have them complete the Creative Expression Activities.

Use Artsource® Performing Arts Package, Lesson 13, for more information about Kurt Jooss and "The Green Table."

John Ramirez

Optional Viewing Selection:
- Artsource® VHS tape, segment 12 (*playing time 12:30*)
- Artsource® audiocassette, segment 3 (*playing time 7:23*)

Setting the Stage

Direct students to read the paragraph about John Ramirez and view the Artsource® video, if available.

Connecting the Arts

Using the Discussion Questions on this page, help students recognize how animation has been used to tell a variety of stories. Possible responses are:

1. An idea or piece of music is given to the storyboard artist, who then sketches a storyboard sequence. These are brought to a creative team whose members make suggestions. The storyboard artist reworks the ideas and they are presented again.
2. Students may mention a theatrical production, a group presentation, space travel, medical treatments. Answers on the effects of technology will vary. Ask students to give reasons for their opinions.
3. Answers will vary.

Extension

- After students have responded to the Discussion Questions and, if possible, viewed the video, have them complete the Creative Expression Activities. Use Artsource® Performing Arts Package, Lesson 14, for more about John Ramirez.

426

John Ramirez

John Ramirez, "Every Picture Tells a Story." Photo: © Craig Schwartz, 1998.

Animator John Ramirez likes to mix art with music. Working with professional musicians such as Paul Tracey, he draws storyboards that bring music and words to life. Ramirez has worked as a storyboard artist for both Walt Disney Feature Animation and Warner Brothers Feature Animation. He loved to draw when he was growing up, especially trains, and felt very proud when his mother would make copies of his work. Eventually, he began to create his own comic strips—a form of storyboarding—and later his own animated films. For every animation project a team of highly creative people come together. The process might begin with the storyboard artist listening to the selected music many times, going with the images that come to mind, and then developing them into a rough storyboard sequence. Ramirez then explains the story line and describes the characters to the other members of the creative team. The storyboard artist then goes back to the drawing board and incorporates the new ideas. This process is repeated over and over until the work is refined. Only then does the animation process begin, usually taking about two years to complete a feature film.

■ Discussion Questions

1. Describe in your own words the basic process required in the making of an animated film.
2. Technology has had a great impact on animated films by enabling animators to produce very complex moving images, such as *Toy Story, Babe,* and *Mulan.* What else can you think of that has been enhanced by technology? How has technology affected communication, work, personal relationships?
3. What about animated films do you find the most intriguing? Why?

■ Creative Expression Activities

LANGUAGE ARTS/ART. Think of a specific topic, such as airplanes, cars, animals or people. Look in magazines to identify all the photos you can find that relate to this theme. Create a simple storyboard, then write a simple storyline which describes or sells an idea or product.

ART. Take a pad of unlined paper or make one by stapling 25 to 50 pages together to make a Flip Book. Choose a simple idea like a bouncing ball or a flower growing. Create a series of pictures in the right hand bottom corner that will show action when you flip through the pages.

APPRECIATING THE PERFORMING ARTS

Animation is all about collaboration. For every film project, a team of creative people works together in much the same way as an orchestra does. Each person is talented in a specific field, and the film director serves as the orchestrator, coordinating the efforts of each player. In an animated film, sometimes the visuals inspire the music; at other times the music gives direction for the visuals. The goal is to create a close interplay of animation, voices, and music so they smoothly carry the story line forward. The animators also take note of the movement and facial expressions of the actors doing the voices and often incorporate these personal expressions into those of the animated characters.

Table of Contents

DRAWING TIPS

1. Making Contour Drawings

When you make a contour drawing, your eye and hand must move at the same time. You must look at the object, not at your drawing. You must imagine that your pencil is touching the edge of the object as your eye follows the edge. Don't let your eye get ahead of your hand. Also, do not lift your pencil from the paper. When you move from one area to the next, let your pencil leave a trail. If you do lift your pencil accidentally, look down, place your pencil where you stopped, and continue.

a. To help you coordinate your eye-hand movement, try this: First, tape your paper to the table so it will not slide around. Then, hold a second pencil in your nondrawing hand and move it around the edges of the object. With your drawing hand, record the movement.

b. If you have trouble keeping your eyes from looking at the paper, ask a friend to hold a piece of stiff paper between your eyes and your drawing hand so the drawing paper is blocked from view. You might also place your drawing paper inside a large paper bag turned sideways. A third method is to put the object on a chair and place the chair on a table. When you are standing, the object should be at your eye level. Then, place your drawing paper on the table directly under the chair. In this way you will be unable to see the paper easily.

c. When you draw without looking at the paper, your first sketches will look strange. Don't be discouraged. The major purpose of blind contour drawing is to teach you to concentrate on directions and curves. The more you practice, the more accurate your drawings will become.

d. As you develop your skills, remember that in addition to edges, contours also define ridges. Notice the wrinkles you see at the joints of fingers and at a bent wrist or bent elbow. Those wrinkles are curved lines. Draw them carefully; the lines you use to show these things will add the look of roundness to your drawing.

e. After you have made a few sketches, add pressure as you draw to vary the thickness and darkness of your lines. Some lines can be emphasized and some can be made less important through the right amount of pressure from your hand.

2. Making Gesture Drawings

Unlike contour drawings, which show an object's outline, gesture drawings show movement. They should have no outlines or details.

a. Using the side of a piece of unwrapped crayon or a pencil, make scribble lines that build up the shape of the object. Do not use single lines that create stick figures.

b. Work very quickly. When drawing people, do the head, then the neck, and then fill in the body. Pay attention to the direction in which the body leans.

c. Next, scribble in the bulk of the legs and the position of the feet.

d. Finally, add the arms.

3. Drawing Calligraphic Lines with a Brush

Mastering the technique of drawing with flowing, calligraphic lines takes practice. You will need a round watercolor brush and either watercolor paint or ink. First, practice making very thin lines.

a. Dip your brush in the ink or paint and wipe the brush slowly on the side of the ink bottle until the bristles form a point.

b. Hold the brush at the metal ferrule so the brush is vertical rather than slanted above the paper. Imagine that the brush is a pencil with a very sharp point—if you press down, you will break the point (Figure T.1).

▲ **Figure T.1**

c. Touch the paper lightly with the tip of the brush and draw a line.

d. When you are able to control a thin line, you are ready to make calligraphic lines. Start with a thin line and gradually press the brush down to make the line thicker. Pull up again to make it thinner (Figure T.2, page 350). Practice making lines that vary in thickness.

▲ **Figure T.2**

lines or dots far apart and bring them closer together. (Figure T.3.)

5. Using Sighting Techniques
Sighting is a method that will help you determine proportions.

a. Hold a pencil vertically at arm's length in the direction of the object you are drawing. Close one eye and focus on the object you are going to measure.

b. Slide your thumb along the pencil until the height of the pencil above your thumb matches the height of the object (Figure T.4).

c. Now, without moving your thumb or bending your arm,

4. Using Shading Techniques
The following techniques help create shading values.

- **Hatching:** Use a series of fine parallel lines.
- **Crosshatching:** Use two or more intersecting sets of parallel lines.
- **Blending:** Use a smooth, gradual application of an increasingly dark value. Pencil lines may be blended.
- **Stippling:** Create shading with dots.

To be effective in forming the shaded areas, your lines and strokes must follow the form of the object. Use lines to show the surface of a flat surface. Let the lines run parallel to one edge of the surface. To show a curved surface, draw a series of parallel curved lines to give the illusion of roundness. The lines should follow the curve of the object.

Lines or dots placed close together create dark values. Lines or dots spaced farther apart create lighter values. To show a gradual change from light to dark, begin with

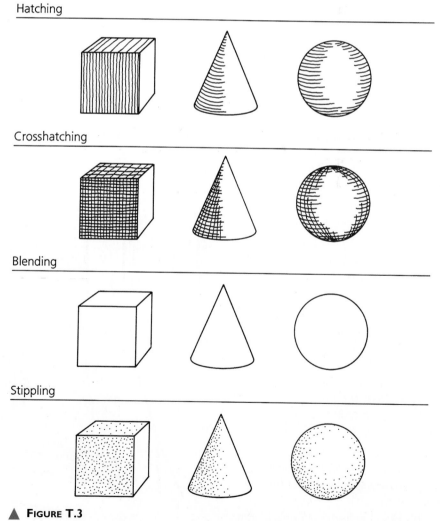

Hatching

Crosshatching

Blending

Stippling

▲ **Figure T.3**

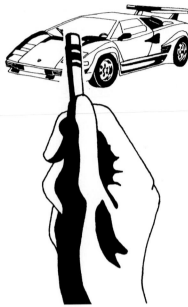

▲ **FIGURE T.4**

subject. Imagine that the opening represents your drawing paper.

c. You can decide how much of the subject you want to include in your drawing by moving the frame up, down, or sideways.

d. You can also move the frame closer or farther away to change the focus of your drawing.

7. Using a Ruler

There are times when you need to draw a crisp, straight line.

a. Hold the ruler with one hand and the pencil with the other.

b. Place the ruler where you wish to draw a straight line.

c. Hold the ruler with your thumb and first two fingers. Be careful that your fingers do not stick out beyond the edge of the ruler.

d. Press heavily on the ruler so it will not slide while you're drawing.

e. Hold the pencil lightly against the ruler.

f. Pull the pencil quickly and lightly along the edge of the ruler. The object is to keep the ruler from moving while the pencil moves along its edge.

hold the pencil parallel to the widest part of the object. Compare the height of the object with its width. You can determine the ratio of height to width by seeing how many times the smaller measure fits into the larger measure. This method can be applied either to different parts of the same object or to two or more different objects. Use one measurement as a base measurement and see how the other measurements relate to it.

6. Using a Viewing Frame

A viewing frame helps you to zero in on an area or object you intend to draw. To make a viewing frame, do the following:

a. Cut a rectangular hole in a heavy sheet of paper (Figure T.5).

b. Hold the frame at arm's length and look through it at your

▲ **FIGURE T.5**

8. Making a Grid for Enlarging

Sometimes you must take a small drawing and enlarge it. To do this, you must first measure the size that the large, finished drawing will be. Then, using proportional ratios, reduce that size to something you can work with.

a. For example: If you want to cover a wall 5 feet high and 10 feet wide, let 1 inch equal 1 foot. Then make a scale drawing that is 5 inches high and 10 inches wide. You may work either in inches or centimeters.

b. After you have completed your small drawing, draw vertical and horizontal grid lines 1 inch apart on the drawing. Number the squares (Figure T.6).

c. On the wall, draw vertical and horizontal grid lines one foot apart.

d. Number the squares on the wall to match the squares on the paper and enlarge the plan by filling one square at a time.

9. Measuring Rectangles

Do you find it hard to create perfectly formed rectangles? Here is a way of getting the job done:

a. Make a light pencil dot near the long edge of a sheet of paper. With a ruler, measure the exact distance between the dot and the edge. Make three more dots the same distance in from the edge. (See Figure T.7.)

b. Line a ruler up along the dots. Make a light pencil line running the length of the paper.

c. Turn the paper so that a short side is facing you. Make four pencil dots equally distant from the short edge. Connect these with a light pencil rule. Stop when you reach the first line you drew.

d. Do the same for the remaining two sides. Erase any lines that

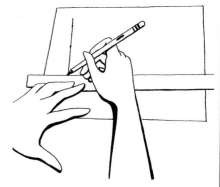

▲ **Figure T.7**

may extend beyond the box you have made.

e. Trace over the lines with your ruler and pencil. The box you have created will be a perfectly formed rectangle.

10. Mixing Paint to Change the Value of Color

You can better control the colors in your work when you mix your own paint. In mixing paints, treat opaque paints (for example, tempera) differently from transparent paints (for example, watercolors).

a. *For light values of opaque paints.* Add only a small amount of the hue to white. The color can always be made stronger by adding more of the hue.

b. *For dark values of opaque paints.* Add a small amount of black to the hue. Never add the hue to black.

c. *For light values of transparent paints.* Thin a shaded area with water. This allows more of the white paper to show through.

d. *For dark values of transparent paints.* Carefully add a small amount of black to the hue.

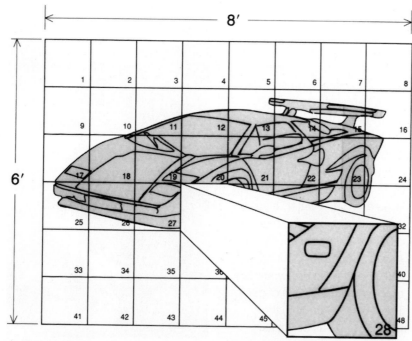

▲ **Figure T.6**

11. Making Natural Earth Pigment Paints

Anywhere there is dirt, clay, and sand, you can find natural earth pigments.

a. Collect as many different kinds of earth colors as you can find (Figure T.8).

▲ **FIGURE T.8**

b. Grind them as finely as possible. If you can, borrow a mortar and pestle from the science lab (Figure T.9). Regardless of the method you use, your finished product will still be a little gritty. It will not have the smooth texture of commercial pigment.

c. For the binder, use one part white glue to one part water. Put a few spoons of pigment into a small container and add some of the binder. Experiment with different proportions of pigment and binder.

d. When you have found the best proportion, apply the mixture to paper with a variety of brushes. Do not allow the brushes you use to dry before you wash them, because the glue will solidify.

e. Keep stirring your paint as you work to keep the pigment from settling. The pigment will keep indefinitely. Mix a fresh batch each time you paint, because the mixed paint is difficult to store for more than a few days.

12. Working with Watercolors

Here are some tips to control watercolor paints.

a. If you apply wet paint to damp paper, you create lines and shapes with soft edges.

b. If you apply wet paint to dry paper, you create lines and shapes with sharp, clear edges.

c. If you dip a dry brush into damp paint and then brush across dry paper, you achieve a fuzzy effect.

d. School watercolors come in semi-moist cakes. Before you use them, place a drop of water on each cake to let the paint soften. Watercolor paints are transparent. You can see the white paper through the paint. If you want a light value of a hue, dilute the paint with a large amount of water. If you want a bright hue, you must dissolve more pigment by swirling your brush around in the cake of paint until you have dissolved a great deal of paint. The paint you apply to the paper can be as bright as the paint in the cake.

13. Cleaning a Paint Brush

Rinsing a paint brush under running water will not clean it completely. Paint will remain inside the bristles and cause the brush to lose its shape. Use the following procedure to help your brushes last a long time.

a. Rinse the thick paint out of the brush under running water.

b. Do not use hot water. Gently "paint" the brush over a cake of mild soap or dip it into a mild liquid detergent (Figure T.10).

c. Gently scrub the brush in the palm of your hand to work the soap into the center of the brush. This will remove paint that you did not realize was still in the brush (Figure T.11).

d. Rinse the brush under running water while you continue to scrub your palm.

e. Repeat steps b, c, and d.

▲ **FIGURE T.10**

▲ **FIGURE T.11**

▲ **FIGURE T.9**

▲ **FIGURE T.12**

f. When your brush is thoroughly rinsed, shape it into a point with your fingers (Figure T.12).

g. Place the brush in a container with the bristles up so it will keep its shape as it dries.

PRINTMAKING TIP

14. Making a Stamp Print

A stamp print is an easy way to make repetitive designs. The following are a few suggestions for making a stamp and printing with it. You may develop some other ideas after reading these hints. Remember, printing reverses your design, so if you use letters, be certain to cut or carve them backward.

- Cut a simple design into the flat surface of a rubber eraser with a knife that has a fine, precision blade.
- Glue yarn to a bottle cap or a jar lid.
- Glue found objects to a piece of corrugated cardboard. Make a design with paperclips, washers, nuts, leaves, feathers, or anything else you can find. Whatever object you use should have a fairly flat surface. Make a handle for the block with masking tape.
- Cut shapes out of a piece of inner tube material. Glue the

shapes to a piece of heavy cardboard.

There are several ways to apply ink or paint to a stamp:

- Roll water-base printing ink on the stamp with a soft brayer.
- Roll water-base printing ink on a plate and press the stamp into the ink.
- Apply tempera paint or school acrylic to the stamp with a bristle brush.

SCULPTING TIPS

15. Working with Clay

To make your work with clay go smoothly, always do the following:

a. Dip one or two fingers in water.

b. Spread the moisture from your fingers over your palms.

Never dip your hands in water. Too much moisture turns clay into mud.

16. Joining Clay

Use these methods for joining clay.

a. First, gather the materials you will need. These include clay, slip (a creamy mixture of clay and water), brush, a scoring tool (such as a fork), and clay tools.

b. Rough up or scratch the two surfaces to be joined (Figure T.13).

c. Apply slip to one of the two surfaces using a brush or your fingers (Figure T.14).

d. Gently press the two surfaces together so the slip oozes out of the joining seam (Figure T.15).

e. Using clay tools and/or your fingers, smooth away the slip that has oozed out of the seam (Figure T.16). You may wish to smooth out the seam as well,

▲ **FIGURE T.13**

▲ **FIGURE T.14**

▲ **FIGURE T.15**

▲ **FIGURE T.16**

or you may wish to leave it for decorative purposes.

17. Making a Pinch Pot

To make a pot using the pinch method, do the following:

a. Make a ball of clay by rolling it between your palms.

b. Set it on the working surface and make a hole in the top by pushing both thumbs into the clay. Stop pushing before your thumbs reach the bottom.

c. Begin to pinch the walls between your thumb and fingers, rotating the pot as you pinch.

d. Continue pinching and shaping the walls of the pot until they are an even thickness and the pot is the desired shape.

18. Using the Coil Technique

Collect all the materials you will need. These include clay, a cloth-covered board, slip and brush, scoring tool, small bowl of water, and pattern for a circular base.

a. Make a base by flattening a piece of clay to about ½ inch thick. Using the pattern, cut the base into a circle.

b. Begin a clay coil by shaping a small ball of clay into a long roll on the cloth-covered board until the roll is about ½ inch thick (Figure T.17). Your hands should be damp so the clay remains damp.

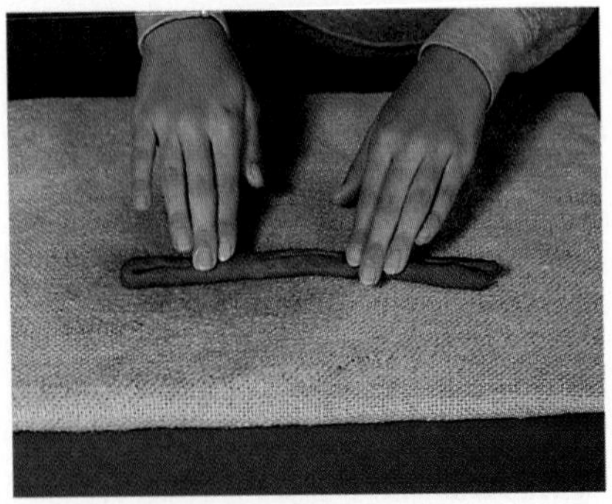

▲ **FIGURE T.17**

c. Make a circle around the edge of the clay base with the roll of clay. Cut the ends on a diagonal and join them so the seam does not show. Using scoring and slip, join this first coil to the base.

d. Make a second coil. If you want the pot to curve outward, place the second coil on the outer edge of the first coil. Place coil on the inner edge for an inward curve. Use proper joining techniques for all coils.

19. Papier-Mâché

Papier-mâché is a French term that means mashed paper. It refers to sculpting methods that use paper and liquid paste. The wet paper and paste material are molded over supporting structures such as a wad of dry paper or crumpled foil. The molded paper dries to a hard finish. Following are three basic methods for working with papier-mâché.

Pulp Method

a. Shred newspaper, paper towels, or tissue paper into tiny pieces and soak them in water overnight. (Do not use slick paper as it will not soften.)

b. Mash the paper in a strainer to remove the water or wring it out in a piece of cloth.

c. Mix the mashed paper with prepared paste or white glue until the material is the consistency of soft clay. Use the mixture to model small shapes.

d. When papier-mâché is dry, it can be sanded, and holes can be drilled through it.

Strip Method

a. Tear paper into strips.

b. Either dip the strips in a thick mixture of paste or rub paste on the strips with your fingers. Decide which method works best for you.

c. Use wide strips to cover wide forms. Very thin strips will lie flat on a small shape.

d. If you do not want the finished work to stick to the support structure, first cover the form with plastic wrap or a layer of wet newspaper strips. If you are going to remove the papier-mâché from the support structure, you need to apply five or six layers of strips. Rub your fingers over the strips so that no rough edges are left sticking up (Figure T.18). Change directions with each layer so that you can keep track of the number. If you are going to leave the papier-mâché over the support structure, then two or three layers may be enough.

Sheet Method

a. Brush or spread paste on a sheet of newspaper or newsprint (Figure T.19). Lay a second

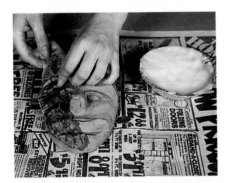

▲ **FIGURE T.18**

▲ **FIGURE T.19**

▲ **Figure T.20**

sheet on top of the first and smooth out the layers. Add another layer of paste and another sheet of paper. Repeat this process until you have four or five layers of paper. This method is good for making drapery on a figure (Figure T.20).

b. If you let the layers dry for a day until they are leathery, they can be cut and molded any way you wish. Newspaper strips dipped in the paste can be used to seal any cracks that may occur.

Support Structures

a. Dry newspaper can be wadded up and wrapped with string or tape (Figure T.21).

b. Wire armatures can be padded with rags before the outside shell of papier-mâché is added.

c. Found materials such as boxes, tubes, and plastic

▲ **Figure T.21**

bowls, can be arranged and taped together to form a base (Figure T.22).

d. For large figures, a wooden frame covered with chicken wire makes a good support. Push and pinch the wire into the shape you want.

▲ **Figure T.22**

20. Making a Paper Sculpture

Another name for paper sculpture is origami. The process originated in Japan and means "folding paper." Paper sculpture begins with a flat piece of paper. The paper is then curved or bent to produce more than a flat surface. Here are some ways to experiment with paper.

• **Scoring.** Place a square sheet of heavy construction paper on a flat surface. Position the ruler on the paper so that it is close to the center and parallel to the sides. Holding the ruler in place, run the point of a knife or a pair of scissors along one of the ruler's edges. Press down firmly but take care not to cut through the paper. Gently crease the paper along the line you made. Hold your paper with the crease facing upward. You can also score curved lines, but you must do this with gradually bending curves or wide arcs. If you try to make a tight curve, such as a semicircle, the

paper will not give. For a tight curve you will have to make cuts to relieve the tension.

• **Pleating.** Take a piece of paper and fold it 1 inch from the edge. Then fold the paper in the other direction. Continue folding back and forth.

• **Curling.** Hold one end of a long strip of paper with the thumb and forefinger of one hand. At a point right below where you are holding the strip, grip it lightly between the side of a pencil and the thumb of your other hand. In a quick motion, run the pencil along the strip. This will cause the strip to curl back on itself. Don't apply too much pressure, or the strip will tear. (See Figure T.23.)

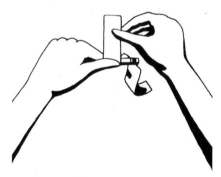

▲ **Figure T.23**

21. Making Paper

Papermaking is a process in which fibers are broken down and reformed as a sheet. In order to make paper, collect all the materials you will need. These include a food blender, two matching stretcher frames approximately 9 x 12 inches each, rustproof window screen slightly larger than the stretchers, staple gun, duct tape, Handi Wipes towels, large pan 5 to 8 inches deep, newspapers, assorted papers, and water.

a. Make the mold by stretching the screen over the frame, stapling it at the edges, and covering the rough edges with duct tape. The second frame is the deckle, the frame that keeps the pulp in place on the mold.

b. Tear paper into 1-inch squares. Put 4 cups water and $1/2$ cup paper scraps into the blender and blend for several minutes until the mixture is the consistency of watery cooked oatmeal.

c. Pour pulp into pan. Continue making pulp until there is

about 4 inches of pulp in the pan. Additional water may be added to aid in the papermaking process.

d. Make a pad of newspapers $1/4$ inch thick. Unfold Handi Wipes towels and lay one on the pad; this is the blotter.

e. Align deckle on top of mold. Stir pulp to suspend paper fibers. Scoop mold and deckle under surface of water and shake to align fibers. Lift to drain excess water.

f. Remove the deckle and flip the mold and pulp onto the blotter, pulp side down against the Handi Wipes towel. Blot back of molds with a sponge to remove excess water and to

compress the fibers. Remove the mold, using a rocking motion.

g. Lay another Handi Wipes towel on top of the sheet of paper and add more newspapers. Repeat the layering process.

h. Let paper dry slowly for 1–3 days. When dry, peel off the Handi Wipes.

i. To clean up, drain pulp through the mold or a sieve. Squeeze excess water from pulp and save pulp in a plastic bag for one to three days or discard it.

22. Basic Embroidery Stitches

The charts below and on the next page show the most common embroidery stitches.

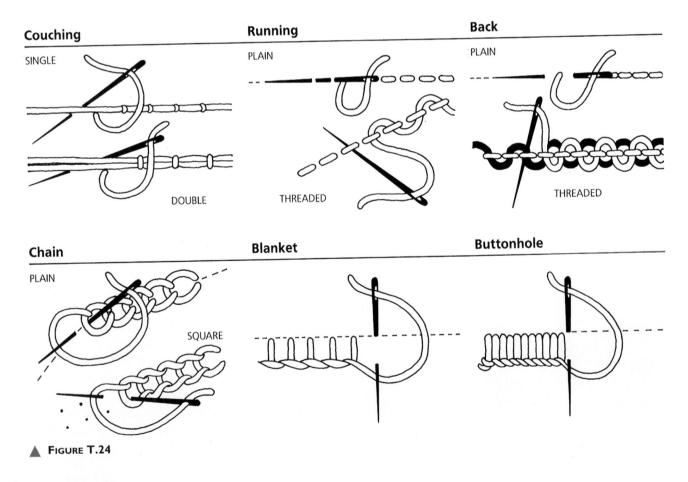

▲ **Figure T.24**

Feather

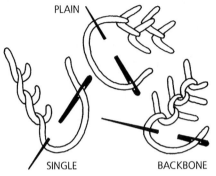

PLAIN

SINGLE

BACKBONE

Outline

Satin

Cross

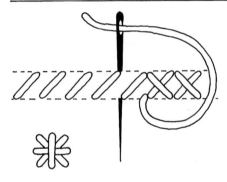

Knotted

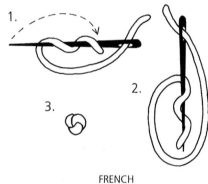

1.

2.

3.

FRENCH

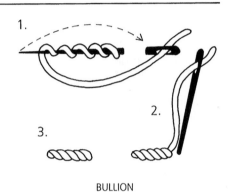

1.

2.

3.

BULLION

▲ **FIGURE T.24 (CONTINUED)**

23. Weaving Techniques

To make a cardboard loom, gather the materials you will need. They include cardboard, ruler, pencil, scissors, strong, thin yarn for warp, various yarns and fibers for weft, tapestry needle, comb, and dowel.

a. Measure and cut notches ¹/₄ inch apart and ¹/₂ inch deep on opposite sides of the cardboard.

b. Tape warp thread to back of loom. Bring it to the front through the top left notch. Pull it down to the bottom of the loom and pass it through the bottom left notch to the back. Move one notch to the right and continue until you reach

the last notch. Then tape the end of the warp thread to the back. (Figure T.25)

c. Start to weave at the bottom of the loom, using a thin yarn. The weft yarns are the horizontal yarns; the easiest way to pull the weft yarn through the warp

threads is to use an over-one-under-one motion. At the end of the row, reverse directions. (Figure T.26)

d. Do not pull the weft threads too tight. Let them balloon, or curve slightly upward (Figure T.27).

▲ **FIGURE T.25**

▲ **FIGURE T.26**

▲ **FIGURE T.27**

▲ **FIGURE T.28**

e. After weaving several rows, pack the weft threads with a comb (Figure T.28). The tighter the weave, the stronger it will be.

f. After there is about 1 inch of tight weave, begin varying weave and materials (Figure T.29). End the process with another inch of thin, tight weave.

g. Before removing the fabric from the loom, weave in the loose ends. Cut the warp threads from the loom carefully and tie two at a time so they will not unravel.

h. Tie or sew the finished fabric to a dowel.

▶ **FIGURE T.29**

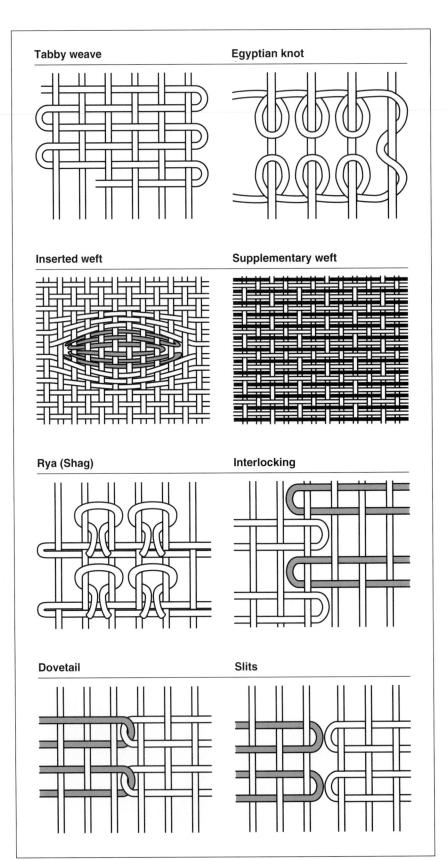

Tabby weave

Egyptian knot

Inserted weft

Supplementary weft

Rya (Shag)

Interlocking

Dovetail

Slits

24. Making a Coiled Basket

Mastering the technique of making a coiled basket takes practice. You will need *core* material (such as heavy cord), weft wrapping materials (such as yarns and fibers), a tapestry needle, scissors, and tape.

Coiling is a stitching technique in which the continuous coils of the *core* material are stitched together with a binding material called the *weft*. The first time you try this your binding and stitches probably will not look neat. Undo the work and begin again. You want to cover the core material completely, and all your weft binding and stitches must be even and tight.

a. Trim the end of the core so it tapers. Thread the tapestry needle with a 3-foot length of weft. Using the loose weft end, begin to wind it around the core starting about 2 inches from the end. Overlap the end as you wind to anchor it. Wind the weft to about 1/2 inch from the tapered end of the core (Figure T.30).

b. Bend the core, catch the tapered end, and make a loop (Figure T.31).

c. Continue winding for about 2 inches, being sure that the tapered core is attached securely to the solid section of core material. Push the tapestry needle through the center of the loop (Figure T.32).

d. Bend the core to form a coil and bring the weft between the core and the coil. (Figure T.33) Begin winding the weft around the core from front to back. You are now ready to begin the Lazy Squaw stitch.

e. Wind the weft around the core from front to back four times.

Then, bringing the weft from behind and over the core, push the needle into the center of the coil (Figure T.34). Pull tightly and hold. Continue to wrap the weft four times around the core and pull the fifth stitch into the center until you complete two coils. Hold them flat between your fingers while you work.

f. As the coiling progresses, you may wrap the weft more than four times between stitches. After the first two coils, you will no longer bring the stitch back to the center; just take it over two coils (Figure T.35). Always insert the needle from the front. This way you can see exactly where you are placing the needle. If you want to create a pattern of long stitches, this is essential.

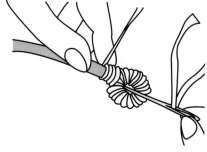

▲ **FIGURE T.32**

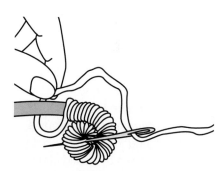

▲ **FIGURE T.33**

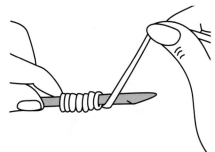

▲ **FIGURE T.30**

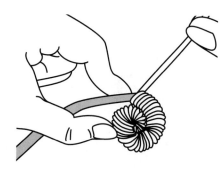

▲ **FIGURE T.34**

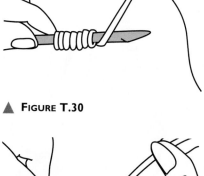

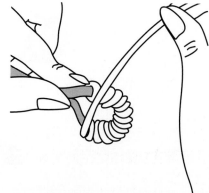

▲ **FIGURE T.31**

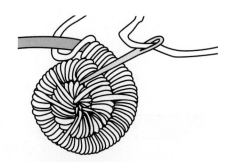

▲ **FIGURE T.35**

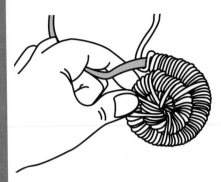

FIGURE T.36

g. Hold the coil with your left hand with the core material coming from the left, and wind the weft with your right hand so you do not tangle it with the core (Figure T.36). If you are left-handed, reverse the process. Always pull the weft very tight.

h. You will need to splice, or invisibly join, the ends of separate materials. To splice the core, taper the cut on the old and the new piece. Before working the weft, secure the spliced ends of the core by wrapping them with sewing thread or tape. Always hold the spliced area carefully until it is wrapped with the weft. Splice the weft during the wrapping, not during the stitching. Hold the tail ends of the old and the new weft together against the core as shown in Figure T.37. Wrap the new weft at least once before making a long stitch.

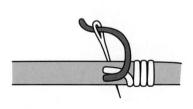

FIGURE T.37

i. When the base is the desired size, it is time to begin making the sides of the basket. If the side is to be perpendicular to the base, lay the first foundation coil directly on top of the last coil. If you want the basket to curve outward, place each new coil on the outer edge of the one below. To make an inward curve, place each coil on the inner edge of the previous coil. Use pressure from the nonstitching hand to keep the coils in place.

j. The best way to finish the basket is to taper the core and make several stitches around the last coil and the tapered coil. Then run the needle back through the wrapping stitches for about an inch and pull the weft thread through. Cut off the excess weft.

k. If you want to make a handle, simply wrap the end of the core until it is as long as you wish.

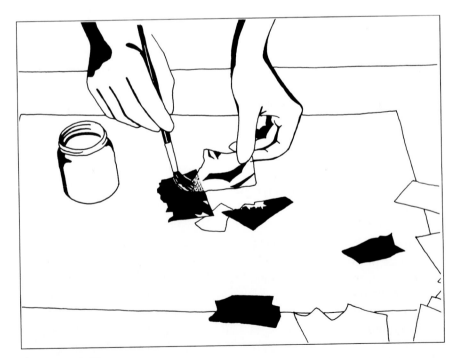

FIGURE T.38

Then attach it to the other side of the top of the basket following the instructions from Step j.

25. Making a Tissue Paper Collage

For your first experience with tissue, make a free design with the tissue colors. Start with the lightest colors of tissue first and save the darkest for last. It is difficult to change the color of dark tissue by overlapping it with other colors. If one area becomes too dark, you might cut out a piece of white paper, glue it over the dark area carefully, and apply new colors over the white area.

a. Apply a coat of adhesive to the area where you wish to place the tissue.

b. Place the tissue down carefully over the wet area (Figure T.38). Don't let your fingers get wet.

c. Then add another coat of adhesive over the tissue. If your brush picks up any color from the wet tissue, rinse your brush in water and let it dry before using it again.

d. Experiment by overlapping colors. Allow the tissue to wrinkle to create textures as you apply it. Be sure that all the loose edges of tissue are glued down.

DISPLAY TIPS

26. Making a Mat

You can add appeal to an artwork by making a mat, using the following steps.

a. Gather the materials you will need. These include a metal rule, a pencil, mat board, cardboard backing, a sheet of heavy cardboard to protect your work surface, a mat knife with a sharp blade, and wide masking tape.

b. Wash your hands. Mat board should be kept very clean.

c. Measure the height and width of the work to be matted. Decide how large a border you want for your work. (A border of approximately 2½ inches on three sides with 3 inches on the bottom is aesthetically pleasing.) Your work will be behind the window you will cut.

d. Plan for the opening, or window, to be ¼ inch smaller on all sides than the size of your work. For example, if your work measures 9 by 12 inches, the mat window should measure 8½ inches (9 inches minus ¼ inch times two) by 11½ inches (12 inches minus ¼ inch times two.) Using your metal rule and pencil, lightly draw your window rectangle on the back of the board 2½ inches from the top and left edge of the mat. (See Figure T.39). Add a 2½-inch

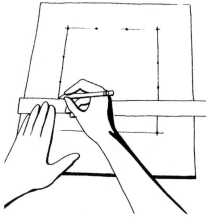

▲ **FIGURE T.39**

border to the right of the window and a 3-inch border to the bottom, lightly drawing cutting guidelines.

Note: If you are working with metric measurements, the window should overlap your work by 0.5 cm (centimeters) on all sides. Therefore, if your work measures 24 by 30 cm, the mat window measures 23 cm $(24-[2 \times 0.5])$ by 29 cm $(30 - [2 \times 0.5])$.

e. Place the sheet of heavy, protective cardboard on your work surface. Place the mat board, pencil marks up, over the cardboard. Holding the metal rule firmly in place, score the first line with your knife. Always place the metal rule so that your blade is on the inside of the frame. (See Figure T.40.) In case you make an error you will cut into the window hole or the extra mat that is not used for the frame. Do not try to cut through the board with one stroke. By the third or fourth stroke, you should be able to cut through the board easily.

f. Working in the same fashion, score and cut through the board along all the window lines. Be careful not to go

beyond the lines. Remove the window.

g. Cut a cardboard backing for your artwork that is slightly smaller than the overall size of your mat. Using a piece of broad masking tape, hinge the back of the mat to the backing. (See Figure T.41.) Position your artwork between the backing and the mat and attach it with tape. Anchor the frame to the cardboard with a few pieces of rolled tape.

▲ **FIGURE T.40**

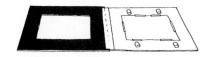

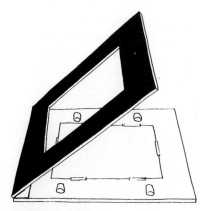

▲ **FIGURE T.41**

27. Mounting a Two-Dimensional Work

Mounting pictures that you make gives them a professional look. To mount a work, do the following:

a. Gather the materials you will need. These include a yardstick, a pencil, poster board, a knife with a very sharp blade, a sheet of newspaper, and rubber cement.

b. Measure the height and width of the work to be mounted. Decide how large a border you want around the work. Plan your mount size using the work's measurements. To end up with a 3-inch border, for example, make your mount 6 inches wider and higher than your work. Record the measurements for your mount.

c. Using your yardstick and pencil, lightly draw your mount rectangle on the back of the poster board. Measure from the edges of the poster board. If you have a large paper cutter available, you may use it to cut your mount.

d. Place the sheet of heavy cardboard on your work surface. Place the poster board, pencil marks up, over the cardboard. Holding the yardstick firmly in place along one line, score the line with your knife. Do not try to cut through the board with one stroke. By the third try, you should be able to cut through the board.

e. Place the artwork on the mount. Using the yardstick, center the work. Mark each corner with a dot. (See Figure T.42)

▲ **Figure T.42**

▲ **Figure T.43**

f. Place the artwork, face down, on a sheet of newspaper. Coat the back of the work with rubber cement. (Safety Note: Always use rubber cement in a room with plenty of ventilation.) If your mount is to be permanent, skip to Step h.

g. Line up the corners of your work with the dots on the mounting board. Smooth the work into place. Skip to Step i.

h. After coating the back of your artwork, coat the poster board with rubber cement. Be careful not to add cement to the border area. Have a partner hold your artwork in the air by the two top corners. Once the two glued surfaces meet, you will not be able to change the position of the work. Grasp the lower two corners. Carefully lower the work to the mounting board. Line up the two corners with the bottom dots. Little by little, lower the work into place (Figure T.43). Press it smooth.

i. To remove any excess cement, create a small ball of dry rubber cement. Use the ball of rubber cement to pick up excess cement.

28. Working with Glue

When applying glue, always start at the center of the surface you are coating and work outward.

- When gluing papers together don't use a lot of glue, just a dot will do. Use dots in the corners and along the edges. Press the two surfaces together. Keep dots at least $\frac{1}{2}$ inch in from the edge of your paper.

- Handle a glued surface carefully with only your fingertips. Make sure your hands are clean before pressing the glued surface into place.

- Note: The glue should be as thin as possible. Thick or beaded glue will create ridges on your work.

Many artists, both students and teachers, come into daily contact with dangerous, possibly deadly materials. The unfortunate truth is that many art supplies contain high levels of chemicals, such as hexane, lead, toluene, and asbestos, and many people are unaware of the danger that these substances pose, both to art students and to teachers. In fact, the danger to art teachers, who are often exposed to toxins for several hours a day for many years, is often greater than to the students. Therefore, it is essential that all art teachers and students become aware of the potential hazards in using art materials.

Many art supplies contain materials that can cause acute illness (that is, a severe sudden illness that can be caused by a single exposure to a toxic substance and result in permanent disability or death). Long-term exposure to materials in many other art supplies can cause chronic illness (which develops gradually after repeated exposure) or cancer. Other chemicals in art supplies are sensitizers, causing allergies, particularly in children. Lead, for example, is acutely toxic and can be found in such commonly used supplies as stencil paint, oil paint, some acrylics, gessoes, ceramic glazes, copper enamels, and automotive paint in spray cans. Many highly toxic hydrocarbon-based solvents, including methyl alcohol, are used in school art programs. Other widely used art materials, such as preservatives, formaldehyde, epoxy glues, and dichromates, can contain dangerous chemicals like cadmium, nickel, silica, and pesticides.

There are three ways in which such chemicals can enter the body: absorption, inhalation, and ingestion. They can be absorbed through the skin from cuts or scrapes, resulting in burns or rashes, or into the bloodstream, moving to and damaging other parts of the body. Chemical irritants can be inhaled, causing lung problems like bronchitis and emphysema. Inhaling small particles, like the free silica in clay dust, can cause pulmonary fibrosis or asthma. Chemicals can be ingested through touching the mouth with the hands or fingers while working with supplies or unconsciously placing tools like paint brushes in or near the mouth. Since hazardous substances can easily enter the body, it is extremely important to make sure that the materials used are safe and that they are used safely.

Labeling

Labeling can provide information on any potentially dangerous art supplies, but teachers need to be aware of what various labels mean. The label *nontoxic,* for example, does not guarantee a product's safety. According to federal regulations, toxicity means that a single exposure can be fatal to adults. The effect on young people, who are more likely to be harmed by dangerous substances, is not considered in this definition. Also, the chance of developing chronic or long-term illnesses is not addressed by the legal definition of toxicity. Repeated exposure to nontoxic materials is not always safe. Many dangerous substances, such as asbestos, can legally be defined as nontoxic. Also, some art supplies, particularly those manufactured by small or foreign companies, may be improperly labeled as nontoxic.

Not all products whose labels provide chemical components, but have no warnings or list no information at all, are safe to use. Since manufacturers are not required to disclose ingredients, products without this information or warnings are potentially hazardous.

For more complete information on the presence of hazardous substances in art supplies, teachers may request a Material Safety Data Sheet (OSHA Form 20) from the manufacturer. This sheet provides information on potential heath and fire hazards, a list of chemicals that might react dangerously with the product, and a list of all ingredients for which industrial standards exist. The manufacturer should supply this sheet on request, and a local public health official or poison control center technician can help interpret the information.

Art teachers can also take advantage of voluntary labeling standards developed by the art materials industry. The Art and Craft Materials Institute (ACMI) administers a voluntary testing and labeling program that helps to insure the safety of those who work with art materials. This system uses the labels CP, AP, and HL.

CP (Certified Product) and AP (Approved Product) labels are used mainly on products designed for younger children, while HL (Health Label) is used on products intended for older students and adults. Products labeled CP, AP, or HL (Nontoxic) are certified in a program of toxicological evaluation by a medical expert to contain no materials in sufficient quantities to be toxic or injurious to humans or to cause acute or chronic health problems. Products labeled CP, in addition, meet specific requirements of material, workmanship, working qualities, and color. HL (Cautions Required) means that the product is certified to be properly labeled in a program of toxicological evaluation by a medical expert. The Art and Craft Materials Institute makes available a list of institute-certified products. For a copy, or for more information on the institute's certification program, teachers can write to:

The Art and Craft Materials Institute
715 Boylston St.
Boston, MA 02116

Safety Rules

There are certain guidelines to be followed in selecting and using art supplies. Perhaps the most important is to know what the materials are made of and what potential hazards exist. If a material is improperly labeled, or if adequate information cannot be obtained about it, don't use it. The following rules are also helpful:

- Be sure that all materials used by younger students (ages 12 and under) have the CP or AP label and that materials used by older students and adults are marked HL.
- Don't use acids, alkalies, bleaches, or any product that will stain skin or clothing.
- Don't use aerosol cans because the spray can injure lungs.
- Use dust-producing materials (such as pastels, clays, plasters, chalks, powdered tempera, pigments, dyes, and instant papier-mâché, except the premixed cellulose type) with care in a well-ventilated area (or better yet, don't use them at all).
- Don't use solvents (including lacquers, paint thinners, turpentines, shellacs, solvent-based inks, rubber cement, and permanent markers) in the art room.
- Don't use found or donated materials unless the ingredients are known.
- Don't use old materials. Many art supplies formerly contained highly dangerous substances, such as arsenic, or raw lead compounds, or high levels of asbestos. Older solvents may contain chloroform or carbon tetrachloride.

Working conditions in the art room also affect safety. A disorderly art room leads to unsafe conditions, particularly when there are many people working close to each other. Controlling the buildup of litter and dust, insuring that tools are in good condition, and keeping workspace reasonably organized not only help prevent common accidents but also make it easier to recognize and eliminate other hazards. An orderly art room is absolutely essential to the students' and teacher's safety.

CHRONOLOGY OF ARTWORKS

Vermeer, Jan, Dutch, 1632–1675, painter
Girl with the Red Hat, c. 1665/1666, 362, Fig.13.13
Vermeer, Jan, Dutch, 1632–1675, painter
The Astronomer, 1668, 128, Fig. 5.38

1700–1799

Watteau, Antoine, French, 1684–1721, painter
Embarkment for Cythera, 1717–19, 363, Fig. 13.14
Hua Yen, Chinese, c. 1682–1765
Conversation in Autumn, 1762, 328, Fig. 12.12
Canaletto, Italian, 1697–1768, painter
Ascension Day Festival at Venice, 1766, 43, Fig. 3.4
Copley, John Singleton, American, 1737–1815, painter
Paul Revere, c. 1768–70, 268, Fig. 10.20
Fragonard, Jean-Honoré, French, 1732–1806, painter
A Game of Hot Cockles, 1767–73, 236, Fig. 9.15
Gainsborough, Thomas, English, 1727–1788, painter
The Blue Boy, c. 1770, 364, Fig. 13.15
David, Jacques-Louis, French, 1748–1825, painter
The Death of Socrates, 1787, 366, Fig. 13.17
Korin, Ogata, Japanese, Edo period (18th century), silk painter
Waves at Matsushima, date unknown, 196–197
Artist Unknown, African, Akan people
Necklace, 19th century, 336, Fig. 12.22

1800–1899

Artist Unknown, Inuit
Mask of Moon Goddess, before 1900, 342, Fig. 12.29
Goya, Francisco, Spanish, 1746–1828, painter
The Third of May, 1814, 365, Fig. 13.16
Hokusai, Katsushika, Japanese, 1760–1849, printmaker, painter
The Great Wave at Kanagawa, 1823–29, 238, Fig. 9.18
Hokusai, Katsushika, Japanese, 1760–1849, printmaker, painter
The Kirifuri Waterfall at Mt. Kurokami, Shimozuke Province, ca. 1831, 226, Fig. 9.1
Turner, Joseph M. W., English, 1775–1851, painter
Snowstorm: Steamboat off a Harbours Mouth, 1842, 368, Fig. 13.19
Bonheur, Rosa, French, 1822–1899, painter
The Horse Fair, 1853–55, 201, Fig. 8.3
Inness, George, American, 1825–1894, painter
The Lackawanna Valley, c. 1856, 11, Fig. 1.9
Delacroix, Eugène, French, 1798–1863, painter
Arabs Skirmishing in the Mountains, 1863, 367, Fig. 13.18
Brady, Mathew, American, 1823–1896, photographer
Civil War, c. 1865, 369, Fig. 13.21
Artist Unknown, Northwest coast region, Haida
Haida totem pole, c. 1870, 343, Fig. 12.30
Straus, Meyer, American, 19th century, painter
Bayou Teche, 1870, 6, Fig. 1.2
Manet, Édouard, French, 1832–1883, painter
The Railway, 1873, 369, Fig. 13.20
Eakins, Thomas, American, 1844–1916, painter
Baby at Play, 1876, 234, Fig. 9.12

Renoir, Pierre Auguste, French, 1841–1919, painter
Madame Henriot, 1876, 177, Fig. 7.7
Cassatt, Mary, American, 1845–1926, painter
The Tea, about 1880, 244, Fig. 9.24
Degas, Edgar, French, 1834–1917, painter, sculptor
The Little Fourteen-Year-Old Dancer, 1880, 181, Fig. 7.12
Black Hawk, Chief, Native American, 19th century, draftsman
Crow Men in Ceremonial Dress, 1880–81, 200, Fig. 8.2
Bashkirtseff, Marie, Russian, 1860–1884, painter
A Meeting, 1884, 301, Fig. 11.21
Morisot, Berthe, French, 1841–1895, painter
In the Dining Room, 1886, 292, Fig. 11.9
Rodin, Auguste, French, 1840–1917, sculptor
The Burghers of Calais, 1886, 297, Fig. 11.14
Rousseau, Henri, French, 1844–1910, painter
Carnival Evening, 1886, 312, Fig. 11.28
van Gogh, Vincent, Dutch, 1853–1890, painter
Café Terrace at Night, 1888, 293, Fig. 11.10
van Gogh, Vincent, Dutch, 1853–1890, painter
Sunflowers, 1888, 178, Fig. 7.8
van Gogh, Vincent, Dutch, 1853–1890, painter
The Starry Night, 1889, 373, Fig. 13.25
Artist Unknown, Native American
Feather Bonnet, c. 1890, 345, Fig. 12.33
Artist Unknown, Native American, Navajo
Saddle blanket, c. 1890, 344, Fig. 12.32
van Gogh, Vincent, Dutch, 1853–1890, painter
Houses at Auvers, 1890, 4, Fig. 1.1
Sullivan, Louis, American, 1856–1924, architect
Wainwright Building, 1890–91, 56, Fig. 3.17
Cassatt, Mary, American, 1845–1926, painter
The Letter, 1891, 350, Fig. 13.1
Gauguin, Paul, French, 1848–1903, painter
Faaturuma (Melancholic), 1891, 372, Fig. 13.24
Monet, Claude, French, 1840–1926, painter
Poplars, 1891, 153, Fig. 6.24
Monet, Claude, French, 1840–1926, painter
The Four Trees, 1891, 153, Fig. 6.25
Homer, Winslow, American, 1836–1910, painter
Sketch for 'Hound and Hunter,' 1892, 47, Fig. 3.8
Homer, Winslow, American, 1836–1910, painter
Hound and Hunter, 1892, 47, Fig. 3.9
Gauguin, Paul, French, 1848–1903, painter
Tahitians, c. 1891–93, 265, Fig. 10.17
Bonnard, Pierre, French, 1867–1947, painter, graphic artist
Family Scene, 1893, 266, Fig. 10.18
Sullivan, Louis, American, 1856–1924, architect
Elevator Grille, 1893–94, 204, Fig. 8.7
Beaux, Cecilia, American, 1863–1942, painter
Ernesta (Child with Nurse), 1894, 294, Fig. 11.11
Cézanne, Paul, French, 1839–1906, painter
The Basket of Apples, 1895, 155, Fig. 6.27
Cézanne, Paul, French, 1839–1906, painter
Apples and Oranges, date unknown,132, Fig. 5.40
Hiroshige, Andō, Japanese, 1797–1858, printmaker
Evening Rain on the Karasaki Pine, date unknown, 330, Fig. 12.15

1900–1949

Cézanne, Paul, French, 1839–1906, painter
Le Chateau Noir, 1900–04, 371, Fig. 13.23

Cassatt, Mary, American, 1845–1926, painter
Margot in Blue, 1902, 140, Fig. 6.8

Picasso, Pablo, Spanish, 1881–1973, painter, sculptor
The Old Guitarist, 1903, 270, Fig. 10.24

Picasso, Pablo, Spanish, 1881–1973, painter, sculptor
The Tragedy, 1903, 145, Fig. 6.13

Matisse, Henri, French, 1869–1954, painter
Femme au Chapeau (Woman with the Hat), 1905, 164, Fig. 6.33

Hodler, Ferdinand, Swiss, 1853–1918, painter
James Vibert, Sculptor, 1907, 240, Fig. 9.20

Kirchner, Ernst Ludwig, German, 1880–1938, painter
Seated Woman, 1907, 35, Fig. 2.9

Munch, Edvard, Norwegian, 1863–1944, painter, printmaker
The Sick Child, 1907, 7, Fig. 1.3

Monet, Claude, French, 1840–1926, painter
Palazzo da Mula, Venice, 1908, 370, Fig. 13.22

Brancusi, Constantin, Rumanian, 1876–1957, sculptor
The Kiss, c. 1908, 104, Fig. 5.9

Wright, Frank Lloyd, American, 1867–1959, architect
Armchair, 1908, 119, Fig. 5.31

Balla, Giacomo, Italian, 1871–1958, painter
Street Light, 1909, 210, Fig. 8.17

Bellows, George, American, 1882–1925, painter, printmaker
Both Members of This Club, 1909, 258, Fig. 10.6

Artist Unknown, Native American, Pueblo
Water jar, 1910, 343, Fig. 12.31

Picasso, Pablo, Spanish, 1881–1973, painter, sculptor
Nude Woman, 1910, 375, Fig. 13.27

Marc, Franz, German, 1880–1916, painter
The Large Blue Horses, 1911, 154, Fig. 6.26

Balla, Giacomo, Italian, 1871–1958, painter
Dynamism of a Dog on a Leash, 1912, 212, Fig. 8.19

Hassam, Childe, American, 1859–1935, painter, printmaker
Jelly Fish, 1912, 157, Fig. 6.29

Huntington, Anna Hyatt, American, 1876–1973, sculptor
Riders to the Sea, 1912, 120, Fig. 5.33

Bellows, George, American, 1882–1925, painter, printmaker
Cliff Dwellers, 1913, 223, Fig. 8.26

Chagall, Marc, Russian, 1887–1985, painter
Paris Through the Window, 1913, 20, Fig. 1.18

Delauney, Robert, French, 1885–1941, painter
Sun, Tower, Airplane, 1913, 134, Fig. 6.1

Marc, Franz, German, 1880–1916, painter
Stables, 1913, 66–67

Chagall, Marc, Russian, 1887–1985, painter
Birthday, 1915, 271, Fig. 10.25

Keyser, Louisa (Dat So La Lee), Native American, 1850–1925, weaver
Basket, c. 1917–18, 218, Fig. 8.24

Picasso, Pablo, Spanish, 1881–1973, painter, sculptor
Still Life, 1918, 316–317

Kirchner, Ernst Ludwig, German, 1880–1938, painter
Winter Landscape in Moonlight, 1919, 34, Fig. 2.8

Stella, Joseph, Italian American, 1877–1946, painter
The Voice of the City of New York Interpreted: The Bridge, 1920–22, 68, Fig. 4.1

Kollwitz, Käthe, German, 1867–1945, painter, printmaker, graphic artist
Self-Portrait, 1921, 374, Fig. 13.26

Lachaise, Gaston, French, 1882–1935, sculptor
Walking Woman, 1922, 272, Fig. 10.26

Brancusi, Constantin, Rumanian, 1876–1957, sculptor
Torso of a Young Man, 1924, 118, Fig. 5.30

Murphy, Gerald, American, 1888–1964, painter
Watch, 1925, 248, Fig. 9.26

Rivera, Diego, Mexican, 1886–1957, painter, muralist
Flower Day, 1925, 229, Fig. 9.5

Bishop, Isabel, American, 1902–1988, painter
Self-Portrait, 1927, 283

O'Keeffe, Georgia, American, 1887–1986, painter
Oriental Poppies, 1927, 2–3

O'Keeffe, Georgia, American, 1887–1986, painter
White Rose With Larkspur, No. 2, 1927, 240, Fig. 9.21

Benton, Thomas Hart, American, 1882–1975, painter
Country Dance, 1929, 79, Fig. 4.18

Hopper, Edward, American, 1882–1967, painter
Early Sunday Morning, 1930. 77, Fig. 4.16

van Alen, William, American, 1882–1954, architect
Chrysler Building, 1930, 206, Fig. 8.9

Wood, Grant, American, 1892–1942, painter
American Gothic, 1930, 12, Fig. 1.10

Calder, Alexander, American, 1898–1976, sculptor
Varese, 1931, 84, Fig. 4.25

Dali, Salvador, Spanish, 1904–1989, painter
The Persistence of Memory, 1931, 375, Fig. 13.28

Orozco, José Clemente, Mexican, 1883–1949, painter
Barricade, 1931, 28, Fig. 2.3

Carr, Emily, Canadian, 1871–1945, painter
Forest, British Columbia, 1931–32, 298, Fig. 11.17

Jones, Lois Mailou, African-American, 1905–1998, painter
The Ascent of Ethiopia, 1932, 386, Fig. 13.42

Albright, Ivan, American, 1897–1983, painter
The Farmer's Kitchen, 1933–34, 177, Fig. 7.6

Münter, Gabriele, German, 1877–1962, painter
Breakfast of the Birds, 1934, 18, Fig. 1.17

Cram, Ralph Adams, American, 1863–1942, architect
Federal Reserve Building (with Ferguson and Goodhue), 1935, 230, Fig. 9.7

Ferguson, American, 20th century, architect
Federal Reserve Building (with Cram and Goodhue), 1935, 230, Fig. 9.7

Goodhue, Betram, American, 1869–1924, architect
Federal Reserve Building (with Cram and Ferguson), 1935, 230, Fig. 9.7

Lee, Doris, American, b. 1905, printmaker, painter
Thanksgiving, 1935, 116, Fig. 5.27

Abbott, Bernice, American, b. 1898, photographer
The Night View, 1936, 202, Fig. 8.4

Ruiz, Antonio M., Mexican, 1897–1964, painter
School Children on Parade, 1936, 214, Fig. 8.22

Wright, Frank Lloyd, American, 1867–1959, architect
Fallingwater House, 1936, 301, Fig. 11.20

Kahlo, Frida, Mexican, 1907–1954, painter
Self Portrait Dedicated to Leon Trotsky, 1937, 239, Fig. 9.19

Matisse, Henri, French, 1869–1954, painter
Purple Robe and Anemones, 1937, 24, Fig. 2.1

Roualt, Georges, French, 1871–1958, painter
Christ and the Apostles, 1937–38, 74, Fig. 4.12

Bishop, Isabel, American, 1902–1988, painter
Waiting, 1938, 282, Fig. 10.32

Escher, M. C., Dutch, 1898–1972, printmaker
Day and Night, 1938, 220, Fig. 8.25

Walkus, George, Kwakiutl, 20th century, maskmaker
Secret Society Mask (Four Headed Cannibal Spirit), 1938, 273, Fig. 10.27

Berman, Eugene, Russian-American, 1899–1972, painter, stage designer
Vendeur de Chapeaux, 1939, 43, Fig. 3.3

Calder, Alexander, American, 1898–1976, sculptor
Lobster Trap and Fish Tail, 1939, 213, Fig. 8.21

Carr, Emily, Canadian, 1871–1945, painter
Above the Trees, 1939, 149, Fig. 6.21

Savage, Augusta, African-American, 20th century, sculptor
Lift Every Voice and Sing, 1939, 209, Fig. 8.15

Apel, Marie, English, 1880–1970, sculptor
Grief, 1940, 119, Fig. 5.32

Davis, Stuart, American, 1894–1964, painter
Hot Still Scape for Six Colors—7th Avenue Style, 1940, 156, Fig. 6.28

Johnson, William H., African-American, 1901–1970, painter
Jitterbugs, c. 1941, 88, Fig. 4.27

O'Keeffe, Georgia, American, 1887–1986, painter
Red Hills and Bones, 1941, 30, Fig. 2.5

Rivera, Diego, Mexican, 1886–1957, painter, muralist
Self-Portrait, 1941, 229

Ernst, Max, German (in America after 1941), 1891–1976, painter
The Eye of Silence, 1943–44, 184, Fig. 7.16

Woodruff, Hale, American, b. 1900, painter
Poor Man's Cotton, 1944, 203, Fig. 8.6

Siqueiros, David Alfaro, Mexican, 1896–1974, painter
Self-Portrait (El Coronelazo), 1945, 264, Fig. 10.14

Lawrence, Jacob, African-American, b. 1917, painter
Children at Play, 1947, 80, Fig. 4.19

Pollock, Jackson, American, 1912–1956, painter
Cathedral, 1947, 14, Fig. 1.13

Tamayo, Rufino, Mexican, 1899–1991, painter
Girl Attacked by a Strange Bird, 1947, 141, Fig. 6.9

Hepworth, Barbara, English, 1903–1975, sculptor
Pendour, 1947–48, 102, Fig. 5.7

Hopper, Edward, American, 1882–1967, painter
First Row Orchestra, 1951, 235, Fig. 9.13

Wright, Frank Lloyd, American, 1867–1959, architect
The David Wright House, 1951, 377, Fig. 13.30

1950–1974

Wright, Frank Lloyd, American, 1867–1959, architect
Stained-glass Window, date unknown, 235, Fig. 9.14

Lange, Dorothea, American, 1895–1965, photojournalist
Migrant Mother, date unknown, 57, Fig. 3.18

Wright, Frank Lloyd, American, 1867–1959, architect
Taliesin West, date unknown, 182, Fig. 7.13

Pereira, Irene Rice, American, 1907–1971, painter
Untitled, 1951, 289, Fig. 11.3

Le Corbusier, Swiss, 1887–1965, architect
Unite d'Habitation, 1947–52, 259, Fig. 10.7

White, Charles, African-American, 1918–1979, painter
Preacher, 1952, 94, Fig. 4.30

Rauschenberg, Robert, American, b. 1925, painter
Red Painting, 1953, 290, Fig. 11.4

Tooker, George, American, b. 1920, painter
Highway, 1953, 96, Fig. 5.1

Shahn, Ben, Russian-American, 1898–1959, painter
The Blind Botanist, 1954, 117, Fig. 5.29

Rothko, Mark, Russian-American, 1903–1970, painter
Orange and Yellow, 1956, 380, Fig. 13.24

Tamayo, Rufino, Mexican, 1899–1991, painter
Toast to the Sun, 1956, 148, Fig. 6.20

Hofmann, Hans, German (born in America), 1880–1966, painter
Flowering Swamp, 1957, 378, Fig. 13.31

Picasso, Pablo, Spanish, 1881–1973, painter, sculptor
Las Meninas (after Velásquez), 1957, 14, Fig. 1.14

Flack, Audrey, American, b. 1931, painter, sculptor
Self-Portrait: The Memory, 1958, 82, Fig. 4.23

Johnson, Philip, American, b. 1906, architect
Seagram Building (with Mies van der Rohe), 1958, 382, Fig. 13.38

Mies van der Rohe, Ludwig, American, 1886–1969, architect
Seagram Building (with Johnson), 1958, 382, Fig. 13.38

Smith, David, American, 1906–1965, painter
Cubi IX, 1961, 101, Fig. 5.6

Dali, Salvador, Spanish, 1904–1989, painter
The Elephants (Design for the Opera La Dama Spagnola e il Cavaliere Romano), 1961, 280, Fig. 10.31

Escher, M. C., Dutch, 1898–1972, printmaker
Waterfall, 1961, 105, Fig. 5.10

Johns, Jasper, American, b. 1930, painter
Map, 1961, 296, Fig. 11.13

Glarner, Fritz, Swiss-American, 1899–1972 painter
Relational Painting #93, 1962, 147, Fig. 6.17

Lichtenstein, Roy, American, b. 1923, painter
Blam, 1962, 379, Fig. 13.32

Marisol, Venezuelan (in America since 1950), b. 1930, sculptor
The Family, 1962, 268, Fig. 10.21

Nevelson, Louise, American, 1899–1988, sculptor
Dawn, 1962, 300, Fig. 11.19

Warhol, Andy, American, 1928–1987, painter, printmaker
Marilyn Monroe's Lips, 1962, 207, Fig. 8.11

Frankenthaler, Helen, American, b. 1928, painter
The Bay, 1963, 111, Fig. 5.16
Loewy, Raymond, French-American, b. 1893, designer
Avanti, 1963, 395, Fig. 14.10
Poons, Larry, American, b.1937, painter
Orange Crush, 1963, 379, Fig. 13.33
Hampton, James, African–American, 1909–1965, sculptor
The Throne of the Third Heaven of the Nations Millennium General Assembly, c. 1950–64, 186, Fig. 7.17
Krasner, Lee, American, b. 1908, painter
The Springs, 1964, 291, Fig. 11.6
Kurelek, William, American, b. 1927, painter
Manitoba Party, 1964, 110, Fig. 5.15
Bearden, Romare, American, 1914–1988, painter, printmaker
Prevalence of Ritual: The Baptism, 1964, 158, Fig. 6.30
Anuszkiewicz, Richard, American, b. 1930, painter
Iridescence, 1965, 146, Fig. 6.15
Magritte, René, Belgian, 1898–1967, painter
The Blank Signature, 1965, 126, Fig. 5.37
Sutej, Miroslav, Yugoslavian, b. 1936, lithographer
Ultra AB, 1966, 288, Fig. 11.2
Evans, Minnie, African-American, 1890–1987, painter
Design Made at Airlie Gardens, 1967, 410–411
Jessup, Georgia Mills, American, b. 1926, painter
Rainy Night, 1967, 302, Fig. 11.22
Safdie, Moshe, Israeli, b. 1938, architect
Habitat, 1967, 382, Fig. 13.39
Stella, Frank, American, b. 1936, painter, sculptor
Agbatana III, 1968, 380, Fig. 13.35
Thomas, Alma, American, 1891–1978, painter
Iris, Tulips, Jonquils, and Crocuses, 1969, 26, Fig. 2.2
Twiggs, Leo, African-American, b. 1934, batik painter
The Blue Wall, 1969, 29, Fig. 2.4
Catlett, Elizabeth, African-American, b. 1915, printmaker, sculptor, painter
Sharecropper, 1970, 48, Fig. 3.10
Hunt, Henry, Canadian Native American, Kwakiutl, 1923–1985, sculptor
K'umugwe' (Komokwa) Mask, 1970, 276, Fig. 10.29
Neel, Alice, American, 1900–1984, painter
Loneliness, 1970, 292, Fig. 11.8
Utzon, Joern, Australian, b. 1918, architect
Sydney Opera House, 1959–72, 286, Fig. 11.1
Estes, Richard, American, b. 1932, painter
Paris Street Scene, 1972, 381, Fig. 13.27
Johns, Jasper, American, b. 1930, painter
Cups 4 Picasso, 1972, 103, Fig. 5.8
Fish, Janet, American, b. 1939, painter
Oranges, 1973, 176, Fig. 7.5
Neel, Alice, American, 1900–1984, painter
Linda Nochlin and Daisy, 1973, 250, Fig. 9.27
Neel, Alice, American, 1900–1984, painter
Still Life, Rose of Sharon, 1973, 74, Fig. 4.13
Ringgold, Faith, African-American, b. 1930, painter, soft sculptor
Mrs. Jones and Family, 1973, 278, Fig. 10.30

Andrews, Benny, African-American, b. 1930, painter
The Scholar, 1974, 81, Fig. 4.20
Flack, Audrey, American, b. 1931, painter, sculptor
Leonardo's Lady, 1974, 192, Fig. 7.20
Paley, Albert Raymond, American, b. 1944, sculptor
Portal Gates, 1974, 78, Fig. 4.17
Thomas Hart Benton, American, 1882–1975, painter
The Sources of Country Music, 1975, 376, Fig. 13.29
Bishop, Isabel, American, 1902–1988, painter
Head #5, no date, 45, Fig. 3.7

1975–

Bearden, Romare, American, 1914–1988, painter, printmaker
Return of Ulysses, 1976, 13, Fig. 1.11
Oldenburg, Claes, American, b. 1929, painter, sculptor
Clothespin, 1976, 261, Fig. 10.9
Chagall, Marc, Russian, 1887–1985, painter
The American Windows, 1977, 136, Fig. 6.2
Houser, Allan, Native American, 1914–1994, sculptor
Coming of Age, 1977, 209, Fig. 8.16
Dillon, Leo and Diane, American, both b. 1933, graphic artists
A Wrinkle in Time (cover illustration), 1979, 38, Fig. 2.11
Goings, Ralph, American, b. 1928, painter, sculptor
Diner With Red Door, 1979, 112, Fig. 5.18
Jimenez, Luis, American, b. 1940, sculptor
Vaquero, 1980, 50, Fig. 3.11
Mitchell, Joan, American, 1926–1992, painter
Dirty Snow, 1980, 179, Fig. 7.9
Fish, Janet, American, b. 1939, painter
Raspberries and Goldfish, 1981, 17, Fig. 1.16
Houser, Allan, Native American, 1914–1994, sculptor
Reverie, 1981, 299, Fig. 11.18
Murray, Elizabeth, American, b. 1940, painter
Painters Progress, 1981, 40, Fig. 3.1
Graves, Nancy, American, b. 1940, sculptor
Zaga, 1983, 51, Fig. 3.13
Haring, Keith, American, 1958–1990, painter
Untitled, 1983, 90, Fig. 4.27
Malangi, David, Australian, b. 1934, Aboriginal artist
Abstract (River Mouth Map), 1983, 92, Fig. 4.29
Steir, Pat, American, b. 1938, painter
The Bruegel Series (A Vanitas of Style), 1982–84, 160, Fig. 6.31
Stella, Frank, American, b. 1936, painter, sculptor
St. Michael's Counterguard (Malta Series), 1984, 383, Fig. 13.40
Torivio, Dorothy, Native American, b. 1946, ceramicist
Vase, c. 1984, 233, Fig. 9.11
Dvorak, Lois, American, 1934–1993, mixed media
Spirit Boxes I, 1985, 304, Fig. 11.24
Naranjo, Michael, Native American, b. 1944, sculptor
Spirits Soaring, 1985, 109, Fig. 5.14
Schapiro, Miriam, American, b. 1923, painter, sculptor
Personal Appearance, 1985, 62, Fig. 3.22

GLOSSARY

This section contains the important words and phrases used in *ArtTalk* that may be new to you. You may want to refer to this list of terms as you read the chapters, complete the exercises, and prepare to create your own works of art. You can also use the Glossary to review what you have learned in *ArtTalk*.

A

Abstract art Twentieth-century art containing shapes that simplify shapes of real objects to emphasize form instead of subject matter.

Abstract Expressionism Painting style developed after World War II in New York City that emphasized abstract elements of art rather than recognizable subject matter, and also stressed feelings and emotions (13).

Acrylic paint Pigments mixed with an acrylic vehicle. Available in different degrees of quality: school and artists' acrylics. School acrylics are less expensive than the professional acrylics, can be washed out of brushes and clothes, and are nontoxic.

Action Painting See *Abstract Expressionism.*

Active Expressing movement. Diagonal and zigzag lines (4) and diagonally slanting shapes and forms (5) are active. Opposite of static.

Aesthetic experience Your personal interaction with a work of art (2).

Aesthetics The philosophy or study of the nature and value of art (2).

Afterimage Weak image of complementary color created by a viewer's brain as a reaction to prolonged looking at a color. After staring at something red, the viewer sees an afterimage of green.

Age of Faith See *Middle Ages.*

Air brush Atomizer operated by compressed air used for spraying on paint.

Alternating rhythm Visual rhythm set up by repeating motifs but changing position or content of motifs or spaces between them (8).

Analog system A system that uses electromagnetic energy to imprint both sound and pictures on videotape (3).

Analogous colors Colors that sit side by side on the color wheel and have a common hue (6). Violet, red-violet, and red are analogous colors. Analogous colors can be used as a color scheme.

Analysis In art criticism, the step in which you discover how the principles of art are used to organize the art elements of line, color, shape, form, space, and texture. In art history, the step in which you determine the style of the work (2).

Animators Artists who create moving cartoons (14).

Applied art Art made to be functional as well as visually pleasing (3).

Approximate symmetry Balance that is almost symmetrical (9). This type of symmetry produces the effect of stability, as formal balance does, but small differences make the arrangement more interesting.

Arbitrary color Color chosen by an artist to express his or her feelings (6). Opposite of optical color.

Arch Curved stone structure supporting weight of material over an open space. Doorways and bridges use arches.

Architect A person who designs buildings that are well constructed, aesthetically pleasing, and functional (14).

Architecture Art form of designing and planning construction of buildings, cities, and bridges (3).

Art criticism An organized approach for studying a work of art. It has four stages: description, analysis, interpretation, and judgment (2).

Artistic style See *individual style.*

Artists Creative individuals who use imagination and skill to communicate in visual form (1).

Ashcan School Group of American artists working in the early twentieth century who used city people and city scenes for subject matter (6). Originally called "The Eight," they helped to organize the Armory Show.

Assembling A sculpting technique in which the artist gathers and joins together a variety of different materials to make a sculpture. Also called constructing (3).

Asymmetrical balance Another name for informal balance, in which unlike objects have equal visual weight or eye attraction (4).

Atmospheric perspective Effect of air and light on how an object is perceived by the viewer (5). The more air between the viewer and the object, the more the object seems to fade. A bright object seems closer to the viewer than a dull object.

B

Background Part of the picture plane that seems to be farthest from the viewer.

Balance Principle of art concerned with equalizing visual forces, or elements, in a work of art (9). If a work of art has visual balance, the viewer feels that the elements have been arranged in a satisfying way. Visual imbalance makes the viewer feel that the elements need to be rearranged. The two types of balance are formal (also called symmetrical) and informal (also called asymmetrical).

Baroque Artistic style that emphasized dramatic lighting, movement, and emotional intensity. It developed after the Reformation in the seventeenth century. Artists used movement of forms and figures toward the viewer, dramatic lighting effects, contrast between dark and light, ornamentation, and curved lines to express energy and strong emotions (13).

Binder A liquid that holds together the grains of pigment (6).

Blending Technique of shading through smooth, gradual application of dark value (3).

Brayer Roller with a handle used to apply ink to a surface.

Buttress Projecting brick or stone structure that supports an arch or vault. A flying buttress is connected with a wall by an arch. It reaches over the side aisle to support the roof of a cathedral.

Byzantine art Artistic style that developed around the city of Constantinople (now Istanbul, Turkey) in the eastern Roman Empire. It featured very rich colors and heavily outlined figures that appeared flat and stiff (13).

C

Calligraphic lines Flowing lines made with brushstrokes similar to Asian writing (4).

Calligraphy An Asian method of beautiful handwriting (4).

Canvas Rough cloth on which an oil painting is made.

Carving A sculpting technique in which the sculptor cuts, chips, or drills from a solid mass of material to create a sculpture. Material is removed until the sculpture is complete; therefore, carving is referred to as a subtractive process (3).

Casting A sculpting technique in which molten metal or another substance is poured into a mold and allowed to harden. Just as in printmaking, an edition of sculptures can be made from the same mold (3).

Central axis A dividing line that works like the point of balance in the balance scale. The central axis is used to measure visual weight in a work of art. It can be vertical (balance between sides is measured) or horizontal (balance between top and bottom is measured) (9).

Ceramics Art of making objects with clay to produce pottery and sculpture. Pottery is fired in a kiln to make it stronger.

Chiaroscuro The arrangement of light and shadow (5). This technique was introduced by Italian artists during the Renaissance and used widely by Baroque artists. Chiaroscuro is also called modeling or shading.

Classical Referring to the art of ancient Greece and Rome. The Greeks created art based on the ideals of perfect proportion and logic instead of emotion. The Romans adapted Greek art and spread it throughout the civilized world (13).

Clay Stiff, sticky earth that is used in ceramics. It is wet, and it hardens after drying or heating (3).

Clustering Technique for creating a focal point by grouping several different shapes closely together (11).

Coil Long roll joined into a circle or spiral. Clay coils are used to make pottery.

Collage An artwork onto which materials such as textured paper and fabric have been attached (7).

Color An element of art that is derived from reflected light (6). The sensation of color is aroused in the brain by response of the eyes to different wavelengths of light. Color has three properties: hue, value, and intensity.

Color-field painting Twentieth-century art created using only flat fields of color (13).

Color scheme Plan for organizing colors. Types of color schemes include monochromatic, analogous, complementary, triad, split complementary, warm, and cool (6).

Color spectrum The effect that occurs when light passes through a prism; the beam of white light is bent and separated into bands of color. Colors always appear in the same order, by wavelengths, from longest to shortest: red, orange, yellow, green, blue, violet. A rainbow displays the spectrum (6).

Color triad Three colors spaced an equal distance apart on the color wheel (6). The primary color triad is red, yellow, and blue; the secondary color triad is orange, green, and violet. A color triad is a type of color scheme.

Color wheel The spectrum bent into a circle (6).

Compass Instrument used for measuring and drawing arcs and circles.

Complementary colors The colors opposite each other on the color wheel (6). A complement of a color absorbs all the light waves the color reflects and is the strongest contrast to the color. Mixing a hue with its complementary color dulls it. Red and green are complementary colors. Complementary colors can be used as a color scheme.

Composition The way the principles of art are used to organize the elements of art (1).

Content The message the work communicates. The content can relate to the subject matter or be an idea or emotion. Theme is another word for content (1).

Contour drawing Drawing in which only contour lines are used to represent the subject matter (4). Artists keep their eyes on the object they are drawing and concentrate on directions and curves.

Contour line A line that defines the edges and surface ridges of an object (4).

Contrast Technique for creating a focal point by using differences in elements (11).

Convergence Technique for creating a focal point by arranging elements so that many lines or shapes point to one item or area (11).

Cool colors Blue, green, and violet (6). Cool colors suggest coolness and seem to recede from a viewer. Cool colors can be used as a color scheme. Opposite of warm colors.

Crafts Art forms creating works of art that are both beautiful and useful. Crafts include weaving, fabric design, ceramics, and jewelry making (3).

Crayons Pigments held together with wax and molded into sticks.

Credit line A list of important facts about a work of art. A credit line usually includes the artist's name, the title of the work, year completed, medium used, size (height, width, and depth), location (gallery, museum, or collection and city), donors, and date donated (1).

Crewel Loosely twisted yarn used in embroidery.

Criteria Standards of judgment (2).

Crosshatching The technique of using crossed lines for shading (4).

Cubism Twentieth-century art movement that emphasizes structure and design (13). Three-dimensional objects are pictured from many different points of view at the same time.

Culture Behaviors and ideas of a group of people. Studying art objects produced by a group of people is one way to learn about a culture (12).

Cuneiform The Sumerian writing system made up of wedge-shaped characters (12).

Curved lines Lines that are always bending and change direction gradually (4).

D

Dark Ages See *Middle Ages.*

Decalcomania A technique in which paint is forced into random textured patterns by pulling apart canvases between which blobs of paint have been squeezed (7).

Dense Compact; having parts crowded together. Dense materials are solid and heavy. Opposite of soft.

Description A list of all the things you see in the work (2).

Design Plan, organization, or arrangement of elements in a work of art.

Design qualities How well the work is organized (2). This aesthetic quality is favored by Formalism.

Diagonal lines Lines that slant (4).

Digital camera A camera that records images digitally. These images can then be downloaded into computer applications where they can be altered and enhanced (3).

Digital system A system that processes words and images directly as numbers or digits (3).

Dimension The amount of space an object takes up in one direction (4). The three dimensions are height, width, and depth.

Distortion Deviations from expected, normal proportions (10).

Divine Proportion See *Golden Mean.*

Dome Hemispherical vault or ceiling over a circular opening. A dome rises above the center part of a building (13).

Dominant element Element of a work of art noticed first. Elements noticed later are called subordinate (11).

Draw program A computer art application in which images are stored as a series of lines and curves. Objects can be resized without distortion in draw programs (3).

Dyes Pigments that dissolve in liquid. Dye sinks into a material and stains it (6).

Dynamism Term used by the Futurists to refer to the forces of movement.

Dynasty A period of time during which a single family provided a succession of rulers (12).

E

Edition All the prints made from the same plate or set of plates (3).

Elements of art Basic visual symbols in the language of art. The elements of art are line, shape and form, space, color, value, and texture (1).

Embroidery Method of decorating fabric with stitches.

Emotionalism Theory that requires that a work of art must arouse a response of feelings, moods, or emotions in the viewer. One of the three aesthetic theories of art criticism, the others being Formalism and Imitationalism (2).

Emphasis Principle of art that makes one part of a work dominant over the other parts (11). The element noticed first is called dominant; the elements noticed later are called subordinate.

Engraving Method of cutting a design into a material, usually metal, with a sharp tool. A print can be made by inking an engraved surface.

Exaggeration Deviations from expected, normal proportions (10).

Expressionism Twentieth-century art movement. A style that emphasized the expression of innermost feelings (13).

Expressive qualities Those qualities that communicate ideas and moods (2).

F

Fabric Material made from fibers. Cloth and felt are fabrics (3).

Fauves French for "wild beasts." A group of early twentieth-century painters who used brilliant colors and bold distortions in an uncontrolled way. Their leader was Henri Matisse.

Fiber Thin, threadlike linear material that can be woven or spun into fabric (3).

Fiberfill Lightweight, fluffy filling material made of synthetic fibers.

Figure Human form in a work of art.

Fine art Art made to be experienced visually. Opposite of functional art (3).

Fire To apply heat to harden pottery.

Flowing rhythm Visual rhythm created by repeating wavy lines (8).

Focal point The first part of a work to attract the attention of the viewer (11). Focal points are created by contrast, location, isolation, convergence, and use of the unusual.

Foreground Part of the picture plane that appears closest to the viewer. The foreground is usually at the bottom of the picture.

Foreshortening To shorten an object to make it look as if it extends backward into space (10). This method reproduces proportions a viewer actually sees, which depend on the viewer's distance from the object or person.

Forms Objects having three dimensions (5). Like a shape, a form has height and width, but it also has depth. Forms are either geometric or free-form.

Formal balance Way of organizing parts of a design so that equal, or very similar, elements are placed on opposite sides of a central axis (9). Formal balance suggests stability. Symmetry is a type of formal balance. Opposite of informal balance.

Formalism Theory that places emphasis on the design qualities. One of the three aesthetic theories of art criticism, the others being Emotionalism and Imitationalism (2).

Free-form shapes Irregular and uneven shapes (5). Their outlines are curved, or angular, or both. Free-form shapes are often referred to as organic (found in nature). Opposite of geometric shapes.

Freestanding Work of art surrounded on all sides by space. A three-dimensional work of art is freestanding. Opposite of relief (3).

Frottage A freshly painted canvas is placed right-side-up over a raised texture and scraped across the surface of the paint (7).

Functional art Works of art made to be used instead of only enjoyed. Objects must be judged by how well they work when used (1).

Futurists Early twentieth-century Italian artists who arranged angular forms to suggest motion (8). They called the forces of movement dynamism.

G

Gallery Place for displaying or selling works of art.

Genre painting Paintings that have scenes from everyday life as their subject matter.

Geometric shapes Precise shapes that can be described using mathematical formulas (5). Basic geometric shapes are the circle, the square, and the triangle. Basic geometric forms are the cylinder, the cube, and the pyramid. Opposite of free-form shapes.

Gesture An expressive movement (4).

Gesture drawing Line drawing done quickly to capture movement of the subject's body (4).

Glaze In ceramics, a thin, glossy coating fired into pottery. In painting, a thin layer of transparent paint.

Golden Mean A line divided into two parts so that the smaller line has the same proportion, or ratio, to the larger line as the larger line has to the whole line (10). Perfect ratio (relationship of parts) discovered by Euclid, a Greek Philosopher. Its mathematical expression is 1 to 1.6. It was also called the Golden Section and the Golden Rectangle. The long sides of the Golden Rectangle are a little more than half again as long as the short sides. This ratio was rediscovered in the early sixteenth century and named the Divine Proportion.

Gothic Artistic style developed in western Europe between the twelfth and sixteenth centuries. Featured churches that seemed to soar upward, pointed arches, and stained-glass windows (13).

Gouache Pigments ground in water and mixed with gum to form opaque watercolor. Gouache resembles school tempera or poster paint.

Graphic designer A person who translates ideas into images and arranges them in appealing and memorable ways (14).

Grattage Wet paint is scratched with a variety of tools, such as forks, razors, and combs for the purpose of creating different textures (7).

Grid Pattern of intersecting vertical and horizontal lines (8).

Griots Oral historians who are also musicians and performers (12).

H

Hard-edge In two-dimensional art, shapes with clearly defined outlines. Hard-edge shapes look dense. Opposite of soft-edge.

Harmony The principle of art that creates unity by stressing similarities of separate but related parts (11).

Hatching Technique of shading with a series of fine parallel lines (3).

Hierarchical proportion When figures are arranged in a work of art so scale indicates importance (10).

Hieroglyphics Picture writing used by ancient Egyptians (12).

High-key painting Painting using many tints of a color (6). Opposite of low-key painting.

Highlights Small areas of white used to show the very brightest spots (5). Highlights show the surfaces of the subject that reflect the most light. They are used to create the illusion of form. Opposite of shadows.

High relief Sculpture in which areas project far out from a flat surface (3).

High-resolution Producing a sharp image.

Holograms Images in three dimensions created with a laser beam (5).

Horizon Point at which earth and sky seem to meet.

Horizontal line Line parallel to the horizon (4). Horizontal lines lie flat and are parallel to the bottom edge of the paper or canvas.

Hue The name of a color in the color spectrum (6). Hue is related to the wavelength of reflected light. The primary hues are red, yellow, and blue; they are called primary because they cannot be made by mixing other hues together. The secondary hues, made by mixing two primary hues, are orange, violet, and green. Hue is one of the three properties of color.

I

Illustrator A person who creates the visual images that complement written words (14).

Imitationalism An aesthetic theory focusing on realistic presentation. One of the three aesthetic theories of art criticism, the others being Emotionalism and Formalism (2).

Implied lines A series of points that the viewer's eyes automatically connect. Implied lines are suggested, not real (4).

Impressionism Style of painting started in France in the 1860s. It featured everyday subjects and emphasized the momentary effects of light on color (13).

Individual style The artist's personal way of using the elements and principles of art to express feelings and ideas (2).

Informal balance Way of organizing parts of a design involving a balance of unlike objects (9). Asymmetry is another term for informal balance. Opposite of formal balance.

Intaglio (in-**tal**-yo or in-**tal**-ee-o) A printmaking technique in which ink is forced into lines that have been cut or etched on a hard surface such as metal or wood. The plate's surface is then wiped clean and the prints are made (3).

Intensity The brightness or dullness of a hue. A pure hue is called a high-intensity color. A dulled hue (a color mixed with its complement) is called a low-intensity color. Intensity is one of the three properties of color (6).

Interior designer A person who plans the design and decoration of the interior spaces in homes and offices (14).

Intermediate color A color made by mixing a primary color with a secondary color. Red-orange is an intermediate color (6).

International style A style of architecture developed after World War II that emphasizes a plain, austere building style (13).

Interpretation In art criticism, the step in which you explain or tell the meaning or mood of the work. In art history, the step in which you do research about the artist (2).

Invented texture A kind of visual texture that does not represent a real texture but creates a sensation of one by repeating lines and shapes in a two-dimensional pattern (7). Opposite of simulated texture.

Isolation Technique for creating a focal point by putting one object alone to emphasize it (11).

J

Judgment In art criticism, the step in which you determine the degree of artistic merit. In art history, the step in which you determine if the work has made an important contribution to the history of art (2).

K

Kinetic A work of art that actually moves in space (8).

L

Landscape Painting or drawing in which natural land scenery, such as mountains, trees, rivers, or lakes, is the main feature.

Layout The way items are arranged on the page (14).

Line An element of art that is the path of a moving point through space. Although lines can vary in appearance (they can have different lengths, widths, textures, directions, and degree of curve), they are considered one-dimensional and are measured by length. A line is also used by an artist to control the viewer's eye movement. There are five kinds of lines: vertical, horizontal, diagonal, curved, and zigzag (4).

Linear perspective A graphic system that creates the illusion of depth and volume on a flat surface. In one-point linear perspective, all receding lines meet at a single point. In two-point linear perspective, different sets of lines meet at different points (5, 13).

Literal qualities The realistic qualities that appear in the subject of the work (2).

Lithography A printmaking technique in which the image to be printed is drawn on limestone, zinc, or aluminum with a special greasy pencil or pencil. Ink is attracted to this material (3).

Location The technique of using placement of elements to create a focal point (11). Items near the center of a work of art are usually noticed first.

Logos Symbols or trademarks that are immediately recognizable (14).

Loom Machine or frame for weaving.

Low-key painting Painting using many shades or dark values of a color (6). Opposite of high-key painting.

Low-relief See *bas-relief.*

Mannerism European sixteenth-century artistic style featuring highly emotional scenes and elongated figures (13).

Manufactured shapes/forms Shapes or forms made by people either by hand or by machine. Opposite of organic shapes/forms (5).

Mat To frame a picture or drawing with a cardboard border.

Matte surface Surface that reflects a soft, dull light (7). Paper has a matte surface. Opposite of shiny surface.

Medieval Related to the *Middle Ages.*

Media See *medium.*

Medium Material used to make art. Plural is media (1).

Megaliths Large monuments created from huge stone slabs (12).

Mexican muralists Early twentieth-century artists whose paintings on walls and ceilings used solid forms and powerful colors to express their feelings about the Mexican Revolution. Also called Mexican Expressionists (13).

Middle Ages Period of roughly one thousand years from the destruction of the Roman Empire to the Renaissance. Culture centered around the Catholic Church. The Middle Ages are also called the Dark Ages (because few new ideas developed) and the Age of Faith (because religion was a powerful force) (13).

Middle ground Area in a picture between the foreground and the background.

Minimalism Twentieth-century artistic style that uses a minimum of art elements (13).

Mobile Moving sculpture (8).

Modeling A sculpting technique in which a soft, pliable material is built up and shaped. Because more material is added to build a form, modeling is referred to as an additive process (3).

Module A three-dimensional motif (8).

Monochromatic A color scheme that uses only one hue and the tints and shades of that hue for a unifying effect (6).

Mortar and pestle Ceramic bowl and tool for grinding

something into a powder.

Mosaics Pictures made with small cubes of colored marble, glass, or tile and set into cement.

Mosques Muslim places of worship (12).

Motif A unit that is repeated in visual rhythm (8). Units in a motif may or may not be an exact duplicate of the first unit.

Movement See *visual movement.*

Multi-media programs Computer software programs that help users design, organize, and combine text, graphics, video, and sound in one document (3).

Mural Painting on a wall or ceiling.

Museum curator Person who oversees the operations of a museum (14).

Negative spaces Empty spaces surrounding shapes and forms (5). The shape and size of negative spaces affect the interpretation of positive spaces. Negative spaces are also called ground.

Neoclassicism New classicism. French artistic style developed in the nineteenth century after the Rococo style. An approach to art that borrowed subject matter and formal design qualities from the art of Greece and Rome (13).

Neolithic period New Stone Age. A prehistoric period stretching roughly from 7000 B.C. to 2000 B.C. (12).

Neutral colors Black, white, and gray. Black reflects no wavelengths of light, white reflects all wavelengths of light, and gray reflects all wavelengths of light equally but only partially (6).

Nonobjective art Art that has no recognizable subject matter (1).

O

Oil paint Slow-drying paint made by mixing pigments in oil and usually used on canvas (3).

Opaque Quality of a material that does not let any light pass through. Opposite of transparent.

Op Art Optical art. Twentieth-century artistic style in which artists use scientific knowledge about vision to create optical illusions of movement (13).

Optical color Color perceived by the viewer due to the effect of atmosphere or unusual light on the actual color (6). Opposite of arbitrary color.

Organic shapes/forms Shapes or forms made by the forces of nature. Opposite of manufactured shapes/forms (5).

Outline A line that shows or creates the outer edges of a shape (4).

P

Package designer Person who produces the containers that attract the attention of consumers (14).

Pagoda A tower several stories high with roofs curving slightly upward at the edges (12).

Paint Pigments mixed with oil or water. Pigment particles in paint stick to the surface of the material on which the paint is applied (3).

Paint program A computer art application in which images are stored as bitmaps. Paint programs are capable of producing more lifelike pictures than draw programs (3).

Palette Tray for mixing colors of paints.

Papier-mâché French for "mashed paper." Modeling material made of paper and liquid paste and molded over a supporting structure called the armature.

Paleolithic period Old Stone Age. Began about two million years ago and ended with the close of the last ice age about 13,000 B.C. (12).

Parallel lines Lines that move in the same direction and always stay the same distance apart.

Pastels Pigments held together with gum and molded into sticks.

Paste-up Model of a printed page. It is photographed for the purpose of making a plate for the printing process.

Pattern A two-dimensional decorative visual repetition (8). A pattern has no movement and may or may not have rhythm.

Perceive To become deeply aware through the senses of the special nature of a visual object (1).

Perspective A graphic system that creates the illusion of depth and volume on a two-dimensional surface (5). It was developed during the Renaissance by architect Filippo Brunelleschi. Perspective is created by overlapping, size variations, placement, detail, color, and converging lines.

Pharaohs Egyptian rulers who were worshiped as gods and held complete authority over the kingdom (12).

Photogram Image on blueprint paper developed by fumes from liquid ammonia.

Photography The technique of capturing optical images on light-sensitive surfaces (3).

Photojournalists Visual reporters (14).

Photo-Realism See *Super-Realism.*

Picture plane The surface of a painting or drawing.

Pigments Finely ground, colored powders that form paint when mixed with a liquid (6).

Plaster Mixture of lime, sand, and water that hardens on drying.

Point of view Angle from which the viewer sees an object (5). The shapes and forms a viewer sees depend on his or her point of view.

Polymer medium Liquid used in acrylic painting as a thinning or finishing material (3).

Pop art Artistic style used in the early 1960s in the United States that portrayed images of popular culture (mass media, commercial art, comic strips, advertising) (13).

Portrait Image of a person, especially the face and upper body.

Positive spaces Shapes or forms in two- and three-dimensional art (5). Empty spaces surrounding them are called negative spaces or ground.

Post-and-lintel A method of construction in which one long stone is balanced on top of two posts. Currently referred to as post-and-beam construction (3).

Post-Impressionism French painting style of the late nineteenth century that stressed a more individual approach to painting, unique to each artist working at the time (13).

Post-Modernism An approach to art that incorporates traditional elements and techniques while retaining some characteristics of modern art styles or movements (13).

Prehistoric Period before history was written down (12).

Principles of art Rules that govern how artists organize the elements of art. The principles of art are rhythm, movement, balance, proportion, variety, emphasis, harmony, and unity (1).

Print Impression created by an artist made on paper or fabric from a printing plate, stone, or block and repeated many times to produce identical images (3).

Printing plate Surface containing the impression transferred to paper or fabric to make a print (3).

Printmaking A process in which an artist repeatedly transfers an original image from one prepared surface to another (3).

Prism Wedge-shaped piece of glass that bends white light and separates it into spectral hues.

Profile Side view of a face.

Progressive rhythm Visual rhythm that changes a motif each time it is repeated (8).

Proportion Principle of art concerned with the size relationships of one part to another (10).

Protractor Semicircular instrument used to measure and draw angles.

Proximity Technique for creating unity by limiting negative spaces between shapes (11).

R

Radial balance Type of balance in which forces or elements of a design come out (radiate) from a central point (9).

Random rhythm Visual rhythm in which a motif is repeated in no apparent order, with no regular spaces (8).

Rasp File with sharp, rough teeth used for cutting into a surface.

Realism Mid-nineteenth-century artistic style in which presented familiar scenes as they actually appeared (13).

Realists Artists in the nineteenth century who portrayed political, social, and moral issues (13).

Real texture Texture that can be perceived through touch. Opposite of visual texture (7).

Recede To move back or become more distant.

Reformation Religious revolution in western Europe in the sixteenth century. It started as a reform movement in the Catholic Church and led to the beginnings of Protestantism (13).

Regionalists Artists who painted the farmlands and cities of the United States in an optimistic way (13).

Regular rhythm Visual rhythm achieved through repeating identical motifs using the same intervals of space between them (8).

Relief printing A printmaking technique in which the artist cuts away the sections of a surface not meant to hold ink. As a result, the image to be printed is raised from the background (3).

Relief sculpture Type of sculpture in which forms project from a flat background. Opposite of freestanding (3).

Renaissance The name given to the period at the end of the Middle Ages when artists, writers, and philosophers were "re-awakened" to art forms and ideas from ancient Greece and Rome (13).

Repetition Technique for creating rhythm and unity in which a motif or single element appears again and again (11).

Reproduction A copy of a work of art (3).

Rhythm The principle of art that indicates movement by the repetition of elements (8). Visual rhythm is perceived through the eyes and is created by repeating positive spaces separated by negative spaces. There are five types of rhythm: random, regular, alternating, flowing, and progressive.

Rococo Eighteenth-century artistic style that began in the luxurious homes of the French aristocracy and spread to the rest of Europe. It stressed free graceful movement, a playful use of line, and delicate colors (13).

Romanesque Style of architecture and sculpture developed during the Middle Ages in western Europe that featured buildings of massive size; solid, heavy walls; wide use of the rounded Roman arch; and many sculptural decorations (13).

Romanticism Early nineteenth-century artistic style that was a reaction against Neoclassicism. It found its subjects in the world of the dramatic and in cultures foreign to Europe. It emphasized rich color and high emotion (13).

Rough texture Irregular surface that reflects light unevenly (7). Opposite of smooth texture.

Rubbing Technique for transferring textural quality of a surface to paper by placing paper over the surface and rubbing the top of the paper with crayon or pencil (7).

S

Safety labels Labels identifying art products that are safe to use or that must be used with caution.

Scale Size as measured against a standard reference. Scale can refer to an entire work of art or to elements within it (10).

Scanner A device that "reads" a printed image and then translates it into a language the computer can use to make a visual image on the screen (3).

Score To make neat, sharp creases in paper using a cutting tool.

Screen printing A printmaking technique in which a stencil and screen are used as the printing plate. The stencil is placed on a fabric screen stretched across a frame and ink is pressed through the screen where it is not covered by the stencil (3).

Scroll A long roll of parchment or silk (12).

Sculpture Three-dimensional work of art created out of wood, stone, metal, or clay by carving, welding, casting, or modeling (3).

Seascape Painting or drawing in which the sea is the subject.

Shade A dark value of a hue made by adding black to it. Opposite of tint (6).

Shading The use of light and dark lines to give a feeling of depth and texture (3).

Shadows Shaded areas in a drawing or painting. Shadows show the surfaces of the subject that reflect the least light and are used to create the illusion of form. Opposite of highlights.

Shape A two-dimensional area that is defined in some way. While a form has depth, a shape has only height and width. Shapes are either geometric or free-form (5).

Shiny surface Surface that reflects bright light. Window glass has a shiny surface. Opposite of matte surface (7).

Sighting Technique for determining the proportional relationship of one part of an object to another (10).

Silhouette Outline drawing of a shape. Originally a silhouette was a profile portrait, filled in with a solid color.

Simplicity Technique for creating unity by limiting the number of variations of an element of art.

Simulated texture A kind of visual texture that imitates real texture by using a two-dimensional pattern to create the illusion of a three-dimensional surface (7). A plastic tabletop can use a pattern to simulate the texture of wood. Opposite of invented texture.

Sketch Quick, rough drawing without much detail that can be used as a plan or reference for later work.

Slip Creamy mixture of clay and water used to fasten pieces of clay together.

Smooth texture Regular surface that reflects light evenly. Opposite of rough texture (7).

Soft edge In two-dimensional art, shapes with fuzzy, blurred outlines. Soft-edge shapes look soft. Opposite of hard-edge.

Soft sculpture Sculpture made with fabric and stuffed with soft material.

Solvent The liquid that controls the thickness or the thinness of the paint (6).

Space The element of art that refers to the emptiness or area between, around, above, below, or within objects. Shapes and forms are defined by space around and within them (5).

Spectral colors Red, orange, yellow, green, blue, violet (6).

Split complementary colors One hue and the hues on each side of its complement on the color wheel (6). Red-orange, blue, and green are split complementary colors. Split complementary colors can be used as a color scheme.

Stained glass Colored glass cut into pieces, arranged in a design, and joined with strips of lead.

Static Inactive (4). Vertical and horizontal lines and horizontal shapes and forms are static. Opposite of active.

Still life Painting or drawing of inanimate (nonmoving) objects.

Stippling Technique of shading using dots (3).

Stitchery Technique for decorating fabric by stitching fibers onto it.

Stone Age Period of history during which stone tools were used (12).

Storyboards A series of still drawings that show a story's progress (14).

Stupas Beehive-shaped domed places of worship (12).

Style See *individual style*.

Subject The image viewers can easily identify in a work of art (1).

Subordinate element Element of a work of art noticed after the dominant element (11).

Super-Realism Twentieth-century artistic style that depicts objects as precisely and accurately as they actually appear (13).

Surrealism Twentieth-century artistic style in which dreams, fantasy, and the subconscious served as inspiration for artists (13).

Symbol Something that stands for, or represents, something else (1).

Symmetry A special type of formal balance in which two halves of a balanced composition are identical, mirror images of each other (9).

Synthetic Made by chemical processes rather than natural processes.

T

Tapestry Fabric wall hanging that is woven, painted, or embroidered.

Tempera Paint made by mixing pigments with egg yolk (egg tempera) or another liquid. School poster paint is a type of tempera (3).

Texture The element of art that refers to how things feel, or look as if they might feel if touched. Texture is perceived by touch and sight. Objects can have rough or smooth textures and matte or shiny surfaces (7).

Tint A light value of a hue made by mixing the hue with white. Opposite of shade (6).

Tonality Arrangement of colors in a painting so that one color dominates the work of art (6).

Totem poles Tall posts carved and painted with a series of animal symbols associated with a particular family or clan (12).

Transparent Quality of a material that allows light to pass through. Opposite of opaque.

Trompe l'oeil French for "deceive the eye." Style of painting in which painters try to give the viewer the illusion of seeing a three-dimensional object, so that the viewer wonders whether he or she is seeing a picture or something real.

U

Unity The quality of wholeness or oneness that is achieved through the effective use of the elements and principles of art (11). Unity is created by simplicity, repetition, and proximity.

Unusual Technique for creating a focal point by using the unexpected (11).

V

Value The element of art that describes the darkness or lightness of an object (4). Value depends on how much light a surface reflects. Value is also one of the three properties of color.

Vanishing point Point on the horizon where receding parallel lines seem to meet (5).

Variety Principle of art concerned with difference or contrast (11).

Vault Arched roof, ceiling, or covering made of brick, stone, or concrete (3).

Vehicle Liquid, like water or oil, that pigments are mixed with to make paint or dye (3).

Vertical lines Lines that are straight up and down (4). Vertical lines are at right angles to the bottom edge of the paper or canvas and the horizon, and parallel to the side of the paper or canvas.

Viewing frame A piece of paper with an area cut from the middle. By holding the frame at arm's length and looking through it at the subject, the artist can focus on the area of the subject he or she wants to draw or paint.

Visual arts The arts that produce beautiful objects to look at.

Visual movement The principle of art used to create the look and feeling of action and to guide the viewer's eyes throughout the work of art (8).

Visual rhythm Rhythm you receive through your eyes rather than through your ears (8).

Visual texture Illusion of a three-dimensional surface based on the memory of how things feel. There are two types of visual texture: invented and simulated (7). Opposite of real texture.

Visual weight Attraction that elements in a work of art have for the viewer's eyes. Visual weight is affected by size, contour, intensity of colors, warmth and coolness of colors, contrast in value, texture, and position (9).

W

Warm colors Red, orange, and yellow (6). Warm colors suggest warmth and seem to move toward the viewer. Warm colors can be used as a color scheme. Opposite of cool colors.

Warp In weaving, lengthwise threads held in place on the loom and crossed by weft threads.

Watercolor paint Transparent pigments mixed with water (3).

Weaving Making fabric by interlacing two sets of parallel threads, held at right angles to each other on a loom (3).

Weft In weaving, crosswise threads that are carried over and under the warp threads.

Woodblock printing Making prints by carving images in blocks of wood (12).

Y

Yarn Fibers spun into strands for weaving, knitting, or embroidery.

Z

Ziggurats Stepped mountains made of brick-covered earth (12).

Zigzag lines Lines formed by short, sharp turns (4). Zigzag lines are a combination of diagonal lines. They can change direction suddenly.

The following is an annotated listing of books dealing with various areas of art and art education. These books can provide valuable assistance to you as you study and work in the visual arts.

ARCHITECTURE

Baker, John Milnes. *American House Styles: A Concise Guide.* New York: W.W. Norton, 1994. An examination of house styles in the United States from the early colonial period to the 1990s.

Erlande-Brandenburg, Alain. *Cathedrals and Castles: Building in the Middle Ages.* New York: Harry N. Abrams, 1995. The story of architecture in the Middle Ages.

Fletcher, Banister, Sir. *History of Architecture.* Edited by Dan Cruickshank. 20th ed. Boston: Architectural Press, 1996. A comprehensive history of architecture worldwide.

Icher, Francois. *Building the Great Cathedrals.* New York: Harry N. Abrams, 1998. A look at those individuals who studied, designed, and built the cathedrals of Europe.

Lepre, J. P. *The Egyptian Pyramids: A Comprehensive, Illustrated Reference.* Jefferson, N.C.: McFarland, 1990. Study of the pyramids and the pharoahs who built them.

COMPUTER GRAPHICS

Cyber Design: Computer-Manipulated Illustration. Rockport, Mass.: Rockport Publishers, 1996. An overview of the art of design using the latest computer technology.

Ziegler, Kathleen and Nick Greco, eds. *Cyberpalette: A Digital Step-by-Step Guide.* New York: Watson-Guptill, 1998. Ten artists who use computer technology discuss their work from the initial idea to the final image.

DESIGN

Designer Posters. Rockport, Mass.: Rockport Publishers, 1996. This book examines over 300 poster designs.

Hiebert, Kenneth J. *Graphic Design Sources.* New Haven: Yale University Press, 1998. A discussion of design creation including form, technique, and communication.

Landa, Robin. *Thinking Creatively: New Ways to Unlock Your Visual Imagination.* Cincinnati: North Light Books, 1998. A discussion of how to think creatively and how designers apply creative thinking to real projects.

Lauer, David A. *Design Basics.* 4th ed. Fort Worth: Harcourt Brace College Publishers, 1995. Organized by the different principles of design using examples from throughout history.

Martin, Diana. *Graphic Design: Inspirations and Innovations.* Cincinnati: North Light Books, 1995. Discusses sources of inspiration including how graphic artists generate ideas and translate them into designs.

DRAWING

Auvil, Kenneth W. *Perspective Drawing.* Mountain View, Calif.: Mayfield Publishing, 1990. A step-by-step guide to perspective drawing.

Bowen, Ron. *Drawing Masterclass.* Boston: Bulfinch Press, 1992. A drawing technique book, including five different drawing strategies.

Goldfinger, Eliot. *Human Anatomy for Artists: The Elements of Form.* New York: Oxford University Press, 1991. A guide to the anatomy of the human body designed for the beginner to the professional artist.

Hammond, Lee. *Draw Family & Friends!* Cincinnati: North Light Books, 1997. A book about drawing shapes and putting those shapes together to create the human form.

Wilson, Brent, Al Hurwitz, and Marjorie Wilson. *Teaching Drawing from Art.* Worcester, Mass.: Davis Publications, 1987. Presents a unique approach to drawing. Masterworks of art are used to motivate drawing activities.

FIBER ARTS

Batik

Roojen, Pepin Van. *Batik Design.* 2d ed. Amsterdam: Pepin Press, 1994. A history of batik design and patterns.

Needlecraft

Guild, Vera P. *Good Housekeeping New Complete Book of Needlecraft.* NY: Hearst Books, 1971. Directions for a variety of needlecraft techniques.

Silk-Screening

Henning, Roni. *Screenprinting: Water-Based Techniques.* New York: Watson-Guptill, 1994. A how-to book for water-based printing, a new approach to silk-screening.

Weaving

Hecht, Ann. *The Art of the Loom: Weaving, Spinning, and Dyeing Across the World.* New York: Rizzoli, 1990. A worldwide examination of the different techniques, colors, and styles of the art of weaving. Includes an introduction on the basics of weaving, spinning, and dyeing.

Floral Arts

Hillier, Malcolm. *The Book of Fresh Flowers: A Complete Guide to Selecting and Arranging.* New York: Simon and Schuster, 1988. Features hundreds of examples of arrangements with instructions.

Rogers, Barbara Radcliffe. *The Encyclopedia of Everlastings: The Complete Guide to Growing, Preserving, and Arranging Dried Flowers.* New York: Weidenfeld and Nicolson, 1988. A book of plant varieties suitable for preservation. Includes information about each plant and arrangement suggestions.

General Crafts

Sprintzen, Alice. *Crafts: Contemporary Design and Technique.* Worcester, Mass.: Davis Publications, 1987. An introduction to traditional and modern crafts, with instructions for beginners.

Stribling, Mary Lou. *Crafts from North American Indian Arts: Techniques, Designs, and Contemporary Applications.* NY:

Crown Publishers, 1975. Techniques and applications of many different crafts using a variety of materials.

Jewelry

McCreight, Tim. *Jewelry: Fundamentals of Metalsmithing.* Madison, Wis.: Hand Books Press, 1997. Handbook of procedures and tools for making metal jewelry.

Phillips, Clare. *Jewelry: From Antiquity to the Present.* New York: Thames and Hudson, 1996. A history of the art and craft of jewelry.

Sprintzen, Alice. *The Jeweler's Art: A Multimedia Approach.* Worcester, Mass.: Davis Publications, 1995. A guide to making jewelry from various materials.

PAINTING

Akiyama, Terukazu. *Japanese Painting.* New York: Rizzoli, 1990. A history of Japanese painting.

Barnhart, Richard M., et al. *Three Thousand Years of Chinese Painting.* New Haven: Yale University Press, 1997. Overview of Chinese painting and its relationship to the social and cultural developments in China.

Davidson, Abraham. *The Story of American Painting.* New York: Harry N. Abrams, 1974. A history of American painting from the colonial period until the 1960s.

Denvir, Bernard. *Impressionism: The Painters and the Paintings.* London: Studio Editions, 1991. A history of French Impressionism.

Freedberg, Sydney J. *Painting in Italy, 1500–1600.* 3rd ed. New Haven: Yale University Press, 1993. An analysis of High Renaissance painting in Italy and the period of Mannerism that followed.

Gair, Angela. *Acrylics: A Step-by-Step Guide to Acrylics Techniques.* London: Letts, 1994. Introduction to techniques and advantages of painting with acrylics.

Gaunt, William. *The Great Century of British Painting: Hogarth to Turner.* 2d ed. Oxford: Phaidon, 1978. A history of eighteenth-century British painting.

Grabar, André. *Byzantine Painting: Historical and Critical Study.* New York: Rizzoli, 1979. An examination of mural painting, frescoes, and mosaics from the Byzantine period.

Haak, Bob. *The Golden Age: Dutch Painters of the Seventeenth Century.* New York: Stewart, Tabori & Chang, 1996. A history of Dutch painting arranged geographically.

Mayer, Ralph. *The Artist's Handbook of Materials and Techniques.* 5th ed. rev. and updated. New York: Viking-Penguin, Inc.,1991. An up-to-date in-depth look at the varied materials and techniques of painting.

Treman, Judy D. *Building Brilliant Watercolors.* Cincinnati: North Light Books, 1998. A guide to the technique of watercolor painting.

PAPER

Innes, Miranda. *Papier-Mâché.* New York: Dorling Kindersley, 1995. Explains the craft of papier-mâché including construction and decoration.

Johnson, Pauline. *Creating with Paper: Basic Forms and Variations.* Seattle: University of Washington Press, 1981. A variety of approaches to paper sculpture.

Stevenson, Cheryl. *The Art of Handmade Paper and Collage: Transforming the Ordinary into the Extraordinary.* Bothell, Wash.: Martingale & Co., 1998. A how-to book for making paper and collage with inexpensive or free materials.

POTTERY

Peterson, Susan. *The Craft and Art of Clay.* 2d ed. Woodstock, N.Y.: The Overlook Press, 1996. A technical guide to both hand-building and wheel-throwing. Includes works from contemporary ceramic artists.

Speight, Charlotte F. *Hands in Clay: An Introduction to Ceramics.* Mountain View, Calif.: Mayfield Publishing, 1995. A history of pottery-making throughout the world and a technical guide to the art and craft of ceramics.

Triplett, Kathy. *Handbuilt Ceramics: Pinching, Coiling, Extruding, Molding, Slip Casting, Slab Work.* Asheville, N.C.: Lark Books, 1997. A guide to the shaping, decorating, and firing of clay.

PHOTOGRAPHY

Filmmaking

Halas, John. *The Technique of Film Animation.* 4th ed. New York: Hastings House, 1976. A look at the history and techniques of film animation.

Harmon, Renee. *Film Directing—Killer Style and Cutting Edge Techniques: A Step-by-Step Guide to Making Your Film.* Los Angeles: Lone Eagle Publishing, 1997. Advice for the movie director on how make a movie that is appealing to the audience.

Lindenmuth, Kevin J. *Making Movies on Your Own: Practical Talk from Independent Filmmakers.* Jefferson, N.C.: McFarland, 1998. A compilation of advice on making a feature film from 25 successful filmmakers.

Lord, Peter and Brian Sibley. *Cracking Animation.* London: Thames and Hudson, 1998. A guide to 3-D animation from simple techniques to making a film.

Still Photography

Craven, George M. *Object and Image: An Introduction to Photography.* 3rd ed. Englewood Cliffs, N.J.: Prentice-Hall, 1990. An approach to photography as a creative medium.

Eastland, Jonathan. *Essential Darkroom Techniques.* New York: Blandford *Press, 1987.* A guide to the techniques of film developing and printing.

Feininger, Andreas. *The Complete Photographer.* Rev. ed. Englewood Cliffs, N.J.: Prentice-Hall, 1978. An excellent overview of basic photographic techniques.

Newhall, Beaumont. *The History of Photography: From 1839 to the Present.* 5th ed. New York: Museum of Modern Art, 1997. A history of photography from its invention.

Rosenblum, Naomi. *A World History of Photography.* 3rd ed. New York: Abbeville Press, 1997. A history of photography worldwide.

PRINTMAKING

Illing, Richard. *The Art of Japanese Prints.* London: Octopus, 1980. A history of Japanese wood-block prints from the early eighteenth century through the twentieth century.

Hults, Linda C. *The Print in the Western World: An Introductory History.* Madison: University of Wisconsin Press, 1996. An introduction to the art of printmaking from its European origins.

Johnson, Una E. *American Prints and Printmakers: A Chronicle of Over 400 Artists and Their Prints from 1900 to the Present.* Garden City, N.Y.: Doubleday, 1980. A survey of artists involved in printmaking in the twentieth century.

Toale, Bernard. *Basic Printmaking Techniques.* Worcester, Mass.: Davis Publications, 1992. Focuses on techniques of relief prints, monotypes, and silkscreen prints.

SCULPTURE

Armstrong, Tom, et al. *200 Years of American Sculpture.* Boston: David R. Godine, 1976. An informative look at the evolution of American sculpture.

Davies, Mike. *Woodcarving Techniques and Designs.* Madison, Wis.: Hand Books Press, 1997. An examination of the art of woodcarving.

Hall, Carolyn Vosburg. *Soft Sculpture.* Worcester, Mass.: Davis Publications,1981. Provides useful information for soft sculpture projects.

Hammacher, Abraham Marie. *Modern Sculpture: Tradition and Innovation.* Enl. ed. New York: Harry N. Abrams, 1988. A history of modern sculpture in Europe and America.

Kleiner, Diane E. E. *Roman Sculpture.* New Haven: Yale University Press, 1992. Overview of both public and private sculpture of Rome.

Meilach, Dona Z. *Box Art: Assemblage and Construction.* New York: Crown Publishers, 1975. A guide to the art of box-making.

Morris, John. *Creative Metal Sculpture: A Step-by-Step Approach.* New York: Bruce Publishing, 1971. This book takes the beginning metalworker through the process of creating various types of metal sculpture.

Pope-Hennessy, John. *An Introduction to Italian Sculpture.* 4th ed. London: Phaidon Press, 1996. Covers Gothic, Renaissance, and Baroque sculpture in Italy.

Stewart, Andrew F. *Greek Sculpture: An Exploration.* New Haven: Yale University Press, 1990. A historical presentation of a selection of large-scale Greek sculpture.

ART HISTORY

Ades, Dawn. *Art in Latin America: The Modern Era, 1820-1980.* New Haven: Yale University Press, 1989. An examination art from a wide variety of Latin American countries.

Arnason, H. H. *History of Modern Art: Painting, Sculpture, Architecture, Photography.* 4th ed. New York: Harry N. Abrams, Inc., 1998. History of modern art in Europe and America.

Barnicoat, John. *Posters: A Concise History.* New York: Thames and Hudson, 1985. This book focuses on the importance of the poster, including its role in various artistic movements.

Berlo, Janet. *Native North American Art.* New York: Oxford University Press, 1998. An overview of the history of art of Native North American cultures arranged by region.

Bloom, Jonathan and Sheila Blair. *Islamic Arts.* London: Phaidon, 1997. A history of Islamic arts from all over the Islamic world.

Camille, Michael. *Gothic Art, Visions, and Revelations of the Medieval World.* London: Weidenfeld and Nicolson, 1996. An overview of Gothic art throughout Europe.

Chadwick, Whitney. *Women, Art, and Society.* 2d ed. New York: Thames and Hudson, 1997. Covers the woman artist in Europe and America; from the Middle Ages to the twentieth century.

Feldman, Edmund Burke. *Varieties of Visual Experience.* 4th ed. New York: Harry N. Abrams, 1992. Examines the relationship between art and life.

Gardner, Helen. *Art Through the Ages.* 10th ed. Fort Worth: Harcourt Brace, 1996. A comprehensive survey of art history.

Harle, J. C. *The Art and Architecture of the Indian Subcontinent.* New York: Penguin Books, 1986. A comprehensive look at art of India, Afghanistan, Pakistan, Nepal, and Sri Lanka.

Harbison, Craig. *The Mirror of the Artist: Northern Renaissance Art in its Historical Context.* New York: Harry N. Abrams, 1995. An overview of Northern Renaissance art, including the art of the Netherlands, Germany, and France.

Highwater, Jamake. *Arts of the Indian Americas: Leaves from the Sacred Tree.* New York: Harper & Row, 1983. Provides an overview of the arts of North, South, and Central Native Americans, including culture and history.

Janson, H. W. *A Basic History of Art.* 5th ed. Upper Saddle River, N.J.: Prentice-Hall, 1997. A history of art for the layperson.

Lee, Sherman E. *A History of Far Eastern Art.* 5th ed. Englewood Cliffs, N.J.: Prentice-Hall, 1994. An in-depth look at East Asian art from prehistory to the nineteenth century.

Paoletti, John T. *Art in Renaissance Italy.* New York: Harry N. Abrams, 1997. Covers art in Italy from the mid-thirteenth century to the sixteenth century.

Patton, Sharon F. *African-American Art.* New York: Oxford University Press, 1998. A look at African-American art from colonial America to Postmodernism.

Phillips, Tom, ed. *Africa: The Art of a Continent.* London: Royal Academy of Arts, 1995. Covers art in all media from a variety of African countries.

Sayer, Chloe. *Arts and Crafts of Mexico.* San Francisco: Chronicle Books, 1990. An overview of Mexican crafts including the history and culture. Richly illustrated.

Taylor, Joshua C. *Learning to Look: A Handbook for the Visual Arts.* 2d ed. Chicago: University of Chicago Press, 1981. A guide to the study of art.

Thomas, Nicholas. *Oceanic Art.* London: Thames and Hudson, 1995. Examines the art of the Pacific Islands and New Zealand.

ARTISTS

Ades, Dawn. *Dali.* Rev. ed. London: Thames and Hudson, 1995. A look at the work and life of this Surrealist artist.

Bearor, Karen A. *Irene Rice Pereira: Her Paintings and Philosophy.* Austin: The University of Texas Press, 1993. An examination of the painting and philosophy of this woman artist.

Brookner, Anita. *Jacques-Louis David.* London: Chatto & Windus, 1980. A look at the life and art of David.

Cachin, Francoise. *Cézanne.* New York: Harry N. Abrams, 1996. A major catalog from the exhibition held at the Philadelphia Museum of Art.

Clark, Kenneth. *Leonardo da Vinci.* Rev. ed. London: Penguin Books, 1993. An important work about this artist and scientist of the Italian Renaissance.

Elderfield, John. *Frankenthaler.* New York: Harry N. Abrams, 1989. An examination of the art and life of Helen Frankenthaler.

Flores d'Arcais, Francesca. *Giotto.* New York: Abbeville Press, 1995. An examination of the first artist of the Italian Renaissance.

Hogrefe, Jeffrey. *O'Keeffe: The Life of an American Legend.* New York: Bantam Books, 1992. A biography of Georgia O'Keeffe.

Levin, Gail. *Edward Hopper: The Art and the Artist.* New York: Norton, 1980. A representative collection of Hopper's work, combined with information about the development of the artist's themes.

Locher, J. L., ed. *The World of M. C. Escher.* New York: Harry N. Abrams, 1988. A catalog of the precise and visually intricate artwork of the Dutch mathematician and artist.

Marnham, Patrick. *Dreaming with His Eyes Open: A Life of Diego Rivera.* New York: Knopf, 1998. A biography of Diego Rivera, an artist known for his mural painting.

Mee, Charles L. *Rembrandt's Portrait: A Biography.* New York: Simon and Schuster, 1988. An examination of the life of Rembrandt.

Paz, Octovio and Jacques Lassaigne. *Rufino Tamayo.* New York: Rizzoli, 1982. A book on the life and art of Rufino Tamayo.

Pollock, Griselda. *Mary Cassatt: Painter of Modern Women.* London: Thames and Hudson, 1998. A close examination of this American artist who studied in France.

Powell, Richard J. *Homecoming: The Art and Life of William H. Johnson.* Washington, D.C.: National Museum of American Art, 1991. An overview of the art and life of this important African-American artist.

Prather, Marla. *Alexander Calder: 1898-1976.* Washington, D.C.: National Gallery of Art, 1998. A catalog of an exhibit held at the National Gallery of Art.

Rubin, William, ed. *Pablo Picasso: A Retrospective.* New York: The Museum of Modern Art, 1980. The catalog of the huge Picasso exhibition at The Museum of Modern Art.

Snyder, Robert R. *Buckminster Fuller: An Autobiographical Monologue/Scenario.* New York: St. Martin's Press, 1980. A thorough examination of Fuller's life and work.

Sweetman, David. *Van Gogh: His Life and His Art.* New York: Crown Publishers, 1990. An examination of the life and art of van Gogh.

Varnedoe, Kirk. *Jackson Pollock.* New York: The Museum of Modern Art, 1998. A catalog of a major exhibition organized by The Museum of Modern Art.

Wardlaw, Alvia J. *The Art of John Biggers: View from the Upper Room.* Houston: Museum of Fine Arts, 1995. A major exhibition of Biggers's artwork organized by the Houston Museum of Fine Arts.

Artists Rights Society

Visual Artists And Galleries Association, Inc. (VAGA)